*To inspire ambition, to stimulate the imagination, to provide the inquiring mind with accurate information told in an interesting style, and thus lead into broader fields of knowledge— such is the purpose of this work*

*The New*
# BOOK OF KNOWLEDGE
*Volume Five*

# Other Famous Works
## of
## Popular Instruction
## by
## the Same Editor

❖❖❖❖

*PRACTICAL KNOWLEDGE FOR ALL*
Six Vols.

*NEW UNIVERSAL ENCYCLOPEDIA*
Ten Vols.

*UNIVERSAL HISTORY OF THE WORLD*
Eight Vols.

*THE SECOND GREAT WAR*
Nine Vols.

*PEOPLES OF ALL NATIONS*
Two Vols.

*COUNTRIES OF THE WORLD*
Two Vols.

*WONDERS OF THE PAST*
Two Vols.

*MANNERS AND CUSTOMS OF MANKIND*
Three Vols.

*OUR WONDERFUL WORLD*
Four Vols.

*WORLD'S GREAT BOOKS IN OUTLINE*
Seven Vols.

*MASTERPIECE LIBRARY OF SHORT STORIES*
Twenty Vols.

Made and Printed in Great Britain by The Amalgamated Press, Ltd.

# PAGEANTRY FROM THE PAST ENLIVENS THE PRESENT

*Keystone*

Much of it based on tradition which has come down unaltered through the centuries, colourful pageantry distinguishes the civic life of the City of London.   A notable occasion in the year is the day when the new Lord Mayor of London is elected ; this takes place at Michaelmas (September 29), and the photograph shows the Lord Mayor arriving at the Guildhall for the election of the man who will succeed him in the following November. In the foreground are trumpeters of the Life Guards blowing a fanfare to greet him, and between them and the Lord Mayor's coach—not the State coach of the ' Show '—is the City Marshal.

# The NEW BOOK OF KNOWLEDGE

## A Pictorial Treasury of Reading & Reference for Young and Old

Edited by
### SIR JOHN HAMMERTON

### COMPLETE IN EIGHT VOLUMES
*Alphabetically Arranged*

OVER SIX THOUSAND ILLUSTRATIONS
OVER 600 IN COLOUR AND GRAVURE

### VOLUME FIVE
## LON—PAP

## THE WAVERLEY BOOK COMPANY LTD.
### Farringdon Street, London, E.C.4

# HERE AND THERE IN THIS VOLUME

*When you are just looking for 'something interesting to read,' this list will help. With it as a guide, you may wander through storyland, visit far-away countries, meet famous people of ancient and modern times, review history's most memorable incidents, explore the marvels of Nature and science—in short, find whatever suits your fancy at the moment.*

# HOW MANY QUESTIONS CAN YOU ANSWER?

*Here are a few of the unnumbered thousands which are answered in each one of our eight volumes. You can use this page as a test of your own knowledge, or you can draw up from it a set of 'posers' with which to puzzle your friends. But odd scraps of knowledge are of little value compared with the result of organized study, and you should refer to the Study Outlines in the Eighth Volume for a reading guide.*

# COLOUR AND GRAVURE PLATES AND PAGES
## IN THIS VOLUME

# WHEN YOU ARE IN NEED OF READY REFERENCE

*In using* THE NEW BOOK OF KNOWLEDGE *as a work of reference, Volume Eight is indispensable. As regards its contents that particular volume is unique, for it is at once a complete Index to the preceding Seven Volumes and an Encyclopedia in itself. Its purpose is fourfold, as indicated below.*

(1) **Through the Year with the N.B.K.** Its opening section takes the form of a Calendar of the Year, giving for each day all the chief events and matters of interest, with references to the pages of THE NEW BOOK OF KNOWLEDGE in which full particulars concerning the event, personality, or other interest of the day may be found. By the intelligent use of this section (a) the young reader can have the daily delight of reading about topics that have special association with the particular day of the year on which he may be making his reference ; (b) father or mother can suggest what would be the most appropriate reading for the day ; and (c) the school teacher can set the lessons for the day with a genuine topical appeal.

(2) **Study Outlines.** This large and important section of the volume provides a simple method of study which should enable any of our young readers to become expert in using THE NEW BOOK OF KNOWLEDGE as an auxiliary manual of home study ; and thus what is learnt in school may be amplified, brought home more vividly, and more securely fixed in the memory.

(3) **The Fact-Index.** Actually this is in itself a complete Encyclopedia. In addition to providing many thousands of references to contents of Volumes One to Seven, it records many more thousands of facts in biography, geography, history, science, the arts, etc.,

that are not mentioned in its seven predecessors. Therefore, if you look in vain for any subject in the alphabetical order of Volumes One to Seven, turn to Volume Eight and you will almost certainly find it there.

*It is a good plan, when using* THE NEW BOOK OF KNOWLEDGE *as a work of reference,* **always** *first to look up any subject in the Fact-Index of Volume Eight.*

(4) **Thousands of Additional Entries.** In the main body of the work all important terms are explained as they arise ; but the scientist in every field of learning uses a "shorthand" of words and terms to convey a more precise meaning and to save repetition. Such words and terms are included in the Fact-Index so as to free the reading pages from a burden of thousands of brief cross-references which a more strict following of the full encyclopedic method would involve. When in doubt, therefore, about the significance of a term, *look it up in the Fact-Index ;* often you will find all the information you want there, but if further explanation is required the Fact-Index will give you page references to that more complete account in the main volumes. Remember that apart from its role as a never-failing source of recreative and entertaining reading, THE NEW BOOK OF KNOWLEDGE is designed to make your school and college learning of treble value by fitting that learning into its place in daily life.

# KEY TO PRONUNCIATION

Most of the subject-headings in THE NEW BOOK OF KNOWLEDGE require no special indication of the way in which they should be pronounced. There are also many for whose proper pronunciation it is only necessary to know which syllable is stressed ; in these cases the stress is shown *after* the syllable, thus, Armadil'lo. Where further guidance is necessary the following signs are employed.

ah = a as in father
aw = a as in ball
ê = vowel sound in fern, word, girl, curl
ow = vowel sound in now, bout
oi = vowel sound in noise, boy
**Unmarked vowels** have their **short sound,** as a in hat, e in bet, i in bit, o in not, u in but, oo in book
**Marked vowels** have their **long sound,** as in hāte, bē, bīte, nōte, tūne, bōōn

**Vowels in italics** have a slurred or obscure sound as in abet (*a*-bet′), recent (rē′-s*e*nt), conform (k*o*n-form′), nation (nā′-sh*u*n), tailor (tā′-l*o*r)

th = first sound in thing, thank
*th* = first sound in the, that
zh = s in measure, leisure
g = hard g, as in good, girl
j = soft g, as in gem, ginger
kh = guttural in loch

# LIST OF ABBREVIATIONS

The abbreviations most commonly used in this work are noted below ; longer lists of abbreviations often met with in reading or conversation are given under the heading Abbreviations in Volume One and also in the Fact-Index that is contained in Volume Eight.

A.D., *Anno Domini* (in the year of our Lord, of the Christian era)
a.m., *ante meridiem* (before noon)
b., born
B.C., before Christ
C., Centigrade
c., *circa* (about)
Co., county, company
d., died
e.g., *exempli gratia* (for example)
etc., *et cetera* (and so forth)
et seq., *et sequens* (and following)
F., Fahrenheit
h.p., horse-power

i.e., *id est* (that is)
lb., pound, pounds (weight)
m., miles
MS., MSS., manuscript, manuscripts
oz., ounce, ounces
p.m., *post meridiem* (after noon)
Pop., population
Pron., pronunciation
q.v., *quod vide* (which see)
sq. m., square miles
St., Saint
U.S.A., United States of America
viz., *videlicet* (namely)
yd., yard

# *Mighty* METROPOLIS *of the* WORLD

*Destroyed by fire in 1666, burned and bombed by the Germans in the Second World War (1939–45), London remains 'the flower of cities all,' greatest in the world in size and population, industry and commerce.*

**London.** Though London with its suburbs now sprawls over nearly 700 square miles, its true heart is to be found within a few miles of Charing Cross. Within the square mile of the City, and within the City of Westminster and the Borough of Southwark, most of the great events of London's history took place; and here stand most of the historic buildings.

**' London Stone,' which stands behind this grille in a church wall in Cannon Street, is said to be a Roman milestone.**

To begin our survey from the oldest part of the City we must start from the Tower of London. Around us is London, the " city of Lud," a king of the ancient Britons who ruled his people in their flimsy huts on the marshy banks of the Thames, in the days before the Romans conquered the land. Here was the first firm ground on which vessels from the sea could land their goods, and here was the lowest point at which the river could be forded or bridged, so roads converged on London and it grew to the mighty giant of today. Romans built the first bridge where we now see Tower Bridge. King Alfred the Great (849–901) added to the city's fortifications, and William the Conqueror (1027–87) built the Tower.

Let us first get the " lie " of the city from the Tower. The Thames sprawls like a great, broad S to the west and south, and winds its course 40 miles eastwards to the sea. When the Tower was built London had about 30,000 people. Today the inhabitants of " Greater London " number about 8,700,000.

What puzzles one at first is the way the streets twist and turn. But you will see that these higgledy-piggledy streets that seem to criss-cross every way really run parallel with the S of the river. When we are at the Tower we are close to the heart of business London, with the Royal Mint and the

*From the reconstruction by Dr. M. Wheeler and A. Forestier in the London Museum*

### RECONSTRUCTION OF THE LONDON OF ROMAN TIMES

This reconstruction shows London much as it must have been during the Roman occupation of Britain. In the foreground is the timber bridge, a little farther downstream than the present London Bridge. On either side of the bridge gate at the London end are wharves. From the bridge a street runs to the Forum and Basilica, the site of which is known from modern excavations. The walls are shown with the towers added to them towards the close of the Roman occupation.

Bank of England, the Stock Exchange, Lloyd's, and Custom House, busy markets like Billingsgate and Smithfield, and banking houses, brokers' and insurance offices. Near by are Tower Hill, grim scene of many an execution, and the magnificent building of the Port of London Authority; away to the east are the docks in which liners plying to Africa and Australia, the sub-continent of India and the East, and cargo steamers which carry a great part of the world's commerce load and unload. There, too, are the slums and poverty of London's sprawling East End.

In the neighbourhood of the Tower you could hardly shoot an arrow without its dropping into a street famous in history or finance. Lombard Street, Threadneedle Street, Cornhill, and Leadenhall Street, are narrow streets famous for banking and finance; Lombard Street being named after the Italian bankers and merchants who settled there in the 14th and 15th centuries. In and near Leadenhall Street are many shipping offices, and in Throgmorton Street is the Stock Exchange. The Bank of England lies north-west of the Tower. It covers perhaps the most important four acres in the British Commonwealth, and is a centre of world finance. It was rebuilt in the 1920s.

Everywhere hereabouts are historic memorials. Alexander Pope, the poet, was born in a little side-street just off Lombard Street. Samuel Pepys, the diarist, who spent his days in the Admiralty offices, lived not far from Tower Street. The Hudson's Bay Company, which dominated half of North America for two centuries, had offices (and have yet) in London, a few hundred yards from the Bank of England. Milton was born in Broad Street, the bakers' quarter, and Sir Thomas More in Milk Street, the site of old dairies. The poet Keats was born near Moorgate, and Thomas Gray, another poet, in Cornhill.

Close to the Bank of England is the Mansion House, the official residence of the Lord Mayor of London; and about a quarter-mile north of it is the Guildhall, headquarters of the Corporation of the City of London. In its hall and library (damaged during the Second World War) many of the City's state functions are held, and Royalties and other distinguished visitors have been entertained there. In the Guildhall the Lord Mayor's Banquet, at which the Prime Minister of the day usually makes an important political speech, is held on Lord Mayor's Day, November 9, after the Lord Mayor has driven in procession to the Law Courts to be sworn in. The Guildhall dates from the beginning of the 15th century; its woodwork was destroyed in the Great Fire, but parts of the hall were untouched and the crypt is intact. It is in this part of London that the halls of several of the City's ancient livery companies are situated.

Half-a-mile west of the Mansion House is St. Paul's, the cathedral of the Bishop of London. Many books have been written about St. Paul's. It is as famous as Westminster Abbey, which we shall visit presently in the West End. Legend says it is built on the site of a temple of Diana, replaced by the Romans with a Christian church, which in turn was torn down by the pagan Saxons. Old St. Paul's, famous in Reformation days, was built about 1160. The present building was planned by Sir Christopher Wren and is one of more than 50 churches constructed by him after the Great Fire in 1666 had destroyed about four-fifths of the London of that day. Wren also built the Monument (near the northern end of London Bridge) to mark the spot where the Fire began.

A host of associations cling round the names of streets in the neighbourhood, such as Paternoster Row, originally inhabited by makers of prayer-

*A. F. Kersting*

**ONE OF WREN'S MASTERPIECES**
In designing St. Bride's, Fleet Street, Sir Christopher Wren bore in mind that the body of the church would be hidden by houses and so made the spire as beautiful as possible. This view was obtained while neighbouring buildings were being rebuilt. The structure was damaged by fire in a German air raid of December 29, 1940.

# CONTRASTING SCENES IN LONDON'S CENTRE

*Topical, The Times*

Visitors to London are always struck by the contrasts visible within quite a small area, and as shown in these two photographs taken in the heart of Great Britain's capital. At the top we see part of the north bank of the River Thames, and the new Waterloo Bridge (completed during the Second World War. 1939–45). Lower is a view of St. James's Park. One of the oldest parks in London, it extends to 93 acres and the lake covers five acres.

beads, but later long associated with the publishing trade ; Watling Street, part of the ancient Roman road between Dover and Wroxeter ; and Cheapside, the historic thoroughfare in which was the Mermaid Tavern, frequented by Sir Walter Raleigh, Shakespeare, Ben Jonson, and other great poets and wits.

In Cheapside, too, stands what the German bombers left of the church of St. Mary-le-Bow, with its famous Bow Bells. Only those born within sound of these bells, it is said, can lay true claim to the title of Cockney; but the original chime was destroyed in the Great Fire, and those that replaced it fell victim to a German raider. The whole area between Cheapside and St. Paul's churchyard was devastated in the air attacks of 1940 and 1941.

Before betaking ourselves to the West End we must glance at Tower Bridge and London Bridge. Tower Bridge is the last bridge crossing the Thames before it reaches the sea, and between the two bridges is the Pool of London, in which ships of as much as 6,000 tons can berth. Such large ships could not pass under an ordinary bridge, so when Tower Bridge was built, between 1886 and 1894, it was necessary that it should open to enable ships to pass. The roadway, therefore, has been made in two sections, which can be raised and lowered by hydraulic power. London Bridge, opened in 1831, stands near the site of a wooden structure which endured for nearly 500 years.

We can make our way westward from St. Paul's either along Fleet Street and the Strand or by the Thames Embankment, which stretches in an almost unbroken line from Blackfriars Bridge to Fulham. The carriageway is over 60 feet wide, and along the pavements there are plane trees with seats beneath.

If we wish to see as many famous buildings as possible we shall choose the Fleet Street and Strand route. These two form the most famous of London's east-to-west thoroughfares. Fleet Street is the heart of newspaperland, and an impressive example of the fine buildings in which newspapers are housed to-day is the office of The Daily Telegraph and Morning Post. Continuing westward, we can visit some of the most famous landmarks of the capital. The first of these is the Temple, lying between the Embankment and Fleet Street, in which there are two of the Inns or societies of the lawyers, the Inner Temple and the Middle Temple. Enemy bombs did great damage to many of the buildings here, wrecking the interior of the Middle Temple Hall (a magnificent Tudor building in which some of Shakespeare's plays were probably first performed), and completely destroying the Library.

In the Temple Church, also seriously damaged, are the tombs of some of the Crusaders; for the Temple gets its name from the crusading Knights Templars, whose stronghold it once was. This is the finest of the four round churches remaining in

**A FAMOUS CHURCH NEAR CHARING CROSS**

*Topical*

St. Martin-in-the-Fields, from which many religious services have been broadcast, is here seen through the columns of the National Gallery. The church, which stands opposite the north-east corner of Trafalgar Square, was built during 1721-26 by James Gibbs, on the site of an older church dating from the time of Henry VIII.

*Keystone*

## LONDON'S SEATS OF IMPERIAL AND LOCAL GOVERNMENT

The top photograph shows the Houses of Parliament from across the Thames. On the extreme right is the Clock Tower while on the left is the Victoria Tower, through an arch in the base of which the King enters for the opening of Parliament. In front of the building is the terrace facing the river. The lower photograph shows the County Hall—headquarters of the London County Council—on the south or Surrey bank of the river; from here the whole of the County of London, except the square mile of the City, is governed. In front of it a row of Thames pleasure launches are moored.

England, and dates from the 12th century. For the rest, the Temple consists of mellow old brick buildings where barristers have their chambers; but much was lost during the Second World War. Goldsmith, Lamb and Thackeray all had chambers in the Temple. The other two Inns of Court are Lincoln's Inn and Gray's Inn.

Farther west, beyond the site of Temple Bar, where the King still asks permission of the Lord Mayor before entering the City (the original archway was removed in 1878), we see the Law Courts, a grey stone building with an imposing frontage on to the Strand. We pass the buildings which house the offices of the Government of Australia, and Bush House, London's biggest office block; and less than half a mile farther on we come to Trafalgar Square, dominated by the Nelson Monument. On the north side of Trafalgar Square is the National Gallery, on the east are the offices of the Union of South Africa, on the west those of Canada, while on the south side Whitehall opens out towards Westminster.

Whitehall and Westminster have been called the heart of the British Commonwealth, for in Whitehall are some of the chief government offices, the Foreign Office, the Home Office, the Admiralty, the War Office (a part of it), the Commonwealth Relations Office, and others. As we go down Whitehall we pass on the right the Horse Guards, whose mounted sentries in their shining steel breastplates attract the attention of every passer-by; and on the left the last relic of the old Palace of Whitehall, the Banqueting Hall, now the home of the Royal United Service Museum (*see* illus., p. 1837).

Whitehall's grandeur dates back to Cardinal Wolsey (*c.* 1475–1530), the favourite of Henry

VIII, for here was Wolsey's London residence as Archbishop of York. After his fall it became Crown property, and was renamed Whitehall. Under the Tudors and the Stuarts it became a palace of regal splendour.

In the centre of Whitehall stands the majestic Cenotaph, erected after the First World War (1914–18), but now a memorial to the fallen of both World Wars. The official residence of the Prime Minister is in Downing Street, which is a turning off Whitehall. On the left, down towards the Thames, is New Scotland Yard, headquarters of the Metropolitan Police.

On the right or south bank of the Thames we see the magnificent hall of the London County Council, and on the left bank the Houses of Parliament by Westminster Bridge ; at right angles to them is Westminster Abbey. The old Parliament building was burned down in 1834 when an impatient servant overheated a flue in burning up wooden "tallies" or receipts, which had accumulated in the Treasury in the course of six centuries. On the site, between the years 1840 and 1852, Sir Charles Barry erected the present Gothic building, covering an area of eight acres. In its chambers sit the House of Commons and the House of Lords amid surroundings of the highest historic significance. Enemy bombers damaged the Houses of Parliament 12 times during the Second World War, and the House of Commons was wrecked.

Topical

**LONDON'S FAMOUS MARBLE ARCH**
Designed by the architect John Nash (1752–1835), the Marble Arch was erected outside Buckingham Palace in 1828, then transferred to the north-east corner of Hyde Park in 1851. When the roadway here was altered in 1908 the Arch was left isolated in the middle of a traffic roundabout.

Westminster Hall, which was begun by the Conqueror's son, William Rufus (c. 1056–1100), and remodelled by some of his successors, now serves as a vestibule to the Houses of Parliament. Here some of the earliest Parliaments were held. The chief English courts sat in Westminster Hall and in buildings on the west side which were erected for the purpose, until the present Law Courts were built. In Westminster Hall the bodies of King Edward VII and King George V lay in state while thousands of their subjects filed past to pay homage.

Just across the street from the Houses of Parliament stands Westminster Abbey, founded by Edward the Confessor (c. 1005–1066) and added to by his successors until it became the magnificent Gothic church that it is today.

We shall not have time to go to St. James's Park, not far from the Abbey, or to visit Buckingham Palace or St. James's Palace—even if we could gain admission. St. James's Palace, long disused as a royal residence, is still the official home of the British monarchy. Foreign ambassadors and Ministers are accredited to the Court of St. James's, and the King still holds his levées and receptions there. There is a fine approach up the Mall to

Topical

**THE VICTORIA AND ALBERT MUSEUM**
In Cromwell Road, South Kensington, is the Victoria and Albert Museum, a vast building designed by Sir Aston Webb (1849–1930), and completed in 1909. Containing one of the finest collections of decorative and ornamental art in the world, it originated in the Museum of Oriental Art established in Marlborough House, Pall Mall, in 1852.

Buckingham Palace, but the frontage is masked by the huge memorial to Queen Victoria.

North of Buckingham Palace is Green Park, and north of that Hyde Park, a vast expanse of 361 acres (636 acres with Kensington Gardens, which adjoin it), one of the royal parks, and now a people's pleasure ground. On Sundays and holidays it is thronged with people. Many of them gather in good-natured knots round the orators, who are allowed to speak freely at a spot in the north-east corner on almost any subject they desire —religious, political or economic ; it is one of the safety-valves of the British constitution. In Kensington Gardens stands Kensington Palace, a former royal residence, in which Queen Victoria was born. Here, too, are the Round Pond, a favourite spot for model yachtsmen, and the Peter Pan statue. Regent's Park with the Zoo lies a mile to the north.

Let us now take a bus and ride up Piccadilly from Hyde Park Corner to Piccadilly Circus, from which six streets, including Regent Street, Shaftesbury Avenue and Coventry Street, radiate, and in the centre of which is a fountain surmounted by the figure of Eros, a memorial to Lord Shaftesbury who did so much to arrest the exploitation of child labour. Here we are in the heart of the great theatrical district of London, while to the north is the foreign quarter called Soho, famous for its restaurants.

The visitor to London will, of course, visit the national picture galleries and museums. After the National Gallery and the British Museum the most important collections are the Tate Gallery at Millbank and the National Portrait Gallery in St. Martin's Place ; the Wallace Collection in Manchester Square, where pictures, furniture and armour are exhibited; the Victoria and Albert Museum, where there are interesting exhibits of furniture and other objects; the Science Museum, Natural History Museum, and Geological Museum, the four last named being at South Kensington. The London Museum, formerly at Lancaster House (which is now used by the Government for important conferences), was reopened in part in Kensington Palace after the Second World War

(1939-45). The Imperial War Museum in Lambeth is a storehouse of exhibits connected with the two World Wars. It is sad to tell that scarcely one of London's museums escaped bomb damage during the Second World War.

We have only touched here and there the central parts of metropolitan London. To the north lie enormous residential areas, such as Highbury, Camden Town and Hampstead. To the east are Greenwich and Woolwich—the one the seat of the Royal Observatory until that was removed to Hurstmonceux in Sussex, the other of the Royal Arsenal. South of the historic river are Battersea (with its great power-station) and Lambeth. Westwards lie Kensington, Chelsea and Hammersmith. The borough of Southwark, south of the Thames, is an industrial district, and you may see there the spot on which stood the Globe Theatre

*The Times*

**PARK LANE ON THE EAST SIDE OF HYDE PARK**
Once noted for its palatial private mansions this thoroughfare runs from Piccadilly to Marble Arch, with Hyde Park on its west side. Hotels, shops and blocks of flats and offices now line the east side. A lane leading to Tyburn (near the site of Marble Arch) in the 18th century, Park Lane became a fashionable place of residence a century later.

in which Shakespeare acted. Here, too, is the George Inn, a famous old coaching house, part of whose galleried courtyard still remains.

London became a place of importance under the Romans, probably first about A.D. 43. It was burnt by the Britons under Queen Boadicea in A.D. 61. From 369 to 412 it was the capital of Roman Britain, being known as *Londinium*. Bede calls it a " princely town of trade " when it was the capital of the East Saxon kingdom. King Alfred restored the city after it had been burnt and the Roman walls destroyed by the Danes. London, already rich and prosperous, sided with the House of York in the Wars of the Roses. The Reformation was welcomed, and the suppression of the monasteries and confiscation of their property made Henry VIII popular.

Under Queen Elizabeth (1533–1603) new openings for adventure and commerce in America and India gave a great impulse to the city's trade. London was a powerful aid to Parliament in the Civil War (1642–48) with Charles I, and the city's " trained bands," made up of Puritan apprentices, fought on many a battlefield. The plague, which had several times visited London, in 1665 destroyed one fifth of the population; and the great fire the following year burned 396 acres of buildings.

London was first lighted by lanterns in 1415; by gas in 1807. The streets were first paved in 1533. Omnibuses began to run on regular routes in 1829 ; the Metropolitan underground railway was opened in 1863, and the first " tube " in 1890. The underground services now consist of about 700 miles of railway, which with buses, trams, trolley-buses and " Green Line " coaches are controlled by the London Transport Executive of the nationalised transport board.

London possesses many important educational establishments, chief among them being London University with its splendid buildings in Bloomsbury and elsewhere. Among public schools are Westminster, St. Paul's, and City of London.

The resident population of the City's square mile (within the Roman walls, the gates of which have given their names to streets like Aldgate and Bishopsgate), is less than 11,000. In addition, London comprises 28 metropolitan boroughs, each administering its own affairs. The London County Council takes care of most matters concerning London as a whole. The " City " is governed by a Lord Mayor, 25 aldermen, and over 200 common councillors.

The administrative county of London and the City together cover over 117 square miles and have a population of 4,863,000. What is known as Greater London includes the City and Metropolitan Police Districts, and covers an area of nearly 700 square miles, with a population of 8,700,000.

When the Second World War (1939–45) came (the first real " war in the air ") London, Britain's great port and commercial centre and focus of the country's vast network of roads and railways, naturally became the chief target of the enemy bombers. In the autumn of 1940 the Germans began the intensive air attacks that came to be called the " Blitz " (from the German word *Blitzkrieg*, lightning war). Night after night and day after day the bombers dropped their deadly cargoes on the capital.

Especially severe was the devastation in the City and in the East End, where the docks attracted the greatest fury of the enemy airmen. When the Blitz was renewed in the spring of 1941, many districts were so severely damaged that even those familiar with them could scarcely trace the streets that ran between the ruined houses. But the great city remained unconquered, its stout-hearted people undaunted. None of the main railway stations or the bridges over the Thames was put out of action for more than a few days at a time.

A great anti aircraft barrage was built up, and fighters of the Royal Air Force attacked the German formations tirelessly as they flew in from the coast. Barrage balloons, shining at the end of their steel cables, protected vulnerable points from low-level attacks. Hundreds of air-raid shelters were constructed both above and below ground, and the tube stations were fitted with bunks where mothers and children could sleep. By the middle of 1941 the first fury of the German attacks was expended. In the summer of 1944 there came to London a new terror—the flying-bombs. Hurried

**CHARING CROSS**
The stone cross in the courtyard of Charing Cross Station is a replica of one set up by Edward I (1239–1307) in memory of his queen, Eleanor. The original was removed in 1647, the copy being erected in 1865.

*Fox*

readjustment of the anti-aircraft defences brought a measure of protection against this new weapon. But there was no means of defence against the next deadly novelty, the rockets which fell from a tremendous height without warning and caused enormous havoc. More of London's famous landmarks, old and new, fell victims to these fearsome new weapons, and the Imperial City was left sadly scarred when peace came in 1945.

From the ruins and ashes of a London battered by nearly five years of air war there began to arise a new city. Where acres of slum dwellings had been destroyed fine modern houses and blocks of flats were planned. In 1948 work began on a great scheme for the south bank of the Thames, with an embankment from Westminster to Waterloo Bridge, featuring a national theatre and a concert hall.

# THE STORIED STONES OF LONDON: WEST & EAST

*Times; Topical*

Piccadilly Circus (upper photograph) is the hub of London's West End, most of the principal shops of this fashionable area and some famous theatres being within easy walk. In the centre of the Circus is the aluminium statue of Eros, one of the masterpieces of Sir Alfred Gilbert (1854–1934). It is a memorial to the 7th Earl of Shaftesbury. The lower photograph shows the Tower Bridge over the River Thames about three miles to the East from Piccadilly Circus; it was built in 1894 on the site of an ancient Roman structure. To the left of the bridge is the Tower of London; it covers 13 acres, was built by William the Conqueror (1027–87), and it has held many prisoners renowned in Britain's past.

# HISTORIC WHITEHALL AND THE ADMIRALTY ARCH

Taking its name from the palace built by Henry VIII and destroyed by fire in 1698, the thoroughfare known as Whitehall (upper) contains some of the principal Government offices. The building with the twin domed towers is the War Office, and on the near side of it is the United Service Museum. Whitehall connects Parliament Street, of which it is an extension, with Charing Cross and Trafalgar Square. At the entrance from Trafalgar Square into St. James's Park is the Admiralty Arch (lower), erected in 1910 as part of the national memorial to Queen Victoria. Designed by Sir Aston Webb (1849–1930), it is connected with the Admiralty offices, and houses the Admiralty library.

# THE CHANGEFUL SCENE IN TRAFALGAR SQUARE

*Times; Barratt's*

Perhaps the best-known of London's many squares is Trafalgar Square, within a few yards of Charing Cross. On the south side stands the Nelson Column (lower photograph), 168½ feet high and surmounted by a statue of the renowned Admiral; four lions sculptured by Sir Edwin Landseer (1802–73) are at the corners of the plinth. This memorial of Nelson's last victory was begun in 1829 and completed in 1867. Busts of Admirals Jellicoe and Beatty on the north wall (upper, right) were added in 1948, when also the fountains were remodelled. The building behind the further fountain is Canada House; the National Gallery occupies the whole of the north side of the square.

# DOWN FLEET STREET AND UP TO ST. PAUL'S

Fleet Street, London, is sometimes called the 'Street of Ink,' from the fact that it is the centre of the area in which almost all the great newspapers of England's capital are published. Here, also, the main provincial papers have London offices. The clock high up in the left foreground marks the Daily Telegraph office, and the light grey building almost opposite houses the international news agency known as Reuters. Fleet Street descends to Ludgate Circus, and the thoroughfare, after passing under a railway bridge, continues as Ludgate Hill to St. Paul's Cathedral, whose dome, crowned by its cupola and lantern with golden ball and cross, is seen in the distance.

## Londonderry.

Covering 816 square miles, this county, more familiarly known as Derry, is one of the six which together constitute Northern Ireland. It is bounded on the west by Donegal and Lough Foyle, on the north by the Atlantic, on the east by Antrim and Armagh, on the south by Tyrone.

Pasture and cultivated areas are about equal, with flax and oats the main crops. Chief industries are flour-milling, distilling, ship-building, tanning, bacon-curing, and the making of linen. Coleraine is the centre of the famous River Bann salmon fisheries. Londonderry, the capital city (population 47,000), was founded in about the year 546 by St. Columba, who called it Doire, " the place of oaks," from which Derry, the city's original name, is derived. The county took the prefix London when in 1609 much of the land was made over to the City of London by King James I. The city of Londonderry successfully withstood a siege by the troops of James II in 1689. The population of the county is 142,730.

## London University.

Though this is the largest university in the world, both in number of colleges and in number of students, a very small proportion of Londoners ever realize that theirs is a university town. This is probably because, apart from occasional " rags," the students living in London never obtrude themselves on the public—and, indeed, are unrecognizable as students, since they do not wear gowns in the streets, like those of Oxford and Cambridge; and partly because the colleges are scattered throughout Greater London, from Hampstead in the north to New Cross Gate in the south, from Kensington in the west to Mile End Road in the east.

London University consists of some 40 schools and colleges, including, among the best-known, King's College, Strand; University College, Gower Street; the Imperial College of Science, South Kensington; Bedford College (for women); Birkbeck College (for evening classes); Goldsmiths' College; the Slade School of Fine Art; the teaching departments of several great hospitals; the former London Day Training College for teachers (now called the Institute of Education); and the London School of Economics.

There is no residential qualification for London University students—they may, and do, live anywhere in the world; comparatively few live in London itself, and only a fraction is housed in the hostels attached to the University. All may sit for the examinations, but those attending a school or college of the University are registered as " internal " students, and those studying elsewhere, or at home, are called " external " students. The number of students in 1947–48 was 50,000.

The University is governed by a Chancellor, Vice-Chancellor, Chairman of Convocation, and Principal, all members of what is called the Court; and by a Senate, which comprises these and the heads of the schools and colleges. The University was founded in 1836, first as an examining university alone, and in 1900 was made a teaching university. In 1936 occurred two great events in its history— the celebration of its first centenary, and the beginning of the removal of certain of its departments to the new London University buildings in Bloomsbury, of which the foundation stone had been laid in 1933 by King George V. These buildings house the administrative offices (removed from South Kensington in 1936), the library, the Institute of Education, Schools of Oriental and Slavonic Studies, Birkbeck College, the Courtauld Institute of Art, and the Students' Union.

London University offers tuition and examination in practically every branch of knowledge. Particulars of its courses and degrees, and of enrolment as internal or external student, may be obtained from the Secretary, London University, W.C.1.

*Fox*

### HEADQUARTERS OF LONDON'S HUGE UNIVERSITY
In Bloomsbury, a district of London to the north of Holborn and New Oxford Street, are the headquarters of London University, the foundation stone of which was laid in 1933 by King George V. Here are housed the controlling and administrative departments of the largest university in the world.

# NORTH AMERICA'S GREATEST POET

*Probably more of Longfellow's verse is known by heart in the English-speaking countries than any other poet's. For we all learn something of his at school, even if it is only The Wreck of the Hesperus.*

**Longfellow,** HENRY WADSWORTH (1807–82). Have you a favourite poet? If it is Longfellow, then Hiawatha is a friend of yours, and King Olaf, that fine strapping hero; you will know all about the village blacksmith; and Evangeline with its "forest primeval" make you feel both sad and happy.

Longfellow was born in Portland, Maine, United States, on February 27, 1807, and was educated at Bowdoin College, Brunswick, Maine. After studying in Europe for three years he returned to Bowdoin in 1829 as professor of foreign languages. In 1835 came his first great sorrow, the death of his young wife. In 1843 he married again, his second wife being the heroine of his Hyperion. Eighteen years of happiness followed, these being also his greatest creative years. A tragic break came in 1861 when his second wife was burned to death. It was long before he recovered from the shock, but his lost years were made happier by the devotion of his five children. He died on March 24, 1882.

He was himself not unlike a child, big and simple-hearted and friendly. He taught young people and helped and encouraged young poets for many years. Everybody loved him, from his great contemporaries like Emerson, Hawthorne and Holmes, to the children he played with.

He did an important service in opening the eyes of his countrymen to the beauties of European legends and literature. He knew French and Italian and German, and his verse translations—especially of Dante's Divine Comedy—brought many foreign poems within the reach of the North American people. His own poetry, too, was often founded on some European folk story or legend, as, for instance, most of the Tales of a Wayside Inn and The Sagas of King Olaf. Others, like Paul Revere's Ride and The Courtship of Miles Standish, were founded on events in American history.

In his famous Hiawatha, Longfellow used material found in old Indian legends. The Iroquois Indians had stories of a great and wise chief named Hiawatha, who lived shortly before the appearance of the white man in America, and who played an important part in bringing together the tribes of the powerful Iroquois League. There were, also, numerous legends among the Indians of the Great Lakes about another hero known by various names. Longfellow became interested in these legends, and decided to embody them in a narrative poem.

The hero, according to Longfellow, was "a personage of miraculous birth, who was sent among them (the Indians) to clear their rivers, forests and fishing grounds, and to teach them the arts of peace. He was known among the various tribes by the several names of Michabou, Chiabo, Manabozo, Tarenyawgon, and Hiawatha." Longfellow gave his hero the name Hiawatha, as this seemed to him the most musical: its cadences may even have suggested the trochaic metre of the poem. Longfellow also wrote shorter poems that are famous, including A Psalm of Life, Excelsior, The Children's Hour, and others. His poems were translated into many European languages.

**HENRY LONGFELLOW**
**Perhaps the best-loved of American poets, Longfellow's work was varied and voluminous. He died on March 24, 1882.**

## LONGFELLOW'S STORY OF HIAWATHA

MANY years ago, by the shores of Lake Superior, which the Indians called Gitche Gumee, the shining Big-Sea Water, there stood the wigwam of old Nokomis, Daughter of the Moon. Here she lived with her grandson Hiawatha, whose beautiful mother had died when he was a baby, and whose father, Mudjekeewis, the West Wind, had gone off and forgotten all about him. Nokomis hushed the little one to sleep in his moss-lined cradle, and told him many a fanciful tale about the moon, the fiery comet, or the rainbow which he saw above the pine trees that cast their shadows about the wigwam.

Almost as soon as he learned to speak the sturdy little Indian boy learned also the language of all the birds, "learned their names and all their secrets," and called them "Hiawatha's chickens." So, too, he learned about the ways of varied beasts of the field and forest:

How the beavers built their lodges,
How the squirrels hid their acorns,
How the reindeer ran so swiftly,
Why the rabbit was so timid,
Talked with them whene'er he met them,
Called them "Hiawatha's brothers."

So Hiawatha grew into a strong, brave and noble man. He was a mighty hunter and had many strange adventures. He wore magic mittens of deerskin with which he could smite rocks asunder, and moccasins which took him a mile at a stride.

One of his great battles was with the fierce Pearl-Feather, a magician who lived in a wigwam among stagnant pools guarded by serpents. Because of a magic shirt he wore, Pearl-Feather could not be harmed. At last Hiawatha, wounded, exhausted, and in despair, had only three arrows left. "Aim your arrows at the roots of his hair, Hiawatha!"

sang a woodpecker to him. Hiawatha did so, and the magician fell dead at his feet. Then, before he took back the furs, wampum (small beads made of shells), and other enemy trophies to divide among his people, Hiawatha stained the little woodpecker's head with blood in honour of his service. That crimson badge the woodpecker wears to this day.

In order that he might bring blessing to his people, Hiawatha once went alone into the forest to fast and pray. On the fourth day of his fasting, as he lay exhausted, a youth dressed in green and yellow garments, with plumes of green falling over his golden hair, came to Hiawatha and bade him wrestle with him. Hiawatha arose and, feeling new life and vigour within him, wrestled with the stranger until he cried, " 'Tis enough! " On the morrow, and again on the next day, the youth Mondamin came and wrestled with Hiawatha. As he departed after the third conflict he said that he would come once again and that this time Hiawatha should conquer him.

On the fourth day, after a long struggle, Mondamin lay lifeless on the ground, his plumage torn, his garments tattered. Hiawatha buried him carefully in the soft earth, as Mondamin had bidden him, where the rain might fall upon him and the sun might warm him. Day by day he watched beside the grave and tended it " till at length a small green feather " shot upward, and then another and another.

> And before the Summer ended
> Stood the Maize in all its beauty,
> With its shining robes about it
> And its long, soft, golden tresses.

Thus it was that Hiawatha gave to his people the great gift of maize or Indian corn.

The Indians saw in Hiawatha the prophet and teacher that Gitche Manito (the Great Spirit) had promised to send them. Hiawatha taught them picture-writing, the art of healing, and other things; and he kept the tribes at peace.

Hiawatha fell in love with Minnehaha, or Laughing Water, the beautiful daughter of an arrow-maker in the land of the Dakotas. To woo her he brought her a fine red deer and, laying it before her, told her of his love. Then the Dakota maiden—

> Softly took the seat beside him
> While she said, and blushed to say it,
> " I will follow you, my husband."

Hiawatha took his bride back to the land of the peaceful Ojibways, where a wedding feast awaited them. He and his bride were very happy together,

**THE LOVELY MINNEHAHA**

**HIAWATHA IN HIS CANOE**

until there came a cold dreary winter, when the Indians could hunt no food in the snow-buried forests, and an epidemic of fever spread among the starving tribes. Then one day Hiawatha strode forth in anguish, praying that he might find food for his beautiful Minnehaha, who lay in the wigwam stricken with fever.

While he was gone Minnehaha lifted up her head. " Hark! " she cried. " I hear the Falls of Minnehaha calling, calling to me! "

" No, my child," said old Nokomis, soothingly. " It is but the night wind in the pines."

" Look! " exclaimed the girl. " I see my lonely father beckoning me! "

" 'Tis but the smoke you see," answered Nokomis.

" Ah," cried Minnehaha. " I see strange glaring eyes—and icy fingers . . . Hiawatha! Hiawatha! "

Far away in the forest Hiawatha heard the cry and, hurrying back, burst into the wigwam. But Death had claimed his beautiful Laughing Water.

Spring came with birds and blossoms to bring comfort to Minnehaha's husband. And with summer there came a morning when from his wigwam door Hiawatha stood looking over the sparkling waters of Gitche Gumee. Suddenly he lifted up his hands toward the sun and smiled, as though he were dreaming a very beautiful dream.

Over the water, with paddles flashing in the sunlight, came a birch canoe filled with white men. Old Iagoo, the traveller, had already brought word of these creatures, and Hiawatha in a vision had seen the pale-faces, sent by the Great Spirit to bring the Indians a message. As the boat grated upon the shore, Hiawatha stepped forward and welcomed them joyously.

" Beautiful is the sun, O strangers," he cried, " when you come so far to see us."

" Peace be with you and your people," answered the white-faced leader, who wore the long black robe of a priest.

The Indian leader welcomed them to his dwelling, where important chiefs and medicine-men of the village gathered to do them honour. After food had been served and a peace-pipe smoked, the priest told his message, the story of Jesus. And the Indians thanked him, saying:

" We have heard your words of wisdom. It is well for us, O brothers, that you come so far to see us."

That evening, at dusk, while his guests slumbered in his wigwam, Hiawatha stole softly out of the door.

" I am going on a long and distant journey," he told Nokomis and his people. " Many winters will vanish ere I again appear, as I am going to the portals of the sunset. See that you guard well these

**'THUS DEPARTED HIAWATHA . . .'**
*Sketches by Honor C. Appleton from The Children's Hiawatha,
published by George G. Harrap & Co., Ltd.*

white strangers and listen to their words. The Master has sent them from the land of light and morning."

Then he stepped into his canoe, turned and waved to the sorrowful group on shore, whispered to his boat, " Westward ! Westward ! " and sailed into the purple and gold of the sunset.

" Farewell for ever, O Hiawatha ! " cried his people. " Farewell ! " sighed the forests and the waves and the heron in the fens.

> Thus departed Hiawatha,
> Hiawatha, the Beloved,
> In the glory of the sunset,
> In the purple mists of evening,
> To the Islands of the Blessed,
> To the Land of the Hereafter.

**Longford.** Situated in the province of Leinster, Longford is one of the smallest counties in Eire ; its area is 403 square miles. The surface is level, except in the north-west, but there is much bogland. Chief rivers are the Shannon on the western boundary, Inny and Camlin. The soil is mainly under grass ; cattle, horses and pigs are raised. Oats and potatoes are main crops. Longford,

the county town, has tanneries and cornmills, and it trades in agricultural produce. St. Mel's Roman Catholic Cathedral is a fine modern edifice.

At Pallas and at Edgeworthstown, Maria Edgeworth (1767–1849), a novelist whose works had considerable influence on Sir Walter Scott and Jane Austen, spent most of her life drawing the characters in her three Irish novels from the local peasantry. The population of the county is 37,100.

**Loom.** The art of weaving fabrics on a loom is very old. It is frequently mentioned in the legends and mythology of ancient Greece. Penelope, wife of Ulysses, was much troubled by many suitors while her husband was absent at the siege of Troy. She baffled them by promising to choose one among them as soon as she had completed a web that she was weaving. Every night she undid what she had woven during the daytime—and so managed to postpone the fateful decision until Ulysses came home and freed her from further importuning, though her stratagem was betrayed at the last.

The earliest looms seem to have been vertical ones, and this type is still much used in the East. The ancient Egyptians used horizontal looms. What is a loom? It comprises some means of stretching tightly a series of parallel threads—the *warp*—and of crossing and interlacing with these threads, in an orderly manner, another set—the *weft*. Examine a piece of coarse fabric, such as sacking or hessian, and you will see the two sets of threads. Or if you look at a handkerchief through a magnifying glass you will see another example.

We illustrate in this page a type of hand-loom used for hundreds of years in Britain. There are two rollers, one at back and the other at front; between them are stretched the warp threads, only a portion being visible horizontally: the rest of the warp is rolled up on the back roller—called the beam, warp or cane roller. The total length of the warp, thus wound, determines how long a piece of cloth can be woven before it is necessary to put on a new warp. The front or breast roller is provided with a ratchet which allows it to be turned, tooth by tooth, without slipping back.

In course of time the weaver, filling in successive " shoots " of weft (the cross-wise threads), gets so close to the comb-like reed hanging from the top frame of the loom that the reed cannot any longer be swung to beat up and lock the weft threads. Then the weaver winds on to the breast roller the cloth he has already woven, and leaves the warp free, further back, for more shoots of the weft.

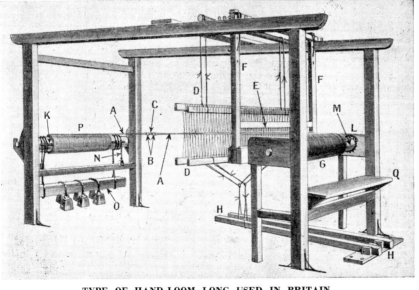

**TYPE OF HAND-LOOM LONG USED IN BRITAIN**
The principal parts are shown. **(A). Warp threads stretching from roller to roller. (B). Lease rods. (C). Porrey cross. (D). Heddles. (E). Reed. (F). Sleigh. (G). Front or breast roller. (H). Treadles. (K). Groove in roller. (L). Pawl and ratchet wheel. (M). Groove in roller. (N). Friction brake. (O). Weight beam. (P). Beam warp or cane roller. (Q). Seat.**

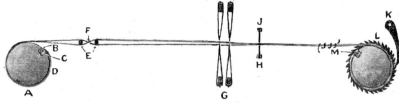

## ESSENTIAL PARTS OF A LOOM

The lettered parts are : A. Beam warp or cane roller ; B. Groove in roller ; C. Cane iron ; D. Portée cross, where there is a cross-over of the warp ; E. Lease rods, over or under which the warp threads pass ; F. Porrey cross ; G. Heddles ; H. Comb or reed ; J. Sleigh or batten ; K. Pawl ; L. Ratchet wheel ; M. Groove in breast roller.

If you look closely at a piece of coarse material you will note that, between each two crosswise threads (of weft), the warp or lengthwise threads go up or down from one face of the cloth to the other side, thus locking firmly the weft threads. This is contrived by means of the heddles and treadles. The threads of the warp are prevented from getting out of order by the two lease rods shown, and by the crossing over of the warp between these rods to form what weavers call the porrey cross.

One thread of the warp will go over the first lease rod and *under* the second rod; the next thread will reverse this order, going under the first and over the second. This simple device keeps the threads separate and apart, and preserves what the weaver calls the shed—or opening between the two sets of warp threads. It is through this shed that the shuttle, containing the thread which will make the weft, is passed from one side to the other—to be brought back again through the shed when opened anew by the heddles.

Following a warp thread as it comes from the back roller, it goes over one and under the other lease rod ; then it goes through an eye in either the back heddle or front heddle (the heddles are looped strands of twine or of wire, hung by a top and bottom lath from the top of the loom), and through a space between two wires or "teeth" of the reed; finally it goes on to the front

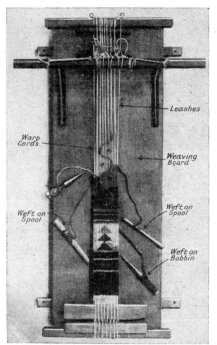

roller. The next thread of the warp follows a similar course, but reverses the path at the porrey cross, going first *under* and next *over* a rod ; it also goes through an eye in the *opposite* heddle to that through which the previous thread was taken. It passes through the *next* space, in order, in the reed. Thus the reed keeps the successive threads separate; if there are only two heddles, all the "even" threads of the warp will go through one, and all the "odd" threads will go through the other heddle.

Each heddle is connected to a treadle by a cord and lever, or by a cord and pulley. By pressing down a treadle, one heddle with its threads is lifted, and the other heddle is lowered. This leaves the opening called the shed. The weaver passes his shuttle through, leaving a thread of weft between the two sets of warp threads. He next swings forward his reed, which is in a weighted framework, and presses each weft thread closely against that already woven.

Next he presses down the opposite treadle: the shed is thus reversed, the warp threads which were at the top now going down, and *vice versa*. This cross-over holds the weft he has just woven, so that each shoot is separated from the last by such a cross-over. The weaving proceeds thus. With two heddles it is possible to weave plain material only. By using four heddles, and leading one-fourth of the warp through each, a, variety of patterns is able to be woven according to the order in which the warp is "entered" and in which the heddles are lifted.

Machine looms have more heddles, and the Jacquard apparatus enables com-

## TWO TYPES OF LOOM FOR HOME USE
The upper picture shows a small board loom, arranged for weaving a narrow piece of tapestry. The table loom (lower) is a portable apparatus, which will take warps up to 33 inches wide. They both work on similar principles—interlacing and interlocking of lengthwise and crosswise threads.

plicated patterns to be woven automatically (*see* Jacquard Loom). But the essential principles of the loom are as we have described. Hand-loom weaving is a favourite hobby; the looms range from a small one, on which braid or neck-ties can be made, to a much bigger one on which we can weave dress material or curtaining. The diagram on page 2024 shows a " standing loom " such as would be used for weaving material up to about 54 inches wide. Of course it takes up a lot of space, and needs a room to itself. Table looms, such as we also show, are compact appliances for home weaving, on which material nearly a yard wide can be made.

Among examples of looms illustrated elsewhere in our volumes are : Persian rug loom, page 706 (the tufts are tied on to a plain warp-and-weft and woven in); and an automatic loom for weaving cotton handkerchiefs, page 920 (on this, the warp is two handkerchiefs wide). Here, then, are the two extremes: a hand-loom differing little from those of the ancients; and a fully automatic loom embodying the latest modern improvements.

**Lorrain,** CLAUDE (1600–82). Many of the world's great painters have been men who from boyhood have followed the profession in which they later found fame; but among those who began life in a very different trade is Claude Gelée, better known as Claude Lorrain. Born in Lorraine, France, in 1600, the son of humble parents, he was trained as a cook, becoming a very able one. As a

cook he went, in an attempt to improve his position, to Rome, and it was there that he first entered the service of an artist, Augustine Tassi. His master soon saw the boy's interest and skill, encouraged him, and enlisted his help in the studio, eventually teaching him to paint. Once started, Claude soon felt confident enough to return to his own country, devoting himself to his new profession. After two years he was in Rome again, where he remained from 1627 until he died, on November 21, 1682.

Fame did not come easily to Claude Lorrain, nor, when it came, did it turn his head. Himself no figure painter, rather than mar his masterpieces he had the figures put in by experts. Although they often give the clue to the titles of Claude's pictures, these figures are small and insignificant; for, above all, he was a painter of classical landscape.

He has never lacked admirers, and his best works are highly prized. One treasure is Claude's Libri di Verità, an album of several hundred monochrome sketches of his chief works, evidently kept by him for reference, with many notes. Like other French painters of his day, Claude Lorrain was also a fine etcher. But it is as the first landscape master, and as the man who set the standard for the British artist Turner (*q.v.*) that he is best remembered.

**Los Angeles.** (Pron. los-ang'-gel-éz, or los-an'-jel-ēz). In California, between the San Gabriel Mountains and the Pacific coast, is one of the largest cities of the United States—Los Angeles.

Within a short distance of the city can be found almost every type of world scenery. This advantage, added to the warm climate and almost perpetual sunshine, has made the city (or, rather, the section known as Hollywood) the centre of the film industry of the United States and of the world.

But Los Angeles is not dependent on the motion picture industry for its prosperity. It is one of the leading ports of the United States, and within the city's boundaries are some of the richest oilfields in the world. In the manufacture of aircraft the Los Angeles area is predominant ; other industries are food processing, the manufacture of tires, machinery, and women's clothes. In the heart of a fruit-growing region, it is a centre from which enormous quantites of oranges and lemons are distributed every year.

Educational and cultural institutions are numerous. There are three Universities—the University of South California, the University of California, and Loyola University, and also the Los Angeles City College. The California Institute at Pasadena is one of the leading scientific and technical schools in the United States.

*Dorien Leigh*

**TOWN OF BEVERLY HILLS, LOS ANGELES**
In the course of its rapid growth the city of Los Angeles has surrounded a number of towns, including Beverly Hills (above) which still retain their municipal governments. Many of the film stars live in Beverly Hills, but the centre of the motion picture industry is at Hollywood, which is a section of the city proper. Los Angeles has an area of 451 square miles, much of which is agricultural land or semi-arid and is but sparsely populated.

Los Angeles was founded in 1781 by a Spanish Governor of California, Felipe de Neve, and named *El Pueblo de Nuestra Señora la Reina de Los Angeles de Portiuncula*—the Town of Our Lady Queen of the Angels of Portiuncula. In 1846 it was taken from Mexico by the United States. The population is 1,504,270.

**Lothians.** There are three Scottish counties to the south of the Firth of Forth named Lothian— West Lothian (area 120 square miles, population 83,900), sometimes known as Linlithgowshire; Midlothian, formerly Edinburghshire (area 370 square miles, population 565,800); and East Lothian, formerly Haddingtonshire (area 267 square miles, population 48,800).

Picturesque ranges of hills cover these counties, including the Pentlands and the Moorfoots in Midlothian, rising in several places to over 2,000 feet, and the Lammermuirs along the southern boundary of East Lothian, giving their name to Sir Walter Scott's Bride of Lammermoor. Besides Edinburgh (*q.v.*), which is the county town of Midlothian, there are few large towns.

Linlithgow (population 3,600) is the county town of West Lothian, with a ruined palace in which Mary Queen of Scots was born. South Queensferry stands at the southern end of the Forth railway bridge, carrying the main line north from Edinburgh. Near Musselburgh, in Midlothian, is the battlefield of Pinkie where the English defeated the Scots in 1547; and in East Lothian is Prestonpans, scene of a defeat of British troops by Scottish rebels in 1745. In East Lothian, Haddington (population

**ORIENTAL LOTUS**
The sacred lotus of the East is this oriental water-lily *Nelumbium speciosum*, with white flowers and round leaves.

4,000) is the county town; while on the coast are several popular holiday resorts, such as North Berwick (with a famed golf-course) and Dunbar.

**Lotus.** When people read in Homer's Odyssey of the magical lotus fruit which caused those who ate it to forget country, friends and home, many think of the Egyptian lotus, the sacred water-lily of the Nile (*Nymphaea lotus*), with its white or rose-coloured petals. But to the ancient Greeks the lotus probably meant a prickly shrub (*Zizyphus lotus*) with a sweet mealy fruit, which is still eaten in some Mediterranean districts and also used for making wine. It is a relative of the British buckthorns. The sacred lotus of the Chinese and Buddhists is a water-lily much like the Egyptian lotus, and so is the lotus of North America.

Then there is the lotus tree of the Romans, probably the species now called nettle tree (*Celtis australis*), which is a relative of the elms. Finally, botanists restrict the term lotus to a genus of the pea family (*Leguminosae*), containing many species of herbs and low shrubs found in temperate regions of the Old World. A common British representative is the bird's-foot trefoil (*Lotus corniculatus*) which is abundant in pasture and wasteland; from a perennial woody rootstock rise tufted stems, bearing leaves divided into four or five oval leaflets, and its clusters of bright yellow, pea-like flowers, blooming all summer, are succeeded by slender curved pods.

A lotus design is conspicuous throughout ancient Egyptian, Indian, Chinese and Japanese art, while many Greek ornaments have a similar derivation.

# A Royal NAME in FRANCE for 1,300 YEARS

*This is the story of the long line of French kings, good and bad, named Louis. Among them are Louis the Fat, the mighty eater ; Saint Louis ; Louis the Sun King, and others of equal interest.*

**Louis,** KINGS OF FRANCE. Throughout 13 centuries this name figures more prominently— sometimes nobly, at other times ignobly—than any other in the history of France. Clovis or Chlodowech (*c.* 466–511), the founder of the kingdom of the Franks, may be considered the first of the numerous French kings to bear the name of Louis. In after years the C was dropped, and the v was written as a u, thus making the modern name of Louis (pron. lōō-ēē). It is the same as the British Lewis and German Ludwig.

But the Louis who is usually reckoned the first in France's royal line was Charlemagne's third son, who succeeded his father as king and emperor, and is called Louis the Pious (778–840). The next four, all of this Carolingian line, call for no mention here.

LOUIS VI (1078–1137), however, was a very different ruler. Although he was rightly called " the Fat," he is the first of the new Capetian

kings (his father, Hugh Capet, ascended the throne in 987) who in any way deserves to be called great. This Louis was a great fighter, a great hunter, and a great eater, and at 46 he became too fat to mount a horse.

But he remained the embodiment of warlike energy. His chief task was to reduce to order the petty nobles of the kingdom, who were truly robber barons. When Louis came to the throne (1108) every lord robbed travellers at will, and it was not safe for even the king to pass along the road. Twenty years of fighting were necessary before the king triumphed, and law and order prevailed. And to make certain that such evils might not recur, Louis ordered every castle that was captured to be destroyed or given to faithful followers.

LOUIS VII (born 1120; reigned 1137–80) is remembered chiefly for the divorce of his wife, Eleanor, who then married Henry II of England;

by this marriage the rich province of Aquitaine in southern France, the dowry of Queen Eleanor, passed from France to England.

LOUIS VIII (1187–1226), son of Philip Augustus, reigned for only three years (1223–26).

LOUIS IX (born 1214; reigned 1226–70), Saint Louis, as he was called, is, perhaps, the most heroic and popular in the whole procession of French monarchs. He was the dutiful, religious son of Louis VIII and his queen, Blanche of Castile. His widowed mother often told him that she would much rather see him dead than have him commit a mortal sin. She herself was a remarkable woman and during her son's minority dauntlessly faced the numerous revolts of the nobles.

In her son she was fortunate, for he possessed all the good qualities and few of the bad ones of the age in which he lived; indeed, his virtues were so remarkable that after his death the Church declared him a saint. His acts of piety, however, such as wearing a hair-cloth shirt, fasting, and waiting on lepers, were known to few. To the world he was a fearless knight, thoroughly trained in the art of war; a conscientious, just, and able king, who was usually good-humoured and kindly, but at times became impatient and angry; and a strong ruler, who greatly strengthened the royal power. He improved the government by appointing local officials who were responsible to him for the administration of justice, the collection of taxes, and the government of their districts. He encouraged the people to appeal to him if the nobles oppressed them, or if his officials proved unjust. He also improved the administration of justice by abolishing trials by combat, and by using in his courts the new lawyers trained in the Roman law, in place of the churchmen who, formerly, alone could read and write. Saint Louis made two Crusades—one to Egypt and the Holy Land (1248–54), when he was captured and held to ransom by the Saracens; the other to Tunis, in 1270, where he died of the plague on August 25.

LOUIS X (1289–1316) ruled for but two years, 1314–16.

LOUIS XI (born 1423; reigned 1461–83) presents a striking contrast to Louis IX. In appearance Louis XI was ugly and unkingly; in character he was unscrupulous, cunning, and underhanded. He firmly believed that "he who has success has honour," and he cared nothing for the way in which he attained success. He made promises only to break them, unless he had sworn by one particular saint. His one ambition seemed to be to extend the boundaries of France, and although he was too mean to buy a new hat to replace the shabby old one he wore, he spent large sums in buying back border cities. In his conflicts with the nobles, especially with Charles the Bold, Duke of Burgundy, he also acquired much territory, so that by the time of his death most of the land of France had been brought under the direct control of the king. The power of the crown in the latter part of his reign was truly absolute over the territory it held. Sir Walter Scott, in his novel Quentin Durward, gives a very fine pen-portrait of Louis XI, as well as an intimate survey of the customs and traditions of the period.

LOUIS XII (born 1462; reigned 1498–1515) is chiefly noted for the Italian wars, begun by his predecessor Charles VIII, and continued after Louis XII by Francis I.

LOUIS XIII (born 1601; reigned 1610–43) is chiefly important for the fact that, in spite of all opposition, he for 18 years kept in power his able minister, Richelieu (q.v.). The first years of the reign, while the king was a youth, were filled with anarchy and disorder. When

*The Panthéon, Paris; photo Bulloz*
**ST. LOUIS CAPTURED BY THE SARACENS**
After the capture of Jerusalem by the Saracens in 1244, St. Louis (Louis IX) of France led the Seventh Crusade to recover the Holy City. Starting in 1248 he invaded Egypt, but was taken prisoner at Mansura, near Damietta, in December 1249. In this painting by A. Cabanel he is seen during his captivity, facing a group of Saracen chiefs.

### LOUIS XIV—THE 'SUN KING'—AND HIS FAMILY

The reign of Louis XIV of France was so brilliant that he was known as le roi soleil (the sun king), and his court certainly shone with a glory never seen before or since in France. In this painting by Nicolas Largillière (1656–1746) the king is seen (seated), with Mme. de Maintenon, once his children's governess and later his wife (left). The other figures in the group are Louis XIV's son, the dauphin or heir to the throne (standing centre) ; his grandson, the Duke of Burgundy (right) ; and the latter's child, Louis XIV's great-grandson, the Duke of Anjou, who became Louis XV.

Richelieu came into power, however, all this was changed. The Huguenots (q.v.) were reduced from a powerful political party to a mere religious body, and the nobles were humbled. National unity and religious peace were secured at home, and France was raised to a great position.

Louis XIV (born 1638; reigned 1643–1715) inherited this power from his father and carried it further. He was styled the *Grand Monarque* and the Sun King, and his brilliant court at Versailles became the model and the despair of other less rich and powerful princes, who accepted his theory of absolute monarchy (*l'Etat c'est moi*, I am the State). Until 1661 the government was largely in the hands of the wily Italian, Cardinal Mazarin. But at the Cardinal's death Louis declared that he would be his own Prime Minister, and from then on he worked faithfully at " his trade of a king."

A passion for fame and the desire to increase French territory in Europe were the leading motives of Louis XIV. His first war (1667–68) was an attempt to enforce flimsy claims to a portion of the Spanish Netherlands. His second (1672–78) was directed against the States-General of Holland, who had balked him of his prey in the first contest. In spite of the great military power of France, the Dutch admiral De Ruyter twice defeated the fleets of the French and their English

allies, and Louis XIV failed ingloriously in his attempt to conquer Holland. The third war (1689–97) also was directed chiefly against Holland, whose ruler had now become King William III of England. The German province of the Palatinate was laid waste, but the Peace of Ryswick brought only slight gains for France.

Louis's last and greatest effort was the War of the Spanish Succession (1701–13), in which the Duke of Marlborough (*see* Marlborough, First Duke of) was the chief leader of the opposing forces. The right to seat his grandson Philip V on the diminished throne of Spain was small compensation for the thousands of lives and millions of treasure which the French king wilfully wasted in the struggle and for the humiliation inflicted on France by the Treaty of Utrecht, which ended the struggle.

Millions more were spent by Louis XIV in building the beautiful palace at Versailles, near Paris, and in maintaining his brilliant court. This extravagance meant a heavy burden of taxation for the people, who were thereby reduced to a misery so great that three-quarters of a century later they rose up in rebellion and drove the Bourbons from the throne.

Louis XIV had the distinction of ruling longer than any other European king; for it was nearly 73 years from the time when he ascended the throne, as a child of less than five, until his death in 1715. He had outlived his son and his son's son, so that he was succeeded by his great-grandson.

Louis XV (1710–74). The luxury of the court of Louis XIV was continued under his weak successor, who also came to the throne at the age of five (1715). The evils from which the country suffered were clearly recognized and the people grew increasingly more discontented with misgovernment; but the king when he grew up was too lazy and selfish to remedy the growing troubles.

Louis XVI (1754–93). The storm broke in the reign of the just but irresolute Louis XVI. He was awkward and timid, and no man could have appeared less like a king than did Louis XVI, who was 20 years old when he became king (1774). Louis realized his defects, and often wished, even before the Revolution, that he were only a common man. When he first came to the throne he entrusted the management of the finances of the kingdom to Turgot, one of the greatest of statesmen, and as long as the king followed his minister's advice the state of the kingdom was improved. But he was more often under the influence of his beautiful but frivolous and extravagant queen, Marie Antoinette, and of self-seeking courtiers. These all opposed any financial reforms, which would threaten their position and salary, their pensions and life of ease, and they soon persuaded the king to dismiss his able minister.

From this time on things went from bad to worse, and in 1789 Louis XVI was forced to call the States-General, a body which had not met since 1614. Its meeting was the first step in the French Revolution (q.v.). Most of the members demanded the granting of greater powers to the States-General which up till then had been little more than an advisory body to the King, and finally they declared themselves a National Assembly or Parliament.

At first the king seemed inclined to work with the Revolution and try to remedy conditions in the country. But the influence of the queen and of the courtiers proved too strong for his feeble will. Encouraged by them, he disregarded the promises he had made, and in June 1791 sought to flee from France, so that he might obtain aid against the revolution from Austria.

This attempted flight was the beginning of the end. The people saw that they could not trust the king and the "Austrian woman," as they called the queen. His disregard of his promises to abide by the newly-established constitution led to the storming of the royal palace of the Tuileries on August 10, 1792.

The king and his family escaped before the mob arrived, and took refuge in the hall of the National Assembly. That body declared the king to be suspended from office, and ordered that he and his family should be imprisoned. They convened a new assembly (the Convention) which decided to abolish the monarchy and declared the king deposed. Louis XVI was tried on the charge of combining with foreign countries for the invasion of France. Almost unanimously Louis Capet, as he was now called, was declared guilty and was sentenced to death. On January 21, 1793, he was beheaded, meeting his fate with courage.

Louis XVI's son, the Dauphin (born 1785), who perished mysteriously in prison, is counted as Louis XVII, though he never ruled.

Louis XVIII (1755–1824). When the Bourbons were restored to the throne of France by the Allies after the defeat of Napoleon Bonaparte in 1814, the younger brother of Louis XVI assumed the crown as Louis XVIII. The difficult task of reconstruction was before the king, but he seemed admirably adapted to meet the situation. He was a lazy man, and his one ambition was to keep his throne. This

### LOUIS XVI AND HIS QUEEN FLEE FROM THE REVOLUTION

In June 1791 Louis XVI and Marie Antoinette, his wife, with their children attempted to escape from Paris, where they had been held virtually prisoners by the revolutionaries in the palace of the Tuileries. This contemporary aquatint shows the arrest of the fugitives at Varennes at eleven o'clock at night. A retired soldier recognized the king from his portrait on a bank note and warned the local authorities. The royal family was brought back to Paris the following day.

*Musée de Versailles, photo, Neurdein*

## LOUIS PHILIPPE TESTS HIS POPULARITY

After the Revolution of July 1830 the French set up a new government, naming the Duke of Orleans (later King Louis Philippe) as lieutenant-general of the realm. The Citizen King, as he was later called, decided to test popular opinion on his acceptance of the office—by driving through Paris from the royal palace to the Hôtel de Ville, the headquarters of the revolutionary government. This painting by Vernet (1758–1835) shows the beginning of the perilous journey.

ambition seemed likely at first to go unfulfilled, for in 1815 Napoleon escaped from his exile on the Mediterranean island of Elba, and Louis XVIII fled in a panic from France. Once again Napoleon was overthrown, this time at Waterloo, and Louis once more returned to Paris.

Until 1820 the king was able to resist the demands of the extreme royalists for vengeance against those who had supported the Revolution. But they became too strong for him. His yielding to their demands for a more despotic form of government marks the beginning of the end of the Bourbons, for 10 years later, under his brother Charles X, they were driven finally from the throne of France.

LOUIS PHILIPPE (1773–1850). Having in 1830 disposed of the Bourbons, the French had to set up a new government. Influenced by Lafayette (*q.v.*) they decided to keep France a monarchy, with Louis Philippe, a member of the Orléans family related to the Bourbons, as king. Louis Philippe was known for his informal habits, and was given the title of the Citizen King. He walked the streets of Paris alone, carrying a green umbrella and talking with strangers, and his children were sent to the public schools. But his government tended to curtail the newly-won rights of the lower classes and the people were no better off than before. Only the wealthy had profited by the Revolution

of 1830. Demands for a government more in keeping with the times were refused by Louis Philippe and his minister Guizot.

When the government forbade a banquet organized by supporters of political reform and which was to be held on February 22, 1848, the Republicans of Paris revolted. Guizot was forced to resign, but this did not satisfy the rioters, and Louis Philippe abdicated on February 24, naming as his successor the Comte de Paris, his grandson, whom the Chamber of Deputies refused to accept. Then Louis Philippe fled to England, where he died on August 26, 1850.

**Louisiana.** (Pron. loo-iz-i-ah'-na). On the Gulf of Mexico at the mouth of the Mississippi river, this southern state of the United States includes the wide delta of the river, on which stands the city of New Orleans (*q.v.*), and also a smaller district to the east of the main stream, containing Baton Rouge (population, 34,710), the State capital. The whole surface of Louisiana, which is generally flat and fertile, is criss-crossed by minor waterways. With an area of 48,523 square miles, it produces sugar, rice, cereals, cotton, oil, timber, natural gas, sulphur and salt. Main industries are sugar refining, the manufacture of carbon black, the processing of food, rice cleaning and polishing, and the preparation of cotton seed cake and oil. Louisiana has had an eventful career, being at first (1682) a French possession, then Spanish, and French again in 1800; in 1803 it was purchased from France by the United States, but was not admitted to the Union until 1812. The population is 2,363,880, of whom 849,300 are of Negro blood.

**Louth,** EIRE. Although the smallest county in Eire, having an area of 317 square miles, Louth is one of the comparatively rich counties of the province of Leinster. The soil is good and well farmed ; barley, potatoes and flax are grown. Lead ore is worked on the boundaries of Armagh and Monaghan. The deep-sea, coastal, and salmon fisheries, centred at Dundalk, give employment to many. In Carlingford Lough there are oyster beds of great value. The main Belfast-Dublin railway crosses the county, with branches to Greenore and Dundalk. The county town and administrative centre is Dundalk (population, 13,000) on the river Castleford. Drogheda, at the mouth of the Boyne, figures in history as the scene of the Cromwellian massacres and as a stronghold of both Danes and Normans. The population of the county is 65,100.

**Louvain.** "In this dear city of Louvain, perpetually in my thoughts, the magnificent church of St. Peter will never recover its former splendour. The ancient college of St. Ives, the art schools, the consular and commercial schools of the university, the old markets, our rich library with its collections,

LOUVAIN'S TOWN HALL
One of the finest buildings in Belgium, the Town Hall in Louvain is a late Gothic work begun in 1448 and completed 21 years later. It survived both World Wars.

its unique and unpublished manuscripts, its gallery of great portraits—all this accumulation of intellectual, of historic, and of artistic riches, the fruits of the labour of five centuries—all is dust." So wrote Cardinal Mercier after the deliberate burning of Louvain by the German army in August 1914. Over 1,200 houses were destroyed.

This picturesque Belgian town is situated on the River Dyle, distant some 19 miles by rail from Brussels. Its chief interest lies in its Town Hall, one of the most beautiful Gothic buildings in the world; the restored cathedral; and the Catholic university, at one time the most noted in Europe.

In the 14th and 15th centuries, when Louvain was at the zenith of its prosperity, it was one of the principal cloth-making centres in Europe. Since then its decline has been rapid and its population has greatly decreased. Brewing and distilling, printing, and the manufacture of tobacco, lace, and starch are the most important industries. During the Second World War (1939–45), Louvain was captured by German forces in May 1940, the library being again destroyed. The city was liberated by British troops on September 4, 1944. The population is about 41,000.

**Louvre,** THE. (Pron. loo'-vr). In Paris is a treasure-house that has no rival. This is the Louvre, formerly a palace of the kings of France, now containing a museum of art and antiquities. It would take two hours to walk, without stopping, through this great building, which adjoins the Jardin des Tuileries on the right bank of the Seine. Many days would be needed to study and absorb the wonder and beauty of its contents.

Even if it were empty this palace would be famous for its own sake. Some of its foundations are as old as Magna Carta (1215); part of it was built by King Francis I of France, who was taken prisoner in war with Spain in 1525; and the last gallery to be finished, much nearer our own time, is not unworthy of the rest of this stately home of art. This gallery alone has 16 statues of great Frenchmen and 63 groups of allegorical statues. The gallery of Apollo, 200 feet long, is one of the finest halls in the world, panelled with priceless tapestries; dating from Louis XIV's reign, it has in it all that is left of the crown jewels of France.

The treasure of the Louvre is beyond all calculation. There are 3,000 ancient sculptures (including the incomparable Venus de Milo), 2,500 pictures and many thousands of drawings by the great artists of all nations. There are the best Raphaels in Europe, Titians in abundance and other masterpieces, like Leonardo da Vinci's Mona Lisa. There are six rooms full of antiquities from Assyria and Phoenicia, five rooms full of sculptures of the Middle Ages rescued from ruined churches at the time of the French Revolution (1789–95), five rooms that speak to us of " the glory that was Greece and the grandeur that was Rome," two halls with relics of the Egypt of the Pharaohs, and five rooms filled with statues representing the work of modern French sculptors.

**Loyola,** IGNATIUS DE (1491–1556). Until his leg was shattered by a cannon-ball at the siege of Pampeluna (1521) in Spain, the future founder of the religious order called the Society of Jesus was known only as a courtly Spanish nobleman and

Once the palace of the French kings, the Louvre in Paris possesses one of the finest art collections in the world. The central view (4) is of the north façade, facing the Tuileries gardens. The other pictures show a few of the more celebrated treasures. (1) Elizabeth Vigée Lebrun's (1755–1842) portrait of herself and daughter; (2) ancient mirror; (3) statue of the goddess Artemis from the Roman town of Gabii; (5) Venus de Milo; (6) antique vase, formerly belonging to the Borghese, a noble Italian family; (7) La Gioconda or Mona Lisa, by Leonardo da Vinci (1452–1519).

**LOYOLA, FOUNDER OF THE JESUITS**
The hollow cheeks and burning eyes of the saint in this likeness from a
Rubens painting bespeak the ascetic and mystic. A holy man himself,
Loyola inspired holiness in others, not least in the members of the Jesuit
Order (or Society of Jesus) which he founded.

soldier. The reading of the lives of the saints during his long convalescence turned him from the quest of military glory and made him a soldier of Christ. His sword and dagger he hung up on the altar of a monastery chapel; his worldly garments he gave to the poor, taking a pilgrim's dress of sackcloth and hempen shoes, with a staff and gourd. Seven hours a day he spent on his knees in prayer and thrice a day he scourged his wasted body.

With difficulty Loyola (pron. loi-ō'-la) travelled to Jerusalem, but he was not allowed by the authorities to remain and labour there as he had planned. Back in Spain, at the age of 32, he again became a schoolboy to learn the Latin needed for his religious studies. The next 10 years he spent at schools and universities in Spain and in Paris. Meanwhile, his plans were taking more definite form. He would found a Society of Jesus—spiritually drilled and disciplined like a military company—to combat all religions other than the Roman Catholic and do missionary work in heathen countries. The members should be bound by vows of poverty, chastity and implicit obedience.

In 1534 Loyola and six companions formed in Paris the beginning of the powerful organization known as the Society of Jesus, or Jesuits as they are called for short. In 1540 its members received at Rome the sanction of the Pope, and Loyola became its first general or commanding officer. The remainder of his life—he died at Rome on July 31, 1556—was employed in working out, with infinite skill, the constitution of his order, and

preparing it for its conflict with the Protestant Reformation. In 1622 Pope Gregory XV canonized him as St. Ignatius Loyola.

**Lucerne.** Also known as alfalfa, this plant, *Medicago sativa*, is a member of the pea, bean and clover tribe, *Leguminosae*. Its purple, pea-type flowers are borne in clusters on tall, hollow, upright stems. In Britain, and elsewhere, it is one of the most valuable crops for fresh green forage, for hay, and for storage in its green state for the winter feeding of cattle. It can be cut two, or three, times in a year; biggest crops are obtained in the third year; and the plants occupy the land for seven or eight years.

Like all members of its order, this perennial is valuable as a nitrate gatherer. The free nitrogen is drawn from the air and stored in nodules, or knots, formed on the roots by certain bacteria. The roots go down very deeply and thus are able to draw upon moisture and nourishment untouched by other crops. On this account it is particularly valuable in drought years, and for use in rotation with crops which draw heavily upon the surface soil. (*See* Nitrogen).

One of the oldest forage crops known to Man, lucerne was grown in central Asia under the name of al-fac-fac-ah, which means "the best feed," and was introduced into Greece at the time of the Persian wars in the 5th century B.C. The Romans carried it from Greece into Italy and then to Spain and southern France. At the time of the Spanish conquests in the New

*International Harvester*
**LUCERNE AND ITS NODULES**
A valuable fodder plant, lucerne (left) also actually enriches the soil. Free nitrogen from the air is transformed into nitrates by bacteria in the root nodules (right), and when the crop is harvested the nitrates remain in the ground.

World it was taken to Mexico and South America. It arrived in California about 1854, probably brought there by gold-seekers from Chile, and then spread throughout the United States. In Britain it may be found growing wild, not as a native plant but as an " escape " from cultivated fields.

**Lucknow.** (Pron. luk'-now). When the storm of the Indian Mutiny broke in June 1857, the British soldier, Sir Henry Lawrence, took refuge with all the European inhabitants and a few troops in the British Residency in Lucknow. He put it into a state of defence, and entrenched the surrounding 60 acres. His force consisted of 1,720 men, of whom 712 were loyal Indian soldiers and 153 British civilians. He had to defend 1,280 old men, women, and children, without artillery or a great supply of ammunition. He died from a wound received in the early part of the siege, which lasted from July 1 to September 25.

On September 25 Generals Havelock and Outram with about 2,500 men joined the defenders, now reduced to fewer than 1,000. The combined forces, however, could not cut their way out and the siege continued. The situation became desperate. Then from the top of the Residency they saw the signals of Sir Colin Campbell, who was advancing to their relief from Cawnpore. Campbell recaptured Lucknow, and on November 17 broke through and joined forces with the weary defenders in the Residency. Havelock died soon after the relief.

Lucknow, which is in the United Provinces of the republic of India, is a great commercial and railway centre, the industries including the manufacture of silk, muslin, glass, cement and paper. There are many schools for European and Indian children, and a university. It is situated on the River Gumti, mainly on the right bank, and is one of the largest cities of the sub-continent of India in point of population, which is 387,000.

# TIMBER'S TALE *from* FOREST *to* SAWMILL

*A picturesque and dangerous life is that of the lumberjack in the forests of the Canadian north, and his work is of the greatest value to mankind. Here we see something of his activities—and what comes after.*

**Lumbering.** The term " lumber," in British usage, means roughly prepared timber; in American phraseology it is used for timber generally, and lumbering means the logging and sawing of timber. That is why, in our text and pictures describing the lumbering industry as it is carried on in North America, and other great timber-growing regions, you will find much which in Britain applies to sawmill operations.

Most timber used in Britain is imported, already in sawn form, as balks, planks, and deals or battens. In our sawmills it is further reduced in size to suit the needs of builders and others ordering the wood. The balk is a log with the outsides cut off and squared in section. The plank is about 10 in. wide and 2 in. thick. Deals are more than 2 in. thick and less than 10 in. wide. Pieces of timber from 1½ in. to 2½ in. thick and less than 9 in. wide are called battens (but this name is used also for sawn timber of about 1 in. to 2½ or 3 in. width, and ½ in. to 1 in. thick). The name " deal " is used in the timber trade for the wood of some firs and of Scotch pine—as well as to specify a certain size of timber, as mentioned above.

Lumbering in Canada includes various processes from opening up the forest to cutting the trees, transporting the logs, and " converting " them into timber in marketable widths, thicknesses and lengths. Each of the great forest regions of the world has methods adapted to the particular conditions that exist there; but it is in the northern woods of America and eastern Canada that lumbering is most picturesque. Here much of the work is done when the forests are locked in the winter's ice and snow. In the spring the lumber workers float the logs downstream to a place where they can be taken to the sawmills—usually not far away.

Not so very long ago, a lumber camp in the northern woods was a settlement of log huts huddled together. The largest of the huts would be one large room with bunks arranged round the walls two or three tiers high. The cooking hut was also one large room with a huge range and cooking table at one end. Here were long tables, laid with dishes, plates, and mugs; there were knives and forks of heavy steel with iron handles.

Then there were the stables, much like the other huts or shanties, but with lower roofs so that the animal heat of the horses and the oxen would help to keep them warm. The blacksmith's shop, the storehouse, and the log hut serving for the office of the camp clerk formed the minor buildings.

Modern lumbering has, in all but the most remote or smallest posts, produced not a camp but a regular town. Transport facilities are so much greater that a far wider area can be covered from one centre, and such a centre can therefore be much more permanent. Thus, not only have the oxen and horses once used for lumber transport been superseded by hundreds of miles of railways but each lumbering town has its schools, churches, cinema, shops, and all the other conveniences which might reasonably be expected where many hundreds of men with their families are working and living together.

Electricity and the internal combustion engine have also changed the lot of the lumberjack. Streams can be harnessed to provide power and light, and the electrically-operated overhead cable-way is now a usual means of transport for logs. Moreover, modern lumbering is organized to do as much as possible of the work on the spot. Often the wood is sawn up into the standard lengths and sizes and prepared completely for the market quite close to where it was felled, so that instead of several stops for various processes between forest and timber-yard there may be only one. Time and money are thus saved and the industry is speeded up.

In spite of all this, the methods of felling have changed but little. A tree which has been marked

# FOUR SCENES IN THE LIFE OF A LUMBER LOG

It is in winter, when the ground is covered with snow, that the woodmen or lumb... ... ... ... The frozen ground makes it easier for men and tractors to penetrate the depths of the forests. All the trees to be felled are marked the previous autumn by experts, who can judge when they are ready to be made into lumber. When it is possible the trees are so felled that they lie pointing downhill, thus making it easier for them to be removed.

How do these immense logs get to the sawmill ? By various means, and like human travellers sometimes they have to 'change.' Here we see one of the ways in which they are moved—a sloping wooden runway in which the logs are placed and hauled by horses. Occasionally the runway is greased ; but when there is snow the work is simple, the first logs packing the snow firmly so that the remainder of them glide really swiftly down the slippery surface.

Here is a method of loading in the summer. The logs are lifted on to motor lorries, in a clearing, by a block and tackle arrangement called a 'skidder,' mounted on caterpillar tracks, the actual hoisting being done by a steam engine which is mounted on the skidder platform. The logs are guided to their place on the load by two men.

Sometimes a convenient mountain stream is harnessed and made to convey logs out of the woods in the manner shown above. A sluice-way is built and the stream, or a portion of it, is turned into the upper part. Then the logs are dumped in, and rush down the slide in the water until they arrive at the collecting point at the bottom of the sluice-way.

for cutting is first notched with the axe. This notch is a foot or more deep on the side towards which the tree is to fall, and governs the direction of the fall. A tree may be completely severed by the axemen, who are so accurate that they can drive into the ground with the fall of the tree a stake set 50 feet from its foot. More usually, however, the felling is done by sawyers, using a long double-handed saw, one man at each end, on the side of the trunk opposite the notch. Steel wedges, driven into the saw-cut, prevent it from closing, and thus binding the saw. Tall trees are usually "topped," by having the top 50 feet or so cut off before the real task of felling is begun. Much felling is done today with power-saws driven by an electric motor or an internal combustion engine.

When the tree falls, the branches are cleared off and the trunk is measured and cut into logs. The cross-cutting is often done with a powered chain-saw, much like a great cycle-chain armed with saw-teeth. The logs are then hauled to the road, which was cut and levelled in the autumn. Sometimes, however, they can be run straight on to a chute or sluice of running water, while in the more highly developed areas they are drawn off by tractors, taken by overhead cable-ways or even loaded, almost directly, on to the lumber railway. When the logs are floated down a river, after the spring thaw, the men travel with them, sometimes along shore and sometimes riding the rafts or even single logs. They watch the logs closely so that they do not get caught in the rapids or jam at a bend of the stream.

When the logs reach a larger river or great lake they are sometimes formed into rafts or booms and towed by a tug. For a long time the River Mississippi was a great highway for lumber rafts, but of late years logging has practically ceased below St. Paul. The River Ottawa in Canada is now the most important stream for this picturesque and adventurous type of lumbering.

In most parts of Canada and America railways are used to handle the log supply. The railway consists of a permanent main line, and of spurs which are projected into the forest and are moved from time to time as the timber is taken out. A steam skidder, operating on the railway track, pulls the logs to the railway line. There they are picked up by a steam loader, which is a crane with a swinging boom, and loaded on flat trucks. On arrival at the mills, logs are probably not needed immediately and they are therefore stored in large ponds or pools, where they will keep almost indefinitely and the seasoning process begins.

A great sawmill—or "lumber manufacturing plant," as it is now more suitably termed—in operation is one of the most interesting places to visit. Formerly circular saws—mounted one above and one below for big logs—were used; but today this type is employed in the big mills only for trimming boards and for similar minor operations. The sawing of logs is done entirely by band-saws. The actual saw is an endless band of tempered steel, with teeth cut in one edge; it is so mounted, on great wheels like pulleys, that it makes a continuous band, travelling at a rapid speed over one wheel above and another below the saw-pit. The wheel mounting is so contrived that the band is under tension. Such saws move at more than 20 times the speed of a "reciprocating" saw, one which moves to and fro. Often a number of band-saws

## WHAT HAPPENS WHEN LOGS REACH THE MILLS

A log from which several boards have been sawn is seen in the left photograph. It rides on a carriage which moves it to and fro against a band-saw. The man at the big lever controls the machinery which shifts the log on the carriage in such a way that the planks or boards are cut the correct thickness. Band-saws are flexible toothed strips of steel, which run over drums. Much of the sawn timber may next go to the planing mill (right) for smoothing. This planed timber is eventually used for flooring, the lining of roofs, joinery, and for many other general building purposes.

**STACKING PLANKS TO DRY**

As it comes from the sawmill, timber is stacked in layers for natural seasoning, to allow air to circulate freely between the boards and so dry them. Here a hand-operated lift is carrying planks up to the men who are building the pile.

are mounted in " gangs," so that the entire operation of sawing the log into boards is done with one forward movement of the log carriage, which presses the log up to the saws. Some band-saws are mounted so that the blade is horizontal instead of vertical; this type is used for cutting off the outside pieces of a log when squaring it into a balk.

Probably most of us have seen the more common type of circular saw, mounted on a bench or platform, along which the piece of timber travels. But there is another sort, which can be swung in its overhead mounting like a gigantic pendulum to cut its way through the log. Circular saws of today often have false teeth! The qualities in steel which are best for the toothed part of the saw are often not so desirable for the inner portion. Also, no matter how carefully the teeth were tempered, the sawing through hardwood logs tended to break them off. So saw-makers now make the teeth separately, and lock them in the blade by means of grooved slots and wedges, so when one breaks or wears out a new tooth is easily inserted.

The product of the old-time sawmill was rough lumber, but now the operation usually does not stop at that point. A planing mill is operated together with the sawmill, and the lumber is cut into smooth-faced boards or shaped into mouldings and like products; for the building trade complete doors, window frames, etc., may be made on the spot. The lumber as it comes from the saw is " green " or wet and must be dried before it is shipped to market. This is done by stacking it in a yard for a long time with slips of wood between to allow a free current of air to circulate. But for such ordinary timber air-drying is giving place to kiln-drying, for example, by putting it through a steam kiln—this method taking a few weeks at most instead of several years. Timber for important uses, and most hardwood, is still seasoned by the slower natural process. (*See* Forests; Timber; Trees).

**Lung-fish.** " Can a fish live out of water? " The answer given by most people would be " No! " But the curator of the aquarium at a Zoo opens a package he has just received from Africa and finds inside a ball of dried mud. It is hard to crack open, so he drops it in a big fresh-water tank. The dried mud melts, and out of the black mass a long eel-shaped creature uncurls and swims away looking for food. This lung-fish, or mud-fish, *Protopterus annectans*, has a close relative, *Lepidosiren*, in South American river swamps, called by the Indian natives lolach; they are about 12 inches long. A more distant cousin in Australia is known as the barramunda.

During the dry seasons the African and South American species, left without water, hibernate in the mud, breathing by means of the air-bladder (*see* Fishes) which, in their case, does duty for lungs; otherwise, when the streams and rivers are flowing freely, they breathe through gills in the ordinary way. The mud " cells " they construct are quite substantial, and together with their hibernating occupants can be dug up and shipped long distances.

The Australian barramunda (*Neoceratodus*), which sometimes reaches a length of several feet, lives in stagnant pools and does not make a mud-cell. When the water-level falls very low it occasionally breathes at the surface through its lung, making a grunting noise that can be heard at a considerable distance.

When the world was several million years younger this family of water creatures was very large, but the three widely separated species are its only surviving members. This class of fish is called *Dipnoi*, meaning 'double breathers. They possess front and back fins of very primitive type and are thought to be survivors of a race of creatures half-way between the true fish and the newt or salamander.

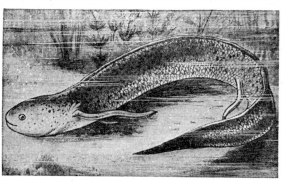

**STRANGE AFRICAN LUNG-FISH**

During the dry season the African lung-fish, left without water, hibernates in the mud, breathing by means of the air bladder which, in this case, acts rather like lungs. This black, eel-shaped creature is about 12 inches long and ordinarily is very active in its movements through the water.

**Lungs.** These are a pair of organs situated one on either side of the chest and they are in charge of that most vital of all animal functions, respiration. This is the taking in of oxygen, without which life and living cannot go on, and the carrying off of carbonic acid gas, which is the product of life and living. The windpipe, or trachea, leading from the mouth and nose by way of the throat, is the main air passage to and from the lungs.

In the upper part of the chest cavity the trachea divides into two main branches—the bronchi. Each enters a lung and is subdivided again and again into the bronchial tubes, which in their turn branch and re-branch as does a tree until small "twiglets" are formed. The smallest divisions of the air sacs, called alveoli, have fine capillaries running in their walls and it is between these juxtaposed walls—so fine that, compared to them, tissue paper would be as the hide of an elephant—that the all-important exchange of gases takes place.

The blood, therefore, does not come into direct contact with the air but, having caught up its load of oxygen through the membranous walls, hurries off with it to feed and build and give energy. Even the most remote tissues of the body give up this oxygen in exchange for a load of carbonic acid gas with which the blood returns to the lung cells for a repetition of the cycle.

LUNGS : ORGANS BY WHICH WE BREATHE

The lungs of the human body are here shown as seen from the front. A portion of the right lung has been cut away to reveal the air tubes and blood-vessels ; the left lung is opened to disclose the interior. A healthy person breathes about 20 times a minute, the air being renewed in the lungs by the action of the diaphragm and the muscles of the chest.

So this goes on unceasingly while the life of the animal lasts, some 20 times a minute in the healthy human being. It is the colouring matter of the blood, the haemoglobin of the red cells, which is responsible for this vital procedure, and it can accomplish it because it has the power to enter into loose chemical combination with both oxygen and carbonic acid gas.

The air is renewed in the lungs by means of the action of the diaphragm and the muscles of the chest. The lungs themselves are passive sacs, but they are filled and emptied like bellows by the action of the respiratory muscles, working in a most complicated mechanical system.

The infant does not breathe until it is born; then it gives a cry and takes its first breath, which opens the air cells of the lungs. Up till then it had received its oxygen, and had got rid of its carbonic acid gas, through the umbilical cord connecting it with the circulation of its mother.

The great stimulus to breathing is not oxygen, but carbonic acid gas acting on the respiratory centre in the brain. This fact is now made use of in giving anaesthetics (q.v.); the patient who breathes badly is often given carbonic acid gas rather than oxygen. Yet this knowledge was long ago in the possession of shepherds. When a new-born lamb did not begin to breathe readily, a shepherd would breathe into its mouth, and so stimulate its lungs to greater activity. How did they find this out ? Folk-medicine—traditional medicine—is full of such customs, many of which modern science now acclaims as justified by reason, not only by observation.

Common diseases of the lungs are bronchitis, inflammation of the bronchi ; broncho-pneumonia, when these bronchi become full of solid matter ; lobar pneumonia, another form of solidity. But all these conditions are now under much better control because of the discovery of the sulpha group of drugs and of penicillin which, between them, inhibit (restrain) the growth of most of the germs causing such diseases.

Tuberculosis is one of the most serious diseases of the lungs, but it comes under control with early treatment of the patient, in which sun and air and good food play a major part.

# The FATHER of the REFORMATION

*Perhaps you think we can owe little in these days to a priest who in the 16th century set Europe aflame with his teachings. Yet had Luther not lived the world today might be far different.*

**Luther,** MARTIN (1483–1546). "Here I stand; I can do no other; God help me! Amen!" These are the words which tradition puts into the mouth of the monk Luther, the originator of the Protestant Reformation, in the year 1521. They were spoken in the bishop's palace of the quaint old German city of Worms, on the River Rhine, when Luther was called to account for his religious teachings. Though it is highly probable that he did not use these words, they sum up fairly well the spirit of the long and elaborate reply he made to the assembly.

The young Emperor, Charles V, had come to his German dominions for the first time in 1520 and now he was holding an assembly or "diet" to regulate the affairs of Germany. Among other weighty topics was the question what to do with Luther, professor in the Elector of Saxony's University of Wittenberg, whose religious teachings, although formally condemned by the Pope's proclamation or " bull " in 1520, still continued to set Germany aflame. Even the Pope's representative, Alexander, who was there to demand that Luther's books be burned and their author sent to Rome for punishment, recognized that there were difficulties. " All Germany is in commotion," Alexander wrote to the Pope. " Nine out of every ten cry ' Luther,' and the tenth, if he does not care for what Luther says, at least cries, ' Death to the court of Rome ! ' " When faint-hearted friends had counselled Luther to distrust the emperor's safe-conduct to Worms, he had replied, "Though there were as many devils in Worms as there are tiles upon the roofs, I will go there."

The refusal which Luther gave to the demand that he should recant was followed by the Edict of Worms, which was issued by the Emperor on May 25, 1521. It condemned Luther and called upon all persons to seize him and give him up to a heretic's death.

His books also were to be committed to the flames. But no attempt was made to carry out this sentence.

Martin Luther, whose teachings thus convulsed Germany, was born of peasant stock in the village of Eisleben, Saxony, on November 10, 1483. His boyhood was spent in poverty, and he sang in the streets for bread, as was the custom of poor students. Later his hard-working father was able to send him to the University of Erfurt to study law. But as a result of an inner religious conflict Luther entered the Augustinian monastery at Erfurt, in 1505. After three years of strict monastic discipline and theological studies he became a professor in the University of Wittenberg, and a few years later was in Rome on business for his order.

Luther's career as a reformer may be said to begin with the nailing of his famous Ninety-five Theses to the door of the castle church in Wittenberg on All Saints' Day, 1517, as an intimation that he proposed to discuss them publicly. Such disputations as the one contemplated were then common in university life. Luther's theses were an attack on the prevailing system of granting indulgences (*see* page 818), and were provoked by the presence of the Dominican monk, John Tetzel, a renowned preacher and seller of indulgences.

When published in pamphlet form Luther's theses attracted much attention, and controversy followed. Cardinal Cajetan was sent as the Pope's representative to Luther, but could not induce him to retract his utterances. The conference held at Leipzig in 1519 between him and the Church authorities widened the breach. In his pamphlets, Address to the German Nobility and The Babylonian Captivity of the Church, Luther broke with the Roman Catholic Church. In 1520 he burned the Pope's bull condemning his publicly expressed opinions, and about the same time he also destroyed a copy of the canon or Church law.

*Pinakothek, Munich*
**MARTIN LUTHER**
**Originator of the Protestant Reformation, Martin Luther was a man of unshakable faith. His translation of the Bible into German had immense influence on German prose.**

*British Museum*

**LUTHER IN THE PULPIT**
**Fearless courage inspired Martin Luther's denunciations of all that he considered insincere or idolatrous in religion. This illustration from a contemporary German MS. shows him preaching against corruption in the Church.**

While returning from the Diet of Worms, Luther was seized by friends and safely hidden in the old castle of the Wartburg, near Eisenach, in Germany. There he remained in disguise, until the emperor's preoccupation with his wars with France made it comparatively safe for him to return to Wittenberg.

In 1525 Luther married an ex-nun, Catherine von Bora. This step emphasized his rejection of monasticism and celibacy for the clergy. The remainder of Luther's life was spent in writing, preaching, and organizing the Reformed Church in Saxony. His translation of the Bible into German remains the standard German version and had an immense influence on the development of German prose; while his numerous hymns—especially Ein' feste Burg ist unser Gott (A Mighty Fortress is Our God)—are still in use. He died at Eisleben, the place of his birth, on February 18, 1546, just as the long-deferred war to put down his teachings was about to break over Europe. (*See* Reformation).

**Lutyens,** Sir Edwin Landseer (1869–1944). The designer of the Cenotaph in London's Whitehall and of the Roman Catholic Cathedral at Liverpool, Sir Edwin Lutyens was responsible for other great public buildings in many parts of the country. He was the architect for the government buildings at Delhi (*see* page 987) ; for this he was awarded the K.C.I.E. in 1930.

It is perhaps for his private houses that Lutyens will be specially remembered. He designed mansions in which the dignity, restraint and simplicity of the Georgian period were coupled with the lightness and brightness demanded by the 20th century. One needs to see their interior to appreciate Lutyens at his best, for it was as a designer of great staircases that he probably excelled.

He was born in London on March 29, 1869, and studied at the Royal College of Art, South Kensington, London, before he began practising as an architect at the age of 19. Lutyens was President of the Royal Academy from 1938 to 1944. Knighted in 1911, he was awarded the Order of Merit by King George VI in 1942. He died on January 1, 1944.

**Luxemburg.** Bounded on the north and west by Belgium, by France on the south, by Germany on the east, the Grand Duchy (a small independent State ruled by a Grand Duke or Grand Duchess) of Luxemburg has an area of 999 square miles. It is mostly rugged forested highland, the northern part being an extension of the Belgian Ardennes with an average elevation of about 1,500 feet. It is a picturesque region, deeply furrowed by the valleys of streams that drain into the Moselle. The southern section is lower, with broad and fertile valleys.

The capital, the city of Luxemburg, with a population of 59,000, is 117 miles south-east of Brussels, the Belgian capital, and part of it is built on a crag 200 feet high. It was once so strongly fortified that it was known as the Gibraltar of the North, but the fortifications were destroyed in 1867.

Small as it is the country has valuable resources, its iron ore mines being the basis of a large iron and steel industry. Stone and slate are quarried. Manufactures include cement, gloves, and leather. Three-fifths of the land is cultivated, oats, potatoes and wheat being the main crops. There are 339 miles of railway and 1,300 miles of State highways. The inhabitants are of mixed origin, but chiefly German, and they speak a dialect akin to Flemish. They are nearly all Roman Catholics.

In the 14th century, when it was almost four times its present size, Luxemburg was a country of considerable importance. At that time its rulers were also kings of Bohemia, and four of them became rulers of the Holy Roman Empire (*q.v.*). From the 15th century Luxemburg was owned in turn by Burgundy, Germany, Spain, France, and Austria. In 1815 it was made a Grand Duchy by the Congress of Vienna and placed under the rule of King William I of the Netherlands ; but in 1830 the western portion was included in Belgium, the eastern part alone remaining in the possession of King William. In 1867, by the Treaty of London the European Powers guaranteed its independence and declared it to be neutral territory. In 1890, upon the accession of Queen Wilhelmina to the throne of the Netherlands, Luxemburg passed to Adolphus of Nassau, whose descendants continued to rule the country.

In the First World War (1914–18) Luxemburg was occupied by German forces until liberated in

Now Lycurgus gave proof of his generosity and greatness, for instead of revenging himself on the youth who had injured him, he took him into his home to live with him. The young man, thus having an opportunity to observe the life of the man he had so hated, became one of his most devoted admirers and followers, and in time was changed from a wild and passionate enemy of the laws of Lycurgus to a sober, discreet, and useful citizen. So runs one of the stories which the Greek historian Plutarch tells us of the great lawgiver.

According to tradition, Lycurgus lived about 800 B.C., and belonged to the royal house of Sparta and might have claimed the throne. When the king's widow proposed to him that they should kill his young nephew Charilaus, who was heir to the throne, so that Lycurgus might reign in his stead, he refused, and pro-

1918. During the Second World War (1939–45) the Grand Duchy was again seized by Germany and this time was annexed to the Reich. It was liberated in 1945, but one-third of the country was devastated in the fighting.

In 1946 Luxemburg, Belgium, and the Netherlands formed a Customs Union for the unification of the Customs duties of the three countries, and for the abolition of the collection of duties from the inhabitants of any of them when crossing their common frontiers. In March 1948 these three States, known as the Benelux countries, joined Britain and France in the formation of the Western Union with a view to co-operating with one another against aggression and in the reconstruction of Europe. The population of Luxemburg, is 281,570.

E.N.A.; Dorien Leigh

**IN THE GRAND DUCHY OF LUXEMBURG**
The capital of the Grand Duchy, the city of Luxemburg was at one time considered to be the strongest fortress in Europe after Gibraltar, but the fortifications were dismantled in 1867. A very small army is maintained, and in the lower photograph a few soldiers are seen exercising in front of the Grand Duchess's palace. Most of the country is hilly and wooded, and oxen are still used as draft animals (upper) on many of the farms.

**Lycurgus.** (Pron. li-kêr′-gus). No really authentic facts are known about Lycurgus, the reputed founder of the Spartan state in ancient Greece, but many stories have been told of him.

An anecdote relates that on one occasion this great lawgiver of Sparta was fleeing for his life before a jeering crowd of fellow-citizens. Stones fell thick about him, but he outran all his pursuers except one vigorous youth. As Lycurgus turned to look back, the youth thrust at him with a staff, putting out one of his eyes. Concealing his pain he waited for the mob to catch up. When they saw what had befallen the greatest man of Sparta their anger turned to shame. They escorted Lycurgus to his home and delivered the youth into his hands.

claimed the child king. Soon after this he set out to travel in foreign lands, conversing with sages and studying the laws of the countries he visited.

When he returned home after many years, he found Sparta in a state of disorder and discontent. With the help of some of the leading citizens, who believed that an entire change of government was the only remedy, Lycurgus made himself master of the city and drew up a new set of laws to govern the lives of the people, so designed as to build up a strong state. Among the measures attributed to him were equitable division of the land among the citizens, the prohibition of gold and silver and the substitution of iron as currency, and the establishment of the strict system of training which gave Sparta military predominance in Greece.

Then, obtaining a promise from his fellow-citizens that they would obey the laws and change none of them until his return, Lycurgus again departed. Being told by the oracle at Delphi that the Spartans would enjoy everlasting prosperity so long as they did this, he decided never to return to Sparta, in order that the citizens might for ever remain bound by their promise.

Lycurgus is one of the great lawgivers of antiquity and ranks with the legendary Manu of the Hindus, with Hammurabi of Babylonia, Moses among the Hebrews, and Solon of Athens.

**Lynx.** So acute is the sight of the lynx that the ancients believed the animal could see even through a stone wall. That is why we speak of sharp-sighted people as " lynx-eyed." This member of the cat family is found in both the Old World and the New. In size it is smaller than the leopard and larger than the true wild cat, and in general appearance is quite unlike any other animal. All species of the lynx have stumpy tails, long limbs, and upright tufted ears. Its eyes contract in the day-time to a narrow slit, for they are adapted for use at night, like the eyes of all cats.

Lynxes live in forests and rocky places, and are fond of resting stretched out on a tree limb in the sun. By night they hunt their prey, which consists of birds and small animals. The cry of a lynx at night is usually a single sharp howl, and it makes use of it in the following way. The creatures on which the animal preys seem to escape notice by lying perfectly still. The lynx crouches down ready for a leap, then suddenly emits its piercing cry. The victim, startled by the sound, cannot help jumping convulsively. Then the lynx pounces upon it and devours it.

The Canadian lynx (*Lynx canadensis*) has heavy grey fur mottled with brown, and its skin is in great demand in the fur trade. It is the most important of the American species. In Europe is found the northern lynx (*L. bore- alis*). There is a Medi- terranean s p e c i e s (*L. pardinus*), and one from Tibet. The c a r a c a l, found in Africa and Asia, is another member of this group.

**Lyons.** Capital of the French department of Rhône, the city of Lyons, which the French call Lyon (pron. lee'-on), is very old and stately. It is built where two rivers, the Rhône and the Saône, meet, the older part of the city being on a point of land between the two. The rivers are bordered by quays, and bridges connect the sec- tions of the city. There is a university, where students are taught law, medicine, and sciences ;

a school of fine arts and other colleges, and beauti- ful old churches and a big municipal library.

The silks manufactured here and in the villages around are famous, and the weaving of them keeps thousands of hand-looms and power-looms hum- ming. Other important manufactures are iron, steel and copper articles, gold and silver ware, chemicals, dyes, wine and cheese.

Lyons became a Roman colony in 43 B.C., and was the starting point of four important highways. During the 5th century it became one of the most flourishing cities of the newly-formed kingdom of Burgundy. In the 13th century the city came under the rule of the King of France; in 1793, during the French Revolution, it was partly destroyed. But Napoleon rebuilt and improved it, since when it has been one of the greatest sources of the wealth of France.

During the Second World War (1939–45) Lyons was captured by German forces, on June 20, 1940. Its factories and railway stations were bombed by the Allied air forces in the spring and summer of 1944 ; and on September 3 of that year the city was liberated by United States troops, the Germans having withdrawn after destroying all the bridges over the Rhône, and all but two over the Saône. The population is 460,740.

**Lyre-bird.** The 16 long and curiously shaped tail feathers of the male give this Australian bird a remarkable appearance. Otherwise both male and female are of unattractive form, about the size of a grouse and of a sooty-brown colour with a few markings of red. The remarkable tail feathers are about two feet long, generally drooping like a peacock's train, but when raised and spread they take the shape of a lyre. The tail does not reach perfection until the birds are three or four years old, and it is shed in the autumn and renewed each

*Fox*

**MANNERS AMONG THE LYNXES**
There seems to be a polite disagreement between these two Asiatic lynxes at a zoo, for while one looks as if it is asking to pass along the branch the other seems calmly determined not to move. Their far northern home makes thick fur necessary. The tufts of hair at the tip of each ear are characteristic of the animals.

*Australian Trade Publicity*

**LYRE-BIRD SHOWS HIS TAIL**
In the male lyre-bird of Australia the two outer feathers of the sixteen long and curiously shaped ones of the tail are curved in the form of the frame of a lyre—an ancient musical instrument—when they are raised and spread.

spring. The male is very proud of his fine feathers and one of his curious habits is that of scratching together little mounds of soil and leaves upon which he stands, spreading his tail, drooping his wings, and calling to his mate to admire him.

Lyre-birds have a mellow liquid note, and are said to imitate the songs of other birds and even animals. The nest is placed on the ground, at the foot of a tree or rock, and is closely woven of fine roots and lined with feathers. About this nest is heaped an oven-shaped mass of sticks, moss and leaves, with a side entrance so that the inner nest and the one egg are entirely concealed. The birds are very shy, and when disturbed escape by running rapidly in the underbrush. They are found at times in trees but they are not good flyers. The best known species is *Menura superba*.

**Lytton,** EDWARD GEORGE EARLE LYTTON BULWER LYTTON, 1ST BARON (1803–73). One of the literary giants of the 19th century, Bulwer Lytton is remembered as the author of novels including The Last Days of Pompeii, Rienzi, The Caxtons, and My Novel. A poem entitled Sculpture was the first of his published works, and it gained for him the Chancellor's prize for verse at Cambridge in 1825.

A contemporary of Dickens and Thackeray and Tennyson, his novels were eagerly sought and read all over the world. His literary output was enormous considering that, besides being an author, he was a prominent figure in society and an M.P. On his Hertfordshire estate at Knebworth, still belonging to his descendants, he often entertained Dickens and other notable Victorians. His library, many of his manuscripts, and other personal belongings, are treasured at Knebworth House.

Bulwer Lytton was born in London on May 25, 1803, and began to write verse at the age of seven. Educated at Cambridge University, he entered Parliament in 1831 and was made a baronet in 1838. He was created a baron in 1866 and was twice Lord Rector of Glasgow University. He died at Torquay on January 18, 1873, and was buried in Westminster Abbey, London.

He was succeeded by his son Edward Robert Lytton (1831–91), who also wrote verse—under the assumed name of Owen Meredith. Born in London on November 8, 1831, and educated at Harrow School and at Bonn University, Germany, in 1849 Lord Edward Robert Lytton entered the British diplomatic service, holding a series of appointments abroad. He became Viceroy of India in 1876 and was created an Earl on his resignation in 1880. From 1887 to 1891 he was Ambassador in Paris, where he died on November 24, 1891. The Earldom then passed to Lord Lytton's son, Victor Alexander George Robert Lytton (1876–1947), who was born at Simla, India, on August 9, 1876, and educated at Eton College and Trinity College, Cambridge. Under-Secretary of State for India in 1920, he was Governor of Bengal from 1922 to 1927, and Viceroy of India, from April to August 1925. He died on October 25, 1947, when the earldom passed to his brother Neville Stephen.

*Portrait by P. F. Poole, National Portrait Gallery*

**LORD LYTTON, ENGLISH NOVELIST**
Widely read in Victorian days, the novels of Bulwer Lytton include The Last Days of Pompeii, perhaps the best known of the many which he wrote. He was made a Baronet in 1838, and created Baron Lytton of Knebworth in 1866.

# M

**McAdam,** JOHN LOUDON (1756–1836). Within a year of each other were born in different parts of Scotland two men who, more than all others, gave us the first-class roads for which our country is famed. One was Telford (*q.v.*), the other was McAdam, the man whose name is perpetuated in the English language by the word "macadam" and its various derivatives, and whom Tom Moore, the Irish poet, called the "Smooth McAdam."

John McAdam was born at Ayr, on September 21, 1756, three years before Robert Burns, the Scottish poet, was born near the same town. At the age of 14 he went to America with his father, returning in 1785 with a small fortune to buy an estate in Ayrshire. Thereafter his hobby became the study of roads and all information concerning them.

Travelling in a closed carriage drawn by two horses, and followed by a Newfoundland dog and a pony, he travelled over more than 30,000 miles of roads between 1798 and 1814 — a remarkable achievement considering the state of the highways and the dangers attendant on travelling in those days. If ever he came upon an unusual type of road he would get down from his carriage, mount his pony, and survey the stretch leisurely from end to end.

From such experiences McAdam gained an immense knowledge of roads, and it became clear to him that the real method of improvement lay in making the surfaces of materials that would absorb surface water, and in cambering them — that is, making them with their sides at a lower level than the crown, or centre, so that surplus water would drain off and not accumulate in puddles as was then usual. To achieve these ends he devised the macadamized system, as it was later called, in which he used broken, angular stones unbound with clay or cement as the surfacing material, instead of the round cemented stones then employed. He also insisted that road-making should be undertaken by salaried officials and carried out by competent labourers instead of being left to parish authorities and pauper labour. He soon became salaried surveyor to 34 different bodies of road trustees and in 1815 general surveyor of the roads around Bristol. Three years later, the House of Commons awarded him a grant of £10,000, and in 1827 he was appointed surveyor-general of metropolitan roads.

*Scottish National Portrait Gallery; photo, Annan*
**JOHN LOUDON McADAM**
It was not until McAdam's system of road construction replaced the old muddy tracks which once served as roads that it was possible for coaches to travel at as much as ten miles an hour.

He died at Moffat, Dumfriesshire, on November 26, 1836. McAdam's grandson William (1803–61), an engineer of considerable ability, was also surveyor-general of roads for many years.

**Macaroni.** Cooked with cheese or served with tomato sauce, this national dish of Italy deserves the widespread popularity it has acquired as a nutritious and palatable food. For macaroni is made from certain varieties of wheat which are rich in gluten and other nitrogenous compounds. The *durum*, or hard wheat, from which most of it is made, is grown principally in southern Europe.

The coarsely ground flour, mixed with hot water, is kneaded to a stiff paste, which is moulded by machinery into various forms: solid strings or hollow pipes (spaghetti and macaroni); fine threads (vermicelli), and other shapes. The dough is put into a cylindrical vessel having a perforated bottom, and a heavy iron plate, driven by a powerful press, forces the paste through in tubes or strips according to the arrangement of the holes. The strings of paste are then hung over rods to dry. True macaroni is hard, has a soft yellowish colour, and is rough in texture. In boiling it swells, but retains its shape.

**MacArthur,** DOUGLAS, GENERAL (b. 1880). In the night of March 11, 1942 (during the Second World War) four motor torpedo-boats slipped away from the fortress of Corregidor, off the island of Luzon in the Philippines, to run the Japanese blockade. In one of them was the American General MacArthur, with his wife and four-year-old son and some of his staff officers. They had been ordered by President Roosevelt to leave Luzon, now almost wholly overrun by the Japanese, for the General had been appointed Allied Supreme Commander in the South West Pacific. "I will return," he promised.

For three months MacArthur's 12,000 American and 35,000 Filipino troops in Luzon had held the Japanese at bay. At last, many times outnumbered, hemmed in on the Bataan peninsula without air support and cut off from reinforcements and supplies, their defence was drawing to a close. Against his personal wishes, General MacArthur handed over his command to General Jonathan M. Wainwright and made his way to Australia.

In two years he returned, as he had promised. His offensive against the Japanese began in the autumn of 1942, with the attack on New Guinea;

by the end of 1944 the Philippines were liberated, and the mighty Allied forces—American, Australian and British—swept on from one island stronghold to the next, until in August 1945 the Japanese were beaten. That same month, General MacArthur landed by air in Japan and set up his headquarters in Yokohama ; and on September 2, 1945, on board the U.S. battleship Missouri, lying at anchor with a great Allied fleet in Tokyo Bay, he received the enemy's unconditional surrender.

General MacArthur's career had been a brilliant one. The son of General Arthur MacArthur, a distinguished commander, he was born at Little Rock, Arkansas, on January 26, 1880, and graduated from the American military school at West Point with the highest honours. During the First World War (1914–18) he rose to command a division in France, and in 1919 was given command of West Point. At 50 he became Chief of Staff, the youngest full General that America had ever known. In 1935 he was sent to organize the defence of the Philippines, and when in 1937 he retired from the American army he stayed on at Manila with the rank of Field-Marshal in the Philippines forces. In June 1941 he was recalled to service by the Americans as commander of the U.S. forces in the Far East.

Made an honorary G.C.B. by the British in 1943 and promoted to General of the Army (American) in December 1944, he became Supreme Allied Commander of the forces occupying Japan (1945–46). On his orders the Japanese carried out radical social reforms, including the granting of votes to women, reform of the system of land ownership, and abolition of the State religion of Shintoism which held that the Japanese emperor was divine.

## Macaulay, THOMAS BABINGTON MACAULAY, BARON (1800–59).

As a child of three, books were Macaulay's constant companions. At four he replied to a lady who inquired how he felt after some hot coffee had been spilled on his legs, " Thank you, madam, the agony is abated." Macaulay was born at Rothley Temple, Leicestershire, on October 25, 1800, and was educated at Trinity College, Cambridge. He was a brilliant student in every subject except mathematics, learning to read books in Greek, Latin, French, German, Spanish, Italian and Dutch.

In August 1825 appeared his essay on Milton, the first of a series which for 20 years made him

famous. No more delightful introduction to history can be found than these brilliantly written and intensely interesting stories of the lives of great men—Warren Hastings and Clive, Pitt and Bunyan, Dr. Johnson, Lord Burleigh, and the rest. Macaulay's gifts as a writer and speaker led him, naturally, into public life. In Parliament, which he entered in 1830, and later in India as legal adviser to the supreme council, he showed gifts of mind that always held men's attention. In politics he strove for the extension of the right to vote to the working classes and supported the Reform Bill for that reason. But he was pleased with the material progress of the time and ignored what he considered necessary economic evils.

During all the busy years of his official life, when writing was just an occasional pleasure and source of income, Macaulay was planning a history of England to begin with the accession of James II to the throne—a history, as he said, interesting enough " to supersede the last fashionable novel upon the dressing-tables of young ladies." He began it in earnest in 1841, and in 1848 finished the first two volumes. Later volumes appeared from time to time, but the work was still uncompleted when Macaulay died, 10 years later.

Macaulay's history had an immediate success—greater, perhaps, than that achieved by any other history. It had a tremendous sale in England and the United States, and was translated into all modern languages. He wrote in his diary at one time: " This is a tough chapter . . . What trouble these few pages cost me ! The great object is that they may read as if they had been spoken off and seem to flow as easily as table talk." His paragraphs achieve their aim, and sweep the reader along.

For a generation Macaulay was read with enthusiasm and respect. In the generation that followed, his fame was not quite so great. His brilliance was unsurpassed; but his insight into the complex character of men and of movements left something to be desired. He saw men's outward actions, but he could not divine their inner motives. He viewed history as a great pageant, a series of pictures in which the doings of the people appear for the first time along with the chroniclings of monarchs, generals, and Parliament. What Scott did with the romantic novel, Macaulay did with history. He made it interesting, first of all, to the average man and woman, and he set a new

**LORD MACAULAY**

The life of Lord Macaulay written by his nephew shows him to have been a man of deep and warm affections, and a devoted son and brother. This portrait of Macaulay by Sir Francis Grant is in the National Portrait Gallery, London.

fashion. So highly was his work appreciated that a body of English workmen wrote to thank him for writing a history, which they could understand. Quite as popular as Macaulay's essays and his history was a little volume of poems entitled Lays of Ancient Rome. These still delight old and young, not merely from their historic interest but because of their stirring rhythm.

In 1857 Macaulay was made a peer, with the title Baron Macaulay. He lived to enjoy this new honour only two years. When he died, on December 28, 1859, the greatest honour that England can show to her illustrious dead was conferred upon him: he was buried in Westminster Abbey, in London.

**Macaw.** The most brilliantly coloured members of the parrot tribe are the macaws. In addition to their vivid plumage they are distinguished by a long wedge-shaped tail, long pointed wings, naked cheeks (in some species) and a short powerful bill. Adults taken into captivity are exceedingly vicious. When caught young they may grow fond of their keepers, but are still given to fits of rage at slight provocation. They do not readily learn to talk, and persist in screaming violently. There are many species, of which the red and blue macaw (*Ara macao*) and the blue and yellow (*Ara ararauna; see* colour plate facing page 2048) are the most brilliantly feathered. These birds, native to Central and South America, average more than 30 inches in length, and feed on fruits or nuts. They often fly at great heights, in flocks. The eggs are laid in holes in trees. (*See* Parrot).

**Macbeth.** This hero of Shakespeare's powerful tragedy of the same name is in command of the armies of Scotland when the play opens,

and has just won a great victory over the Danes. The triumph so fires his ambition that witches, bent on evil, easily implant in his mind the thought that he shall be king. Lady Macbeth still further incites him, until with his own hands he murders the Scottish king Duncan and usurps the throne. From that moment Macbeth goes swiftly to his doom. Ghosts rise to haunt him, Lady Macbeth dies insane, civil war breaks out, led by Malcolm, the son and heir of the murdered king, and, finally, Macbeth himself is slain in battle. Macbeth is to be abhorred for his crimes, but in all that he does and says he excites a tragic pity, as when, informed of the death of the queen, he thus gives utterance to his gloomy thoughts:

> Tomorrow, and tomorrow, and tomorrow,
> Creeps in this petty pace from day to day
> To the last syllable of recorded time ;
> And all our yesterdays have lighted fools
> The way to dusty death. Out, out, brief candle!
> Life's but a walking shadow, a poor player
> That struts and frets his hour upon the stage
> And then is heard no more: it is a tale
> Told by an idiot, full of sound and fury,
> Signifying nothing.

The story of the play is taken from history, the real Macbeth having ruled over Scotland from the year 1040 to 1057. He was the chief of Glamis, and Glamis Castle is the ancestral home of Queen Elizabeth, the consort of King George VI.

**Macdonald,** FLORA (1722–90). In the roll of Scottish heroines, Flora Macdonald, to whose ingenuity, courage and loyalty Bonnie Prince Charlie (Prince Charles Edward, the Young Pretender) owed his escape after his defeat at Culloden on April 16, 1746, occupies a high place.

Charles's defeat was so complete that his loyal Highlanders were scattered and pursued remorselessly and put to the sword by the troops of the English commander, the Duke of Cumberland. The Prince became a fugitive, sleeping by day and fleeing hither and thither by night in the seemingly vain hope of escaping through the military cordon and of evading the numerous parties of soldiers who were searching the Highlands to bring him to London " dead or alive " and so claim the price, £30,000, which the English placed on his head. Just as all seemed lost, after six weeks of fatigue and hunger, there arose to rescue him Flora Macdonald.

She made the Prince dress in woman's clothes, pose as her servant, and accompany her in an open boat from the mainland to the isle of Skye, where she proposed to conceal him among relatives. By skill, luck, and great courage their frail craft was able to evade the

FLORA MACDONALD AND PRINCE CHARLIE

After his defeat by the English at Culloden on April 16, 1746, Prince Charles Edward was forced to seek safety in flight under the guidance of Flora Macdonald. At one time the party had to take refuge in a cave on the isle of Skye. This picture, painted by T. Duncan (1807–45), shows Flora and her attendants watching over the sleeping Prince.

English ships, and they landed safely in Skye. There, with her supposed maid, she dined with Lady Margaret Macdonald, at whose table sat an army officer, stationed there with a party of soldiers to watch for Prince Charles should he attempt to land ! Boswell relates in his Journal of a Tour to the Hebrides how, when Dr. Samuel Johnson visited Skye in 1773, Flora Macdonald told him of this episode, and added that afterwards (when the Prince was safe) she often laughed in good humour with this officer at having so well deceived him !

Shortly afterwards the Prince escaped to France, and Flora Macdonald was taken to London and there detained. In 1747 she was released, and her admirers presented her with £1,500 as a reward for her loyalty and courage to the ill-fated House of Stuart. She died on March 5, 1790.

**MacDonald,** JAMES RAMSAY (1866–1937). Born in a two-roomed cottage at Lossiemouth in Scotland on October 12, 1866, and taught at the local elementary school, the first British Labour

**JAMES RAMSAY MACDONALD**
Thrice British Prime Minister and the first Labour politician to hold that office, James Ramsay MacDonald was a clerk and a journalist before entering politics. He became Premier for the third time in August 1931, and resigned owing to ill-health in June 1935. He died at sea on November 9, 1937.

*Wide World Photos*

866 votes, losing the election, but gaining a wife. Her name was Margaret Ethel Gladstone, the daughter of a professor and a niece of Lord Kelvin. Never was married life more happy. Her death in 1911 left its mark on a man intensely devoted to his home. Her philanthropic work on behalf of poor London children is fittingly commemorated in a beautiful sculpture erected in Lincoln's Inn Fields, London.

Elected Member of Parliament for Leicester in 1906, Ramsay MacDonald was chosen leader of the Labour Party in the House of Commons five years later. During the First World War (1914–18) he became one of the most unpopular men in England owing to his opposition to the war. In 1918 he lost his seat in the House, but returned in 1922. Two years later he was called upon to form the first Labour Government, which lasted less than a year. He became Premier for a second time in 1929, but in 1931 a grave financial crisis, accentuated by world trade depression and rising unemployment, brought about the defection of most of his colleagues, who refused to accept the drastic economies advocated by him. MacDonald remained true to his beliefs in the nation's recuperative powers, provided sacrifices were made, and after obtaining the support of the Conservatives, he became head of the National Government, composed of Conservatives, Liberals and a few Labour members.

The heavy burdens of office, no less than the loss of political friendships, which he endured when he allied himself with the Conservative party to restore Britain's financial prestige, told on his health, and before resigning the Premiership in favour of Stanley Baldwin in June 1935 he had undergone several operations on his eyes. He became a lonely and tired if not disappointed man, and in an endeavour to regain his health, and grasp what he called " that elusive quality, rest," he embarked on a voyage to South America, hoping in these new surroundings to set about writing his political memoirs. After a few days at sea he died from heart failure, on November 9, 1937. His body was brought back in a warship to be buried at Lossiemouth, his first and last home.

Prime Minister displayed from his earliest days of poverty that moral courage which later endeared him to an army of admirers and drew forth the respect of his bitterest opponents. When but an inexperienced boy he journeyed to London in 1884, obtained a job in a warehouse at 12s. 6d. a week, almost starved, and attended evening classes. He studied chemistry, but just when a scholarship seemed within reach, his health broke down. Over-study and underfeeding had taken their toll.

Then fortune smiled on him, rather faintly at first. He became secretary to a Parliamentary candidate at what he then, no doubt, considered the princely wage of 30 shillings a week. In 1894 he joined the Independent Labour Party, and science was abandoned for politics. The future Prime Minister next tried his hand at writing for newspapers, and was successful. He stood for Parliament as a Socialist, but only obtained a mere

**Macdonald,** SIR JOHN ALEXANDER (1815–91). The first Premier of the Dominion of Canada went there at the age of five, a poor Scots immigrant boy ; he was born in Glasgow on January 11, 1815. Poverty ended his schooling at 15, but his insatiable curiosity and love of reading soon made up to a large degree for the lack of formal education. Entering a lawyer's office, he became a qualified solicitor in 1836, and eight years later was elected to the Canadian Assembly (Parliament). Almost at once he became one of the leaders of the

# CHATTY MACAW WITH GORGEOUS PLUMAGE

Especially prized for their ornamental appearance and for their large size—some of the birds are three feet long—the macaws can be trained to talk in a very entertaining fashion.  In a wild state they are noted for the noise that the great flocks of them make in South American forests.  In captivity the blue and yellow macaw (*Ara ararauna*), seen above, is a hardy bird and considered to be the best talker of its family.  Here you can see particularly well its powerful beak and strong, clawed toes.

*To face page* 2048

from a belt, or a metal container. The heavy guns are usually water-cooled, the light ones air-cooled.

The first machine-guns were fired by turning a crank by hand: later models were automatic or semi-automatic (loading and firing themselves after the first shot has been discharged). The automatic types may be divided into those in which the gun is operated by the recoil of shot, and those in which the gun is worked by waste gases of the explosion. The rate of fire depends upon the type of gun and varies from 60 or 75 to 600 or more rounds a minute.

The first practical machine-gun was invented by an American, Dr. R. J. Gatling (1818–1903), in 1861. It consisted of 10 parallel barrels, and could fire 500 shots a minute. The barrels fired in turn as they were revolved around a central axis by a hand-operated crank. The Maxim gun was the first of the automatic type. It was invented about 1881 by Sir Hiram Maxim (1840–1916) and is water-cooled. As the Vickers-Maxim gun it was used by British soldiers in the two World Wars.

The Lewis gun was invented by Colonel Isaac Newton Lewis (1858–1931), an American, but was rejected by the U.S. army and adopted in France, Belgium and Britain, remaining until 1935 the standard light machine-gun of the British army. It fired about 550 shots per minute ; the gun worked by the pressure of the gases from fired cartridges.

After 1935 a new, lighter, and more reliable gun, the Czechoslovakian Bren, was issued to the British army. Of the same bore as the Lewis (·303 inches), it can be used on a tripod (resting the butt on the shoulder) or on a separate bipod, and in certain circumstances can be fired from the shoulder or hip. This gun is air-cooled and gas-operated, the waste gases from the first discharge loading and firing the second round, and so on. Ammunition is fed to the breech from magazines holding 30 cartridges ; the rate of fire, allowing time for the changing of magazines, is about 120 rounds per minute. The gun can be regulated to fire either single or multiple shots.

The Sten carbine, a light automatic weapon, is extensively used in the British Army as an infantry weapon. Introduced during the Second World War (1939–45), it had great advantages—simplicity of design (only 51 parts) and operation and suitability for mass-production. It has a bore of 7·92 millimetres, an effective range of 200 yards, and maximum rate of fire of 500 shots per minute. The carbine is fed by magazines holding 30 cartridges.

## Mackenzie.
The greatest river of Canada, the Mackenzie flows nearly 2,500 miles from its source in the Rocky Mountains to the Arctic Ocean. It drains an area of 682,000 square miles, and in its course it gathers the waters of three immense lakes —Lake Athabaska, Great Slave Lake and Great Bear Lake. Great Bear Lake lies so far north that its surface is frozen for nine months of the year.

From its source to Lake Athabaska, this mighty river is known as the River Athabaska; thence to Great Slave Lake as the Slave river; from there to its mouth as the Mackenzie river. In summer, steamboats of the Hudson's Bay Company ply from Great Slave Lake almost to the river's mouth, where it spreads into many branches flowing through a wide, flat delta. The Athabaska and its other main tributaries, the Peace and the Liard, are navigable for steamboats of shallow draught. Fish abound in the Mackenzie, and its valley contains coal seams, salt deposits, oil, and natural gas. The river was named after Sir Alexander Mackenzie (c. 1755–1820), a fur-trader and explorer, who discovered it.

## Mackerel.
Next to cod and herring, the mackerel is the most important food fish found in the North Atlantic; the various species cover a wide range and are found in shoals, sometimes of immense size, in nearly all tropical and temperate seas. They lay eggs in the open sea, but migrate periodically towards the shore in pursuit of sprats, pilchards and sand eels, which form their principal food. When these are scarce, mackerel live on small crustaceans. The shoals are easily detected, for they swim near the surface and produce " boiling " of the sea.

The common mackerel of the North Atlantic (*Scomber scombrus*) is usually from 14 to 16 inches long and weighs about 2 lb. It sometimes attains a much larger size, but the smaller fish are considered better for the table. Its regular, rather narrow form, bluish-green back with darker bands, its silver underside and fierce, greedy disposition make it typical of the family. In Norway and around the British Isles mackerel fishing is an important industry. Both seine and drift nets are used.

*Schensky*

**A SMALL SHOAL OF MACKEREL**
One of the most handsome of all sea-fish is the mackerel, for its silvery sides are striped with dark, shining blue, in much the same pattern as we see, among animals, in the zebra. The clean, smooth outline, small fins and sharply-cleft tail are other features which make this a striking fish ; and of course it is good to eat.

# Madagascar.

About 240 miles off the south-east coast of Africa, from which it is separated by the Mozambique Channel, is the French island of Madagascar. The fifth largest island in the world, it has an area of 241,094 square miles, with a maximum length of 980 miles and an extreme width of 360 miles. Madagascar lies almost entirely within the Tropics and has rainfall all the year round, with a rainy season from October to March.

The east coast is covered with dense tropical forests, but among the central mountains are large plateaux covered with scattered trees and long grasses. The vast plain to the west is hotter but less moist than the east coast, and has both forests and grassy areas. The south-west coast is flat, sandy and bare.

There are no large native mammals and no true monkeys, but Madagascar is the home of the monkey-like lemurs (q.v.). The largest carnivore is a cat-like relative of the African civets. Remains have been found of a large bird called the *aepyornis*, which lived there until two centuries ago. It was more than nine feet tall, could not fly and resembled the extinct moa of New Zealand. Many of the native animals and plants are different from those of the neighbouring continent of Africa, being more like those of the East Indies. They seem to indicate that at one time Madagascar may have been connected with the Malayan Archipelago.

The natives, called Malagasy, are not related to the Negroes of Africa, but seem to be of Malayan or south-west Pacific stock. No one knows how or when they first came to the island. The most numerous tribe are the Hovas, others being the Betsileo, Betsimisaraka, Tanala, and Sakalava. Each has its own language, but that of the Hovas is generally used.

The chief occupation of the people is agriculture, main crops being rice, potatoes, maize, beans, tapioca, coffee, cloves, cocoa and hemp. Forest trees yield valuable timber, such as ebony, mahogany and rosewood. Immense herds of cattle are kept; frozen meat and hides are among the exports. The mineral resources, which are little exploited, include gold, copper, lead and iron.

Lack of communications within the island makes commerce difficult. Good motor roads are few, and though there are some 16,000 miles of roads, many of them are mere tracks. Few rivers are navigable beyond a short distance from the coast. There are 500 miles of railway, the principal line running from Tamatave, the chief port, to Antanan-

arivo, or Tananarive, the capital, which is situated in the heart of the central plateau.

Although Arabs had visited Madagascar since before the 9th century it was unknown to Europeans until the Portuguese discovered it in 1500. French and Dutch followed the Portuguese, but efforts

*Guy Nind*

**MADAGASCAR'S PLEASANT CAPITAL**

Antananarivo, or Tananarive, the capital of Madagascar, is situated in the centre of the island, and stands at a height of 4,750 feet above sea-level. The city is on a hill 50 feet high, which rises abruptly from a plain completely surrounding it. This photograph shows the prevailing style of architecture of the private houses pleasantly situated on the hillside.

to establish permanent settlements on the island were unsuccessful. About 1700 the French set up military posts, but it was not until well into the 19th century that they really began to control the island. After a series of campaigns against the Malagasy commencing in 1883, Madagascar was subjugated and declared a French Colony in 1896.

After the defeat of France by Germany in June 1940 during the Second World War (1939–45) Madagascar was controlled by the pro-German Vichy French Government until May 1942, when British forces landed at Diego Suarez Bay on the north coast to prevent Japanese and German submarines using the naval station there. Little opposition was encountered and hostilities ceased on November 5, 1942. A provisional British military administration governed the island until, in January 1943, the French National Committee in London sent out a newly-appointed High Commissioner. The estimated population of Madagascar is four million.

# Madeira.

(Pron. ma-dēr'-a). The traveller who approaches the Madeiras, a small group of rocky islands belonging to Portugal, 360 miles off the north-west coast of Africa, sees the finest view in the islands when his steamer enters Funchal, the chief port and the capital of the island which gives its name to the group. Natives—chiefly of Portuguese descent with some Moorish or Negro intermixture—noisy, dark-skinned, and good-humoured, surround the vessel. Their small boats are filled with such wares as cane chairs, basket-work, red bananas, pineapples, custard-apples,

**CAPITAL OF SUNNY MADEIRA**
Funchal, the capital of Madeira, which in normal times is a winter holiday resort, stands in a magnificent situation on the lower slopes of the mountains overlooking the Bay of Funchal. The bay forms a fine natural harbour, seen in the photograph, and even large ships can come close in shore. In the middle distance a rock crowned by a castle rises in the roadstead.

pomegranates and other tropical fruits, and sometimes beautiful lace and embroidery. Within the city one sees, among other strange sights, wooden sledges and other conveyances on runners drawn by oxen, for in the Madeiras wheeled carriages are rare, the streets being very steep.

Madeira is a mountainous island of volcanic origin, 35 miles long and 12 miles wide, with deep narrow valleys and lofty rugged peaks (4,000 to 6,000 feet high). Precipices rise abruptly from the coast, and in parts the scenery is wild and beautiful. The climate is mild and uniform, and the island is noted as a health resort, especially for persons suffering from diseases of the chest.

Absence of rain during the summer, and the rocky, hilly, volcanic nature of the land, have made cultivation difficult. The two staple products are sugar and the Madeira wine which is world-famous. Vegetables and a variety of fruits are grown—oranges, lemons, grapes, figs, bananas, and pineapples—and are exported in large quantities. Madeira is a port of call for steamers plying between Europe and South Africa ; its population is 250,000. It is also an important air and cable station. Funchal has a population of 55,000 ; other towns are Ponta do Sol and Machico. Besides Madeira and Porto Santo, there are three uninhabited islands, all forming the Madeiras.

**Madonna.** The Italian word Madonna (my lady) is applied to a picture or statue of Mary, the mother of Jesus, and sometimes to the Virgin herself. After the 4th century the special homage rendered to the mother of Christ assumed a large place in the minds of the great mass of the people. When the Council of Nicaea in 325 had clearly fixed the place of the Son in the Trinity, He seemed less able to plead with God for mankind, being so much at one with God himself. It seemed natural, therefore, that His mother, the Virgin Mary,

should be a refuge of the faithful, who might pray to her, and thus gain her powerful intercession with her Son. The Roman Catholic Church in its beliefs and doctrines could not remain untouched by this, and the Virgin Mary assumed a larger and larger place in daily worship in the succeeding centuries. So, also, she became the favourite theme of Christian art, from its simple beginnings to its glories in the Renaissance. Such quaint stiff little figures they painted of her in the early days ! Often her arms were extended in prayer, and she always wore a blue robe starred or slashed with gold and draped over her head.

The Madonna became much more natural and beautiful when Italian artists in the 13th century broke away from the old Byzantine forms of representation. Then Fra Filippo Lippi (1406–69), discarding even the gold backgrounds that were then so popular, painted some charmingly life-like pictures of the Mother and Child, and there was scarcely a single Italian artist from the 11th to the 16th century who did not paint one or two such pictures.

All the earthly and heavenly scenes of the life of the mother of Jesus were painted, though, of course, with little respect for time or place, so that the Madonnas of any one period usually wear the clothes of that period. Though striking and beautiful Madonnas have been painted by artists of all lands, there is one painter whose work in this field is supreme—Raphael (1483–1520). " Oh, their Raphael of the dear Madonnas ! " wrote Browning, thinking of the many celebrated Madonnas painted by the Italian master. Raphael's two most famous paintings are that perfect mother picture The Madonna of the Chair (*see* illustration opposite) and the glorious painting of the Madonna descending from the heights of Heaven, clasping her little Son, while below St. Sixtus and St. Barbara kneel in adoration—the world's favourite Sistine Madonna. Another Raphael Madonna is illustrated in page 1777.

**Madras** (Pron. ma-drahs'), INDIA. Occupying the south-east portion of the sub-continent, Madras is a state of the republic of India. To the north lies the state of Hyderabad, to the north-west the state of Bombay, and to the west the states of Mysore and Travancore-Cochin. Its eastern shores, the Coromandel coast, are washed by the waters of the Bay of Bengal ; its western, the Malabar coast, by the Arabian Sea. Divided from it by the narrow, shallow Palk Strait on the south lies the island of Ceylon. Sea breezes help to temper the extreme heat.

Much of the surface of Madras state, which has an area of 126,166 square miles, is flat, but in the south-west the Eastern and Western Ghats

# THE WORLD-FAMOUS 'MADONNA OF THE CHAIR'

The masterpiece of the Italian painter Raphael (1483–1520), who enjoyed in his lifetime general popularity such as has probably never since been accorded to any artist, and who died on Good Friday 1520, on his 38th birthday, belongs to the Pitti Gallery in Florence. This magnificent painting owes its origin to a curious incident. For years the artist had been trying to find a suitable model for the picture which he had in mind. Then one day he happened to encounter a peasant woman, seated and holding a small boy in her lap while another child stood by. She was exactly the type of model that Raphael had been looking for. He had a pencil with him, but nothing else with which to work, so he siezed a smooth barrel head and made his first sketch upon its curved surface. From that preliminary sketch he worked out the picture which has been called ' the most popular painting ever made.' In the whole history of sacred art there is scarcely anything which can be held to compare with it, and its realistic expressiveness is in every way typical of the supreme genius of Raphael at its best. During the Second World War (1939–45), though Florence suffered considerable damage, the art treasures of the city, including the Raphael painting, had been removed to a safe place, out of the fighting zone.

meet in the Nilgiri Hills. The rivers of the Malabar coast are short and unimportant. The lower courses of the Godavari and Kistna, and the middle and lower sections of the Cauvery—all flowing into the Bay of Bengal—are in Madras. Nearly all the smaller rivers are used for irrigation, and the Mettur-Cauvery Dam on the Cauvery river is one of the biggest in the world. The rainfall varies from about 150 inches on the west coast to 20 inches in certain regions east of the Western Ghats.

Forests of palms, banyans, bamboos, sandalwoods, satinwoods, rosewoods, and teak and ebony trees cover about one-sixth of the province. Large mammals include elephants, tigers, bison, leopards, cheetahs, wolves and various species of antelope.

Seventy per cent of the people work on the land. Rice, millet, oilseeds, sugar-cane, tobacco, tea and spices are the chief crops. The most important minerals are beryl, graphite, manganese and mica; gold, iron, copper and lead are also found, but in smaller quantities.

The capital of Madras state and its chief port is the city of Madras, situated on the Coromandel coast and provided with an artificial harbour. It has a population of 777,500 and was founded by the British in 1640, growing up around Fort St. George. There are cotton and rice mills, railway workshops, sugar refineries, tanneries, brickworks, and a quinine factory. Other large towns in Madras are Madura, with its famous Hindu temple, Trichinopoly, Salem and Calicut.

W F Taylor

**TOWERS AND MINARETS OF MADRAS**
Here the skyline of the city of Madras, in the republic of India, is picturesquely broken by towers and minarets. The highest tower seen in this photograph is that of the High Court which, besides being ornamental, serves a useful purpose, for it is used as a lighthouse. It is 160 feet high, and the light is visible 20 miles out at sea.

Madras was visited by the Portuguese in 1498, but the first settlement was established by the British in 1640. In 1746 the French took Madras from the British, but were driven out in 1760. From that time it remained part of British India, until 1947, when the Dominions of India and Pakistan were established. The population of the state is about 50 million.

**Madrid.** When Philip II of Spain made Madrid his capital in 1561, he chose what was then an unimportant town chiefly because of its central position and, perhaps, because his father Charles V had found its bracing climate healthy. Foreign visitors, however, coming from the pleasant south of Spain to a city lying on a plateau 2,400 feet above the sea—scorched by the sun in summer and swept by icy winds blowing from snow-clad peaks in winter, and without suburbs—may think that the gloomy Philip II chose it mainly for its dreariness.

And when they are taken out to Philip's summer palace, the Escorial, 27 miles away to the northwest, their opinion is confirmed. The Escorial is a monastery, a church, and the burial-place of the Spanish kings, as well as a palace. Its unusual shape has led to the fanciful explanation that it is fashioned on the lines of the gridiron on which St. Lawrence was martyred, the courts representing the interstices of the bars, the towers at the corners the legs, and the palace itself the handle.

Although Madrid, which is believed to date from Roman times, was a Moorish outpost in the 10th century and had 30,000 inhabitants at the time Philip made it his capital, it has not the historic picturesqueness of other Spanish cities in whose building the Moors played a principal part. This city represents the new Spain rather than the old, with its wide streets and boulevards, its well-built houses and public buildings, and the splendid bridges that span the meagre trickle of the River Manzanares. It is a standing pleasantry with the Spaniards themselves that these bridges should be sold and the proceeds spent to buy water for the river.

The city centres about the plaza or open space where the Gate of the Sun (*Puerta del Sol*) stood in medieval days. About this are hotels, cafés, and government buildings, and from it radiate 10 important streets, including the Calle Mayor and the Calle de Alcalá. A little further north is the Gran Via, a great thoroughfare cut through the heart of Madrid during the First World War (1914–18).

With its famous old university, Madrid is the chief educational centre of Spain. The new University City on the outskirts of Madrid was largely destroyed during fighting in the Civil War (1936–39). Madrid also possesses in the Prado (near the Retiro or park) the greatest picture gallery in the world, with the exception of the Louvre in Paris. Besides having the most important collection of paintings by the Spanish masters Velazquez and Goya, and fine examples of El Greco's

*Associated Press*

## WHERE SPAIN'S SOVEREIGNS LIVED IN MADRID

Formerly the Palacio Real, or Royal Palace, the huge building with the enormous courtyard in the foreground has been called the Palacio Nacional or National Palace since King Alfonso XIII left the throne in 1931, when Spain was proclaimed a Republic. It is built of granite and limestone and was completed, after 30 years' work, in 1764. The State apartments are of great magnificence, and in the armoury, seen on the left of the courtyard, is the finest collection of armour in the world. During the Spanish Civil War (1936–39) Madrid was besieged for nearly two years.

work, the Prado contains Raphaels, Titians, and Tintorettos that are rivalled only in Italy; also works by Van Dyck, Rubens, Teniers, and other Flemish painters scarcely to be equalled elsewhere. Most of these art treasures were moved to Valencia as a precaution during the Civil War. The old Royal Palace, now the Palacio Nacional, has adjoining it on the south the Armeria, housing probably the world's finest collection of armour.

Madrid is the railway centre of Spain. Manufactures of leather, tobacco, chocolate, shoes, furniture, carpets, glassware and other products are important. During the Civil War which began in 1936, Madrid was the headquarters of the Republican government forces, and was subjected to continual bombardment and siege from the Nationalist forces until hostilities ceased in 1939. The population of the city is 1,413,700.

**Maeterlinck,** COUNT MAURICE (1862–1949). There are some people who think that the world is made solely for Man's use and pleasure, but the Belgian playwright and essayist Maurice Maeterlinck (pron. mah'-ter-lingh) saw a soul in all things. He has just as many wise thoughts to impart when he watches bees, flowers, and dogs as when he tells the story of a wrong-doing king.

Maeterlinck's life, for the most part, had been calm and uneventful and spent in quiet places. He was born in Ghent, Belgium, on August 29, 1862, and was educated with a view to becoming a lawyer. He became interested while at college in the newer

French verse through his acquaintance with Verhaeren, the Belgian poet. Six months in Paris among the younger literary men then turned Maeterlinck's thoughts for ever from the law.

In 1890 he published his first play, La Princesse Maleine. It has an air of unreality; the characters speak simply and repeat their speeches again and again. The critics made fun of the work—that is, most of them, though one Frenchman hailed Maeterlinck as " the Belgian Shakespeare."

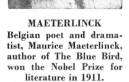

**MAETERLINCK**
Belgian poet and dramatist, Maurice Maeterlinck, author of The Blue Bird, won the Nobel Prize for literature in 1911.

Maeterlinck went on writing in spite of ridicule. Soon people began to see that these plays, which at first some thought so childishly simple, had an elusive beauty of their own, and were full of subtle suggestions of deeper meaning.

The thoughts which he seeks to embody in his plays are not rules for men to live by, or laws for the world to follow, but fleeting ideas, hopes, beliefs which come unbidden to people.

These ideas Maeterlinck expresses clearly and directly in his books of essays. The Treasure of the

Humble (1896) is the simplest of these. In his gentle quiet way he pleads for tolerance for all beings. Amongst his other works may be mentioned Les Aveugles (The Blind), 1890; Monna Vanna, 1903; L'Oiseau Bleu (The Blue Bird), 1909; La Vie des Abeilles (The Life of the Bees), 1901 ; La Vie des Fourmis (The Life of the Ants), 1926. In 1911 Maeterlinck was awarded the Nobel Prize for literature, and in 1932 he was created a Count by the King of the Belgians.

**Magellan,** FERDINAND (1480–1521). " The ocean! The great western ocean! " shouted the Spanish seamen, as their cannon saluted the mighty Pacific for which they had been searching many weary months. " If we live we shall yet discover the new way to the Spice Islands! "

" Thank God our Lord! " exclaimed Magellan (whose real name was Fernão de Magalhaes), their captain. " It is true, Señores, that we have lost two vessels, that our provisions are wasted, and that we may have many more hardships yet to endure. But even if we are reduced to eating the leather on our ships' yards we will go on! "

This was the dauntless spirit shown by that Portuguese mariner who discovered the Strait of Magellan, and who was not only the first European navigator to sail across the Pacific Ocean but also the first person to discover a route over which ships could sail in a complete circle around the world.

Magellan, son of a Portuguese nobleman, early served in the East Indies and Morocco with distinction. Believing that the king of Portugal had not justly rewarded his services, he renounced his nationality and offered to serve Charles V of Spain. This ruler, remembering the discoveries of Columbus and other bold sailors, accepted Magellan's proposal that he should make an attempt to reach the Moluccas or Spice Islands of the East Indies by sailing west instead of east, and on August 10, 1519, Magellan set sail from Seville, Spain, in command of five small vessels. Across the Atlantic and down the coast of South America he sailed until very cold and stormy weather forced him to seek winter quarters. Here mutiny was put down by force.

Sailing on again in the spring (which comes in September in the Southern Hemisphere), Magellan's fleet rounded a promontory, and on October 21, 1520, he sighted what he thought must be the sought-for strait (now named after him) leading to the East. For over a month he battled his way through this stormy 360-mile passage. One vessel was wrecked and another deserted and sailed back to Spain; but still Magellan persevered. On November 28, 1520, he reached the ocean that the Spanish explorer Balboa had discovered seven years before, and which Magellan now named the Pacific.

At first the voyage on the Pacific went well, save for monotony. One of the sources of amusement was a Patagonian, whom Magellan had kidnapped with the idea of exhibiting him in Spain when they returned; and the chronicler of the voyage, an Italian named Antonio Pigafetta, even made progress in setting down the Patagonian language.

After a month of sailing, terrible hardships assailed the fleet. Provisions ran low ; the drinking water turned thick and yellow, and dozens died of scurvy. In all, the fleet sailed 93 days before discovering Guam of the Ladrones, and a week later the Philippines. Magellan established friendly relations with the king of Cebu.

The great navigator, who was induced to undertake an expedition to conquer the neighbouring island of Mactan for the Catholic faith and the king of Cebu, was killed in a fight with the natives on April 27, 1521. The king of Cebu afterwards got into his power several of the explorer's most prominent men and murdered them. The survivors burned one of the three remaining vessels and sailed on to the Moluccas or Spice Islands. Another vessel, becoming leaky, had to be abandoned.

The last remaining vessel, laden with spices, at last rounded the Cape of Good Hope and in melancholy triumph dropped anchor in the harbour of Seville on September 9, 1522.

# The FANTASTIC REALM of MAGIC

**P**rimitive religion, superstition, and magic are closely interwoven. Do you know why some people touch wood to avoid ill-luck ? Why some carry a mascot ? These and other magical practices linger on today.

**Magic.** Our early ancestor, primitive Man, believed that by doing certain things he could influence the health or behaviour of people at a distance, and could even control the forces of Nature themselves by saying certain forms of words or performing certain ceremonial acts. He believed, that is to say, in magic. This belief has survived to some extent down to the present day.

In course of time repeated failure brought proof that there were many things—the changes of the seasons, the vagaries of the weather, and the occurrence of diseases and accidents—which were not controllable by human action. Hence arose the belief in powers greater than Man's, which must be humoured and propitiated. From this belief came primitive religion and idolatry. Put briefly, the difference between magic and religion is that by means of magic Man strove to *compel* the powers of Nature to obey him, whereas in religion he tried to *persuade* the gods to do what he wanted by means of prayer or sacrifice. Neither religion nor modern science has been able to kill the belief in magic, which still flourishes in backward races and has left many traces in the superstitions of educated people.

Among the earliest forms of magic are those connected with the belief that the fate of an individual may be influenced by getting possession of something which once belonged to him. A lock of hair, nail clippings, or a drop of blood might put the person from whom they came completely in the hands of the magician. This is still believed among natives of the Pacific islands and the Patagonians of South America. A bit of clothing stolen from an enemy was also considered a powerful agent of magic. The belief spread to include almost everything which had come in close contact with a

# 'MAGICAL' HATS TO CHARM THE WEATHER

Magic is practised by many very primitive peoples in the full belief that the forces of Nature can be influenced by it. These men, belonging to the Baining tribe who live in the interior of the Gazelle Peninsula of New Britain, in the south-west Pacific, are engaged in a dance of magic significance. The strange hats they wear are made of beaten tree bark and are held in position by long strings. Such hats are supposed to influence the weather. The man on the left is using a crude form of speaking-trumpet.

while white magic was supposed to combat this harm and do good instead.

The special magician or sorcerer has existed wherever a belief in magic prevailed. Under the name of necromancers, wizards, witches, conjurers, medicine-men, soothsayers, astrologers, and other titles, they posed as persons who had unusual powers over the spirit world or could foretell the future or read the secrets of the past. They were everywhere regarded with fearful respect. In Christian countries persons suspected of dealing with the powers of evil were persecuted severely, and thousands were put to death during the Middle Ages.

Studies in magic sometimes led to scientific discoveries, for the sorcerers, in mixing their magic philtres (love potions) and other drugs, stumbled upon new facts in chemistry ; while the astrologers who studied the supposed

task which might be demanded, under penalty of losing honour and reputation. Other spells, like the *tabu* of the Pacific islands, prohibited certain actions. A dwelling might be tabu, in which case no one could enter it, under threat of magic punishment. Various animals or fish, fruits and vegetables might become tabu for certain members of a tribe and not for others. The tabu was often used by native chiefs and priests in place of laws, and it was held in such terror that violations were exceedingly rare.

The word " charm " is also used to describe talismans, amulets, mascots, and any object which is carried to bring good luck. Almost anything may become a charm in this sense. Usually the person discovers the magic properties of the object himself, and while it may be a charm for him it is often supposed to bring bad luck to any other person who may become possessed of it.

The most general use of talismans and amulets is to guard against the " evil eye," the fear of which exists in one form or another in almost all parts of the world. Certain persons are believed to have this evil eye and to bring disaster to anything they gaze at, unless proper magic protection is provided. A surprising number even of educated people retain a belief in charms of some kind, even if it is only a " lucky " penny.

When a charm is believed to be not merely an instrument of magic but the actual dwelling-place of a certain spirit, it is called a " fetish." This belief is very common on the west coast of Africa, and from it the word fetish has come to us. The worship of fetishes is usually regarded as a form of religion, but it has many of the characteristics of ordinary magic. Fetishism plays a large part in the voodoo practices already mentioned.

While most forms of magic are based on the belief that evil spirits are particularly numerous and likely to injure mankind, there arises also a belief in good spirits. Along these lines, the practice of magic came to be divided into black magic and white magic—the former being used to do harm,

**TABU IN PACIFIC ISLANDS**

These curious headdresses, which also serve as masks, are worn by magicians of the New Guinea head-hunters when placing a tabu on fruit trees. In the top photograph, the Maori, a native of New Zealand, rendered tabu by having touched a corpse, has had his hands tied behind him so that he cannot touch anything and thereby spread his own contamination ; meanwhile, the girl is feeding him.

influence of the stars
on human life learned
many a fact about
astronomy. In com-
mon practice, how-
ever, the astrologers'
and sorcerers' skill was
directed toward inter-
preting dreams, or
getting information
about the future from
their "familiar"
spirits and, in almost
all cases, deceiving a
superstitious public
for their own personal
profit. Among the
intelligent their fraud
was usually suspected,
and the Roman Cato
" wondered how one
diviner could meet
another on the street
without laughing."

While modern Man
prides himself on hav-
ing thrown off all such
superstitions, rem-
nants of magical belief
are found even among
fairly intelligent
people. Under this
head come the delu-
sions about touching wood to ward off bad luck, breaking mirrors, walking under ladders, the number 13,
Friday, lucky coins, spilling salt, wishbones, black
cats, opals, and other things that are supposed to
bring good or bad luck. Almanacs for the credulous
will give a list of zodiac (in astronomy, a belt of 12
constellations, each named after an animal) signs,
the appearance of certain planets in which is asserted
to govern the sowing of crops, the treatment of farm
animals, and to perform other functions equally
magical, even to influencing the character and fate
of human beings.

**ONE OF CENTRAL AFRICA'S MEDICINE-MEN**
Among primitive people, magicians or medicine-men gain great influence and often rise to be
chieftains. From this photograph of an African medicine-man we may gather something of the
awe that he commands from the whole village as he goes through the ceremony for bringing
rain, good crops, success in hunting, or victory in battle.

**Magna Carta.** " Why do they not ask
for my kingdom? I will never grant such liberties
as will make me a slave!" Such was the angry
answer of tyrannical King John of England to the
first demand of his barons for a charter of reforms
to secure national liberties.

His tyranny, his wickedness, and his weaknesses
had united against him all classes of his kingdom—
nobles, churchmen and townsmen. And while he
was waging a losing war on the Continent, seeking
to recover his French dominions, the leading barons
of England had secretly met together and sworn to
compel the king to respect the rights of his subjects,
as provided by previous law and custom.

In various ways John sought to break up the
forces that confronted him, but in vain. On June 15,
1215, he met the nobles " between Staines and
Windsor in a meadow which is called Runnymede,"
on the Thames. Deserted by all but a handful of
personal followers, he was forced to affix his seal to
the Great Charter—called Magna Carta (or Charta)
in Latin, the language in which it was written. Four
copies of the Charter still exist. The most complete
is in Lincoln Cathedral, another in Salisbury
Cathedral, and two are in the British Museum.
In page 1196 is reproduced a part of one of these
last copies, together with King John's seal attached
to a fragment of the original document.

It is said that when King John granted the Great
Charter he smiled and spoke pleasantly to the lords
about him, but that when he reached his own
chamber he threw himself on the floor in a mad rage,
gnashing his teeth in fury. Since that day the
Charter has repeatedly been confirmed by succeeding kings of England, and has become a part of
English law and the foundation of the constitution
of every English-speaking nation.

Historical students today agree that the barons
were not so unselfish as was once thought. They
were chiefly interested in securing their own rights,
and they paid little attention to the rights of the
common people or the constitutional liberties of the
realm as a whole. Thus the Charter, in its 63
chapters or sections, deals for the most part with
feudal rights and duties which became obsolete
when feudalism died out. Its chief permanent
importance is that it established the principle that
" the king is below the law " and not above it.
In later days new and more liberal meanings were
read into some of its provisions, and all classes came
to reap the benefits which the barons won for themselves. But legal experts can discover in it no such
guarantees of trial by jury, or the right of the people
to be taxed by Parliament only, as were " read into "
the Charter by 17th- and 18th-century legal writers.
It provided that no man may be punished without
fair trial ; that punishment must be proportionate to
the offence, and that justice may not be denied, nor
delayed, nor sold to any man.

**Magnesium.** Anyone who has seen magnesium ribbon or flashlight powder used for indoor photography knows that magnesium metal can be made to burn with a brilliant white light.

The chemical symbol for magnesium is Mg; its atomic weight is 24·3; its atomic number, 12. Its density is 1·75. Magnesium never occurs free but is present in many minerals, such as asbestos and magnesite, the latter being used as a refractory lining for furnaces. The chloride and sulphate occur in mineral and sea water, the sulphate being better known as the Epsom Salts used in medicine. The metal was first prepared by Sir Humphry Davy in 1808. For a long time manufacture was on a small scale, but immense quantities of the metal are now needed for making the light alloys used in aeroplane manufac-

ture and for other purposes. On the industrial scale, metallic magnesium is obtained by the electrolysis (q.v.) of melted magnesium chloride, which is made by heating magnesium oxide with carbon and chlorine. The magnesium oxide may be obtained by the chemical treatment of sea water. As sea water contains only about one or two parts of magnesium per thousand parts of water, vast quantities of the water have to be treated. Magnesium metal can also be produced commercially by distillation, in a high vacuum, of a mixture of dolomitic limestone ($CaCO_3MgCO_3$) and ferro-silicon. Magnesium has a silver-white colour, which is tarnished by moist air. It is very light, but can be hammered, rolled, polished, and filed. The carbonates, hydroxide, and other salts of magnesium are of value in medicine.

# The MYSTERIOUS FORCE of the MAGNET

*Magnets and magnetism were a ' magical ' mystery to the ancients, and a complete explanation still awaits modern science. What magnetism does is apparent in daily life. An outline of its principles is here given.*

**Magnetism.** If you have ever amused yourself with a toy magnet, picking up nails or iron filings, or watched the behaviour of a compass needle when a piece of iron is brought near to it, you have probably wondered what it is which makes two pieces of metal attract one another. Books tell us that it is due to magnetism—but what *is* magnetism, and what does it do?

Natural magnets were known to the ancients. Plato (429–348 B.C.) gives an account of the " Samothracian Rings " which were used in the ceremonies of the Dactyls, a tribe of roving iron workers who came from near Troy. These rings were iron ones magnetised by contact with natural magnets or lodestones. The name magnetism is said by some to derive from a tribe called Magnetes who came from the city of Magnesia in Thessaly. Others think that it gets its name from a Greek shepherd named Magnes, who found that a particular stone attracted the iron-shod staff which he carried.

Petrus Peregrinus (c. A.D. 1256) carried out some experiments in magnetism; but the first real investigations were made in 1600 when William Gilbert, of Norwich, who was Court Physician to Queen Elizabeth, published his book entitled *De Magnete*. In spite of the fact that magnetism has been observed for many centuries it is still (as in the case of electricity) not easy to explain simply what magnetism *is*; so let us do the next best thing, and see what it *does*.

We can think of a magnet as a piece of material containing a large number of " lines of force " or " magnetic flux," which are concentrated within the material, and which emerge at one " pole " (the positive) to travel back outside the magnet, and to enter at the other pole (negative) just like an electric circuit. If a plate a straight bar magnet under a piece of paper on which iron filings are scattered, the filings will tend to lie along the direction of the lines of force, thus revealing them to the eye; and a pattern (known as a magnetic field) will be shown by the filings (Fig. 1). Notice that the lines of force are concentrated at the poles, while the centre of the magnet shows only a few odd lines. In the case of a horse-shoe magnet (Fig. 2) this concentration is even more marked.

Names are given to the two poles of a magnet. The positive—where the magnetic flux emerges—is called the " North-seeking " or North pole, while the negative (where the flux returns) is called the " South-seeking " or South pole. (These names are explained below, where we deal with the compass.)

If two bar magnets have their North poles pointed at each other the lines of force will " push " against each other, as shown in Fig. 3—and will push with considerable force, if the magnets are powerful ones. This is because *like poles repel.* If, on the other hand, the North pole of one is presented to the South pole of the other, we shall have the condition

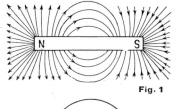

Fig. 1

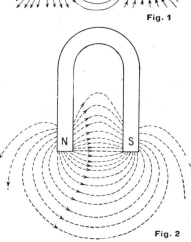

Fig. 2

**TWO MAGNETIC FIELDS**

Fig. 1. In the bar magnet the lines of force are mainly around the ends (' poles '). A horseshoe shaped magnet (Fig. 2) has the field concentrated into the area shown.

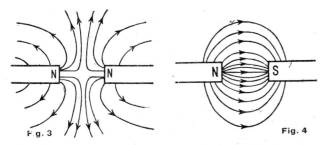

Fg. 3.

Fig. 4

**Fig. 3.** Lines of force from two 'like' poles repel each other ; but when two unlike poles are adjacent (Fig. 4) the lines of force attract each other.

at each end, it has two S. poles in the middle. This is done by magnetising it in a special manner.

If a magnet is put into a magnetic field caused by a second magnet it will, if free to move, align itself with the lines of force of the second field. The earth itself is a giant magnet, with poles nearly (but not quite) at the geographical N. and S. poles, and an external (or "return") field running all down the earth's surface. If we take a magnet which is pivoted at the centre, and free to swing, it will align itself with this field, and point towards the magnetic poles

shown in Fig. 4, where the lines of force are both travelling in the same direction, and there will be a "pull" set up, instead of a push. So we see that *unlike poles attract.*

There is another rule which we must get firmly fixed in our heads before we go any farther. A magnet *must* have two poles. It is not possible to have a North pole without a corresponding South. If we take a bar magnet and break it in two we shall find that extra poles appear at the break (Fig. 5). If we continue to break the magnet into smaller and smaller pieces we shall find that each piece—no matter how tiny— still contains both N. and S. poles.

It occasionally happens that a magnet is found which seems to disregard this rule, and is found to have a N. pole at both ends. This would seem to show that the rule just stated is wrong—but it is not. If we make the field visible with iron filings (Fig. 6), we find that the magnet has what is known as "consequent poles"; and if it has a N. pole

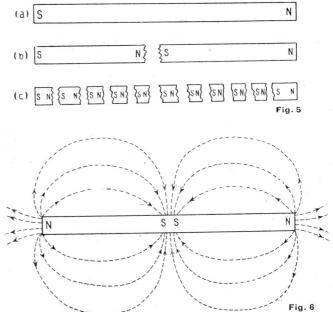

Fig. 5

BAR MAGNET BROKEN IN PIECES

Fig. 6

**Fig. 5.** When a bar magnet (a) is broken across, new poles of opposite polarity appear at the ends (b). This process can be continued indefinitely (c). **Fig. 6.** Magnets can be treated electrically to produce pairs of 'consequent' poles (see text).

(Fig. 7). This is the principle of the magnetic compass for ships. The magnets are made as light as possible, and the card or dial to which they are attached (marked with the points of the compass or with degrees) is pivoted on a needle point; the bowl in which the needle-system rests is filled with liquid, so as to obtain "damping" of the needle, to prevent it swinging wildly, while keeping friction as low as possible. (See Compass).

There is one point to bear in mind, however. What we call the North pole of a magnet could more correctly be termed "north-seeking"—i.e., the pole which points toward the North. Since like poles repel, it follows that the North magnetic pole of the earth really has opposite (i.e., negative) polarity to the N. pole of our compass. This may seem puzzling, but it is easier than trying to call the north-seeking magnet pole the "South," which would lead to endless confusion.

The North magnetic pole does not coincide exactly with the North geographical pole of the earth, nor does it stay in the same place all the

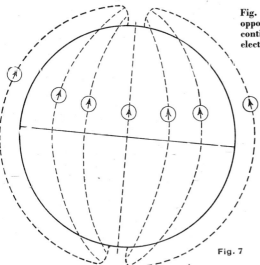

COMPASS IN THE EARTH'S FIELD

**A magnetic compass, placed at any point in the earth's magnetic field, aligns its needle with that field to point towards the Magnetic Pole.**

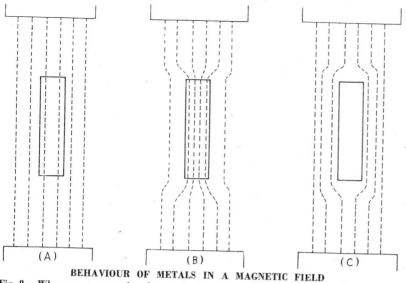

## BEHAVIOUR OF METALS IN A MAGNETIC FIELD

**Fig. 8.** When a non-magnetic substance is placed in the field of a magnet, the field is not affected (A). Ferro-magnetic metals, such as iron and nickel, cause the field to be concentrated on the material (B). Dia-magnetic (anti-magnetic) substances, one of which is bismuth, cause the field to avoid the object (C). *See* text for further explanation.

time. A compass in any part of the earth will point towards the magnetic pole, but we cannot find the true geographical North unless we know the *variation of the compass* for that particular spot. In England, the compass points about 14 degrees West of true North; while in some parts of the world Easterly variation is encountered. On a voyage across the Atlantic the compass course must be corrected every few hours for the change in variation encountered in different parts.

A "magnetic" material is one which is capable of being magnetised, either temporarily or permanently. We cannot magnetise a piece of wood or brass, for example. Any non-magnetic material placed in a magnetic field is completely unaffected (Fig. 8A). The earliest experiments were carried out with lodestones—pieces of a magnetic oxide of iron which is found in Nature, forming natural magnets. The first compasses probably consisted of lodestones, and were known in very early days. A legend states that the Emperor Hoang-ti, of China, in 2634 B.C., used them to track down an enemy.

Iron is the best-known magnetic material, exhibiting magnetic properties very strongly, this quality being known as *ferro-magnetism*, a term which is also applied to other metals than iron (such as nickel and cobalt) which, like iron, exhibit such properties. A ferro-magnetic material placed in a magnetic field concentrates the lines through itself (thus becoming a magnet), as shown in Fig. 8B.

Weak magnetic substances, i.e., materials only slightly more than non-magnetic, are known as *para-magnetic*. There is another class known as *dia-magnetic* (the metal bismuth is an example) which are actually anti-magnetic, and, instead of concentrating the lines of a field, they cause them to diverge (Fig. 8c). These substances are actually *repelled* by a magnet. For ordinary purposes, ferro-magnetic materials are the only ones of any

importance to us, however, and we shall not bother about the others.

The easiest way to regard magnetisation is to think of a piece of iron as being made up of a very large number of tiny magnets, all lying about at random (Fig. 9, top). When the iron is put into a magnetic field these tiny magnets align themselves with the field so that they all point the same way, and all act together instead of against each other. (In fact, the real theory of magnetic "domains," as they are called, is a good deal more complicated than this, but the above is an easy way to think about it.)

Some materials, such as soft iron, exhibit magnetic properties when they are in a magnetic field, but revert to their unmagnetised state when the field is removed. (We use this type of material in the vibrator of an electric bell.) Other materials, such as hard steel and various alloys, once magnetised become permanent magnets. At one time steel was the only material used for magnets of this type; but in the last few years alloys of iron, nickel, cobalt and copper have been developed which are many times more powerful than any steel magnet of the same weight and size. When magnetising a piece of steel, by placing it in a strong magnetic field, it assists the little "domains" of magnetisation to line themselves up in the right direction if the metal is vibrated or hammered.

A certain amount of permanent magnetism is imparted by merely hammering steel in the earth's field. A ship, for example (although it is built of comparatively soft steel which only retains a small amount of permanent magnetism), will become magnetised from the earth's field by the hammering it gets while building; and a ship built on stocks pointing East and West has quite a different "signature" (i.e., its own particular magnetic field) from one which is built pointing North and South.

Demagnetisation of a permanent magnet occurs by hammering or vibration, or with heating, both of which actions tend

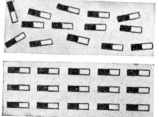

**Fig. 9.** When an iron bar is being magnetised, the 'domains' (like tiny magnets) are gradually aligned so that the North and South poles arrange themselves head to tail. Three successive stages are shown.

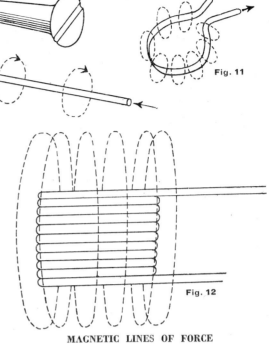

to allow the magnetic domains to return to their " higgledy-piggledy " condition. Demagnetisation also occurs with age, owing to the demagnetising effect of the magnet's own field, which tends to pull the little domains in the centre of the magnet out of line. For this reason bar magnets are usually stored in pairs with the N. pole of one to the S. pole of the other, so as to form a closed magnetic circuit and keep the flux away from the centre of the magnet. Alternatively (in a horseshoe magnet, for example), an iron " keeper " is used which bridges the two ends of the magnet and forms a return path for the flux. Comparing Figs. 1 and 2 we can see that the field of a horseshoe magnet does not approach the centre of the magnet so much, and the demagnetising effect is, therefore, smaller. (That is the reason why the horseshoe form was first adopted.)

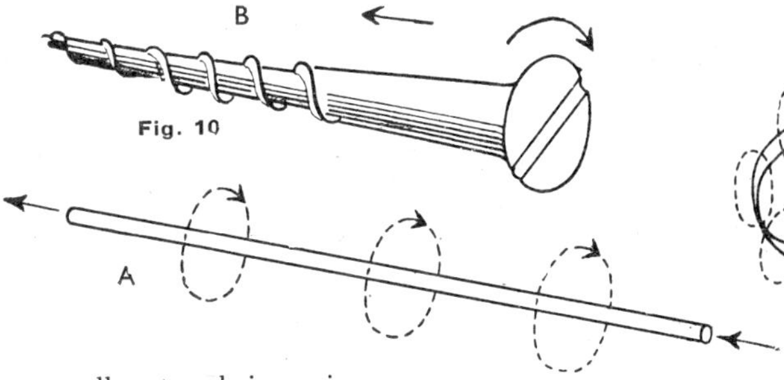

### The Electro-magnet

Magnetism and electricity were for many centuries considered to be separate sciences. In 1821 a Dane, Hans Christian Oersted, discovered that a conductor carrying an electric current affected a compass needle, showing that the conductor produced a field about it. (*See* diagram in page 1132.)

The magnetic field around a straight conductor can be thought of as a large number of small circular lines of force surrounding the conductor (Fig. 10A). The direction which these take is clockwise when looked at from the direction in which the current flows, and may be remembered by the " screw rule " (B) since an ordinary (right-handed) screw, travelling forwards into a piece of wood, turns right-handed or clockwise in the same way.

Carrying this a step further, we can see that if we form the conductor into a loop or " turn " we shall concentrate this field (Fig. 11) and get the effect of a magnet with one pole on each side of the loop, according to the direction of the current. If we extend this loop to a coil of several turns (Figs. 12 and 13), we shall greatly increase the flux, since each turn will contribute its quota; and the total will be proportional to the number of turns. The magnetic effect of a coil is measured in " ampere-turns "; for example, *two*

**MAGNETIC LINES OF FORCE**

Fig. 10. Lines of force around a straight current-carrying conductor (A) follow a clock-wise path (B). By forming the conductor into a loop (Fig. 11) the lines of force are concentrated. By the use of a coil of several turns (Fig. 12) the magnetic flux is greatly increased. (See text).

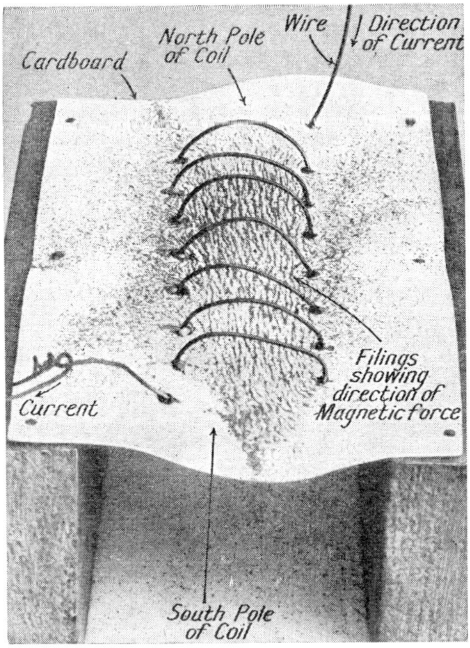

**A MAGNETIC FIELD**

Fig. 13. Make a coil of a few turns of wire, led through a piece of paper (above), and connect the ends to a battery. Sprinkle iron filings over the paper near the coil, and you will see the filings arrange themselves along the lines of magnetic force.

coils of the same size would give the same magnetic flux if one had *four* turns and a current of *one* ampere, and the other had *forty* turns and a current of *one-tenth* of an ampere.

The next step is to put a soft iron " core " inside the coil (Fig. 14), with the result that a greatly increased magnetic effect is obtained for the same number of ampere-turns. The reason for this is that iron has a much greater " permeability " than air. We can think of permeability as magnetic conductivity. Just as copper has a high electrical conductivity, so has iron a high magnetic conductivity. To say that a particular material has a " permeability of 600 " means that a given number of ampere-turns will furnish 600 times as many lines of force with a core of this material, as would be obtained if we had air—i.e., no core at all—for the

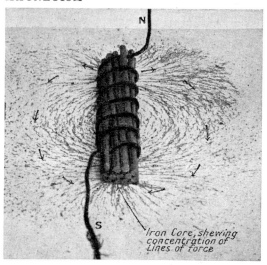

**EFFECT OF AN IRON CORE**
Fig. 14. This is a similar experiment to that shown in Fig. 13 ; but here a core of iron wires is placed within the coil. Sending a current through the coil demonstrates the increased magnetic effect, made visible by the iron filings.

15). When a current is passed through the coil the plunger is attracted into the coil, much like a piston entering a cylinder. Solenoids are made in all sizes—from a tiny coil, perhaps an inch long, which operates a relay requiring a pull of only a fraction of an ounce, to mechanisms for closing Grid switches and giving a pull of several thousand pounds.

There is also a large variety of lifting magnets used in foundries and steelworks in connexion with cranes for picking up all kinds of iron and steel material, either in bars or as lumps of scrap. A great deal of time and money is saved by not needing to have a " slinger " standing by to hook on each separate piece of material to be lifted. (See Electricity).

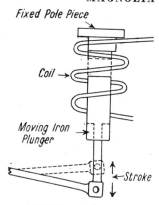

**SIMPLE SOLENOID**
Fig. 15. This is an electro-magnet with a moving iron plunger instead of a fixed core. Current flowing through coil causes plunger to be attracted into coil.

same length of magnetic path, and the same cross-sectional area. The permeability of a material is not a constant figure—after a certain flux density (number of lines of force per square inch) has been reached, the material becomes " saturated," and further increase of the magnetising ampere-turns produces little or no increase in the amount of flux resulting.

The first electro-magnet was made by an Englishman named William Sturgeon (1783–1850), in 1825; he wound a number of turns of wire round a horseshoe shaped iron bar, passed an electric current through the wires and found that this produced exactly the same effects as a permanent magnet, except that it could be " switched off." The electro-magnet is, nowadays, the basis of modern electrical engineering, being used in some form in practically every piece of electrical machinery. The dynamo, the alternator, the electric motor, and practically every scrap of control-gear utilise the electro-magnet either as such or in the form termed a " solenoid." A solenoid is an electro-magnet with a loose core. It consists of a coil with an iron " pole-piece " in one end, and an iron plunger which is free to slide in and out of the coil, and is attached to a lever or other mechanism where a force is to be applied (Fig.

**Magnolia.** Creamy-white blossoms of the evergreen magnolia (*M. grandiflora*), scenting the air in July and August with rich, heavy perfume make this tree a lovely object in parks and gardens.

*The Times*

**MAGNOLIA TREE IN BLOOM**
For all their exotic appearance, species of magnolia are hardy out of doors in some parts of Great Britain and they flower profusely. Taken in mid-April, at Kew Gardens, this photograph shows a magnificent display of large waxy petals, the blooms being cup-like in shape. Native to the Himalayas and other regions in Asia and to parts of Central and North America, the genus is named after Pierre Magnol, a 17th century French botanist.

The large glossy leaves form a fitting setting for the waxy petals and golden cone-shaped heart of the flowers, which are often 8 to 12 inches in diameter. The flowers are succeeded by cone-like fruits, which are reddish when ripe. In Britain, where it has been grown since 1688, this species reaches a height of from 15 to 20 feet. It is a native of the United States. Deciduous species include *M. conspicua*, known also as the Yulan, native to China and Japan; its white flowers are produced in spring, and the tree grows to about 25 feet. Other species vary widely in habit and growth, as well as in colour. The genus is named after Pierre Magnol, a French botanist of the 17th century.

**LOVELY MAGNOLIA BLOOM**
Introduced into the United Kingdom from North America in 1688, the magnolia bears flowers which vary from white to purple. Those of *M. grandiflora* (above) are white.

**Magpie.** A relative of the jay and raven, this handsome bird belongs to the crow family (*Corvidae*). Magpies are from 16 to 20 inches long, with glossy black and snow-white plumage, and a long pointed tail whose feathers are a rich mixture of deep blue, purple and green in colour. The common magpie (*Pica candata*) is plentiful in agricultural districts of the British Isles.

It builds, usually in the top of a tall tree, its nest a large dome-shaped structure of sticks lined with fine roots and dried grass and with an entrance at one side. The eggs (*see* colour plate facing page 440) are pale bluish green or yellowish white, spotted with olive green. The magpie eats snails, slugs, worms, rats, mice, and the eggs and nestlings of other birds; it is easily tamed, and makes a pert and cheerful, if noisy, pet.

**Magyars.** Most of the people living in the Republic of Hungary are Magyars, who are unlike any of the other European races. They are descended from wandering tribes who at some remote time began travelling westwards with their herds of horses from grazing grounds in the Altai Mountains of Mongolia and Western Siberia. A nation of warriors, they conquered many races in the course of their migration, including an Ugrian people whose language they adopted.

At the end of the 9th century they reached the plains of Hungary, where they intermarried with the local population, who were mostly of Tartar extraction. Converted to Christianity in the 11th century they gradually absorbed Western culture, while preserving their Ugrian speech (which somewhat resembles Finnish) and national characteristics.

**Mahogany.** Prized for its beauty, durability, and ease in working, mahogany has long been used for building boats and for making fine furniture. The Spanish colonists found the wood when they settled in the New World and were soon using it to repair their sailing vessels. No one knows when mahogany was introduced into Europe, but by the 18th century it was considered by English cabinetmakers to be the most elegant of all woods.

The mahogany tree is an evergreen and grows in the West Indies and tropical America. It often attains a height of 100 feet, with a trunk 12 feet in diameter and a reach of 60 feet or more to the first limb. Although the supply is abundant, the wood is expensive because of the tremendous labour involved in getting it. There may be only one or two trees to the acre of dense forest, and paths connecting with the main trails must be cleared to each tree before felling can begin. In most places, after the tree is cut, it must be dragged by oxen or tractors to a river bed to wait for the floods to carry it to the coast. In only a few locations can the logs be transported by barge and train.

In colour, mahogany ranges from light reddish tan to deep golden brown. In grain it varies from the plain stripe of the main trunk to the swirling, figured patterns near roots and limbs. It takes a high polish and need not be heavily stained, for it grows darker with age. Since it does not warp or shrink easily and glues well, it is much used for

*John Kearton*

**THE MAGPIE AS A PET**
With its black and white plumage and blue and green tail the magpie is a handsome bird. But it has a reputation as a robber of other birds' nests, eating the eggs and nestlings. Magpies are very inquisitive, and soon become friendly with human beings, making amusing pets.

veneers. Because it can be formed easily and withstands dampness, it is widely used for small boats.

Mahogany is usually sold under the name of the place from which it comes, for example, "Honduras mahogany." But the "Spanish" timber is got from Cuba, Trinidad and Tobago—the former Spanish West Indies. These two belong to the genus *Swietenia*, of the family *Meliaceae*. The species are *S. mahogani* (West Indies) and *S. macrophylla* (British Honduras).

In the timber trade today, other woods resembling the original mahogany are classed as mahoganies. Thus Gaboon mahogany comes from the French Congo and belongs to the family *Burseraceae* (*Aucoumea Klaineana*). African mahogany belongs to the *Meliaceae* family and grows in West Africa (*Khaya grandiflora*). The alternative name for Sapeli mahogany is "Gold Coast cedar," and this is another tree of the *Meliaceae* (*Entandrophragma*, several species).

# The PROPHET of ISLAM and his CREED

*Second only to Christianity as a missionary-religion, Mahomedanism or Islam is the faith of millions in all parts of the world. Here we tell of the Prophet who founded it and of its distinctive beliefs and practices.*

**Mahomet** (570?–632) AND MAHOMEDANISM. Few romances are stranger than the career of this founder of one of the world's historic religions. Born in Mecca, in what is now known as Saudi Arabia, of a good family, Mahomet (or Mahommed, also written Mohammed) was early left an orphan and was brought up by a poor but kind uncle. More than once he went to Syria with trading caravans, and as he grew older, he thought seriously about all that he saw and heard, in the desert and in the cities, as he travelled about.

The matter that caused deepest concern to the thoughtful young man was the ignorance and superstition of the Meccans and other Arabs, who were heathens. Marrying a rich widow named Khadija, he became a merchant but continued to brood on the low moral condition of his people. At that time the Jewish religion and Christianity flourished in some communities of southern Arabia.

Mahomet grew familiar with the teachings and lives of Jesus Christ and the Jewish prophets. He was subject to visions, and claimed that he was directed by God through the archangel Gabriel.

At the very beginning of his mission Mahomet, like other prophets, was fiercely opposed and ill-treated by his own family and relatives ; and from others came persecution so bitter that he was forced to flee from Mecca to the city of Medina, 250 miles to the north, where some of his supporters had already gone.

The date (July 16, 622) of this departure, or *hejira* of Mahomet from Mecca is that from which the whole Mahomedan world reckons time, as we do from the birth of Christ. It was also the turning-point in Mahomet's career. He had proclaimed himself as the true interpreter of God, as a prophet, and persistently preached to the heathen and the followers of Christianity and Judaism. At Medina the Jews were powerful, and Mahomet thought that he could combine with them in furthering his new worship. But the Jews refused.

After winning a powerful position in Medina, Mahomet declared war against both the Jews and the Meccans. When the Arabs began to flock to his standard, he sent messages to neighbouring kings. Some of them accepted Islam, as the Mahomedan religion is properly called (Islam means in Arabic " submission to God and His Divine Will "), while others refused, and wars were first declared against those enemies who persistently tried to check the teachings of Islam.

Mahomet suppressed idolatry, and after the conquest of Mecca, in the eighth year after his flight, all Arabia embraced Islam. Non-Moslems were not allowed to enter Arabia, and he sent letters to all the known kings of Europe and Asia calling upon them to acknowledge that " there is no God but Allah, and Mahomet is His Prophet." He died at Medina, in 632, just 10 years after his departure from Mecca. His tomb at Medina, and also the sacred city of Mecca, are places of pilgrimage for all Mahomedans.

Within 100 years after Mahomet's death, not merely Arabia but Syria, Persia, Egypt, northern Africa, and Spain had been conquered by Mahomet's victorious successors (called caliphs) ; and the followers of Islam were ready to carry their religion to the peoples of Asia Minor, eastern Europe, central and eastern Asia, and the interior of Africa. Today Mahomedanism is the faith of 350–400 millions in Asia, Africa and eastern Europe. There are a few British Mahomedans, too. It ranks third in numbers among the great religions, Christianity, and the religion of the Chinese Confucius having more followers.

Islam's sacred book, the Koran (*q.v.*), teaches the oneness of God in every respect, and strongly condemns idolatry. It lays down clearly the boundary between God and human beings. Its prohibitions include gambling, the drinking of intoxicants, the eating of the flesh of the pig, and the lending of money at a high rate of interest ; it conveys a message of brotherhood and equality to all, whatever their creed or religion may be. It teaches kindness towards the weak, slaves, and orphans. It has raised the status of woman, giving her the right to hold her own property in her own

*E.N.A.*

**MEDINA, WHERE MAHOMET DIED**

Some 250 miles north of Mecca is Medina, the city of Arabia whither the Prophet Mahomet fled in 622 and where he died and was buried 10 years later. His tomb is in the splendid mosque whose minarets are seen here.

name, and inherit from her father, mother, sons, and other relations just as a man can. The Koran states clearly that women have the same rights as have men. It teaches reverence to all past prophets, including Jesus and Moses, and to holy books. No Moslem may deny or dishonour any of them, for the Koran teaches toleration towards every religion. Islam abolished priests, insisting upon direct communication between God and men without the intervention of any priest. The Koran condemns monasticism and lays stress on cleanliness

of body and soul. Every Moslem is commanded to try his best to purify his morals, and recognize the integrity of knowledge, reason and thinking. The Koran teaches Mahomedans to detest ignorance and a blind attachment to their religion.

Every Moslem must pray five times a day, facing towards Mecca. The muezzins, or criers, give the call to prayer at dawn, at noon, and at sunset from the tall minarets of the mosques, or Mahomedan places of worship. One month in the year, called Ramadan, is kept as a season of fasting, when Moslems may not eat between dawn and sunset. As the Mahomedan calendar is a lunar one, the month of Ramadan falls 10 days earlier each year. Polygamy is allowed by the Mahomedan religion, but is limited to four wives at one time, provided the strict conditions laid down are duly observed.

There have sprung up in Islam many sects, which differ only in minor details. Chief of these are the Sunnites, or orthodox Mahomedans, and the Shiites. The Shiites insist that the descendants of Ali, husband of the Prophet's daughter Fatima, are the only legitimate caliphs, or leaders of Islam.

The Saracens, as followers of Islam were called in the Middle Ages, passed from Africa into Spain in 711. At the battle of Tours in 732, exactly 100 years after Mahomet's death, the Mahomedan invasion of France was halted by Charles Martel, ruler of the Franks and grandfather of Charlemagne. Driven back into Spain on the west, and held in check by the Byzantine Empire at Constantinople, the Arabs, Moors, and other Mahomedan peoples settled down in their new-won lands and developed from the 8th to the 12th centuries a culture which far surpassed that of western Europe. Among other centres of this culture were Damascus, in Syria ; Baghdad, on the River Tigris ; Cairo, on the lower Nile ; Cordova, in Spain ; and Delhi, in India.

The Saracens were excellent craftsmen. The sword blades of Toledo and Damascus were world-renowned. Equal skill was shown in the fashioning of vases, lamps, and other articles of copper, bronze, and silver; in the weaving of carpets and rugs, which are still unsurpassed ; and in the moulding of fine glass and pottery. Sweetmeats, syrups, essences, and perfumes were produced. Paper,

E.N.A.

**MAHOMEDANS AT PRAYER**

Followers of the Prophet Mahomet are seen in the upper photograph in the third posture of prayer, in which the forehead must touch the ground as a sign of humility. Mahomedans should be physically clean when they pray, which they are enjoined to do five times a day, the appointed time being announced by a call to prayer given by a muezzin (lower) from the minaret of a mosque.

without which the invention of printing would have been valueless, came to Europe through the Mahomedans. The finest leather goods came from Cordova and Morocco.

In literature, particularly poetry, and in science the Mahomedans attained a high degree of develop-

*Wide World Photos*

**MAHOMEDAN FESTIVAL IN CAIRO**

Every year the Holy Carpet, which is made in Egypt, is carried to Mecca, where it is
used to cover the Kaaba (shrine containing a black stone supposed to be a relic of
Abraham's original shrine) during the ensuing year. Here the carpet, fastened to
a wooden frame, is being taken through the streets of Cairo, Egypt.

them. The University of Cairo at one time had
12,000 students. In Spain in the 10th century a
library of 400,000 manuscripts is said to have been
collected. Learned Arabs did much to preserve
and spread the writings of the great Greek philosopher Aristotle, after he had been all but forgotten
in western Europe. In mathematics and algebra
Mahomedan scholars led the world. The so-called
" Arabic " numerals which we use today were
introduced by them. In astronomy, medicine, and
chemistry they made notable advances. The richness and grace of their architecture are evident in
many lands.

**Maine.** The most easterly state of the
United States, Maine has a deeply indented coastline on the Atlantic Ocean. It is bounded on the
north and east by Canada, on the south-east by the
Atlantic, and on the west by New Hampshire and
Canada. It has an area of 33,215 square miles,
much of it being covered by forests. The State is
mountainous in the north, the highest point being
Katahdin (5,350 feet). There are more than 3,000
rivers and streams, many of them providing water
power, and 1,620 lakes. Maine is one of the chief
summer holiday resorts of the United States.

The State is the chief producer of wood pulp
and paper in the country. It is also first in potato
output, other crops being maize, oats, buckwheat
and apples. The herring, haddock, cod and lobster
fisheries are valuable ; there is shipbuilding at
Bath ; and limestone, slate, sand, gravel, mica and
granite are worked. Maine has a number of rare
minerals, including pollucite (source of the metal
caesium, used in wireless valves), beryl (source of
beryllium, a metal used for alloys of great
strength), and minerals for gems such as tourma-
lines, amethysts, garnets and topazes. Fish, fruit

and vegetable canning, and the
manufacture of textiles and
boots and shoes are main
industries. The State has 1,828
miles of railway, connected
with the Canadian system.
Augusta, with a population of
20,000, is the State capital, but
Portland is the largest city and
chief port.

Sebastian Cabot is believed to
have visited the coast of Maine
in 1496 ; the first permanent
settlements were established in
1622. Massachusetts absorbed
Maine in 1691, and it did not
again become a separate State
until 1820. The population is
about 847,220.

**Maize.** Known also in
Britain as Indian corn, in
America simply as corn, maize
(*Zea mays*) is a half-hardy
annual grass and one of the
most important cereals in the
world. It is grown chiefly in
Britain as a cattle-fodder, also
for decorative purposes in gardens; and in hot summers, when
the plant may reach a height of
six feet, the large heads of
grain (known in America as " corn on the cob ")
ripen so that they can be cooked and eaten. The
grain is also fed to poultry. In some parts of the
world maize flour is used for making bread.

Like the potato and tobacco, it is a New World
plant and probably originated in Central America;
it was introduced into Britain in 1562.

*Dorien Leigh*

**MAIZE PLANTS IN FLOWER**

Cultivated for a variety of purposes, this tall-growing and
very substantial grass is also known in Britain as Indian
corn. Here the upstanding, tassel-like heads of flowers
can be seen ; they will be followed by large heads of grain.

# LIFE *in the* LAND *of* RUBBER *and* TIN

*Within the mountainous, jungle-clad peninsula of Malaya lie a number
of States—some savage and some in a reasonably high stage of civilization.
All of them are under British guidance.*

**Malaya.** Extending from the southernmost part of Siam to the Colony of Singapore, this long and narrow peninsula stretches south and south-east for 750 miles. Much of it is covered with jungle and forest ; roads are few, the many rivers being the main routes of travel.

The rich soil, in one of the hottest and dampest climates in the world, is covered with a tangle of giant trees, creepers, trailing plants, and under-growth so dense that even the wild beasts travel only along well-worn paths. Ferns and rank grasses hide the soil. This tangle of vegetation harbours myriads of leeches, centipedes, scorpions, wasps and stinging flies, pythons and cobras, ants and mosquitoes, parakeets, and many songless birds of brilliant plumage. Black buffaloes with pointed horns, elephants, and tigers are plentiful. There are black leopards and honey-bears, tapirs and deer, the rare Malayan antelope, rhinoceroses and alligators.

Along the swampy banks of the rivers live the people called the Malays. The typical Malay is short and well built, with straight black hair, a dark brown complexion, thick nose and lips, and bright intelligent eyes. He is very suspicious, courageous and, generally, extravagant. Usually a Mahomedan by religion, he is also very superstitious.

He is conservative, proud, and clever but infinitely lazy. He plays at trade sometimes, but almost always fails to make a living at it, because he is so unbusinesslike. His house is untidy, even dirty; but he bathes twice a day and is very fond of gay clothes—especially the coloured cotton and silk *sarong* which both men and women wear draped round the waist to make a sort of skirt.

The Malay village is usually a cluster of huts on piles, built of bamboo and palm leaves or sometimes of wood and thatch. The houses are never close together and are shaded by tall coconut palms and a few fruit trees—the dark-leaved mangosteen, the mango with its brilliant magenta blossoms, and the durian, the latter a tree of magnificent dimensions which produces the golden, spike-studded fruit so relished by the natives. Behind the *kampong* (enclosure) are fields of rice, running back into little valleys, at the foot, perhaps, of the long mountain chains that rise range upon range into the heart of the peninsula. Rice, with fish, forms the staple diet of the people.

About two-fifths of the population of the peninsula are Malays; but the Chinese, who compose another two-fifths of the total, are the labourers, miners, shopkeepers, and contractors. In the mountains are still found about 20,000 of the aboriginal inhabitants—the woolly-haired negroid Semangs,

who support themselves by fishing and hunting, and the Sakais, who build their houses in trees. The Tamils, coming from the southern part of the sub-continent of India, work on the rubber plantations and number about 200,000.

The principal sources of wealth are rubber and tin. Before the Second World War (1939–45) rubber plantations covered more than 3,000,000 acres and 500,000 tons of rubber were exported yearly. Some of the plantations were damaged by the Japanese, who occupied Malaya from 1942 to 1945, but on the re-occupation of the country by the British in 1945 the Government took immediate steps to restore the industry to its former position and by 1948 Malaya was furnishing about half of the world's supply of natural rubber.

After rubber, tin is the most important product of Malaya, the bulk of it coming from the Malay States of Perak, Selangor, Negri Sembilan and Pahang. More than 53,000 tons were exported annually before the Second World War, and after the cessation of hostilities in 1945 the output gradually improved, more than one-third of the world's tin being mined in the peninsula.

Politically the peninsula consists of the southern province of Siam; the Federation of Malaya, which includes the nine Malay States of Perak, Selangor, Negri Sembilan, Pahang, Johore, Kedah, Kelantan, Trengganu and Perlis, and the two British settlements of Penang and Malacca; and the British Colony of Singapore at the tip of the peninsula.

The area of the Federation of Malaya is about 51,000 square miles, and the capital is Kuala Lumpur in the State of Selangor. Singapore Colony is 290 square miles in extent, the city of Singapore (*q.v.*) being the seat of Government.

It was not until the 16th century that the Malay Peninsula became known to Europe through the Portuguese. The British East India Company established trading settlements there in the 18th century, and in 1819 the city of Singapore was founded. The Company's possessions were made a Crown Colony in 1867, and between 1888 and 1896 the Malay States of Perak, Selangor, Negri Sembilan and Pahang came under British control, the protection of the United Kingdom being extended to Kedah, Kelantan, Trengganu and Perlis in 1909.

During the Second World War the Japanese attacked Malaya on December 8, 1941, invading the country from Siam. Despite stubborn resistance from British, Australian and Indian troops, the Japanese advanced rapidly and by the end of January 1942 all troops had withdrawn to Singapore, which surrendered to the Japanese on February 15 of that year. Following the surrender

> **Extent.**—Area of the Malayan Federation about 51,000 square miles ; population 4,800,000. Area of Singapore Colony about 290 square miles ; population about 980,000.
> **Physical Features.**—A vast forest, intersected by countless rivers ; backbone of granite mountains.
> **Principal Products.**—Rubber ; tin ; copra ; palm oil.
> **Chief Towns.**—Singapore, seat of government of Singapore Colony (445,000) ; Kuala Lumpur, seat of government of the Federation of Malaya (141,660) ; Georgetown (101,180).

# SOCIAL CONTRASTS IN PRESENT-DAY MALAYA

*J. Cummins; Malayan Information Agency*

Most Malayan villages are built close to a river, and the houses are raised off the ground (top left) partly to avoid floods and partly to keep out snakes and wild beasts. Bamboo and palm leaves are the principal building materials, and underneath the structures live the family's chickens. Though the Malay is very particular about his appearance and bathes twice a day his home is usually untidy, even dirty. At the top right are two Malayan girls, whose elaborate costumes indicate that their parents are well-to-do. One of the finest buildings in Kuala Lumpur, the capital of the Malayan Federation, is the mosque (lower) which stands beside the Klang river.

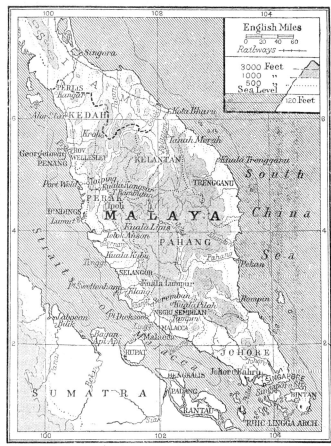

**MALAYA : SOUTHERN EXTREMITY OF ASIA**
That part of the Malay Peninsula south of Siam contains the Federation of Malaya, which is formed by the nine Malay States, the island of Penang, with Province Wellesley on the opposite shore of the mainland, and Malacca. Singapore Colony is at the southern tip.

of Japan to the Allies in August 1945, British forces reoccupied the Malay Peninsula.

In October 1945 a scheme was announced for establishing a Malayan Union, comprising the Malay States and the British territories of Penang and Malacca, Singapore becoming a separate Colony. The Malay rulers, after first accepting the scheme, decided against it on the ground that it deprived them of too much power. A new plan came into effect in February 1948, setting up the Federation of Malaya and including the same territory as the rejected Union. The Federation gave the Malay rulers more power, but Britain is responsible for the defence and external affairs of the Malay States and British possessions. The population of the Federation of Malaya is 4,800,000 ; that of Singapore Colony is about 980,000.

**Mallow.** Plentiful over most of Europe and in Britain, the common mallow (*Malva sylvestris*) has mauve blooms, more than an inch across, on erect stalks, and lobed hairy leaves. It grows to a height of three or four feet, and is a handsome plant when not bedraggled and dust-coated by the side of a country road. The dwarf mallow (*M. rotundifolia*) has smaller flowers. The musk mallow (*M. moschata*), about three feet in height, has pink blossoms in clusters at the top of the erect stems during July and August, and the leaves are divided into narrow segments ; when these leaves are bruised they give out an agreeable odour of musk, hence the name. Though a native wild plant, found in dry meadows and hedgerows, the musk mallow is frequently grown in British gardens, together with a white-flowered variety (*M. moschata alba*). These are all perennial plants. The fruit consists of a number of kidney-shaped seeds arranged in a flattened circular mass like the sections of an orange.

**Malt.** Barley or other grain that has been artificially germinated or made to sprout by moisture and heat is called malt. In the older and simpler method of malting, the grain is steeped in cisterns for from 48 to 100 hours at a temperature of about 55° Fahrenheit. It is then spread on a floor in heaps to germinate for several days, and finally it is further heated and dried in kilns to stop germination. In the malting process various ferments or enzymes are produced, especially diastase, which has the power of changing starch into sugar and is of great importance in the process of digestion.

The greater part of British malt is used in brewing beer, which is made from a mixture of malt (chiefly barley malt), various unmalted grains, hops, and water, to which yeast is added to produce fermentation. It is also used in making malted milk, which is a mixture of powdered milk and powdered malt, and in the manufacture of invalid and baby foods. The starch of the grain is made more digestible in the process of malting ; some of it is actually changed into sugar and other products soluble in water. A solution of malt products, evaporated to a thick consistency until it looks like brown syrup, is used in bread making.

*E. J. Hosking*
**COMMON MALLOW**
Frequently seen by the side of country roads in Britain, the common mallow has mauve flowers veined with darker lines ; these are produced from the axils of the leaves, during June to September. It is at its best when the hairy stems and leaves are not dust-covered.

# A BRITISH STEPPING-STONE to the EAST

*With Gibraltar and Cyprus, Malta forms a chain of British outposts in the Mediterranean and safeguards the shipping routes through the Suez Canal to the East. Thus, though small, it has great importance.*

**Malta.** Fifty-nine miles south of Sicily and about 180 miles from the coast of North Africa, the island of Malta is only 17 miles long and nine miles wide; but near by are the smaller islands of Gozo and Comino, which make the total area of the British Colony of Malta 122 square miles. The climate is mild and healthy in winter, and warm in summer.

Though the surface of Malta is rocky, more than 40,000 acres are normally under cultivation, chief products being potatoes, onions, fruit, wheat, barley and cotton. Goats, pigs and sheep are reared. Soft limestone, of which the houses are built, is the only mineral. Minor manufactures include lace, filigree, pipes, cigarettes and cotton.

The inhabitants are largely descendants of the ancient Phoenicians of Asia Minor and speak a language of mixed Phoenician, Arabic and Latin origin, which is the official language in all the courts of law. The island contains large stone monuments that were erected by a Mediterranean people of the Neolithic period (*c.* 3,000 B.C.). Phoenicians reached the island about 1,000 B.C., and were followed in the 6th century by Carthaginians. Then in succession through the centuries came Romans, Byzantine Greeks, Arabs, Normans and Spaniards, until in 1530 King Charles V of Spain gave the island to the Knights of St. John of Jerusalem, who, driven from the island of Rhodes by the Turks, wanted a new home. Adopting the title of Knights of Malta, they defended themselves successfully against the Turks during the famous siege of Malta in 1565, retaining possession of the island until 1798, when they surrendered without resistance to Napoleon Bonaparte.

In 1800 the French garrison capitulated to the British, the island being annexed to the British Crown by the Treaty of Paris in 1814. With the opening of the Suez Canal in 1869 Malta became an important coaling-station on the shipping routes between Great Britain, India, Australia and the Far

> **Extent.**—Area of Malta, 95 square miles. Area of colony (Malta, Gozo and Comino), 122 square miles ; population of colony, 241,620.
> **Physical Features.**—Hilly islands, with an indented coastline.
> **Principal Products.**—Cotton, wheat, barley, vegetables and fruit.
> **Chief Town.**—Valletta (capital), 48,000.

East, later providing the main base of the British Mediterranean fleet. With the development of air transport, the island was made a staging point on Empire air routes. As an important British sea and air base it has three aerodromes, an up-to-date dockyard, and a fine harbour at Valletta, the capital.

In the Second World War (1939–45), while Germany and Italy had armies in North Africa, aeroplanes and submarines of the Allies from Malta harassed enemy supply ships taking munitions, petrol and food to those forces. In return, the island came under almost constant bombardment from Italian and German aircraft, commencing in June 1940 and continuing until July 1943. At times both the civilian and military inhabitants were on the verge of starvation, and ammunition and petrol were almost exhausted. But Malta held out with the aid of supplies brought from Britain by surface convoys, which suffered heavy casualties in fighting their way through to the beleaguered island, and by submarines.

On April 15, 1942, King George VI awarded the island the George Cross in recognition of the gallantry of its people. The citation, stating how the decoration had been won, reads: " To honour her brave people I award the George Cross to the Island Fortress of Malta to bear witness to a heroism and devotion that will long be famous in history —(signed) George R. I." After being exhibited in the towns and villages of the island the George Cross was placed in St. John's Cathedral, Valletta.

More than 10,000 houses were demolished and 18,000 damaged ; 1,190 civilians were killed, and 3,778 injured by air raids. The British Government granted Malta £10 million to help in the reconstruction of bomb-damaged buildings; and a new form of government, giving the Maltese self-government in home affairs, came into effect in September 1947. The population of the Colony of Malta is 241,620.

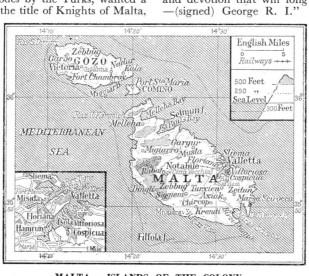

**MALTA : ISLANDS OF THE COLONY**
The British possession of Malta comprises Malta, Gozo, Comino and some other islets, lying between Sicily and the coast of North Africa. Inset is Valletta, the capital of the colony, with its two harbours which serve as a base for the British Mediterranean fleet.

# A GEORGE CROSS FOR THIS VALIANT ISLAND

*Topical; British Official*

In April 1942 King George VI awarded the George Cross to Malta in recognition of the heroism of her people during the Second World War (1939–45). In the lower photograph Lord Gort, V.C., (back to camera) is seen presenting the decoration to the Chief Justice of Malta, Sir George Borg, on September 15, 1942. Sliema Creek (upper photograph) is one arm of the harbour bordering both sides of the promontory on which Valletta, the capital of Malta, is mainly built.

# At the TOP of the TREE of ANIMAL LIFE

*Including all the four-legged and some other creatures—as well as Man himself—
the group at which we glance here comprises animals remarkably different in
many respects yet alike in others.*

**Mammals.** The highest form of animal life in the world, mammals range in size from the elephant to the shrew, and in appearance from the lion to the giraffe, or from the kangaroo to the whale. Certain features they have in common, however, which are not possessed by other forms of animal life.

Birds, reptiles, and insects lay eggs from which their offspring are hatched. Young mammals, on the other hand, are born alive, sometimes blind and helpless, and sometimes able, after a few hours, to run about with their mother. But there are exceptions in the monotremes (primitive types of mammal) such as the echidnas and the duck-billed platypus, or *Ornithorhyncus*, which lay eggs and hatch their young from them. (*See* Duckbill).

Mammals may also be described as four-limbed animals wholly or partly clothed with hair. This in some species forms a thick warm coat which enables them to exist in the coldest climates. In many it is beautifully coloured and marked with bars or spots —for example, the tiger, zebra, giraffe and leopard. It has become a handsome decoration in the mane of the lion, and a very graceful one in the mane and tail of the horse.

How beautifully soft and velvety is the fur of the mole and the seal! The seal and some other mammals have a short, thick, warm under-fur which is covered by a coat of longer and coarser hair. The elephant, the rhinoceros, the hippopotamus, and the pig have only the coarse outer coat and very little of that, and the hair of the pig has become transformed into stiff bristles.

In the hedgehog and the porcupine the hair has become a means of defence: it has been hardened into strong sharp spines. In the rhinoceros, modified hair tissue even forms the large pointed horn or horns on top of its snout.

Again, members of the cat family and some others have long stiff whiskers standing out on each side of the muzzle. These serve as feelers which enable the animal, when it is hunting, to judge, without turning its head, whether an opening in the undergrowth is wide enough for its body to pass through without brushing the plants on either side and so making a noise that would startle its prey.

Whales are mammals, yet many of them have only scanty hair; the thick coat of blubber which is under their skin serves instead to keep them warm. Furthermore, whales have only two limbs—the flippers. They have completely lost their hind-legs. As the whale swims by means of its tail, hind-legs would be not only useless to it but very much in the way. Still, in the skeleton of the whale there are bones which prove that once upon a time it had four limbs. The fore-legs of the whale have been changed into flippers, the bones of the toes being joined and covered by flesh and skin so as to form a flat paddle.

In some other kinds of mammals the fore-limbs have also been changed. Bats use them for flying. For this purpose four of the toes have been very much lengthened, and between them has been stretched a delicate skin, which also extends from the fourth toe to the body and the hind-leg. In monkeys, apes, and also in Man, the fore-legs have become arms with hands instead of feet.

Some mammals walk on the soles of the feet—for example, the bear, the otter, the weasel, and the hedgehog; whereas the dog, the cat, and many others go on their toes. These two types are called *plantigrade* (from Latin *planta*, sole, and *gradi*, walk), and *digitigrade* (Latin, *digitus*, finger) respectively. In some species which depend for safety on speed—for example, the deer, the horse, and the camel—all four limbs are long; these are animals that run swiftly. The kangaroo has another method of escape from its enemies; its fore-legs have become very short and are useless for running, but its hind-legs are large and powerful, enabling the creature to make enormous bounds.

All mammals except the whales have their toes armed with claws or nails. The cats have sharp claws for catching and holding their prey. When not in use, these claws can be withdrawn into sheaths so that the points may not be blunted. The

*F. W. Bond*

**HYRAX, A STRANGE LITTLE MAMMAL**
You would certainly never guess what other mammal is this little creature's nearest relative, nor even to which group it belongs. For the hyrax, although it climbs trees, is a hoofed beast, and its closest relative is the elephant. The above species of hyrax is found in Africa.

# SOME MEMBERS
## of the
## FOUR CHIEF
## GROUPS
## of
## MAMMALS

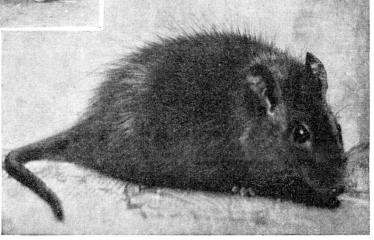

Here are shown representatives of the four chief groups of mammals. At the top is a sable antelope (*Ungulata*); immediately above are two chimpanzees (*Primates*); above right is a snow leopard (*Carnivora*); and on the right below is a black rat (*Rodentia*).

claws of the dog are comparatively blunt, and are used for digging or scratching. The sloth's are long and hooked, and by means of them it hangs upside-down on the branches of trees. The ant-eater's are large, powerful weapons with which it breaks open ant-hills. In monkeys, apes, and Man the claws have become finger-nails.

One large group of mammals, which includes the horse, the deer, the ox, the sheep, and the pig, actually walks on its nails. These have been very much enlarged so that they surround the tip of the toe, and have been given the name of hoof. The full number of toes on the foot of a mammal is five, but many species have fewer. The pig and the deer have four, though they use only two; the sloth has three, the ox and the sheep have two, and the horse has only one.

The tail is used by some mammals as an extra limb. Among the kangaroo tribe it serves as

a support, like a third hind-leg, when the animal is sitting. In the opossum and the spider-monkey it can be twined around a support, and by doing this the animal can swing itself from branch to branch. It is the organ by which the whale is able to swim. Horses and cattle use it to brush flies from their sides.

Mammals are also distinguished from all other animals by the fact that they have different kinds of teeth. Reptiles and fishes have many teeth, but they are all of one kind, sharp spikes by which they can hold their prey. Mammals have four kinds. First there are the chisel-like front teeth, called incisors, which are used for seizing and biting through food. Next, and on each side of them, there are four sharp-pointed teeth, called canines or dog-teeth, with which the animal tears its food. At the back of each jaw are several large teeth with a broad rough surface, which serve to grind food; these are called molars, and between them and the canines there are two or more smaller teeth—premolars—for chewing.

Man, apes and monkeys have all four kinds of teeth, because their food is varied. Tigers, wolves and other flesh-eating animals have small incisors, but large, strong, sharp canines, and narrow molars with sharp points.

The horse and ox and their many cousins which live upon grass and other herbage have large incisors and also big molars (because their food requires much grinding) but only small canines. The rat, the squirrel, the rabbit, and other rodents which gnaw or nibble their food, have long, sharp incisors and no canines. The elephant has no need of incisors, because it picks up food and places it in its mouth with its trunk, but it has incisors which have developed into long tusks.

The canine teeth of the wild boar have in the course of time grown into fierce-looking weapons which curve out of its mouth on each side. One group of mammals, to which belong the sloth, the ant-eater and the armadillo, have, as a rule, no teeth, and some whales, such as the "killer," have a large number of teeth all alike, resembling those of fish.

Top, James; lower, Topical

## MAMMALS THAT LIVE IN THE SEA

The seal (upper), although it spends most of its life in the sea, is actually a member of the carnivorous mammal group, a relative of the cats and their kin. The whales, a stranded shoal of which you see in the lower picture, are members of their own special order, Cetacea, although they are also true mammals in spite of their superficially fish-like appearance.

There is one habit that is practised by all mammals—the mothers suckle their young until they are old and strong enough to eat more solid fare. This is done by no other creatures.

Most mammals are more or less gregarious in habit, and some combine to secure food, or to protect themselves against enemies. Many of the dog family hunt in packs, and there are hoofed mammals that go in herds protected by the old males. Most mammals arrange some kind of home or lair in which to produce and rear their young.

Mammals are classed in groups according to their basic likenesses. In each group we place all those animals which, though remarkably unlike in general appearance, have yet some special habit or type of organ in common. There are three main divisions, of which the first two have only a single group each, as you see from the following table.

(1) *Monotremes* (egg-laying mammals like the duck-billed platypus); (2) *Marsupials* (the kangaroo and other animals which carry their

*W. S. Berridge*

**SLOTH AT REST**

As representative of those degenerate mammals which are grouped together as Edentates (Latin *edentatus*, toothless), because they have no teeth, you see here a sloth, so called owing to its sluggish habits. It hangs back downward from trees.

young ones in a pouch like a pocket of an apron until they are able to fend for themselves); (3) *Placentals* containing all the other groups, as follows : (a) *Ungulata* (all hoofed animals, including elephant, rhinoceros, hippopotamus, horse, pig, deer, ox, and sheep) ; (b) *Sirenia* (manatee and dugong, water animals somewhat like whales) ; (c) *Cetacea* (whales and dolphins); (d) *Carnivora* (flesh-eating animals, such as cat, dog, bear, seal, weasel); (e) *Rodentia* (gnawing animals, such as squirrel, rat, mouse, rabbit); (f) *Insectivora* (insect-eaters—hedgehog, shrew); (g) *Chiroptera* (flying mammals—bats); (h) *Primates* (mammals with hands—lemur, monkey, ape, Man). Besides these there are degenerate groups such as the *Edentata* (ant-eaters, sloths and armadillos).

**Mammoth** AND MASTODON. In various parts of the world are found the bones and other remains of these enormous, prehistoric elephants. Also on cave walls in Europe are drawings which show that men of the Stone Age hunted these

*American Museum of Natural History*

**HUGE MAMMOTHS, HAIRY PREHISTORIC ELEPHANTS**

In this artist's conception of an Ice Age landscape a herd of shaggy mammoths, beasts that roamed the Earth thousands of years ago, is marching across country. We know just what they were like, for in Arctic Siberia carcasses of some of them have been preserved in the frozen soil. For all their size these creatures fell victim to the crude stone weapons of our prehistoric ancestors, as is apparent from their fossil remains found in Great Britain and elsewhere.

monsters. Both the mammoth and the mastodon were about the size of the largest African elephants of today, but their bodies were covered with a kind of reddish wool and long black hair.

The mammoth had long slender tusks which curved upwards and outwards, while those of the mastodon grew out straight in front of it. The fossil remains are found in Siberia and supply large quantities of ivory. The tusks of the mammoth sometimes reached a length of 9 or 10 feet, and a weight varying from 180 to 200 pounds.

The mammoth and the mastodon fed on shoots and cones of pine trees that covered vast areas of the Northern Hemisphere during the Ice Age. Besides being common in Siberia, they were also numerous in England, Central Europe and North America. Some of these extinct monsters apparently came to grief by falling into snow-filled ravines from which they were unable to extricate themselves. It has also been thought that the primitive hunters of those days when mammoths roamed the Earth constructed huge pitfalls for their undoing.

# How MAN became LORD of CREATION

'*What a piece of work is Man!*' *Shakespeare's words have often been echoed by historians and scientists, as well as by ordinary men. And truly Man's history is the most wonderful story one could wish for.*

**Man.** Science can do little more than guess at the period when Man first made his appearance on this earth. Bones buried in ancient soils, rude weapons chipped from stone, carved bits of horn and ivory, pictures of animals long since extinct found on the walls of forgotten caves—these provide the material with which scientists are slowly and patiently piecing together a few details of Man's early existence.

The prehistoric period of Man's existence was vastly longer than the period covered by recorded history. For history, in the restricted sense, does not begin until about 4000 or just B.C., when the art of writing seems first to have appeared, while stone tools or artifacts (objects fashioned by Man) have been discovered which scientists date back many thousands of years earlier. To this we must add the unnumbered generations that elapsed before Man learned to make such tools.

Boucher de Perthes, a French antiquarian, announced in 1846 that during excavations at Abbeville in northern France he had found ancient flint implements in gravel that contained the bones of elephants, rhinoceroses, and other animals that are no longer found in France. His announcement was scorned and discredited for several years. In 1859 Sir Joseph Prestwich, a qualified English geologist, went to Abbeville to see De Perthes's collection and examine the gravel beds. He came away convinced that the flint implements were the work of Man, that they were found in undisturbed ground, that they were associated with the remains of locally extinct animals, and that the period represented preceded historic times.

The scientists who study ancient objects, especially those of the prehistoric period, are called archaeologists, while those who study Man as an animal are called anthropologists. To the aid of these comes the geologist, who knows about the formation of the earth and the age of rocks. He can gauge the age of relics by the amount of soil that time has deposited on them, or by their order in the layers of rock. When fossil bones are found, a palaeontologist supplies facts about the extinct animals, and a highly-skilled anatomist is needed to study and to interpret the human remains.

How evidence on Early Man is pieced together by the co-operation of various scientists, each highly skilled in a special subject, can be illustrated by the story of the Peking Man. In December 1929 news was flashed from China that an undamaged human skull had been unearthed from cave-deposits at Choukoutien, near Peking—deposits which authorities believed to be 500,000 to 1,000,000 years old.

The discoverer of the site was Dr. J. G. Andersson, a geologist from Sweden. The director of the excavations, and the man who actually found the human remains, was W. C. Pei, a member of the Geological Survey of China. The scientist who studied the remains was Prof. Davidson Black, a Canadian anatomist. The archaeologist who co-operated in the work was Père Teilhard de Chardin, a Catholic priest and president of the Geological Society of France. Besides yielding a perfect brain case, these excavations at Choukoutien brought to light human teeth, jawbones, and

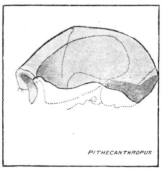

PITHECANTHROPUS

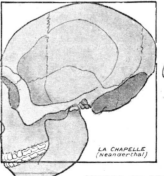

LA CHAPELLE
(Neanderthal)

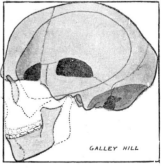

GALLEY HILL

**SKULLS OF PRIMITIVE MAN**

The comparative sizes of skulls of three types of prehistoric Man, based upon fossil remains, are shown. Each side of the ruled squares represents 200 millimetres or 7·87 inches. (See text).

numerous skull fragments from several individuals. Quantities of associated animal bones, the remains of cave-bears, giant beavers, and primitive deer, made it possible to determine the geological age fairly well. Fortunately, too, Dr. Andersson had dated the deposits before the first trace of Man was found, and subsequent discoveries confirmed the first opinion that they must be ascribed to the early Pleistocene, the geological period which preceded the dawn of our modern world, and which began about a million years ago.

The skull has a receding forehead, with massive eyebrow ridges, and its bones are enormously thick as contrasted with the skull bones of modern Man. The teeth are of the human type, but the jaw ridges are very massive, suggesting a powerful jaw mechanism. In brain, the Peking Man was just within the minimum human standard.

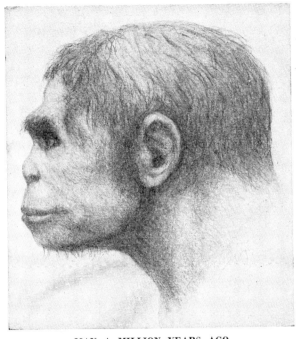

**MAN A MILLION YEARS AGO**
In December 1929 an undamaged human skull was unearthed at Choukoutien, near Peiping (Peking), China. From the shape of the skull A. Forestier made this drawing, to show what the half-ape, half-man, known as the Peking Man, probably looked like some 500,000 to 1,000,000 years ago.

creatures with still more ape-like characteristics are termed pre-Hominids. *Homo sapiens* did not appear on the earth until a good deal later than did the Hominids.

In 1924 the fossil skull of a young child was discovered in Bechuanaland, South Africa, by Professor Raymond Dart, who believed it to represent what Victorian anthropologists called a "missing link," a form between modern Man and the anthropoid apes, filling in a gap in the chain of descent. Later discoveries, in the Transvaal, supplied other examples of these South African apes with remarkably "human" characteristics. As a result, Dart's theory, which aroused much scepticism in 1924, has found supporters since. It has been suggested that these remains belong to the more recent part of the Pliocene geological period, which preceded the Pleistocene.

The search was continued, and artifacts in considerable number were found in the cave, as well as evidence of the use of fire. These discoveries indicate that human life was intelligently organized at the time of the Peking Man. Since then, the remains of about a dozen skulls have come to light.

Previous finds in other parts of the world had made us acquainted with prehistoric types of comparable age, but the evidence submitted was not as complete. Anthropologists tell us that in Java during early Pleistocene times there lived a strange creature known as *Pithecanthropus erectus*, the " erect ape-man." Its existence was recognized by the discovery in 1890 of the top of a skull, three molar teeth, and a thigh bone found scattered in the gravel of a river bed near Trinil in the island of Java. The size of the brain was about midway between the brain of a chimpanzee and the brain of the lowest type of human being alive today. Parts of four more skeletons have since been found belonging to Java Man, who seems to be related in date and structure to the Chinese fossils mentioned above.

Although the near-human remains found in Java and near Peking have been called Java " Man " and Peking " Man " respectively, these individuals had both ape-like and Man-like characteristics, and " ape-men " would appear to be a better name for them. (The scientific term *Pithecanthropus* suggests this difference from " modern " Man, to whom scientists give the name *Homo sapiens*.) Ape-men are classed in the zoological family *Hominidae*, and are called Hominids. Fossil remains of sub-human

The Pleistocene period covers what is called the Ice Age (*q.v.*). During the million years which geologists allot to the Pleistocene there were four great glaciations, in which the ice sheet advanced and then retreated over the northern part of the world. The last glaciation ended probably 25,000 years ago; the first glaciation occurred probably 40 or 50 times as long ago. Between each two ice ages there was a spell of warmer climate known as an interglacial period. The dating of these periods is of course vague; but different forms of Man or of sub-human creatures are ascribed to one or other of them, affording us some approximate notion of comparative age.

The race of Man which anthropologists call " Neanderthal Man " is found in fossil remains over parts of Europe, Africa and Asia. The first fossils of this race or species were discovered in a cave in the district of Neanderthal near Bonn, Germany, in 1856. Many other remains of the same type have since been found in various parts of Europe, from which much valuable information has been obtained. The Neanderthal race is supposed to have lived during the middle Pleistocene. Its members had acquired considerable skill in making stone weapons, lived in rock shelters, used fire, and hunted small game. They buried their dead with some care, in circumstances which suggested a belief in a life after death.

In 1939 Dr. A. C. Blanc, of Pisa University, discovered a well-preserved skull of Neanderthal Man in a cave at San Felice Circeo, about halfway between Rome and Naples. The cave had become blocked, and its contents had remained untouched for between 70,000 and 100,000 years.

The placing of the different species of ancient Man and his relatives in time-order must be left to expert anthropologists, and naturally there is a good deal of controversy about this. It seems that the remains of Neanderthal Man found in different places differ very considerably in characteristics. Some remains approach to *Homo sapiens* in structure, while others are more like *Pithecanthropus*. Neanderthal Man appears even to have inhabited the earth at the same period of geological time as *Homo sapiens*, so we can think of the two as representing different branchings, or lines of development, from an earlier ancestor.

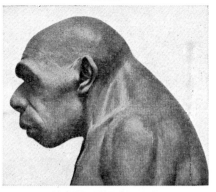

**NEANDERTHAL MAN**

This reconstruction of a Neanderthal Man is based on a skull discovered in 1939 by Dr. A. C. Blanc in a cave at San Felice Circeo, Italy.

In 1888 an interesting discovery was made at Galley Hill, in the Thames valley, though anthropologists of that day did not appreciate its importance. Here there are great beds of gravel, laid down when the Thames flowed 100 feet above its present level. Near the village of Galley Hill, beneath eight feet of this gravel layer and lying under unbroken natural strata, was found an incomplete skeleton of a type resembling modern Man. This would suggest that modern Man—*Homo sapiens*—inhabited the region at a date earlier than that assigned for Neanderthal Man, but the scientists of 1888 were loth to admit this.

Forty-seven years later, in gravel beds near Swanscombe, Kent, remains of a human skull were dug up. Experts date it as belonging to the second interglacial period of the Pleistocene, which would make it about

200,000 years old. It is classed as an individual of *Homo sapiens*. The Galley Hill remains may be twice as ancient. Other equally ancient fossils of " modern " Man have turned up in other parts of the world.

Here, then, are some of the problems of Man's ancestry which anthropologists, palaeontologists and geologists have to contend with. As the years go by other relics of early Man are dug up, and help to fill in gaps in the story—or are just as likely to upset views which have been held till then !

The Neanderthal race seems to have died out before the rise of a people of far higher culture called the Cro-Magnons, from the cave in France where their remains were first discovered (*see* Cave Dwellers). They were tall and strong, and, if we are to judge from their paintings on the walls of their caves as well as from their skull measurements, they were exceedingly intelligent people. The Cro-Magnons appear to have been either driven out of Europe or assimilated by later Stone Age peoples.

Archaeologists divide human history into phases, which are really stages of material culture, but are sometimes conceived of as chronological ages. First, there was the so-called Eolithic Age, or dawn of stone implements. These " eoliths " (Greek *ēos* " dawn " and *lithos*, " stone ") are assumed to be either Man's first crude attempts at tool making or merely pieces of stone of convenient size which show the effect of use. It is difficult to determine whether the eoliths are really artifacts, or were caused by erosion, rock pressure, the pounding of animal hoofs, or other natural forces.

The oldest undoubted human implements are known as palaeoliths (Greek *palaios*, " ancient "), and the men who produced them belonged to the Palaeolithic (Old Stone) Age. This age is further divided into the Upper, Middle and Lower Palaeolithic, each with its typical kinds of artifacts. The older palaeoliths are crude in workmanship and are mostly stones of flint, quartz, etc., shaped chiefly as scrapers or knives by flaking with a hammer-stone. The later palaeoliths show an improved handicraft. Flaking in these was done by pressure instead of by blows, and the implements have a neater and more uniform appearance. The men of the later Palaeolithic Age likewise produced tools of bone, ivory, and horn. The duration of this period is generally estimated at several hundred thousand years, because palaeoliths are found at different depths in the earth, but always in the same order, showing a gradation of cultures from primitive implements to more elaborate, even artistic, craftsmanship.

Next came the Mesolithic Age (Greek *mesos*, "middle"), which was a phase of tran-

**IMPLEMENTS MADE BY EARLY MAN**

Typical flint implements and tools of different epochs are shown. Lower Palaeolithic : 1. Pre-Chellean ; 2. Chellean ; 3 and 4. Acheulean. Middle Palaeolithic : 5. Mousterian ' point,' probably a tool used for many purposes. Upper Palaeolithic : 6. Beautifully made Solutrean implements. For explanation of the names *see* facing page.

# THE TAI

*Direct-colour phot*

The photographs
made by permiss
Chicago. The e
of life-size figures
background. Th
out by Henry F

*Direct-colour photographs of museum groups*

*See text overleaf*

provided warmth on cool nights. They may have collected some of the burning sticks to start a fire of their own, and so learned to keep the flame alive. This need to keep a fire going may have led to Man taking to a more settled mode of life, instead of roaming in search of food. The origin of fire-making is a mystery but must be much later in date.

The savage who noticed that by pounding rocks together sparks could be made to ignite dry leaves or pith, or he who first started a fire by rubbing dry sticks together, made a momentous discovery. With this invention, Man made his first great step towards civilization. The power of making fire gave him a weapon of defence, a source of comfort, and a means of cooking food without being tied to his local hearth. Once more he could be a nomad, a rover, or a far-ranging warrior.

When Man took refuge in caves and rock shelters, and his descendants continued to use the same caves over a period of thousands of years, he unconsciously left his records, chapter by chapter, in the accumulated deposits of rubbish, bones, tools, and so on.

The inhabitants of western Europe at the beginnings of the fourth glacial period were a crude but not a brutish people. They were acquainted with the use of fire. They quarried natural flint nodules, broke them, and trimmed the pieces to make implements of various sorts. They could kill the smaller animals with their axes, spears and clubs, and perhaps hunted some of the large creatures with traps and pitfalls. The dried animal skins were used for clothing; some of the skulls were made into bowls ; the long bones were split and the marrow eaten; smaller bones were turned into tools.

The men of this period already had a rudimentary social life. That these people had certain religious ideas is attested by skeletons found in their burial

**A VERY EARLY BRITON**

An artist's idea of the appearance of the very first inhabitant of Britain is reproduced above. An animal's skin forms the man's only clothing and he carries in his left hand a spear with a flint head. Such a man as this was among our ancestors of perhaps 200,000 years ago.

places, interred with implements and food, indicating ceremonial burial and belief in a spirit world. During the period called the Middle Stone Age men equipped themselves with newer and keener tools. They fitted barbed ivory points to their wooden spears and invented a throwing stick to hook round the butt of the spear so as to discharge the weapon with greater speed and power. They also invented the bow and arrow. Now Man was more than a match for the savage cave-bear, the mammoth, and sabre-toothed tiger. Now, too, he was assured of abundant food. The women learned to scrape and cure skins until they were soft, and to sew them with bone and ivory needles into more serviceable garments. An astonishing fact is that these early hunters could carve and draw, and even paint with skill.

One of the most important innovations of the Late Stone Age was the invention of pottery. This great discovery enabled men to cross the gap between savagery and what we call barbarism. For with pottery came the means of boiling food. This added

*From Régouen, L'Anthropologie*

**MASTERPIECE OF A PRIMEVAL SCULPTOR**

These models of bison in the cave of Tuc d'Audoubert, French Pyrenees, have been preserved through the ages owing to a near-by subterranean river which kept moist the clay of which they are composed.

to men's bill of fare, and the simmering pot became the community centre. It was also discovered that stone tools might be ground and thus become sharp axes, chisels, and knives. With these men could fashion more comfortable dwellings, boats, and wooden utensils.

Early settlements of the Late Stone Age are to be found in Denmark. There, along the sea-coast, prehistoric men built their wattle huts, erected on a foundation of stone and constructed of interwoven reeds plastered with clay. In simple boats they ventured out from shore to gather oysters and other shellfish, and on land hunted the wild boar and the wild bull. After feasting by the fireside, they would toss aside the shells, bones and other refuse, which accumulated into e x t e n s i v e heaps. From these " kitchen-middens " archaeologists have recovered thousands of stone tools, weapons, fragments of pottery, and other relics of the life of these early people.

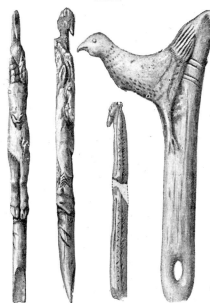

*From Mas d'Azil, after Breuil and Piette*
**HORN SPEAR-THROWERS**
Many Magdalenian (late period of the Upper Palaeolithic Age) spear-throwers were richly carved (above). The realistic grouse (right) and the chamois (left) are carved from reindeer horn.

The Late Stone Age people of Switzerland were even further advanced than the prehistoric Norsemen. To make themselves s a f e from attack, they erected comfortable wooden dwellings out over the water of the Swiss lakes (*see* illustration in page 1237, and also the colour plate and its text facing page 2081). Quantities of wooden furniture, implements, and pottery have been recovered from the sites of these " pile-dwellings."

With agriculture and the domestication of animals there arose two methods of living. Some of the people settled in one place, devoting themselves to agriculture, while others took care of the animals, following the pasture according to the season. The shepherds might go to the north side of the mountains in the summer and to the south in the winter, living on milk and meat from their herds. Such wandering tribes we call nomads. They were very hardy

*From a diorama in the London Museum*
**MAN'S EARLIEST ATTEMPTS AT WORKING METALS**
Copper was first successfully worked by mankind more than 5,000 years ago, and this illustration shows the methods of mining and smelting. The ore was broken from an outcropping seam with stone hammers (top right) and then pounded in a mortar. The pulverised ore was melted in a clay furnace (bottom right), the molten metal then being conveyed in ladles to moulds of clay or stone (left). Broken moulds and finished axe-heads are in the left foreground.

*From the drawing by A. Forestier in the London Museum*

**WHEN MAN FIRST LEARNED TO CARVE**

The earliest carvings made by Man served some useful purpose and were not merely decorative ; bone and horns were the materials used. The man on the left, armed with a short spear, is carrying the horns of a reindeer ; the other is showing him an implement he has made.

being followed some 1,500 years later by the Age of Bronze. Iron came into use in Europe during the thousand years before the beginning of the Christian era.

**Man,** ISLE OF. In the Irish Sea, nearly equidistant from England, Ireland and Scotland is the Isle of Man or Mona. With a length of 33 miles and a breadth of 12 miles, it has an area of 221 square miles. The coast is in the main rugged and the interior is hilly, the highest point being Snaefell, 2,034 feet. The climate is mild, and the island is noted for its breed of tailless cats.

The soil is not very fertile, but much of it is cultivated, oats, barley, wheat and turnips being the chief crops. Dairy farming is carried on, and much of the land affords pasture for cattle, horses and sheep. The island, especially Douglas, the capital, is one of the most popular holiday resorts in the British Isles. A railway system of about 50 miles links up the principal towns ; there is regular steamboat communication with Liverpool, Glasgow, Dublin, Belfast and other places.

Part of the British Commonwealth, the Isle of Man has its own Government, although the British Parliament exercises certain powers over it. The island is governed by a Lieutenant-Governor appointed by the British Sovereign, a Council consisting of certain high officials, and the House of Keys, an elected body of 24 members. The Council and the House of Keys together form the Court of Tynwald of which the Lieutenant-Governor is the president. The population of the island is 49,300.

**Manchester.** Many centuries ago this Lancashire city on the River Irwell was noted, as it still is, for its textile manufactures. At first it specialized in woollen cloth, which was produced by Flemish weavers who settled there in the Middle Ages. Now it is the world centre of the cotton trade, having grown with enormous rapidity since the inventions that revolutionized the cotton industry in the 18th century. The factories, however, are not so much found in the city itself as in the outskirts and ring of neighbouring towns.

Manchester and the surrounding district are the most populous industrial section in England. Hundreds of thousands of workers are employed in the cotton industry, to which the moist climate is peculiarly adapted, and in the numerous factories, which are able to obtain a plentiful supply of fuel from neighbouring coalfields.

Since 1894 Manchester has been not only the industrial and commercial centre of this region, but, with the opening of the Manchester Ship Canal, a seaport as well. This waterway, which extends to the mouth of the River Mersey, a distance of 35 miles, has enormously increased Manchester's importance. Not only textiles but glass, clothing,

and often made raids on the farmers. The conflict between nomads and townsmen, begun so many ages ago, recurs periodically through the history of the human race.

Besides Swiss lake dwellers there existed elsewhere in Europe other settled communities, the remains of some of which are still traceable. These people lived in fortified towns and near by erected impressive tombs, built of blocks of rough stone and covered with earthen mounds. They also erected circles of enormous natural stones. It must have required organization and leadership and a knowledge of engineering to raise the mighty megaliths (Greek *megas*, "great") at Stonehenge or drive in the 50,000 piles at Wangen, Switzerland.

After the Stone Ages came the Age of Metal (the precise dating of these events is not possible). Copper implements and ornaments were apparently the first metal objects to be made. The Age of Copper began in Egypt perhaps 5,000 years ago,

*From Abbé Breuil, Caverne d'Altamira and Caverne de Font-de-Gaume*

ne prehistoric men were artists whose work achieved a very high standard. Remarkable examples of these early paintings have n found in the Altamira cave in Cantabria, in the north of Spain, and in the Font-de-Gaume cave in the Dordogne, in the south 'rance. The running boar, hind, and bison are in the Altamira cave; the two reindeer (bottom) are at Font-de-Gaume.

# MANCHURIA

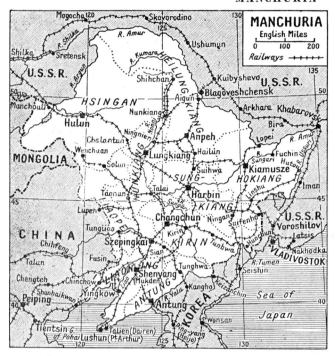

**CHINESE TERRITORY OF MANCHURIA**
The nine north-eastern provinces of China together form the territory known as Manchuria, through which pass the railways linking China with the rest of Asia and Europe. One of the most fertile regions of eastern Asia, Manchuria also possesses considerable mineral wealth.

and east respectively, with peaks ranging from 3,000 to 8,000 feet. They are rich in timber and minerals, especially coal. The climate is one of extremes, very hot in summer and intensely cold in winter. All the rivers freeze-up for several months in winter, and only the southern ports of Dairen and Lushun (Port Arthur) are ice-free all the year. The north is drier than the south, and the far west is too nearly rainless to be of any use except as pasture land.

The central plain, with its rich black soil, is one of the world's granaries, soya beans, kaoliang (sorghum), millet, wheat, maize, hemp, tobacco and oats being among the main crops. In western Manchuria horses, cattle, sheep and goats are raised, and from there also come such furs as sable, ermine, leopard, lynx, marten, squirrel and fox.

The extraction of bean oil and the manufacture of bean cake, as fodder for cattle, are important industries. The most valuable mineral is coal, which is widely distributed, though much of it is poor in quality. Deposits of oil have been found ; and some of the coal seams are overlain by oil shale, from which oil is extracted. Most of the iron ore is found around Mukden, other mineral resources of the country being gold, silver, lead, copper, manganese, salt, and limestone. Iron and steel works were built

Keystone

**IN CHANGCHUN, CITY OF CENTRAL MANCHURIA**
In 1933 the Japanese established the State of Manchukuo, which roughly corresponded to Manchuria and of which Changchun (then known as Hsinking) was the capital. Under Japanese rule concrete buildings were erected and wide avenues constructed. Above is Tatung Avenue, a boulevard lined with fine structures ; that on the left is a department store. When Japan surrendered to the Allies in August 1945 (during the Second World War), Manchukuo ceased to exist, Manchuria again becoming Chinese territory, and being then divided into nine provinces.

by the Japanese between 1932 and 1945, but the equipment was removed by the Russians in 1945–1946, when they occupied the country at the end of the Second World War (1939–45). Chemical, aluminium and synthetic rubber factories were similarly despoiled.

Manchuria has 7,380 miles of railway and about 3,800 miles of motor-roads. In normal times there are air services between the principal cities. The capital is Changchun in the province of Kirin. Other large cities are Mukden, Harbin, Dairen (chief port), Antung and Kirin.

In 1644 the Manchus, a wandering people akin to the Mongols, conquered China, the Manchu Emperor moving his capital from Mukden to Peiping. For many years the Chinese were not allowed to settle in the homeland of their conquerors, but in the beginning of the 20th century Chinese immigrants swarmed into the country. After a brief war with China in 1894–95 Japan obtained the Liaotung Peninsula, at the tip of which Dairen is situated. The Japanese developed roads and railways, and after a bomb outrage on the South Manchurian Railway in 1931 they occupied Mukden and other important cities all over Manchuria.

Early in 1932 the Japanese established the State of Manchukuo, which comprised the three north-eastern provinces of China—Liaoning, Kirin and Heilungkiang—together with the province of Jehol. In 1934 they installed Henry Pu-yi, the exiled Emperor of China, as the ruler of Manchukuo, but he remained entirely under Japanese domination. Japan retained her hold on this vast region until August 8, 1945, when Russia declared war on her, sending three armies into Manchuria. Hostilities ceased on August 15, 1945, when Japan surrendered to the Allied Nations ; China regained possession of Manchuria, but the Soviet Union were granted the right to use the port of Dairen as a naval base, and as the Russian forces withdrew in 1946 they removed most of the industrial equipment from the factories built by the Japanese in Manchuria.

Civil War between Chinese Communists and the Government of General Chiang Kai-shek, President of China, broke out in 1946, and by 1948 the Communists had gained control of Manchuria. The population of the territory is estimated at 43,233,950.

**Manganese.** This metallic element is used for making some very important alloys, such as manganese steel, which contains about 12 per cent of manganese, and which, being very hard and tough, is used for making things like railway points and rock crushers. Manganese bronze is an alloy of copper and manganese with some tin or zinc. Being hard, and resistant to the action of sea water, manganese bronze has been used for propellers and other ships' fittings. The chemical symbol of manganese is Mn ; its atomic weight is 54·9 ; atomic number, 25. Its density is 7·4.

Manganese resembles iron, but it is not magnetic. It has a greyish lustre, faintly tinged with red, and rusts rapidly in moist air. Pure manganese is only a chemical curiosity. " Spiegeleisen " and ferromanganese are alloys of iron and manganese. " Spiegeleisen " contains five to 20 per cent of manganese; ferromanganese contains about 50 per cent of manganese. Both these alloys are used during the manufacture of special steels.

Some salts derived from manganese are used in chemistry, medicine, and the arts. Because of their readiness to part with their oxygen, potassium and sodium permanganate are sometimes used as antiseptics and disinfectants, the liberated oxygen being a potent killer of germs.

Russia is the greatest producer of manganese, India and Africa ranking next.

**Mango.** One of Man's greatest triumphs in improving wild plants is the cultivated mango. In its home in India, this evergreen tree originally

*Queensland Govt.*

**MANGO TREE IN FRUIT**
Although it is a native of India and Malaya the mango is grown in other parts of the tropics and sub-tropics. Here is a fine specimen in full fruit, growing in Brisbane, Queensland. The fruit has been vastly improved by cultivation from the original wild species.

had a small plum-like fruit, with a turpentine flavour. Centuries of cultivation and selection have produced a luscious fruit somewhat like a small melon. Many varieties are now grown in Florida, U.S.A., the Caribbean region, and elsewhere in the tropics and sub-tropics. Green mangoes are used for pickles and preserves, and so the name has come to be applied also to those made from melons, peppers, and cucumbers.

The tree grows from 40 to 90 feet high. It has large glossy leaves, and in Florida the pinkishwhite flowers bloom from December to April. The mango (*Mangifera indica*) belongs to the cashew family or *Anacardiaceae*.

**Mangrove.** The mangrove, *Rhizophora mangle*, is highly adapted to tropical and sub-tropical seashores, where most trees cannot live because their roots cannot get air from the soil. The mangrove overcomes this difficulty by dropping vinelike roots from its trunk and branches to the surrounding mud and these aerial roots take in air through their pores at every low tide. Seeds germinate while on the tree, and do not break away until they have sent down a "breathing" root to win a foothold in the mud.

Dense groves of these trees, which reach a height of about 20 feet, grow in the coastal swamps. The tangle of roots catches rubbish and mud, and thus helps to build new land. Some species have heavy, close-grained wood. The bark is used for tanning and as a fever medicine, and the sweet fruit is edible.

**MANGROVE TREE**
Remarkable for its aerial roots, the mangrove contrives to grow where most other trees cannot.

**Manila.** Situated on the west coast of the island of Luzon in the Philippine Islands at the entrance of the Pasig river into Manila Bay, Manila is the capital and chief seaport of the Republic of the Philippines. Manila exports hemp, copra, sugar and tobacco. Chief industries include foundries, machine shops, boot and shoe and furniture factories, flour mills and shipbuilding yards ; but much damage was done to these during the Japanese occupation of 1942-45.

Manila was founded by the Spaniards in 1571, and by the beginning of the 17th century it had become one of the centres of commerce and culture in the Far East. On the south bank of the Pasig the Spaniards established the old walled city, with the Cathedral, University, Government buildings and churches. At the conclusion of the Spanish-American War of 1898-99 the Philippines came into the possession of the United States. In the ensuing years the harbour was greatly improved, electric lighting and tramway systems were provided and the drainage entirely remodelled.

During the Second World War (1939-45) the Japanese captured Manila on January 2, 1942, and occupied it for three years. United States forces recaptured the city in February 1945, but the Japanese had destroyed every large building in the old walled city and blown up all the bridges over the Pasig. The population is 684,800.

# CANADA'S CENTRAL PRAIRIE PROVINCE

*Unbroken by hills or deep valleys, the grain-land region of Manitoba stretches for five hundred miles across the heart of Canada—field after field of waving corn, as far as the eye can see.*

**Manitoba.** (Pron. man-i-tō'-ba). The Red Indians of the prairies believed that the region now included in the Canadian province of Manitoba was especially favoured by the Great Spirit, and that around the narrowest part of Lake Manitoba his voice might be heard. Therefore they called the region Manito-Waban (Great Spirit's Narrows), from which its present name is derived. The inhabitants of today agree with the red men in regarding the province as " God's Country," and for proof they point to the broad prairies of the south-west, covered with fields of grain, which form one of the world's greatest grain regions.

The area of the province is 246,512 square miles, of which 26,789 are water. The southern part is prairie or lightly wooded, the northern section hilly and rocky with swift-flowing rivers draining into Hudson Bay. Manitoba lies between the provinces of Ontario and Saskatchewan, with the United States on the south and Hudson Bay on the north. The chief rivers are the Red, which comes from the United States ; the

Assiniboine which, rising in Saskatchewan, flows into the Red river at Winnipeg; and the Nelson, which carries the waters of Lake Winnipeg to Hudson Bay.

The largest body of water is Lake Winnipeg (area, 8,555 square miles), nowhere more than 70 feet deep. The province enjoys an invigorating climate, though variations are sudden and of great range. The winters are severe and the summers very hot. The great heat of midsummer causes the grain to ripen quickly, and there is little rain at harvest time, so that crops are seldom spoilt by getting damp. Occasional early frosts rarely affect the yield. The soil and climate are adapted not only to producing a large quantity of wheat but also to growing a fine quality, so that " Manitoba hard " has become the standard for the highest grade of wheat sold. Cattle and pig raising, dairying, and bee-keeping are also important occupations in the province.

The northern part of Manitoba is too cold for agriculture, but it is in this section that the hunter and the trapper find the numerous fur-bearing animals—

**Extent.**—North to south, 760 miles ; east to west, 495 miles. Area, 246,512 square miles, nearly 27,000 of which are water. Population, 729,700.

**Physical Features.**—Great prairies in south-west and south, with broken and hilly land of the Laurentian country in the north and east. Higher elevations, Riding and Duck mountains. Lakes Winnipeg, Winnipegosis, Manitoba, and Dauphin and numerous small lakes. Principal rivers : Red River of the North, Assiniboine, Saskatchewan, and Winnipeg, draining into Lake Winnipeg ; Nelson, draining Lake Winnipeg into Hudson Bay ; Churchill and Hayes, also emptying into Hudson Bay.

**Products.**—Wheat, oats, barley, rye, potatoes, flax, hay ; live-stock and dairy produce ; copper, zinc and gold ; building materials (brick, cement, stone, gypsum) ; lumber ; fur and game, fish.

**Principal Cities.**—Winnipeg (capital, 221,960), Brandon, St. Boniface.

the mink, musk-rats, martens, foxes, and others—whose skins command such a high price. Here also, and in the western part of the province, are forests of spruce, which yield valuable timber and material for the paper and wood-pulp industries. Another source of wealth is the rich deposits of gold and copper, zinc, and silver. The numerous lack of transportation, until recent years has been but little known and seldom visited. Now the Hudson Bay railway and its branch lines as well as air services are making this region more accessible. For years Manitoba has been famous for its wildfowl shooting, and some of the largest wildfowl breeding grounds in America are located in the province.

*Canadian National Rlys.*

### MANITOBA'S PARLIAMENT BUILDINGS

At Winnipeg, the capital of the province of Manitoba, are the provincial legislative buildings, seen above. These were completed in 1923, replacing an older building on the same site, near the Assiniboine river. They form an imposing edifice in the best modern style, and are surrounded by well laid-out grounds.

In the 18th century Manitoba was a region inhabited only by fur traders. Regular colonization began in 1812, with the establishment of the Red River Settlement. The land was controlled by the Hudson's Bay Company until 1869, when it was purchased by the Canadian Government. The French *métis*, or half-breeds, feared that their language and religion (Roman Catholic) would not be respected, and there followed the Red River Rebellion of 1870, which was quickly suppressed. It was the building of the Canadian Pacific Railway that changed Manitoba to the prosperous province of today. The opening up of the country by the new line brought thousands of settlers from the older parts of Canada, from the United States, and from Europe, with the result that the white population increased rapidly from 1,565 in 1870 to its present total of 729,700.

lakes in Manitoba furnish large catches of excellent fish. These products and the wheat from the south all find their way to Winnipeg, the capital and an important railway centre.

Although Manitoba is referred to as a prairie province more than three-quarters of its area is wooded, providing excellent cover for moose, deer, bear and wolf. Noted big game areas include the south-eastern portion along the Whitemouth river and lake, and east to the Ontario boundary and the territory bordering the Riding Mountain National Park and the Duck Mountain forest reserve.

The north of the province is virtually a vast natural game reserve which, owing to

*Canadian Official News Bureau*

### PLOUGHING THE PRAIRIE FOR GRAIN

Western Canada is one of the great granaries of the world and could, with intensive ? be made to supply the needs of practically the whole British Commonwealth. S? wheat is grown in Manitoba, where this picture was taken of a motor-tracto? that look a mile long, and where, later in the year, golden ears of grain ?

**Mantis.** Perhaps no living creature has such a strange appearance and a more bloodthirsty disposition than the "praying mantis."

With the front part of its body raised up in a prim pose, the hind part reminding one of the flounce of an old-fashioned skirt, and with its fore-limbs beneath its small triangular head, the mantis does indeed look like an old lady at her prayers. But concealed on the inside of those arms are sharp spines, and that head, cocked now to the right, now to the left, has two large eyes on the look-out for unwary victims.

Perhaps a fly ventures too near. Suddenly the mantis springs; the long arms shoot out, and the fly is caught on their curved barbs. Then one leg after another of the captive is eaten; the body is sucked dry; and the mantis awaits another victim.

Members of the family *Mantidae* are found in southern Europe and in nearly all tropical countries. European species range up to about three inches in length; tropical ones vary from three-quarters of an inch to five inches. The eggs are laid in tough cases attached to twigs, and as soon

*H. Bastin*

**THE MANTIS AT ITS 'PRAYERS'**
One of the queerest insects, the praying mantis (above) has been so called from the 'prayerful' attitude it adopts while waiting for its victims to come within reach of the barbed fore-limbs, with which it seizes flies and other living food. The mantis is found in nearly all tropical countries and in southern Europe. Since ancient times it has been held in superstitious awe.

as the young hatch they start killing small insects. Their life-history is similar to that of grasshoppers and others of the order *Orthoptera*, which do not pass through the chrysalis stage. The word mantis is a Greek one and means soothsayer or prophet.

**Manuscripts,** ILLUMINATED. Among the most beautiful of all early works of art in the western world are the lovely illuminated manuscripts which were produced in monasteries and other seats of learning during the Middle Ages. Some of these have individually become world-famous, while as a whole they show the highest form of art that graced those far-off times. Illumination, as the art itself is called, consisted in the ornamentation of the covers and pages of the manuscripts, religious or otherwise, produced for patrons or religious houses. At first the illumination consisted simply of making the capitals and initials more and more complicated, and illustrating the text with small drawings. Gradually the ornamentation spread until the decorations around a single initial might occupy the margin of a whole leaf of vellum and extend into the text as well. While brilliant colours were used for the decorations—though the actual initials themselves often remained in red—gold was extensively used for the backgrounds.

*British Museum*

**A BEAUTIFUL MEDIEVAL MANUSCRIPT**
... of a page from an illuminated manuscript, done in France during the ... Observe the lovely little miniature above the ornate capital letter, ... drolleries ' which help to form the margin. Work like this was ... all over Western Europe during the Middle Ages.

Every country of civilized Europe had its own schools of illuminators, with their own

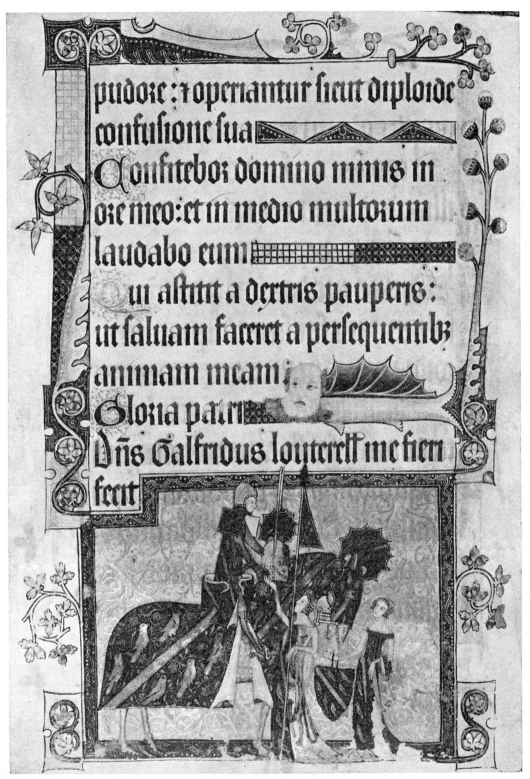

Few illuminated manuscripts are so interesting as the Luttrell Psalter, which is in the British Museum, London. It was done about 1342 for Sir Geoffrey Luttrell, an English knight, whom you see in the miniature at the bottom of this page. He is setting out for a tournament, his wife handing him his helmet and a pennant, while another lady holds his shield. On this, as on his horse's trappings, are the Luttrell arms.

styles, so that an expert can tell at a glance where any manuscript comes from and about when it was executed. One of the earliest and most remarkable of these schools was that which flourished in the Byzantine era (*see* Byzantine Empire). There was another in Ireland during the 8th and 9th centuries which produced the art known as Irish Romanesque. The origin of this school, so different from any other and yet growing to perfection in so isolated a spot, is still something of a mystery, but it certainly shows the influence of Spanish art of that period. It is remarkable for the complexity of the decoration, its richness, and the manner in which whole sheets of vellum may be filled with intertwining designs. The lettering of this period was also very lovely, and a feature of these illuminated manuscripts were full-page drawings of the Evangelists. This Irish school spread to England, and flourished in the monasteries of the north. The Book of Kells containing the Gospels is its greatest masterpiece; this is preserved in Trinity College, Dublin. (*See* page 510).

In England, the Winchester school was later pre-eminent. In this a very different style was evolved, the colours being pale and pure. This type of work is illustrated in our pages 1177 and 1194. In East Anglia, again, another school flourished, producing not only very beautiful

manuscripts but also some of surpassing interest, though of less artistic merit. An example of this is the famous Luttrell Psalter, which is illustrated with a lovely series of miniatures showing country life of the early 14th century. That is why these miniatures and those from similar works, are often reproduced in history books, for they alone often provide a clue as to how our ancestors lived in the late Middle Ages. (*See* illus., page 2091).

In France, in Flanders, and in Italy there were many notable schools of illuminators, each with its particular style. France, especially, has produced some lovely works, principally the outcome of the great age of Gothic art, and done during the 13th-15th centuries. Each figure, illuminated in fine colours against a background of gold-leaf, is framed in a design similar to that of the stone-work surrounding a Gothic church window.

A further feature of these manuscripts is the inclusion in the margins of weird beasts and monsters of all sorts; these are known as " drolleries." The art of illumination declined in the 16th century with the coming of printing.

# Maple.

Members of this group of trees, comprising the genus *Acer*, are notable for their brilliant autumn tints. The two species most often seen in Britain are the sycamore, or great maple, *A. pseudoplatanus*, and the field maple (*A. campestris*). The latter, known by its soft, woolly leaves, is seldom a large tree, and is most common in the hedgerow. When left to grow in the open or in an uncut hedge, it can reach a height of 30 feet. Also grown in Britain are the Norway maple (*A. platanoides*) and the ash-leaved maple or box elder (*A. negundo*).

The chief of the family in North America is the sugar maple (*A. saccharum*), which not only yields maple sugar, but also produces the finest wood for furniture of any member of this family. Other common American species are the silver maple (*A. saccharinum*), whose branches are long and drooping; the red, scarlet, or swamp maple (*A. rubrum*), whose autumn colour is especially wonderful; and the lovely Japanese maples, with their deeply-cut, delicate leaves. Canada has adopted the maple leaf as its national emblem, and one of its national songs is entitled The Maple Leaf For Ever.

Although all of the maples have sweet sap, the sugar or rock maple is the source of practically all the maple syrup and sugar that is marketed. Maple sugar production, however, is commercially important only in the north-eastern United States and the neighbouring parts of Canada. Sugar maples grow slowly, and are seldom good sap producers before they are 40 years old. They yield the greatest amount after they are 80. The sap begins to run in very early spring and flows for about three weeks, each tree producing about 10 gallons of sap. Boiled down, this yields a quart of syrup, or two pounds of sugar.

The tapping is done carefully so as not to cause permanent damage to the tree. Each year it is tapped in a different place, so that

**CANADA'S MAPLE TREE**
The sugar maple, one of the most handsome and valuable members of its tribe, will grow to a fair size in Great Britain under favourable conditions and the one seen above is a good example. A native of North America, this is the tree from which comes maple syrup, and the leaf of which is Canada's national emblem.

**MAKING MAPLE SUGAR IN A NORTH AMERICAN FOREST**

In the maple forests when the sap is running, the great fire is never let out night or day as long as the season lasts. Somebody is always cutting wood to feed it ; somebody is busy most of the time gathering in the sap ; somebody is required to fill the kettles and to see that they do not boil over. It is not the boy, however ; he is otherwise engaged !

during the summer the cut bark may grow over and heal the slight wound. Before drilling the hole for tapping, the workers vigorously brush down the trunk to remove dirt and loose bark; then, with a brace and bit, a hole is drilled about three-eighths of an inch in diameter, slanting up into the tree. Into the hole a spout is driven, each having a hook from which the sap bucket hangs; in some places a system of pipe lines made of tin tubing has replaced the buckets.

The sap is made into syrup by boiling out the excess water, this being done at the camp. To make maple sugar, the syrup is boiled for a further period, sugar forming as the thick liquid cools.

# REPRESENTING *the* GLOBE *on* PAPER

*Over 4,000 years ago there were maps—on Babylonian clay tablets. In all that time the difficulties of map-making have not been entirely overcome, though cartographers now have 'flying cameras' to assist them.*

**Maps.** It is easy to show the earth's surface on a globe, but it is difficult to do so on the flat surface of a map. You will see why if you cut the skin of an orange into half-separated strips and remove them as a single piece. The result, when flattened out, will resemble Fig. 1. One encounters this problem of adjusting a flat surface to a sphere when one tries to cover a ball with a piece of leather; it can only be done by cutting the leather into shaped pieces and sewing them together.

But it *is* possible to cover the surface of a cone with a continuous piece of paper, or other material, and make it lie flat. One way of making maps, therefore, is to imagine

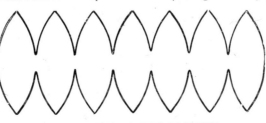

**THE 'ORANGE PEEL' PROBLEM**

Fig. 1. The nearest to a flat surface you could get by peeling a globe of the world would be a shape something like this, as you can find out by trying it with an orange.

the earth as being composed of two cones which have the Equator as their common base. In this way is prepared a conic projection which is fairly satisfactory for single states and other small sections of the globe's surface. Figs. 2 and 3 show how a conic projection is made. Such a projection is easily recognizable by the fact that the meridians are all straight lines diverging from a common centre, and the parallels are arcs of concentric circles. In what is called a polyconic projection the meridians are slightly curved, and the parallels are not always concentric arcs. This is because a separate cone is used for each parallel.

Imagine a cone of paper fitted over the top of a

globe touching the surface at, say, the 40th parallel of north latitude, as in Fig. 2 ; this is then the " standard " parallel. Meridians are drawn at equal intervals on the paper as straight lines from the apex of the cone to its base; and, from above, the parallels appear as concentric circles drawn with the apex as a centre.

When the paper cone is unrolled it appears as in Fig. 3. In conic projections the scale along every meridian and along the standard parallel is correct;

Fig. 2 (top). How a conic projection is made.
Fig. 3 (lower). The completed conic projection.

but north and south of the standard parallel, latitude and longitude are progressively distorted. This defect makes these projections useless as sailing charts.

For showing the whole surface of the globe on a single map, what is called Mercator's projection (after its originator the Fleming, Gerard Mercator, 1512–94) is frequently used. In making this projection the globe is imagined as enclosed in a paper cylinder (Fig. 4). If the cylinder were of the same height as the globe, the east-and-west distances near the poles would be enormously exaggerated while the north-and-south distances would be practically correct.

To remedy this distortion of shape, a corresponding distortion north and south is introduced. Projection lines are drawn from the centre of the globe at regular intervals of latitude and continued until they meet the surface of the cylinder.

Thus the distance between the 60th and 75th parallels of latitude becomes enormously greater than that between the Equator and the 15th parallel, and the poles cannot

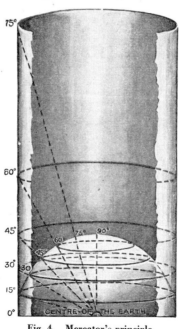

Fig. 4. Mercator's principle.

be shown at all on these maps. Fig. 4 explains how the Mercator's projection is formed, and Fig. 5 (see page 2096) what it looks like when it is completed. In spite of its great exaggeration of areas towards the top and bottom of the map this projection is very useful, especially for sailing charts. All meridians and parallels are straight lines crossing at right angles, and a compass course between any two points is the straight line connecting them.

There are other types of map projections, but these are among the simplest. No map, it should be remembered, can ever represent the surface of the earth as accurately as a globe. If you examine a map on a conic projection, and then one of the same area on a Mercator's projection, you will see a great difference in apparent size and shape. And yet each is an accurate representation according to its system of projection. Without projections we could not have the world mapped in a convenient atlas.

Maps which show the character of the *surface* of the ground are of several kinds, such as relief, topographic or contour maps. An example of a contour map is given in Fig. 6. Such maps show the detail of the earth's surface by joining with contour lines all points which have the same altitude above sea level. In this case the planes are 20 feet apart. Lines very close together indicate a sharp rise. In Fig. 7 we see how a profile sketch can be made from the contour map in Fig. 6 (page 2096).

The earliest-known maps were designed either to guide travellers or to illustrate contemporary ideas on the nature and extent of the world. The oldest maps in existence are thought to be those on Babylonian clay tablets, now in the British Museum, London. These date from about the year 2300 B.C.—over 4,000 years ago.

As men journeyed over more and more of the earth, so their maps became larger and more accurate. Those of the Egyptian geographer Ptolemy (c. A.D. 150), are extraordinarily good considering the period in which he lived. But his ideas of a spherical earth were eventually discarded, and cartographers (from Latin *charta*, map ; and Greek *graphē*, description) represented the world on " wheel maps," with Jerusalem or some similar city as the supposed centre of the world.

Today nearly every quarter of the globe is mapped in detail. The official organization for map-making in Britain is the Ordnance Survey, which is constantly charting the country and revising

# MAPPING THE EARTH FROM AN AEROPLANE

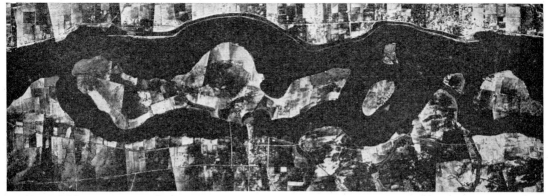

*Courtesy of the Royal Aeronautical Society*

A general view of the land to be mapped has a grid of white lines placed over it (lower left), so that any foreshortenings in photographs taken at an angle can be corrected. Then the area is traversed by an aeroplane and photographed in detail. When the photographing has been completed, the developed prints are roughly pieced together (lower right). In the top picture 150 photographs have been corrected and put together to form a mosaic, making an accurate photographic map; below it (centre strip) is an actual chart drawn from the mosaic, the area shown being roughly 11 square miles, and the very small figures indicating the depth of water in fathoms.

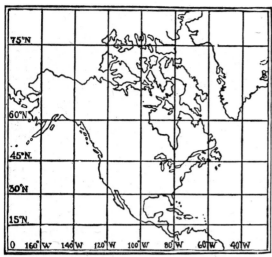

Fig. 5.   Mercator's projection completed.

ward to the ground.  They give a very accurate plan of the area, but have the disadvantage of not always being easy to understand, as there is little indication of height.  The oblique photograph is taken at an angle, being very similar to one of the surrounding country taken from the top of a hill.  Very often a combination of the vertical and oblique methods is used.

As each photograph is taken there is automatically recorded upon the side of the film certain items of information, which include the number of the photograph, whether the aircraft was flying level or not when the picture was taken, the height and the time.  It is very useful to know the exact time at which a photograph was taken, because then it is possible to calculate from the length of the shadows on the ground the heights of buildings, trees and hills, and similar prominent features.

An immense amount of time is saved by making maps from the air, especially in countries where distances are great and natural difficulties formidable.  An air survey was made in Egypt over an area of 120,000 square miles; this particular region would have been exceedingly difficult to map from the ground, and the work might have taken 15 years to complete.  The whole district was photographed from the air and maps prepared in 18 months.

old maps.  The scale of maps published varies considerably, but one inch to the mile is a fairly common one.  This scale, also given as 1 : 63,360, means that one inch on the map represents one mile or 63,360 inches on the actual surface of the earth.

An atlas often gives various special maps, such as those illustrating rainfall, temperature, religions of the world, races, density of population, languages, communications and industries.  In addition, it is usual to provide both physical and political maps of every land.  Motoring maps are a specialized form.  In them the classes of roads and places of interest are particularly emphasized and distinguished from one another.

Aeroplanes are now used extensively in mapmaking, automatic cameras taking photographs of strips of the ground.  The first thing that has to be done is to take a complete set of photographs of the ground which is to be mapped.  These photographs are afterwards pieced together, rather like a huge jig-saw puzzle, and from them maps are finally drawn.  To make certain all the ground is covered a definite course is marked out for the pilot, and photographs are taken at regular intervals while he is flying that course, the intervals being so arranged that each photograph overlaps the previous one.  If a part of the ground has been missed, the error will be observed when the photographic mosaic is fitted together.

There are two kinds of photographs taken for air survey work, the vertical and the oblique.  Vertical ones are taken with the camera fixed in the aeroplane so that the lens points straight down-

## Marat, JEAN PAUL (1744–93).  Notorious for his violent character and on account of the dramatic nature of his death—he was murdered in his bath—Marat (pron. mah-rah') has gone down in history as one of the fiercest, or inhumanest leaders of the French Revolution of 1789.

He was born at Boudry in the canton of Neuchâtel, Switzerland, on May 24, 1744.  He studied medicine at Bordeaux and Paris but in 1786 he gave up his practice, devoting himself to politics and journalism.  When the French Revolution broke out in 1789 he was one of its most ardent supporters and his speeches and writings did much to bring about the Reign of Terror.  His policy of denouncing as traitors all those in authority made him many enemies, and his advocacy of the use of more extreme measures against opponents of the Revolution made him increasingly dangerous to the Government.

Though Marat was feared and disliked by the leaders of the Revolution he was popular with the people, and after his assassination (by a former revolutionary named Charlotte Corday, on July 13, 1793) he was buried with considerable pomp, his bust replacing figures of the Virgin in the streets.  In 1795 his remains were placed in the Panthéon at Paris, but popular feeling turned against him and four months later they were removed.

Fig. 6.   Contour map of a coast-line.

Fig. 7.   Profile sketch from contour map.

## Marathon.

(Pron. ma′-ra-thon). On the little plain of Marathon, in Greece, about 26 miles north-east of Athens, may be seen a mound nearly 50 feet high. Beneath it lie the remains of 192 Athenians who gave their lives, more than 2,400 years ago (490 B.C.), to preserve their city and all Greece from conquest by the Persian hordes of Darius the Great. The mound, raised by their grateful fellow-citizens to receive their bodies and commemorate their heroism, was excavated in 1890, and the sacred relics were brought to light for the first time since the day of their glorious victory. (For the story of the battle *see* under Persia).

The famous Marathon Race (covering 26 miles and 385 yards, the distance from Marathon to Athens) was founded in Greece in honour of the runner Pheidippides, who brought news of the victory to Athens, and died shouting " Rejoice ! We conquer !" A marathon race forms part of the English Amateur Athletic Association championships, and has been one of the classic events of the modern Olympic Games ; it is still run over the same distance.

## Marble.

We owe most of our supply of the beautiful crystalline rock called marble to countless millions of tiny sea animals, whose mineral remains accumulated on the floors of ancient seas during periods of time running into millions of years. These deposits of marine animal remains eventually became hardened to form limestone (*q.v.*). True marble is merely limestone which has been altered or " metamorphosed " by the action of heat and pressure ; but other hard limestones, which can be polished, are often called marble, and the fossil remains of

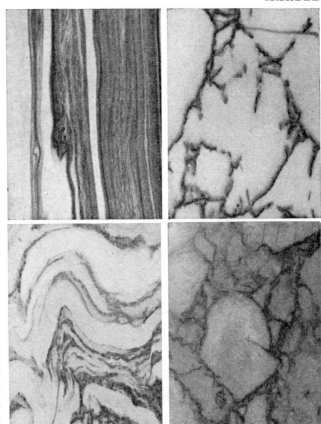

*Courtesy of Art Pavements and Decorations, Ltd.*

**FOUR KINDS OF MARBLE**

The figure and texture of marble vary considerably. The four varieties shown are Swiss Cippolino, a banded marble, Pavonazzo (from Carrara), Arni Alto, and Escalette (from the Pyrenees).

larger animals, such as sea shells, can often be seen in the polished slabs of these marbles used for ornamental purposes.

The colour of marble depends on the purity of the limestone from which it is made. If considerable quantities of materials other than calcium carbonate or magnesium carbonate are present, the colour varies according to the nature and distribution of these impurities in the rock. Pure marble is white, but impurities may make it red, brown, yellow, black, etc.; or, if the impurities are irregularly distributed, it may be mottled. or beautifully veined. Onyx marble (which must not be

**MOUNTAIN SOURCE OF ITALY'S MARBLE**

Some of the most famous marble quarries in the world are those at Carrara in the Apennines, Italy. These quarries have been worked almost continuously for 2,000 years, since the days of the Roman Empire, and Carrara marble has been used for buildings and statues all over the world. Pavonazzo marble (*see* illus. above) comes from Carrara.

confused with true onyx, a variety of agate) is formed by the precipitation of calcium carbonate from solution, usually from the waters of springs, its colours including white, yellow, and green.

Marble has always been a favourite material with sculptors and architects because of its beauty. The exquisite statues of the Greeks were made chiefly from the so-called Pentelic marble, from the quarries on Mount Pentelicus in Attica. The Elgin Marbles in the British Museum were carved from this fine stone. The beautiful Venus of Milo in the Louvre at Paris, dating from the 2nd to 3rd century B.C., was made from the Parian marble quarried on the island of Paros, in the Aegean.

The marble most used by sculptors still comes from the famous quarries of Carrara, in northern Italy, which furnished the material for the Pantheon at Rome. Marble is used for monuments, buildings, statues, and for many other purposes. In dry climates and when sheltered from rain, it is very durable, but otherwise the surface is liable to crumble from the effects of weathering.

# The MAN who MASTERED WIRELESS

*We owe more to Marconi's pioneer work in wireless communication than is perhaps realized. It robbed sea travel and, later, air travel of some dangers. It led to broadcasting, and knit the whole world together.*

**Marconi,** GUGLIELMO (1874–1937). In a dusty little room of an old Newfoundland barracks, on December 12, 1901, Guglielmo Marconi sat among some queer-looking instruments, his eyes sparkling, nerves taut, a telephone headpiece clamped to his ears. Outside a violent North Atlantic storm whipped the sea into huge waves. Several men stood by watching Marconi. They had faith in him, even though his purpose seemed fantastically impossible. He was trying to receive a telegraphic signal out of thin air from across the Atlantic Ocean.

Everyone was tense, alert. For a time, nothing happened. Then suddenly there came a sharp tap. Marconi raised his hand, listened a moment, then handed the headphones to his assistants for them also to hear the distinct clicks of the letter " S."

These signals were being sent from Poldhu on the Cornish coast, 2,000 miles away. Wireless communication across an ocean had been established.

The inventor was happy, but not surprised. The marvellous accomplishment was merely the fulfilment of theories he had held since 1895, when he began experiments in methods of sending and receiving the electrical impulses known as Hertzian waves. These theories were not entirely new. Other men, like Hertz, and Clerk-Maxwell, had laid their foundations.

Marconi was born near Bologna, Italy, the son of an Italian country gentleman and an Irish mother. He was educated in both Italian and English schools, gaining his scientific training at Leghorn and Bologna. Even as a small boy he was keenly interested in anything to do with electricity.

At Bologna he watched eagerly the experiments of Prof. Righi with electromagnetic waves and went on to make some investigations of his own. In 1895 he set to work in earnest. He substituted a vertical wire for the Hertzian form of resonator (*see* Hertz, Heinrich Rudolf), improved the Branly coherer which he used as a detector, and invented an electric tapping device. With this apparatus he could send messages more than a mile. The next year he went to England and took out a patent—the first ever granted for a practical system of wireless telegraphy. In 1897 a company was formed to exploit wireless commercially.

By constant and patient work he continued to invent and improve the basic devices, sending messages farther and farther. In 1910 he was able to receive signals at Buenos Aires from Clifden, Ireland, and in 1918 sent a message from England

*Marconi's Wireless Telegraph Co., Ltd.*

**WHERE WIRELESS BRIDGED THE ATLANTIC**
In this room in a hut at Signal Hill, St. John's, Newfoundland, Marconi received the first wireless signals coming across the Atlantic from Poldhu in Cornwall, some 2,000 miles away, on December 12, 1901. The inventor is here seen sitting before the actual instruments used on that historic occasion.

*Marconi's Wireless Telegraph Co., Ltd.*

**MARCONI'S FAMED EXPERIMENT**

**In December 1901 Marconi erected his kite-flown aerial outside the barracks at St. John's, Newfoundland. This was the aerial that picked up the first wireless signal—the letter S in Morse—to be sent across the Atlantic Ocean.**

beam, and thus to send them in one direction only. "Beam transmission," perfected in 1922, is now employed by most world-wide wireless communication systems. Marconi sponsored and developed many special applications of his beam system. Among his inventions to help to save lives at sea is a beam lighthouse that can direct signals to give ships their shore bearing in a fog. In 1934 he successfully demonstrated transmitter equipment that makes " blind " navigation of ships possible.

He applied wireless waves less than one metre long to a wireless telephone for communicating over moderate distances. In 1932 this system was adopted for telephonic communication between Vatican City and the Palace of the Pope near Rome.

Marconi was awarded the Nobel Prize for physics in 1909. The same year the King of Italy nominated him a member of the Italian Senate. A motor accident cost Marconi the use of his right eye in 1912, but he did not let this handicap interfere with his work or his favourite sports of yachting, motoring, cycling and hunting. He served in both the Italian army and navy during the First World War (1914–18). In 1919 he was appointed plenipotentiary delegate to the Paris Peace Conference. In 1929 he was created a *marchese* (marquis). He died on July 20, 1937.

**Marcus Aurelius Antoninus,**

ROMAN EMPEROR (A.D. 121–180). In the second century of our era the peace and happiness of the civilized world depended largely upon whoever happened to be the Roman emperor. He

to Australia. When Sir Ambrose Fleming invented the thermionic valve and made wireless telephony possible, broadcasting was successfully established and wireless communication made familiar to everyone. One of the first practical applications of wireless came in 1898, when Marconi followed the Kingstown Regatta races in a tug and flashed the results to a Dublin paper.

As early as 1904 Marconi had established a ships' news service, which has grown so much that today ships thousands of miles out at sea receive bulletins of what is happening on shore almost as soon as it occurs, and passengers may receive and send personal messages or may even speak directly to persons on shore by radio-telephone.

In 1916 Marconi began extensive experiments to confine wireless impulses to a directed path, instead of letting them spread in all directions, as in ordinary broadcasting. By using a parabolic reflector behind the aerial, Marconi and his engineers were able to concentrate and focus short wireless waves in the form of a

**MARCONI IN HIS FLOATING LABORATORY**

**Devoted to life on the sea, the Marchese (or Marquis) Marconi carried out much of his finest research work when many miles from civilization. He claimed that he could obtain ideal conditions for his experiments only when at sea. This photograph of him was taken in the cabin of his yacht Elettra, when he was at the height of his fame.**

ruled Rome, and Rome ruled the world. But the ruler of Rome had a task of appalling difficulty. Generations of ease and luxury had made the upper classes flabby and selfish. The middle class was rapidly being reduced to slavery and despair. Germanic barbarians were pressing at the borders, and few Romans seemed willing to fight in defence of their country. The armies themselves were recruited largely from barbarians. These were the conditions which Marcus Aurelius faced when he became emperor in A.D. 161.

Marcus had been marked for this task almost from birth. It was usual at that time for Roman emperors who lacked sons to adopt kinsmen as their successors and train them for imperial duties. Marcus was adopted and educated by his uncle, who later became the Emperor Antoninus Pius; and when Antoninus died, Marcus succeeded him. Marcus Aurelius had been trained in the Greek Stoic philosophy, and followed it throughout his life. Although the wealth of the Mediterranean world was at his disposal, he chose to dress plainly, live frugally, and work from early morning to midnight. " Blot out vain pomp; quench appetite; keep reason under its own control," was his advice to all.

He placed the good of society before his own individual comfort. " What is not good for the swarm is not good for the bee," he wrote. He put good government into effect, limited the gladiatorial games, and passed laws benefiting slaves, heirs, women and children. This pagan emperor, by the nobility of his principles, attained something like the loftiness of Christianity ; but he persecuted the Christians themselves, for fear they would destroy the Roman Empire. Though he loved peace he was a good warrior, and throughout his life defended the empire's border provinces against invasion.

In his few spare moments, whether between battles or in the noisy amphitheatre, he jotted down in Greek the rules that guided his own conduct. The resulting volume of Meditations is one of the world's great books of wisdom. Worn out by war and burdens of State, he died on March 17, 180.

*Studio Lisa*
**PRINCESS MARGARET**
Margaret Rose, the second daughter of King George VI and Queen Elizabeth, was born on August 21, 1930.

**Margaret,** PRINCESS (born 1930). The second daughter of King George VI and Queen Elizabeth, this British Princess was born at Glamis Castle, in Angus, Scotland, on August 21, 1930, and christened Margaret Rose. Brought up with her elder sister Princess Elizabeth, Duchess of Edinburgh, she joined the Girl Guides in 1937, later continuing her training as a Sea Ranger. In February-April 1947 she accompanied her parents and sister on a Royal tour of the South African Union.

**Margarine.** A prize was offered by the French government at the time of the Franco-Prussian War (1870) to anyone who could produce a good substitute for butter. The prize was won by Mège-Mouries, a French chemist, who originated a process for making a product from beef fat called margarine, or oleo-margarine. This proved to be a good substitute, for it had the appearance of butter, contained similar amounts of fat and other food elements, though lacking certain factors since discovered, and was cheaper than good butter and more wholesome than poor grades.

Since those pioneer days the manufacture of margarine has developed into one of the largest of our food industries. Research directed towards the improvement of its nutritional value, appearance and flavour, has so transformed margarine that the flavour is equal to that of butter.

The oils and fats which furnish the basis of the industry are largely of vegetable origin. This was made possible by the discovery of a process for introducing

*Capitoline Museum, Rome; photo Anderson*
**MARCUS AURELIUS IN TRIUMPH ·**
Philosopher and soldier, Marcus Aurelius (121–180) was the last of the ' five good emperors ' whose reigns mark the golden age of the Roman Empire. In this relief he is seen riding among his guards, and receiving the submission of barbarian chieftains whom he had conquered.

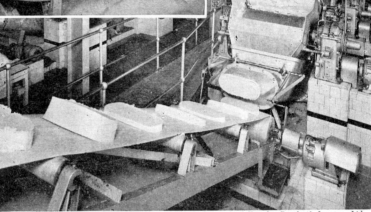

*Courtesy of Van der Berghs & Jurgens, Ltd.*

**HOW MARGARINE IS MIXED**

Most kinds of margarine are made from vegetable oils, expressed from copra, soya beans, etc., and mixed with milk. In the upper picture the mixture is being kneaded by a machine which gives it its proper consistency. From the 'kneader' the mixture passes to the 'multiplexing' machine (lower) from which it emerges in solid slabs.

hydrogen (*q.v.*) into them, thereby raising their melting-point, as without such processing they would remain liquid at ordinary temperatures. Ground nuts, coconuts (copra), palm kernels, soya beans, and other oil-bearing fruits are used in vast quantities. They are crushed between rollers, and the oils are extracted and refined to a point of absolute purity. Milk is the other major raw material. It is pasteurized, then inoculated with a standardized culture of the lactic ferment, and kept under carefully-controlled conditions so that the butter aroma may develop.

The refined oils and fats are blended and churned with the conditioned milk. The result is a cream-like emulsion which passes over great revolving cooling drums and is thus solidified. It is kneaded to give consistency to the texture. Salt is added, and the margarine is ready for the weighing and packing machines.

All brands of margarine in Great Britain today contain the fat-soluble vitamins A and D, giving them an equal vitamin value with butter. (*See* Fats).

**Maria Theresa,** EMPRESS. (1717–80). Difficulties surrounded Maria Theresa when at the death of her father Emperor Charles VI in 1740, at the age of 23 she was proclaimed Archduchess of Austria and Queen of Bohemia and Hungary. The young and beautiful but inexperienced queen was surrounded by a circle of enemies. The unscrupulous Frederick the Great of Prussia took advantage of her youth and sex to seize the rich province of Silesia. Bavaria and Saxony claimed Austria's lands with France's support, and Spain threatened her Italian provinces. The result was the war of the Austrian Succession (1740–48).

Maria Theresa was not one to sit idly by while her lands were torn from her, and the Hungarian people and nobles came to the rescue of their young queen. Her most dangerous enemy, Frederick of Prussia, made peace in 1742, and though he re-entered the war in 1744 his interest centred exclusively in Silesia. By the treaty of Aix-la-Chapelle in 1748, Maria Theresa had to submit to the loss of Silesia to Prussia, and to give up some of her Italian possessions to Spain, but she retained the rest of her lands. Meanwhile her husband had been elected Emperor as Francis I.

The loss of her possessions hurt Maria Theresa, and she set herself industriously to win France from its 200 years' enmity to Austria, in order that she might recover them. An alliance with France was brought about in 1756 by her clever minister, Kaunitz. This she sealed later (1770) by the marriage of one of her 11 daughters, Marie Antoinette, to the heir to the French throne. Great Britain at that time decided to abandon her old Austrian alliance, and formed a new one with Prussia. When, therefore, the "third Silesian war" broke out in 1756 Maria Theresa found herself, in spite of an alliance with Russia and the desperate straits to which Frederick was reduced, still quite unable to force Prussia to loosen its hold upon Silesia. She died on November 29, 1780.

# Marie Antoinette. (1755-93).

QUEEN OF FRANCE. Somewhere about noon on October 16, 1793, a cart rumbled slowly through the Paris streets amid the howls and jeers of the

*Versailles Museum: Photo Mansell*

**MARIE ANTOINETTE**

The tragic queen of Louis XVI of France, who, with her husband, met death by the guillotine in the French Revolution, is here seen portrayed by Madame Vigée Lebrun (1755-1842), with her three children. Her extravagance, though rumour exaggerated it, helped to bring about the Revolution.

populace. In it sat a woman in a ragged white dress with hands bound behind her, yet with traces of majesty in her stricken bearing and of beauty in her wasted face. At the Place de la Révolution the victim alighted, then mounted the steps of the scaffold, and lay her prematurely-whitened head beneath the knife of the guillotine. Such was the end of an empress's daughter, once the gayest and most beautiful princess in Europe.

Marie Antoinette (pron. ma-rē-ahn-twah-net'), fourth daughter of Maria Theresa of Austria, was born in Vienna on November 2, 1755, and was married at 15 to Louis XVI of France, then dauphin or heir to the throne. A frolicsome, reckless, extravagant child, she shocked the more sober members of the French court by her disregard of etiquette. When she became queen (1774), her open furtherance of Austrian interests and her enmity towards the statesmen Turgot and Necker, who wished to check the extravagance of the Court, aroused distrust.

Meanwhile she had become an obstinate woman who forced the king to resist all reforms, and when the Revolution came in 1789 it was she rather than the King who was blamed for the misgovernment of the country. The King and Queen fled from Paris in 1791, but were stopped at Varennes and brought back to the city, in the belief that they were seeking foreign aid and inviting invasion.

In August 1792 charges of treachery brought against the Queen for her conduct in the war with Austria led a revolutionary mob to storm the Tuileries palace, seize the royal family, and send them as prisoners to the Temple. From there the king was led in December to trial, and in January 1793 to execution. The queen was taken in August 1793 to the prison of the Conciergerie, where common criminals were confined. Amid insults and brutality she bore herself with dignity and patience at her trial, but was convicted of treason, and her execution by the guillotine followed, on October 16, 1793.

# Marigold.

In the Middle Ages various golden-yellow or orange blossoms that grew in profusion throughout southern Europe were dedicated to the Virgin Mary and called " Mary's gold " or marigolds. A native of the Mediterranean region, this hardy annual herb is the marigold referred to by Shakespeare as " the marigold that goes to bed wi' the sun, and with him rises weeping "—for it closes its petals at sunset, and in the early morning dewdrops rest on the bloom. It was formerly used for making marigold vinegar and for flavouring soups. The scientific name of the common garden marigold is *Calendula officinalis*. Robust and bushy, it grows about 12 inches in height, and belongs to the order *Compositae*.

The African and French marigolds belong to a different genus and are natives of Mexico. The African species (*Tagetes erecta*) attains a height of from two to three feet; its flowers are usually solid in colour, varying from pale yellow to deep orange. The French marigold (*Tagetes patula*) is a bushy plant about a foot high; the blossoms are usually golden yellow with red markings. These are grown as half-hardy annuals in Britain, and there are a number of improved varieties. The so-called marsh marigold is not a marigold but a buttercup.

*H. Bastin*

**CORN MARIGOLDS**

One of the worst weeds of the cornfield is this marigold whose yellow daisy-like flowers are seen during the summer months. Above is a crop of oats in which there seems almost as great a growth of marigolds as of the cereal itself.

# A WONDERLAND beneath the WAVES

*Divers and marine biologists have discovered a world full of life and colour thousands of feet beneath the sea's surface. From their descriptions of what they have seen a vivid picture of it can be painted.*

**Marine Life.** Nearly three-quarters of the surface of our globe is covered by the sea. So vast is the area of the ocean that even the great continents of the earth are but islands in its midst, the Pacific Ocean alone covering some 64 million square miles. The volume of salt water upon the earth is even more stupendous, because the ocean has an average depth of about 12,000 feet, and is more than five miles deep in some places.

**BEADLET ANEMONE**
Brown, green or red beadlet anemones are common inhabitants of sea pools on rocky shores of Great Britain.

Wonderful is the sea with its tides and waves and currents, its calms and terrible storms, its rocks and reefs, its icebergs and water-spouts. But a thousand times more wonderful is its teeming and varied life. Incomplete as our knowledge of the sea and its inhabitants is at present, we do know enough to convince us that the forms of life in the sea are as varied and as wonderful as the infinite and diverse species of animal and vegetable life which are found on the dry land.

Not only has every sea its distinctive inhabitants, but in all but the shallowest waters each stratum of depth is like a storey of a house, with different creatures living on each floor. On the ocean bed there is as varied a salt-water vegetation as can be found in the terrestrial forests of all the lands of the earth. And in the same way as our woods and forests shelter and support millions of inhabitants of thousands of species of animal life, so amid the thickets and jungles of the sea-floor, and floating and swimming in the waters above it, are myriads of creatures which are the descendants of similar animals and fishes that have populated these same waters since the beginning of life—for, according to most theories, it was in the sea that life began, billions of years ago.

These creatures of the sea are of every size and shape, varying in structure, in colour, and in habits of life just as widely as do the insects and animals of the dry land. Hundreds of living creatures, so tiny that a single drop of salt water may contain thousands of them, have been identified by scientists with the aid of the microscope, and every part of the sea from Pole to Pole, and from the surface to 30,000 feet and deeper, is teeming with these minute forms of life.

Some idea of the numbers of the lowest forms of life in the ocean, and their use in Nature through the ages, can be obtained when one bears in mind that such enormous depths of chalk as now underlie the south of England and elsewhere, as well as the older and harder limestones, were built up by the depositing on the bottom of the sea of the shells and debris of microscopic creatures that lived in far-back ages. Similar deposits are being built up in our own time on the bed of some of the oceans by the same slow-working agency, and in the great depths each layer of ooze has its own name and is composed of distinct types of animalcule. The term plankton is given to these minute organisms.

From the microscopic the orders and species of marine life ascend in the scale step by step to the gigantic. If we omit some of the intermediate forms, marine life may be classified upwards from the protozoa (lowest and simplest forms, mostly consisting of a single cell) through the sponges, corals, anemones, starfishes, molluscs, worms, crustaceans, fishes, turtles, dolphins, whales, and, finally, to the highest of all—the seals.

In such a wonderland of sea life it is but natural to find remarkable creatures, and many intensely interesting facts are connected with even the commonest and most familiar of them—the fishes. Not only do the creatures of the sea find all their food therein, but the sea also furnishes food to myriads of sea-birds and animals that live on its shores, and also no inconsiderable amount of the sustenance required by Man. It is true that the area of the sea from which mankind takes his toll of fish is very small compared with the vast extent of the ocean, and yet millions and millions of edible fish are caught every year, even within a few miles of the coasts of Great Britain. Despite continuous fishing for centuries, and the fact that many mature fishes and even seals and sea-birds, continually prey upon the food fishes used by Man, the supply did not appear to be appreciably diminished—until Man

*E. A. Botting*

**TINY SHELLS FROM OCEAN OOZE**
At the bottom of the deeper seas there is a thick layer of ooze, the debris of centuries of life from the waters above. Here is a sample of this ooze, consisting of innumerable tiny shells (very highly magnified) of the minute creatures which are called Foraminifera.

little workers occupy a position between the plant and animal kingdoms in the sea. The coral animal is born from an egg, and for a time it swims, like a marine worm; then it adheres to some object, becomes a fixture like a plant in the soil, and henceforward lives the life of a marine plant, generally in great communities, which in time build up reefs and islands of coral rising above the sea.

The struggle for existence is as intense among marine life as it is in the animal kingdom on land—indeed, more so. Certain kinds of whales and large fish follow shoals of such fish as herring and prey

so improved the efficiency of his fishing methods that the balance of nature was disturbed.

Under-fishing of a fishing ground also may do harm: the fish population increases; the ground becomes overcrowded, and the fishes' food supply diminishes. There is then a bigger proportion of older fish; owing to crowding and the fiercer struggle to get food, the fish do not grow so large and vigorous. (Note what we said, in the story of Ecology, about Man's interference with the deer population of the Grand Canyon National Park of the U.S.A.) Marine biologists who study the conditions in the fishery industry aim at taking each season the biggest catch of any particular group of food-fish which is "safe," having

Prof. W. H. Longley

## LIFE AMONG FLORIDA'S CORAL REEFS

Conditions are seldom satisfactory for taking direct underwater photographs, but here are two examples from Florida, where among the coral reefs the water is perfectly clear. In the upper, a shoal of yellow goat-fish are searching for food among the corals. Below are some dark-barred pork-fish, keeping just above the long spines of sea-urchins which rest on the bottom.

in mind the ability of the fishing grounds to continue to yield up abundantly, year after year, this valuable food for Man.

Among the innumerable strange and wonderful creatures that inhabit the sea few are more remarkable than the coral-making animals (*see* Coral *and* Plate facing page 908). These extraordinary

on them incessantly; while swarms of other species not only devour the food fishes that have been caught in the fishermen's nets but cause considerable damage to the nets, too.

Some fish are furnished with remarkable weapons which make them terrors of the sea. In nearly every museum one may see the bony sword of a

*Painting by* ELIE CHEVERLANGE

*See text overleaf*

# SOME OF HIS UNDER-WATER PORTRAITS

KEY TO COLOUR PLATE

THE picture on the preceding page was painted from life by Elie Cheverlange while the artist was studying fishes in the waters surrounding the island of Tahiti, where for long he made his home. The creatures portrayed can be identified with the aid of the small key-picture at the left. At the top are two members of the *Chaetodon* family, small, lively colourful swimmers of the South Seas, sometimes called " butterfly fish." The two species shown are *Chaetodon citrinellus* (1) and *Chaetodon juniula* (2). Below them with great outspread feelers rests *Palinurus penicillatus* (3), a tropical relative of the crawfish (*Palinurus vulgaris*) found in the Mediterranean and off Britain's southern coasts. These are sometimes called rock, or spiny, lobsters, but do not have the formidable pincers of the true lobster (*Homarus vulgaris*). Like his Mediterranean cousins, the Pacific crawfish is considered a table delicacy.

The still life in the painting includes whip coral (4), stony coral (5), and green calcareous alga fringing the bottom of the frame.

No less interesting than the details of the picture itself is the manner in which the artist gathered his material on the ocean bottom. The plate facing page 2104 shows him on one of his under-water tours of exploration and observation. The painting for that plate was specially made to illustrate the unique procedure he followed in producing the pictures which have won for him a high place among the relatively few Nature painters who combine fine artistic ability with scientific method.

His odd appearance in this self-portrait is due to the faithful representation of two items—the common clothes-peg he is wearing on his nose, and the hair of his head which, with its tendency to float, seems to be standing on end.

More information about this artist's method of working under water will be found on the back of the first plate.

*To face page* 2105

Dr. Graf Zedtwitz

## SEA-ANEMONES WITH THEIR POWERFUL TENTACLES

Few objects found around our shores are so attractive as the sea-anemones, those 'flowers' of the rock pools whose colours and habits are so fascinating. Those you see above have been catching food, and their tentacles are gradually closing inwards, a sign that they are going to retire 'into themselves' while they digest the little fish or other creatures which they are swallowing. Like corals, sea-anemones belong to the class of Anthozoa ('flower-animals').

sword-fish. This fish has been known to thrust the sword-like prolongation of its upper jaw through the oak timbers of large sailing ships with such fury that the sword has broken. This is no relative of the saw-fish, whose blade has projections like saw-teeth along either edge.

Another fearsome monster of the deep is the octopus, which has eight long arms each provided with suckers. Lurking in a hole among the rocks at the bottom of the sea, the octopus uses its tentacles to seize its prey.

Amongst the higher orders of marine life are the seals, of which there are many varieties. These are not fish but mammals, and although some of them are able to move along the ground on their flippers and tail, they live an aquatic life. They are for the most part inhabitants of the Arctic and Antarctic seas.

Whales, which belong to the same order as the porpoise, the grampus and the narwhal, are the largest of all marine creatures. The whale is a mammal ; its young are born alive. There are various kinds of whales, the most valuable from a commercial point of view being the large blue whale of the Antarctic seas, which yields quantities of oil and sometimes measures 100 feet in length.

**Mark Antony** (c. 83–30 B.C.). The story of Marcus Antonius—the Roman statesman and soldier commonly referred to as Mark Antony— and Cleopatra (q.v.), is one of the famous romances of history. After a mis-spent youth, he gained distinction as a military leader in many campaigns; he led the left wing of Julius Caesar's victorious army against Pompey at the battle of Pharsalus in 48 B.C. Before he was 40 Antony became joint consul of the Roman Empire with Caesar himself.

After the assassination of Caesar, in Shakespeare's tragedy Julius Caesar, Antony makes his famous speech : " Friends, Romans, countrymen . . ."

In alliance with Octavian, Caesar's adopted son, Mark Antony defeated Brutus and the other conspirators who had plotted against Caesar, becoming ruler of the eastern portion of the Roman Empire, while Octavian took the western regions. Later Antony fell in love with the Egyptian Queen Cleopatra, spending most of his time in Egypt. In 31 B.C. he and Octavian quarrelled over the division of the Roman Empire, and Antony was defeated at the naval battle of Actium. He fled to Egypt, whither Octavian followed him in 30 B.C. And there Antony killed himself to avoid falling into the hands of his enemy.

**Marlborough,** John Churchill, 1st Duke of (1650–1722). When John Churchill at 15 became page of honour to the Duke of York (later King James II), he was almost unknown ; but at his death, nearly 60 years later, he had been made Duke of Marlborough (pron. mawl'-brê) and was renowned throughout Europe as the greatest general of his age and one of its best statesmen. The friendship between the Duke of York and Churchill's sister Arabella won for him his appointment as page, and later, at the age of 16, a commission in the army. He learned the art of war while serving under the famous French soldier Marshal Turenne against the Dutch. His rise at Court was further aided by his marriage in 1678 with Sarah Jennings, the clever, beautiful, imperious attendant and friend of Princess Anne, the younger daughter of James II, who later became Queen Anne.

Churchill was born at Ashe, near Axminster, Devonshire, probably on June 24, 1650, and was educated at St. Paul's School, London. He entered the household of James, Duke of York, but soon afterwards received a commission in the Guards. He was made a Baron in 1682 and on the accession of James to the English throne in 1685 was promoted Major-General. When the follies and tyranny of his old patron turned all England against James II, Churchill took a leading part in the "Glorious Revolution" of 1688, the result of which was to make William of Orange king of Great Britain and Ireland.

For the assistance he then gave he was rewarded by being made Earl of Marlborough. He was of great service to William III in conquering Ireland, which supported James II, and as commander against the French in the Netherlands. But he was never wholly trusted by the new king; and not without reason, for while ostensibly supporting William III Marlborough was in correspondence with the exiled James II.

When Queen Anne came to the throne, in 1702, she showered favours upon Marlborough and his wife. These included the title of Duke and the position of commander-in-chief of the English forces. His abilities were equal to his opportunities. A Frenchman once said that he never besieged a fortress that he did not take, never fought a battle that he did not win, and never carried on a negotiation that he did not bring to a successful close.

During the War of the Spanish Succession (1702–14) in which England's chief interest was to prevent France from obtaining Spain, with its vast colonies and dependencies, Marlborough showed his unrivalled generalship in some of the most brilliant campaigns in English history. On August 13, 1704, as commander of the Dutch and English forces, acting with Prince Eugene of Savoy, the Austrian commander, he won a victory over the French at Blenheim (q.v.), in southern Germany. This battle stamped Marlborough as the first general in Europe. It broke the spell surrounding the power of France under Louis XIV, and ensured the continued exclusion of the Stuart line, as represented by the descendants of James II, from the English throne. The victory also helped to lay the basis for English rule both in North America and in India.

In 1706 the battle of Ramillies, in 1708 that of Oudenarde, and in 1709 Malplaquet, continued Marlborough's career of victory. And as a result of these victories England was able to negotiate the profitable Treaty of Utrecht in 1713, and that of Baden in 1714, which ended the war.

Marlborough, however, had fallen from power in 1711. The Queen had grown heartily tired of being domineered by his wife and dismissed her. Then Marlborough's enemies accused him of misusing public moneys, and he was deprived of all his appointments. But when George I came to the throne in 1714 Marlborough was restored to his military posts. He died on June 16, 1722, and was

*National Portrait Gallery, London*

**THE GREAT DUKE OF MARLBOROUGH**

The first Duke of Marlborough was one of the greatest generals of all time, and won every battle that he fought in command of the armies of the Grand Alliance against France. This portrait of him is by Sir Godfrey Kneller (1646–1723). As was often the way of artists of that period the painter has surrounded Marlborough with allegorical figures, one of whom is placing a crown of laurels on his head.

buried in Westminster Abbey, London. Later his remains were removed to the chapel at Blenheim, the magnificent palace which had been erected for the Duke at Woodstock, near Oxford, at the nation's expense before his fall from favour.

**Marlowe,** CHRISTOPHER (1564–93). Before he perished tragically in a drunken brawl, aged 29, Marlowe had written both plays and poems that rank among the glories of English literature.

Born on February 6, 1564, at Canterbury, Kent, where his father was a shoemaker, he was educated at the King's School in the cathedral city and at Corpus Christi College, Cambridge. Little is known about his career after he left the University, except that he was friendly with Shakespeare and other leading Elizabethan men of letters.

His earliest drama, Tamburlaine the Great, was written in 1587, followed by The Tragical History of Dr. Faustus (1588), The Jew of Malta (1590), and Edward the Second (1593). He also wrote several translations of Greek and Latin authors, and composed original poetry.

Marlowe in his dramas handled English in a way that had never been attempted before. There is no earlier author who writes such deep, resounding verse, and of later writers Shakespeare alone surpasses him in poetic feeling and dramatic power.

Unfortunately Marlowe held views which were regarded by the authorities as dangerous, and in 1593 a warrant was issued for his arrest on some unknown charge. Marlowe learned of this in time to escape, and reached the little village of Deptford, now part of London. But there he became involved in a quarrel, and was stabbed to death, in May 1593.

*Barratt*

**MEMORIAL TO MARLOWE**

This monument in Canterbury was erected to Christopher Marlowe's memory in 1891, when Sir Henry Irving unveiled it near the Cathedral. It now stands in the Dane John. The small figures in niches round the plinth represent the plays, the one visible here being Tamburlaine.

**Marquette,** JACQUES (1637–75). One of the French explorers of North America in the 17th century, Jacques Marquette (pron. mar-ket´) was born at Laon, France. Joining the religious order of the Jesuits, he was sent to Canada in 1666 as a missionary and worked amongst the Red Indians living around the Great Lakes, until 1673.

On May 17 of that year he set out with a few followers to re-discover the Mississippi, traversing Lake Michigan in birch-bark canoes and paddling up the Fox river. Ascending that waterway nearly to its source, they carried their canoes across country for 50 miles to the Wisconsin river, down which they paddled for eight days before they floated out into the mighty stream of the Mississippi. They were the first white men to gaze upon the Mississippi since the Spaniard de Soto discovered it 130 years previously. Marquette died on a missionary journey, on May 18, 1675.

**Marriage.** A man and woman, having become " engaged to be married " or " betrothed," have the choice of two different forms of marriage procedure—a religious ceremony, in a church or a nonconformist building; or a " civil " ceremony before the Registrar in a Register Office. Many buildings belonging to religious bodies other than the Established Church are " registered " for marriages by the State, and a Registrar of Marriages attends the ceremony. Where the minister of a nonconformist building, or some other official, is authorised under an Act of Parliament, he can register the marriage, and a Registrar need not be present.

If the parties prefer not to have a religious ceremony, they can attend a District Register Office where, in the presence of the Registrar, they solemnly declare that they take each other as husband or wife. Two witnesses must be present. The marriage must be solemnised between the hours of 8 a.m. and 6 p.m., with open doors. Each of the parties must declare that he or she knows of no lawful impediment to the marriage.

The usual procedure for a marriage in church is that notice is given " by banns." This means that, for three Sundays preceding the day of the marriage, the particulars are read out in church, giving the names of the parties. If parties reside in different parishes, the banns must be " published " in each parish church. The purpose of banns is to allow any person who may know of an impediment to the marriage to declare it to the minister. (For example, it may be that either party has a husband or wife still living, and has not been divorced.)

By obtaining an " ordinary " marriage licence from the ecclesiastical authorities, on payment of a fee, the publication of banns can be dispensed with; in this case one of the parties must make an affidavit (a written statement, confirmed on oath before an official) that there is no legal impediment to the intended marriage. A " special " licence may be granted by the Archbishop of Canterbury. This is much more costly, and allows a marriage at any place within the district and at any time. (Such a licence might be desirable if one of the parties had to go abroad at short notice, for example.)

The State has an interest in the marriage, for unless there were proper safeguards lawless persons might misrepresent themselves and go through forms of marriage which were fraudulent. An "infant" may not marry without the consent of his or her parents or guardians; infant here means a person under the age of 21. No marriage may take place if either party is under the age of 16. We have seen that the publication of banns is designed to prevent "bigamy," or the "marrying" of a second spouse while the first one is still alive.

Another way in which the State protects its citizens is in laying down strict laws for the recording and registration of marriages. No matter how many years may elapse, one can procure a marriage certificate which is a copy of the entry in the Register of the church, or of the Register Office. There are carefully preserved, at Somerset House, London, the local registers, which go to the Registrar General for safe keeping. On payment of a small fee a copy of any entry can be had.

In Scotland, both regular and irregular marriages are recognized. The first is celebrated by a minister of religion or an authorised Registrar after publication of banns or the giving of notice. The irregular marriage, until the passing of an Act of 1939, need have been merely the exchanging of consents by the parties, so long as one of them had his or her usual place of residence in Scotland, or had resided there for 21 days beforehand. Nowadays an irregular marriage is recognized only if the parties live together as husband and wife, and if they are held as such by the "general repute of the neighbourhood."

Even then, before such a marriage can be registered a decree of the Scottish Court must be obtained.

In 1770, the English marriage laws were tightened up, and for many years afterwards foolish or romantic couples wishing to get married hastily—for example, to circumvent opposition by parents or guardians—fled over the border to Scotland. At Gretna Green, a village of Dumfriesshire near the little River Sark, that divides England from Scotland, they found a compliant blacksmith or innkeeper who "celebrated" the marriage, according to Scottish custom. But in 1856 the law of Scotland made 21 days' residence necessary, and eloping couples who wanted a Gretna marriage had then three weeks in which to think things over ! Probably many of them repented of their rashness.

Many and diverse are the customs connected with marriage in different lands. Though marriage by capture is rare today, and practised only by certain primitive peoples, the custom of mock-capture lingers. In some Australian tribes the husband stuns his intended bride before taking her off. Among the Yakuts the bride will be carried away on horseback, while the "angry" relatives follow in mock pursuit. Refined down to a show of reluctance by the bride, mock-capture is seen among some central and eastern European peoples.

Marriage by purchase is still common; its relic, in the insistence on a sizeable dowry by the bride's parents, is a feature of marriage arranging in many lands. On the other hand, the husband or his

*Keystone*

A MARRIAGE CUSTOM OF OLD JAPAN

When a marriage is contemplated in Japan the matter is often placed in the hands of a professional ' match-maker ' or marriage-broker. He arranges for the young couple to meet in a tea-house, formerly the favourite meeting-place for everyone in Japan, and there makes the arrangements. If the pair like each other well enough, the bride-to-be serves her future husband a ceremonial cup of tea (seen being drunk in this photograph), in token of their marriage.

**MARRIAGE ROOM AT THE SMITHY, GRETNA GREEN**          *Topical*
In 1770 the English marriage laws were made more strict, and so couples wishing to wed hastily fled over the Scottish border to Gretna Green, where they could be married at the blacksmith's shop (above) without delay, according to the Scottish custom. The practice died out in the latter half of the 19th century.

Vegetable marrows grow to a great size, specimens sometimes weighing as much as 50 pounds, but consisting very largely of water. The flowers are large, trumpet-shaped, and bright yellow or orange; the straggling stems bear big rounded leaves, whose main veins are armed with spines or hooks, as are the stems themselves.

**Marryat,** FREDERICK (1792–1848). Immense numbers of people have been thrilled by Captain Marryat's vigorous stories of the sea with their inimitable accounts of fights, chases and expeditions. Many a schoolboy might well envy the life of this sailor-novelist; for previous to settling down to writing his numerous stories of nautical life he passed years of exciting and dangerous service in the Navy in many parts of the world.

He was born at Westminster, London, on July 10, 1792, and as a child he tried several times to run away to sea. In 1806 his father entered him as a midshipman in the Royal Navy. He saw a great deal of service, both in European and American waters, and held a command during the Burmese War of 1824–25. Retiring in 1830, Marryat died at Langham, Norfolk, on August 9, 1848.

The best of Marryat's books rank as classics in English literature. They include Frank Mildmay

parents may demand the equivalent of a purchase price before agreeing to a marriage. Marriage by service, in which the would-be husband had to give his labour to the bride's parents for a certain period, was another ancient custom. Jacob served Laban for 14 years in order to get Rachel, the bride of his choice.

Betrothal customs are equally ancient and widespread. Infant betrothal is very common, two children being plighted to each other; in fact the betrothal of two babies even before they are born is common with some primitive races. Some of the customs are indeed strange. A Nigerian bride-to-be may be sent to a fattening house; while a betrothed woman of the Orinoco may have to stay some long time in a fasting hut! Even worse is the fate of a bride in New Ireland, who may have to spend five years secluded in a leaf-cage before she is married.

An engagement is the formal recognition that the man and the woman have " plighted their troth "—pledged their word—that they intend to marry. The engagement lasts until the day of the wedding. It is the custom for the man to give his bride-to-be an engagement ring, and quite often she gives him a ring in exchange. Usually the engagement is celebrated by some social function such as a dinner party, in which the parents and relatives on both sides get to know one another if they are not already acquainted. A public announcement of the engagement is sometimes made in the newspapers.

**Marrows.** These plants and their relatives are members of the family *Cucurbitaceae*, which flourishes especially in tropical regions. One well-known member is the cucumber (*Cucumis sativus*), another, the melon (*C. melo*). But the vegetable marrow is really the typical member of the family, belonging to the genus *Cucurbita*, together with the pumpkin (*C. pepo*); these are grown in Britain as half-hardy annuals.

*R. A. Malby*
**VEGETABLE MARROWS**
The large yellow (female) flowers of the marrow plant are succeeded, after fertilization, by fruits commonly known as vegetable marrows—variously coloured and shaped, and sometimes reaching a large size and weight.

(1829); Peter Simple (1834); Mr. Midshipman Easy (1836); Japhet in Search of a Father (1836); Masterman Ready (1841); The Settlers in Canada (1844); and The Children of the New Forest (1847).

**Mars.** Next in importance to Jupiter in the Roman religion was Mars, the god of war. He was regarded as the father of the Romans through his son Romulus, the legendary founder of Rome, and was extensively worshipped. He was in early times also a god of Nature and fertility. The month of March (Latin, *Martius*) was dedicated to him.

The Greek god Ares is identified with Mars; but the Greeks thought of Ares only as a sender of war and pestilence, a quarrelsome god, delighting in the slaughter of men and the destruction of cities. He was not widely worshipped, though the Areopagus, the sacred hill of Athens, was named after him.

In astronomy the name Mars is given to the fourth planet in order from the sun—supposedly because of its red and angry countenance. (*See* Planets *and* the Plate facing page 280).

**Marseilles.** (Fr. mar sǎlz'), French On the shores of the Mediterranean lies the second city and chief seaport of France—romantic, busy

**FREDERICK MARRYAT**
Author of many thrilling books, Marryat was an officer in the Royal Navy until he retired in 1830, his own exciting experiences providing him with material for his nautical stories. He died on August 9, 1848.

Marseilles. In the harbour, which was enlarged in 1933, when the canal to Arles was completed, ships from all parts of the world can be seen. Southwest of the harbour lies the tiny island called Château d'If, made famous by Dumas's story, The Count of Monte Cristo.

Marseilles was one of the most picturesque cities in the world until, in January 1943, its famous old port and the surrounding quarter were blown up or transformed into fortifications by the German invaders. The new port, begun in 1844, is connected with the Marseilles-Rhône Canal and in normal times is used annually by 8,000–9,000 vessels. The city is the centre of French trade with East and North Africa. Chief industries of Marseilles are the making of soap, glass and chemicals, and shipbuilding.

The most impressive buildings include the Palais de Longchamps (containing several museums), the Byzantine Cathedral, and the Church of Notre Dame de la Garde, standing on a 300-feet hill and surmounted by a statue of the Virgin visible from far out at sea. The Town Hall dates from the 17th century and the Church of St. Victor from the 10th to the 13th century. Marseilles contains an observatory, and zoological and botanical gardens.

*New York Times Photos*

**MARSEILLES : FRANCE'S VAST MEDITERRANEAN PORT**

Capital of the department of Bouches-du-Rhône, and France's biggest seaport, Marseilles is situated on a large bay of the Mediterranean coast. The Old Port (above) is used mainly by fishing vessels, and here a vast crowd gathered on April 19, 1948, to hear a speech by General de Gaulle. In the background is the church of Notre Dame de la Garde, on the summit of a hill 300 feet high, with a 150-foot tower carrying a gilded statue of the Virgin Mary.

There in 1792 supporters of the French Revolution sang a new march which under the name of The Marseillaise became the French national anthem. The history of Marseilles goes back to about 600 B.C. when Greeks settled there, calling it Massalia. Though long remaining a centre of Greek civilization, it was successively captured by the Germanic Visigoths and Ostrogoths, and the Franks. Its development as a modern port really dates from the opening of the Suez Canal in 1869.

During the Second World War (1939–45) Marseilles was occupied by German forces in November 1942, following the Allied landings in French North Africa. The city was liberated in August 1944. The 1946 population was 636,264.

GEORGE MARSHALL

U.S.A. Secretary of State (Foreign Minister) during 1947–49, Marshall announced the plan named after him and designed to help Europe recover from the Second World War.

*Planet*

**Marshall,** GEORGE CATLETT (born 1880). To the distressed nations of Europe in 1947 came the news of a plan for American aid, the Marshall plan, named after its originator, George Marshall, the United States Secretary of State. Soviet Russia and the nations under her influence denounced the plan as a scheme to further American imperialism, but the Western countries accepted it.

George Marshall was born in Unionstown, Pennsylvania, on December 31, 1880, and chose the Army as his career. He was commissioned in 1901 ; fought in France during the First World War (1914–18) in 1917–8, and reached the rank of Brigadier-General in 1936. Appointed Chief of Staff on September 1, 1939, he had the task of expanding the United States Army in the Second World War (1939–45).

In December 1944 General Marshall was promoted to the rank of General of the Army, equivalent to a British Field-Marshal. In November 1945, on his retirement from the Army, he was appointed United States ambassador to China, charged with the mission of bringing about peace between the National Government and the Communists. He arranged a meeting between the two leaders, and a pact was signed, but the terms were not observed and fighting broke out again. In March 1946 he was sent as ambassador to the Soviet Union. But he did not remain there long; on January 7, 1947, his nomination as Secretary of State (Foreign Minister) was announced.

On June 5, 1947, Marshall, in a speech at Harvard University, Massachusetts, announced his plan which provided for American aid for Europe in the form of food, fuel, raw materials and equipment if the nations of Europe would unite in planning their economic reconstruction. The United Nations supported the scheme, and the Governments of Great Britain, France, the Netherlands, Belgium, Luxemburg, Italy, Iceland, Denmark, Norway, Greece, Turkey, Austria, Eire, Western Germany, Switzerland and Portugal expressed themselves as being willing to co-operate

in the plan. In 1948 aid from the United States began to flow into Europe, with a view to making the countries who had accepted the Marshall Plan self-supporting by 1952.

**Marsupials.** These animals are so named from the Latin word *marsupium*, meaning a pouch, on account of the curious pocket in which they keep their young. In former ages marsupials were met with all over the earth, but today they are found chiefly in Australasia. Besides the kangaroo, the principal marsupial of Australia, they are the bandicoot, wallaby, cuscus, phalanger, banded ant-eater, Tasmanian wolf or thylacine, Tasmanian devil, and certain pouched dog-like and bear-like animals such as the koala and wombat. Outside of Australasia the only marsupials which now exist are the opossums, found in South America and in the southern United States.

**Marten.** Members of the weasel family, martens have fur of a reddish-brown colour and a long bushy tail. The outer fur is long and glossy, the under-fur thick and soft. They have long slender bodies and short legs, and live mostly in trees, leaping from one to another like squirrels. They vary from 17 to 40 inches in length.

The European pine marten, *Mustela martes*, is the only species that occurs in the British Isles, where it used to be common, but is now confined

*Frances Pitt*

RARE PINE MARTEN

One of the rarest of British wild animals, and in many parts now extinct, the pine marten is a large, tree-haunting relative of the weasel, as its sharp snout, alert look and long, slender body show. It is trapped for its fur and because of the damage it does in game preserves.

to the wilder regions, for it has been much persecuted as injurious to game. The beech marten or stone marten is another variety, with hair inclined to greyish-brown, and pure white on the breast. It is found in most parts of Europe south of the Baltic, and also in Asia.

The North American species include the American pine marten or Canadian sable, which is about the size of the large house cat. It has a soft deep fur of rich brown, lighter-coloured underneath, with a tawny spot on the throat. Another is the fisher marten, black marten, or pckan, as it is variously called, the largest of the group. It is from two to three feet long, with a bushy tail a foot or more in length ; greyish-brown, with dark markings, it has a black tip to its tail. The furs of these animals are all valuable commercially.

**Martinique.** (Pron. mar-ti-nēk′). Visitors to Martinique, one of the small group of French islands in the West Indies, find two spots of historic interest. The first is the ruins of the quaint old house in which the unhappy Empress Josephine, Napoleon's first wife, was born. The other is the scene of desolation which marks the site of the once beautiful St. Pierre, the city which was destroyed in 1902 by the eruptions of Mont Pelée, when that volcano's molten lava and poisonous gases killed nearly 40,000 people.

Mont Pelée, about 4,500 feet, is the highest point in a lofty, thickly-wooded mountain ridge, which gives the hot, damp little island most of its picturesqueness. Of volcanic formation, Martinique is irregular in shape, with indented coasts, high and rugged. Its area is 385 square miles; the capital is Fort-de-France, whose population is 52,000.

Somewhat more than a third of the island is under cultivation. Sugar, rum, cocoa, coffee, and tobacco are leading products. The farms are served by well-built roads, and some of the sugar-cane plantations have light railways.

Discovered by the Spaniards in 1493, Martinique was colonized by the French in 1635. They have held it since that time, save for three occupations—in 1762, from 1793 to 1801, and from 1809 to 1814—by the British. Since 1947 it has ranked as a department of France. The population of about 247,000 consists chiefly of Negroes and half-castes, the whites amounting to only about three per cent of the total.

**Martyrs.** CHRISTIAN. "The blood of the martyrs," wrote one of the early Christian Fathers (ecclesiastical writers of the first centuries of the Christian era), "is the seed of the Church." For, by the heroic courage with which they endured persecution and died for their faith, they won thousands of converts, and so Christianity triumphed over paganism.

"Martyr" comes from the Greek *martur*, meaning a witness. Stephen, who was stoned to death at Jerusalem in the days of the Apostles (*see* Acts vii) was the first of the Christian martyrs. Altogether about 14,000 martyrs are included in the records of the Roman Catholic Church. Among the most famous are St. Lawrence, who is said to have been roasted on a gridiron about the year 258, during the persecution of the Emperor Valerian; and St. Sebastian, a captain of the Praetorian (Imperial) Guard under the Roman Emperor Diocletian, who was condemned to be shot by a troop of archers for his faith. Sebastian's martyrdom has been a favourite subject with painters, who represent him as a beautiful youth bound to a tree and pierced by many arrows. In 1563 an English clergyman named John

*Painting by Sir John Millais, Tate Gallery; photo, Mansell*
**THE FIRST CHRISTIAN MARTYR**
Brought to trial Stephen made a speech (reported in Acts vii), and 'when they heard these things, they were cut to the heart, and they gnashed on him with their teeth ... And cast him out of the city, and stoned him ... And he cried with a loud voice, Lord, lay not this sin to their charge. And when he had said this he fell asleep.'

Foxe published his History of the Acts and Monuments of the Church, commonly referred to as the Book of Martyrs, commemorating those who had died for Protestant beliefs.

**Marx,** Heinrich Karl (1818–83). The theories of this revolutionary were adopted by the Russian Social-Democrats and Bolsheviks ; when the Bolsheviks seized power in Russia in 1917 they made Marx's tenets the keystone of their system of government. So it came about that Marxism became the dominant " faith " of Russian Communists and of other Communists throughout the world, in East and West, who followed the Russian line of thought. Karl Marx, as he is generally referred to, could hardly have imagined such a widespread influence for his political and economic theories.

Marx was born at Trier (Trèves) in the Rhineland on May 5, 1818, the son of a Jewish lawyer. He studied history and philosophy at the universities of Bonn and Berlin, but then gave up the idea of an academic career to become the editor of a Liberal newspaper, the Rhenish Gazette (1842). For its outspoken views this journal was suppressed by the authorities a year later. Marx went to Paris and wrote for publications of advanced political views, and it was there that he began his life-long friendship with Friedrich Engels (1820–95). He associated with the French Socialists, but scorned their sentimental idealism. At the request of the Prussian government the French authorities expelled him, and he settled then at Brussels where he drew up his Communist Manifesto, which was published in 1848—known as the " year of revolutions."

In this document, which is claimed as making Marx the founder of modern Socialism, he sets out his theories briefly. In his book Das Kapital (Capital) these ideas are fully expounded. The first volume was published in 1865 ; the author died on March 14, 1883, leaving the work unfinished ; but it was completed and edited by Engels, and the other two volumes appeared in 1885 and 1895. Marx returned to Germany in 1848 to take part in revolutionary outbreaks in the Rhineland ; but he had to leave Germany and then settled in London, where he lived until his death. He was buried in Highgate Cemetery, in North London.

Marx's basic theories are somewhat difficult to explain. He took an ancient philosophic method of disputation or argument called " dialectics " (from a Greek word meaning the art of debate), in which the dispute proceeds by solving a series of contradictions. But Marx applied this to his view of historical development, called historical material-

KARL MARX
The writings of the German Socialist Karl Marx have had a profound influence on modern political thought, and the Communist creed is based on his theories. Marxism is the keynote of the system of government established in Russia by the Revolution of 1917.

ism. According to Marx, every class of society develops by this method of dialectics—or the growth of an opposing class which in the end is bound to destroy the original class.

Thus Capitalism, involving (according to Marx) the exploitation of the workers by their masters, produced that association of organized working-class people which in the end would destroy Capitalism and take over the means of production. Later, since there would be no " masters," and no differentiation of classes into an exploiting and an exploited class, a " classless society " would come about. Marx held that the organized workers would succeed because they were better fitted to utilise to the full the means of production. Instead of government of a subject class by an upper class, the resources in wealth and means of production would be administered for the general benefit of all.

Marxism is both a political and an economic system, founded on Marx's own theory of historical development. There can be no real " democracy," according to Marxists, as long as a Capitalist system of economy exists and one class is " exploited " by another. But this interpretation of democracy is very different from that cherished by such countries as Britain and the United States, or by Switzerland. (See Democracy; Government).

In the U.S.S.R. the Russian interpretation of Marxism has led to a form of government in which every important activity of the workers is controlled by the State. Private ownership of shops, farms, factories, transport, communications has been or is being abolished. Art, literature, science, the Press, the theatre—all are rigidly controlled. It is by no means a classless society, for there are wide variations of income, privilege and opportunity between the mass of the workers and the myriad officials, great and small, necessary to exercise this iron control of the rest of the people. (See Russia).

**Mary,** Queens of England. In the long list of rulers of England and Britain there are only five women, and two of these bear the name Mary.

Mary I, called Mary the Catholic or Mary Tudor, reigned from 1553 to 1558. She was the daughter of Catherine of Aragon and Henry VIII, and was born at Greenwich, London, on February 18, 1516. At first she was a favourite with her father, but when none of Catherine's other children lived, and this retiring, sickly daughter was left as his sole heir, he grew to dislike her. After his divorce from Catherine she was forced to sign a declaration acknowledging the union of her parents to have been illegal. During the rest of Henry's life, and the reign of Edward VI, Mary was harshly treated, for she was a staunch supporter of the Roman Catholic Church.

When her young half-brother Edward VI died in 1553, almost all England rejoiced that the attempt to put Lady Jane Grey in Mary's place as the heir to the throne was defeated. Indeed, at her accession Mary was one of the most popular rulers that England ever had, though before the end of her reign she had come to be one of the most hated.

In part, her loss of popularity was due to her marriage in 1554 with Philip II of Spain, the champion of the Catholic party in Europe. Englishmen disliked this marriage, partly because they did not like foreigners, but still more because they feared that it would force England to take an active part in the wars between

*National Portrait Gallery, London*

**CATHOLIC AND PROTESTANT MARYS OF ENGLAND**

Known for her persecution of Protestants as Bloody Mary, Queen Mary I (left) was a much misunderstood character ; for, though a devout Roman Catholic, she had the welfare of England at heart. Mary II (right), the daughter of James II and wife of William of Orange, was an ardent Protestant, to which fact, indeed, she owed her throne.

France and Spain. These fears were justified, and in the struggle England lost Calais, which had been an English possession since the days of Edward III (1312–77). This was a great grief to Mary, who declared that when she was dead the word " Calais " would be found graven on her heart.

Much of her unpopularity came from her persecution of the Protestants and her attempts to restore the authority of the Pope in England. Because of the many Protestants who were burned at the stake or otherwise executed during her reign, she is sometimes styled Bloody Mary. In the midst of the struggle between the Roman Catholic and Protestant Churches, Mary herself—childless, sick, neglected by her husband, and one of the saddest figures of that age—died on November 17, 1558.

MARY II (1662–94), the elder daughter of James II by his first wife, Anne Hyde, was born in London on April 30, 1662. She married William, Prince of Orange, on November 4, 1677, and when the revolution of 1688 drove her father from the throne she and her husband were proclaimed joint sovereigns of England (*see* illustration in page 1208), the coronation taking place on April 11, 1689. The management of affairs of State was left in the hands of William, but it was Mary who made the reign popular by her good heart, pleasing manners and staunch adherence to the Protestant faith. She died from smallpox on December 28, 1694, leaving no children. William reigned alone until his death in 1702.

**Mary,** QUEEN (born 1867). No Queen Consort in English history has been better beloved by the people than Queen Mary, wife of King George V, and none has had greater influence for good on the social conditions of her time.

Queen Mary was born at Kensington Palace, London, on May 26, 1867. She was the eldest

*Hay Wrightson*

**MARY, CONSORT OF GEORGE V**

Equally with King George V, Queen Mary shared in the love and loyalty of the whole Empire—especially, perhaps, at their Silver Jubilee celebrations in 1935. Her dignity and true queenliness set a high standard and example for her successors and her subjects

child and only daughter of the Duke of Teck and his wife, Mary, a daughter of the first Duke of Cambridge and a granddaughter of George III. The Princess was baptized Victoria Mary Augusta Louise Olga Pauline Claudine Agnes, and was known in the family circle as May.

In 1891 the Princess Mary was betrothed to the Duke of Clarence, the heir, after his father, the Prince of Wales, to the throne. He died, however, on January 14, 1892. On May 3, 1893, the engagement of the Princess and the Duke of Clarence's brother, the Duke of York, was announced, the marriage being celebrated on July 6, 1893, in the chapel of St. James's Palace, London. The Duke and Duchess lived at York House, London, and York Cottage, Sandringham, Norfolk. Her husband was made Duke of Cornwall on his father's accession as Edward VII in 1901, becoming Prince of Wales in November of the same year.

As Princess of Wales, Queen Mary became widely known to the country by her performance of many public duties. She accompanied her husband on his tours in the Dominions and India. She became Queen Consort on the accession of her husband to the throne in 1910, and was crowned in Westminster Abbey, London, on June 22, 1911, her

coronation as Empress of India taking place at Delhi in December of the same year.

During the First World War (1914–18) Queen Mary did invaluable work for the women's organizations. She started in August 1914 the Queen's Work for Women Fund, to provide employment for women made workless by the war ; and in the same month inaugurated Queen Mary's Needlework Guild, to provide clothes for those made destitute by the war. She was a constant visitor to hospitals, and accompanied King George V on his visits to the wounded in France and Flanders. In 1934 she named and launched the liner that bears her name. After the death of King George V in 1936 she continued to appear at public ceremonies, but was able to devote more of her time to her hobby—the collecting of old furniture and china. During the Second World War (1939–45) she lived at Badminton, Wiltshire, the home of the Duke and Duchess of Beaufort, returning to London in 1945.

**Mary Stuart,** QUEEN OF SCOTS (1542–87). It was with tears and heart-broken cries of farewell that Mary Stuart set sail from France for Scotland in 1561. A girl of 19, returning like an exile from the French Court, where she had been brought up and where she had met her late hus-

*From a painting by Eugene Siberdt*

### MARY STUART FACES HER FAVOURITE'S MURDERERS

Although Mary's Italian secretary, David Rizzio, had always been his devoted supporter, Lord Darnley (Mary's second husband) was persuaded that the Italian was stealing the Queen's heart, and helped to plan his murder. On March 9, 1566, a party of Darnley's friends burst into the Queen's room at Holyrood, Edinburgh, seized the terrified secretary, and dragged him outside to his death. The murderers were outlawed, and Darnley, a year later, was himself murdered.

band, to her homeland for which she had not a single affectionate thought—a queen approaching her throne as Cinderella might have crept back to her ashes!

Mary, the daughter of James V of Scotland and the French princess Mary of Guise, was born on December 8, 1542. Seven days later the king died, leaving Scotland and its infant queen as prizes to be fought over, not only by England and France but also by Scots lords and clerics. In 1547 the English demanded that the infant queen should be pledged to marry Edward VI of England, and to avoid this Mary was sent to France to live with her mother's kinsfolk the Guises.

Married to the Dauphin, the heir to the French throne, in 1558, at the age of 15, Mary became queen of France, as well as of Scotland, when her husband ascended the throne as Francis II in 1559. A year and a half later she was left a childless widow, and journeyed back to Scotland

But the Scotland to which she returned was very different from the one she had left. Her mother, who had acted as regent in her absence, had just died; French influence had waned as English power under Elizabeth had grown, and the Protestant Reformation, for which John Knox (q.v.) and others had long laboured, was now established.

*Painting at Hardwick Hall; photo, Annan*

**MARY, QUEEN OF SCOTS**

**Held a prisoner by Queen Elizabeth for 18 years, Mary Stuart is one of the most tragic figures in history. This painting shows her in 1578 when she was detained in Sheffield Castle.**

As granddaughter of Henry VIII's elder sister, Mary was heiress to the crown of England if, as might be expected, Queen Elizabeth should die without issue. Mary's second marriage, in 1565, to her cousin Lord Darnley, who also had pretension to the English crown, was meant to strengthen this claim.

But Darnley's insolence and Mary's attachment to Catholicism produced discord between her and her Protestant subjects. Darnley's natural jealousy was fostered by many Scots lords, Mary's enemies, who pointed to the rapid advancement with which the queen favoured her Italian secretary, David Rizzio. Darnley became a party to a conspiracy of nobles, which resulted in Rizzio's murder in Mary's presence on March 9, 1566. The queen pretended to pardon Rizzio's murderers, and there was even a formal reconciliation with Darnley. On June 19, 1566, Mary's son—afterwards James VI of Scotland and James I of England—was born. Then in February 1567 she induced her husband, who was ill with smallpox, to take up his residence in a house called Kirk o' Field, near Edinburgh. One night the house was blown up, and Darnley's murdered body was found near by the next morning.

Suspicion against the queen flared into open denunciation when, three months and six days afterwards, Mary was married to the Earl of Bothwell, who had been exposed as the chief of Darnley's assassins. The nobles rose in arms and took her prisoner at Carberry Hill on June 15, 1567. While Bothwell fled to Denmark, she was forced to abdicate in favour of the boy James. Escaping from prison at Loch Leven (May 2, 1568), she hastily rallied around her a little army. When this was defeated by the regent Moray's forces at Langside, Glasgow, Mary fled across the English border and cast herself upon the mercy of her cousin, Queen Elizabeth, who promptly made her a prisoner. For the next 18 years English Catholics formed plot after plot to liberate her and place her on the throne of England. The Babington conspiracy, named after the ringleader Anthony Babington, was the last and fatal link in a series which at length induced Elizabeth to bring Mary to trial. She was convicted of complicity in the plot for Elizabeth's assassination. So long as Mary lived there could be no safety for Elizabeth, and after a delay of some months she was prevailed upon to sign the death-warrant. On February 8, 1587, Mary Stuart, arrayed in black velvet and bearing herself as befits a queen, was beheaded in Fotheringhay Castle, Northamptonshire.

**Maryland.** One of the 13 original states of the United States, Maryland has Pennsylvania on the north and Delaware on the east. The western boundary is Virginia, and on the south is the Atlantic Ocean. The state has an area of 10,577 square miles and is divided into two parts by Chesapeake Bay. In the east the surface is low and marshy, but to the west it is hilly.

Agriculture is important. The fisheries are invaluable, particularly the oyster trade. Mineral resources include iron ore, coal, clay and asbestos. Shipbuilding and the manufacture of aircraft are leading industries. Annapolis, the capital (named after Queen Anne), has a population of 13,000, and contains the United States Naval Academy. The largest city and industrial centre is Baltimore (q.v.). Within the boundaries of Maryland is the District of Columbia, with Washington, the seat of the United States Government.

The state was settled by English Roman Catholics in 1634 and named Maryland after the wife of Charles I, Henrietta Maria. It became a State in 1776. The population is 1,821,240.

**Masaryk,** JAN GARRIGUE (1886–1948). The son of Thomas Masaryk (pron. mah'-sah-rēk), the first President of the Republic of Czechoslovakia, Jan Masaryk was born in Prague, now the capital of the Republic, in 1886 and was educated there. He emigrated to the United States in 1907. When the Czechoslovakian Republic came into being in 1918 (at the end of the First World War) he entered its Ministry of Foreign Affairs, going to Britain as ambassador in 1925.

In 1939 he resigned, partly as a protest against the Munich agreement, under the terms of which Germany was granted parts of Czechoslovakia, and partly because in March 1939 the German Government annexed Moravia and Bohemia. He became Foreign Minister in the provisional Czechoslovak Government which was set up in London in 1940 during the Second World War (1939–45), and was deputy Prime Minister during 1941–45.

With the re-establishment of the Republic in 1945 he was appointed Foreign Minister and led his country's delegates at the San Francisco conference of the United Nations in the same year He retained his post after the Communists came into power in February 1948, but committed suicide in Prague on the following March 10.

**Masaryk,** THOMAS GARRIGUE (1850–1937). One of the most respected statesmen in Europe, Masaryk devoted himself ceaselessly to freeing the Czechs and Slovaks from Austrian domination and, when independence was achieved, he raised the new state of Czechoslovakia to a position of influence in the councils of Europe. His energy of mind and body was unbounded, and he was a man of deep knowledge, and an excellent linguist.

Thomas Masaryk was born on March 7, 1850, at Hodonin, in Moravia (then part of Austria), the son of a coachman. Apprenticed to a locksmith when he was 14, and later assistant to the village blacksmith, by dint of hard study he became a professor at Prague University in 1882. Elected a member of the Austrian Parliament in 1891, he resigned two years later but was re-elected in 1907.

When the First World War broke out in 1914 Thomas Masaryk saw that his opportunity had arrived, and although over 60 he set himself the task of winning independence for his country. Escaping from Austria, he travelled widely, visiting the Netherlands, Italy, France, England, Russia, and the U.S.A. in his efforts to arouse sympathy for his countrymen. In 1915 he was professor of Slavic studies at King's College, London. He then worked in Paris, and was active in gaining the support of the Allies. When in 1918 the Czechoslovak republic was formed, he was

**PRESIDENT MASARYK**
The first President of the Republic of Czechoslovakia, Thomas Masaryk was responsible for freeing the Czechs and Slovaks from Austrian domination in 1918. He is here seen with his youngest grandson. He died in 1937.

elected president, and re-elected in 1920, 1927 and 1934, failing health causing him to resign in 1935. He died on September 14, 1937.

Thomas Masaryk would have been notable for his literary career alone, for he wrote much on philosophical, sociological and political matters

**Masefield,** JOHN EDWARD (born 1875). The life of a poet is generally supposed to be if not a quiet one at least unlikely to have been spent in dangerous places, in sailing the seas, or in the slums of great cities. Yet this is how the poet laureate, John Masefield, spent his early life. Born at Ledbury in Gloucestershire on June 1, 1875, he served on the Conway, a training ship for the Mercantile Marine, and sailed round Cape Horn. He joined the White Star Line, but after several years left the sea and lived for a time in the United States, gaining the hard experience he was later to write about. All the while he had been practising writing and his Salt-water Ballads were published in 1902. A Mainsail Haul in 1905 and his edition of Dampier's

**JOHN MASEFIELD**
Poet, dramatist and novelist, John Edward Masefield was first widely acclaimed in 1911 on the appearance of his narrative poem, The Everlasting Mercy. He became poet laureate in 1930.

Voyages in 1906 enabled him thenceforward to devote himself to a literary career in England.

Many of Masefield's earlier poems, as seen in the volumes of 1902–05, and in Ballads and Poems (1910) were marked by bold rhythms resembling those of Rudyard Kipling. His reputation was consolidated upon the publication, in 1911, of the first of his long narrative poems, The Everlasting Mercy, recounting in somewhat rough-and-ready verse the story of a village drunkard's conversion. It was followed by similar works, unequal but vivid in style: The Widow in the Bye-Street (1912), remarkable for its stark realism and haunting pathos; The Daffodil Fields (1913); and Dauber (1913). In 1912 he was awarded the Edmond de Polignac prize for poetry.

Biography (1912), one of Masefield's less-known poems, shows the poet concerned with that ceaseless striving after an ideal beauty which forms the subject of the series of grave and characteristic sonnets in the volume entitled Lollingdon Downs (1917). With Reynard the Fox (1919) and Right Royal (1920), pictures of the sporting life of the English shires, Masefield resumed his narrative poems. Enslaved was published in 1920.

Versatile as he is, he also writes plays, which include The Tragedy of Nan, a finely dramatic dialect play (1909) and The Coming of Christ, which in 1928 was performed on the chancel steps of Canterbury Cathedral. His novels, mainly about the sea, include Lost Endeavour (1910); Sard Harker (1924), Odtaa (1926), The Bird of Dawning (1933); The Taking of the Gry (1934) and New Chum (1944). He also wrote a study of Shakespeare (1911), and the Old Front Line (1917). Masefield succeeded Robert Bridges as poet laureate in 1930 and was awarded the Order of Merit by King George V in 1935.

**Massachusetts.** The site of the first settlement founded by the Pilgrim Fathers, this north-eastern State of the United States is bounded on the north by New Hampshire and Vermont, on the east by the Atlantic Ocean, on the south by Rhode Island and Connecticut, on the west by New York. It has an area of 8,257 square miles. Its irregular coastline is broken by Cape Cod, Massachusetts Bay, Buzzard's Bay, and scores of lesser inlets. The highest elevations, about 3,500 feet, are in the west, in the Berkshire Hills, where the scenery is not unlike that of the English Lake district. There are many rivers, the chief being the Connecticut, Merrimac, Charles, Housatonic and Hoosac. There is a vast amount of water-power, both developed and potential.

Hay, potatoes and maize are the chief crops. Tobacco is grown, and much land is under fruit. Fishing is an important industry, Boston being the leading fishing port in the United States. In the second half of the 19th century Massachusetts was transformed from an agricultural to a manufacturing State, the industries including the making of boots and shoes, textiles, paper, watches, machinery and leather. Boston, the capital, with a population of 771,000, is the largest city; other towns of importance are Worcester, Springfield, New Bedford, Somerville, Lowell, Lynn and Lawrence. At Cambridge, near Boston, is Harvard University, founded in 1636 and generally regarded as the oldest college in the United States.

The landing of the Pilgrim Fathers near Cape Cod in 1620 marked the beginning of the history of Massachusetts. In 1629 they secured possession of the land around their first home from the king of England and, known as Plymouth colony, other settlements were made in it. Thus was established the first self-governing community of white people in

*W. Fiske-Moore*

**A SCENE FROM JOHN MASEFIELD'S MIRACLE PLAY**

One of the most memorable works of John Masefield is the miracle play, The Coming of Christ. It is in the style of the old miracle plays which were acted in the Middle Ages and were the earliest form of dramatic representation in England.

The Coming of Christ was performed in 1928 on the chancel steps of Canterbury Cathedral, in a beautiful setting in keeping with the simplicity of the play. This photograph shows one of the scenes, with angels adoring the infant Jesus.

*Harvard University*

**HARVARD UNIVERSITY IN MASSACHUSETTS**
**Senior university in the United States, Harvard was opened at Cambridge, near Boston, Massachusetts, in 1637. It is named after one of the founders, John Harvard, an Englishman. Despite its age many of the buildings are comparatively modern, both Sever Hall (right) and the Memorial Hall, with its clock-tower, dating from the latter half of the 19th century.**

acid act on the chemicals in the head; or the match-head was crushed by a pair of pliers.

About 1836, white phosphorus began to be used for match composition, along with potassium chlorate; such matches ignited when rubbed on a hard substance. The action was rather explosive, owing to the " fierceness " of the potassium chlorate, so this chemical was replaced later on by another such as red oxide of lead or manganese dioxide—both of which yielded up oxygen freely. White phosphorus is sometimes called yellow phosphorus; it is white when first prepared, but turns yellow later. It is exceedingly poisonous, and its fumes caused an ailment, known as "phossy jaw," among workers in match factories. Another drawback was that matches tipped with a composition containing white phosphorus took fire too easily, and were dangerous because they were apt to ignite accidentally.

America. Many Puritans emigrated there during the reign of Charles I (1625–49). One of the 13 original States of the American Union, Massachusetts joined the Federation of United States in 1776. The population is 4,316,720.

**Matches.** The indispensable little light-giving sticks we use today usually without a thought of their origin are " friction matches," and the first of this type were not invented until 1827. Even then they were very different from our familiar matches, as you can see from the picture in page 1279 ; the match-head had to be drawn through a folded piece of sandpaper to ignite it. The head was tipped with a composition made of (1) potassium chlorate, a substance rich in oxygen; and (2) antimony sulphide, a substance which easily combines with oxygen; gum was added to bind the composition. When gentle heat was generated by the friction against the sandpaper, the composition was raised to the ignition point (*see* Heat) and burst into flame.

In page 1279 are pictures of two other early kinds of match: one was tipped with potassium chlorate and sugar, held together by gum; it was ignited by touching the head with a drop of concentrated sulphuric acid from a bottle in the little " Instantaneous Light Box " which contained also the matches. The other kind of match, called a " promethean," after Prometheus, the Greek god of fire, had on the end of its wooden splint a tiny vesicle of glass containing the acid; around this was the composition, similar to that of the match just described. One lighted the promethean by a light blow which crushed the glass and let the

Instead of white phosphorus, the red form of this chemical then came to be used, prepared by heating the white form in an atmosphere of some inert gas such as nitrogen. In Britain the manufacture, importation and sale of matches containing white phosphorus was forbidden after 1908–9 ; similar laws were passed in most other enlightened countries. Red phosphorus is much less poisonous, and takes fire less readily.

" Safety " matches were introduced about 1853; no phosphorus was put on to the match-head, for which the composition consisted of antimony sulphide and red lead or potassium chlorate. Red phosphorus formed part of the composition with which the side of the matchbox was coated, which also contained antimony sulphide and gum, along with some abrasive such as powdered glass. This match was " safe " because it would not light by friction alone; it had to be struck on the prepared surface, from which it picked up a trace of phosphorus, and then the heat caused by friction was enough to ignite it. You may have found out that even a safety match can sometimes be struck by drawing it quickly over a sheet of glass. This is because glass is such a bad conductor of heat that the match-head can absorb sufficient heat from the friction to start the oxidation reaction, and ignite the composition.

The kind of match which " strikes anywhere "— but strikes better on the sandpaper-covered side of the matchbox—is now tipped with a composition containing phosphorus sulphide (non-poisonous) with lead oxide or some other such substance rich in oxygen. It will ignite by friction alone. Originally white phosphorus was used instead of the sulphide, but was abandoned for the reasons which have been given earlier.

Some matches have circular sticks, while most of them have square-section splints. They are made from seasoned blocks of white pine, aspen, or similar woods. The blocks are first soaked in a chemical solution to hinder smouldering and the falling away of the head and tip of the match after striking. The cylindrical sticks are formed by hollow dies; the square ones are cut by special machines which turn out about a million in an

hour. The next step in match-making is to feed the loose splints to a machine which inserts them in the myriad holes of a travelling band composed of pierced metal plates linked together. (This is why the untipped end of a square match stick is rounded.) On the travelling band the splints go first to a bath of melted paraffin, into which they are dipped to make them take fire more readily.

On goes the band then to the place where the splints are given the coating of composition. After this they pass in a lengthy travel over drying drums, continuing until, dry and ready for boxing, they

arrive at the stage where they are stripped automatically from the metal plates and pass on to the box-filling appliances. Meanwhile, boxes by the hundred thousand are being made by automatic machinery from chip or paper-board, and the paper labels affixed. Now the boxes are filled, and go to a packaging machine where they are made into parcels of a dozen.

**Mathematics.** Far back in the dim ages when men first started to count, even on their fingers, the first of the sciences, mathematics, began to develop.

Mathematics may be defined as the science of number and quantity. Elementary mathematics includes arithmetic, algebra, geometry and trigonometry—all of which are described in three volumes under their own headings. Analytic and differential geometry, the theory of probabilities, differential and integral calculus, and the analysis of complex quantities constitute higher mathematics. Then we have what is called applied mathe-

### THREE OPERATIONS IN THE MANUFACTURE OF MATCHES

This method of making square-section match sticks consists in slicing off from a block of wood a veneer of match thickness (upper), which is afterwards cut into strips and then into sticks. After being dipped into the composition which enables the match to be ignited, the sticks are carried around revolving drums to dry (lower left). Box-filling machines pack the matches into containers (lower right), which go to another appliance to be made up into packages of a dozen.

matics, *i.e.*, mathematics used in such sciences as mechanics, electricity, optics and astronomy.

It was the Greeks who developed geometry, principally as an intellectual exercise. Because number and quantity seemed so tremendously significant, many of the ancients believed that number was the stuff from which the world was made, or at least a key to its meaning. This seems almost a foreshadowing of what modern physical science has discovered—that every invariable numerical relation between physical substances is a clue to facts of the greatest importance.

Thus when Galileo (1564–1642) discovered that the velocity of falling bodies increases in a definite ratio with every stage of their fall, he had made an important step in the discovery of the law of gravitation. Then, too, when Dalton (1766–1844) found that chemical combinations only took place in definite ratios, there was born the atomic theory of matter, and with it the wonders of modern chemistry.

Mathematics has an over-riding importance in life. It is the one exact science from which spring all other mechanical and physical sciences. Without it such callings as engineering could not exist, and a mathematical training is essential for all those who would adopt such professions.

## Mauretania.

Two famous British liners have borne this name, the earlier being launched in September 1906 and owned by the Cunard Line. With a displacement of 31,938 tons and a designed speed of 25 knots, she won the " blue riband " of the Atlantic (fastest crossing by a passenger vessel) in 1907, with an average speed of 23·69 knots, a record that stood until broken by the German liner Bremen in 1929. Used as a transport in the First World War (1914–18), she was broken up in 1935.

The second Mauretania, of 35,677 tons, was launched in 1938 for the Cunard-White Star Line and had a designed speed of 23 knots. Used as a troopship during the Second World War (1939–45), she was completely refitted and returned to the Atlantic passenger service in 1947.

## Mauritius.

Known also as Île de France, the British island-colony of Mauritius is in the Indian Ocean about 530 miles east of the island of Madagascar. It is 39 miles long and 29 miles wide, with an area of 720 square miles. Surrounded by coral reefs, it is a rugged, hilly mass of volcanic origin, the chief heights being Black River Peak (2,711 feet) and Pieter Both (2,676 feet), with valleys of great fertility. Sugar is the chief export and to it the island owes its prosperity. Tropical fruits, vanilla plants, and hemp are grown, most of the inhabitants being engaged in agriculture. There are about 120 miles of railways. Port Louis, the capital, with a population of 66,460, has the only good harbour ; it is an important link on the sea route to India.

*Courtesy of F. H. Vallancey*

**' POST OFFICE '**
Here is the ' Post Office ' Mauritius stamp, one of the greatest prizes of the collector and worth thousands of pounds.

Mauritius was discovered by the Portuguese in 1505, but they soon abandoned it, the Dutch occupying the island in 1598 and giving it its present name in honour of Prince Maurice of Orange-Nassau. The Dutch left in 1710, and five years later the French established a settlement there, renaming the island Île de France (Isle of France). The British conquered Mauritius in 1810. In literature it is famous as the scene of the French novelist Bernardin de Saint Pierre's story entitled Paul and Virginia. The island was once the home of the dodo, a bird which became extinct in about the year 1700. The population of Mauritius is 424,450.

## Mayflower.

In the last three centuries thousands of ships have made their way to North America, bearing from the Old World many of the men and women who have populated the United States and whose genius and industry have developed her enormous natural resources and welded her into a great nation. Compared to most of these vessels, the Mayflower,

*Roger Halbwachs; courtesy of The Crown Colonist*
**PORT LOUIS, CAPITAL OF MAURITIUS**
All the sea-borne trade of the British island-colony of Mauritius in the Indian Ocean passes through Port Louis, whose harbour (above) is one of the finest in the East. The exports include sugar, copra (dried coconut) and raw hides.

of 180 tons, was but a cockle-shell. Yet no other ship's arrival was fraught with such significance as that of this little sailing vessel, which carried the Pilgrim Fathers North to America in the year 1620.

To understand who these Pilgrims were and why they went to America, we must go back to Elizabethan England round about the year 1600. Then it was that a group of men and women began to gather together in secret for religious devotion at the home of William Brewster, which was the old manor-house of the little village of Scrooby in Nottinghamshire. They were called Separatists, because they wished to have a separate Church instead of conforming to the Church of England favoured by Elizabeth (see Puritans). In thus following the dictates of their conscience, they defied the laws of the realm, and for this they suffered heavy penalties.

Because of these persecutions they were driven at last to leave England. There was one country where they knew they would be allowed to practise their own form of worship—that was Holland; and to Holland they went in 1608. From Amsterdam, where they landed, they went to Leiden (Leyden), and there established a church under the leadership of their minister, John Robinson.

But though they found freedom in Holland, it was not really home to them. Life there was very hard. Most of them had been farmers, and they were now forced, in this industrial and commercial community, to follow occupations to which they were unaccustomed, and by which they could earn only a bare subsistence. Worse still, their children were in danger of falling away from their faith, and were growing up partly Dutch instead of wholly English, a natural result of environment which they might have foreseen. So, after long discussions, it was decided to make the long voyage to the New World, where they might preserve their native language and customs and have complete freedom to worship as seemed right to them.

In 1620 they set sail in a little ship called the Speedwell. At Southampton, Hampshire, they found another ship awaiting them, the Mayflower, having on board a number of Separatists from London, who wished to join the expedition. The vessels had proceeded only a short distance when the Speedwell began to leak. Twice they were forced to turn back, and finally, abandoning the ill-fated Speedwell, they sailed from Plymouth harbour, Devonshire, on September 6, 1620, on the Mayflower.

For two months and five days the weary voyage continued. At last they reached the bleak and desolate shores of Cape Cod, in what is now the State of Massachusetts, and the evening of November 19 found them anchored in the sheltered harbour just within the tip of the cape. But their troubles were far from over.

" Being thus passed the vast ocean, and a sea of troubles," writes William Bradford, one of the leaders of the Pilgrims, in the quaint language of that time, " they had now no friends to wellcome them, nor inns to entertaine or refresh their weather-beaten bodys, no houses or much less townes to repaire too, to seeke for succoure. And for the season it was winter, and they that know the winters of that countrie know them to be sharp & violent, & subjecte to cruell & fierce stormes, deangerous to travill to known places, much more to serch an unknown coast. Beside, what could they see but a hidious and desolate wilderness, full of wild beasts and wild men? and what multitudes there might be of them they know not "

According to their agreement with the Virginia Company of London, they were to settle on land that is now part of New Jersey, but they had disembarked north of that region. They wished to sail south to the River Hudson, but the master of the ship refused and declared they must remain where they were. Such a site as they sought for their settlement was found at Plymouth, on Cape Cod Bay, and to that harbour the Mayflower was then moved.

Before leaving the ship as "loyall subjects of our dread soveraigne Lord, King James," the heads of the Pilgrim band set their hands to the famous Mayflower agreement. In this they promised to "combine ourselves togeather into a civill body politick, for our better ordering and preservation and furtherance of the ends aforesaid; and by vertue hereof to enacte, constitute, and frame such just and equall lawes, ordinance, acts, constitutions, and offices, from time to time, as shall be thought most meete and convenient for the generall good of the Colonie, unto which we promise all due submission and obedience."

**Mayfly.** Those delicate-winged insects, with long threadlike tails, which appear suddenly in great swarms in the late spring or early summer and then perish, are also known as shad flies or day flies. The adult Mayfly is incapable of taking any food, either liquid or solid; hence its life is brief. They were once believed to live only a single day, but

J. J. Ward

**THE ADULT MAYFLY**
Both approximately natural size, these two photographs show what an adult mayfly looks like. When full grown the insect leaves the water, bursts out of the sub-imago skin (left) and flies away. The right-hand specimen is set out to display the wings, antennae and ' tails.'

# WITH THE PILGRIM FATHERS IN THE MAYFLOWER

Reproduced from a painting by W. F. Halsall, this picture shows the Mayflower lying at anchor in the harbour at Plymouth, Massachusetts, while a party of the Pilgrim Fathers is rowing ashore to explore the land and prepare shelters for the settlement. In the winter the colonists lived on shipboard, until they had built log cabins for all the company.

The signing of the famous Mayflower Compact, one of the most memorable events in the history of America, took place in the tiny cabin of the Mayflower, the day before the ship came into a harbour where Provincetown now stands. Here one of the Pilgrim Fathers is putting his name to the historic document by which the colonists bound themselves to obey such laws as they might make for their general welfare as a self-governing community.

more careful study showed they might remain alive for periods varying from a few hours to a few days. But if the final stage of their life is short the early stages are long. The nymphs of the 300 or more species of Mayflies may spend from one to three years actively swimming in lakes and streams after hatching from the eggs.

The eggs are laid in large numbers in the water and sink to the bottom. The larvae are strong and active creatures which spend their time swimming about, crawling on the bottom, or burrowing in the mud in search of the smaller forms of animal and vegetable life on which they feed. When full grown they rise to the surface, burst their skins, and fly away in huge swarms. Fish devour Mayflies greedily, and many of the artificial flies used by anglers are imitations of these insects.

Mayflies belong to a very ancient and primitive type, fossils of their ancestors having been found in the deposits of the Coal Age. They are interesting to scientists chiefly because they pass through what is called a *sub-imago* stage —that is, after the winged adults emerge from the water they shed their skin again, the full imago often coming forth in colours very different from those of the sub-imago. This is a habit found in no other insects.

**Mayo.** In the extreme west of the province of Connaught in Eire, its long seaboard washed by the Atlantic Ocean, is Mayo. It is the third largest Irish county, covering 2,084 square miles. Achill, Clare, Inishturk and other islands belong to Mayo, and in parts the cliff scenery is wild and magnificent. It is drained by the Moy, Owenmore and several smaller rivers, and contains loughs Mask, Conn, Carra, and Beltra. The surface is fairly level in the east, but mountainous in the west, with Muilrea, Nephin, and other heights over 2,500 feet.

The soil is poor, but cattle, sheep and pigs are raised, and oats and potatoes grown. Trout and salmon are caught in the rivers and loughs; the coastal fisheries are also important. Castlebar is the county town. The population of Mayo is 148,200.

**Mazarin,** JULES (1602–61). The most famous European diplomat of the early part of the 17th century, this Italian was the virtual ruler of France during the infancy of Louis XIV (1638–1715). Born at Piscina, Italy, on July 14, 1602, Mazarin (pron. ma-zah-ran′) was educated by the Jesuits, entered the service of the Pope, and was sent on a diplomatic mission to France in 1634. There he attracted the attention of Cardinal

**GIUSEPPE MAZZINI**
An Italian revolutionary, Mazzini was one of the three rulers appointed under the Republic of 1848. When united Italy became a monarchy in 1861 he refused to accept the new form of government, and plotted for its overthrow until his death in 1872.

Richelieu, the French First Minister of State (Prime Minister), and in 1639 he took service with Louis XIII, and became a naturalized Frenchman.

Mazarin was made a Cardinal in 1641, and on Richelieu's death in 1642 was appointed First Minister. After the death of Louis XIII in 1643, though Louis XIV's mother, Anne of Austria, acted as Regent, Mazarin was the real ruler of the kingdom, bringing the Thirty Years' War (1618–48) to an end and concluding a series of treaties all of which greatly enhanced the prestige of France. He suppressed a rebellion of nobles in 1653, and set about the creation of that strong royalist party which was to prove the main source of power of Louis XIV.

Mazarin's greatest failing was his love of money. Though he died a millionaire (at Vincennes, France, on March 9, 1661), he left the finances of France in a state of chaos.

**Mazzini,** GIUSEPPE (1805–72). Italy was divided into a number of small States when Mazzini (pron. mat-sē′-nē), Italian patriot and author, founded a movement with the object of making it a united nation. He was born at Genoa on June 22, 1805. Educated for the law, he became interested in politics and, abandoning a promising career as a lawyer, joined a revolutionary group that was working for the deliverance of Italy from Austrian domination.

He founded a society called Young Italy, whose aim was to unite Italy into one country with a central Government. Sentenced to exile in 1830 for his revolutionary activities, he went to Marseilles, France, where he organized a small band of conspirators to spread the doctrines of Young Italy. In 1832 he moved to Geneva, Switzerland, and to England in 1837. He did not cease working for Italian unification, and in April 1849 he established a republic in Rome; but this was crushed by French troops in the following June and Mazzini returned to England.

Ardent patriotism, heroic self-sacrifice and unconquerable faith in the final triumph of his ideas made Mazzini a notable leader of men. In 1861 Victor Emmanuel was declared King of Italy; and though Mazzini despaired of unifying Italy under a Republican Government, he continued to plot against the monarchy until his death at Pisa on March 10, 1872.

**Meat.** The word meat is generally used to describe the flesh of cattle, sheep, pigs and deer used for human food. To the meat derived from each of these sources distinctive names are given, e.g. veal

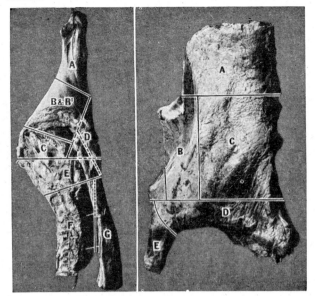

**HOW A SIDE OF BEEF IS CUT**

Two quarters marked to show the cuts for market. Left, hind-quarter : A. Leg ; B. Topside ; B.1. Underside ; C. Aitchbone ; D. Thick flank ; E. Rump ; F. Loin ; G. Flank. Dotted lines show direction of cut on the other side. Right, fore-quarter : A. Fore-rib ; B. Brisket ; C. Middle piece ; D. Clod and sticking ; E. Shin.

from the calf, beef from the bullock or cow, mutton from sheep, pork and bacon from pigs, and venison from deer. These again are subdivided into other categories, according to the particular part of the carcass from which the meat is cut, or the different processes it undergoes before being offered for sale in the shops.

For example, the carcass of the bullock is first cut by the butcher into fore and hind-quarters, after which each quarter is cut into a certain number of joints, each having a specific name. Thus, the two fore-quarters are divided into " cuts " or joints called the fore-rib, middle-piece, brisket, clod and sticking, and the shin, while the two hind-quarters are cut into the flank, rump, loin, aitchbone, underside, topside, thick flank, and leg.

The carcass of the pig is split lengthwise, and, when used for bacon, the several cuts, beginning from the fore end, are named the fore-hock, collar, thick streaky, back and ribs, thin streaky, long loin, flank, gammon hock, and corner hock. When used for pork, the joints, in the same order, are named the hand, belly, loin, and leg.

The butcher cuts the sheep's carcass quite differently, the various cuts being known as the leg, loin, breast, neck, and shoulder.

For veal, the calf's carcass is divided into the leg, loin, breast, and shoulder. For venison the only cuts used are the haunch, which includes the loin and the leg, the shoulder, breast, and neck.

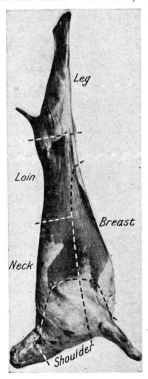

**MUTTON**

Carcass of a sheep, showing the several joints into which it is cut by the butcher.

**Meath.** In the province of Leinster, Eire, between county Dublin and Louth, the county of Meath contains some of the most fertile land in the whole of Ireland. It is largely a level area, though there are hills in the west. Chief rivers are the Boyne and its tributary the Blackwater. The county has an area of 903 square miles, and a coastline of about 10 miles on the Irish Sea.

Agriculture is the sole industry, oats and potatoes being grown. Cattle, sheep and pigs are raised. Trim is the county town; at Kells monks wrote the famous Book of Kells, the most beautifully illuminated volume in the world (*see* illustration in page 510).

Meath was the name of one of the ancient kingdoms of Ireland, and in the valley of the Boyne on the hill of Tara are the ruins of the royal palace celebrated in the lines of the poet Thomas Moore (1779–1852) beginning "The harp that once through Tara's halls." There, too, was fought, on July 11, 1690, the battle of the Boyne, in which James II was defeated by William III of England. The population of Meath is 65,300.

**Mecca.** Capital of the Kingdom of the Hejaz, part of Saudi Arabia, and a holy city of the Mahomedans, Mecca lies in a narrow valley surrounded by hills about 45 miles east of Jidda, which is its port on the Red Sea. Although non-Mahomedans are strictly forbidden to enter the city, it has been visited by several Christians, who went there either in disguise or protected by a temporary profession of Mahomedanism. The city presents one of the most remarkable sights when, in the 12th month of the Mahomedan year, some 100,000 pilgrims from all over the world converge on it, making the journey that every believer is supposed to undertake at least once in his lifetime.

By way of the Suez Canal come Egyptians, bearing their gift of costly black brocade for covering the sacred Kaaba, the cube-shaped stone sanctuary in the court of the great mosque. From Jidda, camel caravans or motor transport carry the pilgrims across the desert to Mecca. Long before the city appears in view, the pilgrim shaves his head and puts on two white seamless garments in place of his travelling clothes. He wears these until after he has kissed the sacred black stone that is built into the south-eastern corner of the Kaaba, and performed the other intricate ceremonies which occupy the next few days and reach their climax in a pilgrimage to Mount Arafat, a half-day's journey away.

There the pilgrim takes his stand at noon on the ninth day of the pilgrimage month and recites prayers and texts till sunset. This is the most important ceremony of the whole pilgrimage, and the one which alone entitles him to the coveted title of

# WHEN MAHOMEDAN PILGRIMS REACH MECCA

In this view of Mecca during the pilgrim season notice the hundred of tents set up to shelter the many thousands of people from all over the world, who have come to pay homage at the shrine of the Prophet. The first ceremony consists in kissing the Black Stone set in the wall of the Kaaba shrine, shown in the lower picture. Then they circle the shrine seven times, three times running and four times walking. Next they run up and down some of the sacred hills you see here, visit Mount Arafat, and throw stones at the devil in the village of Mina. Once the ceremonies are complete the pilgrims acquire the honourable title of Hajji, with the right to wear a special green turban.

Dense crowds of pilgrims gather about the Kaaba shrine (above) in the courtyard of the Great Mosque at Mecca, the vast enclosure being said to be capable of holding 30,000 worshippers. According to legend, the Black Stone set in one corner of the Kaaba is a relic of the original shrine built by Abraham and is supposed to have been given him by the angel Gabriel. The Kaaba is covered with a carpet of black brocade brought from Cairo as a gift from Mahomet's Egyptian followers. It is toward the Kaaba that all Mahomedans are supposed to turn when they pray.

*Hajji* (pilgrim) for the rest of his life. At Mina, on the journey from Arafat back to Mecca, the pilgrims sacrifice an animal, throw stones at three pillars which are believed to represent Satan, then shave their heads again and put on ordinary clothing.

Mecca was a place of pilgrimage long before the rise of Mahomedanism. When Mahomet was born, in A.D. 570, it was a commerical town of some importance, lying on the ancient incense trade route from southern Arabia. It was also the centre of a religion then widespread in Arabia; the Kaaba was surrounded by 360 idols, one for each day of the ancient Arabian year. Mahomet retained some of the ancient rites but did away with the idols. Old Mahomedan legend attributes to Abraham the building of the first Kaaba, and affirms that the Black Stone (probably of meteoric origin) came from the Garden of Eden with Adam and Eve.

Mecca, as part of the province of Hejaz, was under nominal Turkish rule until the successful revolt of the Arabs during the First World War (1914–18). In 1924 Ibn Saud, sultan of Nejd, took Mecca, and two years later he was declared king. The population of Mecca is about 130,000.

# *The* SCIENCE *of* BODIES *in* MOVEMENT

*Mechanics is a branch of science which has great interest, for our own movements and those of all the machines which we use, or which transport us from place to place, are governed by its laws. Here is an outline of the subject.*

**Mechanics.** From its name one might think that mechanics is the study of machines and the way that they work. This, however, is only partly true, since it is the branch of science most closely related to our every-day experiences—that in which forces take a part. Riding a bicycle, throwing a cricket ball, or merely sitting in a chair, all involve the interplay of forces which are governed by the laws of mechanics. Sir Isaac Newton, the great 17th century scientist, was the first man to state those laws clearly, and they have proved to be of such wide application that, on the one hand, they guide the designers of our steam engines and jet aeroplanes, and on the other, astronomers with their aid can calculate the orbital paths of the planets.

There are many different types of force. When we sit on a chair our weight exerts a force on it, and, since the chair does not move, it must also be pushing us upwards with an equal force. If we try to push a heavy crate sideways on the ground and it does not move, there must be a force of friction acting in the opposite direction. Again, on a roundabout we experience an outward centrifugal force due to the rotation. Mechanics can be roughly divided into two parts : that dealing with forces which are balanced and produce no motion is known as statics, while cases in which the forces do produce motion come under the heading dynamics.

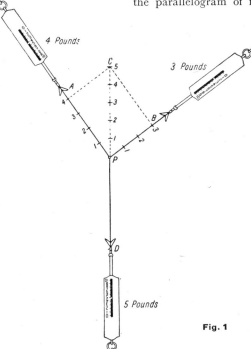

4 Pounds

3 Pounds

5 Pounds

**Fig. 1**

**PARALLELOGRAM OF FORCES IN MECHANICS**
Three forces (represented by spring balances) are acting in different directions upon a point P. If we know the amount of two of the forces and the angle between their directions, we can compute the amount of the third force by drawing a parallelogram like that here shown. A 3-pound force is acting along string PB ; so we mark three graduations of one inch along that string. Similarly we mark off four inch-graduations along string PA to represent the 4-pound force acting there. Next we draw line AC, parallel to PB ; and line BC, parallel to PA, thus completing the parallelogram. The length of the diagonal PC will represent the 'resultant' force (5 pounds) acting downwards.

We have seen that if a body acted on by forces remains stationary, the forces must be equal and opposite. This was expressed by Newton in his statement : " Action and reaction are equal and opposite." If the forces do not all lie in the same direction they can be added together by means of the parallelogram of forces, explained in Fig. 1.

The "resultant" of forces pulling in different directions at an angle can be found by adding lines to complete a parallelogram as shown : the diagonal represents the resultant. The engineer who builds a large bridge has to calculate the forces in each strut of the bridge so that he knows how strong to make it ; and he does this by applying the force parallelogram at each joint of the bridge. For instance, the suspension bridge in Fig. 2 is really a roadway slung from two large chains supported by stone towers. The engineer must arrange that there is no sideways force on the towers tending to pull them over, and he designs the chains so that they hang at equal angles on both sides of the tower. The diagram (Fig. 3) shows that the resultant force is vertically downwards.

Another example of the balancing of forces according to the parallelogram law explains how an aeroplane is able to fly. In Fig. 4 the weight of the aeroplane and the forward force pulling it along are balanced against the suction force caused by air flowing past the wing. The force due to

The lever finds countless applications in everyday life. When we use a bicycle tyre lever to prise off the outer cover of the tyre, we are exerting a much greater force on it than could be done with the unaided muscles. The brake levers on the bicycle enable us to apply, in a convenient manner, a large force to the brake

the weight of a body acts downwards at its centre of gravity. This centre of gravity must lie above the base of the body, or else the body will topple over. In riding a bicycle we are continually adjusting our centre of gravity so that it will be above the wheel-base. Again, the centre of gravity of a motor-car or other vehicle is arranged to be low down so that it can be tilted through a large angle before falling over sideways (see illustration under heading Gravitation, page 1514).

Before the working of a complicated piece of machinery can be properly understood, we must first study the working of its components. The lever, the inclined plane, the wheel-and-axle, the pulley and the screw are all simple machines whose purpose is to convert small forces into larger ones. These machines have been used for thousands of years, to supplement Man's own weak muscles, but it is only with the invention of artificial power that they have been developed and combined to a high degree.

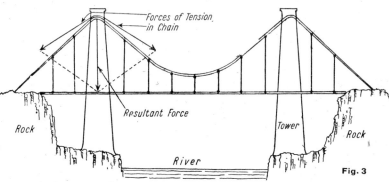

ILLUSTRATING THE MECHANICS OF A SUSPENSION BRIDGE

The photograph shows the Menai suspension bridge, built by Thomas Telford (1757-1854) and opened in 1826. The diagram indicates the forces acting on such a structure at one of the supporting towers over which the suspension chain is slung. Compare this diagram with the parallelogram of forces in page 2127. (See further, Bridges.)

The forces acting upon an aeroplane wing can be resolved by a parallelogram in the manner shown. (See p. 2127).

Fig. 4

block in the same way. It is obvious that the greater the ratio of the lengths of the two arms of the lever, the greater will be the mechanical advantage, or multiplying power, of the lever. The hinge of a lever, or fulcrum, as it is known, can have three alternative positions in relation to the load and effort applied, giving rise to the three classes of lever in Fig. 5. Note that the third class of lever actually has a mechanical disadvantage, and for this reason it is employed in designing a blow-off safety valve for a steam boiler. The steam pressure has to be very great before it can push up the small piston and lift the weight at the end of the lever arm. The biceps muscle on our forearm is also a lever of the third class, but in this instance the mechanical disadvantage is not a help. Archimedes first made known the principle of the lever. " Give me a long enough lever and a place to stand on," he said, " and I will move the world."

The inclined plane is said to have been used by the Egyptians in building the Pyramids. Draymen now use it in loading barrels on to wagons. Here again there is a mechanical advantage, for although the men have to push the barrel farther up the ramp than lifting it straight up, the force they exert is much less. The wedge is a double inclined plane, at the back of which power is applied ; and we use it in knives, axes, chisels, and other tools. Some common applications are illustrated in page 2129.

The wheel-and-axle, turning about their centre, form mechanically a special form of lever. A small force applied to the rim of the wheel will balance a large force on the axle. Gear wheels are really two linked levers which can act continuously in

## THE SIMPLE MECHANICAL POWERS IN DAILY USE

The three 'machines' known as the primary mechanical powers were, in their simplest form, the first mechanical aids that Man used to help him in his work. They are the lever; the pulley or grooved wheel, with a rope passing over it; and the inclined plane. Other devices have been derived from these three, the wheel-and-axle being an adaptation of the lever.

transmitting power. The pulley is a device for changing the direction of a force, and can also be used to multiply forces, when several pulleys are used together in a pulley block (*see* Pulley). The screw is a form of inclined plane, wound as a helix around a cylinder; its many applications are dealt with under its own heading.

Unbalanced forces, which produce motion, are exemplified by the steam pressure acting on the piston of a steam engine. This force is transmitted by way of simple machines such as cranks, belts and pulleys, or cog wheels, to a machine tool; or, in the locomotive, it is used directly to cause a train to move. If there were no force of friction such a tool or train would speed up indefinitely, but, of course, the speed actually adjusts itself so that the frictional force equals the driving force.

The simplest instance of an unbalanced force producing motion is that of an unsupported weight falling to the ground. If the effect of air resistance

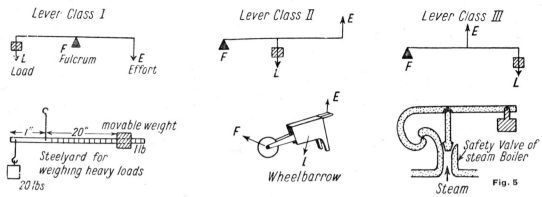

Fig. 5

### MECHANICS OF DIFFERENT CLASSES OF LEVER

Levers are ranged in three classes according to the respective position of the fulcrum and those of the load and the effort. Class 1 is well illustrated by the steelyard, that ancient implement for weighing heavy loads. For Class 2 the common wheelbarrow will serve as an everyday example. Class 3 levers work at a mechanical disadvantage. One type of safety valve is an example ; the biceps muscle of the forearm is another, but here the mechanical disadvantage is not a help, as it is in the safety valve illustrated. Other applications of levers are shown in page 2129.

is neglected, it is found that the speed increases at a uniform rate—that is, with a constant acceleration. Starting from rest, the weight falls 16 feet in the first second, 64 in the second, 144 feet in the third, and so on. Its velocity increases at the rate of 32 feet per second every second. The distance fallen may be expressed by the formula :

$S = u\,t + \frac{1}{2}\,a\,t^2$, where $S$ = distance travelled, $u$ is the initial velocity, $t$ the time taken, and $a$ the acceleration.

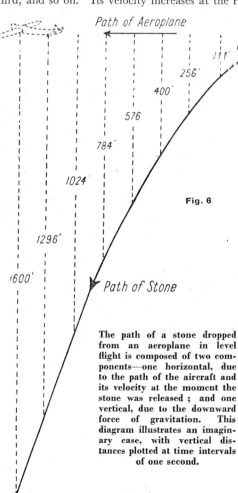

Fig. 6

The path of a stone dropped from an aeroplane in level flight is composed of two components—one horizontal, due to the path of the aircraft and its velocity at the moment the stone was released ; and one vertical, due to the downward force of gravitation. This diagram illustrates an imaginary case, with vertical distances plotted at time intervals of one second.

With this formula the distance that a stone dropped from an aeroplane after any time may be found. In Fig. 6 the path, or trajectory, of the stone is drawn. Whereas its vertical speed is increasing all the time, due to the gravitational force, its horizontal speed remains the same as that of the aeroplane. Trajectories of rockets and of shells fired from guns may be found in a similar way, using the simple laws of mechanics. That is how artillery-men can calculate where their shots are going to fall.

Newton summed up the way in which forces cause motion of a body in the following laws :

1. Every body stays at rest, or continues moving uniformly in a straight line, unless acted on by an outside force. That is, matter has *inertia*.

2. If a force acts on a body, the body *accelerates* at a rate proportional to the force, and inversely proportional to its mass.

3. To every force there is an equal and opposite reaction.

Although experience tells us that if we keep pushing a heavy truck it will not speed up indefinitely, as Law 2 would indicate, it must be remembered that on the earth frictional forces are always acting to oppose us. It is only in the motion of the heavenly bodies that perfectly free motion can take place, and the planets are found to " obey " Newton's laws very accurately. Scientists also use Newton's laws of dynamics to explain the motion of electrical particles in radio valves, the vibration of the molecules in a gas or liquid, and the propagation of waves in water, air and the ether.

These are a few of the interesting features about Mechanics. Space will not permit more examples, but our story should open your eyes to hundreds of other applications which you can see every day as you go about your work or play. School text-books will elaborate the information which we give here in a necessarily brief form.

## Medes.

In ancient times (about the 9th century B.C.), when the mighty Assyrian Empire was at the height of its power, there grew up on its borders, in the mountainous land south-east of the Caspian Sea, another power which steadily became more dangerous—the kingdom of Media. In contrast to the Assyrians, who were Semites (group of peoples including Hebrews, Arabs, and others), the Medes belonged to the great Indo-European family, from which practically all the peoples of Europe except the Jews are descended.

Once subject to the Assyrians, these people, simple in their habits and strong in body, had won their independence and were gaining in strength, while their former masters became weakened through wealth and luxury. At length the Medes in 612 B.C. swept down on Nineveh, the Assyrian city on the River Tigris, and, with their Babylonian allies, laid it in ruins.

For a brief time the Medes were the greatest power in western Asia. Among their vassals were the Persians, another Indo-European people, who were, like the Medes, followers of the religion of Zoroaster, a form of sun-worship, and who had the same language and customs. And now again the subject state became the ruler, for Cyrus the Great, king of Persia, about 558 B.C. seized the throne of the Median king Astyages. In course of time the two peoples were merged into one as Medes and Persians. Because their laws could not be changed, the phrase " the laws of the Medes and Persians " became a synonym for something which is unalterable.

## Medici.

(Pron. med′-i-chi). In the stirring days of the Renaissance, which began in the 15th century, many families rose to power in Italian cities by force of arms, intrigue and assassination. The Medici of Florence, on the other hand, owed their position largely to the great wealth derived from their activities in commerce and banking.

Giovanni de' Medici (1360–1429) was the real founder of the wealth and power of the family. His son Cosimo (1389–1464) did vast banking and commercial business by means of branches in Rome, Venice, Geneva, Bruges, London, and elsewhere; at the same time, while remaining nominally a private citizen, he was the ruler of Florence, friends in influential positions carrying out his

**CATHERINE DE' MEDICI**
Daughter of an Italian banker, Catherine de' Medici married Henry II of France in 1533, and was largely responsible for the massacre of the Huguenots in August 1572.

orders. Cosimo was a generous patron of art and literature.

With Cosimo's grandson, Lorenzo the Magnificent (1448–92), the glory of the Medici reached its height. He escaped the fate of his younger brother Giuliano, who was stabbed to death in 1478 as the result of a plot of their Florentine enemies. Lorenzo continued his grandfather's policy and even excelled him in the magnificence of his patronage of men of letters and artists, including the youthful sculptor Michelangelo.

Lorenzo's influence enabled him to secure the election as cardinal, at the early age of 14, of his second son Giovanni. Later this son became Pope, as Leo X (1475–1521), and gained fame for his patronage of fine arts.

The later Medici—from 1530—bore the title of Duke of Florence. In 1569 Cosimo the Great received from Pope Pius V the title of Grand Duke of Tuscany. The Medici continued to rule until 1737, when the family died out.

Catherine de' Medici (1519–89), great-granddaughter of Lorenzo the Magnificent, became the wife of one French king (Henry II) and the mother of three others—Francis II, Charles IX, and Henry III. She was chiefly responsible for the terrible St. Bartholomew's massacre on August 24, 1572, when thousands of Huguenots were slain. (See illustration on page 195).

Marie de' Medici (1573–1642), a daughter of Francesco de' Medici, was born at Florence on April 26, 1573, and in 1600 married Henry IV of France. After Henry's death in 1610 she became Regent for their son Louis XIII. An ambitious and unscrupulous woman, with the aid of the Minister of State, Cardinal Richelieu, and an Italian family named Concini, which she had brought with her from Florence, she gained supreme power.

Her great extravagance and abuse of her position as Regent turned the nobles against her, and in 1617 Louis had the Concinis murdered, and exiled his mother to Blois (a town on the Loire river, France) where she remained until 1619. She was then liberated, and made several attempts to regain power, which, though at first successful, were eventually brought to naught by Richelieu, whom she had offended. In 1631, forced to leave France, she went to Cologne, a German city on the Rhine, where she died on July 3, 1642.

**LORENZO DE' MEDICI**
Known as the ' Magnificent,' Lorenzo de' Medici lavished his wealth on Florence, in the 15th century. The painting, of which this is a reproduction, was in the Uffizi Gallery, Florence.

# MAKING *and* KEEPING *the* BODY HEALTHY

*Out of the groping and fumbling practice of primitive Man, befogged by magic and superstitious rites, has developed the art of healing as we know it today—in its twin branches of Medicine and Surgery.*

**Medicine and Surgery.** These are the two dominant arts of healing as applied to human beings ; Veterinary Medicine and Surgery are the corresponding arts applied to the treatment of animals.

Medicine concerns itself with the prevention of disease, its cure, or its relief. Surgery concerns itself in the " mechanical " work—with the setting of broken bones, the removal of diseased parts, and the like. So wide is the field of medicine and of surgery today that few men can be both physician and surgeon, though at the beginning of a student's training he has a grounding in both branches. He will begin his studies by reading Botany and Zoology, grasping thereby how all life, vegetable and animal, is part of the same scheme. Then he will read Physics and Chemistry, learning the great unchanging laws which control gases and liquids and the stresses and strains of matter; and how matter and material are formed and interchange and rebuild their substances. Anatomy will show him the formation of the body down to the most minute tissue. Physiology will demonstrate these parts at their proper specialized work. Pathology deals with these parts when diseased and functioning wrongly. Midwifery traces the development of the embryo from the two single cells and treats of the safe delivery of the mature foetus.

On this wide base the student will begin to practise the art of Medicine and the craft of surgery. A great modern subdivision of Medicine is Preventive Medicine— not allowing a disease to gain ground. For example, malaria and yellow fever, so common in tropical countries, are well known to be conveyed by the bite of a mosquito from some animal host to Man. But instead of curing the man or hunting the animals or chasing the mosquitoes, preventive medicine drains the swamps where the mosquitoes breed, so controlling the situation. Public Health departments follow the same interests, seeing that milk is not contaminated, nor wells ; nor tainted food allowed to be sold. Most infectious diseases are notifiable by law. Should an outbreak of, say, scarlet fever or typhoid fever occur, the quick action of the Public Health departments in tracking down the source of infection and in segregating the contagious patient prevents much illness and suffering.

**THE FATHER OF MEDICINE**
Hippocrates (*c.* 460 B.C.) was the earliest medical man whose name has come down to us. He practised both as a physician and surgeon, though the Greeks objected to dissection.

Vaccination against smallpox could come in this category. The patient is deliberately given a mild form of the virulent disease so that he is thereby protected against it. The great number of preventive vaccines challenge the defence mechanisms of the body by the injection of a measured amount of poison derived from killed germs. The body is then armed and prepared should the real live invader alight, for the cells of the body " remember," in some extremely mysterious way, the enemies against which they have been armed or have fought. The common cold, typhoid fever and cholera come in this class.

Diagnosis—the finding out of what is wrong with the patient—is of paramount importance. The history of the patient, of his habits, work, environment, as well as of the present illness, is taken carefully. What the patient complains of is known as a " symptom"; what the observer notes is termed a " sign." Thus, pain is a symptom, and a high temperature is a sign. Diagnosis is helped by methods such as X-ray findings ; and results worked out on the laboratory bench give valuable information as to germs, reactions of the body fluids, and so forth.

Once the condition is recognized accurately, it is in a fair way to be cured—or at least to be alleviated. Rest, warmth and fluid are indeed distinguished " physicians," but added to these are numerous substances which help the patient to combat the disease. For example, there are digitalis to strengthen his heart-beat, strychnine to deepen his breathing, various purges to aid the bowel in its task of eliminating waste matter—the list of such remedial substances is endless. Penicillin and the sulpha group of drugs control between them the germs of many common and often dangerous complaints. These drugs stop the germs from breeding, and during this respite the patient gathers strength to win through. Some drugs, however, are the specific answer to specific diseases, *e.g.* quinine for malaria, and salicylate for rheumatism.

How has all this knowledge grown ? Since the earliest times there have been doctors working by magic and by spells—the witch doctors—still to be found in primitive tribes over the world. Then it was gradually observed that this herb or that mineral achieved a certain result, though the reason

# MEDICAL PIONEERS IN THE FIGHT AGAINST DISEASE

In this book some of the greatest practitioners of medicine and surgery, such as William Harvey and Joseph Lister, are considered and illustrated under their own headings. Here and in the next page we put on record others whose discoveries have been of lasting benefit to mankind. Left, Sir James Young Simpson (1811–70), who experimented with chloroform in childbirth and surgical operations, and introduced the art of practical anaesthesia. Right, the German professor Robert Koch (1843–1910), who ranks with Pasteur as the founder of bacteriology, isolated the comma bacillus of cholera and the tubercle bacillus, and was the discoverer of tuberculin ; this drawing is from life.

E.N.A

Left, Sir Patrick Manson (1844–1922) specialised in parasitology (the science of parasites), and his hypothesis that the malaria parasite was carried by the mosquito led to the later discoveries of Sir Ronald Ross (1857–1932) and the control of those tropical scourges malaria and yellow fever. Right, Sir Frederick Grant Banting (1891–1941) who in conjunction with other research workers discovered insulin, a curative drug for diabetes. Awarded the Nobel prize for medicine in 1923, he was knighted by King George V in 1934. Early in the Second World War (1939–45) Banting made investigations into the strains imposed on airmen by high-altitude flying and dive-bombing.

# SURGEONS WHO EARNED MANKIND'S DEEP GRATITUDE

Ambroise Paré (1510–90), called the father of modern French surgery (left), was primarily a military surgeon and introduced the ligature in place of the red hot cautery to stop bleeding. Right, Sir Astley Paston Cooper (1768– 1841), surgeon at Guy's Hospital, London, and Professor of Comparative Surgery at the Royal College of Surgeons, London, was famed for his operation of tying the aorta (main artery) for aneurism (local dilatation of an artery).

John Hunter (1728–93) was a particularly daring surgeon (left). His collection of anatomical specimens, known as the Hunterian Museum, is in the care of the Royal College of Surgeons. This picture of him is from the painting by Sir Joshua Reynolds (1723–92). Right, Sir James Paget (1814–99) was a surgeon at St. Bartholomew's (Bart's) Hospital, London ; his lectures as Professor of Anatomy at the Royal College of Surgeons became a standard text-book.

of the result was ungrasped ; this knowledge came down from father to son. The whole art and practice of medicine has its very roots in folk-lore. What a far cry from all this to the coveted degree of Bachelor of Medicine (M.B.) and Bachelor of Surgery (B.Ch. from the old way of spelling Surgery, Chirugerie), granted by a university after some five years of study at desk and at bedside.

Much that has been said about medicine applies to its sister, surgery, dealing with those " mechanical " conditions which menace health and, like medicine, practised since the earliest times. Ancient skeletons coming to light after countless ages show holes bored in the skull to relieve pressure, much as is done today; and bones splinted with metal even as now. But sepsis, the invasion of wounds by germs, hindered the surgeon however skilled; and throughout past generations the patient died of blood-poisoning and in misery all too often. Two discoveries belong to our era and have revolutionized surgery in the most complete sense of that word. Pasteur, in France, demonstrated the power of micro-organisms to cause change in tissue ; and Lister, the famous English surgeon, jumped to the right conclusion that it was these micro-organisms which invaded wounds and caused disaster and death. Lister had all the surroundings of the patient sprayed with carbolic, and even this crude method of asepsis gave him hitherto unheard of results of recovery.

Then in the middle of the 19th century Simpson, a Scottish doctor, produced the general anaesthetic we call chloroform, a contribution to humanity never to be over-estimated. Now when an operation is to be done the chief dread of the patient is the anaesthetic. How it was in the old days, in terms of pain and fear, does not bear thinking of. The surgeon now is not in haste. Within wide limits, in the warm aseptic theatre, he has all the time he needs for meticulous workmanship.

Pasteur, Lister, Simpson—these three had what is known as the scientific imagination. Their minds, brooding and working over the facts in their possession, flung forward to fresh and dazzling facts deduced from those earlier ones.

## Mediterranean Sea.

Thousands of years ago the Mediterranean was the centre of the known world and upon its waters many races learned the art of seamanship. Today the Mediterranean is once again the centre of the world's interest, the large quantities of oil obtained in the Middle East making the control of this sea in time of war a matter of the greatest military importance.

The sea is 2,400 miles long ; 1,200 miles at its broadest, from Venice in Italy to the Gulf of Sidra in Tunisia, and 300 miles on an average; and, at the highest estimate, 1,145,000 square miles in area. The Mediterranean is virtually tideless and is almost entirely enclosed by Europe on the north and north-west, Africa on the south, and Asia on the east, with a narrow opening into the Atlantic at the Straits of Gibraltar and another into the Black Sea at the Dardanelles. For convenience of description it is sometimes divided into (1) the Western Mediterranean, or that part west of Sicily and Malta; (2) the South-eastern Mediterranean, east of Malta; (3) the Adriatic Sea, the large arm

### A VISIT TO THE DOCTOR IN THE MIDDLE AGES

This illustration of a doctor's house is from a 15th-century manuscript. The doctor is wearing a robe trimmed with fur and, as is not uncommon in drawings of this time, the artist, wishing to show two separate actions, has drawn the same man twice in one picture—attending to the injured arm of a young man, and preparing a potion for another patient. The right of the picture depicts two more men arriving to have their injuries attended to.

**INDENTED COAST OF THE MEDITERRANEAN, VAST INLAND SEA**

between Italy and Yugoslavia; and (4) the Aegean Sea, lying between Greece and Asia Minor.

There are really only two basins, however, divided by the Italian peninsula, which reaches out towards Cape Bon in Africa, with Sicily in between.

Here is a centre of volcanic activity, marked by Vesuvius in Italy, Etna in Sicily, and Stromboli in the Lipari Islands. The greatest depth in the eastern basin is 14,400 feet, between Malta and Crete; in the western basin, 12,200 feet, east of Sardinia. At Gibraltar the depth is 3,000 feet, yet just outside the Strait in the Atlantic it is only 1,200. The chief islands of the western division are Sicily, Sardinia, Corsica, and the Balearic group; and in the eastern, Cyprus, Rhodes, Crete, the Ionian Isles and Malta.

Were it not for the water flowing in from the Atlantic, the Mediterranean would no doubt dry up in a short time to a salt desert like the former seas of Asia, for it loses three times as much by evaporation as it gains from the few great rivers that flow into it—the Ebro, Rhône, and Po from Europe, and the Nile from Africa. From the Black Sea—fed by several large rivers—there is also a strong current. The Suez Canal connects it by way of the Red Sea with the Indian Ocean.

Sponge, tunny and sardine fisheries are important, and red coral is found off the coasts of Provence, the Balearic Islands, Sicily, Tunisia and Libya.

**Meerschaum.** (Pron. mēr'-sham). The name of this mineral is derived from two German words, *meer*, meaning sea; and *schaum*, foam. It is a white or cream-coloured clay-like substance, which, when dry, will float on water. When first dug from the earth it is soft, like soap, makes a lather in water, and will remove grease marks from materials ; chemically it consists of hydrated magnesium silicate. In Europe it is found in Spain, and the Crimea; and in Asia Minor there are large beds of it. It is also found in South Carolina and New Mexico in the United States.

The best quality comes from Asia Minor. It is mined in blocks about a foot square and is packed in cotton to avoid damage in transit. Meerschaum is fashioned into pipe bowls, the material being coloured by the burning tobacco and taking a high polish.

*Australian News and Information Bureau*
**MELBOURNE'S STATE HOUSES OF PARLIAMENT**
In Spring Street, Melbourne, the capital of Victoria, Australia, are the State Houses of Parliament (above), which were completed in 1891. When the neighbouring gold-fields were opened in 1851, and what was then Port Phillip province became the colony of Victoria, Melbourne (which was founded in 1834) was made its capital.

**Melbourne.** Until the discovery of the neighbouring gold-fields in 1851, the growth of the town of Melbourne had been slow. Within the next 10 years its development was so rapid that it had become one of Australia's leading cities, second in size only to Sydney.

Capital of the State of Victoria, the city lies on the banks of the River Yarra, which flows into Hobson's Bay, an inlet of Port Phillip. The planning of the city was done with great care; the principal strccts, 99 feet wide, run at right angles to each other, and the public buildings, among the finest of any city of equal size in the world, include the Houses of Parliament, Exhibition Building, and the Town Hall, with an assembly hall holding 2,500. There are also a national art gallery, a technological museum, a university and an observatory.

The industrial centre of Victoria, Melbourne has foundries, flour and woollen mills, boot and clothing factories, potteries, soap works and tanneries. Gold, meat, wool and fruit are main exports. Railways and air services afford communication with all the other State capitals.

First occupied by white settlers in 1835, Melbourne was named after Lord Melbourne, Prime Minister of England in 1834 and 1835–41. When Victoria was proclaimed a colony in 1851, the city was made its capital. The population is 1,226,920.

**Melon.** Generally an oval-shaped fruit, growing on trailing plants, the melon is a member of the family *Cucurbitaceae*. A tough outer skin covers the thick fleshy pulp, which in turn encloses numerous seeds. The surface may be smooth or grooved, and the flesh may be green, white or orange. Many varieties are cultivated in warm and temperate regions throughout the world In addition to their use as fresh fruit, melons are also used as an ingredient of various pickles and jams.

The two most common types of melon are the water and the musk varieties. The water-melon (*Citrullus vulgaris*) is a native of tropical Africa and has a dark-green spotted or striped rind, the colour of the pulp ranging from pink to scarlet, though it may be yellow or white. It probably gets its name from the large quantity of watery juice it contains. The musk-melon (so named from its delightful flavour suggestive of musk) is a native of the sub-tropical parts of Asia and was grown by the Israelites and Egyptians.

Most important of the varieties is the cantaloup or rock-melon, named after the town of Cantalupo,

**A CENTURY OF PROGRESS IN MELBOURNE**
The city of Melbourne was founded in 1835, two years before Queen Victoria came to the throne. The drawing (lower) was made five years later and shows what is now Collins Street, with the River Yarra on the left. Today the 99-feet-wide Collins Street (upper) is the principal thoroughfare in the business part of a great modern city with a population nearing a million and a quarter, capital of the State of Victoria.

*Australian Trade Publicity*

Italy, where it was first cultivated in Europe about 1570. The nutmeg or netted melon has a softer rind than the cantaloup, the whole surface being covered with a network of lines. Nutmeg melons have salmon, golden or green flesh. The cassaba, a variety of musk melon, was first grown at Cassaba in Asia Minor. The flesh is white or green.

**Memnon.** In Greek mythology, Memnon, king of Ethiopia in North Africa, was the son of Eos (Aurora), goddess of the dawn. He came to the aid of Troy against the Greeks towards the end of the Trojan War, slew Antilochus, the son of Nestor (one of the Greek leaders), in single combat, and was himself slain by Achilles (*q.v.*). The colossal statues of King Amenhotep III of Egypt and his consort erected near Thebes in Egypt were believed by the Greeks to represent Memnon. One of them, after its partial destruction by an earthquake in 27 B.C., produced musical notes at sunrise, according to numerous Greek and Latin inscriptions on the statue. Modern science has ascribed this sound to the rapid passage of the air through the pores of the stone when heated by the sun. Septimius Severus (193–211) repaired the statue with large blocks of sandstone, after which the plaint was never heard.

**CARGO OF MELONS FROM ASIA MINOR**
Some varieties of melon are native to Asia, and are still grown to a large extent in Asia Minor, whence the fruits are exported to Europe. Here is a cargo of them of varying size and colour, that has just come across the Sea of Marmara to Istanbul, where they find ready purchasers.
*L.N.A.*

**Memory.** "Remembering" is one of the most important functions in living. Yet ordinarily remembering is done with so little effort that it is difficult to realize how complicated it actually is. Memory has been defined as the knowledge of an event or fact of which, meantime, one has not thought, coupled with the further knowledge that the particular event or fact concerned has been experienced in the past.

It is estimated that some 600 million nerve cells, linked up by countless nerve fibres, build up this tremendous, little-understood, filing cabinet of memory — implying the retention of an event and the reproduction of it. To understand memory, one must split up the process into its several phases or parts. Of these the first is called *association*. This means the coming together of the two experiences so that the thought of one brings up the thought of the other. That is how "habit" is formed—repeated suggestion sets groups of cells acting in unison. This is how the typist knows where the keys on her typewriter lie; it is the principle underlying all "specialist" knowledge such as that of doctor or lawyer or mechanic.

**FAMOUS 'COLOSSI OF MEMNON'**
*Donald McLeish*
These two huge figures which stand on the west bank of the Nile at Thebes, Egypt, were erected about 3,000 years ago, and represent Pharaoh Amenhotep III and his consort, though by the Greeks and Romans they were associated with the mythical Memnon. The one on the right is said to have emitted at sunrise a musical note, since attributed to the action of the sun's heat on the cold stone. The figures are about 65 ft. high.

The second phase of memory is known as *retention*, and refers to the power to retain associations in the mind. It varies from individual to individual, and seems to be based upon a natural quality of the nervous system. The opposite of retention is forgetting. One forgets most in the first hour, less in the next, less in the third, and so on. After the first 24 hours the rate of forgetting is relatively slow.

A person studying French, for instance, finds that he may learn the meaning of 50 French words in one day; the next day most of the words will be forgotten. If, however, he practises the forgotten words the next day and on succeeding days in the course of time he will master the list completely. Repetition is the soul of memory.

In school one does not study arithmetic for one whole day, grammar the next day, and geography the next day ; but rather one studies arithmetic, grammar, and geography each day for short periods. This is in order that the memory bonds, which have been weakened through the rapid forgetting that takes place during the first 24 hours, may be reinforced.

The third phase of memory is usually spoken of as *recall*, and refers to the ability of the individual to call up, under the appropriate circumstances, that which has been associated and retained. The ability to recall under appropriate circumstances is obviously the test of memory. Thinking of the answer to a question in an examination paper after the paper is handed in is of little value in comparison with thinking of the answer when the question was being dealt with. The ability to recall depends in large part upon the number of associations which have been formed with the particular fact to be recalled. Herein lies the great opportunity for improving memory. Each association forms a " handle " by which to pick out of the storehouse of the brain the wanted fact.

The fourth phase of memory is called *recognition*, and refers to the " labelling " by which an experience is assigned a place in earlier life. It is the feeling of "pastness," or familiarity. Ordinarily, recall and recognition go hand in hand ; occasionally, however, recognition occurs without recall. A face may be familiar yet may call no name immediately to mind.

Persons differ in the kinds of things they remember easily. Some remember things they have seen better than things they have heard, according as the eye or ear is the dominant sense. Generally it is the eye in Man. In good teaching an attempt is made to present the material to the student in various ways: he reads about it in a book, he discusses it in classes, he looks at diagrams and illustrations, and in some courses he actually works with the material in the field, the laboratory or the workshop.

The cinema, with its powerful impact on visual memory, is a modern method; and gramophone records assail the hearing centres of the brain. All these methods multiply the " handles " of association, with which a person can remember the required fact when need arises.

Instead of complicated systems for improving the memory which have been devised in the past, modern psychologists rely on a few simple principles. Of these the first is that repetition tends to fix associations. But repetition is not sufficient. It is necessary to concentrate the whole attention upon the task in hand. Perhaps the foremost principle of efficient memorizing is the principle of recall during memorizing. If, after reading, the student closes the book and tries to recall what he has read, his ability to retain will increase steadily.

The memory becomes impaired and changed with age. This is due in most part to a thickening of the little arteries which feed the " tablets of the memory," and resulting in a poorer blood supply. The time to learn is in youth, when these tablets are " wax to receive and marble to retain." Recent memory in the aged is blotted out. The old man remembers with difficulty the happenings of yesterday; but he has a clear-cut picture of the happenings of his childhood and youth.

There is, as the psychologist Freud has pointed out, no such thing as " forgetting." All those 600 million cells see to that. The smallest experience is registered somewhere. If unpleasant it can be pushed down into the subconscious, but it is far from being " forgotten "; and in the subconscious it can burrow and fret, causing a sick personality. Psychologists know this; they go in search of such thrust-under memories and fish them out. The very remarkable fact is that when they are found and discussed their power for mischief often vanishes.

Today not only are the memory processes of the individual studied but a greater and more mysterious memory is acknowledged—the memory of the race or tribe. When one sleeps on a problem, or, as the French say, " takes counsel of the night," it is really this universal memory or subconsciousness one is consulting for wise help. One communes again with the boundless deep from which the life of the mind has sprung.

**Mendel,** Gregor Johann (1822–84). When Darwin and Huxley were astounding the worlds of science, philosophy, and religion by expounding the principles of evolution set out in Darwin's Origin of Species (1859) and The Descent of Man and Selection in Relation to Sex (1871), an Augustinian monk and lecturer in natural history, at Brünn, Austria, was formulating and proving fundamental laws of heredity which, had they been known to Darwin

*E.N.A.*

**GREGOR MENDEL**
Monk and scientist, Mendel by his experiments on plants established important laws of heredity, though they remained unnoticed until 25 years after his death in 1884.

and his fellow scientists, would have changed the course of biological science in the 19th century.

The name of this monk was Gregor Johann Mendel, and the natural laws of heredity he

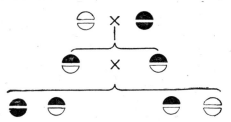

**MENDEL'S THEORY OF HEREDITY**
The hybrids resulting from the union of two individuals (above) show the dominant character (black). The other character (white) is recessive, and will lie dormant in the offspring of the first generation. The progeny of the hybrids will show pure white, pure black, and hybrids.

discovered are always spoken of as the " Mendelian Laws." He was born at Heinzendorf, Silesia, on July 22, 1822, and, studying for the priesthood, became an Augustinian monk in 1843. He was made abbot in 1860, and for 15 years taught biology in the monastery school while pursuing his own researches into hereditary characteristics—that is, the qualities passed on from parent to offspring.

Seeking to record the reappearance in successive generations of " unit characters," Mendel chose for his experiments two contrasted types of the garden pea, the green and the yellow. And he found that by crossing one variety with another, i.e. by " cross-fertilization " he produced hybrids or crosses in which only the one colour, yellow, appeared. He thereupon called yellow the *dominant*, and green the *recessive* character. Mendel found, by further cultivation, that in the offspring of his first crosses 25 per cent showed pure dominant (yellow) character, 25 per cent pure recessive (green) character, while the remaining 50 per cent were hybrid like their parents, with yellow still dominant and green recessive. Moreover, he discovered that the 25 per cent yellows reproduced only pure yellows and the 25 per cent greens only pure greens.

In other words, characteristics are either dominant or recessive. The offspring of the *first* generation tend to inherit the dominant characteristics, the recessive characteristics lying dormant and appearing in the *second* and later generations. If individuals possessing recessive characteristics unite, recessive characteristics become in turn dominant in their offspring. This is why marriage between cousins may be unwise if there is a flaw in the stock : two " recessive flaws " may breed a " dominant flaw."

Thus Mendel established the principle of " segregation " in heredity, or the law which maintains pureness in the unit characters of a family. The offspring is not intermediate in type between its parents, but throws clear to one or the other in physical or mental characteristics. These characteristics may appear, " leaping down " many generations, but they are always clear-cut, not modified. Mendel's laws, discovered by his experiments on peas, have since been found to hold good for many highly specialized plants and animals, and for Man himself.

While Mendel's laws do not apply to all characters of plants and animals, they are known to be of sufficiently wide application to be of very great importance in the improvement of domestic plants and livestock.

Unfortunately for science, Mendel's discoveries, which he published in 1866 and distributed to the chief scientific societies of the world, received no recognition, and it was not until 1900, when they were " discovered," that their immense value to agriculture and horticulture were fully realized. It was then seen that the Mendelian Laws gave to breeders and growers definite guidance, and completely revolutionized all previous knowledge of heredity. As with many great men his discoveries were not appreciated until after his death.

**Mendeléev**, DMITRI IVANOVITCH (1834–1907). Mendeléev, a Russian chemist, was one of the discoverers of the periodic law, and gave his name to Mendeléev's Periodic Table (*see* Chemistry). Some of the earlier chemists had tried to classify the chemical elements in such a way as to bring together elements of similar properties, but a very important advance was made by Mendeléev, and, independently, by Lothar Meyer, a German chemist. Mendeléev's periodic law states that when the elements are arranged in order of atomic weights, then similar elements occur at regular intervals in the list. While we now know that atomic *numbers* are more fundamental properties of atoms than are atomic *weights*, yet the Periodic Table of today is very similar to Mendeléev's.

Born at Tobolsk, in Siberia, Mendeléev was the youngest of 14 children. His father's blindness made the family dependent on the mother, who fed and educated all these children by establishing a glass works. Young Dmitri studied in St. Petersburg (now Leningrad), became a science master, and in 1866 was made Professor of General Chemistry in St. Petersburg University. He

*E.N.A*
**DMITRI MENDELÉEV**
Professor of Chemistry at St. Petersburg (Leningrad), Mendeléev announced his theory of periodicity in 1869. Many of his predictions of the future discovery of then unknown elements have since been realized and the gaps in the Table filled.

was interested mainly in the philosophical and physical aspects of chemistry, such as his law, and the properties of liquids, solutions, and gases, and in trying to explain how natural petroleum was formed. He died on February 2, 1907.

## Mendelssohn, JAKOB LUDWIG FELIX

(1809–47). Most noted musicians have become famous in the face of handicaps, but in the case of Mendelssohn-Bartholdy (to give him his full name) there was never a day when he lacked anything that money or friends or education could supply. The son of a wealthy Jewish banker, Felix Mendelssohn (pron. men'-del-son) was born at Hamburg, Germany, on February 3, 1809. At the age of four his lessons in music began, and when nine he composed pieces for the family orchestra. In 1826 he wrote his wonderful overture to Shakespeare's play A Midsummer Night's Dream.

In 1829 he paid the first of many visits to England, where he obtained inspiration for his Scottish symphony and Hebrides overture. His Italian sym-

**MENDELSSOHN**
At the age of 18 Felix Mendelssohn was one of the leading composers of his time.

phony was completed in 1833. The University of Leipzig honoured Mendelssohn by conferring on him the degree of Doctor of Philosophy. At Leipzig he directed concerts, taught music and worked on his oratorio Elijah, the first performance of which he conducted at Birmingham on August 26, 1846. He died at Leipzig on Nov. 4, 1847.

No composer has enjoyed more general popularity, and the list of his compositions is long. His best-known works, besides those already mentioned, include the Saint Paul oratorio, the overture Ruy Blas, the violin concerto, and 48 songs without words—among which are the Spring Song and the Bees' Wedding.

# The SIMPLE ART of MEASUREMENT

*H*iding under the name of mensuration is the branch of arithmetic dealing
with measuring lengths and surfaces and the volumes of solids. Here are
given some hints on this kind of calculation.

**Mensuration.** That branch of applied mathematics which deals with lengths, areas, and volumes we call mensuration (from Late Latin *mensuratio*, measuring). By the use of the tables and formulae of mensuration we may determine the area of a tract of land, the mass of a pyramid, or the weight of water in a large tank. We may ascertain the cost of painting the outside of a building, the number of bricks required to build a wall, or the amount of gravel needed to surface a road.

In measuring distances, and solving problems dependent on distances, linear measure is used, and in all cases it is necessary to reduce all figures to the lowest common measure. Thus, if the problem is set in rods, yards, and feet, it will be found easier to reduce all to feet :—

| | |
|---|---|
| 12 inches (in.) | =1 foot (ft.) |
| 3 feet | =1 yard (yd.) |
| 5½ yards | =1 rod (rd.) |
| 40 rods | =1 furlong (f.) |
| 8 furlongs | =1 mile (m.) |
| 5280 feet | =1 mile |

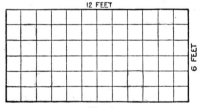

12 FEET

6 FEET

**Fig. 1**

*Problem.* How many feet of wire are needed to make a fence 6 wires high around a field 30 rds. long and 20 rds. wide ?

*Solution.* $2(20+30) \times 16 \cdot 5 \times 6 =$ length of wire in feet.

*Problem.* How many trees can be set, 20 ft. apart each way, in a field 40 rds. long and 200 yds. wide ?

*Solution.* $\dfrac{40 \times 16 \cdot 5}{20} \times \dfrac{200 \times 3}{20} =$ number of trees.

Plane surfaces (like a floor) are measured by finding the number of square units each contains, according to this table :

| | |
|---|---|
| 144 square inches (sq. in.) | =1 square foot (sq. ft.) |
| 9 square feet | =1 square yard (sq. yd.) |
| 30¼ square yards | =1 square rod (sq. rd.) |
| 40 square rods | =1 rood |
| 4 roods | =1 acre (A.) |
| 640 acres | =1 square mile (sq. m.) |

*Problem.* Find the area of a carpet 12 ft. long and 6 ft. wide. Look at Fig. 1 ; how many square feet are there in the upper row ? How many rows are there ? How many square feet in the six rows ?

*Solution.* $6 \times 12$ sq. ft.$=72$ sq. ft., the area of the carpet. We see therefore that to find the area of a rectangular surface we must multiply the length by the width : area$=$l.$\times$w.

*Problem.* The area of a floor is 192 sq. ft. ; one side is 12 ft. Find the other side.

*Solution.* Divide the area by the given side thus: $192 \div 12 = 16$ ft.

A practical application of surface measure is seen in this problem: What will it cost to make a concrete path 6 ft. wide and 150 ft. long, at 10s. a sq. yd. ?

*Solution.* $\dfrac{6 \times 150 \times 10}{3 \times 3} =$ cost of path

The area of the path is 6 times 150 sq. ft., or 900 sq. ft. ; divide by 9 to change to square yards. The area is 100 sq. yds. The cost is 100 times 10s., or £50.

A parallelogram has opposite sides equal. In a parallelogram like Fig. 2 the width is not the

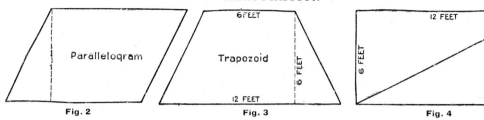

Fig. 2        Fig. 3        Fig. 4

side, but the dotted line, which is called the *height* or *altitude* (alt.). The formula for finding the area of a parallelogram is: area = base × alt.

A trapezoid, Fig. 3, has two sides parallel. Its area is alt. × mean (or average) of the two bases.

*Problem.* Find the area of a trapezoid whose bases are 12 ft. and 6 ft. and altitude 6 ft.

*Solution.* $\dfrac{12+6}{2} \times 6 = 54.$  The formula for finding the area of a trapezoid is: area = ½ sum of bases × alt.

We see that the rectangle (parallelogram), Fig. 4 is divided into two equal triangles. The area of the rectangle is 6 × 12, or 72 sq. ft. The area of each triangle is ½ of 72 sq. ft., or 36 sq. ft.

The formula for finding the area of a triangle is: area = ½ base × alt.

The circumference (C) of a circle is about three times the diameter (D). To be more exact, it is 3·1416 times the diameter. (The usual symbol for the number 3·1416 is the Greek letter *pi* or $\pi$.) The formula for the circumference of a circle is C = $\pi$ × D. Conversely D = C ÷ $\pi$. A tree whose circumference is 8½ ft. has a diameter of 8·5 ÷ 3·1416, or 2·7056 ft.

FINDING THE AREA OF A CIRCLE. We may think of a circle as made up of a number of triangles which may be cut apart and then fitted together as in Fig. 5. If we take enough triangles, we shall have almost a parallelogram, with one half of the circle's circumference for base and its radius for altitude, and equal in area to the circle. Pushing this to the limit, to "flatten" the base, we can consider the result exact. The area then is ½C × R. But ½C = ½ × 2$\pi$R, so the area = $\pi$R².

*Problem.* How much ground can a horse, tethered by a rope 100 ft. long, graze over?

*Solution.* 100 ft. is the radius of the circle over which the horse can graze. The area of this circle equals $\pi$ multiplied by the radius squared: 3·1416 × 100 × 100 = 31,416 sq. ft.

To FIND THE VOLUME, OR CUBIC CONTENT, OF A RECTANGULAR SOLID. In the rectangular solid represented by Fig. 6 we see that there are 5 layers of cubes of 1 cu. ft., and each layer consists of 12 small cubes (4 times 3 cu. ft.); in the five layers there are 5 times 12 cu. ft., or 60 cu. ft.

Cubic Measure is:

    1,728 cu. ins. = 1 cu. ft.
       27 cu. ft. = 1 cu. yd.

*Problem.* What will it cost to make the excavation for a basement 45 ft. long, 30 ft. wide, and 7 ft. deep, at 5s. a cu. yd.?

*Solution.* The volume of the earth removed is 45 × 30 × 7, or 9,450 cu. ft. This, divided by 27 cu. ft., equals 350 cu. yds. The cost is 350 times 5s., or £87 10s.

We can see that the volume of a cylinder (Fig. 7) is equal to the area of the base multiplied by the altitude, or height, remembering that the base of the cylinder is a circle.

*Problem.* Find the amount of water held in a cylindrical tank with a diameter of 6 ft. and a length of 12 ft.

*Solution.* $\pi$ times the square of the radius (3 ft.) equals the area of the base; 12 times the area equals the volume, or the quantity of water the tank contains. 3·1416 × 3 × 3 × 12 = 339·2928 cu. ft.

We may wish to paint a cylinder. Its total surface consists of two circles and the equivalent of a rectangle (the lateral surface unrolled).

*Problem.* Find the cost of painting the outside of a cylinder 15 ft. high and 8 ft. in diameter, at 3d. a sq. ft.

*Solution.* 2 (3·1416 × 4 × 4) + (3·1416 × 8) × 15 × 3d. = cost. The area of each base (circle) is $\pi$(3·1416) times the radius (4) squared, or 50·2656 sq. ft.; the two bases, 100·5312 sq. ft. The circumference of the base ($\pi$ × D) is 3·1416 × 8 ft. or 25·1328 ft. Multiplying this by the height (15) gives us the area of the side surface of the cylinder, or 376·992 sq. ft. Adding this to the area of the two bases, we have the total surface, 477·5232 sq. ft. Multiplying 3d. by this number gives the cost of painting, £5 19s. 4d.

A pyramid is a solid whose base is a polygon (figure bounded by three or more straight lines)

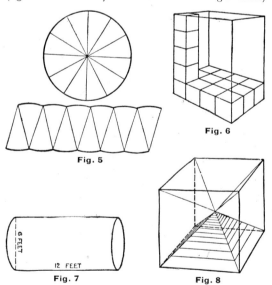

Fig. 5

Fig. 6

Fig. 7        Fig. 8

and whose sides are triangles meeting at a point called the vertex. The cube in Fig. 8 is divided into six equal pyramids. Now the volume of each pyramid must be ⅙ the volume of the cube, and the volume of the cube is the area of one side multiplied by the height. But the height of each pyramid is only half the height of the cube. Therefore the volume of each pyramid is $\frac{1}{3}$ the area of the base times the altitude.

*Problem.* Find the volume of a pyramid 5 ft. square at the base and 12 ft. high. Solution: $\frac{1}{3}(5 \times 5 \times 12) = 100$ cu. ft.

Find the area of the sides (external surface) of a pyramid 8 ft. square at the base, and having a slant height of 10 ft. Each of the four sides is a triangle, its area is $\frac{1}{2}$ (base × alt.); but the altitude of each side is the slant height of the pyramid. Hence, the area of all sides (convex surface) equals $\frac{1}{2}$ the slant height times the perimeter (the sum of the sides) of the base. $\frac{1}{2}(4 \times 8 \times 10) =$ area of external surface $= 160$ sq. ft.

A cone is a solid having a circle for a base and tapering uniformly to a vertex. Think of this as being a pyramid with an infinite number of sides to its base. Obviously then the volume of a cone will equal $\frac{1}{3}$ the area of the base times the height.

*Problem.* How much earth is needed for a conical mound 42 ft. in diameter at the base and 12 ft. high?

*Solution.* $\frac{1}{3}(3.1416 \times 21 \times 21) \times 12 = 5541.7824$ cu. ft. We multiply $\pi$ by the radius (21) squared, multiply that result by 12, and find $\frac{1}{3}$ of this result.

We considered the surface of a circle to be made up of a large number of triangles. Similarly, we may think of the curved surface of a cone as made up of small figures that are almost triangles. Hence, the area of the curved surface of a cone is equal to $\frac{1}{2}$ the slant height of the cone (which is the altitude of height of each triangle) times the perimeter of the base (a circle).

*Problem.* Find the area of the curved surface of a cone which has a slant height of 10 ft. and a diameter at the base of 12 ft.

*Solution.* $\frac{3.1416 \times 12 \times 10}{2}$ sq. ft. $= 188.496$ sq. ft.

Suppose a pyramid or cone is cut through in a plane parallel to its base. The remainder below is known as the frustum of the pyramid or cone. Let us elaborate the frustum of a pyramid into the form of a solid whose base and top are formed by parallel polygons, and whose sides are therefore triangles or quadrilaterals. Such a solid is called a prismoid, the term including among other things pyramids and frustums of pyramids. The formula for finding the volume of a prismoid is of the greatest importance, since it holds true in many instances when the sides of the prismoid have become curved surfaces, as in a sphere, cylinder, cone, or frustum of a cone; it can be used to find the volume of many irregular objects.

To find the Volume of a Prismoid. Ascertain the area of the base and top surface; let us call them A and $a$ respectively. Call the area of the mid-section M, which is the area of the plane midway between, and parallel to the base and top. Call the height H.

Then the volume $= \dfrac{H\,(A+a+4M)}{6}$

Volume measurements may be used to find the capacity of a bin or a tank and to determine weight of materials.

*Problem.* Find the number of bushels (bu.) that can be put into a bin 10 ft. long, 8 ft. wide, and 6 ft. deep, allowing .8 bu. to the cu. ft.

*Solution.* $10 \times 8 \times 6 \times .8$ bu. $= 384$ bu.

*Problem.* Find the number of gallons (gal.) of water that can be stored in a cylindrical tank 14 ft. in diameter and 11 ft. deep, allowing 231 cu. in. to the gal. The solution is as follows:

$$\frac{3.1416 \times 7 \times 7 \times 11 \times 1728}{231 \text{ cu. in.}} = 12,666.93 \text{ gals.}$$

What is the weight of this water, at 62.5 lb. to the cubic foot? $3.1416 \times 7 \times 7 \times 11 \times 62.5$ lb. equals the weight of the water in the tank, or 105,832.65 lb.

The weight of any mass is the weight of an equal volume of water times the substance's specific gravity.

*Problem.* Find the weight of a cylindrical section of marble 4 ft. in diameter and 6 ft. high, the specific gravity of marble being 2.688.

*Solution.* $\dfrac{3.1416 \times 2 \times 2 \times 6 \times 62.5 \times 2.688}{2240 \text{ lb.}}$

equals the weight of the marble in tons. After finding the cubic contents of the marble we find the weight of an equal volume of water, then multiply by 2.688. Reduce this to tons by dividing by 2240. Answer 5.663 tons.

Think of a sphere (or ball) cut into two hemispheres (half spheres) which rest on their flat sides. The area of the curved surface of each hemisphere is just twice the area of the circular base. Hence the area of the curved surface of the whole sphere is equal to 4 times the area of this flat base of the hemisphere. This area we can find from the diameter of the sphere.

*Problem.* Find the area of the surface of a sphere whose diameter is 6 ft.

*Solution.* $4 \times 3.1416 \times 3 \times 3 = 113.0976$ sq. ft.

We may think of a sphere as made up of a large number of pyramids whose height is the radius of the sphere, and the sum of whose bases is the surface of the sphere. Hence, its volume is $\frac{1}{3}$ of the area of the surface times the radius.

*Problem.* Find the volume of a sphere whose radius is 8 ft.

*Solution.* $\frac{1}{3}(4 \times 3.1416 \times 4 \times 4) \times 4 = 268.08$ cu. ft. We first find the area of the surface, get $\frac{1}{3}$ of that, and multiply the result by the radius.

**Mercerising.** In 1844 John Mercer, an English chemist, announced the discovery of a process by which cotton could be given a sheen resembling that of silk, and his name is perpetuated in the trade term "mercerised cotton." When cotton fabric or thread is kept stretched and immersed in a solution of caustic soda, the material after it has been rinsed takes on the characteristic sheen of silk. Cotton cloth thus treated becomes softer and stronger, and takes more brilliant colours when dyed.

**Merchant Navy.** The progressive development of the shipping industry is one of the wonders of modern civilization. In the first quarter of the 19th century there were not more than 100 steamships owned in the United Kingdom; and it was not until 1819 that the first paddle steamer crossed the Atlantic. Yet in the year 1938 Britain alone possessed 3,881 ocean-going vessels, manned by more than 159,300 seamen. And in spite of huge losses suffered during the Second World War (1939–45) the tonnage of shipping operating under the flag of the United Kingdom amounted to over 15 million in 1947. In the same year the tonnage of the seven largest merchant services in the world totalled 81 million, of which the United States owned over 33 million.

The importance of what was once called the mercantile marine to Great Britain can hardly be exaggerated; and in recognition of its services to the Empire King George V, in April 1928, changed the title to that of the Merchant Navy, creating at the same time the office of Master of the Merchant Navy and Fisheries, the then Prince of Wales being the first Master.

The Merchant Navy is responsible for a large part of what are termed invisible exports, i.e., services rendered in all parts of the world by

**Standard Cap Badge of Merchant Navy.**

British ships that are paid for in goods or money by the countries concerned. For example Argentina needs locomotives and steel rails, which she orders from Britain. These are shipped to Buenos Aires in a British vessel, which on arrival is chartered (hired) by an Argentine firm to carry a cargo to England or to some other country. In any case the ship will earn money for services rendered; and in this way British shipping provides employment for thousands of seamen and earns many millions of pounds annually.

To maintain the high standard of efficiency of the Merchant Navy owners and shipbuilders are continually constructing better vessels to compete with the mercantile marines of the rest of the world, and its sea-going personnel are highly-trained.

The Merchant Navy offers four classes of employment: service as a navigating officer, as an engineer, and in the catering and the wireless departments. To become a navigating officer it is customary either to serve an apprenticeship with the company concerned or to undergo preliminary instruction at one of the recognized officers' training establishments. A marine engineering officer is required to serve an apprenticeship in general engineering ashore, after which he is eligible for employment as a junior engineer officer. Beginners in the catering department are also encouraged to undergo preliminary training ashore. Prospective wireless officers must hold the Postmaster-General's certificate of proficiency in wireless telegraphy.

The flag worn by British merchant vessels is the Red Ensign, or, in ships manned by a stipulated proportion of Royal Naval Reserve officers and ratings, the Blue Ensign.

During the Second World War (1939–45) the Merchant Navy was employed in conveying troops, munitions and food to and from all parts of the world, and severe losses were suffered from attacks by enemy submarines, surface craft, and aircraft. Ships (excluding the fishing fleet) lost by enemy action numbered 2,426, with a gross tonnage of over 11 million. In addition 136 fishing vessels were lost.

## 'Merchant of Venice, The.'

In this comedy Shakespeare opposes the magnificent womanhood of Portia to the malignant power of Shylock, the Jew. Bassanio, soldier and scholar, and the " best deserving of a fair lady "; Gratiano, the madcap wit in Bassanio's following; Jessica, that " most beautiful pagan, most sweet Jew," daughter of Shylock; and the " merchant of Venice " himself—Antonio, " the kindest man " —are the chief characters in this enthralling play.

The main plot concerns the discomfiting of Shylock, who wishes to enforce against Antonio the latter's bond to give one pound of his flesh in default of payment of a loan. Portia discovers a law forbidding a Jew to shed Christian blood, and successfully pleads in court that the bond cannot be

*P. A.-Reuter*

### TRAINING SHIP FOR FUTURE OFFICERS OF THE MERCHANT NAVY

Moored in the Thames off Greenhithe, Kent, is H.M.S. Worcester (painted black and white), the training ship of the Thames Nautical Training College. Formerly named Exmouth, she is the third Worcester in which cadets have been prepared for service as officers in the Merchant Navy. At the left is the Cutty Sark, also the property of the College, which was once the smartest and fastest windjammer in the world, bringing tea from China and grain from Australia.

*From the water-colour by Sir John Gilbert; Victoria & Albert Museum*

**A SCENE FROM 'THE MERCHANT OF VENICE'**

In the first scene of the third act of Shakespeare's play 'The Merchant of Venice,' Shylock (right) meets Salanio and Salarino, friends of Antonio, in Venice and tells them of his determination to enforce his bond against Antonio. The bond provided that if Antonio did not return Shylock's loan of 3,000 ducats, the forfeit would be ' an equal pound of your fair flesh, to be cut off and taken in what part of your body pleaseth me.'

enforced. " If the scale do turn but in the estimation of a hair, thou diest," she warns Shylock. This play contains some of the finest passages in Shakespeare. One of these is Portia's matchless lines in reply to Shylock:

The quality of mercy is not strained,
It droppeth as the gentle rain from heaven
Upon the place beneath: It is twice blest:
It blesseth him that gives, and him that takes:
'Tis mightiest in the mightiest: it becomes
The thronèd monarch better than his crown:
His sceptre shows the force of temporal power,
The attribute to awe and majesty,
Wherein doth sit the fear and dread of kings;
But mercy is above this sceptred sway,
It is enthronèd in the hearts of kings,
It is an attribute of God himself,
And earthly power doth then show likest God's
When mercy seasons justice. Therefore, Jew,
Though justice be thy plea, consider this,
That in the course of justice none of us
Should see salvation: we do pray for mercy,
And that same prayer doth teach us all to render
The deeds of mercy.

**Mercury.** This is the only metallic element that is fluid at ordinary temperatures. It is from this fact that it receives its common name " quicksilver," meaning live or fluid silver. The name mercury is given it from the fleet-footed Roman god Mercury.

Pour a little of this silvery-white metal on a piece of paper, and you will readily see how the name fits it. No matter how much you pour out, it will not spread like water but clings together in a flattened ball. If you break up this ball, the portions promptly form smaller balls. If you bring the portions near one another again they will run together and form larger balls, because they have a strong attraction for one another. Though quicksilver is a liquid, it will not wet paper.

This liquid metal is very dense, being about 14 times as heavy as water. Only gold and a few of the rarer metals surpass it in density. Its chemical symbol is Hg, a contraction of the Latin name *Hydrargyrum*. The atomic weight of the element is 200·61; atomic number, 80.

Heat expands mercury, and cold contracts it regularly down to its freezing-point, which is about 39° below zero (Centigrade). This fact—its fairly constant expansion at ordinary temperatures — explains the common use of mercury in a thermometer, the range being about 400° Centigrade between its boiling- and freezing-points. Mercury is evaporating at all times, just as water evaporates, but the vapour is invisible, and the rate of evaporation is much slower than that of water. Nevertheless, mercury is being used in place of water in some power-generating boilers.

Native mercury is found in small quantities, usually associated with other mercury ores. These ores, of which the most important is called cinnabar, are burned in a furnace, and the sulphur which they contain passes off as sulphur dioxide ($SO_2$). The mercury is collected in a condensing chamber. It is then filtered through chamois-skin to purify it, and packed in iron " bottles " for the market. The Greeks and the Phoenicians procured cinnabar from Almaden, Spain, where a mine is said to have been worked since 800 B.C. Spain, Italy, Mexico, Russia, Czechoslovakia, China and the United States now produce it.

Mercury readily unites with other metals to form what are called amalgams, and this property was, for a long time, made use of in extracting gold and silver from their ores. The amalgam of mercury and tin was formerly employed for silvering mirrors, while other amalgams are used in electric batteries and in filling teeth. Mercury is used largely in making instruments such as barometers and thermometers. Since mercury is a good conductor of electricity, it is used for making contacts in thermostats and for power control switches. Mercury vapour is used in electric lamps of the ultra-violet ray type; it acts as the generator of these rays in fluorescent lamps, and so causes the " phosphors " in the tube to become luminescent.

Other industrial uses are in the manufacture of fulminates used in detonators for cartridges and other ammunition; in making pigments, such as vermilion red (which has been used by the Chinese for over 1,000 years); in fireworks; for wood preservatives; and for anti-fouling marine paints used on ships' hulls.

Drugs and chemicals account for a large part of the total consumption of mercury. A familiar example is calomel (mercurous chloride: HgCl). This should not be confused with the bichloride of mercury ($HgCl_2$), called corrosive sublimate, one of the most powerful antiseptics and also one of the deadliest poisons known.

In Roman mythology Mercury was the god of merchandise and of merchants. He was identified with the Greek god Hermes (*see* illus. page 1619). The innermost planet of the solar system is named after him. (*See* Planets).

**Meredith,** GEORGE (1828–1909). This great English novelist and poet was born at Portsmouth on February 12, 1828, and died on May 18, 1909, in the cottage on Box Hill, near Dorking, Surrey, where he had spent his later years.

The extraordinary length of his working life as a writer is shown by the fact that his first literary contribution to appear in print was accepted 60 years before his death, having been published in Chambers's Journal in 1849. It took him many, many years to gain recognition; indeed, for a very long time he was neglected by the reading public, although younger writers recognized him as one of England's foremost men of letters, and were much influenced by his individual philosophy.

In old age he was accorded the recognition long denied him; deafness and partial paralysis did not impair the brilliance of his mind, and in 1905 he was awarded the Order of Merit by King Edward VII. English literature would be immeasurably poorer without such masterpieces as The Ordeal of Richard Feverel, The Egoist, and Diana of the Crossways—to mention only three of his works.

**GEORGE MEREDITH**
Among the leading literary figures of late Victorian times, Meredith greatly influenced the younger writers of his day. He was awarded the Order of Merit in 1905.

**Merionethshire.** County of North Wales, facing the north end of Cardigan Bay, Merioneth contains some of the most beautiful mountain scenery in the principality. The estuary that stretches between Barmouth and Dolgelly, in particular, furnishes a wonderful panorama of mountains and placid water, and the walk between these two towns has been described as the finest in Great Britain. Cader Idris, nearly 3,000 ft. high, and Aran Mawddy, are the highest peaks; there are a number of others over 2,000 ft. The rivers include the Dee, which has its principal source in Lake Bala, and the Dovey.

The county, which has an area of 660 square miles, is very mountainous, and agriculture is backward. Slate, limestone and manganese are quarried, and woollens are manufactured. Dolgelly (population, 2,260) is the county town; other towns are Barmouth, Festiniog, Harlech (famed for its ruined castle and its place in national song), and Towyn. Population of the county is about 43,000.

**Mermaids.** Even to this day some credulous people believe in the existence of "sea-maidens," and fancy that they have seen them coming up from the deep, or seated on the rocks. The mermaid is usually represented as a lovely woman with a human head but a body ending in the scaly tail of a fish. Among sailors she was often imagined as sitting on a rock combing her hair and singing, her appearance being supposed to portend a storm. Many stories are told of mermaids enticing human lovers to the depths of the sea. One of the legends told of the Lorelei rock on the River Rhine is of a singing siren. There are also tales of their leaving their ocean home and assuming a human form.

**Mesopotamia.** Now known as Iraq (*q.v.*), this is the land lying north-west of the Persian Gulf between the Rivers Tigris and Euphrates. It is a fertile plain originally formed from the silt brought down by those two rivers. Tradition has it that the Garden of Eden was situated in this region.

So fertile was Mesopotamia that the wandering tribes of the Arabian Desert on the west and of the uplands of what are now Iran and Turkey on the east and north looked upon it with greedy eyes. Successive tribes overran it, founding kingdoms and falling before more powerful foes. (*See* Babylonia).

In the southern part of Mesopotamia archaeologists have found remains dating from about 4000 B.C. In that era the Sumerians, who probably came from the mountainous north, settled there, building houses, constructing irrigation systems and creating what was, perhaps, the first civilization. They invented cuneiform (wedge-shaped) writing, and were the first people known to have used the potter's wheel. There was early connexion with Egypt, whose civilization seems to have owed some of its elements to the Sumerians.

After the Sumerians came the Semites from Arabia, who established themselves at Akkad on the Tigris, gradually absorbing Sumerian civilization. About 3000–2500 B.C. ancient Babylonia, or Southern Mesopotamia, was divided into numerous city-states, warring with each other. A second wave of Semites founded the Babylonian Empire, their King Hammurabi (2123–2081 B.C.) formulating the earliest known code of laws. In the 13th century B.C. Assyria overthrew Babylonia, becoming the dominant power in Eastern Mesopotamia.

In 612 B.C. the Medes (*q.v.*), with their Babylonian allies, captured the city of Nineveh, the

## MESOPOTAMIAN FLOODS

The two chief rivers of Mesopotamia (now Iraq) are the Tigris and the Euphrates, and the level of the land under normal conditions is very little higher than the rivers. Above, the Tigris in flood at Baghdad.

Assyrian city in Northern Mesopotamia, destroying that empire. Babylon then had a brief revival until 539 B.C., when it was taken by the Persians, who ruled there until 333 B.C. Then the Macedonian king, Alexander the Great, defeated the Persians. Alexander died at Babylon in 323, and Seleucus, one of his generals, secured the central part of his empire, including Mesopotamia. In A.D. 115 the Romans invaded the land, but were driven out by the Persians.

In 637 the Persians were decisively beaten by the Arabs, who annexed Mesopotamia in the following year, ruling the country for the next 400 years and making their capital, Baghdad, the cultural centre of the Middle East. Mongol invasions began in the 11th century, continuing for nearly 200 years. In 1516 Mesopotamia came under Turkish rule, and so remained until the Turkish defeat in the First World War (1914–18). The country first became known as Iraq in 1919, when the Arab kingdom of that name was established.

Valuable archaeological discoveries have been made at the Sumerian city of Ur by the British Museum and the Pennsylvania University joint expeditions.

### RECOVERED FROM MESOPOTAMIA'S DUST

Life in the Mesopotamia of 3,500 years ago is continually being made more real to us by archaeologists' discoveries. For instance, in a royal tomb 74 bodies were found and the floor was strewn with gold and silver ornaments, including this headdress. Experts reconstructed it and mounted it on a head moulded over a female skull of the period to show us what a lady of the court of Ur, a Sumerian city, may have looked like.

# Metallurgy. (Pron. me-tal'-êr-ji). This

is the science concerned with the study of metals, their extraction from ores, their purification, their physical and alloying properties, their microscopic and chemical structure, and the effects of temperature changes and mechanical treatment on their properties, etc. Quite a large subject!

The first man who discovered by accident how to extract a metal from a piece of stone may be said to be the first metallurgist, but the date when this happened is not known. Gold is found in Nature as the metal, and it was undoubtedly one of the earliest metals to be used by Man. Gold was known to the Ethiopians, and the Ancient Egyptians extracted the metal from its mixture with quartz, and made it into gold wire for embroidery.

Iron, which can be extracted from its ores only by mixing the ore with charcoal, wood, coal or coke, and strongly heating the mixture, was no doubt discovered later than gold, though steel was known to the Chinese as far back as 2220 B.C. and they knew also how to " temper " it.

These ancient men laid the foundations of what was much later to become our science of metallurgy. Today no enterprise of any importance connected with the manufacture, working and use of metals is begun until metallurgists have explored the possibilities and have reported on them. The smelting of ores, and the compounding of various metals into alloys; the many forms of heat treatment; the testing of metals and alloys, and the physical and chemical examination of them—all these fall into the province of the metallurgist He may be called upon to design new plant for new processes, and to preside at the inauguration of new methods in dealing with old problems.

Large concerns which make or use metals employ metallurgists constantly on research and investigation. The National Physical Laboratory (a Government institution) has a Metallurgy Division staffed by scientific and experimental officers. (See Alloys; Iron and Steel; Metals).

# Metals. About three-fourths of the chem-

ical elements are classified as metals. To the chemist, an element is a metal if its oxide forms a base with water, as do sodium and iron; and it is a non-metal if its oxide forms an acid with water, as do sulphur and phosphorus (see Acids and Alkalis). Yet the line cannot be sharply drawn between metals and non-metals, for some elements, like arsenic and antimony, have properties characteristic of both.

Ordinarily we think of metals as having certain properties, such as weight, hardness, malleability, ductility, and as having a crystalline structure capable of taking a polish, and as being good conductors of heat and electricity. But not all metals have these properties. Mercury is a liquid; antimony and bismuth are brittle; sodium and potassium are extremely soft; lithium weighs little more than half as much as water. Metals vary greatly in their melting-points, from mercury, which melts from the frozen state to a liquid at 37° F. below zero, to tungsten, which is believed to melt at about 5,900° F. They also vary in chemical activity; some metals, like potassium and sodium, combine vigorously with even cold water; some, like gold and platinum, react only with the strongest and most active chemical agents.

Many metals have properties in the pure state that are undesirable to Man, and as a consequence most of the metals we see in common use are either alloys or compounds. Table silver, pennies, solder, bronze, the metals of tools and machinery, of buildings and locomotives, are alloys. Pure iron, for example, is too soft to be of much value; therefore steel, an alloy, is more generally used. Other metals such as chromium are sometimes alloyed with steel for hardness, and for resistance to corrosion.

Some metals are found in the pure state, but by far the greater part of them are in combination with other elements in the form of sulphides, oxides, carbonates, and silicates, usually mixed with rock and earthy materials (see Minerals). Lead, zinc, iron, copper, chromium, nickel, and mercury are among the common metals found in combination in ores. Some metals are quite rare, and tons of ore must be treated to recover even a small amount of the pure metal. Among these are rubidium, caesium, and radium.

The correct blending of metals to produce alloys (q.v.) having any desired properties forms a part of the science of metallurgy (q.v.). Until fairly recent times, iron and copper were the two important metals used in alloys for engineering purposes; but nowadays aeroplanes, motorcars, and other machines, as well as domestic utensils such as saucepans, kettles, and preserving pans, are being made from alloys of aluminium and of magnesium. Some of these alloys, though much lighter than steel, are as strong as steel itself.

Now that the arrangement of the atoms in metals has been studied by means of X-rays, we understand more clearly why metals and their alloys have certain properties, and why those properties can be changed by heat treatment (e.g. the " tempering " of steel).

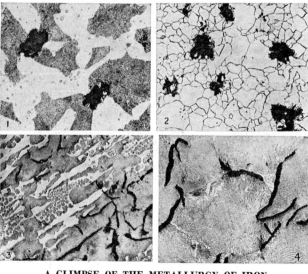

**A GLIMPSE OF THE METALLURGY OF IRON**
Sectional microphotographs of four kinds of iron reveal striking differences in their composition. Fig. 1, Whiteheart malleable ; Fig. 2, Blackheart ; Fig. 3, Mottled ; Fig. 4, Grey cast-iron.

*R. L. Mitchell*

**HOW METALLIC SALTS AFFECT GROWTH**
The badly developed lamb in front (above) has been grazing on herbage deficient in cobalt. The larger animal in the background, kept in the same pasture, has been receiving supplementary doses of cobalt salt in solution.

Some metals are necessary to plant and animal life. Iron is present in the red colouring matter (haemoglobin) of blood; calcium phosphate forms the greater part of bony structure; sodium, in the form of sodium chloride (NaCl), is an essential constituent of blood and other body fluids; potassium and magnesium play a part. In addition to these metals, needed in relatively large quantities by animals and plants, we now believe that minute quantities of other metals are necessary to maintain good health.

For example, it seems that the body cannot assimilate iron from our diet, to form haemoglobin, unless a very small quantity of copper is also present; and lambs fed on grass entirely free from cobalt do not develop properly (*see* illustration). Zinc, molybdenum, and manganese are among other metals which must be supplied in very small quantities if plants, and the animals which feed on the plants, are to thrive. As research progresses, we may have to add to this list of "trace" metals, necessary to plants and animals, including Man.

**Meteorology.** The study of atmospheric conditions and the physical processes at work there is called meteorology; in turn this is a branch of the wider science of physics. An idea of the extent of the variation in the properties of the air (*see* Air) may be conveyed from the fact that, within a few feet of the ground, the temperature has ranged from about $+130°$ F. on a summer afternoon in the Libyan desert to $-95°$ F. during a Siberian winter night. Ten miles above the equator it is even colder, and a temperature of $-130°$ F. has been recorded.

Scientific investigations, carried out during the Second World War (1939–45), showed that at this height the atmosphere is extremely dry and contains only a minute fraction of the water required to produce saturation, i.e. a relative humidity of 100 per cent. Even if the air were saturated the proportion of water vapour present would still be comparatively small, since cold air cannot hold as much as warm air. The highest clouds seen over England are seldom more than six or seven miles above the surface. About three-quarters of the total weight of air is contained in this column. Thus, at a height of seven miles the atmospheric pressure is only one-quarter of that at ground level.

The beginnings of the study of weather can be traced to the ancient civilizations, where weather entered into the daily life. For example, the Greeks—to whom we owe the word "meteorology"—observed the winds because of their practical use in navigation. In the course of time men learnt to associate certain phenomena with certain types of weather. The originators of such weather-lore were probably the fisherman, the farmer, and other out-of-doors folk, who before going to the sea or harvesting the corn, tried to deduce from the appearance of the sky what the day's weather would be like.

With the general development of scientific instruments in the 17th century there began a gradual transition from the descriptive to the exact. In this new era, the thermometer (*q.v.*) of Galileo and the barometer (*q.v.*) of Torricelli provided the means of measuring the temperature and pressure of the air. The meteorological elements whose values are normally required to specify atmospheric conditions are, in addition to temperature and pressure, humidity, wind, precipitation (rain, snow, etc.) and clouds.

**Distinction Between Weather and Climate**

While the term "weather" is used to denote the changes which occur at any place from hour to hour or day to day, by "climate" we mean a summary of the weather, averaged over each month or season of the year. Every major country of the world has now a well-established network of observing stations which are representative of the different regions, and which regularly transmit reports of observations made at fixed times to a central Meteorological Office. In the British Meteorological Service there are several hundred stations at which complete observations are available at hourly intervals; at more than 5,000 other places in the United Kingdom rainfall is recorded.

One of the aims of the meteorologist is to forecast the course of the weather for some time to come. The first daily weather report, based upon observations obtained simultaneously, was made possible by the invention of the electric telegraph, copies of this novel publication being on sale at the Great Exhibition, in Hyde Park, London, in 1851. A feature of present-day synoptic meteorology, as this branch of the subject is known, is the rapid exchange, by radio, of the fundamental observations between the various countries, in order to enable each major forecasting centre to have the maximum amount of material on which to base its forecasts.

The duties of the International Meteorological Organization, which was formed towards the end of the 19th century, include the standardizing of observations and the co-ordinating of the procedures in the countries taking part; this body, whose membership is composed of the heads of the official meteorological services, is truly world-wide, as it sets going any necessary measures for the development or improvement of international meteorology.

Weather charts normally consist of the observations (made at a particular time throughout the area concerned) plotted on a suitable map, thus giving a geographical distribution of the prevailing elements. Definite meteorological "systems" are recognized, such as the depressions and the anti-cyclones, which are in effect series of closed isobars (i.e. lines of equal pressure) encircling regions where the barometric pressure is respectively lower or higher than the surroundings. These systems may retain their identity for days at a time, and frequently travel long distances carrying their own characteristic weather with them.

### Back to the Wind in Two Hemispheres

The relation of the wind to the pressure distribution was discovered, in 1860, by the Dutch meteorologist Buys-Ballot, who stated that if one stands with one's back to the wind in the northern hemisphere pressure will be lower to the left than to the right; in the southern hemisphere the reverse conditions hold. A glance at a weather map is sufficient to verify the truth of this law. In the northern hemisphere the winds blow counter-clockwise round centres of low pressure, spiralling inwards slightly; and they blow clockwise round centres of high pressure.

If charts are prepared showing, for the entire globe, the distribution, over each of the 12 months, of the mean pressure, temperature, and so on, a picture is obtained of the general circulation of the atmosphere. These may be regarded as the background upon which are overlaid the local, short-lived circulations with which the day-to-day forecaster is concerned. Amongst other features such general charts demonstrate the tendency, in the northern hemisphere, for anti-cyclones to form over the continents in winter and over the oceans in summer; and for low pressures to form over the oceans in winter and over the continents in summer.

The atmosphere of the earth may be compared to a gigantic heat engine. When the sky is cloudless, solar energy heats the ground without much interference from the atmosphere and, in turn, the ground warms up the neighbouring layer of air. Unlike the radiation from the sun, that from the earth is readily absorbed by water vapour ; hence the great importance of this constituent. Substances which are good absorbers of heat, however, are also good radiators; and, at a certain height, a layer will be reached where the loss of heat exceeds the gain. It is here that the cold source of the heat engine will be located, as compared with the hot source found in the tropics or middle latitudes. In the cold regions the air will sink and in the warm ones it will rise, thus leading to a flow of air horizontally. The clouds serve to regulate the temperature at the earth's surface, since they are capable of reflecting solar energy away from the upper surfaces and, at the same time, of preventing terrestrial energy from escaping to space.

It is the depressions and anticyclones, in effect huge whirls in the easterly and westerly air streams, which are responsible for the interchange of air between the cold polar and warm tropical masses. And, according to the so-called frontal theory, developed by the Norwegian school of meteorology, weather is mainly caused by such interactions of air masses of different geographical origin, which are involved in the wind systems. The boundary regions between these air masses are " fronts."

At a warm front, the warmer air is forced to climb up over the underlying cold air, and its approach can therefore be detected by steadily descending clouds, finally producing a wide belt of rain. At a cold front, the heavier cold air approaches and undercuts the lighter warm air, forming towering clouds, showery rain, and sometimes thunderstorms, which arrive not ahead of, but simultaneously with, the front.

Instrumental measurements of atmospheric conditions are not confined to the earth's surface. In 1898 Teisserenc de Bort discovered that the normal upward decrease of temperature with height (roughly 1°F. per 300 feet) ceased at a certain level, above which the temperature was either constant or even increased slightly. It is not known how far the *stratosphere*—as this upper region is termed—extends upwards, but there is good reason to believe that at 20–25 miles above the sea the temperature begins to rise again at about the same rate as it falls in the *troposphere*, as the lower region is termed. The base of the stratosphere is variable. On the average, it is at 10 miles in the tropics and six miles at the poles. Since the greater height through which the temperature decreases can offset the higher temperatures at the equatorial surface compared with that at the poles, it may be said that the coldest known region is 10 miles above the equator (−130° F.).

With few exceptions the formation of cloud and rain is confined to the troposphere, and the absence of weather in the stratosphere commends it to long distance aviation flights. Not infrequently the decrease of temperature with height is interrupted by layers in which the temperature is either constant or rising. Such a layer is known as an inversion and is associated with stable conditions in the atmosphere. On the other hand, should the rate of decrease exceed a certain limit (e.g. as a result of strong heating at the earth's surface) the atmosphere becomes unstable and thunderstorms may develop.

### Getting Information of the Upper Air

Radio-sonde methods are now largely employed to obtain upper air information, and in the British service four ascents to the stratosphere are made each day at selected stations. Miniature weather stations, carried by balloons filled with hydrogen, automatically transmit signals which are representative of the values of temperature, pressure and humidity, at the various levels. Radar targets, attached to the balloons, are followed from the ground; in this way the strength and direction of the upper winds can be deduced.

Meteorology has applications of vast economic importance. Commercial, agricultural and engineering projects frequently are dependent upon meteorological knowledge. Nowhere, perhaps, is the connexion so intimate as with aviation; questions regarding the icing of aircraft, lightning risk, winds, fog on airfields, are vital to the airman.

The mariner has long contributed to, as well as received benefits from, weather science. The meteorological observations made regularly on ships and reported to the official services have now been supplemented by a network of Ocean Weather Ships which, to all intents and purposes, are stationary in the Atlantic and carry out a full programme of surface and upper air observations. They are also equipped for air-sea rescue work.

The atmosphere is the meteorologist's laboratory, and since the Second World War many new instruments and techniques have been developed, e.g. apparatus for the detection of thunderstorms, the application of radar to the study of the distribution of the sizes of water droplets in clouds, and the artificial stimulation of rain.

**Meteors** AND METEORITES. On many clear nights when there is no moon you may see " shooting stars "—those objects that flash brightly across the heavens for a brief moment and are gone. Actually they are not stars at all, for stars are great bodies like the sun, while " shooting stars," or meteors, are tiny bits of matter, often no bigger than a grain of sand. But they are travelling so fast—26 miles a second on the average—that when they strike the earth's atmosphere they grow flaming hot, and

are entirely consumed as a rule before they reach a distance of more than 30 miles from the ground. There is little doubt that some meteors are particles of comets which have broken up.

One proof of the connexion between comets and meteors is that swarms of meteors travel on orbits or paths which were once occupied by comets. When the earth passes through one of these orbits we have meteoric " showers."

Since most meteors are individually very small, it is believed that their total masses amount only to 350 tons in a year. Most of this is added to our atmosphere in the form of gases, but part of it is probably deposited on the earth as ash or small particles.

Objects similar to meteors sometimes strike the earth. These are known as meteorites or aerolites, and it is probable that they are meteors which are large enough to get through the atmosphere before being burned up. Meteorites may weigh from a few ounces to many tons. They are mostly of a stony character, though about one in every ten is composed principally of iron. This iron is combined with nickel, cobalt, copper, etc., in a way different from any combination found on earth.

Armour plate was first made as a result of the knowledge gained through analysis of meteorite

**A  METEOR'S  FIERY  COURSE  ACROSS  THE  SKY**

Usually a meteor travels quietly along on its regular orbit through space (upper). But when it nears a planet, such as the Earth, it plunges toward its vastly larger neighbour, its passage across the sky often being followed by a noise like distant thunder. Heat generated by friction with the Earth's atmosphere ignites the rushing mass (lower), so that it is seen as a streak of fire. But the flaming trail lasts only a few seconds, because the meteor is soon consumed.

### VAST CRATER CAUSED BY A METEORITE'S CRASH

Meteorites, which are distinct from meteors, sometimes reach the Earth. Here is shown a tremendous pit near Winslow, in Arizona, United States, believed to have been made by a meteorite. The crater is four-fifths of a mile wide and 570 feet deep, and meteoritic iron is scattered within a radius of five miles. Drillings from the southern rim (in shadow) struck what scientists consider may be the meteorite itself, at a depth of 1,400 feet.

composition. In cutting up iron meteorites it was found that those having 90 per cent of iron and about 10 per cent of nickel were very hard and extremely difficult to slice. By mixing iron and nickel in the same proportions a steel was made which was harder and tougher than any known at that time.

A meteorite weighing some 70 tons was found in Tanganyika in 1931. Near Winslow, in Arizona (U.S.A.), is Meteor Crater, 570 feet deep, believed to have been caused by a huge meteor. The largest meteor so far recorded is the one that struck central Siberia in 1908, laying waste an extensive area of forest land—fortunately uninhabited. This probably consisted of a shower of meteorites weighing altogether several hundred tons.

Many swarms of meteors seem to fall from a single point in the sky which is called the " radiant," and the various swarms or groups are named from the constellation in which the radiant appears to lie. Thus we have the Leonids, Perseids, etc. The Leonids are active in November; other groups appear in August, April, September and October. Nowadays these meteor showers (or rather the clouds of conducting gas they produce in the upper air) can be detected by radar, for they reflect radar waves just as aeroplanes do.

**Meters.** If you use gas or electricity in your home there is sure to be a measuring instrument called a meter fixed in some convenient place. This meter is " read " periodically by an official of the supply company, and the amount of gas or of current used since the previous reading is charged in the next bill. Many householders use a prepayment meter, having a coin-box into which they can insert shillings or pennies to pay in advance.

It is seldom that water meters are installed in houses, since water is paid for usually by means of the " water rate," a fixed percentage on the annual value of the house, charged by quarterly or half-yearly bills. But factories and similar concerns pay for their water by the quantity consumed, and then, of course, a meter is interposed between the supply main and the building.

The induction type of electricity meter for alternating current is the commonest. It is really an electric motor, of which the revolving member, or armature, is a metal disk. The current used in the house passes around the coils of the electromagnets which drive the disk. The latter is geared to the tiny shaft of the registering mechanism, which consists of a number of ten-toothed gear wheels and is, in fact, a calculating machine (q.v.). The speed of the disk is proportional to the amount of current passing through the meter, so the number of revolu-

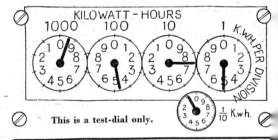

This is a test-dial only.

| DATE | READINGS | UNITS USED |
|------|----------|------------|
| July 1st | 8090 | |
| Oct. 1st | 8724 | 634 |
| Jan. 2nd | 9475 | 751 |

### READING AN ELECTRICITY METER

To find out how much electricity has been used since the last reading, look first at the dial on the right. Write down —in order of units, tens, hundreds and thousands—the lower of the two figures between which the indicator may be pointing (if between 9 and 0, read 9). Do the same for the other dials. Subtract from the figure obtained the reading on the last quarter's bill, and you have the number of kilowatt-hours or Board of Trade Units used.

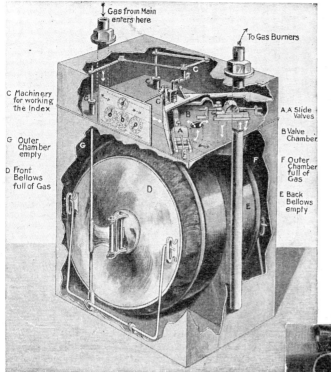

C Machinery for working the Index

G Outer Chamber empty

D Front Bellows full of Gas

Gas from Main enters here

To Gas Burners

A, A Slide Valves

B Valve Chamber

F Outer Chamber full of Gas

E Back Bellows empty

### HOW GAS IS MEASURED IN A METER

The measuring chambers are the two bellows (D, E) and the two lower compartments (F, G) in which they work. The valves and valve-ports which, in turn, allow gas to enter and leave the different receptacles are housed inside a gas-tight chamber seen on the right of the top compartment. It is the movements of the bellows, as they expand and collapse with the passage of gas through them, which turns the counting wheels of the recording mechanism at the top (see detailed description in the text). The dials, shown below, are read like those of the electric meter described on the preceding page, except that the right-hand dial shows hundreds instead of units.

| 10,000 | 1,000 | 100 |
|---|---|---|

| WRITE DATE HERE | | 5 | 3 | 8 | 0 | 0 |
|---|---|---|---|---|---|---|
| 5—20 | READING THIS MONTH | 5 | 3 | 8 | 0 | 0 |
| 4—20 | READING LAST MONTH | 5 | 2 | 2 | 0 | 0 |
| | DIFFERENCE | | 1 | 6 | 0 | 0 |
| | (Showing number of cubic feet of gas used during current month) | | | | | |

motor disk and the first gear wheel, are made to measure the current in the way desired. Electricity is sold in Board of Trade units, or kilowatt-hours; such an unit represents 1 kilowatt (1,000 watts) of electric power used for 1 hour. Therefore the primary gearing is designed so that the meter reads in kilowatt-hours (abbreviated kWh.). In heating, 1 kWh. is equivalent to 3,415 British Thermal Units.

Gas meters are of two main types, the "wet" and the "dry." We shall only describe the dry meter. It consists of a sheet-metal box with a small upper compartment (for the registering mechanism) and two larger compartments below, for the meter proper. Fixed to each side of the partition between the two lower compartments is a bellows made of circular plates and leather sides. Inside a gas-tight casing over part of the top compartment are valve-ports and valves which communicate with the insides of the bellows, and with each lower compartment outside the bellows. In passing through the lower compartments, and the bellows inside

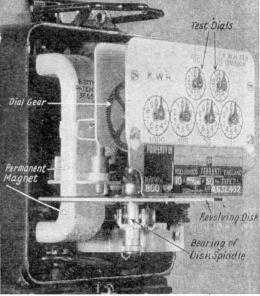

Test Dials

Dial Gear

K.W.H.

Permanent Magnet

Revolving Disk

Bearing of Disk Spindle

*Ferranti, Ltd.*

### HOW AN ELECTRICITY METER WORKS

Here you see the instrument which measures the electricity your lights use. The current passes through electro-magnets, causing rotation of the disk, the speed of which is controlled by the permanent magnet on the left. The spindle of the disk turns the pointers on the dials.

them, the gas is measured; the movements in and out of the bellows operate rods and levers and a crank, thus causing gear wheels in the top registering mechanism to move round and count up the amount of gas passing through the meter. The mechanism is shown in the diagram at top of page.

Gas first enters the triangular chamber (B), which is cut away to show the valves (A). The back valve (A) is open and admits gas to the back chamber

tions recorded on the dials indicates the amount of current used.

As in the calculating machine, the first ten-toothed wheel, in completing one revolution, moves on the next wheel a step; and the second wheel in turn (at the end of its revolution) moves on the third one a step. Thus the revolutions of the disk are counted up, and by suitable gearing between the

(F). In this chamber is a bellows (E) with its interior connected through a valve to the pipe supplying the burners. As soon as a burner is opened, releasing gas from inside the bellows, the pressure in the chamber (F) forces the diaphragm of the bellows inward. As it moves in, it pushes out, by means of a connecting rod, the diaphragm of the front bellows (D), which now sucks in gas from the front chamber (G). This chamber has been filled by a previous stroke of the meter. When the back bellows has been emptied in the manner described, the back valve in the triangular chamber (B) closes, and the front valve opens, admitting gas in the chamber (G). This forces the front bellows inward, and so the pumping goes on, like a mechanical heart. The system of rods (C) records the movements of the bellows on the dials and tells you how much gas has passed through the meter.

The price of gas is today based on its calorific or heating power, and unless we know the calorific value of any particular gas supply we cannot gauge its value. This value has to be declared by the company making the gas. The unit of heating power is the British Thermal Unit (abbreviated B.Th.U.). The unit by which gas is sold is the therm, consisting of 100,000 B.Th.U. One B.Th.U. represents the quantity of heat required to raise the temperature of 1 lb. of water by 1 degree Fahrenheit. Let us suppose that the declared calorific value of the gas you burn in your home is 450, and that your meter shows that you have consumed 11,300 cubic feet of gas since the last meter reading.

Then you multiply gas consumed (cubic feet) by the declared calorific value, and divide by 100,000, thus :

11,300 cubic ft. $\dfrac{11,300 \times 450}{100,000} = 50.85$ therms.

Originally gas was valued by its illuminating power, burnt in an open-flame burner. But since today we always use it in a Bunsen burner, whether for lighting, cooking or warming, it is the heat value which matters.

Water meters are of various types. The kind used for measuring the comparatively small quantity consumed by private concerns consists usually of a casing containing two pistons working in cylinders of known capacity. The water passes through each cylinder in turn, and the movement of the pistons is transmitted by levers and gearing to a registering mechanism not unlike that of the gas meter.

When large flows of water are to be measured a mechanism of a very different type is installed. It is generally one which utilises the "Venturi" principle, and as this is of some importance in physics it is worth while to describe it. The name is that of the 18th century Italian physicist who propounded the "Venturi law": Fluids under pressure in passing through *converging* pipes gain velocity at the expense of static pressure; and vice versa in passing through *diverging* pipes. In 1750 the Swiss scientist Daniel Bernouilli (1700–82) noticed that a liquid flowing through a pipe with a narrowing in its bore (forming a convergence on one side and a divergence on

the opposite side) increased in velocity at the narrowest point, and lost velocity again after passing this point.

The *total energy* of the flowing stream is the same in both the wide and narrow portions; but it is evident that, as the same amount of water must pass, the *rate of flow* must become speeded up through the narrow part of the pipe. The only way for this to happen is for some of the potential (or pressure) energy to become converted into energy of movement (kinetic energy). This conversion causes a drop of pressure at the narrowing in the tube, or "Venturi throat." So if we insert a vertical pipe into the throat or narrowing itself, and insert another vertical pipe at the "upstream" side of the throat, before the narrowing begins, the water in these two verticals will rise to different heights. In scientific terms there will be a drop in the "hydraulic gradient" between the tapping taken from the wide part of the pipe and that taken from the Venturi throat itself.

The diagram given below explains this, and shows how the vertical pipes each enter the bottom of a float chamber, and raise floats to different heights. Cords from the floats go to the recording mechanism; between them they actuate a pen which rises and falls, and traces a curve on a chart wound upon a drum turned regularly by clockwork. The chart is ruled with vertical lines to indicate time elapsed; and with horizontal lines for rate of flow. Further, the total flow of water is recorded on dials by wheels connected to the float mechanism.

**Metric System.** This system of measures and weights, based on the metre, was born of the French Revolution. The National Assembly of France, seeking to do away with the confusion arising from the many different systems of measurement used in different countries, set up a commission to devise some "natural" standard. The new measure was to be one which could easily be re-determined at any time ; it was also one which was to be invariable.

The commission decided to make the standard of length one ten-millionth of the distance from

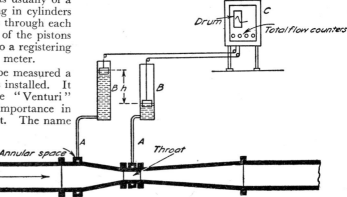

**METER FOR LARGE FLOWS OF WATER**
**Water flowing** through a narrowing of the pipe gains velocity and loses pressure (*see* text). By taking a tapping vertically from the wide part of the pipe, and another tapping from the narrowest part, or 'Venturi throat,' and leading these pipes to the bottom of the float chambers (A, A), we get a difference of water level. Cords take the float movement to the recorder (C), where dial mechanism translates it into rate-of-flow readings.

the Equator to the North Pole, measured on the meridian of Paris. This unit they called the metre (from the Greek word *metron*, " measure "). So much for the measure of *length*. Then, for a unit of *capacity*, the commission chose the volume of a cube each side of which was one-tenth of a metre in length; this unit they called the litre, intended to be equal to 1,000 cubic centimetres—or cubic hundredths of a metre. Next they established a standard of *mass*, which was to have the same weight as a litre of water at its temperature of maximum density—39 degrees Fahrenheit, or 4 degrees Centigrade. This unit they called the kilogram, equal to 1,000 grams.

Note that the standards of length, capacity and mass are related, derived from one single basic unit—the metre. It was a far-sighted scheme, admirable in introducing logical order into the confusion then existing. But, above all, the commission thought, there need never be any doubt about this basic unit, even if all standards made from it were lost or destroyed. One could always re-determine, they thought, the length of the quadrant of the meridian which, subdivided, gave the metre.

But as scientific methods of measurement developed it was found that the original determination of the length of the quadrant had been inaccurate. Today the " mean " distance from the Equator to the Pole (measured on the meridian of Paris) is taken as 10,002,100 metres, or 2,100 more than the original measurement. As a result, the metre is no longer a " natural " standard; it is defined as the distance, at the melting point of ice, between two marks engraved upon a metal bar made of platinum-iridium and kept at the International Bureau of Weights and Measures in the Pavillon de Breteuil at Sèvres, near Paris. This bar, made of metals selected for their resistance to corrosion and to temperature changes, is of X-section in order to avoid warping, etc, Exact copies of the bar have been made and are kept in the Weights and Measures departments of other countries which use the metric system.

Modern scientific research has established that the length of the quadrant of the meridian is not constant but changes slightly. It was discovered, also, that the volume of a kilogram of pure water (which ought to have been 1,000 cubic centimetres) was actually 1,000,028 c.c., so the intended relationship between the kilogram and litre no longer held good. Today, scientific measurement of volume is not by cubic centimetres, but by centilitres, or thousandths of a litre. But these inaccuracies are so tiny that they do not affect the value and inter-relation of the metric units for practical purposes. The metric system was legalized by the French Republic in 1795, and its use soon spread to other countries. For scientific purposes it is universal, and is the basis of the " C.G.S."—centimetre-gram-second—system of units.

The simplicity of the metric system, with its unit base of 10, renders it ideal for all purposes of calculation. The fundamental metric unit of length is the *metre*, which is 39·37 inches. Dividing the metre by 10, 100, and 1,000 gives the smaller units, distinguished by the Latin prefixes, *deci-*, *centi-*, and *milli-*; multiplying by the same numbers

gives the larger units, distinguished by the Greek prefixes *deca-*, *hecto-*. and *kilo-*, as in this table :

| 10 millimetres (mm.) | = | 1 centimetre (cm.) |
|---|---|---|
| 10 centimetres | = | 1 decimetre (dm.) |
| 10 decimetres | = | 1 metre (m.) |
| 10 metres | = | 1 decametre (dam.) |
| 10 decametres | = | 1 hectometre (hm.) |
| 10 hectometres | = | 1 kilometre (km.) |

The units most used in actual measurements of length are the *millimetre* (about 1·25 inch), the *centimetre* (about $\frac{2}{5}$ inch), the *metre*, and the *kilometre* about $\frac{5}{8}$ mile—(3,280·9 feet).

In surface measure the most common unit is the *hectare* (10,000 sq. metres = 2·471 acres).

A hollow cube measuring 10 *centimetres* on each edge would hold 1 *litre*, the basic unit of capacity in the metric system. It is just over $1\frac{3}{4}$ pints. It is divided and multiplied to make the smaller and larger units, respectively, viz. :

| 10 millilitres (ml.) | = | 1 centilitre (cl.) |
|---|---|---|
| 10 centilitres | = | 1 decilitre (dl.) |
| 10 decilitres | = | 1 litre (l.) |
| 10 litres | = | 1 decalitre (dal.) |
| 10 decalitres | = | 1 hectolitre (hl.) |
| 10 hectolitres | = | 1 kilolitre (kl.) |

The *litre* and the *hectolitre* are the units in this table chiefly employed. Dry and liquid measures are identical in the metric system; but where the metric system is employed in commerce there is the same tendency to buy and sell by weight instead of dry measure.

The *gram* is the basic metric unit of weight. Multiplied and divided for larger and smaller units, it gives :

| 10 milligrams (mg.) | = | 1 centigram (cg.) |
|---|---|---|
| 10 centigrams | = | 1 decigram (dg.) |
| 10 decigrams | = | 1 gram (g.) |
| 10 grams | = | 1 decagram (dag.) |
| 10 decagrams | = | 1 hectogram (hg.) |
| 10 hectograms | = | 1 kilogram (kg.) |
| 10 kilograms | = | 1 myriagram |
| 10 myriagrams | = | 1 quintal (q.) |
| 10 quintals | = | 1 metric ton (t.) |

The *milligram* and *centigram* are chiefly used in exact scientific work. The units most used in ordinary transactions are the *gram*, ·035 ounce; the *kilogram*, about $2\frac{1}{5}$ pounds (2·2046 pounds avoirdupois); the *quintal*, about 220 pounds; and the metric ton (·985 ton avoirdupois).

**Metz.** Capital of the Moselle department of France, Metz stands on the River Moselle in an agricultural and wine-growing district. It has shoe, jam and tobacco factories, and is an important railway junction. The most impressive building in the city is the Gothic Cathedral of St. Stephen which, begun in the 13th century, was not completed until the 16th century.

The capital of Lorraine in 843, Metz was a city of the Holy Roman Empire from the 13th century until 1552, when it was captured by Henry II of France. Heavily fortified by the French in the 17th century, it was unsuccessfully besieged by the Allies in 1814–15 in their campaign against Napoleon Bonaparte. The city surrendered to the Germans during the Franco-Prussian War (1870–71) and at the conclusion of hostilities passed to Germany, together with much of Lorraine.

After the First World War (1914–18) Metz became French once more and was regarded as one of

France's main military strongholds. Occupied again by the Germans on June 17, 1940, during the Second World War (1939–45), Metz was liberated by United States forces in November 1944. The population is 70,100.

**Meuse,** RIVER. This river of western Europe rises in north-eastern France and flows northwards into Belgium, where it receives at Namur its chief tributary, the Sambre, which almost doubles its volume. Flowing north-east across Belgium, it enters the Netherlands at Maastricht, being known at that point as the Maas. Curving to the west it joins the Waal, an arm of the Rhine, then divides again, flowing into the North Sea by several mouths.

A curious feature of the Meuse is that it disappears below ground for some three miles shortly before it enters Belgium. The direct distance between its source and its mouth is only 230 miles, but because of its many windings its actual length is 575 miles, of which 305 miles are in France, 120 miles in Belgium, 150 miles in the Netherlands. It is navigable up to a point near Verdun, and is connected by canals with the Marne, the Rhine and the Saône.

The river came into prominence in the fighting in the First World War (1914–1918), a battle between French and Germans taking place on its banks around Liége towards the end of August 1914; and again in the Second World War (1939–1945), for it was at Sedan, a town on the banks of the Meuse, that the Germans broke through in May 1940 and so succeeded in out-flanking the Maginot Line. After the Allied landings in Normandy in June 1944, United States troops crossed the Meuse at Sedan on August 31 unopposed, the Germans then being in rapid retreat.

# REAL LIFE *in* ROMANTIC MEXICO

*M**ost of us are familiar with the aspect of the Mexican cowboy, with his flashing teeth, his ear-rings and sombrero, for we have seen him on the 'pictures.' But life in the republic is not all romance.*

**Mexico.** Land of Cortes and the Aztecs, of silver mines and rolling plains, vast cattle-ranges, pieces of eight and stilettos, of caballeros and señoritas—such is Mexico, the great republic lying between the United States and the republics of Central America. It has an area of 763,944 square miles—greater than that of Great Britain, Germany, and France combined. Its shape is, appropriately enough, much like that of a horn of plenty. The coastline extends a distance of 1,727 miles on the Gulf of Mexico, and for 4,574 miles on the Pacific.

Majestic mountains, rising abruptly from the shores of the Atlantic, greet the eye of the traveller entering the magnificent harbour of Vera Cruz. In general, however, the land surface rises gently from the east and west coasts and from the Rio Grande to the broad tableland of the interior, where most of the mining and the agriculture are carried on, and where most of the people live.

There are no good natural harbours on the east coast, but much money has been spent to make Tampico and Vera Cruz serve the needs of the country. Progreso is the great sisal shipping port of the State of Yucatan. Excellent harbours abound on the west coast, however, among the more important being Mazatlan, Salina Cruz (the terminus of the railway across the Isthmus of Tehuantepec), Acapulco, Guaymas and La Paz.

The boundary between Mexico and the United States is 1,833 miles long, of which 1,136 miles are constituted by the Rio Grande river. South of the border are majestic mountain ranges known as the Sierra Madre Oriental (Eastern) and the Sierra Madre Occidental (Western). These mountain chains form a link of the great Cordilleran system, and contain some of the grandest scenery in America. Several of the highest peaks are found in Mexico, among them being the extinct volcanoes of Popocatepetl (17,520 feet), Orizaba (17,400 feet), and Ixtaccihuatl (16,960 feet).

The climate of Mexico varies widely with the height above sea-level. Hot weather prevails generally on the coasts, and hurricanes may occur between August and October. As one penetrates farther into the interior, however, the weather becomes delightfully cool and bracing. One finally reaches the region of perpetual spring at an elevation of 3,000 to 6,000 feet, a region where extremes of heat and cold are unknown. So slight is the variation of temperature that wheat and sugar-cane are grown side by side. From an elevation of 6,000 feet upwards extend the *tierras frias*, or cold lands. During the rainy season, from the middle of May to October, torrential storms drench the southern half of the republic, but the mountain ranges bordering the plateau prevent the moist winds from reaching the interior, so that nearly all the farming land requires irrigation.

Most fruits flourish in Mexico, and nearly every variety of grain grows luxuriantly in the rich soil. More than half the farming land is devoted to maize, from which the favourite flat cake of the Mexicans, the tortilla, is made. Millions of acres bear trees whose woods are the most valuable in the world for industry.

---

**Extent.**—Greatest length (north-west to south-east) more than 1,900 miles ; width, from 1,800 miles along the northern boundary to 134 miles at the Isthmus of Tehuantepec. Area, 763,944 square miles (including island groups off the coast). It is divided into 28 States, one Federal District and three Territories. Population 22,178,490.

**Physical Features.**—Mountain ranges : Eastern Sierra Madre and Western Sierra Madre (highest peaks, Orizaba, 17,400 feet, and Popocatepetl, 17,520 feet) ; central plateau 6,000 to 9,500 feet high. Principal rivers : Rio Grande, Conchos, Sonora and Yaqui.

**Chief Products.**—Petroleum ; silver gold, copper, lead, zinc, antimony ; maize, cotton, wheat, sisal hemp, coffee, beans, sugar-cane, tobacco, fruit ; live-stock ; sugar and tobacco manufactures, textiles, spirits and wine.

**Principal Cities.**—Mexico City (capital ; population 1 468,420), Guadalajara (227,730), Puebla (137,970), Monterey (125,100), Mérida (98,630).

---

## MEXICO : ONE OF THE WORLD'S RICHEST TREASURE LANDS

Lofty mountains, rising from coastal plains, hem in the central plateau of Mexico on three sides. That portion of the New World called Latin America begins at the United States-Mexican frontier, with great differences not only in language but in culture and tradition. Mexico is young as a nation, but its distinctive culture is old, for it is essentially an Indian nation. The country is rich in mineral resources, but large areas are undeveloped because of transport difficulties.

The mountains form one vast deposit of valuable minerals. Nearly all the famous mines of Mexico are situated on the south central plateau at an elevation of 5,500 to 9,500 feet. Silver is found in all the States, but more than half has come from Zacatecas, San Luis Potosi, and Guanajuato. The Veta Madre lode of Guanajuato is one of the richest veins ever discovered. Enormous quantities of lead are found, in association with the silver. Gold, copper, antimony, quicksilver, vanadium, bismuth, zinc, manganese and graphite are among the other mineral resources, and tin has been found at Chihuahua. Iron is abundant. Engineers estimate the amount of ore in sight on the famous Cerro del Mercado at 500,000,000 tons. So far, lack of fuel has made it impossible to work much of it.

The history of oil in Mexico makes a veritable romance. Although the presence of oil and asphalt in great quantities had been known for many years, attempts on the part of Mexicans to extract this wealth failed. In 1883 wells were sunk in Tabasco without result. Repeated failures discouraged investors until 1901, when operations were begun at Ebano. The Americans then opened up the Casiano district and drilled the greatest oil-gushing well the world had ever seen, known as Casiano No. 7. Much of the petroleum is now refined in Mexico, though formerly most of it was shipped abroad for purifying. The wells were acquired by the Mexican Government in 1938.

Hundreds of thousands of acres on the northern plateaux are devoted to stock-raising. Here may be seen the Mexican cowboy—a magnificent horseman and a colourful figure in his wide-brimmed hat, embroidered jacket and big silver spurs. Many of these riders use saddles and bridles heavily ornamented with silver. Cotton-milling is a great industry, and overshadows the woollen mills, since the local demand is chiefly for cotton garments. The numerous fibre plants support a considerable rope and cordage industry. There are many soap and cotton-seed oil factories.

The manufacture of iron and steel products, including rails and the smaller agricultural implements, has grown considerably, especially around Monterey, in recent years. Rubber is manufactured where the guayule plant grows. Mexican cigar and cigarette factories not only supply all local needs but export manufactured tobacco and cigars to Europe and the United States. Soap is made in considerable quantities. There are many flour mills and sugar mills, and the manufacture of native drinks forms a large adjunct to the country's internal commerce. Oranges, bananas, guavas, avocado pears, and custard-apples are grown in abundance. The most important Mexican plant, however, is the agave or maguey; its fibres are used to make paper and rope, and its huge leaves serve as thatch for native houses.

The yield of maize. wheat, and other cereals in orderly times is large, but has been seriously interfered with by revolutions. The Mexican bean, the frijol, is grown in every State of the republic, and with maize forms the staple diet of the people. The forests contain many rare and valuable woods. Logwood and other dyewoods are largely

On May 19, 1822, a Spaniard named Augustin de Iturbide proclaimed himself Emperor of Mexico and independent of Spain. He was dethroned the following year and later put to death. Half a

The floating gardens of Xochimilco, 10 miles from Mexico City, existed long before the arrival of the Spaniards in 1519. In the shallow lake are floating masses of water-plants which support soil and are attached to poplar stakes that take root in the bed of the lake, thus anchoring the islands. On them are grown fruits and flowers for the city.

exported. Huge quantities of henequen, or sisal hemp, are exported from Yucatan, making it one of the richest states in Mexico.

For centuries Mexico has been the cradle of wars—wars of conquest, wars of defence, civil wars. In prehistoric times one native race after another dominated the country. When the Spaniards under Cortes (q.v.) invaded and conquered Mexico (1519–21) they found the Aztecs in power, under Emperor Montezuma (see Aztecs). In 1810, after three centuries in which Spain ruthlessly exploited the country and ill-treated the natives, Miguel Hidalgo, a parish priest, led a revolt; but he was captured and shot in 1811. Others kept the flame of revolt alive.

## THINGS TO SEE IN MEXICO
Just south of Mexico City a line of volcanoes crosses the country, one of them being Popocatepetl (above), whose name means Smoking Mountain. Like most volcanic countries Mexico is sometimes shaken by earthquakes.

century of civil war and revolution followed. For 30 years the dominant figure was General Antonio Lopez de Santa Anna, who was president when Texas revolted and again during the war with the U.S.A. Texas won its independence from Mexico in 1835, but 10 years later boundary disputes with the United States resulted in another war. Santa Anna's rule ended with his exile in 1855.

When President Juarez announced a two-year suspension of payments on foreign loans in 1861, France, under the Emperor Napoleon III, attacked and overthrew the Mexican government. The French troops suffered a severe defeat on May 5, 1862, whence comes the Mexican national holiday known as the Cinco de Mayo

(5th of May). In 1863 France declared Mexico an empire with Maximilian I, an Austrian archduke, as Emperor. The United States protested against this violation of the Monroe Doctrine, and at the close of the American Civil War France withdrew its troops.

The leader of the Mexican patriots, Porfirio Diaz, then captured Mexico City, in 1867, and took Maximilian prisoner. The latter was tried by court-martial, and shot. In 1877 Diaz secured the presidency after overthrowing Juarez's successor. The progress of Mexico between 1884 and 1911, while Diaz ruled as a benevolent dictator, was perhaps greater than the sum total of the progress achieved by Mexico in all the centuries of its previous history.

*Dorien Leigh*

**THE OLD SPANISH CATHEDRAL OF MEXICO CITY**
In most of the principal cities of South America there are Roman Catholic cathedrals, some of them dating back to the days of the Spanish Conquest in the 16th century. One of the most remarkable of these is that of Mexico City, standing in the Plaza de la Constitución. It was begun in 1573, and was built on the site of the Aztec war-god's temple destroyed by Cortes, the conqueror of Mexico, in 1521. The church was not completed until 1730.

Between 1911 and 1934 there were no fewer than 17 presidents; but in spite of almost constant civil war a great deal of beneficial work was done in developing the land. By a new constitution, set forth in 1917, the great estates were broken up. Over 65 million acres were let among 1,600,000 peasants.

Archaeologists are finding relics of the advanced Mayan and Aztec civilizations that flourished centuries ago, and Mayan art and architecture are having an influence on modern work. The twentieth-century revival of Mexican art has brought recognition in foreign lands to such painters as Diego Rivera and José Clemente Orozco. Mexican craftsmen, under conditions that still remain primitive, are turning out pottery, woven goods, feather work, and leather work which show the artistic skill that is their racial heritage.

Mexico is a federated republic, and the president is elected for a term of six years. The country is divided into 28 states, three territories and a federal district. The prevailing religion is the Roman Catholic, though none is officially recognized by the State. Education is provided free and is compulsory.

**Mexico City.** The picturesque capital of the Republic of Mexico lies almost mid-way between the east and west coasts, on the great central plateau of Mexico, about 7,400 feet above sea-level and 200 miles north-west of Vera Cruz. To the south tower the rugged Ajusco Mountains, and to the south-east the snow-clad Popocatepetl and Ixtaccihuatl peaks. The 30-mile Canal del Desague, completed in 1900, with its many branches drains the lake area to the east, and removes the sewage of the city.

The city is laid out with almost unbroken regularity. On the western side are the better residential sections; on the east lie the poorer districts. The buildings are low because of the frequent earthquake shocks. The commercial and political centre of the city is the Plaza Mayor. Facing this are the Spanish Renaissance cathedral (16th century), the national palace, and the municipal palace. North of the national palace is the national museum, which houses an almost priceless collection of Aztec antiquities. Leading from the public gardens is the magnificent boulevard Paseo de la Reforma, over three miles long.

Mexico City, the oldest city in North America, was founded about 1325 by the Aztecs, who built a village of mud and rush dwellings on little islets in Lake Texcoco and called it Mexitli, in honour of their god of war. It grew rapidly, and in the 15th century the crude dwellings were replaced by stone structures. The town had reached the height of its glory when, in 1519, the Spaniards under Cortes appeared and practically destroyed it. It was rebuilt by natives under the direction of the conqueror. The city's population is 1,468,420.

**Mica.** A piece of this mineral an inch thick can be split into about a thousand sheets, each as thin as the thinnest tissue-paper. For its familiar use in the doors of stoves and as chimneys for incandescent gas-burners, it is split into sheets about as thick as heavy paper. These sheets are tough, elastic, and resistant to heat, and those made from the variety of mica called "muscovite" or "white mica" are almost as transparent as glass. The name muscovite, or muscovy glass as it used to be called, came from the fact that this mica was used for windows in Russia.

The chief use for mica today is as an insulator in electrical apparatus, since it is a poor conductor of electricity. Broken into small sparkling bits it is also much used as "spangles" to produce glittering effects on stage costumes, Christmas trees, and some wall papers. Ground mica is used in some paints, is sometimes added to rubber to act as a filler, and has other industrial uses.

All the members of the mica family of minerals are complicated silicates of aluminium and potassium. Other metals may be present, e.g. paragonite contains sodium; lepidolite contains lithium, and is an important commercial source of this metal; biotite, or black mica, contains iron and magnesium. The colours of micas vary with the metals they contain, and may be white, brown, yellow, green, rose red, or black.

Examination of mica with X-rays has shown that the atoms (*see* Atom *and* Chemistry) are arranged so as to form sheet-like structures, and that is why micas so readily split into sheets.

Most of the world's supply of sheet mica comes from India; but if we include both "scrap" and sheet mica, then the United States are the biggest producers, followed by Russia, India, South Africa, Canada, Madagascar, and Argentina. Many rocks, such as granite, contain mica; and during the Second World War (1939–45) usable supplies of mica were found in Great Britain. Such supplies, however, are uneconomic to work under peace-time competitive conditions. (*See* Minerals.)

# Michelangelo Buonarroti.

(1475–1564). On a scaffolding high above the floor of a chapel in Rome lay a man, painting with fast strokes on the plaster of the ceiling which stretched its 5,000 square feet of surface above him. He was Michelangelo (pron. mī-kel-an'-je-lō), the greatest genius of the Italian Renaissance, who between the years 1508 and 1512 decorated the ceiling of the Sistine Chapel, revealing his wonderful vision of the world's creation.

Today we gaze in awe at the nine scenes depicting the story of Genesis from the Creation to the Flood, and we can understand why artists call this "technically the most extraordinary piece of work ever accomplished." Not only are we thrilled by

*The Louvre, Paris; photo Giraudon*

**MICHELANGELO BUONARROTI**

**Upon this bronze head of Michelangelo, Italian artist, poet, architect and engineer, are stamped some of his essential qualities—immense strength, uncompromising honesty and tragic gloom.**

Michelangelo's lofty conception and by his masterly technique; we are stirred by his indomitable will and almost superhuman energy and courage to endure the "great hardships, illness, and overwhelming labour" that accompanied this work.

Michelangelo was born on March 6, 1475, at Caprese, a small Tuscan town of which his father was governor. The Buonarrotis were a poor but noble family of Florence. He grew up in Florence, and soon began covering the walls of his home with charcoal drawings and carving with chisel and mallet.

At the age of 13 he was apprenticed to Ghirlandaio, the painter, who was soon compelled to admit "This boy knows more than I do." A year later Michelangelo joined the School of Sculpture which Lorenzo de' Medici, merchant prince and patron of art, had established in his palace gardens at Florence. There, amid a famous collection of old Greek and Roman sculpture, Michelangelo began to work, showing such skill in copying the head of a laughing faun that Lorenzo took him to live in the palace. He worked there untiringly until he was 17. Then Lorenzo died, and two years later Michelangelo was in Rome, making great progress with sculpture, the art he loved best. The pietà, the statue of the Virgin Mary holding the crucified body of her son, was sculptured during his stay there, and its fame spread so rapidly that the young sculptor was recalled to the city of Florence.

There at the age of 26 he retired into a workshop built round an 18-foot marble block which had been discarded as useless after being mutilated by other sculptors. When he removed the covering two years later the artistic world gasped, for out of that marble block he had created his wonderful "David"—one of the world's greatest statues.

The year 1505 found Michelangelo again in Rome, this time at the request of Pope Julius II, who wished the young genius to design for him a tomb. It was to be a magnificent three-storeyed tomb, representing art and victory; but political upheavals, jealousies, and changes of plan after the Pope's death interfered with the work. In the end Michelangelo completed only a few figures for the much reduced tomb. Among them were the majestic "Moses" (*see* illustration, page 1783), which is part of the memorial as it appears today, and the "Slaves," now in the Louvre. By common consent these rank among the supreme triumphs of the sculptor's art. With them are the figures of Dawn and Dusk, Night and Day, and the portrait statues which Michelangelo carved for the Medici monument.

More than 20 years after he painted his ceiling frescoes for the Sistine Chapel, Michelangelo began his enormous Last Judgement, 60 feet in height, on the wall of the chapel behind the altar. It has over 100 more than life-size figures. In its vast proportions, technical excellence and daring conception it is a fitting companion for the ceiling paintings. Completed in 1541, it has been called the most famous single picture in the world.

Besides these masterpieces, Michelangelo left other significant works in both painting and sculpture. Nor did these twin arts even absorb all his many-sided genius, for he used his vast powers in many fields. In 1527, when Florence revolted against its ruler the Duke of Florence, he was appointed director of fortifications, superintending the building of the city's defences. He wrote a collection of impassioned sonnets which in their impetuosity and vigour remind us of his work in marble. And he left us the greatest architectural achievement of the Italian Renaissance, the dome of St. Peter's in Rome, designed, at the request of Pope Paul III, during the artist's last years.

"Death plucks me by the cloak!" he cried when he was 89 years old, and the brush fell from his hand. He was buried in the church of Santa Croce, the Pantheon of Florence. Honoured as " more than mortal, angel divine," Michelangelo outlived his illustrious contemporaries Raphael, Leonardo da Vinci, and Correggio. Except for Titian, he was the last great figure of Italy's golden age of art. A stern and lonely dreamer, in the loftiness of his inspiration and in the number and variety of his amazing works Michelangelo still stands unrivalled. He is typical of the universal genius which the Italian Renaissance produced beyond any other epoch in the world's history (*see* Renaissance). In him were summed up the vigour of mind and body, the restless energy, the boldness of spirit, the freedom of action and expression, the curious combination of worldliness and religious zeal, which marked that period.

**THE BOY DAVID**

*Academia, Florence; photo Anderson*

At the age of 26 Michelangelo created this masterpiece—the statue of David carved from a discarded block of marble.

**Michigan.** This northern member of the United States borders on lakes Superior, Michigan (which lies wholly within the United States and divides Michigan State into two parts), Huron and Erie. It covers 58,216 square miles, of which 1,194 are water. In the hilly northern peninsula copper, iron, magnesium, gypsum, silver and timber are produced; in the south, farming and manufacturing are the chief concerns, the city of Detroit being the main centre of the United States motor-car industry, Other cities are Grand Rapids, Flint, Saginaw, and Lansing (population 78,000), the capital. The population of the State is 5,256,000.

**Micrometer.** A difference of $\frac{1}{1000}$ of an inch may not seem important, but some parts of a motor-car or a sewing-machine have to fit even closer than this. In certain types of scientific apparatus, moreover, a discrepancy as great as this would render them useless. To ensure perfectly fitting work, engineers employ devices called micrometers (from two Greek words meaning small and measure). The commonest type is operated by a screw having 20 threads to the inch. Each turn of the screw, then, moves the measuring spindle $\frac{1}{20}$ or $\frac{50}{1000}$ of an inch. A scale revolving with the screw is divided into 50 parts, and thus indicates the fractions of a turn in units of $\frac{1}{1000}$ of an inch. Sometimes such a micrometer carries in addition a " vernier " scale with which a movement of $\frac{1}{10000}$ of an inch can be read. Micrometer readings are usually written as decimals; for example, the thickness of an ordinary sheet of newspaper is about ·0035 or $\frac{35}{1000}$ of an inch.

Even more delicate devices are sometimes attached to microscopes and telescopes. Some consist of simple scales ruled on glass with a fine-pointed diamond. These rulings are themselves made by " dividing engines " regulated on the micrometer principle, having a slide moved by a very accurate long screw, and capable of marking as many as 120,000 lines to the inch. A common unit for such scales in scientific work is the micron

*The Vatican, Rome; photo Anderson*

**MICHELANGELO'S PAINTING OF ADAM**

Executed between 1508 and 1512, Michelangelo's paintings on the ceiling of the Sistine Chapel, Rome, depict the story of Genesis from the Creation to the Flood. In the fourth section is this figure of Adam, with God's outstretched finger causing life to stream through his veins.

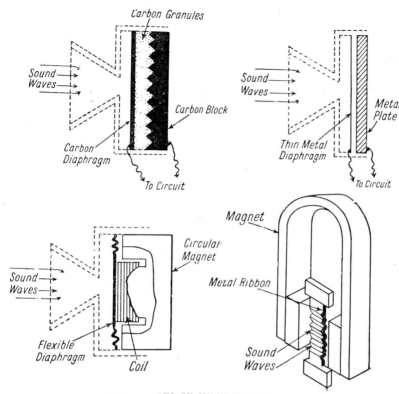

Carbon Granules

Sound Waves→

Carbon Block

Carbon Diaphragm

To Circuit

Sound Waves→

Metal Plate

Thin Metal Diaphragm

To Circuit

Magnet

Circular Magnet

Metal Ribbon

Sound Waves→

Flexible Diaphragm

Coil

Sound Waves

FOUR TYPES OF MICROPHONE

Millions of telephone instruments contain a carbon microphone (top left), which is cheap but not so effective as the condenser microphone (top right). The moving coil type (lower left) uses the principle of electro-magnetic induction, as does the ribbon microphone (lower right), which has no diaphragm.

to vary some electrical quantity—current, voltage, capacity, etc.—in a way which exactly corresponds to the sound waves which it "hears" at all audible frequencies. If it does not do this, i.e. if the amount of its "response" differs at different frequencies, it will introduce distortion of the sounds. (Actually, there is no microphone which does not distort to some extent, but some are better than others.)

*Resistance Microphones.* One principle on which a microphone can work is by changing its resistance (and therefore varying the current flowing in the circuit) in accordance with the sound waves. The waves which are directed on to a diaphragm (a plate of thin material which will move or "whip" under the varying air pressures produced) is connected so as to vary the pressure between electrical contacts as it moves. The earliest type, due to David Edward Hughes (1891 1900), consisted simply of an iron nail laid across two other nails which were connected to a battery and telephone receiver. The nails lay on a box which acted as a sounding board or diaphragm.

The best-known type of microphone is the carbon microphone. One wire of the circuit is connected to a carbon block, while the other is connected to a thin carbon diaphragm, the space between the two being filled with small granules of carbon. When the diaphragm vibrates, the pressure between the granules varies, causing considerable changes in resistance and, hence, in the current flowing. The carbon microphone has many advantages: it is cheap, and will stand quite a lot of hard usage, and is employed on millions of telephone instruments. But it has not a very even response, and it gives a hissing background-noise to speech. The working principles of the four chief types of microphone are illustrated in the diagrams at the top of the page.

The invention of the thermionic valve amplifier made it possible to use other methods which gave greater purity of sound, although the electrical changes made were so minute that they could not be detected without an amplifier.

*Condenser Microphone.* As explained in the story of Electricity, the capacity of a condenser varies according to the spacing of the plates. If we were to make a small two-plate condenser with one plate thin and "whippy" so that it could act as a diaphragm, the electric charge taken by the condenser would vary with the movements of the diaphragm, and this could be used to operate an

($\frac{1}{1000}$ of a millimetre or about $\frac{1}{25000}$ of an inch). The object to be measured is compared with this scale, both being equally enlarged. Another device moves the image of the object across a hairline consisting of a spider's thread or a quartz fibre, in the eye-piece of the instrument. The distance moved is indicated by the turn of a micrometer screw.

With the aid of such micrometer controls, gauge blocks can be made that are accurate to $\frac{1}{1000000}$ of an inch at standard temperatures. Such blocks have been used in adjusting instruments for measuring the velocity of light. Similar gauges, though not necessarily so exact, are employed to check the accuracy of tools and dies in motor-car and aeroplane factories.

**Microphone.** A microphone is a device for translating sound waves—the voice, or music, or in fact any sounds—into electrical impulses so that they can be carried away electrically, either over a wire or on wireless waves, to be translated back again elsewhere into sound impulses, by a telephone or loudspeaker (*see* Telephone; Radio). It was first used as a detector of small sounds (its name is derived from two Greek words *mikros*, "little"; *phone*, "sound"). Whatever its use, whether it be for detecting small sounds, for an ordinary Post Office telephone, for addressing a large crowd by means of loudspeakers, or for broadcasting an orchestra, a microphone is required amplifier. That is, in fact, what happens with the modern condenser microphone, which has better characteristics than the carbon type.

*Moving Coil Microphone.* Faraday's principle of electro-magnetic induction (*see* Electricity ; Dynamo) is also used. If we attach a small coil of wire to a flexible diaphragm and place a strong magnet around it the tiny movements of the coil in the field of the magnet will generate tiny voltages proportional to the movement, and these can be used to operate an amplifier, giving a very good reproduction.

*Ribbon Microphone.* This uses the same principle as the moving coil type, but consists of a single conductor, in the form of a very thin corrugated metal ribbon moving in a magnetic field. It differs from all other types of microphone in that it does not have a diaphragm but operates on the air particles flowing past the ribbon; for this reason it is often called a " velocity " microphone to distinguish it from the " pressure " microphones which operate with the air pressure on the diaphragm.

*Crystal Microphone.* In our story of Electric Clocks we refer to " piezo-electricity," or the property of certain crystals to generate a minute voltage when they are squeezed; or to vibrate when an alternating voltage is applied. This principle is made use of in the crystal microphone, by arranging that the movement of the diaphragm shall compress the crystal, and that the tiny voltages thus generated shall operate an amplifier.

*Directional Microphones.* Most microphones are to some extent directional—i.e. they are more sensitive to sounds of the same loudness arriving from a particular direction. This is an advantage for some purposes and a disadvantage for others. It is, for example, inconvenient to have a microphone which " fades " considerably when a speaker merely turns his head. On the other hand, it is often very convenient to have a microphone which will pick up comparatively faint sounds from the desired direction and ignore a louder noise closer at hand.

The positioning of microphones is of importance. Where the source of sound covers a large area—as, for example, an orchestra or a theatre stage—no one microphone will give good results over all the area. It is customary for this reason to use several microphones each picking up a part of the sound, and to allow them to feed into a " mixer " unit, where the amount of sound contributed by each one is regulated by a control engineer to give a natural and pleasing overall result. In public address work the microphone must not be located where one of the loud-speakers can feed straight into it, or they will feed back into each other, producing a continuous howl.

**BINOCULAR MICROSCOPE**
*R. & J. Beck, Ltd*
**The great advantage of a binocular microscope is that it affords freedom from eyestrain, both eyes being used.**

**Microscope.** This is the scientific instrument most familiar to the ordinary man or woman, and indeed the knowledge gained by its use affects our lives directly. Physicians use it extensively in tracking diseases to their sources in various forms of bacteria, and the microscope has led to the conquest of many of them.

Surgeons determine by microscopic examination of a section of tissue whether severe operations for new growths in the body are necessary. Botanists, biologists, and bacteriologists rely on it in their study of living things; whilst the structure of metals, chemical crystals and rocks is also determined by its use. With all these applications it is no wonder that the microscope has been perfected to a degree far greater than that of any other scientific instrument. The recent development of the electron microscope has further widened the scope of microscopic studies.

Ordinary magnifying glasses, or simple microscopes—convex lenses used for obtaining a magnified view of an object—were apparently known, at least as curiosities, from remote times; but the compound microscope was invented some time between 1590 and 1610. To Galileo, the famous astronomer, has been assigned the honour of inventing first the telescope and then the microscope.

Remarkable discoveries in anatomy and biology were made by use of the microscope in the 17th and 18th centuries. For example, the Dutch scientist Leeuwenhoek, sometimes known as " the father of microscopy," showed that weevils, fleas, and other minute creatures are not " spontaneously generated," but come from eggs. And the Italian, Malpighi (1628–94), was the first to see the capillary circulation of the blood previously inferred by Harvey (*q.v.*). Our modern microscope owes its perfection largely to the 19th century German scientist Ernst Abbé (1840–1908), who thoroughly explored the workings of the instrument.

A " simple " microscope may be a simple lens, or a set of lenses, used to view the object directly. Its action is explained in the article on Lens. A " compound " microscope uses (1) " a lens called the object glass, or objective, to produce a reversed magnified image ; and (2) another, called the eyepiece or ocular, to magnify this image. Both objective and ocular, in actual practice, are composed of several lenses because simple lenses are subject to various defects called aberrations, which distort or blur the image. Of these defects spherical aberration and astigmatism are corrected by compounding lenses whose faces have different curvatures; while chromatic aberration—that which makes the image look coloured at the edges—is overcome by making the component lenses of different types of glass. A convex lens of crown glass and a concave lens of flint glass are matched together so that both chromatic and spherical aberration are eliminated. In better microscopes the objective and eyepieces may consist of more than two lenses.

The high-power microscope needs to be very accurately adjusted when it is used to view small objects. These are mounted on a slide clamped to a movable stage, or platform, and they are focused by varying the distance between stage and objective lens, by means of a micrometer screw adjustment. For very high magnifications, the object is mounted in oil between a cover glass and the lens, and it is illuminated by a strong beam of light reflected into the microscope through a condenser lens, used to concentrate the beam. Nowadays most microscopes are fitted with binocular (double-eye) eyepieces, to relieve eye-strain, and these can be replaced by a camera attachment to photograph the magnified object if necessary.

The power of a microscope depends on the power of the object glass, the power of the eyepiece, and the distance separating eyepiece and objective— the greater the separation the greater the power. Powers of enlargement of more than 2,000 diameters are attainable for visual use; and photographs of very minute objects enlarged 5,000 diameters have frequently been produced.

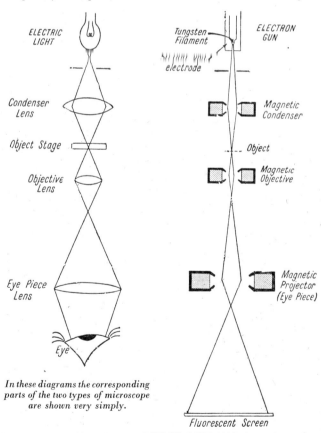

*In these diagrams the corresponding parts of the two types of microscope are shown very simply.*

### LIGHT AND ELECTRON MICROSCOPES

**The object viewed in a light microscope (left) is illuminated by a strong beam of light reflected into the instrument through a condenser lens. An electron microscope (right) may be four or more feet in length ; the electron gun has high voltages applied to it to speed up the electrons.**

When the working of the instrument has been thoroughly mastered it is best to try the microscope for the first time on an object which does not need a very great deal of preparation. The leg of an insect placed in a small drop of water on the slide and examined in plenty of light makes an extremely interesting subject; and the beginner will be astonished at the great pincers, the thick joints, and the numerous hairs with which it is provided.

The professional microscopist uses various methods to make the different parts of his object stand out in relief from one another. If biological specimens are stained with a dye, only certain tissues " take " the dye, leaving the others un-coloured. Again, a mineralogist uses polarised light in his microscope for the same purpose. The different minerals in the thin section of rock which he examines take on different colours in this way. If an object is illuminated from the side, so that only the light scattered from it enters the micro-scope, this will also help to increase the contrast. " Dark-ground illumination," as this is called, is obtained by using a special type of condensing lens. There is also a recent development in micro-scopy which enables two transparent substances to be distinguishable from one another.

Is there any limit to the powers of the micro-scope? Can we not obtain ever greater and greater magnification, so that at last we can peer into those minute particles, the molecules, atoms and electrons ? There are certain practical difficulties, the chief of which is not the imperfection of the instru-ment (which is small) but the very nature of light and vision. We see non-luminous objects by the light they reflect, and light is composed of waves of a certain definite length. If the detail in an object is much smaller than the wavelength of the light, then the light reflected from the object will not be capable of showing it up, or " resolving " it.

Now atoms, and even the largest mole-cules, are far below the size of light waves; and as for electrons, they are far smaller still. Using ordinary light, we shall only be able to distinguish two separate points if they are more than about a micron ($\frac{1}{1000}$ millimetre) apart; but this does not prevent our *detecting* particles many times smaller. Any ultra-microscopic particle— that is, a very tiny particle—if brightly illuminated from the side, will show up as a point of light against a dark back-ground, just as dust particles in the air scatter light from a searchlight beam, enabling us to see its path. In the ultra-microscope, so called, such particles are illuminated by a shallow intense beam of light, transverse to the microscope. Their irregular dancing movements, or " Brown-ian movement " (*q.v.*), confirms our belief in the molecular constitution of liquids and gases.

Since the resolving power of a micro-scope increases when the wavelength of the light becomes smaller, it is only natural to try to make microscopes em-ploying shorter wavelengths. This is

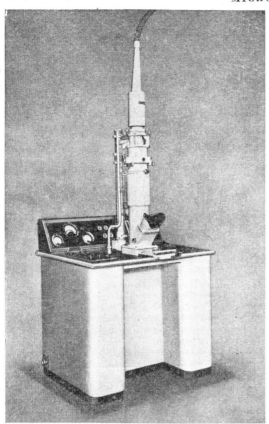

microscope; and after striking and being scattered by the specimen under examination, they are subjected to the action of two or three magnetic lenses, in order to acquire the necessary magnification. The final image is viewed on a fluorescent screen, which glows green at the points where electrons hit it. Or a photographic plate can be exposed to the electron beam, and a photo-micrograph taken.

The instrument is usually arranged " upside down," compared with a light microscope, with the electron gun at the top and fluorescent screen below. It is often four feet or more in length, so that sufficient magnification can be acquired ; and the whole microscope tube, including the specimen to be viewed, has to be pumped free of air down to a high vacuum. This is because electrons can only travel freely when there are no gas molecules for them to collide with. The electrons are derived from a hot tungsten wire, similar to the filament in a radio valve, and are speeded up by attracting them to a high-voltage plate with a hole in it, so that most of them shoot straight through. This electron gun has voltages of 50,000 or more applied to it to give the electrons sufficient speed.

Magnifications of 100,000 times and greater can be obtained with the electron microscope, and the instrument is proving of invaluable use in many branches of science. In medical research, viruses, which are invisible in the ordinary microscope, have been observed ; and it has been found that bacteria have even smaller parasites living on them. Chemists have already been able to see very large molecules and " invisible " colloidal particles ; while metallurgists have detected fine structure in metal surfaces. Here a special technique for making a

done in the " ultra-violet microscope," which uses ultra-violet instead of visible light. This radiation has a wavelength of about half that of the visible light, so we get double the resolving power. Glass lenses cannot be used in such a microscope, since glass does not transmit the ultra-violet, and so quartz lenses are used instead. The eyes, too, are not sensitive to ultra-violet light, so the magnified image has to be photographed every time.

Recently the revolutionary idea that a microscope could be made, using a beam of electrons instead of a beam of light, has resulted in the development of the electron microscope. The French scientist Louis de Broglie showed, in 1924, that high speed particles behave in many respects like waves; and further, if the particles are the negatively charged very light particles called electrons, that their wavelength will be many thousands of times smaller than that of visible light. This means that a much greater resolving power can be achieved by their use.

Although the electron microscope magnifies objects by means of lenses in a similar manner to the light microscope, its construction differs in many respects. The lenses used are not glass ones, but are circular electro-magnets surrounding the main tube of the instrument. Electrons are shot down this tube from an electron " gun," which corresponds to the lamp used in an ordinary

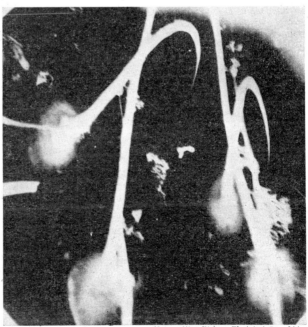

*Metropolitan-Vickers Electrical Co., Ltd.*

**WONDERS OF AN ELECTRON MICROSCOPE**
The lenses of an electron microscope (upper) are circular electro-magnets surrounding the main tube of the instrument ; magnifications of 100,000 can be obtained. The high power of this type of microscope reveals new facts about natural objects. For example, examine the hairs (lower) on the wings of a fly, with their hooked ends.

replica of the surface in some plastic material has to be used, since the electrons cannot penetrate thick layers of metal. The ultimate aim of the electron microscope design, not yet achieved, is to see the atoms and molecules themselves.

**Midas.** According to mythology, Midas, a king of ancient Phrygia, in reward for a kind act was promised by the god Dionysus (or Bacchus) whatever he should ask. Midas asked that everything he touched might turn to gold. When the request was granted he found to his sorrow that there are many things more necessary, for even his food became gold before he could swallow it; and he begged the god to take back the gift.

According to another story, told by Ovid, Midas once decided a musical contest between Pan and Apollo, giving the prize to Pan. Apollo in revenge gave Midas a pair of ass's ears. King Midas hid these ears under a cap, but his barber discovered the secret and was so excited by it that he dug a hole in the ground and whispered into it: " King Midas has ass's ears ! " A reed was said to have grown from this hole, which, when moved by the wind, divulged the secret of the king's misfortune.

# *From* DARKNESS *to* DAWN *in* EUROPE

*When Roman civilization crashed before the onset of Teutonic barbarians, there followed a thousand years of rebuilding until the modern age dawned with the Renaissance. The story of those years is reviewed here.*

**Middle Ages.** History is continuous like a stream, and just as a stream has rapids and waterfalls so has the stream of human life. One waterfall, so to speak, in the stream of European history was in the 4th and 5th centuries, when the Roman Empire crumbled and fell; after that until the 15th century the stream flowed on with no strikingly abrupt changes.

The years between those centuries are known as the Middle Ages, although, in fact, they were no more " middle ages " than any other historical period. The term " middle ages " was applied to them some 300 years ago, and has clung to them ever since. The name is somewhat misleading, for it suggests that these years were peculiarly uneventful; whereas the truth is, as students of history have found, they were years of considerable significance for the development of many important features of our social and political life. No one can understand some of our existing institutions without knowing something of the life and customs of the Middle Ages.

If we go back in imagination along the stream of history till we come to the 4th century, we shall find the Roman imperial government ruling over the entire Mediterranean basin, and over some regions beyond it. The Romans had conquered the Greeks, the Gauls, the Carthaginians, the Egyptians, and various other peoples. Roman civilization was made up of many mingled elements held together by the army, the roads, the trade, the law and the government of the empire. (*See* Roman History).

A number of religions flourished in the empire, for the Romans, when they conquered a city or a region, allowed the people to keep their own religion and merely required them to pay homage to the emperor. In a remote province there grew out of the religion of the Jews the Christian faith. The Christians believed the payment of homage to an earthly ruler was akin to idolatry, and that other religions were false and should be destroyed. In the resulting struggle the Christians were persecuted as enemies of the State, but their courage and zeal enabled them to survive. In the early 4th century the emperor, Constantine (ruled 306–337), sought their aid against his enemies, and in return decreed the toleration of Christianity in the Western Roman Empire. By the end of the 4th century the em-

peror, Theodosius (ruled the Eastern Roman Empire 379–395), had outlawed all other religions. (*See* Christian Church).

At this time the Eastern Roman Empire was threatened with invasion by hordes of barbarians. On the north were many tribes of Teutons, so barbarous, as the Roman historian Tacitus wrote about A.D. 100, that they had no word for autumn or harvest. This shows that they were still merely hunters and fishermen, and had not advanced to the agricultural stage of civilization. However, they were bold and warlike and were learning of the wealth to be found in sunny Mediterranean countries and of the growing weakness of the Roman Empire. To the north-east of the Black Sea and the Caspian, tribes of fierce nomads wandered with their flocks and herds. Among these were the Huns, who were of the Mongolian type, small in stature, with yellowish skin, straight black hair, and slanting eyes. Moving westward between the Ural Mountains and the Caspian Sea they met the Goths, who were Germans. Some of the Goths, fleeing before the Huns, crossed the River Danube in 375 and settled within the boundaries of the Eastern Roman Empire. Soon they quarrelled with the Romans, and in the Battle of Adrianople, in 378, decisively defeated them. Not only Huns and Goths but Vandals, Burgundians, Lombards, Franks, Angles, Saxons, and various other tribes attacked both the Eastern and Western Roman Empires, pillaging, fighting, sacking Rome, and hastening the downfall of the Western Empire. " The whole world," wrote St. Jerome (*c.* 340–420) " is sinking into ruin."

The Roman world, indeed, was sinking into ruin; yet, in the midst of these troublous times, several forces kept society from falling into complete disorder. One of these was the Byzantine Empire, the eastern or Greek portion of the Roman Empire. It survived the barbarian invasions; and the armies of the Emperor Justinian (ruled 527–565) even for a time reclaimed Italy and Northern Africa from the invaders. In Constantinople, the capital of the Byzantine Empire, art and industry flourished. Justinian's architects built one of the world's finest structures—the cathedral of St. Sophia. His lawyers collected, edited, and summarized the system of Roman law. Throughout the Middle Ages the people of Italy carried on extensive trade with the Byzantines and brought back to the West much of the culture of antiquity and of the East. (*See* Byzantine Empire).

Among the barbarous tribes that invaded the empire in the West, the Franks differed from the others by merely extending their Rhineland territory. Most of the other tribes, instead of expanding, migrated. The Vandals, for instance, moved all the way from North Central Europe to North Africa, where they established a short-lived kingdom. The kings of the Franks included Clovis in the late 5th century, Charles Martel, conqueror of the Mahomedans at Tours, in 732, and Charlemagne, who in 800 was crowned emperor of the Holy Roman Empire by Pope Leo III. These rulers, although often brutal, helped to rescue the age from lawlessness and disorder. Important invasions, in addition to those of the Franks, were made by the Angles and the Saxons, Germanic tribes that began to settle in England at the opening of the 5th century. They established several kingdoms, out of which grew the system of shires, or counties. Basic elements of English, German, and French civilizations are traceable, respectively, to the Anglo-Saxons, the East Franks and the West Franks.

Clovis was converted to Christianity in 496, and he and his successors allied themselves with the Bishop of Rome, who was known as the Pope; and the peoples they conquered obeyed the Roman bishop as head of the Church.

In these years of invasion and uncertainty the monasteries did much to preserve knowledge of the arts, crafts, industries and literature of Roman times. They were also important in providing a discipline and a bond of union which helped to hold society together in an age when it was threatened with destruction or with reversion to savagery. (*See* Monks and Monasticism).

However, even during the reign of Charlemagne, his dominions, which included nearly all of Central and Western Europe, were endangered by new invasions. From the south-east came the Arabs; from Central Asia, the Avars, the Bulgars, and the Hungarians ; from North-Eastern Europe, the Slavs; and from the Scandinavian peninsula, the Northmen or Vikings. After the death of Charlemagne in 814 his empire soon collapsed, and in its place there grew up a large number of feudal states, their rulers acquiring power as organizers of defence against invaders. (*See* Feudal System).

Many people still longed for a vast and powerful empire such as that of the ancient Romans. These ideas found expression in 962 in the crowning of the German king, Otto I, at Rome as emperor of the Holy Roman Empire (*q.v.*). The emperor was regarded as the ally of the Pope and the protector of the Church. But emperors and Popes soon came into conflict over the question of the appointment of the bishops of the Church, each claiming that the right was his.

While this long struggle was weakening Italy and Germany, in France and England the kings were

*From Les très riches heures du Duc de Berry: Musée Condé. Chantilly; photo, Giraudon*

### LAVISH HOSPITALITY IN THE MIDDLE AGES

Towards the end of the 15th century the rich nobility of Europe dispensed hospitality on a grand scale. This picture, reproduced from a French manuscript of about 1460, shows a noble host sitting under a canopy in his banqueting hall. His steward with his wand of office stands at his right hand, and on the other side of the table is his carver with a towel flung over his shoulder. Despite all this magnificence, fingers were used instead of forks.

gradually extending their powers. In each country the ruler had a council consisting of his vassals, and at first all government was carried on by the king and this council. When public business became more complicated, various institutions grew out of the council. Many of these still exist. Why, for example, does the British Parliament consist of two Houses—the Commons and Lords ? This system dates from the Middle Ages. The nobles were members of the king's council because they were his vassals. In the 13th century, when the kings decided to call on the wealthy townsmen and the lesser landlords for money they were permitted to be represented in the council, and there arose the custom of sending out orders (writs) to the sheriffs of the counties, calling on the wealthy middle classes (commoners) to elect representatives to sit with the nobles in the council. They preferred,

Mahomedans, were travelling to and from the East, bringing new ideas, new customs and new products to Europe. These centuries saw the rise of commerce and the growth of the towns. They witnessed the development of universities and an intellectual and artistic re-birth that was to mature in the centuries that followed. Later, the horizon of Europeans expanded to include even the Far East—India and China and the Spice Islands. From all these new influences came the Renaissance, or revival of learning, and the dawn of modern history.

**Middlesex.** One of the smallest counties in England, and entirely inland, the whole of Middlesex is included in Greater London. Even Brentford (*q.v.*), the county town, is only 10 miles west of Central London. In Saxon times there was a " great forest of Middlesex " in the north of the county, but now the only rural area is in the west, where there are market-gardens and orchards. The county, covering an area of 233 square miles, is flat, with the exception of the "northern heights" of Highgate a n d Harrow-on-the-Hill—the latter notable for its public school.

MIDDLESEX GUILDHALL IN LONDON
Though the county town of Middlesex is the old town of Brentford on the western outskirts of London, most of the county business is transacted at the Middlesex Guildhall, in Broad Sanctuary near Westminster Abbey. It is a fine Renaissance style building, completed in 1913. The statue in front is of Abraham Lincoln.

Towns in the county include Acton ; Ealing ; Enfield, where is a small-arms factory ; Hendon and Heston, with their aerodromes ; Staines, where the [illegible]; Twickenham, headquarters of Rugby Union football, and a borough which now includes Hampton with its magnificent palace—a royal residence for over 200 years—and Teddington, h o m e of the National Physical Laboratory ; Wembley, with its vast stadium where the Football Association Cup Final and other sporting events are held ; and Willesden.

Many factories line the Great West Road, the principal artery from London to the west. An ancient and still important highway is Watling Street, leading to the north-west. The population of Middlesex is 1,629,000.

Middlesex Hospital, in Mortimer Street, London, W., was founded in 1745. It has over 700 beds, including a cancer wing, and research laboratories.

however, to sit separately, and so the House of Commons was formed. Some other modern institutions and practices are fully as old. Among these are counties and county courts, towns or parishes, and constables, writs, juries, circuit judges. Then, too, our system of law and of procedure in the courts goes back as far as the 12th century.

This brief account of the Middle Ages has been confined to the framework of society, and especially the institutions of government and religion. This framework was built up as a defence against invasions and other dangers of the period, and was adapted to a simple, self-sustaining farm life.

In the 12th and 13th centuries, when a greater measure of peace and order had been established, the era of rapid change in the political, social, and intellectual life of Europe began. It was the age of the struggle for power between the Papacy and the Holy Roman Empire, and it was the time of the Crusades, when hordes of Christians, fired by a common desire to rescue the Holy Land from the

**Midnight Sun.** One of the most wonderful of natural phenomena is seen at the Arctic and Antarctic Circles on their respective Midsummer Days (June 21 and December 22). The sun does not set at all on this day, but sinks only to the horizon, and the sky is suffused throughout the night with an eerie glow.

Within the Polar regions the Midnight Sun continues for several days or even months. At North Cape in Norway (a country known as the " Land of the Midnight Sun ") the sun is visible at midnight from May 12 to July 29. By contrast, the sun does not rise above the horizon at this point during two whole months of the winter.

E.N.A.

## WHERE THE SUN SHINES ALL NIGHT AT MIDSUMMER

The midnight sun is something which can be seen only in extreme north and south latitudes. It may be witnessed at any point on the Arctic Circle at the summer solstice, June 21, or on the Antarctic Circle on December 22. Within these circles the length of time the sun is in the sky day and night increases according to the latitude. In latitude 70°, for instance, the duration of the midnight sun is 65 days, and in latitude 80° it is 134 days. At the poles the sun does not set for six months. At midnight, however, it is not high above the horizon, and all the colours of sunset are seen, as in this photograph taken in Norway.

H. J. Shep

## WHEN THE SUN SHINES AT MIDNIGHT

IN this photograph there are not really seven suns, though it looks like it; but the same photographic plate was exposed seven times during the " night " of June 21, the time when the sun never sets on the Arctic Circle. Its nearest approach to setting is the slight declination seen in the middle of this string of suns; then, on the right, it begins to rise again. This strange phenomenon of the Midnight Sun might be seen at any point on the Arctic Circle, and northern Norway is a favourite spot from which to view it. This photograph, however, was taken in North Greenland, and the exposures were made at half-hour intervals. Like the seasons of the year, the Midnight Sun is due to the tilting of the Earth's axis. The same sight is visible at the " other end " of the Earth, for the Midnight Sun is seen on the Antarctic Circle at the summer solstice in the Southern Hemisphere, December 22.

## Midsummer Night's Dream, A.

According to the plot of this fanciful comedy, written by Shakespeare, the King of the Fairies, Oberon, and Puck or Robin Goodfellow, his elfin lieutenant, set out to bewitch Titania, Oberon's Fairy Queen. Discovering two pairs of lovers wandering in a wood near Athens, they include them also in their enchantments, as well as a company of workmen who have come into the wood to rehearse a rustic play with which to win the favour of the Duke of Athens on his wedding-day.

Queen Titania falls absurdly in love, under the enchantment, with Bottom, the weaver, the chief of the clownish actors, on whom the mischievous Puck has placed an ass's head. In a highly comic scene her attendant fairies scratch Bottom's donkey-head and otherwise take care of him, while their fond mistress kisses the " fair large ears " of her " sweet love."

The wandering lovers wake to find their loves reversed, and charming Hermia is ready to scratch out fair Helena's eyes.

Puck, being a mischievous sprite, watches this sport in glee, but Oberon soon takes pity on them all, releases Titania from her foolish fancy, gives Bottom back his own foolish head, and the lovers their proper loves.

Then at daybreak all the human folk hasten back to Athens, the lovers to be wed, and Bottom and his workmen friends to present their play—the oft-told story of Pyramus and Thisbe, two lovers who kept apart by their parents, yet conversed through an opening in the wall that separated their houses. One night they planned a secret meeting. Thisbe, startled by the roar of a lion, ran away, dropping her veil. When Pyramus arrived and found the veil torn by the lion's blood-stained jaws, he imagined Thisbe had been slain and stabbed himself. Thisbe, returning, found the body of her lover and ended her life with the same weapon. As presented by the rustics, the tragedy becomes a laughable burlesque. After this " tragical mirth " the court retires to bed, and the play ends with the entry of the fairies to bless the house.

Mendelssohn (q.v.) wrote some beautiful, really fairy-like, music to preface and accompany the Midsummer Night's Dream. This music was first performed in Berlin, in 1843.

## Mignonette. (Pron. min-yon-et').

It was the French who bestowed upon this delightfully fragrant plant, Reseda odorata, the familiar name mignonette—which means " little darling." In Africa and Asia Minor R. odorata is a plentiful weed. It was introduced to British gardens from Egypt in the 18th century. It grows up to two feet in height, and there are varieties with white, golden or red spikes of flowers.

Two forms of " wild " mignonette are native to Britain: R. lutea, whose pale yellow flowers are scentless; and R. luteola, with greeny-yellow flowers. The latter plant yields a beautiful yellow dye, and was once cultivated extensively.

## Migration, ANIMAL.

The migration of animals is among the most wonderful things in Nature. You probably know most about migration of birds, bringing some species in winter, others in summer; it brings the swallows and cuckoos in spring, and sends them back to the South in autumn. Most creatures, in one way or another, migrate.

L.N.A.

**' A MIDSUMMER NIGHT'S DREAM ' IN REGENT'S PARK**
The Open Air Theatre in Regent's Park, London, provides an ideal setting for Shakespeare's A Midsummer Night's Dream, which has always been one of the most popular of his plays. Here you see Bottom with Titania, the fairy queen, and her retinue, the natural surroundings adding considerably to the effectiveness of the scene.

Insects—some kinds of butterflies, for example—migrate across the Channel, and go to warmer climates in winter; an American butterfly, the Monarch, is found in Alaska in the summer and in Mexico in the winter; salmon migrate from the sea to the headwaters of certain rivers to lay their eggs; eels, on the contrary, lay eggs in the sea, only their young returning to the rivers, as " elvers "; and red deer descend from the hills to the shelter of the woods in winter.

Where in all the Book of Nature will you find anything to compare with the journey of some storks and swallows, marked specimens of which have been proved to migrate from Northern Europe to South Africa, a distance of 6,000 miles ? Not all birds migrate in this sense of the word, but almost all make some regular seasonal movements from one place to another. Thus, woodland birds may leave their thickets and take up their quarters, temporarily, in gardens. Moorland species, like the curlew, descend from the bleak hillsides to feed in the estuaries and the salt marshes.

Most of the long migrations are performed by night; and on cloudy nights, when the birds are passing low to escape flying in the clouds, one may hear them as they call to one another. The distance travelled in any one night or on any one continuous flight is ordinarily not more than 200 or 300 miles; but certain birds (such as storks and swallows, as already mentioned) are known to travel enormous distances, apparently without stopping. The American golden plovers appear to migrate from Alaska to the Hawaiian Islands, a distance of 2,000 miles, with no stopping-place between the two points on the direct route.

Perhaps even more remarkable than the distances travelled by these birds is the fact that they are able to find their way over the sea without landmarks to guide them. An instinct for home, preferably the place of their own birth, is apparently the cause of their return year after year to the same region for nesting purposes, but just *how* the bird finds its way is a mystery. Many theories have been advanced as to *why* birds migrate, but this also is an unsolved problem.

Higher animals also afford interesting examples of seasonal migration. Deer, goats, sheep, antelopes and the like, in many parts of the world, regularly leave the plains for the mountains in early summer to escape the flies and to find new grass and safer solitudes. In winter they seek the valleys and plains again.

Many fishes and reptiles also perform long and complex wanderings. In the spring there are great migrations of herring, salmon, trout, mackerel, and other fishes from deep water to shallow.

## Migration, HUMAN.

Mass movements in the animal world have their counterparts in the migrations of peoples that have often changed the course of history.

Migration sometimes occurs in great surges; sometimes in a slow, thin stream. It may take place within the boundaries of a country, or it may extend into distant countries. The impetus most frequently comes from over-crowding in one country. Migrations may also be necessitated by changes in weather; the advancing ice-cap over Northern Europe in glacial times drove Man southward. The attraction of a place may be so strong that people are lured to it; such a motive started the gold rush to the Yukon in 1898. A desire to gain political or religious freedom has inaugurated migrations. And there have been large-scale enforced migrations during time of war.

The wanderings of prehistoric Man gradually took him from his place of origin, which was perhaps in Central Asia, to nearly all parts of the world except the Americas. The Stone Age culture spread into Western Europe, first around the Mediterranean and up the Atlantic coast, then inland by way of the river valleys. Long residence in diverse and widely-separated regions brought about variations in physical characteristics, and Man became separated into widely different races.

At length, in regions suitable for agriculture and where large numbers could live in comfort, men began to come together in communities or towns. The first of these grew up along the banks of the Nile in Egypt, and in the valley of the Tigris and Euphrates in Mesopotamia (now Iraq). This civilization lasted about 3,000 years, and was finally wiped out by a great migration of energetic shepherd folk from the grasslands bordering the Caspian Sea. We call these people Indo-Europeans because they flocked into both India and Europe. They were our ancestors.

The Indo-European parent people pushed out branches in several directions. A group of tribes swept south-east to the plateau of Iran or Persia, and came to be named " Aryans." This group later split up into two: the one developed the great empire of the Medes and Persians; the other colonized India. Meanwhile another group advanced across the Aegean Islands into the rocky peninsula of Greece. Not long after, others invaded the Italian peninsula and founded the empire of Rome. Some tribes swung southward, coming into collision with the Semites, whom they drove into Arabia and Africa. Others spread northward over the plains of Russia and became the Slavs, while those who went up the valley of the River Danube became the Celts, later followed by the Teutons, who settled around the Baltic.

These migrations from Asia were irregular, and sometimes took centuries to accomplish. The young and vigorous peoples who came into Europe in wave after wave developed new and different civilizations by the combination of the customs of different peoples. It was this intermingling of civilizations that speeded up progress.

For more than a thousand years Greece and Rome were the centre of culture. In time Rome became over populated and had also to protect herself against invading barbarians. So it was that Roman armies extended the sway of the empire over much of Europe, subjugating Greece and the countries round about the Mediterranean.

During the 5th century A.D. came the great migrations of the Goths, Vandals, Alemanni, Franks, and others—barbarous tribes living in Eastern and Central Europe. Stirred into activity by inroads of Huns from Asia, they begun to flood the civilized world, and put an end to the supremacy of Rome. Out of the break-up of the Roman dominion appeared the kingdoms and nations that gradually gave rise to modern Europe. Early migration from Europe to America was chiefly from Spain and England. Japan and China today are over-populated, and their peoples have spread into neighbouring lands.

During the Second World War (1939–45) the Germans carried out forcible migrations of masses of the population from the Soviet Union, Poland, France, the Netherlands, Belgium and Norway, the majority of these displaced persons being used as slave labour in Germany's war industries. Jews of the enemy-occupied countries also were subjected to mass deportations, being taken to concentration camps or to special centres where they were massacred. At the end of the war the Allies estimated that there were nearly eight million people, known as displaced persons, awaiting repatriation (return to their homelands).

## Milan, (Pron. mil-an´), ITALY.

Standing on the River Olona in the midst of the fertile plains of Lombardy, Milan from the earliest days was the natural axis round which turned the stirring history of Northern Italy. Its position, which placed the city in the path of invaders armed with

# HOW SPRING AND AUTUMN MIGRANTS REACH BRITAIN

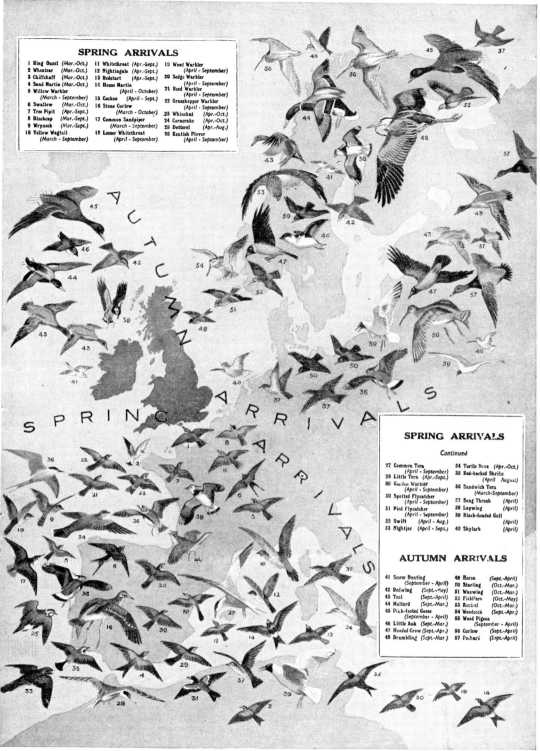

## SPRING ARRIVALS

1 Ring Ouzel (Mar.-Oct.)
2 Wheatear (Mar.-Oct.)
3 Chiffchaff (Apr.-Oct.)
4 Sand Martin (Mar.-Oct.)
5 Willow Warbler (March - September)
6 Swallow (Mar.-Oct.)
7 Tree Pipit (Apr.-Sept.)
8 Blackcap (Mar.-Sept.)
9 Wryneck (Mar.-Sept.)
10 Yellow Wagtail (March - September)
11 Whitethroat (Apr.-Sept.)
12 Nightingale (Apr.-Sept.)
13 Redstart (Apr.-Sept.)
14 House Martin (April - October)
15 Cuckoo (April - Sept.)
16 Stone Curlew (March - October)
17 Common Sandpiper (March - September)
18 Lesser Whitethroat (April - September)
19 Wood Warbler (April - September)
20 Sedge Warbler (April - September)
21 Reed Warbler (April - September)
22 Grasshopper Warbler (April - September)
23 Whinchat (Apr.-Oct.)
24 Corncrake (Apr.-Oct.)
25 Dotterel (Apr.-Aug.)
26 Kentish Plover (April - September)

## SPRING ARRIVALS

### Continued

27 Common Tern (April - September)
28 Little Tern (Apr.-Sept.)
29 Garden Warbler (April - September)
30 Spotted Flycatcher (April - September)
31 Pied Flycatcher (April - September)
32 Swift (April - Aug.)
33 Nightjar (April - Sept.)
34 Turtle Dove (Apr.-Oct.)
35 Red-backed Shrike (April - August)
36 Sandwich Tern (March-September)
37 Song Thrush (April)
38 Lapwing (April)
39 Black-headed Gull (April)
40 Skylark (April)

## AUTUMN ARRIVALS

41 Snow Bunting (September - April)
42 Redwing (Sept.-May)
43 Teal (Sept.-April)
44 Mallard (Sept.-Mar.)
45 Pink-footed Goose (September - April)
46 Little Auk (Sept.-Mar.)
47 Hooded Crow (Sept.-Apr.)
48 Brambling (Sept.-Mar)
49 Heron (Sept.-April)
50 Starling (Oct.-Mar.)
51 Waxwing (Oct.-Mar.)
52 Fieldfare (Oct.-May)
53 Kestrel (Oct.-Mar.)
54 Woodcock (Sept.-Apr.)
55 Wood Pigeon (September - April)
56 Curlew (Sept.-April)
57 Pochard (Sept.-April)

In this specially-prepared picture are shown the more common birds which reach the shores of Britain as migrants in spring and autumn, together with the routes by which they come. Some of the migrants are included in both groups, for when our breeding birds go south for the winter, others of the same species often take their place in Britain. There are, too, many 'passage migrants'—birds which pass over Britain on their way south in autumn, and again on their return in the spring. Still other birds migrate from north to south within our own shores as the seasons change. The established routes are followed year after year, generation after generation.

fire and sword, also made of Milan the gateway for commerce, and prosperity; and while the need of self-protection developed courage and independence in the Milanese they also waxed rich and powerful.

Milan today is the centre of the financial life of Italy and the second largest city in the kingdom, surpassed only by Rome. Ever since it was taken from the Gauls by the Romans in 222 B.C. the city has continued to grow, despite the fact that it was sacked and burned once by the Huns, twice by the Goths, and once by Frederick Barbarossa as late as 1162.

After Milan had been rebuilt, following its destruction by Barbarossa, the city suffered a century of civil strife. It then fell under the rule of the House of Visconti. The last Visconti duke died in 1447, and three years later began the rule of the Sforzas, continuing to 1535. Most of the ancient beauty of the city is due to those two famous houses. When the Sforza line died out, Spain seized Milan and held it until 1714. It was under Austrian rule until Napoleon created his short-lived kingdom of Italy and made Milan its capital in 1805. After Napoleon's final defeat in 1815, Milan was restored to Austria, but in 1859 it became part of United Italy.

The famous cathedral is on the Piazza del Duomo—the centre of the city's life. It is the third largest in Europe, surpassed only by St. Peter's at Rome and the Cathedral of Seville. Forty thousand people can worship in Milan Cathedral at the same time. Its foundation-stone was laid in 1386, but it was not completed until 1812. The cathedral is 486 ft. long and towers 356 ft. from the ground. The style is Gothic, very elaborately decorated, and there are more than 3,000 statues in its niches. The building is faced with marble (see illus. page 1236). Second in importance among the many churches is that of Sant' Ambrogio, built by St. Ambrose in the 4th century, but twice destroyed and rebuilt; it was again seriously damaged in an air-raid in 1943. Here St. Ambrose, who was bishop of Milan, baptized St. Augustine (q.v.).

Milan has always been a seat of art and learning. Its artistic and literary life centred about the Brera Palace, the home of the Academy of Fine Arts and Science. Here was one of the finest picture galleries in Italy, containing paintings by Raphael and other great masters. The palace was severely damaged during the Second World War, though fortunately the pictures and other treasures had been removed to a place of safety. The city has famous libraries, a large government school of agriculture and commerce, and the second largest opera-house in Europe, the Teatro della Scala, erected in 1778. Its academy of music is one of the oldest and finest in Europe.

The largest factors in Milan's modern industrial life are textiles and machinery. Locomotives and other railway equipment, also motor-cars, electrical supplies, carriages, and rubber goods are important articles of manufacture. Here are centred the silk, artificial silk, and cotton industries of Italy. Milan has an airport and a huge railway station—claimed to be the largest in the world.

After the surrender of Italy to the Allies in September 1943, during the Second World War (1939–45), the Germans continued to use that country as a battle-field. Milan, an important military centre, was heavily garrisoned by German troops, and suffered a number of bombing attacks by Allied aircraft, many famous buildings being damaged. In April 1945, Italian patriots, encouraged by the rapid approach of the Allies, rose against the Germans, and the city was liberated on April 27. The population is 1,268,000.

**MILAN'S MAGNIFICENTLY DECORATED CATHEDRAL**
Architecturally, the principal glory of Milan is its Cathedral dedicated to the Virgin Mary (see also page 1236). The city, the second largest in Italy—surpassed only by Rome—is the richest commercial and industrial town in the country. Its products include motor-cars, machinery, locomotives, electrical equipment and furniture.

**Mildews** AND MOULDS. We frequently find small downy or velvety patches on the surface of leaves, fruit, damp cloth, moist foodstuffs, and other substances. Sometimes the growth covers a large area with a very thin film of soft cottony tissue. By using a magnifying glass we discern that the growth is composed of a great number of tiny plants. Under a high-powered microscope we can see the structure of these tiny plants, and we discover that their threadlike bodies cover the surface on which they grow with a network of delicate cobweb-like strands (the *mycelium*), of which the branches are called *hyphae*.

Mildews and moulds are members of the *fungi*, which include toadstools, mushrooms, and similar forms. Like all fungi, they are either parasites, living upon the bodies of other plants larger than themselves; or else they are saprophytes (Greek *sapros*, " rotten," and *phuton*, " plant "), living upon dead vegetable and animal matter. The name m i l d e w s should be restricted to those " blights " of which the mycelial threads form a film over leaves and shoots of plants, while their hyphae attack the cells of the surface layers.

" Downy mildews " do a great deal of harm to the stems and leaves of plants, drying them up and making them curl and twist. One of the best-known of these is the rose mildew, familiar to most gardeners from its frequent appearance, in the form of white patches, on the leaves and stems of rose trees.

If a piece of bread is soaked in water and then left in a warmish room for four or five days, while under cover, white patches of mould will appear on the surface, and we say then that the bread is " mouldy." One of the most common of these moulds is named *Mucor mucedo*. It is quite likely that a green mould will also grow on the bread, belonging to the genus *Aspergillus* or *Eurotium*. At first these moulds also are white, but turn green as they develop. A blue mould known as *Penicillium glaucum* attacks almost any form of dead organic matter. If present in a sugary solution it will, like yeast (*q.v.*), which is also a fungus, cause fermentation and produce alcohol.

From another mould of the *Penicillium* genus (*P. notatum*) is obtained the wonder-working germ-killer penicillin (*q.v.*). This mould is grown on a solution of sugar with various salts; it forms tiny quantities of penicillin, which pass into the solution and have to be extracted by rather complex procedure. Moulds are potent for evil as well as for good, and some cause diseases in Man and the animals. (*See* Fungus).

*J. J. Ward; E. A. Botting*
**MOULD AND MILDEW MAGNIFIED**
The left-hand picture shows the spore-bearing heads of the common blue mildew (*Penicillium glaucum*), which is referred to in the text. On the right is seen the extraordinary appearance of a tomato attacked by the mould *Mucor*. Both these pictures are very highly magnified.

**Milk.** In infancy and in its corresponding stage, milk is the food of all the higher animals, or mammals (i.e. animals whose young are suckled at the breast). The breast contains special glands for secreting milk, manufactured by Nature from the ordinary food eaten by adult female animals. The food elements needed to build all the various tissues are found in milk—and found, generally speaking, in the most easily digestible and usable form for the growing creature.

While the milk of its mother is usually the best food for the young animal until the stage of " weaning " (gradually changing to more like adult food), sometimes the milk of the human mother does not agree with her offspring; or perhaps she has not a large enough quantity for its growth and health. Then a substitute has to be found. Today there are many such substitutes, generally prepared from cow's milk with certain additions or with special treatment to make it more like the food Nature supplies. However, the milk from the mother's breast has inherent in it some protection against many of the diseases she herself has had, and she passes on this protection to her child. This is why even a few feeds from the mother's breast are of great value, even when they have to be supplemented by other foods.

For the adult, milk is a valuable food if other food is scarce. If, however, varied food is plentiful, milk is often not a wise addition to the diet, as its digestion falls largely to the liver, leaving the liver too fatigued to grapple with its innumerable other important functions. Milk is essentially the food of the young vigorous growing animal, not of the sedentary grown-up; and, indeed, it does not agree with all children. Nowadays all patients, however young, with asthma, chronic catarrh, hay fever, eczema, and the like type of disease, are taken straight off raw milk as a routine treatment.

Among English-speaking people the cow furnishes by far the largest share of the milk supply; the Laplander drinks the milk of reindeer; the Beduin of the desert get their milk from the camel; the roving Tartar drinks mare's milk. Sheep, goats, asses, buffaloes, and even zebus contribute, in one region or another, to the world's milk supply. The milk of goats and ewes is rich in fats and is used in making some of the most famous European cheeses. The raising of milch goats is a prominent industry in Switzerland, and is being encouraged in England and the U.S.A.

Whatever its source all milk contains the same valuable food elements, though in different pro-

# MILK

portions. In good cow's milk there is about a quarter of a pound of food solids to every quart—as much as in three-quarters of a pound of beef. The most important of these solids are: (1) butter fat, the chief constituent of butter; (2) casein or curd, which forms the body of cheese; (3) milk-sugar, or lactose, which is less sweet than cane-sugar; (4) mineral salts, which build bone.

Milk is the hardest food to replace in the diet of children, because it is a rich source of calcium, which few other foods have. The vitamin content of milk, especially vitamins A and D, is important, and particularly necessary to the growth and vigorous health of the young. But this content depends on the cow being much on pasture land eating fresh grass. Milk from stall-fed cows can be poor in this vitamin content, and their foodstuffs are now often irradiated to replace it (*see* Vitamins). The casein of milk, moreover, is more easily digested than any other protein, and milk-sugar is more readily assimilated than any other kind of sugar.

Of the many milk products, butter (*q.v.*) is the most important, because it is largely made up of the valuable fats. Cheese (*q.v.*), which is made in a great variety of ways in various countries, is rich in casein as well as fats. Ice-cream is a valuable food, since it contains all the milk solids, unless it has been prepared from cornflour or such like cheaper materials. Evaporated milk is whole milk with part of the water removed. Condensed milk is similar, but with sugar added as a preservative. To make powdered milk, the heating is continued until nearly all the water is evaporated and the thickened milk is then sprayed into hot air so that the dried milk falls in fine powder. Besides taking up less room than fresh milk in storage and shipment, evaporated, condensed, and powdered milk can be kept indefinitely and be shipped long distances. By simply adding water to powdered milk, a product is obtained closely resembling fresh milk. After the removal of fats and casein to make butter and cheese, the whey still contains milk-sugar. This is removed for use in the making of infant foods and " sugar-coated " pills.

Butter-milk, the fluid which remains after churning for butter, is a valuable drink. It gets its acid flavour from the conversion of much of its sugar into lactic acid. There are several fermented milk drinks, the best-known of which is the koumiss originally made by the Tartars from mare's milk.

4/5 lb. of Beefsteak

1¼ lbs. of Chicken

½ lb. of Ham

2⅓ lbs. of Codfish

8 Average Size Eggs

1½ lbs. of Beans

2⅔ lbs. of Peas

6⅔ lbs. of Tomatoes

Water 87%

Mineral Salts 0.75%
Protein 3.35%
Sugar 4.90%
Fat 4%

## THE VALUE OF MILK AS A PRODUCER OF ENERGY

Food serves a variety of purposes—to build body tissue, to supply fuel for body heat and activity, and to maintain a reserve of fat. This diagram shows how valuable milk is as an energy producer—that is, for making ' body fuel.'

The quart of milk in the centre of the picture is equivalent in ' energy value,' measured in calories, to any of the other quantities of foodstuffs shown. Its efficiency as a body builder, arising from its protein content, is also high.

This is now made on a large scale from cow's milk in Europe and America for invalids. Malted milk is made by mixing whole milk with the liquid obtained from a mash of ground barley, malt, and wheat flour, and drying into a product like powdered milk.

Casein has a wide use in the industrial arts in addition to its use as a food. It is employed in the manufacture of coated papers to produce the smooth surface necessary for fine half-tone printing. It also enters into the manufacture of glues, cements, oilcloth, water paints, and various kinds of enamels. Hardened by a special process, it makes a material which can be moulded, and is used for buttons, electric insulation, combs, and other articles.

*After G. F. Watts; National Portrait Gallery*
**JOHN STUART MILL**
**Famous son of a famous father, J. S. Mill was the greatest economist of the Victorian Era. That he was interested in other things than economics is clear from his Autobiography.**

When the Second World War broke out in September 1939, the British government made special arrangements for maintaining and then increasing the supply of cow's milk, which in the phrase used by the official account of wartime agriculture was " Priority Food No. 1." Owing to the stoppage or diminution of oversea supplies of eggs, butter, meat and fruit, farmers were urged and aided to produce more milk.

Invalids and young people were assured of extra supplies; arrangements were made to sell milk at cheaper rates to the poorer members of the community—or they were even able to get it free. During the war years Britain's milking cows were increased in number by 300,000. In the year 1944–45 the number of dairy cows was nearly three million. The total milk output increased during the war period from 1,300,000,000 gallons per year to 1,400,000,000 gallons.

**Mill, JOHN STUART** (1806–73). One of the foremost thinkers of the 19th century, and a political economist whose writings are still often quoted, John Stuart Mill was born in London on May 20, 1806.

The son of James Mill, himself a philosopher and historian of great learning, John Stuart was very carefully educated. It is said that he could read Greek at three years of age, and that by the time he had reached the age of 14 he had a good knowledge of an extraordinary number of subjects. He entered the service of the East India Company, in which his father held a high position as a clerk, and remained there for 33 years, eventually occupying his father's old post. He wrote extensively for the reviews, and published many books on political economy. He also entered Parliament, and corresponded with all classes of people, from Carlyle down to labourers, on public questions.

Mill was a man of very liberal views and a recognized leader of the Utilitarian school of political philosophy, i.e. of those who held, with Jeremy Bentham (*q.v.*), that the " happiness of the greatest number " should be the object aimed at in legislation. Though his views on political economy (or economics as we usually call it today) are now somewhat out of date, his books On Liberty, Representative Government, and The Subjection of Women —particularly the first—are still perhaps the best on their particular subjects. Not the least of Mill's claims to be remembered is that he was one of the first to advocate votes for women. He died at Avignon, France, on May 8, 1873, and is buried there beside his wife.

**Millet.** One-third of the world, it is estimated, relies for its staple food on the seeds of the cultivated grasses called millets. Originally the name applied only to the true Egyptian millet (broomcorn millet), but today it covers a wide variety of grasses with seeds large enough to be ground into flour by peoples who lack the larger grain crops. Millet flours are not so palatable as most other breadstuffs, but most of them are very nutritious and the plants can be grown in regions where other cereal crops will not flourish because of scanty rainfall or extremes of temperature. They are extensively cultivated in China, India, and Africa. The seeds are ground up for meal, or parched, or even eaten raw. From the seeds also a great variety of beers and other fermented drinks are made.

In the United States the millet grasses are usually grown only for hay, for silage, for poultry food and bird seed, or as a crop to be ploughed in, as " green

**PORTUGUESE MILLET HARVEST**
**One of the chief cereal crops, millet is a grass of which various types are cultivated. That shown here has long seed-heads, which are being swept in great masses into a barn.**

manure," to enrich the soil. Millets are very prolific, and have been cultivated in the Old World since prehistoric times. Ordinary millet seeds are smaller and far more numerous than those of the more common cereals.

**Millet,** JEAN FRANÇOIS (1814–75). Amid rural scenes in Normandy the great artist of peasant life, Millet (pron. mē'-yā), spent his early days; and the love of Nature and the life of the peasants that in later years he put on canvas were the priceless heritage of his own upbringing. His parents were farmers. He was born at Gruchy, on October 4, 1814, and as soon as he was old enough he had to work in the fields. But the noon rest hour gave him a little time in which to draw, and at night he read and studied. When he was 18, the family savings were put together and he

was sent to near-by Cherbourg to study. In 1836 he went to Paris with an art scholarship.

After living in various parts of Normandy and in Paris, Millet settled in 1849 in the little village of Barbizon, on the borders of the forest of Fontainebleau, near Paris. There, living once more among the peasants, he produced that famous series of pictures, The Man with the Hoe, The Water Carrier, The Sower, The Gleaners, and The Angelus. (*See* illustration page 1372).

Artists and students understood Millet and his pictures, but he was not publicly appreciated for many years. Yet through him arose the famous group of painters known as the Barbizon school (*see* France, Art of). Just when he was becoming generally recognized his health failed, and he died on January 20, 1875.

# GREAT MAKER *of* MAJESTIC VERSE

*E*ngland's second greatest poet was John Milton, the most lasting product *of the Puritan period and writer of the most memorable epics in our language. His life below is followed by the story of Paradise Lost.*

**Milton,** JOHN (1608–74). Milton was born December 9, 1608, eight years before the death of Shakespeare. To quote his own words: " I was born in London, of a good family, my father a very honourable man." His father was a cultivated gentleman, although Puritan in sympathy, a distinguished musician, and a well to do "scrivener" (a sort of attorney and financial agent).

Like his father, John came to be an accomplished musician; he is said to have had " a delicate tunable voice, and great skill." By his ninth year he was writing verse, and under private tutors perfecting his Latin and Greek. At 12 he was entered at St. Paul's as a day scholar. After that age, he tells us, he scarcely ever quit his lessons before midnight. The brilliant boy was trained to the limit of his capacities and beyond the limits of his health and eyesight. By the time he left school for Cambridge, in his 17th year, he was well acquainted with French, Italian, and Hebrew, as well as Greek and Latin.

Milton was at Cambridge until his 24th year. He was a strikingly handsome young man, far advanced in his studies beyond most of his fellow students. His early biographers agree that he " was a very hard scholar at the University, and performed all his exercises there with very good applause." He left the university in July 1632. His father, who was almost 70, had taken a country house at Horton, a Buckinghamshire village.

*Courtesy of the Duke of Buccleuch*
**JOHN MILTON**
**The truth of the report that the poet John Milton was a very handsome young man is demonstrated by this miniature. He became blind at the age of 46, and died in 1674. (*See* also page 1212).**

There Milton settled to the attempt to write "things unattempted yet in prose or rhyme." There in trial flight, as he called it, he wrote L'Allegro, Il Penseroso, Comus, Lycidas, and some of his sonnets.

In 1637 his mother had died. Approaching his 30th year, with such stupendous hopes and, he thought, with so little yet accomplished, alone at Horton with his aged father, he began to be irked by solitude and obscurity, and he set out on a Continental tour. From Paris, where the English Ambassador entertained him, he moved on to two months in Florence, where " I found and visited the famous Galileo, grown old, a prisoner of the Inquisition." After two months in Rome he moved on to Naples, where he was checked by news that civil war was likely in England and gave up his plans to visit Sicily and Greece. " I thought it disgraceful, while my fellow citizens fought for liberty at home, to be travelling for pleasure abroad." But he took his time in returning home, spending six more months in Italy, and tarrying a while in Geneva.

Milton had been away 15 months. He found that in those troubled times the household at Horton had been broken up and the family fortunes sadly depleted. " I hired for myself and my books a large house in the city (London), where I happily resumed my interrupted studies." There, about to embark on " the troubled sea of noises and hoarse dispute " as a writer of pamphlets, he undertook the education of the two sons of his sister, Mrs. Phillips. Later he took other pupils as well. The Long Parliament was called in 1640. In 1641 Milton launched the first of his pamphlets—the gun that opened his 20 years of political warfare, attacking the corruptions of State and Church and upholding the ideals of the Puritans.

In the spring of 1642 (or possibly 1643) Milton visited a Royalist family that lived near Oxford. He returned a married man—a 35-year-old husband with a pretty 17-year-old bride, Mary Powell. It was an unhappy marriage. Mary, says an early biographer, " found it very solitary; no company came to her." After about a month she went back to her family, promising to return soon. She was away three years. Under the spur of his unhappy situation he wrote a pamphlet on The Doctrine and Discipline of Divorce, advocating freedom of divorce. In passionate language, often of haunting beauty, he set forth ideals of marriage that even today sound rather " advanced." The pamphlet was greeted by a storm of insult, and by an attempt to prosecute him for unlicensed printing. In reply he wrote the masterfully eloquent Areopagitica, the most able defence of the freedom of the press that has ever been written.

From 1645 to 1649 Milton rested his pen and remained a silent witness of the Civil War. But a few days before the execution of Charles I Milton's voice again arose—it was the first to rise—upholding the right of the people to execute a guilty sovereign. With astounding courage (or the audacity of desperation) he published the Tenure of Kings and Magistrates, in January 1649. In March of the same year he was appointed secretary for foreign tongues under Cromwell. His duties were to conduct correspondence with foreign States and to

**MILTON'S COTTAGE**

To this 'pretty box' in the Buckinghamshire village of Chalfont St. Giles the gifted Puritan poet retired · in the summer of 1665, when the Great Plague swept through London. It is now a Milton museum.

write pamphlets setting forth the views of the government. To that task he deliberately sacrificed his eyesight. Complete blindness came to him in 1652.

Worse even than blindness was the shattering of all his ideals and hopes with the downfall of the Commonwealth in 1660. The House of Commons ordered him to be arrested and that all copies of his pamphlets defending the execution of Charles I should be burned by the hangman. Through the good offices of powerful friends at court he escaped prosecution, but he was actually taken into custody and released only after the payment of large fees.

Now in his 52nd year, blind, embittered, and cramped by the loss of a considerable part of his fortune, Milton was free to resume the poetic task which he had given up 20 years before. His

**ANDREW MARVELL GREETS MILTON AT CHALFONT ST. GILES**

This is The Meeting of Milton and Andrew Marvell at Chalfont St. Giles, a painting by G. Boughton, R.A. In fine weather Milton delighted to sit outside his house to receive his visitors. Marvell, who achieved fame as a poet and satirist, had been of service to the blind poet when he was Latin Secretary to the Council of Foreign Affairs.

household consisted of three daughters, borne to him by his first wife, who had returned to him in 1645 and had died seven years later. His second wife, Katharine Woodcock, whom he had married in 1656, had died within two years. His motherless daughters, we are told, gave him much trouble, rebelling against the drudgery of reading to him and writing at his dictation. His complete egotism made him unlovable, but in 1663 he won domestic peace by taking a third wife, Elizabeth Minshull, a woman 30 years his junior.

With dauntless courage Milton set about the task which he had long meditated. Nothing in literature is more magnificent than the picture of the blind Puritan dictating day after day the superbly rolling periods of his great epic, Paradise Lost. During the Great Plague of 1665 Milton retired to a cottage, still preserved, at Chalfont St. Giles, and in 1667 the world received the book which has had an influence on English thought and language surpassed only by the influence of the Bible and the plays of Shakespeare. The remaining seven years Milton devoted to his second epic, Paradise Regained, and to his tragedy, Samson Agonistes. He died on November 8, 1674, and was buried in St. Giles's, Cripplegate, London.

# THE STORY OF PARADISE LOST

IN this great Puritan epic Milton tells the story—

> Of Man's first disobedience, and the fruit
> Of that forbidden tree whose mortal taste
> Brought death into the World, and all our woe,
> With loss of Eden . . .

The poet plunges right into the heart of the great events which led up to the expulsion of Adam and Eve from Paradise. He takes us first to the abyss of Hell, into which the hosts of Heaven had hurled Satan and the other rebellious angels,

> Hurled headlong flaming from the ethereal sky,
> With hideous ruin and combustion, down
> To bottomless perdition, there to dwell
> In adamantine chains and penal fire,
> Who durst defy the O... 'present to arms.

There they lie stretched out in their vast length along the burning lake, until Satan, concealing his despair, boasts that they will be successful in a second war on Heaven. God in Heaven hears his speech, and lets the flames die down so that Satan may "heap on himself damnation" by a second trial. He rises on huge pinions above the lake, alights on the shore, and proclaims defiantly to the dreadful realm of Hell:

> Receive thy new possessor—one who brings
> A mind not to be changed by place or time.
> The mind is its own place, and in itself
> Can make a Heaven of Hell, a Hell of Heaven.

The rebel chief then marshals his forces, and in an hour builds a huge palace of gold and bronze and marble, more beautiful than any palace of Babylon. A council of war is held at once, and Satan tells the assembly that he has heard rumours of a new world and a new race called Man whom God is about to create, and that perhaps these beings may be seduced to revolt. No one else is bold enough to undertake the perilous mission of finding this new world, so Satan takes it upon himself. He passes out by the gates of Hell, guarded by the foul monsters Sin and Death, after promising them the new race for their own.

Through the dreadful abyss of "Chaos and ancient Night" the Fiend wings his way, skirting the wall of Heaven and finally alighting on the Sun. There he takes the form of a "stripling cherub," in whose face "youth smiled celestial," so completely disguising himself that the Archangel Uriel, whom he meets, shows him the way to the Earth.

Triumphantly Satan speeds thither, alighting on a mountain-top not far from the Garden of Eden, the Paradise of delight in which God had placed the newly created parents of the human race. He then finds his way to the Garden and, disdaining the gate, leaps over the barrier. After admiring the gentle beauties of hill and vale, the rich verdure, the "odorous sweets," he finds the Tree of Life— the forbidden tree—and sits upon it like a bird of prey. He looks out upon the wonders of the place, the living creatures, "new to sight and strange," and—

> Two of far nobler sight, erect and tall,
> God-like erect, with native honour clad
> In naked majesty . . .
> For contemplation he and valour formed,
> For softness she and sweet attractive grace,
> He for God only, she for God in him.

These beings are Adam and Eve, who lead blissful and happy lives in Paradise, which yields them "nectarine fruits" to eat as they sit—

> On the soft, downy bank damasked with flowers.

About them, frisking harmlessly, the animals play—

> Sporting the lion ramped, and in his paw
> Dandled the kid ; bears, tigers, ounces, pards,
> Gambolled before them; the unwieldy elephant,
> To make them mirth, used all his might, and wreathed
> His lithe proboscis.

In the shape now of a lion, now a tiger, now some other animal, the vengeful Fiend stalks round the happy couple and overhears the secret by which their downfall is to be worked—that the one command God has placed on them is not to eat of the fruit of the Tree of Knowledge. When Satan hears this he exultantly says to himself :

> O fair foundation laid whereon to build
> Their ruin! . . .
> . . . . . . . Live while ye may,
> Yet happy pair; enjoy, till I return,
> Short pleasures; for long woes are to succeed!

Soon Adam and Eve retire to rest, for—

> Now came still Evening on, and Twilight grey
> Had in her sober livery all things clad;
> Silence accompanied; for beast and bird,
> They to their grassy couch, these to their nests
> Were slunk, all but the wakeful nightingale,
> She all night long her amorous descant sung.

When all has sunk to rest Gabriel, who guards the gates of Paradise, sends two angels to search the garden. They find Satan crouched, "squat like a toad," at Eve's ear, trying to corrupt her mind by dreams. They drive him forth, but the Fiend's work had already been done. On awaking, Eve tells Adam of the dream in which Satan had told her that the forbidden fruit would make her a goddess. Adam comforts her distress, and they sing a hymn of praise.

The Almighty, understanding the stir that Satan had raised in Paradise, and his baleful schemes, summons Raphael, " the sociable spirit," and bids him visit Adam and warn him of danger. The winged spirit perceives Adam sitting at the door of his cool bower, while Eve is preparing dinner within. Hospitably they invite the heavenly guest to share their meal of the choicest fruits of Paradise. Seated on mossy turfs about a table of raised turf, they hold a long conversation.

Raphael tells his hosts the story of Satan's rebellion and defeat, and relates the story of Creation. He tells how, after the rebel angels had been hurled into Hell, God had made a new world and a new race to take the place of Satan and his hosts. Adam in turn tells of his first experiences, how he had awakened to find himself lying on a bed of grass, amid the warbling of birds and the murmur of streams. And he describes how God, to relieve his loneliness, had taken from his side a rib, which He had fashioned into a creature—

> . . . so lovely fair
> That what seemed fair in all the world seemed now
> Mean . . .

After warning Adam against the wiles of the Evil One, Raphael departs. Meanwhile Satan has been circling the Earth, and has decided to take the shape of the Serpent.

In the morning Eve asks Adam to let her work apart from him that day. Adam is fearful of danger, but at last consents ; and Satan, greatly to his joy, finds Eve alone, " veiled in a cloud of fragrance." He goes towards her, " his head crested aloft and carbuncle his eyes." He

> Curled many a wanton wreath in sight of Eve,
> To lure her eye.

Eve hears the rustling of his folds among the leaves, and is astounded that he uses the speech of Man. He tells her that she should be admired by all the world—here in Eden there is only Adam to know how beautiful she is; and that he (the Serpent) had received his power of speech by eating the fruit of a certain tree.

Eve answers:

> Serpent, thy overpraising leaves in doubt
> The virtue of that fruit, in thee first proved.
> But say, where grows the tree? . . .

Satan leads her to the tree, and she recognizes it as the forbidden tree that bears the one fruit they must not taste, lest they die. Satan says that threat is false; and he has eaten and has not died. If Adam and Eve eat, they shall be as gods. Eve listens to the tempter and eats the forbidden fruit. It seems to her that she has never tasted such delight, and she decides that Adam shall share with her in it;

## ADAM AND EVE BEFORE PARADISE WAS LOST

John Milton's grandest poem is based on the Bible story of Adam and Eve in the Garden of Eden. But whereas the Genesis account is in the stately prose of Tudor England, Milton's is penned in sonorous blank verse. This picture, reproduced from a painting by John Martin (1789-1854), illustrates an incident in the poem that is not in the Bible. Adam and Eve, emerging from a glade of the garden, are confronted by the dazzling shape of the Archangel Raphael.

Adam is horrified, but resolves to eat the fruit and, if needs be, die with her, since without her he cannot live. And then, though

> Sky loured, and, muttering thunder, some sad drops
> Wept at completing of the mortal Sin,
>
> . . . . . . . . . .
> They swim in mirth and fancy that they feel
> Divinity within them breeding wings
> Wherewith to scorn the Earth.

But soon their high spirits droop and they quarrel. Sleep does not refresh them, and they are ashamed of their nakedness. They make for themselves girdles of leaves, and then soon—

> . . . The voice of God they heard
> Now walking in the Garden.

God asks them why they hide, and they confess their guilt. Adam says :

> She gave me of the Tree, and I did eat.

Eve, " with shame nigh overwhelmed," replies:

> The Serpent me beguiled, and I did eat.

God pronounces punishment first upon the Serpent, decreeing that he shall thenceforward creep on his belly and shall be hated by woman evermore. Eve's doom is to be always subject to her husband's will, and to bear children in sorrow. Adam's is to till the ground in the sweat of his brow.

Rejoicing in his successful villainy, Satan meanwhile returns to Pandemonium and boastfully relates his deeds before the assembly of the fallen angels. He waits for their applause in his yearning and dismay his ears are filled instead with the sound of hissing from innumerable tongues. Amazed, he looks about, and sees that God has changed the rebel hosts into a den of swarming serpents with forked tongues, and—crowning horror !—Satan himself crawls on his belly, a monstrous serpent.

Overwhelmed with grief, Adam and Eve at first wish for death; but gradually courage and hope return, and they resolve to bear their lot submissively. Prostrate they fall on the spot where God had judged them—

> . . . And both confessed
> Humbly their faults, and pardon begged, with tears
> Watering the ground.

The Son of God presents their prayers to the Father and intercedes for them. God accepts their repentance, and consents to the ultimate redemption of the race, but decrees that they must leave Paradise. The Archangel Michael leads them forth from the Garden by the hand, while the fiery sword waves behind them and the Cherubim take their stations to guard the Paradise they had lost; and so they depart.

> Some natural tears they dropped, but wiped them
> soon;
> The world was all before them, where to choose
> Their place of rest, and Providence their guide.
> They, hand in hand, with wandering steps and slow,
> Through Eden took their solitary way.

**Mind.** Whatever men mean by the word " I," when they say, " I know or believe, I suffer, or rejoice," this is the mind of Man—it is that part of him which thinks, remembers, reasons, feels or wills.

The dictionaries tell us that mind is " conscious intelligence " or the " faculty of knowing." The brain is the main seat of the mind, yet mind can scarcely be said to be absent from any tissue in which feeling resides, and some, with Herbert Spencer, the Victorian philosopher-scientist, have even assumed the existence of a "mind dust" diffused with matter throughout the universe. Certainly an inter-relationship exists between the physical body and the mind, and this is so nicely balanced that for either to be well and normal the other must be well also. Thus the old Greeks were not wrong when they set up as their ideal " a sound mind in a sound body." Psychology is the science which deals with study of the mind. The modern tendency is to emphasize behaviour, or what the individual does, rather than conscious states, or what he is thinking.

There are differences of opinion as to how far down the animal scale what is usually called mind can be traced. Some writers hold it to be characteristic only of human beings; others see in the human being only a more complex manifestation of what is present to some extent in all animals.

**Mineralogy.** This is the science of minerals (q.v.). A mineralogist identifies minerals by studying their properties, such as composition, crystalline form, colour, hardness, specific gravity, and optical properties when examined with the microscope. He is also interested in the ways in which minerals occur in Nature, the places where they are found, and their uses.

In identifying minerals, the modern mineralogist obtain very much assistance from the chemist and the X-ray expert. (See Crystals).

**Minerals.** The solid part of our earth, known as the earth's crust, is composed of rocks (see Rocks ; Chemistry), and these rocks are made up of " minerals." Many rocks contain several minerals ; an ordinary piece of granite can be seen with the naked eye to contain at least three minerals —dark coloured flakes (mica), pinkish crystals (feldspar), and a glassy material (quartz). But some great masses of rock material are made up almost entirely of one mineral only ; examples of such masses are natural rock salt (common salt, sodium chloride), and gypsum (calcium sulphate). Gypsum is used to make plaster of Paris.

All these substances that make up the rocks of the earth are called minerals ; some, such as our quartz, rock salt, and gypsum, are pure or almost pure chemical compounds ; others, such as the mica and feldspar of granite, vary in chemical composition, but are homogeneous (consisting of the same substance throughout), just as a solution of sugar in water, though a mixture, is quite homogeneous. Minerals like mica (q.v.) are complicated silicates ; there are many micas of different chemical composition, but they all have similar internal arrangements of the atoms, and similar properties, such as the ease with which they can be split into thin sheets. Thus the name mica is given to a whole family of minerals having similar physical properties. There are many other families, e.g. the feldspars.

Silicate minerals are of great importance to Man, for not only are they the materials of which roadstones and many building stones are composed, but some of them have other important uses. For examples, mica is used in large quantities in the electrical industries; feldspar is used during the manufacture of glass and pottery; quartz, in the form of sand, is used in glass manufacture and for many other purposes. Crystals of quartz are employed in radio-communication to fix the frequency of broadcasting stations. We see then that our three friends, the minerals found in granite, have many uses. There are other useful silicate minerals, such as talc, which is added to toilet-powders, paints, paper, etc.; and asbestos, which is used to make fireproof materials, such as safety curtains and firemen's rope and clothing.

All our precious stones, such as diamond (pure carbon), amethyst (a form of quartz, silica), and ruby (aluminium oxide) are minerals; and the precious metals gold and platinum are found in Nature in the metallic form as " native " gold and " native " platinum. The commoner metals, much used by Man, such as iron, zinc, and aluminium, are obtained chiefly from minerals which are compounds of the metal with other elements. Iron is mined mainly as haematite (oxide), limonite (hydrated oxide), siderite (carbonate), and magnetite (magnetic oxide); zinc is found mainly as zinc blende (sulphide), smithsonite (carbonate), and hemimorphite (silicate); aluminium occurs mainly as bauxite (oxide).

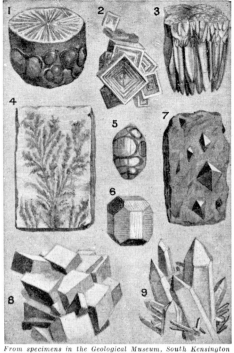

From specimens in the Geological Museum, South Kensington

**MINERAL CRYSTALS**
**1. Marcasite, showing internal radial structure. 2. Hopper-shaped crystals of salt. 3. Haematite, with nodular exterior and crystalline internal structure. 4. Dendritic pyrolusite. 5. Olivine crystal. 6. Pyrite. 7. Octahedral crystals of magnetite in schist. 8. Crystals of fluorspar. 9. Quartz crystals.**

Many minerals, such as diamond and quartz, are found in the form of beautiful crystals (q.v.); while other minerals, such as bauxite and limonite, do not appear crystalline to the naked eye, though the X-ray tells us that their atoms are arranged in a definite pattern.

Even clay is composed of minerals, though it was not until the X-ray was used to explore their inner secrets that the nature of the " clay minerals " began to be understood. By heating clay, Man makes bricks; and by heating clay with limestone (q.v.) he makes Portland cement.

The sand you find in sand pits and on the sea shore is usually composed mainly of rounded grains of quartz, though other minerals, such as feldspar and magnetite, may be present.

Coal, which is largely made up of carbon, hydrogen, and oxygen, is classed among our mineral resources; but, being of variable composition and not homogeneous, it is not a mineral in the strictly scientific sense.

Without minerals we could not have acids, salts, and other chemicals; glass, porcelain, pottery, brick; pigments such as ochre and umber; some writing materials; some plant fertilizers; bicycles, motor-cars, machinery and the many things made by machines; and a whole host of articles that we take for granted in our everyday life.

# EXTRACTING WEALTH *from the* EARTH

*The world is dependent to an enormous extent on the products of mining. How the prospector and the miner go about their important and often difficult tasks varies in accordance with the mineral concerned.*

**Mines and Mining.** The most important basic industries are agriculture and mining; between them they produce nearly all the raw materials required in modern life. But they differ in one fundamental respect. The products of agriculture are replenished by seasonal growth but the products of mining cannot be replaced, and so it is necessary to search for new mineral deposits continually if the exhaustion of those already being worked is to be made good.

Geological exploration, or prospecting, is therefore a most important branch of mining. This is now being done with the aid of scientific instruments and special tools, but the prospector can often tell from the appearance of the rocks if they are likely to contain useful minerals. The best

opportunities for such observations are generally to be found along the beds of streams and rivers where the rocks are exposed to view. In the course of time the rivers have not only washed away the soil but they have also worn down the rocks to some extent, and the resulting silt and gravel which collect in the alluvial deposits on the flat reaches of many streams and rivers are found to contain gold and other valuable minerals in a finely divided state.

The recovery of minerals from alluvial deposits is called placer mining, and it has been going on for thousands of years. The existence of gold in the river beds was known in very early times, and the ancient practice of placing a sheepskin in the stream to catch the heavy gold particles which became entangled in the wool—may have given rise to the legend of the Golden Fleece (see Argonauts). This method is still employed at gold mines in South Africa and other parts of the world, where the crushed ore is carried by water over woollen blankets or corduroy fabrics in which the coarser pieces of gold are caught. Much more elaborate methods are employed to extract the remainder of the gold from the ore.

The prospector uses a shallow metal pan for testing samples of silt and gravel. The sample is stirred with water in the pan to enable the gold or other heavy mineral particles to settle at the bottom, and the upper layers of dirt are washed away by repeatedly adding water and pouring off the surplus until only the minerals remain in the pan. The familiar phrase " How did it pan out ? " owes its origin to this practice.

Placer mining is carried out by digging, dredging or hydraulicing. In the latter, the gravel bed is

**HEWING COAL IN A SOMERSETSHIRE MINE**
*Fox*
Deep down in the bowels of the earth this miner follows his dangerous trade, hewing out the coal which is the very basis of Britain's industrial activity. The seam in which he is working is but two feet high, and his only light is the small lamp fixed in his cap.

broken down by means of powerful water-jets directed on to the vertical sides of the deposit in the same manner as a fire-hose is used on the walls of a building. The water not only breaks up the gravel, it also helps to separate the minerals from the dirt. Dredging is widely used, and most of the tin produced during recent years has been obtained by this method from alluvial deposits in the rivers and lakes of Malaya.

Prospectors are mainly concerned with discovering the rocks from which the minerals came originally. Gold and other precious metals are usually found in the metallic state in the minerals which contain them ; but the base metals—copper, lead, zinc, tin, etc.—are never found as such but as constituents of various chemical compounds containing oxygen, sulphur and other elements, and the metals have to be extracted from these compounds by smelting and refining processes after the ores have been taken out of the mine.

Minerals which are rich enough to be used for the extraction of metals are called ores. The

ores of most metals, with the exception of iron and aluminium, are found in the form of elongated or lenticular bodies of variable thickness and inclination in the rock structure of the earth. Iron and aluminium ores sometimes occur in very large irregular masses, and sometimes in stratified beds similar to the beds of limestone and chalk which are to be seen in seaside cliffs and in railway cuttings. Miners refer to the first type of ore bodies as veins, lodes or reefs.

When the existence of a lode or ore-body has been discovered, the prospector or his employer completes the legal formalities required for the acquisition of mining rights; and he then proceeds to test the quality and the extent of the ore by putting down boreholes by means of a diamond drill. If possible, he also examines the upper portions of the lode by trenching or by digging shallow pits. The diamond drill consists of a long metal tube with black diamonds riveted into the end to act as cutters ; as the tube rotates a core of rock of a few inches in diameter is bored out, and this is brought to the surface in successive lengths for examination. Additional lengths of tube are screwed on as boring proceeds until the hole in some cases reaches a depth of more than a mile.

The method of mining depends on whether the ore-body is near the surface or deep in the earth, or whether it is in a mountain or under level ground. If it is sufficiently near the surface it is extracted by the open pit or open cast method. This mode of mining is similar to that used in stone quarries, and it is often used for getting coal as well as ores. If the ore-body is in a mountain, it is reached by driving adits, or tunnels, into it from different levels. The adits are given a slight upward inclination from the outlet inwards, so that any water encountered in the workings may run out of the mine. When the ore-body is below the general land surface it is reached by vertical or inclined shafts from which cross-cuts, or tunnels, are driven into it at different levels (see the diagrams of a coal mine and a gold mine in opposite page).

The ore is extracted between the successive levels by underhand or overhand stoping; that is, by breaking the ore from above downwards, or from below upwards, with the aid of pneumatic drills and explosives. The working places in a metal mine are called stopes, but in a coal mine the working place is referred to as the coal-face.

The distance from one level to the next in a metal mine is about 120 feet and the levels are connected at frequent intervals along their lengths by vertical shafts called winzes, which are necessary for ventilation and to give access to the stopes. The broken ore falls from the stopes to timber chutes on the level below, from which it is loaded into the mine cars in which it is taken to the shaft; there the cars are tipped into a large pocket, or bunker, from which the ore flows into the skip, or container, attached to the winding rope which lifts it to the surface. The lode or reef is usually inclined at a steep angle, and the stopes in a metal

# MINES THAT ARE LIKE THE HOMES OF GIANT ANTS

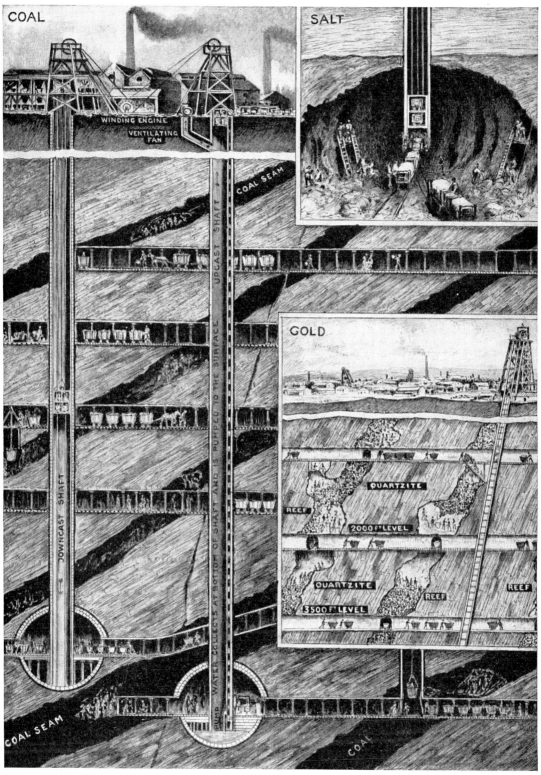

In diagrammatic form is shown how men work in getting coal, salt and gold out of the earth. The general principle is much the same, the excavated material being brought to a shaft and hoisted to the surface. In a drawing such as this it is not possible to show things to scale; for example, the diameter of a shaft is considerably greater than the thickness of a seam. With the increase of mechanical working, ponies are used in fewer numbers.

mine stand one above the other so that the miners work on different levels.

A coal seam, on the other hand, is usually flat or only slightly inclined, and the workings thus spread out laterally from the shaft. In the course of many years the workings of a coal mine may extend to a distance of several miles from the shafts. In Great Britain the coal is removed along a continuous face and each miner is allotted so many yards, up to about 12, of the face as his working place. This mode of working is called the longwall method. In the U.S.A. solid pillars of coal are left between the individual working places as the face advances; and these pillars are subsequently removed, the inner ones being removed first and the rest in succession.

In all cases the roof, or strata above the seam, collapses into the " goaf," or open space left after the coal has been removed, and great skill is needed to control the rate of subsidence to prevent serious accidents. To minimise the effects of subsidence the goaf is filled, as far as it is possible to do so, with waste rock as the coal face advances. Steel or timber props are also inserted to support

leading to the face. The cars are then marshalled to a point where they are formed into trains, which are hauled to the shaft by locomotives or by wire ropes operated by stationary engines installed near the bottom of the shaft. The employment of ponies and horses for haulage in mines is rapidly giving way to these mechanical methods. At least two shafts are necessary in a mine to enable air to be circulated through the workings and to provide an alternative means of escape in case of accidents.

Metal miners formerly used candles and carbide lamps for illumination, and coal miners used the oil safety lamp on account of the danger of igniting methane, or firedamp, which is nearly always present in a coal mine (see illus. page 1889). But portable electric lamps are now in general use at all mines, and electric lighting from the mains is also largely used on the principal roadways.

The amount of coal still left in the earth at a workable depth is estimated to be seven million million tons, and the rate of production throughout the world is 1500 million tons per annum. The position with regard to other minerals cannot be estimated, because new discoveries are being made from time to time. The ores of some metals are, however, getting dangerously near to exhaustion, particularly those of lead and zinc.

The maximum depth to which Man can go to extract minerals is also being approached at some mines in South Africa, India and America. The temperature of the rocks increases with depth, and at a mile or so below the surface it becomes too hot for miners to work. Some of the gold mines near Johannesburg have reached a depth of about 9000 feet, and to enable men to work the air is cooled by powerful refrigerators to nearly the freezing point of water before it enters the mine. (See Coal; Gold).

The Sphere

**DETECTING GERMAN TELLER (' PLATE ') MINES**
These field mines had a sprung top plate, which, when pushed down, fired the charge. They were used in large numbers by the Germans during the Second World War (1939-45). The Russians detected them by using a magnetic ring on a pole (above) which was waved over a suspected area, the presence of a mine being indicated by a dial on the handle.

the roof above the face while the miners are at work there.

Much of the heavy work done in mining is now carried out by machines. Coal-cutting machines working on the principle of the band-saw travel along the face and make cuts about five feet deep under the seam, and at the same time the coal is sheared at the back of the cut in a vertical plane by another cutter attached to the machine. The coal as it falls is gathered by a loading device which transfers it to a conveyor which carries along the face to the mine cars on the roadways

## Mines in Warfare.

The word " mine " has several meanings, and we must be sure which we mean when we use it. The military mine was at first a tunnel made beneath the walls of a besieged fortress, to allow the attackers to gain an entry. Then it denoted next an underground gallery leading to or beneath an enemy's position. It was charged with gunpowder, a fuse was laid back to a point whence the explosive could be safely detonated, and at the chosen moment the fuse was lit. We can see how this meaning was derived, for making the tunnel is merely a special form of " mining." Then the navy has its own " mine," defined as a receptacle filled with explosive and sunk, for example, at the entrance to a harbour which it is intended to block. Submarine mines was the name given to such machines; a coastal fortress might be protected by many such mines laid in its approach waters; they would be connected with the fortress by electric cables, and ignited by pressing buttons if an enemy warship came within striking distance of them, since their position was marked on a chart.

One of the earliest uses of explosives, apart from propelling cannon balls, was for demolishing enemy fortifications, the explosives being placed underneath the stronghold by excavating underground passages. From this, the name mine came to be given to almost any type of explosive charge which is placed in position—in contrast with one (such as a shell or a bomb) which is propelled.

During the First World War (1914–18), which was largely fought in trenches and fixed defence points, the old type of mine was used, and elaborate systems of tunnels (or " saps," as they were called) were dug, often taking months to complete before the charge was laid and fired.

In the Second World War (1939–45), fast transport and tanks made the conflict largely a war of movement, and there was little time or need for such lengthy and elaborate means; mines therefore became little more than buried bombs. About the size of a large soup-plate, they contained an explosive charge set off by a firing mechanism which operated under pressure. When buried in large numbers a foot or two beneath the surface of the ground, they were capable of killing men or wrecking lorries, and were a formidable obstacle to advancing troops. Methods of dealing with them included trained mine recovery squads of brave men who crawled over the minefield with mine

detectors, electrical instruments which could detect the presence of buried metal. When the mines were located, the men dug them up. Another method was to use a " flail tank "; this had a pole projecting in front carrying a revolving wheel which lashed the ground with lengths of steel chain, thus exploding the mines in front of the tank.

### Modern Mines at Sea

The use of " water-petards " or " water-mines " fitted to damage enemy ships below the water-line dates from the siege of Antwerp where, in 1585, the Dutch used clockwork firing mechanisms on their " explosion vessels." The first mine to explode by contact—i.e., on touching a ship—was used by an American, David Bushnell (1742–1824), during the War of Independence (1777), and contact mines have been a feature of sea warfare ever since.

The modern contact mine consists of a steel globe, filled with explosive, which floats below the surface of the sea, being moored by a long wire rope to a heavy " sinker " on the sea bottom; the length of the rope is set when the mines are laid by being dropped overboard from a "minelayer" (ship specially fitted for the work). The contact firing arrangement usually consists of a number of soft lead " horns " which project at various angles from the exterior of the mine. These horns enclose glass tubes containing acid. When a ship bumps against the mine, one of the horns is sure to get bent. The glass tube is broken, and the acid released to form the electrolyte in a battery. The small voltage thus generated is used to fire the explosive.

The Second World War produced a large increase in the use of non-contact or " ground " mines. These were not moored, but lay on the bottom of the sea, and were exploded underneath a ship by various devices, chief of which were the " magnetic " and the " acoustic." The magnetic mine

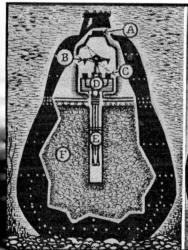 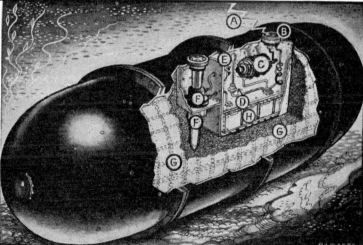

### TWO KINDS OF SEA MINE SOWN BY GERMAN AIRCRAFT

Dropped into the sea at night, the German magnetic and acoustic mines sank many Allied vessels in the Second World War (1939–45). At the left is a sectional diagram of a magnetic mine, which is harmless until the seal (A) has dissolved. Then a ship passing over it deflects the balanced magnet (B), so that one end completes an electric circuit at (C). A weak current, strengthened by the relay (D), fires the detonator (E), which sets off the explosive charge (F). At the right is shown the operation of an acoustic mine. Sound waves (A) from a ship's propeller affect the hydrophone (B) and set the trembler (D) and the electro-magnet (C) vibrating. When the ship is near, the trembler touches the contact (E), setting off the detonator (F) to explode the charge (G). The battery is shown at (H).

contained a delicate magnetic needle, like a compass needle (*see* Magnetism), which was sensitive enough to operate on the change of the magnetic field when a ship passed over it, thus closing electrical firing contacts. The acoustic mine (from the Greek word *akouō*, "I hear") contained a microphone (*q.v.*) mechanism which closed a firing relay operated by the noise made by a ship's propeller when the ship was over the mine.

The clearing up of sea mines is carried out by ships known as "minesweepers." Moored mines are swept by towing a serrated sweep-wire, supported at the other end by what is known as an Oropesa float and a "kite" which causes the wire to swim out in a kind of "J" shape, instead of towing straight astern of the sweeper. The serrated sweep-wire rubs against the mooring wire of the mine, and cuts through it, thus causing the mine to bob up to the surface, where it is either sunk or exploded by gun or rifle fire.

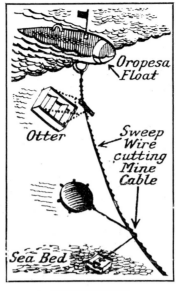

**MINESWEEPING**

**Moored mines are swept by cutting the mooring line with a serrated sweep-wire, supported by an Oropesa float.**

Magnetic sea mines are exploded as they lie on the bottom by special minesweepers which tow a long cable astern of the vessels. Through this cable a heavy electric current is passed, thus producing an artificial magnetic field which is sufficient to explode a mine. The sweeper is herself protected from being blown up by a "de-gaussing" device. This, invented to protect ships from the magnetic mine, consists of a number of turns of cable, wound in a coil round and round the ship, through which a carefully measured current is passed. The magnetic field set up by this coil neutralises the ship's own field, thus preventing the mine from detecting any change in magnetic field when the ship passes over. The only protection from the acoustic mine is to make so much noise (by means of special underwater noise-making devices) that the mine will explode *before* the ship reaches it.

Ground mines were laid by parachute from aeroplanes, as well as by minelaying ships. During the period of the heavy air raids which characterised the Second World War, many ground mines were dropped on land by aircraft, to act as ordinary bombs, detonating by impact.

**Mink.** One of the most popular and luxurious furs worn by women comes from the mink, a long-bodied, slender, brown animal related to both the weasel and the marten. It is found in widely scattered regions of North America, from the Gulf of Mexico to the Arctic Circle, and in northern Europe and Asia. The American mink (*Mustela vison*) is about two feet long, including its eight-inch bushy tail. It has small ears, a long neck and short legs. Its fur is thick and soft, with long, stiff, shiny hairs, which are plucked out by the furrier. The minks of northern regions have the darkest coloured and most lustrous fur. The European species (*Putorius lustreola*) is somewhat smaller than the common American mink and is also distinguished

by its white upper lip. The Siberian mink is tawny brown.

The mink lives along the banks of streams and ponds in the woods or on the plains. It is a skilful swimmer and diver, and hunts its food both in water and on land. It is fond of birds and sometimes climbs trees to rob nests; it also eats frogs, fish, lizards and grubs. In winter it chases rabbits and muskrats over the snowy ground. It is wonderfully agile in spite of its short legs and can elude almost any pursuer. When cornered, a full-grown mink is a foe to be reckoned with. It fights fiercely, and gives off a disagreeable odour.

The young begin life in a nest prepared in a hollow log or in a hole among rocks. There is only one litter a year, with usually five or six young, although there may be from three to ten. Mink-raising on fur farms is a growing industry both in Europe and America. It is profitable and the animals are not difficult to raise in captivity. A mink coat is expensive, for a full-length garment takes from 60 to 70 skins. The fur wears exceptionally well. The "Japanese mink" of commerce is the pale yellowish-brown fur of the Itashi weasel, and is always dyed.

**Minnesota.** Some of the world's finest wheat-growing land and most productive iron ore mines are in this northern State of the United States. Minnesota is bounded on the north by Canada, on the west by North and South Dakota, on the south by Iowa, on the east by Wisconsin and Lake Superior. It has an area of 84,068 square miles and contains some 11,000 lakes, including Lake Itasca, the source of the Mississippi. Other waterways include the Minnesota, St. Croix and the Red river, all of which are navigable and are utilised to supply water-power.

Chiefly an agricultural State, Minnesota produces enormous quantities of maize, wheat and oats. Dairy-farming and meat-packing are also

W. S. Berridge

**THE VALUABLE MINK**

**One of the most important fur-bearing animals is the mink, found wild in various parts of the world and bred in large numbers for the fur trade. Notice its fine, long coat and big tail, and its general resemblance to the weasel and stoat.**

important industries. The Mesabi range, in the north-eastern corner of the State, is the world's richest iron ore district, St. Paul, the capital, stands on the Mississippi, opposite Minneapolis, the largest town, which has the world's biggest flour-mills. The chief educational institution is the University of Minnesota at Minneapolis. The population of the State is 2,792,300.

**Mint.** The fragrant herb we call mint preserves the name of the nymph Mintha. The goddess Persephone, so the old Greek myth runs, in a fit of jealous rage turned her beautiful rival into the plant now highly prized for its odour and flavour. These qualities are due to essential oils secreted in glands in the leaves, which when distilled give the widely used mint flavours. The flowers, which according to species vary from lilac to purple, appear in August and September.

The commonest example of this plant is the spearmint of gardens, *Mentha viridia*. Species native to Britain include peppermint, *M. piperita* ; penny-royal, *M. pulegium* ; marsh-mint, *M. sativa* ; horse-mint, *M. sylvestris* ; round-leaved mint, *M. rotundi-folia* ; and corn-mint, *M. arvensis*. All are perennials, with creeping root-stocks ; and with the exception of corn-mint, which grows in corn-fields and dry waste places, they flourish in wet ground.

**Mint.** ROYAL. The Royal Mint stands on Tower Hill in London. It has been on its present site only since 1810, but for centuries there has been a mint in London. One existed before William the Conqueror landed; and, in even earlier times, the Romans and the Anglo-Saxons had mints in London. For some centuries prior to 1810 the Mint was situated within the Tower of London. In early days there were a number of provincial mints, notably at Bristol, Derby, and Winchester, but these gradually came under the power of London, and during the reign of Edward VI they came to an end.

The office of Master of the Mint has since 1870 been held by virtue of his office, by the Chancellor of the Exchequer. The executive head is the Deputy Master and Comptroller, who is also engraver of His Majesty's seals.

The Royal Mint is the only institution in Great Britain authorized to strike coin. It executes the coinage not only of Great Britain, but of the colonies and of certain foreign countries. The standard of craftsmanship is very high. A well-struck and ably designed coin is in keeping with the dignity of the State and it also renders difficult the task of the counterfeiter. Counterfeiting is a serious crime—a felony punishable with penal servitude, the minimum sentence being three years.

Gold and silver are no longer used for making Britain's coins. Two World Wars have resulted in great changes. No gold coin has been struck for general circulation since 1917, although some sovereigns were struck in 1925 for the Bank of England to use in its transactions with other countries. For hundreds of years Britain's silver coins contained 92½ per cent of silver, but in 1920 the proportion of silver was reduced to 50 per cent. In 1946 it was decided to abolish the silver coinage and to replace it with a cheaper one made of cupro-nickel—an alloy of copper 75 per cent and nickel 25 per cent. Cupro-nickel coins are still loosely referred to as " silver " in common speech.

The " copper " coins are made of bronze, which is practically all copper with just a little zinc and tin added. The " nickel " 12-sided yellow 3d. bits contain only 1 per cent nickel, with 79 per cent of copper and 20 per cent of zinc.

The first step in making the coins is to get the different metals in their right proportions for the alloy required. About two cwt. of the mixture is then put in a cauldron which is placed in a gas furnace and brought up to a heat nearly 10 times greater than that of boiling water. When the metals are melted, samples are taken to make sure that the

*A. W. Dennis*

**WILD PEPPERMINT**
This is one of the species of mint found growing wild in Britain, and it is easily recognized by its scent. Its general features—opposite leaves and spikes of pale purplish flowers—are common to most of the mint tribe.

mixture or alloy is correct. After about two hours in the cauldron the metal is poured into moulds and when cool, is taken out in strips about two feet long, two or three inches wide and perhaps one inch thick.

The strips are too thick to be made into coins, so they are passed between very powerful rollers until they are of the exact thickness for the coin required. A half-crown, for instance, is thicker than a sixpence.

The strips are next passed through a machine which cuts them into disks or blanks. The metal left over is remelted and used again. The rolling has made the metal very hard, and the blanks are now softened by being heated in another furnace from which they are ejected red-hot into water. The disks are now black and dirty so they are washed in a mixture of water and acid, rinsed in fresh water and dried by hot air. The disks, shining bright, are now ready for the last stage of their manufacture into coins.

They are next taken into the coining room and one by one they are placed between the jaws of a powerful coining press. These jaws close with a pressure of about 70 tons and in one blow the press

# HOW MONEY IS MADE AT THE MINT

*Fox*

Five stages in the manufacture and handling of money at the Royal Mint, in London, are recorded in these photographs. (1). Cutting coin blanks (disks from which coin can later be struck) from a metal strip; (2). Examining 12-sided threepenny pieces; (3). Cleaning coin blanks before striking them into coin; (4). A coining press, which will strike both head and tail on a coin blank at one blow; (5) Newly-minted money being weighed in bulk.

makes the impression of the " head " and " tail " or, to use the official terms, the " obverse " and the " reverse." For cupro-nickel coining the milling is effected by the same blow. Each coining press can strike about 100 coins a minute.

Cupro-nickel coins are then weighed individually on very delicate automatic balances. These balances are ingenious devices. They pass coins that are of correct weight but others are rejected—the right ones being thrown to one side and those that are overweight to the other.

The coins are then put on to a moving band and pass under the skilful eye of scrutineers, who at once detect and remove any piece imperfectly cut or bearing any blemish. They are now ready to pass into circulation, but they are first counted by a telling machine which will fill canvas bags with any required amount. Silver is made up into bags of £100, the yellow 3d. bits into those of £20, and bronze in bags of £5.

The Royal Mint strikes coins to meet public demand, and no very large stocks are kept in its own vaults. Cupro-nickel coin is sent to the Bank of England, which issues it to other banks. Bronze and the nickel 3d. bits are sent direct to the banks.

Although the most scrupulous care is taken in striking coins in the Royal Mint they are subject to a further searching test. Every year a selection of coins is examined by a special jury drawn from members of the Goldsmiths' Company. The coins are weighed and chemically examined to ensure that they are in every way correct. This examination, called the Trial of the Pyx, dates back many centuries, to the times when the King could not always trust his moneyers, and it is probably our oldest monetary institution.

Although cupro-nickel has displaced silver for coins in ordinary circulation, the old standard silver —92½ per cent fine—has since 1947 once again been used for Maundy money—those tiny silver coins for 1d., 2d., 3d. and 4d., given to the aged poor by the King at Westminster Abbey each year on Maundy Thursday, the day before Good Friday.

In 1947 the Royal Mint struck 176,321,691 British (or Imperial) coins and 165,136,400 Dominion and foreign ones. The most numerous coin was the penny, of which 52,220,400 were struck. The sixpence headed the list of cupro-nickel coins at 25,428,059.

## Mirabeau, COUNT (1749-91).

To the nobles of France, in 1789, the brilliant but dissolute Honoré Gabriel Riqueti Mirabeau (pron. mēr-ah-bō) must have seemed a traitor to their class, for in the States-General (parliament) of that year, to which he was elected, he acted as a leader of the Third Estate or common people. But Mirabeau had learned by personal experience something of the evils of the old form of government under which the king ruled without Parliament; and when the nobility refused to elect him as a representative he turned to the Third Estate, so that he might not be prevented from helping to obtain the reforms so badly needed.

The son of a nobleman, Mirabeau was born at Bignon in Provence, France, on March 9, 1749, and in his youth was a notorious rebel against social and moral conventions. In the States-General, Mirabeau first attracted attention by openly defying the king. Louis XVI had sent a command to the members of the Third Estate to retire from the hall in which they were sitting to their former place of meeting. But Mirabeau replied to the messenger: " Go tell your master that we are here by the will of the people, and that we shall be removed only at the point of the bayonet." From that time his influence in the assembly was great.

In 1789 he saw clearly the dangerous direction in which the French Revolution was going. In order to save the country from impending disasters, he undertook secretly to advise the king with counsels of moderation. But the king and queen, who detested Mirabeau because of his former life and because he took money for his advice, refused to be guided by his counsels. Thus his attempt to establish a parliamentary form of Government similar to that of England failed.

Worn out by his work and weakened by his dissipations, Mirabeau died on April 2, 1791. His death removed the one statesman who could have guided the Revolution through the coming troublous times, a fact which Mirabeau clearly recognized when he exclaimed just before his death: " I carry with me the ruin of the French monarchy! " (See illustration, page 1394).

## Miracle Plays.

In the Roman Catholic Church the celebration of the Mass and the special services for festivals have many dramatic elements. In the Middle Ages these services were made more popular and more instructive for uneducated people by the use of living pictures or tableaux—as, for instance, the representation of the Child in the Manger with the Wise Men.

It was a natural step from tableau to acting, first in dumb show and then with appropriate songs and dialogues. This was the origin of the " mysteries " and " miracle plays." As far back as the 10th century simple plays of this kind were performed, though the earliest mentioned by name is the Play of St. Katherine, produced in England in the 12th century.

At first the language used was Latin, but later this was changed to the language of the people— English or French or German, as the case might be. As the plays grew in length and elaborateness they were transferred from the church to the churchyard, and then to the village streets. Once outside the church, secular and comic elements were added. In the 13th century these plays came little by little to be taken out of the hands of the clergy, and by the latter part of the 14th century they were acted almost entirely by the different guilds, or unions, of craftsmen.

The Creation, Noah and the Flood, Adam and Eve, Abraham and Isaac, and other stories of the Old Testament were presented, as well as incidents in the life of Christ. Strictly speaking, these representations of stories from the Bible were " mysteries," while miracle plays dealt with the lives of the saints, but this distinction was not always observed. Closely associated with these were the " moralities," in which moral lessons were taught by representing virtues and vices as persons.

Most of these plays, which originated as a means of religious and moral instruction, became so corrupted by jests and vulgarities that they were

# MIRAGE           MIRAGE                                                                  MIRROR

## THE HEART-BREAKING MIRAGE OF THE DESERT

There are stories of thirst-maddened travellers in the desert suddenly seeing a tempting vision of an oasis, which vanishes at their nearer approach. Usually the mirage is accompanied by an inverted duplicate, which looks as though it were mirrored in the sand (above). A phenomenon like the mirage is sometimes seen at sea, the inverted images of ships appearing in the air. 'Looming' mirages are often seen in the Strait of Messina, between Italy and Sicily.

condemned by the Church, and after the 15th century they almost ceased to be given. But the pure type of "mystery" is still preserved in the beautiful Passion Plays, the most famous of which is performed periodically at Oberammergau, Bavaria.

**Mirage.** (Pron. mer'-ahzh). Travellers in a desert sometimes think they are nearing an oasis because they see in the distance green palms growing about a lake. But as they draw nearer the vision fades: for it is only a reflection, or air picture, of an oasis far away below the horizon. This is a mirage.

To understand the cause of a mirage it must be remembered that we see an object by rays of light reflected from it to our eyes and in the straight line in which the rays enter the eye. Ordinarily these rays come to the eye in straight lines from the object and we see only objects above our horizon.

Now, in the case of a desert mirage the rays of light passing upward from an object below the horizon are reflected back from a layer of denser air above the hot light air next the sand. This higher layer of dense air acts as a mirror, and, as it is above the object it reflects, this object appears above the horizon and in the field of vision of the traveller, when in reality the place seen in the reflection is miles away and out of sight. The air layers vary in density and sometimes reflect a double image, one part being upside-down.

In an ocean mirage a vessel below the horizon is plainly reflected in the upper air. A most remarkable mirage of this kind was seen in 1854 on the Baltic, when an English fleet 30 miles away appeared to be floating in the air. The case of the ocean mirage, which occurs in cold northern waters, is just the opposite of the desert mirage, for the cool dense air is close to the water and the reflection is caused by a warmer layer of air above it.

Still another form of mirage is known as "looming"; objects are seen magnified and sometimes,

when the sun is in the right position and other conditions are favourable, are set against a background of coloured mists. This form of mirage is common in the Strait of Messina, between Italy and Sicily. People in Reggio, looking towards Sicily, may see houses, trees, and men suspended above the sea. This vision is a reflection of the city of Messina, though for long years it was thought to be a city of fairy castles and was given the name Fata Morgana (fairy Morgana) the fairy known in English legend as Morgan le Fay who was supposed to build the phantom towns.

**Mirror.** The making of mirrors is not a recent craft. The Egyptians, Greeks and Romans used mirrors of highly-polished metal, usually bronze. Rather similar are our "unbreakable" mirrors made of chromium-plated steel. Not until the 13th century, however, were mirrors of glass with backs of tin or lead manufactured; and these were greatly improved by the Venetians, in the 17th century, by mixing mercury with the tin, or "amalgamating" it to form the reflecting surface. The process was long and dangerous, due to the poisonous mercury fumes and many workmen died as a result. The modern process, using nitrate of silver, was patented in 1855, and is in general use for backing ordinary mirrors.

An ordinary looking-glass mirror, of any size, can be made in about an hour. For the best mirrors, plate-glass about a quarter of an inch thick is used. It is first cut to size with a diamond tool, then bevelled with sand and water in a "roughing mill," then the edges are ground with emery and polished with rouge-covered felt pads. Next, in the silvering department, it is cleansed and placed on heated and blanketed tables. A dilute compound of silver nitrate, ammonia, and tartaric acid is poured over it, and a silver layer deposits on and sticks to the glass. The silver back is dried, and coated with a special paint to protect it from the atmosphere.

2190

Silver is the best material for making a mirror, since its reflecting power—that is, the fraction of the light which the surface reflects—is very high, about 90 degrees. However, in many modern scientific instruments it is necessary to form the reflecting surface on the front surface of a plate of glass, and if silver is used it will soon tarnish in the air. For this reason other metals, such as aluminium or the rare metal rhodium, are used. They are deposited by evaporating, or " boiling off " the metal by heating it in a vacuum, and allowing it to condense on the glass plate.

In the ordinary flat-surface or plane mirror the image of an object appears erect, and as far behind the mirror as the object is in front of it. This is illustrated in Fig. 1, which shows the path of the rays. Note that the image is a " virtual " one—that is, it is not possible to throw it on to a screen, and that, although it lies the right way up, the left-and-right sense is reversed.

Curved mirrors are used in a number of ways, for everyday use and more especially in optical instruments. The convex mirror forms part of the surface of a silvered glass sphere, and it has the property of forming a much-reduced image of an object placed in front of it. Fig. 2 shows how this comes about; rays striking the mirror obey the ordinary laws of reflection (*see* Light). Once again we see that the image is virtual and erect. Convex mirrors are used as the driving mirrors of cars, for they enable the driver to see a wide expanse of road behind him in a relatively small mirror.

Concave mirrors are also spherical in shape, but are viewed from the " inside." The images which they form lie in front of the mirror, and are inverted; they are also real images, which fact can be demonstrated by throwing the image of the sun on to a piece of paper, held in front of the mirror. The paper will burst into flames, owing to the concentration of the sun's rays, just as a convex lens or " burning glass " does this. The way in which the real image is formed is shown in Fig. 3.

Most large astronomical telescopes are " reflectors," using a concave mirror to image the stars and planets. The largest telescope in the world, on Mt. Palomar in America, has a concave mirror 200 inches in diameter. This huge

mirror was first cast in glass, which had to be cooled down over a period of months so that it should be strain-free, and then ground and polished to an accuracy of a hundred-thousandth of an inch, and finally silvered. Mirrors for astronomical telescopes of this type are not quite spherical, but like the mirrors used in searchlights and car head-lamps are parabolic in cross-section.

**Mississippi.** The mightiest river in North America and one of the longest in the world, the Mississippi, whose Red Indian name means Father of the Waters, has a basin which includes two-fifths of the United States and is second in size only to the valley of the Amazon. The greater part of this vast region is very fertile, a fact which, combined with the latitude, elevation, and rainfall, makes the Mississippi valley an ideal dwelling-place for Man. Sixty million people dwell in the States drained by this river, which flows into the Gulf of Mexico through the delta—this being a marshy impassable area of more than 12,000 square miles.

As it issues from Lake Itasca (the usually accepted source) in Minnesota, the Mississippi is only a little stream 10 or 12 feet wide and about two feet deep. For a time it flows north, but after much twisting and turning its course becomes south-easterly. Tributaries, often as large as the main stream itself, join it, until it reaches a width of 1,200 feet at the Falls of St. Anthony. Here the river descends about 65 feet in three-quarters of a mile, forming rapids, in the midst of which is a precipice over which the river once plunged in a beautiful cascade. Now this water-power has been used to build up the manufacturing interests of Minneapolis. The banks of the stream presently rise in rocky bluffs, sometimes as high as 500 feet, and continuing almost to the junction with the River Ohio. At Cape Girardeau, 38 miles above the mouth of the Ohio, the bluffs cease and the alluvial valley, built by the river, begins. There are in the Mississippi system 250 tributaries and their branches, making 14,000

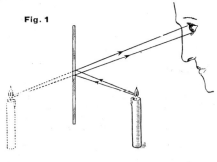

Fig. 1

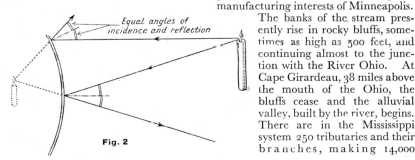

Equal angles of incidence and reflection

Fig. 2

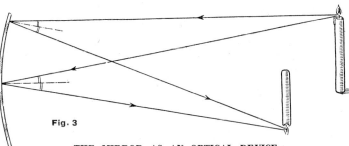

Fig. 3

**THE MIRROR AS AN OPTICAL DEVICE**
In a flat mirror (Fig. 1) the object reflected is seen erect, and the image appears to be as far behind the mirror as the object itself is in front of the glass. A convex mirror (Fig. 2) forms a much-reduced image of the object placed in front of it. A concave mirror (Fig. 3) forms an inverted image, but this is a ' real ' one. (See text for a fuller explanation.)

**HEADWATERS OF THE MISSISSIPPI AT LAKE ITASCA**

As it issues from Lake Itasca in north-western Minnesota, ~~United States, the Mississippi is only a stream 10 or 12 feet wide, and about two feet deep (above). This is the~~ birthplace of the largest river of North America, with a length of 2,460 miles. In spring, melting snow from the Rocky and Appalachian mountains raises the water-level ~~along the lower reaches ... embankments, or levees, have been built to control these~~

miles of navigable water and a drainage basin of 1,240,050 square miles. The Mississippi itself is 2,460 miles in length, and, with the Missouri, its longest tributary, 3,988 miles. There are great variations in the river's width and depth. At the junction of the Illinois it is just over a quarter of a mile wide, but below the mouth of the Missouri it is a mile and a half from bank to bank.

Floods occur on the Mississippi almost every year, usually in the spring when melting snow and rain swell the tributaries and the waters come down in a great torrent, which brings disaster to vast stretches of lowland along its lower course. In a flood in 1927 more than 200 lives were lost and nearly 700,000 people were driven from their homes, and the cost of the damage amounted to £80 millions.

From Cairo (at the junction with the Ohio) to the sea the river is confined within a levee or embankment system, the most extensive work of its kind in the world. There are about 2,000 miles in the present system, of which all but 70 miles have been constructed since 1905. The first levee was built at New Orleans early in the 18th century, to protect the new settlement. Among the chief cities along the banks of the Mississippi are Minneapolis, St. Paul, St. Louis—18 miles below the junction with the Missouri (*q.v.*)—Cairo, Memphis, Baton Rouge and New Orleans.

Early Spanish explorers saw the mouth of this river and named it the River of the Holy Ghost. But Fernando de Soto is usually considered its discoverer, for he crossed the Mississippi in 1541. More than 100 years passed before other white

men saw it, when, in 1673, two Frenchmen, Marquette and Joliet, descended it as far as the mouth of the River Arkansas. It remained for the French explorer La Salle and his party, in 1681, to follow it to the Gulf of Mexico. A few years later Louis Hennepin, sent by La Salle, explored the upper river from the mouth of the Illinois to the Falls of St. Anthony. Not until 1832 was the Mississippi proper traced to its source in Lake Itasca in Minnesota.

The State of Mississippi, with a coastline of 85 miles on the Gulf of Mexico, is bounded on the north by Tennessee; on the east by Alabama; on the south by the Gulf of Mexico and Louisiana; on the west by Louisiana and Arkansas, the Mississippi forming the western boundary line. Its area is 46,716 square miles. The climate is sub-tropical.

Agriculture is the main industry, with cotton the most important crop. Other products include maize, fruit, wheat, oats, sweet potatoes, sugar-cane, ground-nuts and rice. The mineral resources are limestone, gypsum, coal and clay. Vast forests contain much valuable timber, chiefly pine, the timber industry being second only to agriculture in importance. Jackson, the capital, has a population of 62,000; other large towns are Meridian, Vicksburg, Hattiesburg and Laurel.

Mississippi was first settled by the French in 1699, and it became British territory in 1763. At the end of the American War of Independence (1776–1782) it formed part of the United States, and was admitted to the Union as a State in 1817. The population of Mississippi State is 2,183,800.

# MODERN LIFE ON 'THE FATHER OF WATERS'

*Keystone; Galloway; Three Lions; American Barge Line; Army Engineer*

1. This new type of Mississippi steamboat is streamlined but still flat bottomed. 2. Buttons are cut from the shells of river clams and the remains (shown here) are ground up for poultry feed. 3. Oil, coal, and other heavy cargoes move up and down the river in great barges pushed by powerful tugs. 4. Air map of the river mouth showing the channel that is kept open across the mud-filled delta. 5. The Mississippi catfish grow to a great size.

# Missouri.

From its source in the Rocky Mountains in south-west Montana, United States, to its junction with the Mississippi above St. Louis, the mighty river Missouri (Red Indian word meaning " mud river ") winds through a distance of 2,723 miles, while the Missouri-Mississippi is 3,988 miles long.

Beginning at the meeting-point of the Jefferson, Madison, and Gallatin rivers, the Missouri flows almost due north through a beautiful mountainous region. Sixteen miles east of Helena, Montana, it passes through a narrow canyon or gorge, with walls 1,200 feet high, called the Gates of the Rocky Mountains, where the beauty and grandeur of scenery are almost unequalled. Farther along, about 350 miles from its source, are the Great Falls of the Missouri, where the river descends nearly 400 feet in 16 miles, by a series of cataracts, the highest of which has a fall of 90 feet.

Turning east and then south-east at Kansas City it flows eastward again until it reaches the Mississippi. With its tributaries it drains an area of some 528,000 square miles.

Marquette and Joliet were the first explorers to discover the mouth of the Missouri, as they came down the Mississippi in 1673, but it was not till 1819 that the first steamboat was seen on the river.

The State of Missouri is bounded on the east by the Mississippi, on the south by Arkansas, on the west by Oklahoma, Kansas and Nebraska, on the north by Iowa. The State is cut in two by the Missouri river, which forms the northern part of the western boundary line. Its area is 69,674 square miles. The climate varies from temperate in the north to sub-tropical in the south. In the north and west are fertile prairies; in the south the plains give way to densely forested slopes of the Ozark Mountains.

Agriculture is an important industry, maize being the chief crop. Wheat, hay, oats, cotton, fruit and potatoes are grown in large quantities, and stock-breeding is carried on in the south, the State being specially famous for its mules and horses. Missouri is one of the world's main sources of lead; other minerals are coal, zinc, copper, granite, limestone, marble and clay. Among the manufactured products are machinery, tinned foods, tobacco, boots and shoes, buttons, glass and pottery. Jefferson City is the capital, with a population of about 20,000. St. Louis is the largest town, with a population of 816,000. The population of Missouri State is 3,784,700.

# Mistletoe.

Do you know that this familiar Christmas decoration, with its waxen white berries and evergreen leaves, never takes root in the ground but is a parasite that grows on the branches of trees? It belongs to a genus of which there are about 20 species, all of them parasitic. Of these only the mistletoe proper (*Viscum album*) is a native of Europe.

The mistletoe appears as a bushy growth with many forking branches, often reaching four feet long. It has oval leaves, and tiny yellow blossoms, which are followed by sticky white berries. It grows on both deciduous and evergreen trees. In England it grows in greatest abundance on the apple tree. It is rarely found on the oak. The birds eat the pulpy berries, and thus the seeds are conveyed to other trees, where they become lodged in the bark and in due course germinate.

Mistletoe is prominent in European folklore as a magical plant credited with a number of virtues. It was said to bring happiness, safety and good fortune so long as it did not touch the ground; perhaps that is why we hang it up. The Celts held it in veneration, especially when found on an oak tree; and it was sacred to the Druids (*see* page 1048). Mistletoe is supposed to have been the " Golden Bough " which played so important a part in the strange rite celebrated at Diana's temple at Lake Nemi, near Rome (*see* pages 1387–88).

# Models.

The making of small replicas of engines, boats, and machines is an absorbing hobby, especially if these models are " working " ones. Some grown-ups devote time and often a good deal of money to making and building " scale " models of such things as locomotives, every item and component, almost, being made to a scale bearing a fixed relation to the dimensions of the prototype. This hobby usually calls for the use of a lathe and other machine-tools, since the model-maker works from castings and from materials in the rough. The finished model may be powerful enough to haul a couple of youngsters on a garden railway.

Another similar pastime is the modelling of replicas of historic ships, such as famous galleons, or the Mayflower, complete with sails and rigging, guns, etc. Or you can make little " waterline "

*H. Bastin*

## MISTLETOE LEAVES AND BERRIES

Growing as a parasite on the branches of living trees, the mistletoe plant makes a mass of bushy growth sometimes four feet long. Birds eat the sticky white berries and convey the seeds to other trees, where some of the seeds germinate and form new plants.

models of our own warships of today; a collection of these bring home very vividly the meaning of the Navy. When we come to aircraft there is scope for the home modeller who is satisfied with realistic small replicas of leading types; and for the youngster who builds and flies bigger craft, fitting them with petrol engine or Diesel engine, and taking them at week-ends to commons to compete in miniature flying trials. Less ambitious modellers can do quite a lot with aircraft powered by nothing more than twisted strands of rubber.

So much for modelling as a pastime; but the subject is much wider than this. Shipbuilders and aircraft manufacturers carry out many experiments with scale models before committing themselves to building the real craft. Model ships are towed along a big tank in which the conditions at sea are simulated. Scale models of experimental aircraft are tested in a wind-tunnel—an horizontal enclosed gallery in which the model is suspended in the air-stream produced by very powerful fans.

In another class are models made for display or demonstration purposes. The great shipping companies usually display in their office windows models of passenger liners; while railway companies will show models of famous expresses. An architect commissioned to prepare a scheme for a great building may model it, or have it modelled by a firm

which specialises in such work, in light wood, plaster or cardboard. An entire estate may be shown thus, with roads, houses and churches.

During the Second World War (1939–45) the crews of bombing or of torpedo-carrying aircraft

Barratt's; Bassett-Lowke Ltd.; Associated Press

## MODELS OF SHIPPING AND ARCHITECTURAL MODELS

When a model sailing ship is inserted in a bottle (top) the masts are flat on the deck and are attached to a thread or wire which is pulled to raise them after the model is in position in the bottle. At centre is a group of models of types of landing craft used in amphibious operations during the Second World War (1939–45). The model of the Bankside power station (bottom, foreground)—a great electric generating plant for erection on the south bank of the River Thames—shows its position in relation to St. Paul's Cathedral (domed building on the far bank).

were "briefed" by reference to elaborate and realistic models of the ships, dockyards or munition works or other targets in enemy countries which they were to attack. These models showed the targets as they would appear from the air. When plans were made for Commando raids, and for the great invasion landings in France towards the end of the war, models of the enemy-held beaches, and of the country beyond, were used to instruct our soldiers and sailors.

Yet another use of models is in preserving for the future student the likeness of ships, engines, machines and apparatus which illustrate the history

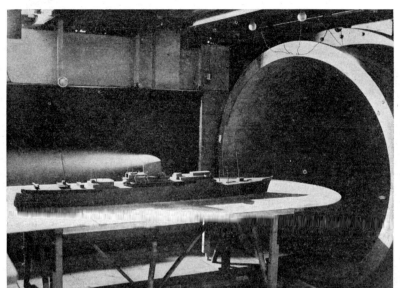

of invention and progress. In the great collection owned by the nation at the South Kensington Museums, London, are models of all kinds—many which "work" by compressed air when you press a button; others which show in perfect miniature the appearance of present-day or by-gone mechanisms. Whether the reader is an aircraft "fan," a railway enthusiast, or a lover of ships, he will find at the Science Museum a collection, the proper study of which would need days and days of inspection.

Models, then, mean a great deal to us, in work and in play—in peace-time and in war-time. The hobby of model-making is a very old one—far more ancient than the day of the sailor home from the sea who, a hundred and

fifty years ago, carved a tiny model of a schooner and then fitted it by a rather mysterious process, into a glass bottle, with a neck far too narrow to admit it, it would seem. How *did* he manage it?

**Mole.** Destined to spend its whole life in darkness, digging, digging, digging, in order to build its home and to obtain the food necessary for its existence, the mole is a queer little creature, scarcely able to see or hear, and yet marvellously adapted for the part Nature has designed him to play in the world.

You can always find the mole by the long ridge of cracked earth that zigzags across fields—the roof of his tunnel. It is lively work to dig him out, for he may be at either end, anywhere along the route, or in a side chamber. In your hand he lies helpless, a flat ball of fine, velvety, mouse-coloured fur, about six inches long, with a naked, pink tail about an inch long. He has no neck; his ears are only little openings concealed in the fur; his dim eyes are tiny points covered with skin. If you put him on the ground, he scrambles about frantically until he finds a soft spot. Then he begins to dig with his strong spadelike forefeet (details of which are shown in the illustration in page 1572) and in less than one minute the animal has disappeared

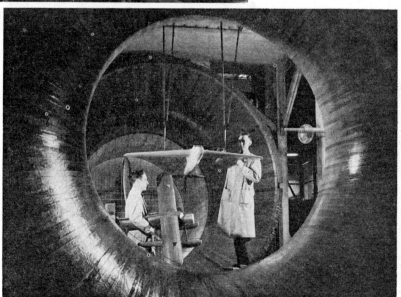

*Fox; Central Press*

**DESIGN TESTED BY THE AID OF MODELS**
At the National Physical Laboratory at Teddington, Middlesex, a scale model of a proposed liner is seen undergoing tests as to the deflection of gases from the ship's funnel in a high wind (upper). Flying qualities of aircraft are tested by means of models, or parts thereof, suspended in a wind-tunnel (lower), where they are subjected to hurricanes of velocities up to 160 miles per hour; here a model is being placed in position.

# TRIUMPHS OF THE MODEL-MAKER'S ART

John Brown & Co., Ltd.; Fox

One of the many practical uses of models is in determining the relative merits of various scientific designs by observing the behaviour of scale models under artificially-produced conditions. In the top photograph an 18-foot model of the liner Queen Mary is supposed to be encountering a gale : it is riding waves formed by special wave-making apparatus in an experimental tank. Built by R. R. Callingham at Beaconsfield, Buckinghamshire, the famous model town of Bekonscot (lower) has a railway, an airport, docks, and houses, a miniature lake and convalescent home.

**MOLE ABOVE GROUND**
If you should find a mole above ground you will have a chance to note the strong little digging ' hands,' the sharp nose, and the close fur of the queer little animal that makes mole-hills in fields and gardens.

*S. Crook*

into a burrow in the ground. The speed with which a mole works is almost incredible. In a single night one has been known to tunnel more than 75 yards. It almost " swims " through the soil—and sometimes it has need to go hurriedly backwards. So that the mole's movements either forward or backward shall not be impeded by its fur the latter grows short and thick and upright. The pile of the velvety little coat therefore lies either very slightly forward or backward according to the direction of the animal's movements underground, and consequently does not become clogged with earth. Nor, during the life of the mole, does the coat become stained but is always immaculate in appearance. The paws (which do the digging) are devoid of the soft fur; they are covered with thick, bare skin.

Moles are found both in the Old and the New World in the Northern Hemisphere. The common mole (*Talpa europea*) disfigures lawns, pastures, and gardens extensively by the ridges and furrows it makes hunting food, but it pays for some of the damage it does by eating root-destroying larvae, insect pests, and occasionally even field mice, but its chief food is earthworms. The mole ordinarily lives in a colony, in a more or less planned " home." In little hillocks of earth, called molehills, there may be constructed a central chamber surrounded by two ringlike galleries, one above the other. These circular galleries are connected by vertical passages and the upper one has openings into the central cavity. From the lower gallery a number of alleys or runs lead off in different directions toward the feeding grounds.

It is a pity that these little animals have to be destroyed by farmers and gardeners. But the professional mole-catcher makes a profit, and the skins are in demand for ladies' coats.

**Molière.** (1622–73). What Shakespeare was to English literature, the comic dramatist Molière (pron. mōl-yăr) was to France. Molière, though he portrays his own countrymen and his own era, belongs, like Shakespeare, to all lands and all ages.

Jean-Baptiste Poquelin—for that was his real name—was born in Paris in January 1622, the son of a prosperous furniture-maker who held the office of upholsterer to the king. Instead of following his father's calling the son chose the uncertain life of a strolling player, and it was at that time that he took the stage name Molière. As an actor and theatrical manager he learned the art of the stage, and gained that perfect mastery of dramatic structure for which his plays are noted. He also learned to know human nature, especially men's vanities and follies, and one outstanding human weakness is usually emphasized in his plays.

Harpagon in L'Avare (The Miser), and the hypocritical Tartuffe, are immortal creations of his genius; and few characters have aroused the world's laughter so much as Monsieur Jourdain in his comedy Le Bourgeois Gentilhomme (The Tradesman turned Gentleman).

Molière's last play was Le Malade Imaginaire (The Imaginary Invalid), and in this he himself played the leading part, that of Argan. Though the character was suffering only from an imaginary disease, the actor himself was really very ill. In the midst of the play he fell into a violent fit of coughing, and died half an hour after the performance, on February 17, 1673. It was Molière's last jest.

His chief plays are Les Précieuses Ridicules (The Ridiculous Blue-stockings), 1659 ; Tartuffe

**PLAN OF THE MOLE'S HOME**
In this plan you see the features that may be found in mole-hills, although no one hill will have all of them, nor will it be quite so complicated or well-designed. Often it is as simple as the nest you see on the left and may show little if any sign of planning.

(1664) ; Le Misanthrope (The Hater of Mankind) 1666 ; Le Médecin Malgré Lui (The Physician in spite of himself) 1666 ; L'Avare (The Miser) 1668 ; Le Bourgeois Gentilhomme (The Tradesman turned Gentleman) 1670 ; Les Femmes Savantes (The Learned Ladies) 1672, and Le Malade Imaginaire (1673). (See illustration in page 1381).

## Molluscs.

The large group (or phylum) of animals called molluscs, or *Mollusca*, comprises all those creatures which are known usually as shellfish. Most molluscs are provided with hard, limy, or chitinous shells, which are either carried on the outside or are partially or wholly enclosed by a sheet of shell-forming muscular tissue called the mantle. They live on land and in water, both fresh and salt. There are four principal groups or classes.

The first, the most highly developed of all molluscs, are the *Cephalopods*, or head-footed molluscs, so called from the fact that the head is surrounded by a circle of eight or 10 sucker-bearing tentacles. In some ways the cephalopods approach in intelligence and in complexity of structure the vertebrates, or animals with a backbone. They have often been the subject of poem and story, and the beauty of colouring in some forms is so striking as to merit the attention of the artist as well.

Cephalopods include the nautilus, the argonaut, the octopus, the cuttle-fish and the squid. The nautilus is the only member of the group now living which carries an external skeleton or shell. But long before human history began—millions and millions of years ago—there were many shelled cephalopods in the sea, all of which, except the nautilus, became extinct. They included many forms with all sorts of curious shells, as well as the whole group, as well known as fossils, of the Ammonites (*q.v.*).

All cephalopods which have survived and become large possess either a small internal skeleton or no skeleton at all. The shell of the beautiful paper nautilus, or argonaut, is not a skeleton at all but a mere case used by the female for the protection of her eggs.

The second group of molluscs, *Lamellibranchia*, is given its name became the gills (*branchia*) are composed of a series of flat, leaf-like plates (*lamellae*). The members of this group have a " foot " shaped like a stone axe, which serves as a burrowing organ, and from this they are sometimes called *Pelecypods* (Greek *pelekys* meaning hatchet; *pous*, foot) or hatchet-footed molluscs. They are popularly known as bivalves because the shell has two halves or "valves," one on each side of the body. This group includes the oyster, cockle, mussel and scallop. The body is enclosed by the two lobes of the mantle, which in turn is covered by the two half-shells.

P. Mignard, Musée Conde, Chantilly; photo, Giraudon
**MOLIÈRE**
**Court entertainer to Louis XIV (1638–1715)**
**Molière produced the world's best comedies of character, presenting a perfect picture of the French society of his time.**

This group of molluscs supplies Man with a large amount of food as well as with other articles. Oysters, clams and mussels are eaten in enormous quantities in many parts of the world; the shells of fresh-water mussels are manufactured into buttons. Pearls of fine quality have been found in mussels, as well as in oysters. Mussels are of service as scavengers, for they devour decaying organic substances in lakes and streams which otherwise would pollute the water.

The *Gastropods*, stomach-footed molluscs (gastropod is derived from the Greek *gaster*, stomach; *pous*, foot) which form the third group, are typified by the snail and the whelk. They have a distinct head, which bears one or two pairs of sense organs—the tentacles or horns, the two eyes being placed on the tentacles. When there are two pairs of tentacles the eyes are placed on the hind pair. The foot is a muscular disk underneath the body, on top of which is a twisted hump covered by the mantle and containing the digestive organs.

When at rest the animal is sometimes entirely covered by its shell, the form of which is determined by the hump. If this is twisted or coiled, the shell also is twisted. In some forms, as in the limpet, the shell is a simple cone. Many of the gastropods, like the periwinkle, close the mouth of the shell with a trap-door on retiring into it. The gastropods are found throughout the world, and furnish more than half of the 60,000 known species of living molluscs. Some forms have lost their shells more or less completely, and these are known by another name—slugs.

The fourth group, called *Amphineura* (Greek *amphi* meaning on both sides; *neura*, nerves) because of the doubling of their nerve-cords, contains the chitons, which are molluscs with a small shell, formed only on the upper surface, consisting of a number of overlapping plates. The body is usually oval, and there is no distinct head. The feet constitute the entire lower part of the body. (*See* Cockles and Mussels; Cuttle-fish; Oyster; Scallop ; Shell ; Snails and Slugs).

## Molotov,

VYACHESLAV MIKHAILOVICH (born 1890). Educated at the St. Petersburg (Leningrad) Polytechnic, this Russian politician (whose surname was originally Scriabin) organized revolutionary groups of students while he was completing his education. In 1917, shortly after the Bolshevik Revolution, he became a member of the Petrograd (Leningrad) Soviet Executive Committee, which was the governing body of the city and of the surrounding district.

Molotov was appointed chairman of the Council of People's Commissars (Premier) in 1930, and was nominated Foreign Commissar (Minister for Foreign Affairs) in 1939. In 1941 he resigned the chairmanship of the Council, and was succeeded by Joseph

Stalin (*q.v.*), but retained the office of Foreign Commissar (Minister). During and after the Second World War (1939–45) he acted as Stalin's right-hand man, leading the Russian delegation at the conference of the United Nations at San Francisco in 1945.

The Soviet Union's principal delegate at most of the major international diplomatic meetings, he became notorious for his obstinate attitude. In 1947 he gathered the eastern European nations into a " block " dominated by the Soviet Union. He ceased to be Foreign Minister in 1949 but remained a vice-premier.

**Monaghan.** This inland agricultural county of Eire, with an area of 498 square miles, lies within the ancient province of Ulster. The border between Northern Ireland and Eire marks the limit of its northern and north-western boundaries. Its north-eastern boundary is the River Blackwater.

Partly in the central plain of Ireland to the north-west, the county is rugged and barren in the south and east. Oats, potatoes and flax are main crops. Cattle, sheep, pigs, goats and poultry comprise its important livestock industry. There are few manufactures, the chief being linen and lace, the town of Carrickmacross giving its name to a special type of lace which has been manufactured there since 1820. Limestone and slate, near the surface, are cheaply quarried in considerable quantities, and there are some small coal-mines.

The county town is Monaghan (population 4,000). A magnificent modern Roman Catholic cathedral stands on a hill just outside the town. Clones (population 2,500), is a busy market centre and has historic and archæological interest. Other places are Castleblayney and Ballybay. The population of the county is 57,200.

# The USE of MONEY in the WORLD TODAY

*P*ieces *of metal, paper, shells, cattle and many other things are used—or have been used—as money ; that is, as a means of trading or exchange. There is a wealth of interesting and useful information here.*

**Money.** Several purposes are served by money in our economic life. It is the yard-stick by which we measure the values of goods and services. It is the medium by which we make nearly all our exchanges. It also serves as a convenient way to store up purchasing power for later use. As a measuring device, money is almost indispensable in our present economic society. Let us take a few examples.

Suppose a certain family has an income of £50 a month. It is spending £15 for rent and dividing the balance among food, clothing, light, heat, savings, and miscellaneous expenses. At every turn it measures the cost of one desired article against another, and the cost of all desired articles against the total family income. The family may consider whether it should try to move into a better house at £20 or £25 a month and cut down other expenses. On one occasion it may decide to spend £30 on furniture. Many articles may be desired, but most of all a wireless set and an Oriental rug. A shopping tour may show that the Oriental rug would take all of the £30. But a satisfactory domestic rug can be bought, say, for £10, leaving enough to buy a wireless set.

Such experiences illustrate the use of money as a *measuring device*. The family is able to compare the cost of shelter, a rug, a wireless, and other articles because it can express these costs in terms of a common denominator—that is, a money unit. It can also compare its total wealth and its total monthly income with the cost of things that are desired, because all of these can be expressed in a common unit. That common unit is for us the pound sterling. When we think of money in this way we are thinking of it as a *unit of measurement*. It is like a foot-rule, or a pound weight.

Now for an illustration of a second use of money. Suppose I have a carthorse which I no longer need. I desire a horse for riding. I may search for a man who has a hack and who wants a carthorse of equal value. If I find him, an exchange may be made.

But it is far simpler to work through a medium—i.e., to sell my carthorse for money and with the money to buy a hack. Thus I may bring about the exchange, even though the man who has the hack does not want a carthorse, or if the two are of very different values. In other words, *by having some common medium which everyone will accept, trading or exchange is made easy.* When some type of article or commodity will be generally given in return for goods or services and will be generally accepted as payment for goods and services, that type of article or commodity is serving as money in the sense that money is a medium of exchange. A government may declare that a certain commodity, or representatives or *tokens* of it (such as pennies and halfpennies), shall be taken as payment for debts. A government thus makes such money *legal tender*.

Barter, which is direct trading without money, is supposed to have existed in many parts of the world before money was thought of. Even now barter has not completely disappeared, for sellers frequently take things in " part exchange," but in such cases the things are valued in money.

To appreciate the importance of money as a medium of exchange, we must recall the extent to which we today carry on production by division of labour—*specialization*. Only a few people produce completed articles. Most of us contribute only some part of a specialized article or service. We have to exchange our specialized contributions, which often have no tangible form, for the many things we use. The values of these goods and services are measured in money units. Without money, we could hardly have so high a degree of specialization.

There are several ways in which one can " store up " savings. One way is to buy goods which last, such as buildings or land. A second is to accumulate claims against the future income of others. This may be done by lending money to individuals, or by buying shares or stocks of companies (*see* Stocks and Shares), or by taking out an endowment

# MONEY

policy, or by putting money into a bank or into National Savings. A third way is merely to keep the savings in the form of money, i.e. to " hoard " the money. Money thus used is said to be serving as a " store of value." One's stock of money represents a claim against the community in general.

Many different things have been used as money. Some of these things have had no intrinsic value except from their use as money. Shells, beads, tobacco, furs, skins, hatchets, salt, rice, tea, dates, and ivory are among the types of money used by primitive peoples. Sparta used iron; many nations have used copper or brass. The early Romans, as have many other peoples, measured their wealth in cattle, and their word for " money " was *pecunia*, from *pecus* (meaning " cattle ") ; hence our word *pecuniary*. White and purple " wampum " beads, made of sea shells, were the money of the North American Indians, as cowrie shells were of the natives of Africa and Hindustan. The value of this shell money was due at first to its attractiveness for ornament, but it was greatly increased by its usefulness as money.

Metals, it was found, make the most satisfactory money. Silver or gold, or both, came to be used for large payments, and copper for smaller payments. Now various metals, including nickel, bronze and antimony are used in " token " coins ; that is, coins whose value is greater than that of the substance of which they are made.

Gold and silver have many advantages. They are easily recognizable, and can be cut or moulded into ingots of convenient size. They do not deteriorate with age, and are not easily damaged or worn. Their value is sufficiently high for amounts suitable for ordinary transactions to be handled easily. And they are more stable in value than are most commodities, because the demand for non-monetary uses is steady and the stock in existence is so large that it is not affected by sudden changes in production.

At first gold and silver passed by weight, as gold dust often does still in mining communities. Several of the common units of money were originally names of weights—as the Hebrew " shekel " and the Anglo-Saxon " mark," the later English " pound," the older French " livre," and so on. Indeed, coinage was originally merely a way of certifying the weight and fineness of an ingot of precious metal, so that payments could be made by count. The earliest known coins were those of the Lydians in Asia Minor, dating from the 7th century B.C. China and India may have had coins even earlier. Even after coining began the coins were often weighed, because dishonest people clipped or filed the coins to obtain the particles of gold or silver. To prevent such " theft " modern gold and silver coins are made with raised and " milled " edges.

In the ancient world, and also throughout the Middle Ages, money circulated on the basis of its metallic content. True, kings sometimes " debased " the currency by putting out new coins smaller than those issued in the past or by putting in more alloy; thereby they cheated their creditors when government debts were paid, and incidentally gave all debtors something

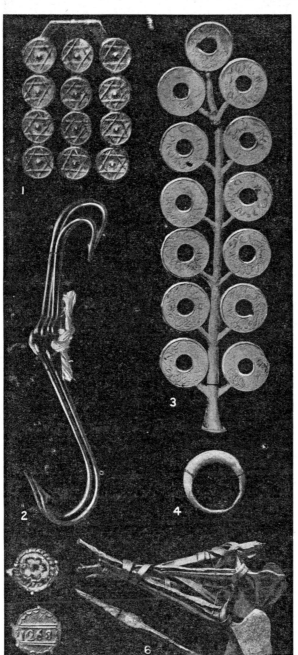

From the Zerbe Collection

**MONEY OF PRIMITIVE FOLK**

In different parts of the world strange things are used as money. Above, for instance, are : 1. Moroccan coins cast in a mould and divisible (5) for small change ; 2. Fish-hook money from islands off Alaska ; 3. Tin ' tree ' money from Malacca with detachable coin branches ; 4. Zulu ring money ; 6. Primitive African money in the shape of miniature weapons.

2201

2 R 5

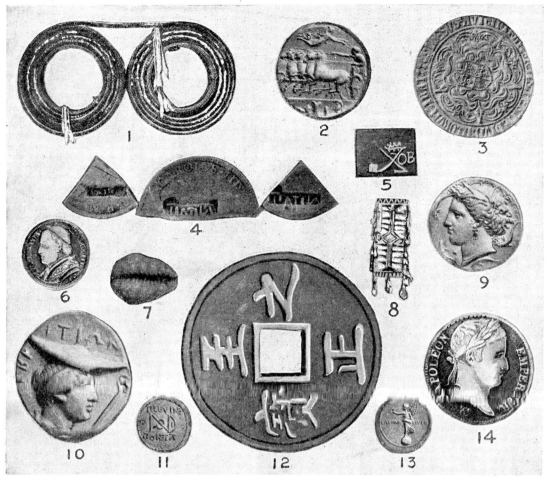

MONEYS OF DIFFERENT CLIMES AND TIMES

Here is a further selection of money used amongst peoples widely separated in geography, time and degree of civilization. 1. Feather money of Melanesia ; 2. Ancient Greek coin from Syracuse, Sicily ; 3. Gold sovereign of Henry VIII of England ; 4. Spanish coin, cut in halves and quarters for use in Peru ; 5. Swedish oblong money of the 17th century ; 6. Lira issued by Pius IX, Pope 1846–78 ; 7. Cowrie shell used in the South Sea islands ; 8. Wampum (strings of shells), ornament and currency of the Red Indians ; 9. Coin of the city of Amphipolis (ancient Greece) ; 10. Head of Hermes, god of commerce, on a coin of Sybrita, a Cretan city ; 11. Coin of Alfred the Great ; 12. Chinese cash ; 13. Roman coin of Octavian (63 B.C.–A.D. 14) ; 14. Twenty-franc piece (napoleon), with head of Napoleon I.

at the expense of their creditors. But in the early modern period it was discovered that a *promise* to pay money, if there was general confidence in the maker of the promise, would serve most of the purposes of real money. Goldsmiths, merchants, and money-lenders began to issue notes—written promises to pay cash on demand. This *credit currency*, being in the form of paper, was more convenient and safer to handle than the gold for which it could be redeemed. It was also less expensive to transport and to store. The issuing of such bank-notes became one of the important activities of the banking business.

Another form of credit money is the *bank deposit*. The banker merely gives a receipt for money deposited, and allows his customers to transfer these deposits among themselves by cheques instructing him to transfer amounts from one account to another. (*See* Banks and Banking).

In most countries paper money now circulates instead of, or in addition to, coins. Sometimes it is issued by the Treasury of the Government, but usually by the Central Bank as the Treasury's agent. Such paper money may be made out in the form of a promise to pay—a £1 Bank of England note has on it the words, " I Promise to pay the Bearer on Demand the sum of One Pound "—but the promise really now has no meaning, for the holder of such paper money in most countries is not entitled to receive gold in exchange for his notes. It used to be thought improper for governments or central banks to issue notes unless they had an equivalent amount of gold as a " note reserve " to back them. This belief has weakened, however, since the First World War (1914–18), and most governments during the Second World War (1939–45) met a large part of their expenditure by issuing paper money instead of raising taxes.

If this is done too much, the notes begin to lose much of their former power to buy goods; that is, prices of most commodities rise. This increase of prices itself increases the expenses of the government, and may call for additional paper money. So prices continually rise as the quantity of paper money in circulation increases. This condition is called *inflation*. Inflation can cause paper money to become practically worthless, for the value of paper money that is not freely exchangeable into gold depends really on the willingness of people to accept it in exchange for goods, in the belief that they will be able to exchange the money for goods.

If traders lose faith in the money and refuse to part with their goods in exchange for it, terrible misery can ensue. This was so after the 1914–18 war, particularly in Austria and Germany. Vast numbers of people whose claim to wealth or to income was expressed in a fixed number of German marks or French francs or Italian lire were ruined.

The value of any article expressed in terms of money is known as its *price*. The value of money is not stated as a price, since that would only be stating the value in terms of itself. The price of standard money, if we used the term, would never vary; but when its *value* goes up, the prices of other things fall; and when it loses value, other prices rise. As prices of different commodities do not move exactly alike, it is customary to measure the changes in the value of money by taking an average of the prices of a large number of commodities. Such an average is called an *index number*. A succession of such averages for different dates is called a series of index numbers. By looking at such a series one can see the changes in the value of money for that period.

Such index numbers show that the value of money, that is, its power to buy goods, varied considerably from time to time, even when gold coins circulated. When paper money circulates and is not exchangeable for gold, it becomes necessary to " manage " the currency in order to keep prices relatively stable. The government, in conjunction with the central bank, must adapt its taxes, the current rates of interest, the amount lent by banks to their customers, etc., in such a way as to adjust to the circumstances the total money available for spending. Lord Keynes (1883–1946) was the chief advocate of managed currencies, and his teachings are now widely accepted and practised.

Nevertheless, by the Bretton Woods Agreement of 1944 the United Kingdom, the United States of America, and numerous other countries that later joined the International Monetary Fund, linked their currencies to gold by stating that the standard (e.g. the pound or the dollar) would represent a certain amount of gold ; so the old belief in gold as a basis for money has by no means lost its attractiveness, in spite of the vast volume of paper money now in use throughout the world.

After the British withdrawal from India in 1947 the sub-continent was divided between the Dominions of India and Pakistan, and ceased to form part of the British Empire. Accordingly, in 1948 King George VI renounced the title of Emperor of India (Latin *Indiae Imperator*), and it was decided to omit the words *Ind. Imp.* from future issues of British coins.

*Keystone; Fox*

**THE DESIGNS ON BRITAIN'S COINS**

New British money struck in 1949 includes half-crown, two shilling, one shilling, and sixpenny pieces (top row), the words *Ind. Imp.* being omitted. In the second row, from left to right, are a penny, halfpenny, farthing, and threepenny piece showing the obverse. There are two different designs for the reverse of the shilling, the left-hand one being introduced in 1937 as a tribute to Queen Elizabeth. The lower photograph shows a pile of the twelve-sided threepenny pieces.

**Mongolia.** Between Siberia and China, with Manchuria to the east and the Chinese province of Sinkiang to the south-west, lie the vast plains and mountain ranges of the indefinite tract of land called Mongolia, which is about 1,875,000 square miles in extent. It forms a gigantic basin-like plateau, from 3,000 to 4,000 ft. above sea-level, surrounded by mountains and steppes or prairies.

The whole region can be divided into three main geographical areas, of which the highest is the mountainous tableland of North-Western or Outer Mongolia; the second is the Gobi desert (260,000 square miles); the third is the enormous plain of South-Eastern or Inner Mongolia.

The boundaries of the political divisions of Mongolia are not clearly defined. Inner Mongolia is a province of China; but the Outer Mongolian People's Republic situated between Inner Mongolia

**MONGOLIAN WOMAN'S HEADDRESS**

In Outer Mongolia the women wear their hair threaded through a headdress shaped like the horns of a mountain sheep and ornamented with jewelled metalwork. Once the coiffure is complete it remains in place for weeks. Two red spots on the cheeks indicate high rank.

and Siberia, is nominally an independent State, with a government organized on Soviet lines. The largest city in the whole of Mongolia is Ulan Bator Khoto (formerly Urga), which is also the capital of the Outer Mongolian People's Republic and has a population of about 100,000. It is the centre of the caravan trade between China and Siberia, and has a wireless station and an airport. In the north-western corner of Outer Mongolia is the Republic of Tannu Tuva, which is under Russian domination.

The climate of Mongolia is one of extremes and is rendered more trying by the high winds that blow continuously. The heat in summer is well-nigh unbearable, but in winter the temperature may fall as low as −40° F. In the Gobi Desert, and in the less fertile areas of Inner Mongolia, the people live a wandering life. Finding water is their greatest problem, and they

**MONGOLIA'S SITUATION IN THE DESERT AREA OF ASIA**

About 4,000 feet above sea level, Mongolia is an enormous plateau, with the Gobi Desert toward the centre. The political boundaries in this region are not clearly defined; but Inner Mongolia is nominally under Chinese control, while Outer Mongolia is an independent Republic. On the east is Manchuria, which from 1932 until the end of the Second World War (1945) was known as Manchukuo. In 1928 Peking was named Peiping by the Chinese Government.

**CARAVAN ON THE MONGOLIAN STEPPES**

Mongolia, one of the least-known and yet one of the largest regions of the world, has been throughout historic times the home of wandering tribes of hunters. Horses and camels are their beasts of burden, and here is a camel being loaded with furs secured by its master.

plains. In the early 13th century Jenghiz (Genghis) Khan (1162–1227), the Mongol Emperor, having drilled his wild tribes into a strong and efficient fighting machine, turned it first against the neighbouring Tartars, whom he amalgamated with his own people, and then against the already collapsing Kin dynasty of China. He took Peking (now Peiping) in 1214, and subdued almost all China. Then, turning his armies westward against peoples who had never even heard of the Mongols, he swept over Turkistan and Persia, and reached the southern part of the Principality of Kiev in Russia, penetrating as far as the River Dnieper.

Kublai, a grandson of Jenghiz, who became Great Khan or Emperor in 1260, completed the conquest of China and founded the Yuen dynasty, which ruled there for over 100 years. Sovereign or

seldom use it to wash their bodies or clothes. The rainfall of between eight and 12 inches a year supports grass and stunted shrubs ; but agriculture is impossible over most of the country. As water and grass fail in one locality their herds are moved on to another grazing ground. Because they never stay long in one place, they live in movable tent-like dwellings and make their household utensils of wood instead of breakable earthenware.

From their herds the Mongolians obtain almost everything they need. The sheep provide mutton, cheese, butter, clothing, and wool for making the felt to cover their homes and for bedding. Goats and horses are kept. A fermented drink, called *koumiss*, is made from mares' milk. Sheepskin outer garments are worn in winter, cotton clothes in summer. Both men and women like to wear brightly coloured material, and on special occasions the women appear in gorgeously ornamented headdresses, as illustrated in the facing page.

Furs, hides, wool, camels' hair and animals are exchanged for tea, flour, sugar, tobacco, cotton cloth, saddles, boots and jewelry. Camels are used to carry loads and sometimes to draw high-wheeled carts, but horses are the chief means of transportation. The population of the whole of Mongolia has been estimated at about two millions.

**Mongols.** The story of these slant-eyed wandering people, with their flat, yellow faces and straight black hair, is a strange one. A barbarous, almost unknown tribe or group of tribes, learning the art of war in obscure struggles with each other and with their Chinese overlords, then suddenly blazed forth in the 13th century under brilliant military leaders as conquerors of much of Asia and eastern Europe, supplanting many native rulers. After making the Mongol name a world terror for centuries, they sank back again into obscurity as subjects of realms in which once they had ruled.

Squat, wiry horsemen, hunters, and herdsmen, the tent-dwelling Mongols roved over the mountain region south of Lake Baikal and the open steppes or

*From A. Waley, Introduction to Chinese Painting*

**KUBLAI KHAN, A MONGOL EMPEROR**

From the Black Sea to the coast of China spread the domains of Kublai Khan, one of the greatest rulers of the Middle Ages. His court, as Marco Polo witnessed, was highly civilized.

overlord from the Black to the Yellow Sea, Kublai Khan was ruler over more human beings than had ever before owed allegiance to one man. The first of his race to evince traits of benevolence or magnanimity, or any interest in arts or culture, he had travellers from as far west as Constantinople and even Venice among his ministers, generals, governors, envoys, physicians and astronomers. It was during the reign of Kublai Khan that the first reports of the wonders of "far Cathay" (China) came to the ears of an astonished and incredulous Europe through the tales, on his return to Venice, of Marco Polo (c. 1254–1324).

In the 14th century a Mongol chieftain from Turkistan, said to be of Jenghiz Khan's blood, though not a direct descendant, began a series of conquests covering Persia, Afghanistan, northern India, Mesopotamia (Iraq), and the greater part of Asia Minor. This

*Bibliothèque Nationale, Paris; Ancien fonds persan, 98*

**EDUCATION OF A MONGOL PRINCE**
The great attention paid to education by the Mongol rulers of India is attested by this picture of a prince (right) at lessons with his tutor. It is an illustration from the Persian poet Firdausi's Book of Kings.

*Victoria & Albert Museum*

**MONGOL RULER OF INDIA**
From 1556 to 1605 ruler of India, the Mongol, or Mogul, Emperor Akbar did much to unite that country into one empire and was the first Indian monarch with whom England had dealings. Here he is seen seated in state upon his imperial throne, giving audience to a traveller.

was Timur i Leng or Tamerlane (Timur the Lame), whose career was used by the Elizabethan dramatist Christopher Marlowe (1564–93) as the basis for his tragedy entitled Tamburlaine the Great. Timur's crowning achievement was his conquest of Asia Minor from the Turks in 1402. His empire broke up soon after his death in 1405, though his descendants for a time retained some slight authority in Persia.

About 100 years later one of Timur's descendants, Babar (1483–1530), ruler of a petty kingdom in what is now the Russian Soviet Republic of Turkmenistan, became the Mahomedan conqueror of northern India, the empire he established being known as the Mogul or Mongol.

At Babar's death his empire was divided between his two sons. Humayun and Kamran, India being assigned to Humayun. The latter had neither the martial spirit nor resolution of his father and by 1540 had been driven out of India by Sher Shah, the Afghan ruler of Berar. He was succeeded by his son Akbar, who was only 14 years of age when he came to the throne.

Young as he was, Akbar declared war on Sher Shah and within four years had established his authority across northern India from Afghanistan to the mouth of the Ganges. Besides being a skilful general he was a good administrator and wise statesman. He was also a keen advocate of education and declared that every boy should read books on morals, arithmetic, geometry, physical science, agriculture and the rules of government.

Akbar had no prejudices with regard to Europeans, and in his reign England first entered into relations with India. He was the Great Mogul to whom Queen Elizabeth sent a letter. None of his descendants had his ability, though his grandson Aurungzebe extended the limits of the Mogul Empire. This fell to pieces after Aurungzebe's death in 1707, the British becoming dominant in India.

The Mongols of the present day are one of the chief branches of Asiatic peoples. They are divided into the East Mongols, living in Mongolia and Tibet ; West Mongols or Kalmucks, living in Mongolia and Siberia ; and Buriats, living around Lake Baikal, Siberia. They are still mostly tent-dwellers and wandering herdsmen. Most of them are Lamaistic Buddhists ; a few are Mahomedans ;

*E.N.A.*

**THE MONGOOSE LIKES AN EGG**

Although it is famous chiefly as the enemy of snakes, which it kills and eats, the mongoose is also very fond of eggs and poultry. The name is derived from the Tamil (language of southern India) *mangus*.

cobra. The destruction of snakes is a characteristic of these small carnivorous animals. Members of the family *Viverridae*, the mongooses are found in Africa and Asia. They are generally about 16 inches in length, and have thick greyish fur, with a long bushy tail.

The Egyptian mongoose was held sacred by the ancient inhabitants of that land, probably because it killed poisonous snakes. The Indian species (*Herpestes mungo*) is easily tamed. When introduced into the British island of Jamaica in the

and some of the Buriats still hold to their ancient form of spirit worship, Shamanism. There are estimated to be about two million Mongols today.

**Mongoose.** Readers of Kipling's Jungle Book will know about Rikki-tikki-tavi, the mongoose that displayed such wonderful skill in killing a

West Indies, the mongoose multiplied so quickly as to become a serious pest, killing game, poultry and birds, as well as snakes and rats. Although the mongoose is not immune to the bite of a snake, its agility and thick fur render it more than a match for its deadly foe.

# HERE and THERE in MONKEY-LAND

*So quaint are the monkeys in their looks and ways that there is always a crowd around their house in a zoo. In this chapter we make the acquaintance of some members of the tribe.*

**Monkey.** Although the word " monkey " probably conjures up for you a picture of a small, hairy agile individual with a long tail, these animals are actually among the most various of all creatures. Some monkeys are as small as squirrels and others are as large as cocker spaniels. There are monkeys with long curly tails, with straight tails, bushy tails, stubby tails, or no tails at all. Some have very hairy, and others nearly naked, faces. There are dog-faced and purple-faced monkeys; monkeys with white cheeks, with turned-up noses, with tufted ears, with whiskers, mufflers, and bonnets. Most of them are black, grey, or some shade of brown, from silver-fawn to seal ; but there are dandies with green coats and orange vests.

*Gambier Bolton*
**The proboscis or long-nosed monkey is at home in the East Indies island of Borneo.**

Many people include the big apes—the gorillas, chimpanzees, orang-utans — under the name " monkey." But these higher forms are usually called *apes*, for there is as much difference between apes and monkeys as between apes and Man.

You would not suspect that the word " monkey " comes from *monna,* a contraction of " madonna,"

which is Italian for " my lady," though this is one of various suggested derivations. The name was given to certain lower forms of the order Primates (Man-like animals, a group including the apes, lemurs, and Man), perhaps because of their fancied resemblance to old women.

Monkeys inhabit the warm regions of both hemispheres. They are found in China, Japan, India, and southern Asia, including also the Malay islands, and in all parts of Africa except the deserts. In Europe they are found only at Gibraltar. The New World monkeys are found in the tropical regions of Central and South America, east of the Andes.

A monkey in captivity is happier in a cage with a number of other monkeys. " The more the merrier " is the rule in monkey-land, and nearly every kind of monkey lives in a " village " in the trees when he is at home. There is a wise old male for a chief. He and the older males keep trespassers away from a chosen feeding-place, and he leads his followers to a new home when they move. Early in the morning and late in the evening seem to be playtime among them. Monkeys love the dense forests of very hot countries. In the tropical forests along the River Amazon in South America they make their homes in boughs in the trees. They live in thousands on the tropical islands, and only a few are found in colder countries.

No matter how much monkeys may differ in other things, they are all alike in having four *hands*. The bear, the lion, the elephant, the dog—nearly all the animals you can think of—have four *feet*. Humans, of course, have two hands and two feet. A foot has

# MONKEY

**' FOLLOW MY LEADER '**
The extraordinary agility of monkeys is seen in this photograph taken in a zoo. A cable stretched between two
trees provided an aerial crossing : first one monkey
climbed to the start of the cable, then up went the others
after him, across and then down.

*Topical*

a long sole and short toes, usually, and the toes
cannot grasp and hold things. A hand has a nearly
square palm, fingers much longer than toes, and a
thumb. In the " best " kind of hand the fingers
have three joints each, and can all be brought
together, and even closed into a fist.

All four of a monkey's feet are really hands,
with grasping fingers and more or less perfect
thumbs. That is why a monkey is so clumsy
on the ground. Usually he walks on the outside
edges of the palms of his hands, with fingers
and thumbs curled in, which gives him a bow-
legged look. But watch him on a tree or a perch,
and he is as much at home as a squirrel.

The monkeys of the Old and New World have
been separated geographically for so long that they
have several distinct features. Thus, if you give an
Old World monkey nuts he will stow them away in
cheek pouches like a squirrel. He can put a surprising number away, for those pouches stretch like
rubber balloons. He has a flat nose with the
nostrils close together. And when he goes up to a
perch to eat his nuts he does not use his tail in
climbing or for holding on.

### Monkeys of the New World

A South American monkey's nostrils are far
apart. He has no cheek pouches, but heaps as
many nuts as he can carry in his two front limbs.
He can keep other monkeys from taking his nuts
when he climbs, for he uses his long curly-tipped
tail as a fifth hand. With *five* hands for grasping, the
South American monkey is a wonderful trapeze
performer. The tree-squirrel climbs faster, the
flying-squirrel leaps farther, the bat clings better
with his wing-hooks; but no other animal can climb,
leap, and swing across a gap, 40 feet from the
ground, as the South American monkeys can.
They do not leave the trees except in case of
necessity, and they drink while clinging to a bough
which overhangs the water. They feed on leaves,
fruits, insects, eggs, young birds and honey. The
American monkeys seldom damage Man's property, but they are hunted for their flesh and fur.

One kind of South American monkey is a small
rusty-brown animal, about the size of a toy terrier.
He has a curved hair-covered tail, good thumbs,
a whistling chatter, and a care-worn, anxious face,
as if he expected nothing in life but bad news. In
captivity he is bright and obedient, and soon learns
tricks and performs them willingly. Another
favourite is the Capuchin monkey. You may know
him by the way the hair grows round his face,
like a monk's hood or cowl.

Unlike the other South American monkeys, the
marmoset, the smallest and prettiest of them all,
cannot use his tail in climbing. He is only eight
inches long, with a furry body and a foot-long
bushy tail that he carries like a plume. If it wasn't
for his almost human face and hands, and his wing-
like tufted ears, you might think him a squirrel.

There is a squirrel monkey in South America
only a little larger than his nut-cracking namesake.
He has a grey face and a black nose, and long hind
legs so that he leaps somewhat like a kangaroo.
In his home in the Amazon forests it rains torrents
sometimes, as if the bottom had fallen out of the
clouds. When caught in such a storm a troop of
these squirrel monkeys huddle together in the

# STRANGE MEMBERS OF THE MONKEY FAMILY

*F. W. Bond; W. S. Berridge*

Some idea of the great variety of form and appearance shown by monkeys is given here. At the top left is a Humboldt's woolly monkey, a native of the South American forests. At the top right, a pig-tailed macaque with its baby ; these are found in southern Asia, North Africa and Gibraltar. The white-tailed colobus (lower left) lives in Africa. At the lower right is the curious white-headed saki, which is found only in Guiana and the valley of the Amazon, in South America.

**HANUMAN MONKEY OF THE EAST INDIES**

Known also as the langur, the hanuman monkey is three or four feet in length, with cream-coloured fur and black hands and face. There are several species in the sub-continent of India and south-east Asia. They feed mainly on fruit, leaves and the tender shoots of trees. This female is nursing her nine-days-old baby. *See also illustration opposite.*

So many of the Old World monkeys have only little stubs and lumps of thumbs that scientists class them in one family of " cut-off-thumb " monkeys. If you see a monkey with a very fine, long-haired silky coat, particularly if he has cheek pouches and makes no use of his tail, look for shrunken little thumbs. His coat makes monkey-skin collars and muffs for humans. One monkey of the mountains of Abyssinia, where it is cold, looks as if he were wearing furs himself. He has a fringe of white down on either side of his jet-black velvet body, a white tippet under his chin, a white edge to his cap, and a white tip to his tail. A monkey of the hot west coast of Africa wears the hair on top

thickest tree they can find and put their tails around one another's necks for company and comfort.

The marmosets and squirrel monkeys have some of the noisiest neighbours— the " howling " monkeys. These have a larynx or voice-box with six pockets, which reflect the voice and give it unusual strength. They begin howling at sunrise, keep it up until the next sunrise, and then make a fresh start. The woods ring and echo with their howls. They travel all the time through the high branches of the trees, the males leading and the mother monkeys following, each with one or two babies clinging to her neck with fingers and tails. They swing by their tails and catch the next limb with a hand. The brown howler is bad enough, but the red howler makes even more hideous cries.

Another South American monkey is the saki. He has a ruddy back, and an almost human habit of cupping a hand and scooping up water when he wants to drink. He is so delicate that he seldom lives long in captivity, so you may never see him. But you are sure to see the spider monkey. He has such long, slim arms and tail and such a small body that he looks like a big, hairy spider. In captivity he is gentle and even affectionate. He has tiny stumps of thumbs that are of little use to him, and he is not as agile as some other monkeys. A mother spider monkey likes to sit down quietly in a corner and cuddle her baby.

*W. S. Berridge*

**THE GROTESQUE MANDRILL**

Few creatures in the world of mammals are so grotesque in appearance as the mandrill, largest and most powerful of the baboons. The colour of the nose and eyebrows is brilliant red, and the cheeks are bright blue

of his head in a crest, with a parting on each side; he also has whiskers under his chin.

The African guenon is a small, graceful creature with fine hands, long thumbs and tail, big cheek pouches, and large hairless " callosities " on his " seat." He is a lively, merry monkey, doing much damage by raiding cornfields, most of the crop being spoiled by his attempts to select the choicest ears for eating.

Among the brightly-coloured species there are a red-faced and a purple-faced monkey; a Diana monkey, with a white crescent like a new moon on the forehead, a white beard and neck scarf; and one with a blue moustache above yellow whiskers—hence his name, "moustache" monkey. The

E.N.A.

**FEEDING THE SACRED MONKEYS AT A HINDU TEMPLE**
In the sub-continent of India hanuman monkeys (see also illustration opposite) occupy a privileged position, because the Hindus regard them as sacred to Hanuman the monkey god. One of the attendants of a temple in the State of Jaipur, Dominion of India, is here seen feeding the sacred monkeys which come down from the hillside for their daily ration.

green monkey, whose home is in the region of the Nile, is quite a dandy in dark green and black, set off with dull orange whiskers, throat band, breast-plate and tail tip.

The hanuman monkey, common in India, is a little spider-legged animal three or four feet long, with cream-coloured fur and black hands and face. In his native land he is sacred to Hanuman, the monkey god, and so he is never interfered with. He goes in troops into the villages, helping himself to grain, fruits and nuts in shops and houses. Stories are told of tribes of the hanuman monkeys swarming into dining-rooms and feasting. In some Hindu communities these monkeys live in the top storeys of the homes of the natives. If one native bears another a grudge, he places rice or corn on the enemy's roof during the rainy season. When the monkeys see this they eat the grain that is within reach, then tear up the roof to secure particles which have fallen into the crevices, so that the house is opened to the rain.

Another mischievous monkey is the Barbary ape or magot of north-western Africa and Gibraltar. He is about as big as a terrier. He and all his relations will go to a fruit garden and set sentinels in trees and on rocks to watch, while the others eat melons, figs, grapes, oranges and almonds until an alarm sends them flying.

The street strollers of India, Japan, and northern Africa lead about the macaque (ma-kahk') or " bonnet " monkeys. These are sturdily built, with short tails, and their hair grows in a frill round the face. Some of these monkeys love crabs so much that they have learned to swim and dive for this article of diet. The pigtailed bonnet monkey of the East

India islands is used on plantations to climb up the tall palms and pick coconuts. In the East Indian island of Borneo is found the long-nosed or proboscis monkey, a slender species with the nose of the adult male long and beak-like. His nose is not only movable in all directions but it can be retracted or protruded at will. The fur is red, thick, and soft, and about the neck it is nearly a foot long, forming a heavy collar.

The baboons or dog-headed monkeys are among the ugliest. In size and habits they come between the true apes and the tree-dwelling monkeys. They are made especially hideous by large bare spots, often brilliantly coloured, on their hind quarters. Their long blunt muzzles, with nostrils at the extreme end, and the great canine teeth give their faces a dog-like appearance. They run swiftly on all fours and climb trees with difficulty. They hunt in great droves, and, led by their old males and guarded by sentinels, will defend themselves against other wild beasts. Their food is chiefly insects, small animals, vegetables and fruits. In their raids on plantations they often do great havoc.

About a dozen different kinds of baboons are known, of which the mandrill is the largest and fiercest. This brute, said to be the most hideous of all animals, is larger than a mastiff; it has short legs, a heavy body, immense canine teeth, and a stump of a tail less than two inches long. It is especially remarkable for the brilliant flower-like hues of the hairless portions of its face and body. Its cheeks are an intense blue, the central line of the nose a brilliant scarlet. It is immensely strong.

The powerful hamadryad (ham-a-dri'-ad) baboon of Arabia and north-eastern Africa was worshipped by the ancient Egyptians, and its solemn appearance gained it credit for great wisdom. It is remarkable for the shaggy coat of greyish-green hair that covers its head and shoulders, and the flaming red of its callous spots.

Amazing stories are told of the intelligence of the chacma baboon of South Africa, which is nearly as large as the mandrill but is much more gentle in early life. In several instances chacma baboons are said to have been trained to act as shepherds, driving their woolly charges to and from pasture and protecting them; in defence of their own young or their females they do not hesitate to attack leopards, pythons, and even men. Their span of life is thought to be nearly equal to that of human beings.

# MONASTIC LIFE: PAST and PRESENT

*In their devotion to religion men throughout the ages have cut themselves off from the world, living either as solitary hermits or in disciplined communities. How the monastic system grew up is described here.*

**Monks** AND MONASTICISM. The word "monk" (from Greek *monos*, meaning alone) originally meant a solitary, or one who lives alone, but in course of time it came to mean a member of a religious community. Similarly the word "monastery" meant a cell or hut, and then came to mean a building in which lived a number of men devoted to the service of God and obeying a code of rules.

**All large monasteries had a scriptorium—a room where books could be copied by hired scribes or monks.**

In the early days of Christianity there lived in the Egyptian desert called the Thebais numbers of solitaries or hermits (from the Greek *eremites*, a dweller in the desert). The most celebrated of these was Paul of Thebes, who lived towards the middle of the 3rd century. These hermits were remarkable for their self-denying or ascetic mode of life.

The first monastic organization dates from the year 305, when St. Anthony established a monastery near Memphis, on the Nile. This, however, was not a monastery in the strict sense, as the brethren had separate huts; and, though under St. Anthony's direction, they lived a life which was largely suggested by individual fancy. The first community of monks living under a common roof was established by Pachomius in A.D. 340, at Tabennisi, an island of the Nile. He compiled the first monastic rule. The difference between the monks of St. Anthony and those of Pachomius was chiefly this, that the former spent all their time in the reading of the Scriptures, in prayer and fasting; while the latter led an active life in which religious exercises and the reading of the Scriptures alternated with daily labour in the fields.

From Egypt monasticism spread into Asia Minor and Syria; and about the year 360 St. Basil established a monastery near Neo-Caesarea, in Pontus, a country on the southern shores of the Black Sea. He is regarded as the founder of Eastern monasticism, of which the famous monastery at Mount Athos in Greece is a modern representative. St. Basil laid down the principle that a monk must not live for himself alone, but must do good to his fellow-man. In order to give his monks an oppor-

tunity to put this into effect, he established hospitals, hospices (rest-houses) and orphanages near the monasteries under his care. He also provided schools for the education of boys, not necessarily with a view to their becoming monks. He discouraged excessive asceticism, and taught that work is of greater value in the monastic life than self-imposed hardships or punishments. Accordingly, the time of the monks was divided between the duties of prayer, good works, and the reading of the Scriptures.

Monasticism was introduced into Italy directly from Egypt at an early date, and monasteries for men and nunneries for women soon became numerous throughout the Italian peninsula, especially in the neighbourhood of Rome. Thence the movement spread into Gaul when St. Martin of Tours founded the monastery of Ligugé, near Poitiers, in 360. Even more celebrated than Ligugé was the monastery of Lérins on an island in the Mediterranean off Cannes, France, which gave to the Church of Gaul some of its famous bishops and saints. St. Patrick, the Apostle of Ireland, was trained there, and under him and his successors many monasteries were founded in Wales and Ireland. Undoubtedly the chief glory of Celtic monasticism was its missionary work, the results of which are to be found all over north-western Europe. There is little known of Spanish monasticism before the close of the 5th century.

The greatest name in the history of western monasticism is that of St. Benedict of Nursia in Italy, who was born about the year 480. He detailed the essentials of monastic life in a way that had never been done before. According to St. Benedict's idea, the disciplinary force for human nature is work—the first condition of all growth in goodness. The religious life as conceived by St. Benedict is therefore essentially social, where prayer alternates with the daily tasks and social duties.

The influence of Benedictine monasticism was evidenced in many ways during the Middle Ages— in the conversion of the barbarians and the civilizing of Europe, in the development of agriculture, in the encouragement of learning and the teaching of crafts and trades, such as painting, wood-carving, working in metals, carpentry, weaving, tailoring, and the tanning of leather. Study is an essential part of the work with which the Benedictine monk must occupy himself, and from its foundation the order has been distinguished for its learning and its promotion of education. Most of the older universities grew out of Benedictine schools.

Nearly all the monastic orders of the Middle Ages were founded on the Benedictine plan. The most notable of these were the Carthusians, founded by St. Bruno at Chartreuse, France, in 1086; the Cistercians, or White Monks, founded by St. Robert at Molesme, France, in 1098; and the Premonstratensians, or Norbertines, who were established at Prémontré, France, in 1120 by St. Norbert. The Benedictines were formerly known as the Black Monks, from the colour of their habit.

The monasteries were all self-contained communities, with the abbey church as the centre. In all monastic churches the plan was governed by certain common necessities : (1) A choir had to be provided for the chanting of the canonical hours by the monks. The canonical hours are fixed forms of prayer which Catholic priests are bound to recite daily, viz., matins, lauds,

British Museum
**PRIOR OF A MONASTERY**
An abbot was the head of an abbey of monks, and he appointed as his second-in-command a prior, who was responsible for order and discipline.

prime, tierce, sext, none, vespers, and compline. (2) A certain number of altars was necessary, so that the priests of the monastery might be able to celebrate Mass at fixed hours. (3) Arrangements had to be made for processions, which were held every Sunday.

Next in importance to the church was the cloister, which was an enclosed space surrounding all four sides of a rectangular court known as the " garth." Here the older monks laboured at appointed duties, such as copying manuscripts and writing; here, too, younger members of the community studied under the supervision of teachers. Then came the refectory, or, as it is called, the "fratry" or common dining-hall, which was always some distance from the church. Close to the refectory was the kitchen; the dormitory was usually near the cloister. In early times the dormitory was an open apartment without

**CISTERCIAN MONKS AT WORK AS FARMERS**
History records that some monasteries have been retreats for the lazy and incompetent, but these were the exception. The founders of the chief monastic orders were all convinced that idleness is a great source of evil, and they laid down rules which would entail that the monks in their establishments should be always busy—in church or study, in the various workshops, in tending the poor and sick, in teaching, or (as seen here) in tilling the monastery fields.

screens. Later, partitions were introduced, and each monk had a small room as bedroom and study.

A most important feature of every monastery was the infirmary or house for the sick and the aged. It was placed near the dormitory and close to the garden, or "herbarium," where herbs used in compounding medicines were cultivated. The care of the sick was especially enjoined upon the superior or abbot of every Benedictine monastery. A guest-house was a necessary part of the establishment; and near the gate of the monastery there was invariably a shelter for travellers. Every religious house had an almonry, or place where the poor could receive alms, in the name of Christ. To the almonry was usually attached a free school for poor boys. Near the cloister there was a common-room or "calefactory" (warming place), where the monks might resort in winter to warm themselves at the common fire, which was lighted on the Feast of All Saints, November 1, and kept burning till Easter.

**A CLUNIAC MONK**
The order of Cluniac Benedictines was founded in 910. In place of the manual labour of the Benedictines, this order substituted prolonged church services. The order is so called from the town of Cluny in France, where it originated.

Manuscripts and copied books were carefully preserved in lockers or cupboards in the church or in the cloister. By the 15th century, however, libraries as we know them were common, many of them very large and splendidly arranged, with cubicles or small writing-rooms. In addition to the foregoing parts of the monastery there were numerous buildings set apart for various kinds of work, such as carpenter-shops, book binderies, forges, mills, bake-houses and barns. All were under the supervision of a chamberlain, or procurator.

All the inmates of a monastery were under an abbot or a prior. Next to the abbot (in an abbey) came the prior; and then his assistant, the sub-prior.

*Fitzwilliam Museum, Cambridge MS.22*
**SERMON BY A MENDICANT FRIAR**
Dominicans were specifically the order of preaching friars, but missionary work in the world was the purpose of all the mendicant (begging) orders, and they were in great demand as preachers. They might not, however, encroach upon the privileges of the clergy, nor preach without leave in the parish churches.

The daily life of a monastery was very carefully arranged. The day between sunrise and sunset was divided into 12 equal parts or *horae* ("hours"), and likewise the night, or from sunset to sunrise, into 12 equal *horae*. The hour for rising was about 2 a.m., when the monks went to the church, or oratory, for a service. Meditation and other prayers followed. Prime was said at sunrise, after which they went to their appointed work till 10 o'clock. Tierce was then said; and from 10 till 11.30 they read. Then sext was recited, followed by dinner, which was over shortly after midday. The dinner, or *prandium*, usually consisted of vegetables, possibly eggs, or fish, salad, bread and wine; but no meat was allowed. In Italy, because of the hot climate, there followed a *siesta*, or afternoon nap; but elsewhere the monks went to the fields, the workshops, or the bake-house and worked until vespers at 5 o'clock. Supper, or the *coena*, was at 5.30; then the reading of the last service of the day, and to bed at 6.30.

We must distinguish between monks and friars (from the French *frère*, brother), though both are members of religious orders, and are known as Regular clergy, as distinct from the Secular. Seculars are not bound by the vow of poverty as are Regulars; they follow no special rule, and may hold property as individuals. Retirement from the world, and solitude, are the essential characteristics of monks; hence it is that most monasteries are far from cities or towns. Friaries are usually found within or near city limits as friars engage in parochial and other ministerial work, and come in close contact with the outside world. Friars originally depended on alms or offerings of the people for their subsistence; hence the term mendicant (from the Latin *mendicare*, to beg) was formerly applied to them. The chief orders of friars are the Dominicans (Black Friars), the Franciscans (Grey Friars), the Carmelites (White Friars), and the Augustinians, the popular names being derived from the colour of their habits.

In the early Middle Ages there were established many communities of nuns in France, Italy, Spain, England and Ireland, whose organization was, with a few exceptions, similar to that of monks. Heading each community was an abbess, who had complete jurisdiction in matters of administration. Today there are many such communities of nuns (convents), the abbess being now called the Mother Superior. In both the Roman and Anglican churches there are also orders of women, such as the Sisters of Charity and Sisters of Mercy, living under religious rule but not enclosed in convents; members of these devote their lives to good works, helping the poor and nursing the sick.

**Monmouthshire.** One of the English counties, though for certain legal purposes it is considered part of Wales, Monmouthshire is bordered on the west and north-west by Wales proper, on the north-east by Hereford, on the east by Gloucester, on the south by the Bristol Channel. The county, area 546 square miles, is generally hilly, especially in the north and north-west, where several summits exceed 1,500 feet, the highest being the Sugar Loaf (1,955 feet). The chief rivers are the Wye, the valley of which is famous for its scenery, Usk, Ebbw, Rhymney and Monnow.

In the western part of Monmouthshire coal-mining and iron-working are the main industries. Agriculture is carried on in the east and south, and there are extensive sheep farms in the upland districts. Monmouth (population 4,700) is the county town; industrial centres include Newport, Ebbw Vale, Tredegar, Abertillery and Pontypool.

Numerous Norman castles were built in the county to check the incursions of the Welsh into England, and of these there are several ruins, including those at Chepstow, Raglan, Caldicot, Monmouth and Abergavenny. The county contains Tintern Abbey and Llanthony Abbey; and at Caerleon, near Newport, there are remains of a Roman amphitheatre. The population of Monmouthshire is 434,900.

# The MARVEL of SETTING our TYPE

*If this book had been printed not so very long ago, it would have been 'set up,' letter by letter, by hand. But actually it was 'tapped out' on a machine very much like a kind of typewriter—a 'Monotype' Keyboard.*

**'Monotype.'** To the patient monk in his "scriptorium," spending years in making a single copy of a book, printing from movable types must have seemed almost a miracle. How stupefied with amazement he would have been if prophetic vision could have shown him 'Monotype' machines of today which produce thousands of type each hour —cast, set, and "justified" by nimble machines.

Strictly speaking, there are *two* machines—a keyboard "composing" machine and an automatic type-caster. At the keyboard of the "composing" machine (Fig. 1) an operator punches a paper ribbon into a pattern of holes. This perforated ribbon, called the "controller paper," is the code of instructions to the caster-machine.

When the controller paper is inserted in the caster (Fig. 2), that knowing machine casts one type after another, with spaces of the proper thickness, in order to "justify" each line to the given length; it assembles one line after another and delivers them on galleys, exactly as if the type had been set by hand. Unlike 'Linotype' machines (*q.v.*), which produce solid bars or "slugs" of metal, each having a line of type characters on its face, 'Monotype' machines cast each character separately.

A 'Monotype' keyboard has more than 260 keys, because the casting machine carries five or more different alphabets. With those five alphabets on the keyboard, the operator can make the con-

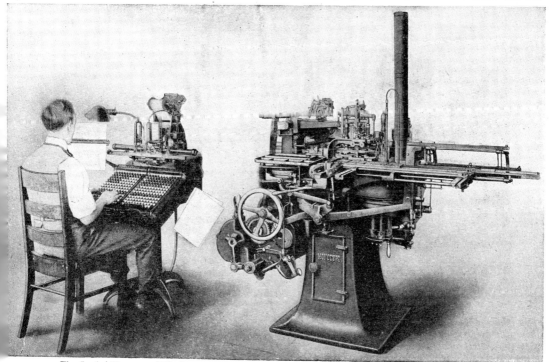

Fig. 1. A 'Monotype' Keyboard.          Fig. 2. A 'Monotype' Casting Machine.

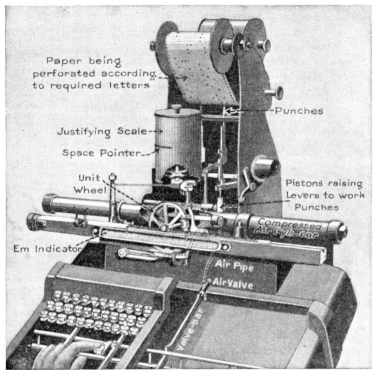

Fig. 3. How the controller paper is perforated.

that must be used to fill out the line. The operator presses the red spacing keys on the keyboard as the pointer tells him; that is all. The caster, thus instructed by the perforations, which this makes in the controller paper, will do the rest.

Fig. 3 shows how the controller paper receives its perforations. When a key is pressed the valve-bar opens an air-valve, and by means of the piston, lever, and punch, one or more holes are made which stand for that letter or character. Those perforations then become the instructions to the automatic caster to cast that type or character. In the picture, parts of this wonderful machine are removed in order to make clear the principle on which it operates.

Now let us look at the caster diagram (Fig. 4). It consists essentially of the following parts: (a) a pot of molten metal heated electrically or by a gas flame; (b) above the melting-pot, a mould for a single type, into which the molten metal is driven at the right instant by a pump; (c) face down over the mould, a matrix case (Fig. 5) in which are locked 225 matrices in which the faces of the type are formed; and (d) a compressed-air supply, contained in a cylinder, with outlet valves which control the mechanism that does the casting.

When the perforated controller paper is placed in the caster, and the machine is set going, what happens is briefly this. Each set of perforations

troller papers that enable the caster to produce hundreds of different faces of types of various sizes.

Both keyboard and caster are controlled by compressed air. When you touch a key on the keyboard, a complicated system of valves, pipes, levers, and punches perforates the moving paper ribbon (see diagram, Fig. 3). Each key controls a particular combination of perforations, which is made by no other key; each set of perforations made by any key, therefore, stands for the character on that key and for no other. The code, however, is one of position, like the code of letters and numbers that help to find places on an indexed map.

One interesting feature of the keyboard deserves particular notice. This is the " justifying scale," the swinging cylinder above the keyboard, round which run row on row of figures. Printed matter, as you know, must be " justified " or spaced so as to fill out each line and leave no ragged edges. When the operator nears the end of a line, a warning bell rings as it does on a typewriter. The operator looks at his copy and finds, let us say, that his next word (one of six letters, like " pledge ") cannot be divided, and he has not enough space to put it in. What does he do ?

Ask rather what the machine does. The operator looks at the justifying scale; the space-pointer on it, which has been keeping watch on every letter, points to figures indicating the spacing

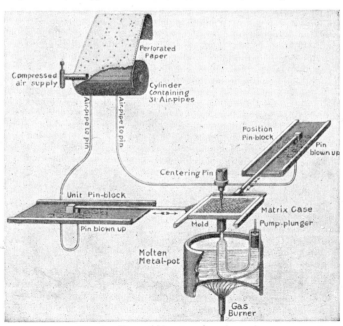

Fig. 4. How a ' Monotype ' caster works.

in the paper, as it comes opposite the row of holes in the air cylinder, releases air into little tubes or pipes, and by a system of pin-blocks and rods the matrix case is instantly shifted, so that the matrix for the corresponding letter or character is brought directly over the type mould. As soon as this is centred over the mould, molten type metal is forced by the pump-plunger into the mould, and the type is cast.

Automatically the width of the type-mould alters with the size of the letter that is to be cast, so that a capital letter M, for example, will have a wider body than an I. The operation of adjustment and casting is repeated as each new combination of perforations passes over the compressed-air outlets. By an exceedingly ingenious arrangement the spaces between the words in each line are cast thicker or thinner, as a result of the spacing indications, so that each line of type when completed exactly fills the page or column measure.

So entirely independent of each other are keyboard and caster that a keyboard in London or Manchester may prepare a controller ribbon from which a caster in Glasgow or Edinburgh may cast and set type—and set it just as well as if the two machines were in the same room. And because the caster, like the hand compositor, sets movable type, its work may be corrected or altered by hand, letter by letter, instead of having to reset a whole line as is the case with 'Linotype' machines.

Joan Beard

CASTER OF A 'MONOTYPE' MACHINE

One of the advantages of a 'Monotype' machine is that the caster casts and sets movable type, so its work can be corrected or altered by hand, letter by letter, instead of a whole line having to be reset as with Linotype machines. Here the operator is about to place a piece of type metal in the melting pot.

'Monotype' machines are specially suited for setting books and magazines. You need not look far for an example of the work of these machines, for the whole of the text of this book was set up by 'Monotype' machines.

This wonderful machine was invented and patented in 1887 by Tolbert Lanston, for many years a clerk in the Pension Office in Washington, U.S.A. Improvements and innovations are continually being made, one of the most recent being a supercaster which casts type up to 72-point (that is, large enough for using in bills and advertisements), fancy rules, borders, ornaments and all

Fig. 5.   Matrix case.

necessary spacing material. The Monotype Corporation have revived some beautiful old types like Jenson, Garamond, Caslon, and Plantin. They have also had new types specially made. The type known as " Gill Sans," now seen everywhere, was originally designed for the Monotype Corporation by the famous sculptor, Eric Gill, who also designed other type for them.

**Monsoon.** The atmosphere over continental land-masses far removed from the sea is very warm during the summer months, and becomes much colder in winter. As a result of this summer warming, the pressure of the air over the land is reduced below the pressure over the surrounding seas, and winds blow in over the land during summer. In winter the opposite conditions prevail: the winds blow outwards from the land towards the sea, where pressure of the atmosphere is then lower than over the continental mass.

Monsoons (from Dutch *monssoen*, perhaps derived from Arabic *mausim*, " season ") is the name given to these winds changing with the seasons. In the sub-continent of India the hot season lasts usually from about February until June, but some time may elapse before the summer monsoon begins to blow, from the south-west. Then there is stormy weather, the wind reverses suddenly from its former north-east direction of the winter monsoon, and until about October the rain-laden summer monsoon continues to blow. This is the rainy season, during which anything from six to nine tenths of the yearly rainfall may be expected.

The winter monsoon, coming from the land masses, is a drying wind, and rain is slight during its blow. It has much less strength than the summer monsoon. Only over parts of Asia (such as India and China) do the monsoons have such importance, affecting the agriculture and day-to-day life of the inhabitants of those regions. They occur less strongly over equatorial Africa and over Australia, with less marked changes of direction at the seasons. America scarcely knows the monsoon; and in Europe it can be discerned very slightly over the Spanish peninsula only.

Should the summer monsoon "fail," so that the customary rainfall does not come to revive the parched agricultural land, famine and plague may follow. For the Indian peasant the important economic event of the year is the "bursting" of the clouds which the wind rolls over the Indian sub-continent from the Arabian Sea. (See Wind).

**Montaigne,** MICHEL D'EYQUEM, SIEUR DE (1553-92). The first essayist in point of time, this French writer has appealed to people of every disposition and belief. Although he lived in an age of religious strife and political upheaval, he was open-minded about most matters and able to appreciate other people's points of view. He wrote clearly and naturally, with delightful touches of humour. In his essays there are accounts of his own clumsiness, of how he could not harness a horse, and the difficulty he had in distinguishing between a lettuce and a cabbage in his garden. Many a time he mentions ideas much more serious and complicated than his own domestic troubles, but he never takes himself too seriously.

Montaigne (pron. mon-tān'-ye) was born near Bordeaux, France, on February 28, 1553, and in accordance with his father's views on education was taught Latin by a tutor who knew no French. He studied law, probably at Toulouse, and became a magistrate. Succeeding to the family estate near Bordeaux, he gave up his magistracy and, to indulge his love of solitude, he had a tower built separate from his house, where he worked and to which not even his wife was admitted. The first two books of his Essays appeared in 1580 and the third in 1588.

Montaigne had no very high opinion of the

*Condé Museum Chantilly; photo. Giraudon*
**MICHEL DE MONTAIGNE**
The first great essayist, Montaigne was so wise and witty that his works appealed to the people of many lands. This picture is a reproduction of a painting by a contemporary.

intelligence of women, but a mocking Fate so arranged it that a young female admirer, Marie le Jars de Gournay, whom he met in 1588, should edit his essays after his death on September 13, 1592.

**Montana.** Texas and California are the only States of the U.S.A. bigger than Montana, which has an area of 147,138 square miles. It is bordered on the east by North and South Dakota, on the south by Wyoming, on the west by Idaho, on the north by Canada. In the west are the Rocky Mountains; the eastern portion is mostly rolling plains. The headwaters of the Missouri and Columbia rivers rise in Montana; and the Yellowstone, Milk and other tributaries of the Missouri help to drain the State.

Agriculture is the most important industry; wheat, oats, flax, barley, rye, maize, fruit, and potatoes are the main crops. Dairy-farming and stockbreeding are among the leading occupations, Montana being second only to Texas in the number of its sheep and in wool production. The mineral wealth includes copper, zinc, lead, silver, coal, gold and oil. Helena, the capital, has a population of 15,000. Other cities are Butte, Great Falls, Billings, Missoula and Anaconda. The population of the State is 559,000, of whom some 17,000 are Red Indians. The majority of the latter are located on six reservations.

**Montcalm de St. Véran,** LOUIS JOSEPH, MARQUIS DE (1712-59). In the Seven Years' War (1756-63) the name of Montcalm de St. Véran (generally shortened to Montcalm), the commander of the French troops in Canada, is linked with that of General Wolfe, who led the British forces in the campaign which decided that Canada was to become a part of the British Empire.

Though Montcalm was defeated and mortally wounded in the final battle on the Plains of Abraham outside Quebec, his reputation stands almost as high as that of his conqueror. In Quebec there is a monument to the two heroes, bearing this inscription in Latin: "Valour gave them a common death, history a common fame, and posterity a common monument."

Born near Nîmes, France, on February 29, 1756, Montcalm entered the French army at the age of 14 and had risen to the rank of colonel by the time he was 24. In 1756 he was appointed commander of the French forces in Canada. Taking Fort William Henry from the British in 1757, he successfully defended Fort Ticonderoga against a superior British army in

1758. Then the tide turned. French strongholds were lost, and Montcalm retired to Quebec and prepared to defend it against the British under Wolfe. In the battle fought on the Plains of Abraham on September 13, 1759, the French were defeated. Wolfe was killed and Montcalm mortally wounded.

**Monte Carlo.** The picturesque seaside town of Monte Carlo in the Principality of Monaco is situated on the Bay of Monaco, close to the point where the frontiers of France and Italy meet on the coast of the Mediterranean. In normal times it is one of the most frequented resorts in the south of France and is noted for the gaming rooms in the large Casino, which, built in 1878, is adorned with statuary and paintings. The gambling yields so large a revenue that no taxes are paid by the people of Monaco, who are not allowed to take part in the games of chance.

Monte Carlo, with the two smaller towns of Monaco and La Condamine, covers almost all the territory of the Principality of Monaco, which is ruled by the Prince of Monaco, and has an area of eight square miles. The population of Monte Carlo is 11,000.

**Montenegro.** Formerly the smallest independent kingdom in Europe and the only part of the Balkan Peninsula which was never really conquered by the Turks, Montenegro is a province of Yugoslavia. It is a barren mountainous region with an area of 3,733 square miles, lying on the eastern shore of the Adriatic Sea, just north of Albania.

Maize, tobacco and wine are produced, and cattle are reared on the uplands. Cetinje and Jakova are the only towns of any size. The people are of the Slavic race and belong mainly to the Greek Orthodox Church.

After the defeat of the Serbians by the Turks at Kossovo in 1389, Montenegro still maintained its independence despite perpetual conflict with Turkey, who subjugated the other Balkan States. In 1910 the country became a kingdom, and in 1914, at the outbreak of the First World War (1914–18), Montenegro went to the aid of Serbia, which was attacked by Austria and overrun by Austro-German forces. It was freed in 1918, and in November of that year joined the new Kingdom of Yugoslavia.

In the Second World War (1939–45) Montenegro was occupied by German troops in April 1941, and was liberated by the Allies early in 1945. The population is 360,000.

**Montesquieu,** Charles Louis de Secondat, Baron de (1689–1755). The importance of this French writer lies in his sociological (dealing with human society) works, which influenced the political thought of the 18th century.

*Donald McLeish*

**MONTE CARLO, THE GAMBLERS' PARADISE**

The most famous winter resort on the Mediterranean is Monte Carlo, the chief town of the little principality of Monaco. Here it is seen from across the harbour. The building with twin towers across the water is the Casino, from which is derived Monaco's main source of revenue. Behind the town is the hill of La Turbie, an outcrop of the Maritime Alps.

Montesquieu (pron. mon-tes-kyê) was born at the chateau of La Brède, near Bordeaux, France, on January 18, 1689, and was educated at Juilly, near Meaux, and afterwards at Bordeaux.

In 1716 he succeeded his uncle Jean Baptiste de Secondat, whose wealth, title and high legal office in the parliament of Bordeaux he inherited. His *Lettres Persanes* (Persian Letters), published in 1721, pretend to be the outspoken comments of two Persians on a visit to Europe, and are a wonderful satire on the manners and customs of the age. He went to live in Paris in 1726 and was admitted to the French Academy in 1728.

A long visit to England, 1729–30, greatly impressed him, and on his return to France he managed his estate at La Brède in the same way as an

English landowner. In 1734 appeared his *Considérations sur les Causes de la Grandeur et de la Décadence des Romains*, which shows the workings of a powerful and original mind, strengthened by wide reading. This book is almost the first important essay in the philosophy of history.

Montesquieu's greatest work was *L'Esprit des Lois* (Spirit of Laws), published in 1748 and consisting of 31 books. An amazingly comprehensive review of the social order, it is equally notable for its learning, broad-mindedness and wisdom. Montesquieu died on February 10, 1755.

**Montessori,** MARIA (born 1870). Most progressive schools of today emphasize liberty, pupils being given the opportunity to follow their own bents, and urged to concentrate on the activities that especially appeal to them. The credit for this forward step in education belongs to Dr. Montessori, who was the first woman in Italy to be granted a medical degree, and who has given her entire life to the study of education.

Liberty is the central principle of the Montessori school. Dr. Montessori believes that the child can develop its individuality and grow in self-reliance and in appreciation of the rights of others, only if it is allowed to work at subjects of its own choosing. The teacher is not to be a dictator, but a supervisor and a guide. The interest of the pupil in his work is sustained by the pleasure which he has in doing it rather than by orders, rewards, or punishments. Concentration on attractive occupations results in the development of self-control.

A second characteristic of this system is emphasis on sense training. Through appropriate exercises the child learns to distinguish between various sights, sounds, feels, smells and tastes. A third point is the "exercises of practical life," through which the child learns to dress itself, to sweep, to wash, to polish, and to perform other tasks.

To carry out these principles Dr. Montessori devised what she calls "didactic apparatus." This material is supposed to teach the child without the assistance of the teacher. For example, puzzles, each piece of which can be fitted into only one other piece, teach the child differences in shape and thickness. Dressing is taught by means of buttoning- or lacing-frames. In 1907 she founded a school at Rome which she called *Casa dei Bambini*, or House of the Children. Within a few years the Montessori system was being imitated throughout the world.

Many educationists consider that the Montessori method does not lay enough emphasis on the play element in education. Experience, they urge, gives better preparation for practical life than does formal apparatus. The imaginative side of the child is largely ignored. Stories and musical interpretations are not widely used, though a few games are included.

Dr. Montessori was born near Ancona, Italy, on August 30, 1870, and took her medical degree at Rome University in 1894, becoming assistant doctor at a clinic for mentally deficient children. Experience there led her to evolve the Montessori method of education, and later she founded other clinics in Barcelona, Spain; Laren, the Netherlands; and London. She was appointed Inspector of Schools by the Italian Government in 1922.

**Montevideo.** (Pron. mon-tā-vē-dā'-ō). About one-third of the inhabitants of the South American Republic of Uruguay live in Montevideo, the capital and only large city of the State. It is situated at the mouth of the Rio de la Plata, or River Plate, and has one of the few good harbours on the South American continent.

Because of its beautiful gardens Montevideo is sometimes called the City of Roses. Cobbled streets and quaint houses form the old quarter near the harbour. The newer sections of the city have wide boulevards and palm-shaded squares, lined with fine stone buildings. The Plaza Constitución is the very heart of the city's life, and there are the Cathedral and the old Houses of Parliament. Montevideo handles the trade of a

*Courtesy of the Little Felcourt School, East Grinstead*
**AT A 'MONTESSORI' INFANTS' SCHOOL**
**At modern infants' schools learning is largely practical, thanks to Maria Montessori, whose methods have revolutionized the teaching of the very young. In schools run on her principles freedom is the keynote. The children in this picture are performing domestic tasks free from strict supervision.**

E.N.A

**MONTEVIDEO'S CENTRAL SQUARE**

In the centre of the oldest part of the city of Montevideo, the capital of Uruguay, is the Plaza de la Constitución. It is surrounded by clubs, hotels, and business houses, and a large part of one side is occupied by the cathedral, seen on the right. Compared with the cathedrals of some of the other South American cities, this is a modern building. It was first consecrated in 1804, becoming a cathedral in 1869, but the present façade dates only from 1905.

large grazing and agricultural region, exporting meat, wool, hides and flax seed.

Founded by settlers from the Argentine in 1726, it became the capital of Uruguay when that country was recognized as an independent State in 1828. In Montevideo harbour the German battleship Admiral Graf Spee took refuge from British warships after the battle of the River Plate on December 13, 1939, during the Second World War (1939–45), and it was scuttled by the Germans just outside the harbour four days later. The population of Montevideo is 730,000.

**Montfort,** SIMON DE (c. 1208–65). That the British Parliament should owe its birth to a foreigner is one more of the many strange things we meet so often in English history. To this stern and warlike knight, a Frenchman by birth who had become Earl of Leicester in England, historians credit the origin of the House of Commons. At first the English barons distrusted him as a foreigner, and, although he had married a sister of King Henry III, he was often out of favour with Henry.

In 1258 he assumed the leadership of those among the barons who wished to end Henry's misgovernment. In 1259 Henry was forced to accept a scheme by which the Government of England was placed in the hands of baronial committees. When in 1261 the King announced the abolition of these committees, Montfort and the barons took up arms. In the first battle, fought on the downs above Lewes, Sussex, on May 14, 1264, the barons were not only victorious but they took captive King Henry and his son Edward.

During the time that Simon de Montfort exercised power he

*British Museum*

**MONTFORT'S SEAL**

To Simon de Montfort, thus depicted on his seal, is credited the origin of the British parliamentary system, with commons, nobles and clergy.

made a change in the Great Council or Parliament for which he will always be remembered. In calling a meeting in 1265 he summoned not only the barons and rulers of the Church, who had always attended, but also two knights from each shire and two townsmen from each of those cities and boroughs which could be depended upon to support his reforms. This is usually called the first Parliament, because it was the first in which the Commons (as opposed to the clergy and nobility) were represented.

Soon after this meeting Prince Edward, King Henry's son, escaped from captivity and rallied about him many of the nobles who were jealous of Earl Simon's power. He showed much skill in forcing Simon to fight in an unfavourable position at Evesham in Worcestershire on August 4, 1265. When the Earl saw Edward's army approaching in great numbers and excellent order he said: " They come on skilfully, yet it is from me that they have learned this order of battle. God have mercy on our souls, for our bodies are Prince Edward's ! "

True to his prediction Simon and his barons were defeated. Simon himself was killed, but the reforms which he had begun were continued by the wise Prince Edward, who later became Edward I.

**Montgomery,** BERNARD LAW MONTGOMERY, 1ST VISCOUNT (b. 1887). Of all the Allied leaders in the Second World War (1939–45) none earned greater renown than " Monty "—Field-Marshal Lord Montgomery, whose colourful personality and unbroken record of victory made him one of the great generals of military history. Everyone was familiar with the spare figure in battledress, whose black beret bore two, sometimes even three, badges.

Bernard Law Montgomery, son of an Anglican bishop, was born on November 17, 1887, in County Donegal, Ireland. He went to St. Paul's School, London, and the Royal Military College, Sandhurst, and in 1908 became a Second Lieutenant in the Royal Warwickshire Regiment. He fought in France in the First World War (1914–18), winning the D.S.O. in 1914, and being twice wounded. Promoted Major-General in 1938, he commanded the 3rd Division when the Second World War broke out in September 1939. He fought in Belgium and France, and after Dunkirk was appointed Commander-in-Chief of South-Eastern Command. There he earned a reputation for his tireless energy, for the importance he attached to physical fitness, and for the realism he infused into the training of his men.

In August 1942 " Monty " took over the 8th Army at El Alamein, in the Western Desert of Egypt. Two months later, having beaten off an attack, he launched the first battle of an offensive that was to continue to the end of the war, pursued the Germans and Italians for 13 weeks across the desert, and wiped them out at Mareth, in Tunisia. Following up these victories in North Africa, he led the 8th Army in the invasion of Sicily and of Italy. In December 1943 he was recalled to England to prepare for his greatest task.

On January 2, 1944, General Montgomery assumed command of the forces which were to assault the " fortress of Europe." On D-Day, June 6, he was in command of all the land forces. By August 30 enough American troops had landed to constitute a separate army group, and General Montgomery, on that day promoted to Field-Marshal, was placed at the head of the British and Canadian contingent which now formed the 21st Army Group. He directed the gallant air-

borne attack on Nijmegen and Arnhem, and played a major part in stemming the German counter-offensive in the Ardennes in December 1944.

From the crossing of the Rhine in March 1945, the Allied advance was unchecked. Field-Marshal Montgomery's troops, on the left flank, liberated Holland, captured Bremen, Hanover and Hamburg, and reached the River Elbe at Magdeburg. On May 4, 1945, in his tent at the 21st Army Group headquarters at Luneburg Heath, the Field-Marshal received the unconditional surrender of all German forces in Holland, North-West Germany and Denmark.

Field-Marshal Montgomery became the senior British member of the Allied Commission in Germany and commander-in-chief of the British occupying forces. In June 1946 he succeeded Lord Alanbrooke as Chief of the Imperial General Staff. He relinquished that office when in October 1948 the Governments of the Western Union (Great Britain, France, Belgium, the Netherlands and Luxemburg) who were pledged to assist each other against any aggressor nation, appointed him permanent Military Chairman of the Commanders-in-Chief Committee, so that he became the virtual commander of the Union's armed forces. He was knighted in 1942, received the G.C.B. in 1945,

*British Official; Keystone*

**FROM ALAMEIN TO GERMANY HE LED THE EMPIRE'S MEN**
1. ' Monty ' addresses his troops who outflanked the Mareth Line, Tunisia.  2. In June 1944 on the Normandy beaches he discusses the position with an officer.  3. Greeting Marshal Rokossovsky at Wismar, Germany, on May 7, 1945, after the link-up between 21st Army Group and the Russians.  4. In Brussels, Monty addresses the Belgians.  5. A typical portrait.

and was made Knight of the Garter by King George VI in 1946. Created a Viscount in January 1946 he chose, in memory of the battle that won him fame, the title of Lord Montgomery of Alamein.

## Montgomeryshire.
This inland county of North Wales, with an area of 797 square miles, is almost entirely surrounded by mountains, and is itself a hilly region. The best-known ranges are Plynlimmon (where five rivers have their source, including the Wye and Severn) and the Kerry Hills. In the county is the artificial lake Vyrnwy, which supplies water to Liverpool.

There are many remains of ancient British and Roman camps. It was at Machynlleth that the Welsh rebel Owen Glendower (c. 1359–1416) set up a parliament and was crowned Prince of Wales, and there his senate (parliament) house is still to be seen.

Sheep and horses are reared, the Kerry Hills giving their name to a breed of sheep whose fleece is brownish-red. Oats are the chief grain crop. The county town is Montgomery (population 900). The population of the county is about 48,000.

## Month.
The word "month" comes from *mona*, the Old English word for moon, the length of a month being the time that elapses between consecutive new or full moons. This is called a lunar month (from the Latin *luna*, moon). It is usually reckoned as 28 days, but the actual average duration is 29 days, 12 hours, 44 minutes, and 2·7 seconds. Calendar months, which are those recognized by almanacs, differ in length, as is indicated in the old rhyme, of which one version runs—

> Thirty days hath September,
> April, June, and November;
> All the rest have thirty-one,
> Excepting February alone,
> Which has twenty-eight days clear
> And twenty-nine in each leap year.

A solar month is one-twelfth of the time taken by the earth for its revolution round the sun.

The origin of the names of the months is of interest. January was named after Janus, the two-faced Roman god who was the patron of births and of the first steps in all human activities; and February after the Latin word *februare*, to purify, in allusion to the Lupercalia, a festival of atonement held on February 15. Before January and February were introduced into the calendar, the Roman year had only 10 months, and March (named after Mars, the Roman god of war) was thus the first month. Spring officially begins on March 21, known as the vernal (spring) equinox, the date when days and nights are of equal length. The old weather saying is that " If March comes in like a lion it will go out like a lamb."

April, month of fickle weather, derives its name from the Latin *aperire*, to open, and it certainly opens the gates to the summer months ahead. The first of May has for long been a gala day, May Day celebrations originating in the Roman festival of Flora, goddess of flowers. In some countries it is now a day of political demonstrations. Various Roman origins have been suggested for May, including the goddess Maia, and it may be connected with the word *maior* meaning greater (increase), as *junior* (youth) is associated with June. Others derive June from Juno, queen of heaven, or from Junius Brutus, one of Julius Caesar's murderers. July, we know, was named after Julius Caesar, and August after the later Emperor Augustus. These two months were previously called *Quintilis* and *Sextilis* by the Romans—meaning the fifth and sixth months. In the same way September, October, November and December were once the seventh, eighth, ninth, and tenth months respectively of the Roman year.

## Montreal.
(Pron. mon-tri-awl'). The name of the largest Canadian city is derived from Mount Royal (French *Mont Réal*), the towering mass of rock rising 753 feet high from the river behind the town. The city stands on the south-

*Canadian Official News Bureau*

**LOOKING DOWN ON MONTREAL FROM MOUNT ROYAL**

A magnificent view of Canada's Montreal is obtained from Mount Royal, the fine pleasure park which lies some 770 feet above the city. In this photograph we are looking out across the St. Lawrence river, spanned on the right by the Victoria Jubilee bridge built in 1898–9. Like the cities of the United States, Montreal is now a city of skyscrapers.

east side of the island of Montreal at the junction of the Ottawa and St. Lawrence rivers, and although it is nearly 1,000 miles from the Atlantic ocean-going vessels can be accommodated at the port. A canal system connects it with the Great Lakes, and it is linked by rail with the rest of the Dominion.

As one of the largest seaports of the North American Continent, Montreal exports enormous quantities of grain, chiefly to Great Britain. Its industries include meat-packing, the manufacture of boots and shoes, railway rolling-stock, paper, flour, clothing, cement, steel and machinery.

The city has numerous ecclesiastical buildings. The church of Notre Dame is built after the style of the famous Notre Dame in Paris; St. James's Cathedral is a replica of St. Peter's, Rome. Chief of the educational institutions are McGill University and L'Université de Montréal.

Montreal's first records date from 1535, when the site of the city was visited by the French explorer Jacques Cartier. It was founded in 1642 by a group of French settlers led by Sieur de Maisonneuve, the early years of its existence being marked by constant struggle against hostile Red Indians. During the Seven Years' War (1756-60), when Britain and France fought for possession

**MONTROSE**
James Graham, Marquess of Montrose, brilliant Royalist leader in the Highlands, who was executed in 1650.

of Canada, Montreal was the last place to surrender to the British—in September 1760. One of the most important factors in the growth of the city has been the constant deepening of the shipping channel of the St. Lawrence river, thereby enabling the import and export trade to expand. The population is about 900,000, three-quarters of whom are French.

**Montrose,** JAMES GRAHAM, 1ST MARQUESS OF (1612–50). Son of the 5th Earl of Montrose, he was born in 1612 and was educated at St. Andrew's University, Scotland. In 1637 he took an active part in drawing up the National Covenant, whose signatories bound themselves to maintain the Presbyterian faith as the religion of Scotland, in opposition to the plans of King Charles I.

He soon found himself in complete antagonism with the Presbyterians, and when the Scottish army entered England in alliance with the English Parliament in 1644, Montrose raised an army of Highlanders on behalf of the King. Created a Marquess, he conducted a series of brilliant campaigns until his defeat at Philiphaugh on September 23, 1645.

Montrose escaped abroad, but later returned, landing in Caithness, Scotland, in April 1650. He found few supporters, was captured and tried as a traitor and was hanged in the High Street, Edinburgh, on May 21, 1650.

# *Our* NEAREST NEIGHBOUR *in the* SKY

*Because there is no atmosphere around the moon there is no life, animal or vegetable. In some ways, not all of them understood, this dead satellite exercises tremendous power over the Earth.*

**Moon.** The moon is one of the smallest of the heavenly objects, but because it is relatively near to us, and is, in fact, a " satellite " of the earth, it appears to be the largest, next to the sun, and we know more about it than of any of the planets or stars. With a telescope we can actually see its mountains and ravines, its craters and broad expanses or plains, which early observers thought were seas. We know the general physical geography of that part of the moon which we can see, nearly as well as we know that of the earth; and all its principal mountain ranges and craters and " seas " have been named. Among the ranges are those called the Caucasus, the Apennines, the Alps, and the Carpathians, some of whose peaks rise as high as 20,000 feet. Among the craters are Apollonius, Archimedes, Julius Caesar, and Tycho, and among the " seas " are Mare Serenitatis (Serene Sea), Mare Imbrium (Rainy Sea), Oceanus Procellarum (Hurricane Ocean), and so on.

But such names are merely fanciful. There are no seas because there is no water, not even vapour, and there are no storms such as ours because there is practically no air or atmosphere. Indeed, we might almost say that nothing ever happens on the moon. There are no winds to stir the dust, or waters to moisten it. No cloud ever moves in

the airless sky, no flash of fire comes from an erupting peak. The land is cold and dark, and over all hangs a terrible silence.

With nothing to breathe and nothing to eat or drink, human life or any form of animal life (as we know it) could not exist on the moon. Even if it could, life would not be very pleasant there from our standpoint. The lunar day—that is, the time from sunrise to sunrise—is about a month long. Two weeks of scorching sunlight are followed by two weeks of frigid darkness. During the period of sunshine the temperature may go up to boiling point, but during the long lunar night it probably goes down to nearly 250 degrees below zero.

In ages past the moon was doubtless the scene of violent " moonquakes " and volcanic eruptions. Whether the volcanoes evolved the craters, some of which are 100 miles in diameter, is not known; the craters may possibly be the result of collisions with huge meteorites. In any event it is supposed that the moon is now a dead planet.

The area of the moon is 14,685,000 square miles. Its diameter (2,160 miles) is about a quarter of that of the earth, and it would require 49 moons to equal the earth in volume and 81 to equal it in weight (or mass). The moon's average distance from the earth is about 239,000 miles, whereas the

In these two drawings, based on scientific data, the artist Lucien Rudaux shows what the heavens would look like seen from the moon. Just before the sun rises, or just after it sets, the chromosphere with its red flames and streaming silvery corona is visible, as in the top drawing. When at various intervals the sun is eclipsed by the earth passing between it and the moon, as illustrated in the lower picture, the resultant corona effects are even more colourful and spectacular.

A day on the moon is nearly as long as 15 days on the earth, for it lasts approximately 354 hours. During that time one side of the moon is lit up by bright sunshine. These two drawings show sunrise on the moon when, at the beginning of the long day, the first rays of the sun shine upon the summits of the mountains and craters. As the moon has no atmosphere, the sunlight is very much brighter and its heat far more intense than that which reaches the surface of the earth sun is 400 times as far away. It would take an aeroplane travelling 300 miles an hour somewhat more than one month to reach the moon.

The moon is the earth's only satellite. It revolves around the earth because it is held in leash by the force of gravity exerted by the superior mass of the earth. The moon itself reacts on the earth, causing the tides. (*See* Tide).

The phases of the moon—" new," " half," and " full "—result naturally from its various positions with respect to the sun and earth. The moon is " new " when it is between the earth and the sun; it is " full " when it is on the side of the earth away from the sun. Solar eclipses occur only when the moon is new, and lunar eclipses when the moon is full. (*See* Eclipse).

# THE VAST AND SHINING SOLITUDES OF THE MOON

WHO is not moved by that picture of the moon which Sir J. A. Thomson has given us ? We may say of the moon, in his words, that " it was earth's only child, and it died ! "

Several different theories have been advanced as to the origin and history of the earth-moon system. One of the most interesting of these was advanced by Sir George Darwin, who sought to show that the moon and the earth were originally one mass and that they have come to their present state through the influence of the tidal action of each on the other. According to this theory the earth, it is said, was once shaped like a pear, and as it spun round the small end of the pear broke off and spun round independently. For ages it went round the sun side by side with the earth; but slowly it got farther away, until at last it is where it is, as far away from us as 10 times round the world. This happened, it is said, millions of years ago, when the earth was cooling down from its molten state and a crust about 30 miles thick had been formed; and the part which broke away equalled about 5,000 million cubic miles of matter.

A more recent theory suggests that the moon was formed by the drawing together of a great number of small masses about a larger one which attracted the smaller ones by reason of its greater mass. These small masses were probably of the same sort of material as those from which the earth and other planets were built up. In all probability the earth and the moon were formed in the same way, at the same time, of material which came from the sun as the result of some cosmic explosion.

## Extremes of Heat and Cold

The pull of the earth on the moon and the pull of the moon on the earth have never failed; and today they travel together and revolve together, so that the other side of the moon has never yet been seen by anyone on earth. But we know, from the face that we see, that the moon has had an amazing history since it was first formed. The sun pours down its light and heat on it unceasingly through a day 354 hours long. No life like ours could exist in the heat that reaches the side turned to the sun; but on the opposite side the moon is much colder than ice, and no life like ours could endure a cold like that. A man living on the moon would spend his long day in the tropics and his long night in the Arctic. He would have to endure alternately such heat and cold as human beings have never known.

No atmosphere envelops the moon, so the fierce heat of the sun pours down on it unchecked. There is no " blanket " to break its heat, no ocean of air to diminish its intensity or soften its dazzling light. And as there is no atmosphere there is no " sky light," so that the sun shines on the moon from a dense black sky. It would look like a great white ball shining in pitch-black night. When the sun withdraws its light and the moon is wrapped in night, the darkness there must be as in the darkness of a pit. A day and a night on the moon are equal to a month on earth, so that for 14 of our days a man of the moon would live in light and heat unknown to us, and for another 14 days in unimaginable blackness and cold.

We can hardly think of a world like that as anything but dead, and if the moon was born when the earth was born we may ask why it has died so soon.

### Why there is No Life on the Moon

Why is the earth covered with green trees, and carpeted with flowers, and throbbing with the life of a myriad living things, while the moon is dead and bare ? It is because the moon is smaller. If the earth were small like the moon, our air would gradually be left behind as the earth travelled through space. With the air would go our water; and with air and water gone, no life would be possible on earth. We would have the same great heat of the lunar day, the same extreme cold of the lunar night.

On the moon, all life and water and air have passed away, all sound has gone. If we should shoot an explosive rocket against the moon its impact would be silent, for sound is carried by air, and over the moon's surface, as between it and the earth's atmosphere, there is a vacuum.

Weird and strange indeed are the scenes on this dead world, and it is one of the triumphs of the human mind that we know them well. Long before we reached the North Pole of the earth men knew the North Pole of the moon. Men find their way about the moon by telescope almost as easily as about the earth. It was the first thing Man began to study in the heavens. It is these craters that seize a man's imagination. They are the handwriting on the moon. They are gigantic beyond anything seen on earth, and the forces that made them are beyond our understanding. There are hundreds of them, and from some of them vast quantities of matter have been flung for more than 20 miles.

Their walls rise up miles high, and some of them are so wide that two men standing one on each side would be 50 miles apart. The walls rise sheer like walls of houses, but they fall away outside, and for 100 miles at times we can trace the vast extent of those tremendous forces which flung up burning lava in molten streams from the furnace

# BARREN WASTES OF THE LUNAR LANDSCAPE

This striking photograph was taken with the 100-inch reflector at Mt. Wilson, California. It shows the moon in natural position, and not upside down as it would be seen through a telescope. The smooth area in the centre is the Mare Imbrium (Rainy Sea), bounded below at the right by the Apennines. The shallowest and most prominent of the three craters at the right near the mountains is Archimedes. Directly above Archimedes, on the margin of Mare Imbrium, is the black, ring-like plain known as the crater Plato. If you look closely in the lower left-hand corner you can make out the dimly outlined crater Copernicus, one of the hugest of all. It is 46 miles across and is rimmed in by mountains 12,000 feet high. The smaller crater to the right and above Copernicus is that called Bullialdus.

of the moon. These craters, according to one theory, are the remnants of volcanoes; but to what can we compare the mighty cataclysms which tore the very heart of the moon to pieces and left it yawning with chasms and stricken with death?

It is believed that sometimes, in these explosions on the moon, a single eruption may have sent forth, crashing out of the red-hot depths, hundreds of cubic miles of matter. In some craters there are gaps across the surface a mile wide and 150 miles long, and deeper than from the top of our highest mountain to the bottom of our deepest sea, or more than 10 miles below the surface.

And, as chasms are deeper and craters wider, so mountains are higher on the moon. A grain of mustard seed on a globe three feet across would represent the highest mountain on the earth; but a grain of seed on a globe one foot wide would stand for the highest mountain on the moon. Cliffs are much steeper than on the earth, and the mountain scenery, if we could see it as we see the Alps or the Rocky Mountains, would be far grander than our own.

Perhaps you have not thought of it, but as the sun keeps our atmosphere in constant circulation through the winds, so the moon does with the waters. The power of gravitation runs from moon to earth and earth to moon, and the pull of the moon on the sea brings the tides up on the shore twice a day.

In 1945 the British astronomer, P. Wilkins, completed the most detailed lunar map ever made. It is 25 feet in diameter, and took 13 years to make.

**Moore,** SIR JOHN (1761–1809). Born in Glasgow, on November 13, 1761, Moore joined the British army when he was 15. He saw service in America during the War of Independence, then fought against the Irish rebels, in the Netherlands, and in Egypt, before being knighted and promoted lieutenant-general. In 1806 he was sent to the Mediterranean, and led a division in an unsuccessful attempt to help Sweden. Returning home in 1808 he was immediately sent out to Portugal, and soon became supreme commander of the British forces against Napoleon there. He had to move his troops to Salamanca, in Spain, to assist his Spanish allies, but was compelled to retreat in face of enemy superiority in numbers. The port of embarkation was Corunna, in the north-west, and Moore's retreat to the coast over 250 miles of difficult country in mid-winter has become a classic of military history.

In a last heroic stand, at Corunna, on January 16, 1809, Moore was mortally

*Painting by Sir T. Lawrence, National Portrait Gallery*
**SIR JOHN MOORE**
**Killed in a victorious rearguard action with the French at Corunna, Portugal, in 1809, Sir John Moore was buried on the field of battle. The scene is described in a poem by Charles Wolfe (1791–1823), entitled The Burial of Sir John Moore.**

wounded; but his army had driven back the French in much confusion. Moore died the next day. During the night Sir John Hope, his next in command, withdrew the British force. Charles Wolfe's famous poem, The Burial of Sir John Moore, graphically describes the scene at the general's graveside.

**Moors.** When the Arab armies swept across northern Africa in the 7th century, they found in the north-western corner of the continent a white race of ancient origin called the Berbers. These they converted to Mahomedanism after a sharp struggle at the beginning of the 8th century. Then Berbers and Arabs joined in invading and conquering Spain, and a mixed race sprang up called the Moors.

The name Moor comes from the Greek *Mauros*, the name for the Berber inhabitants of the old Roman province of Mauretania, now Morocco. It is applied today chiefly to the people of mixed blood inhabiting the sea-coast of the so-called Barbary States. The typical Moors of Morocco are a handsome race, with olive skin, black eyes, and black silky hair. The women are beautiful in early youth, but soon grow fat, a quality much admired by their own people. The Moors are courteous and intellectual, but often cruel and revengeful. Of the pirates who infested these coasts in former days, the mild-mannered cut-throats were most feared.

The Moors reached the height of their power in Spain. After the conquest of the Visigoth kingdom in 711, and a period of great disorder, the Arab caliphate of Cordova was formed which lasted until 1031. Following the collapse of the caliphate, the Moors (Berber-Arabs) who had obtained control of north-western Africa crossed to Spain and wrested the power from the pure-blood Arabs already there.

After the battle of Navas de Tolosa in 1212, in which Alphonso VIII of Castile broke the Moorish power in central Spain, the Moors still ruled the kingdom of Granada, which rose to a splendour rivalling the former caliphate of Cordova. It was not until 1492 that its power was shattered by the Spanish armies.

The Mahomedan Moors were then expelled from Spain, to the great economic and intellectual loss of that country. Many Moors adopted Christianity and remained. About 60,000 of their descendants, called Moriscos, dwell in Spain today. Remains of the days of Moorish greatness are still found in Spain, chief among which is the Alhambra palace at Granada. (See illustration page 119).

**Moose.** The largest living deer common to the northern regions of the Old and the New World is the elk or moose, for the latter is merely the American counterpart of the European elk. The elk is found right across the Old World from Scandinavia to Siberia, and the moose is found from the United States northwards, though its chief American home is in Alaska. It has long legs, and a big bull stands six feet high; it has a huge head with broad muzzle and large nostrils. The average weight is about 700 pounds, while unusually large specimens attain twice that weight.

The moose can be distinguished from all other deer by the magnificent antlers of the male, which sometimes have a spread of more than six feet. Each antler is like a broad hand, with the palm curved and held upward, and with the margins set with prongs. An average full-grown pair of antlers, with the skull, weighs 70 pounds. They grow gradually; the first year they are knobs an inch high, the second year they grow to about a foot in length, and the third year they take on their palm-shaped character. The fully formed horns are shed in December and new ones sprout in April, reaching their full size in June. It is remarkable that these enormous horns should be shed annually and produced again in so short a time.

The moose feeds on willow-tips, on the slender shoots of the maple and other trees, and on bark. It often wades in water up to its neck, to escape flies and mosquitoes and to feed on succulent water-plants. When enraged a bull moose strikes vicious blows with its front feet as well as with the heavy antlers, and is a dangerous foe for Man or beast. Moose are rapid runners, and have a sharp sense of hearing and of smell; as a result they are difficult to hunt. In winter they herd in small troops for protection. Moose-hide is sometimes used for leather.

**Morayshire.** Washed by the broad waters of the Moray Firth, this Scottish county was formerly called Elginshire for all official purposes, although the natives often referred to it as Moray, a Gaelic word meaning "among the seaboard men." This name was formally adopted in 1920.

Comprising just over 476 square miles, with a population of about 44,000, it is one of the finest farming districts in all Scotland. Favoured with a rich soil, equable temperature both in winter and in summer, and a moderate rainfall, its lowlands yield big harvests of wheat, barley, potatoes and oats. Livestock breeding is another profitable side of farming, large numbers of the famous Aberdeen-Angus beef cattle and Leicester and Black-faced breeds of sheep being reared. Other industries are whisky distilling, and deep-sea fishing. The fleets of Findhorn, Burghead, Hopeman and Lossiemouth (where Britain's first Labour Prime Minister, J. Ramsay MacDonald, was born) are among the oldest in the herring, haddock, and cod fisheries of the North Sea. There is much natural beauty in Moray, particularly among the Cromdale Hills and along the courses of those famous salmon rivers the Spey, Findhorn and Lossie.

Elgin (population 9,000), the county town, on the Lossie, five miles above Lossiemouth, is of great antiquity and historical interest. Its castle housed Edward I of England in 1296 and 1303, in his campaigns to subjugate the Scots. And the cathedral of Moray, founded in 1224, was almost destroyed in 1390 by the "Wolf of Badenoch," as a son of King Robert II of Scotland was styled. Elgin manufactures woollens, tweeds, and plaid cloths.

**More,** Sir Thomas (1478–1535). "I say no harm, I think no harm; but I wish everybody good," once declared Sir Thomas More, the great English statesman, scholar and author. This was no idle boast, for the man who made it was a lovable man, with warm affections and a kind heart. Yet he wished it engraved on his monument that as Lord Chancellor he was "the scourge of thieves, murderers and heretics."

Son of a prominent London barrister who became a judge, young Thomas More was born on February 7, 1478, and reared as a page in the household of Cardinal Morton. As a student at Oxford, More came under the influence of the New Learning, and later formed a close friendship with the Dutch scholar Erasmus, who was captivated by his charming personality. Erasmus speaks of More's home as "school and exercise of the Christian religion. No wrangling, no angry word was heard in it; no one was idle; every one did

**HUGE-ANTLERED AMERICAN MOOSE**
Largest member of the deer family, an American bull moose may stand six feet high at the shoulder. The European species, which is called an elk, is somewhat smaller. The cow moose has no horns ; the colour of both sexes is very dark brown shading to black.

his duty with alacrity and not without a temperate cheerfulness." These two, with John Colet, Dean of St. Paul's, were the leaders of a group of scholars and religious reformers in England since known as the "Oxford Reformers," who did much to promote the Renaissance in England.

Entering his father's profession of law, More early attained distinction; but for a time religious piety led him to fast, pray, and scourge himself as a preliminary to entering the priesthood. He gave up this plan, but religious motives remained supreme in his life.

In 1504 More earned the enmity of Henry VII by opposing, as a member of Parliament, the King's exorbitant demands for money. The accession of Henry VIII brought More into high place at court. The young King was attracted by the rising lawyer's learning, wit and geniality, and employed him on various embassies. He knighted him, promoted him to various official posts, including that of Speaker to the House of Commons, and on Cardinal Wolsey's fall from power, in 1529, More was made Lord Chancellor—the first time that the office had been held by one who was not a clergyman.

When it appeared that Henry had resolved on a divorce from his queen, Catherine of Aragon, More, as a loyal churchman, resigned his office on the plea of ill-health. He refused to acknowledge Henry's claim to be head of the English Church, and for this defiance the King had More—together with Bishop Fisher and others—committed to the Tower on a charge of treason. Against the pleadings of his favourite daughter, Margaret Roper, his wife, and his friends, More stood firm, and on July 6, 1535, he was beheaded.

Even in his death More's wit did not desert him. Climbing the scaffold where he was to die, he said to the officer in charge: "I pray you see me safe up; as for my coming down, let me shift for myself." When the axe was about to fall he asked the executioner to wait a minute until he had pushed his beard aside, observing, "Pity that should be cut, which has never committed treason."

More is famous as the author of Utopia, a romance written in 1516. "Utopia" (meaning "nowhere")

**SIR THOMAS MORE**
Author of Utopia, and appointed Lord Chancellor by Henry VIII in 1529, More was beheaded on a charge of treason on July 6, 1535.

is the name of an imaginary island which More represents as the abode of a happy society, free from all cares, anxieties and miseries. All men are equal, and everyone may worship as he chooses. None is allowed to become rich through the oppression of others, property is held in common, and all are required to perform the same amount of labour. The book had a political object, for the evils which it depicts as remedied in Utopia are those which then afflicted England. From the title of this book we get the adjective "utopian," which is applied to plans for the improvement of society that are considered visionary and impracticable. In 1935 More and Bishop Fisher were canonized—the first English saints to be created since the breach between Henry VIII and the Pope.

**Morgan,** SIR HENRY (c. 1635–88). While still a boy Henry Morgan was kidnapped at Bristol and sold as a slave in Barbados, eventually joining the pirates who then had their headquarters in Jamaica. His first important expedition was as a ship's captain in the attempted capture of Curaçao in 1666. When his chief, Edward Mansfield, was captured and put to death by the Spaniards, Morgan was elected "admiral" by the buccaneers. He became the most feared man on the Spanish Main.

Two successful expeditions led by Morgan, with a commission from the Governor of Jamaica, are worthy of particular mention. These were the sacking of Panama in 1668, and, in the following year, his capture of the town of Maracaibo (now in Venezuela) and subsequent astonishing escape from the pursuing Spanish fleet. Morgan was sent home

**CAPTAIN MORGAN DEFEATS THE SPANIARDS**
Like many pirates, Henry Morgan gained fame at home primarily for his privateering activities against his country's enemies, for he rarely attacked ships belonging to England or her allies. In this old woodcut his ships are seen defeating the Spanish fleet off Maracaibo in 1669. He then held the town, on that part of the South American mainland now known as Venezuela, to ransom and sacked it, obtaining a rich haul of gold plate, jewels and silver.

in disgrace in 1672, but managed to find favour with King Charles II, who sent him back to the West Indies as Colonel Sir Henry Morgan, Lieutenant-General of Jamaica. Morgan died at Port Royal, in August 1688.

**Mormons.** The term "Mormons" is really a nickname for members of the Church of Jesus Christ of Latter-Day Saints, an American religious sect.

Joseph Smith (1805–1844), founder of Mormonism, received his first heavenly manifestation, it is said, at the age of 14. Other visions followed, including those which revealed to him the Book of Mormon, which purports to be a record of the early inhabitants of America—three groups of people, one of whom had come from Babylon at the time of the confusion of tongues, and the other two from Jerusalem about 600 B.C. He organized the Church of Jesus Christ of Latter-Day Saints with six members at Fayette, in New York State, in 1830. Missionaries were sent out and branches were started in various states and in Europe. Following trouble with non-Mormons, the Mormon leaders were thrown into gaol at Carthage, Illinois. On June 27, 1844, a mob stormed the gaol and killed Joseph Smith and his brother.

The Mormons then decided to go to the Far West. On their 1,000 mile trek to the valley of the Great Salt Lake, one of the notable migrations in history, they were led by Brigham Young (1801–77). They arrived in July 1847. This first band of Mormon pioneers, who founded Salt Lake City consisted of 143 men, three women and two children. Because four per cent of their membership believed that a man might have more than one wife,

the Mormons were once the subject of much notoriety. Since 1890 the policy of the Mormon church has been against plural marriages.

**Morocco.** During the opening years of the 20th century the Mahomedan country of Morocco, in the north-west corner of Africa, was a perpetual menace to the peace of Europe. Bounded by Algeria, the Mediterranean, the Atlantic, and the Sahara, and with an area about the size of France, it was a land of fine agricultural possibilities, and with unknown mineral wealth. But never was a realm so amazingly misgoverned as this independent sultanate. There was practically no law except the Sultan's whim. He appointed a horde of greedy ministers or viziers, who in turn appointed governors of provinces, who in their turn selected the town officials and village sheiks. No salaries were paid. The lesser officials grabbed what they could by bribery and extortion from the poverty-stricken population. They were then forced by the higher officials to disgorge much of their loot, whereupon the Sultan extracted the lion's share from these latter. The decisions of the judges in the " courts of justice " were bought and sold; the man who bid the highest was always right.

Powerful bandits were allowed to infest the country. In 1905, for instance, the notorious Raisuli captured Ion Perdicaris, a naturalized American citizen, and demanded about £14,000 ransom. In this case the Sultan of Morocco was compelled to pay the ransom himself.

The rival interests of European powers—France, Germany, and Spain especially—gave rise to what was called " the Morocco question." France came to be regarded as having special interests in the country because of the dangers to French capital invested and to French rule in Algeria from the continued anarchy in Morocco. In 1905 Germany demanded a reconsideration of Moroccan affairs, and her threat of war produced a conference at Algeciras in Spain in 1906.

Then, in 1911, Germany again brought Europe to the verge of war by sending her gunboat Panther to Agadir (on the Atlantic coast), in violation of what France considered to be her right in the country. France and Germany were almost on the point of mobilization when Great Britain let it be understood that she would support France, and Germany stated that no threat was intended. Thus the matter was adjusted and

**MORMON TEMPLE AT SALT LAKE CITY**
*H. J. Shepstone*
Headquarters of the Mormons is Salt Lake City in the State of Utah, United States, and the 10-acre enclosure here seen holds all that is most sacred to the members of that faith. In it are the Temple (the building with the six pinnacles on the right), the Tabernacle with its curious domed roof, and the Assembly Hall on the extreme left. In the foreground is the Pioneer Monument, surmounted by a statue of the Mormon leader, Brigham Young.

summits, the Moroccan seaboard has a delightful climate, but the regions beyond the mountains suffer from intense heat in summer and bitter cold in winter.

The country produces quantities of grapes and nearly all kinds of European and tropical fruits. Grain growing is on the increase, wheat, barley, oats, and beans having been added to *durra*, the native millet. Sheep, goats, cattle, and horses are raised. The future of Morocco is believed to lie in its rich mineral resources; copper, lead, silver, and gold have been found. Iron ore is exported.

The inhabitants consist chiefly of Berbers, Arabs, and Jews. Of these the Berber mountaineers are the hardiest, most numerous, and most indus-

honour and wealth before him. But he chose to disappear into a little shop in New Haven and live through years of poverty, obscurity, toil, and ridicule in pursuit of his scientific vision. He lived alone in his shop, sleeping on a camp-bed, cooking his own food, often going hungry. In 1837 he applied for a patent on " The An Telegraph," but this was

He went to Europe seek but in vain. He ev United States Congress ir sufficient capital to buil Washington to Baltimore. 1844, the first message w

From that time the grov tric telegraph was rapid. A men of science, in Europe had worked at the problen tem became the basis of m graph systems. The code dashes he invented, with the Vail, is still known as the " The first attempt to lay an was made in 1857 by Morse Field. Four cables parted was laid in 1866 (*see* Ca died in New York on April

**Mosaic.** (Pron. mō-things show better how beautiful than their efforts floors, ceilings, and walls, ments, of their homes and te

Germany agreed to recognize a French protectorate over Morocco, in return for the cession to Germany of a large area of French territory in central Africa. The aggressive party in Germany remained dissatisfied, however, and the war cloud of 1911 helped to produce the First World War (1914–18).

The French protectorate in Morocco is still in force, but there are also a Spanish zone in a strip running 200 miles eastward from the Strait of Gibraltar and a special international zone round the port of Tangier. Tribes known as the Riffs, led by Abd el Krim, gave much trouble after the First World War, until their commander surrendered to French and Spanish forces in 1926.

The Sultan of Morocco resides in the French zone—normally at Rabat, but sometimes at Marrakesh or Morocco City (population 190,000), Fez (144,000), or Meknes. Casablanca (258,000) is the largest city. The effective government is in French hands, with a Resident-General at the head. In the Spanish zone the Sultan's powers are given to a Khalifa, chosen by the Sultan. The principal town in the Spanish area is Tetuan (49,000). The total area of Morocco is estimated at 231,000 square miles (of which 220,000 square miles comprise French Morocco), and the total population at nearly nine million.

Morocco is divided into two parts by the Great Atlas Mountains, which sweep parallel to the seacoast from the Atlantic to the east coast of Tunis. Jebel Ayashi (15,000 feet), the loftiest peak in northern Africa, rises in central Morocco. Protected from the hot winds of the desert by snow-clad

**IN TWO MOROCCAN CITIES**

Other gates formerly quite as beautiful as that seen in the upper photograph grace the walls of Marrakesh, but they have been allowed to fall into disrepair. Marrakesh is one of the three cities in which the Sultan has a palace, the other two being Rabat and Fez. The latticed roof over a bazaar in Fez (lower) serves to keep out the heat of the midday sun. Fez, the capital of northern Morocco, is one of the sacred cities of Islam.

*Top, Felix; lower, E.N.A*

trious. The mixed population of the coast towns are known as Moors ; mostly descendants of the Moslems who were driven out of Spain in 1492, they formed a large proportion of Gen. Franco's troops during the Spanish Civil War (1936–39). The large Jewish population also traces its origin to the Spanish exiles of an earlier period.

In ancient times Morocco was known as Mauretania, and its early Berber natives were subjects first of Carthage and then of Rome. In 429 the country was overrun by the Vandals, who introduced piracy, which lasted for 15 centuries.

In 682 the Arab armies, carrying the green banner of Mahomet, seized Morocco. From that

time a long and c[...]
the Berber chiefs a[...]
rule of the Sultan[...]
Sahara Desert to T[...]
and disorder set i[...]
period of French o[...]

In the Middle [...]
learning and indu[...]
university as early [...]
of goat skins, was [...]

**Morris,** Wr[...]
should put his hea[...]
should be the kind[...]
the creed of the E[...]
Morris, a practical [...]
and versatility who[...]
literary, artistic an[...]

Morris, born in l[...]
remembered by sc[...]
" a thick-set strong[...]
and black curly ha[...]
with a fearful tem[...]
doing things with hi[...]
and of telling long [...]

During quiet Ox[...]
began a life-long f[...]
Jones. Both Morri[...]
a passion for a re[...]
that of the Middl[...]
Dante Gabriel R[...]
Edward Millais, M[...]
the group called th[...]

In 1859 Morris [...]
beauty whom he l[...]

**DESIGN B[...]**
At Kelmscott Manor,[...]
William Morris used th[...]
were designed by him a[...]
The verses on the val[...]
chief aim in life was[...]

of the anti-religious drives of the revolutionary leaders. The old walled monasteries, the hundreds of churches with their bright and bulbous domes, the turreted palaces, the myriad bells that pealed hymns at evening—these gave Moscow its individuality. But many of the churches have now been converted to other uses, or pulled down to make room for new buildings.

There are business blocks of skyscrapers built in the bold, rectangular German style, and on the outskirts are modern buildings to accommodate the tremendous increase in population, which doubled between 1926 and 1939. However, Moscow still has many of the towers and bulging cupolas which make it look like a dream city.

*Planet News*

**YOUNG RUSSIA IN MOSCOW'S RED SQUARE**
Forty thousand athletes from the 16 Republics of the Soviet Union are giving a display on the Red Square at Moscow (above) to celebrate the anniversary of the Bolshevik Revolution of November 1917. The square stone building on the right is Lenin's tomb, in front of the Kremlin wall. At the far end of Red Square is the Cathedral of St. Basil, with its many painted domes.

Dominating the city are the pink walls and battlements of the Kremlin. This fortress is an imposing city in itself—a large triangle enclosed in walls about 65 feet high. There are 19 towers and five gates; the loveliest, perhaps, is the Gate of the Redeemer, which in the old days was a shrine no man might pass without removing his hat. The Kremlin, which was erected in the 15th century on the site of a fort built in 1156, was the ancient residence of the Tsars and the headquarters of the Russian Church. Now it is the residence of the leaders of the Soviet Union, and it houses some of the Government departments. Within the walls of the Kremlin is an array of historic cathedrals and convents, sacred relics, big cannon, tombs and priceless collections of jewels and works of art.

The most ambitious and at the same time the oddest structure is the Palace of the Soviets, erected outside the Kremlin and close to Red Square on the site of the former Church of Christ the Saviour, the latter being an unattractive monument to the Napoleonic War of 1812. Begun in 1935, the building itself is a little more than 1,000 feet high, and the foundations cover an area of 24 acres. The famous chapel of the Iberian Mother of God—formerly the most venerated shrine in the city—was demolished to make way for new streets in accordance with the 10-year plan put into operation in 1935 for the reconstruction of the Soviet capital. Other streets, such as Gorky Street, were widened by moving back buildings bodily.

East of the Kremlin is the Kitai Gorod, or Chinese city, so called because the Mongols built the wall surrounding it. It was once the residence of merchants, just as the Kremlin contained the homes of the aristocracy. Red Square, which was called Red long before Russia came to be known as Red Russia after the Bolshevik Revolution of 1917, is in the Kitai Gorod. It was repeatedly used as a camp by the Mongols, was a forum (place where political speeches were delivered) and place of execution under the Russian monarchs, and under the Soviet government it is the centre of national demonstrations. Dominating the square is the imposing Lenin mausoleum, where crowds wait in long queues to view the khaki-clad body of their former leader. Three of the principal streets meet here, as do most of the city's bus and tramway routes.

One of the most noteworthy buildings in the square is the Cathedral of Saint Basil, built by Ivan the Terrible in the 16th century. Legend says the Tsar had the architect blinded so that he could never reproduce its 12 painted domes, some twisted, some scaled, each topped with a heavy cross. It was later a museum. Moscow guards everything of educational or artistic value and has many museums. Homes of the former aristocracy have been converted into schools, hospitals or day nurseries. The city is proud of its artistic productions —its lavish opera and ballet and the drama of the Moscow Art Theatre.

Always an important centre of trade, Moscow is now a meeting point of the Russian railways and of air routes connecting with the principal cities of European and Asiatic Russia. An underground railway, or Metro, was opened in 1935. A canal links Moscow with the Baltic, the Black Sea, the White Sea, the Caspian, and the Sea of Azov.

Moscow's history as a city dates back to the 12th century. It was the capital of all Russia from 1480 to 1712, when it was superseded by St. Petersburg (Leningrad), regaining the position of capital in 1918. A striking event in its troubled history occurred during Napoleon's invasion in 1812, when the burning of the city forced the French to begin the disastrous " retreat from Moscow." In the Second World War (1939-45) Moscow was raided by German aircraft, but was successfully defended against the attacks of the German army. The population is 4,137,000.

**Moses.** Among all lawgivers there is one supreme name, that of Moses, the great leader and lawgiver of the Hebrews. The story of his life as told in the Bible is full of wonders. In the land of Egypt, where the Hebrews were held as slaves, Pharaoh ordered that every male child born to them should be cast into the Nile. But Moses's mother put her small son in a box made of bulrushes and laid it in the reeds by the river's brink. There Pharaoh's own daughter found him, and cared for him. Thus Moses was saved for his destined work of delivering his people from oppression and of founding a nation.

From Egypt Moses led his people through the Red Sea and the desert wilderness to Mount Sinai. There, according to the Biblical account, amidst flashes of lightning that enveloped the mountain top, God gave to Moses the Ten Commandments, written upon two tablets of stone. These laws, often called the Decalogue (from the Greek *deka*, ten, and *logos*, word), formed the foundation of the civil and religious laws of the Hebrews (Exodus xx, 2-17). They turned the people away from the idolatry that they had learned from the Egyptians to a purer faith and a higher moral order. In these simple commandments are the fundamental elements of all moral law, and they have had a tremendous in-

*From the picture by Sir John Millais, P.R.A.; Manchester Art Gallery*

**MOSES IN THE DAY OF BATTLE**

This illustrates the Bible story of Moses ensuring the victory of the Israelites, under the leadership of Joshua, over the Amalekites. When Moses held up his arms the Israelites prevailed and when he let them down the Amalekites prevailed. Towards the end of the day Moses's strength failed, and his arms were supported by Aaron (left) and Hur.

fluence not only on the Jews, for whom they were framed, but on mankind as a whole.

Moses, who had led the people for 40 years in the wilderness, did not live to see them established in the Promised Land, but through the laws which he gave them and the ideals he held before them the little band of wandering shepherds was transformed into a nation, destined to bring moral and spiritual light to the world. Among the heroes of the nations, few exhibit such a combination of strength and spiritual nobility as Moses. He had the courage to defy the great Pharaoh of Egypt, and yet he was " very meek, above all men that were upon the face of the earth." He led his people " as a father carries his child."

The first five books of the Bible—Genesis, Exodus, Leviticus, Numbers, and Deuteronomy—or the *Pentateuch* (meaning " five books ")—are sometimes called the five books of Moses, from the fact that their authorship was attributed to him, though it is now thought that others contributed. Among the Jews they are known as the *Torah*, or law, because they contain the Mosaic law. They tell, too, the story of Moses's life.

recognized way of controlling the insects. The pupae, too, swim about by means of leaf-like appendages at the tail-end of their bodies. In due time the perfect insect emerges on the surface of the water, and when its wings are dry it takes to the air.

We do not, luckily, suffer much from the malaria mosquito in Britain, though there were times when such marshes as those along the south bank of the Thames, where now is situated Battersea Park, were among its breeding haunts. But in places on the Continent a very great battle has had to be fought against the insects. In Italy, the marshes between Rome and the sea were uninhabitable for hundreds of years because of the mosquito plague; now they have been drained and are in consequence quite healthy to live in.

Gnats or mosquitoes are represented by 29 different kinds or species in Britain. Only four of these belong to the *Anopheles* or malaria-carrying group. The others are members of the *Culex* group which do not carry disease-organisms in Britain. You would have difficulty in distinguishing the two kinds without a magnifying glass, unless you were an expert. But there are ways of telling which is which, even when both specimens are not there at the same time for comparison; and it is worth while being able to, so that you may know whether the insect that has just " bitten " you is a dangerous one or not. When resting on a wall, or elsewhere, mosquitoes of the *Culex* type hold the body parallel with the surface to which it is clinging. *Anopheles* lies with its body at an angle with the supporting surface. Also, the female *Culex* has the palps (feelers) much shorter than the proboscis, whereas in *Anopheles* they are of about the same length as the proboscis. The larva of *Culex* hangs head downwards from the water surface, while that of *Anopheles* lies horizontally at the water surface. In all mosquitoes the female is the one responsible for the " bites "; the male is harmless, being a drinker of vegetable juices only.

**Moss.** The mosses which form beautiful green carpet-like expanses on the forest floor, or appear like brilliant green rosettes on decaying logs, wet boulders, and dripping cliffs in ravines and gorges, are masses of very small plants, each of which by itself has a separate stem, and little leaves growing out from it all the way from base to tip.

Each moss plant is held firmly fixed in the soil, and obtains its nourishment, by means of a number of little thread-like *rhizoids*, which take the place of the true roots of the higher plants. Some mosses, instead of standing erect, trail over the ground like tiny velvety vines, which interlace and form a thick dense mat. Mosses as a rule delight in moisture, and their habit of growing compactly together makes them able to hold large quantities of water in storage for use during dry periods.

Mosses were called by botanists " flowerless " plants, because they do not have the blossoms which we are accustomed to see on the seed-bearing plants. The process by which mosses reproduce is quite different from that of seed-bearing plants. Each moss plant grows up from a tiny green thread-like trailing structure, known as the *protonema;* this sends up here and there little buds which develop into the moss growths with which we are familiar. In the tips of some of these moss plants grow structures called *archegonia*, in which eggs develop. In other moss plants grow still other structures, called *antheridia*, in which are developed free-swimming male cells (sperms).

When the moss plants become covered with a film of water, the little sperms go swimming, by means of tiny hair-like appendages (called *cilia*), over to the archegonia and there fertilize the eggs. From the egg there then grows another sort of plant, which takes root right in the top of the archegonial plant where the egg was developed. This plant is known as the *sporophyte* (spore-plant).

On top of this sporophyte grows a little case which contains spores. Spores are more or less equivalent to the seeds of higher plants, but they are very minute, so that a mass of them together resembles a little cloud of dust. When the sporophyte is ripe, the little case at its tip opens and the spores are scattered about by the wind. From each spore, if it alights on favourable soil, there may grow a new protonema, completing the cycle.

Mosses (*Musci*) are sometimes confused with the liverworts (*Hepaticae*), which, with them, form the group *Bryophyta* in the plant kingdom, and which usually prefer even damper situations, and are green or yellow in colour. Most of them may be distinguished from the mosses by their thicker leaves, which usually lie flat on the ground. (*See* Liverworts).

**LOVELY DETAILS OF THE LOWLY MOSSES BENEATH OUR FEET**
If you look at moss under a magnifying glass you will see that it is far more than a carpet of green woolly stuff. Sometimes it has a beautiful flower-like growth, as shown by *Mnium hornum* at the left. Or perhaps you may discover a curious ' fruit,' such as that on *Bryum capillaris* (centre). Other mosses look like a miniature forest, as *Hypnum tamariscum* (right).

" Irish moss " is not a moss, but a seaweed, and " Iceland moss " is a lichen (*see* Lichens). " Florida " or " Spanish moss " is a flowering plant. Some 5,000 species of true mosses are known, distributed all over the world, and of these the sphagnum or bog mosses are of considerable value to Man. Their pale sponge-like leaves, filled with hollow cells, absorb liquids with great rapidity, and for this reason the moss has been used as a surgical dressing.

The sphagnums grow in large patches in damp meadows, bogs and swamps. When they occur along the shores of a lake or pond, they often gradually fill up the whole area with their spongy growth. Such a filled-up pond is called a quaking bog, because, like some enormous sponge, it trembles and quakes when one walks upon it, while the oozing of the water is heard on every side. Some such bogs are as dangerous as quicksands, and have been known to drown men, horses and cattle. Growths of sphagnum accumulating through thousands of years helped to form the deposits of peat found in England, Ireland and other countries.

At the present time mosses seem rather humble members of the plant kingdom. But they played a great part in making the land fit for animal habitation. After the most primitive plants (algae and fungi) had carpeted the bare rocks, and by heaping up their dead bodies provided a little store of nutritive soil, the mosses and liverworts appeared and took up the work. In time their remains provided a rich soil, and thus made possible the growth of higher plants. The mosses and the higher plants together formed the material which supported animal life on land.

## Mother Goose.

Who was Mother Goose ? Nobody knows, yet everyone is acquainted with her rhymes. One story declares that the original Mother Goose was a certain Elizabeth Goose (or Vergoose), a widow of Boston, U.S.A. It is claimed that she sang these ditties to her infant grandson, and that the boy's father, who was a printer, published them in a book in 1719. No trace of such a book, however, has ever been found, and long before that date the name " Mother Goose " was used in France in connexion with various popular stories.

The first mention of this French " Mother Goose " is to be found in a French poem of the year 1650. In 1697 a Frenchman, Charles Perrault, published a book of fairy stories under the title Tales of Past Times, by Mother Goose. It contained stories such as The Master Cat (our Puss in Boots), Little Thumb (our Hop o' My Thumb), Sleeping Beauty, and Bluebeard. In 1760 a London publisher, John Newbery, transferred the name Mother Goose from the fairy stories to a collection of old nursery jingles which he called Mother Goose's Melodies, and the rhymes have ever since borne the name of this author.

## Motor, Electric.

It will assist the reader to understand better the following explanations if he or she has already read our stories of Dynamo and Electricity. The article on Transformer also contains information related to the present one. The story goes that the electric motor, the most convenient source of power which it is possible to imagine, was discovered by accident when, owing to a workman's error, a running dynamo was connected to a stationary dynamo, which promptly commenced to rotate. One can hardly believe that this was really the first inkling that anyone had of the fact that the electro magnetic effect is reversible, since Oersted's experiment, which you can read about in our story of Electricity, had shown *before* Faraday made his first dynamo, that a current-carrying conductor would move in a magnetic field.

In order to understand why a conductor moves in a magnetic field when a current passes, look at Fig. 1, A, which shows a conductor *not* carrying a current, at rest in a magnetic field (of which only a few lines are shown to make it easier to follow). When a current passes through the conductor, it sets up its own magnetic field around the conductor (*see* Magnetism). This interacts with the field due to the magnet, stretching and distorting the lines (Fig. 1, B). We can think of lines of force as being elastic, i.e., they try to take the shortest possible path, having due regard to all the forces acting on them. These lines, then, try to " snap back " into their straight paths again, and the only way in which they can do so is to push the conductor out of the field (Fig. 1, C). If the conductor is bent back on itself to form a loop, as we imagined in the case of the dynamo (*see* Fig. 2, in page 1061), and both sides are taken through the field, one side will be pushed up, and the other pushed down. The loop will have a turning or twisting force on it, and if we enlarge the loop into a coil of several turns, the effect will be greatly increased.

The direct current motor, like the dynamo, is a development of this principle. A powerful electro-magnet is used for the field ; the loop becomes a number of coils each of many turns, wound round an iron core to make a solid rotating armature, and is supplied with current through the segments of a commutator. Thus, as the coils rotate, the current in each coil-side is reversed so that the force always acts in the same direction and we get a constant torque or turning effect.

There are three main methods of connecting the field magnet (Fig. 2). In *shunt* connexion, the field coil consists of a large number of turns of fine wire and is connected in parallel with the armature (A). This has the effect of " shunting off " a small portion

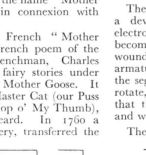
Fig. 1

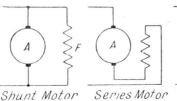
Shunt Motor   Series Motor

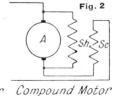
Compound Motor

Fig. 2

**INSTRUMENT PANEL OF A MOTOR-CAR**

*The Standard Motor Co., Ltd.*

**Fig. 1.** Nearly every new piece of equipment fitted to a car means another knob or switch for the driver to operate. Above is a typical modern instrument panel of the Standard 'Vanguard,' which includes the controls of a wireless set. (*See* also illustrations in page 2245).

even be made in another country. But, owing to standardization, they fit.

Mass production of motor vehicles is accomplished by progressive assembly on the "conveyer-belt" system. (*See* illustrations in page 897).

In a typical plant the steps of construction are as follows: First, the chassis begins to take shape: the two long side members are fastened together by the cross members, and this bare frame is placed on a moving platform which is drawn steadily forward along a chain or belt. As it moves along its route, workmen attach the various parts—springs, brackets for the running boards, silencer, axles, and many other things. A spray of naphtha cleans the frame of any dirt or grease it may have accumulated, and it is then spray-painted in less than a minute. The frame is next passed through a drying room built over the assembly line. When it reappears on the other side, it gets a coat of varnish and is sent again into a hot room to dry. When cooled, it resumes its journey along the assembly line.

box or other portion of the car mechanism. The principle of "interchangeability" was not applied, and the parts and components were individually fitted, a tedious and lengthy process.

This is a much more complex and far-reaching alteration than may appear. Each little part of an engine is made to gauges dimensioned in thousandths of an inch; *all* these dimensions are standardized for *all* cars of a particular make. Very strict and careful inspection rejects parts which do not conform to the gauges. Thus it is that different engine parts may be made, perhaps, in engineering works many miles away from each other; some may

Now the wheels are slipped on to the axles; the engine comes along another track, is swung down from above, and is fastened securely in its proper place in the frame. Next, the electrical system units and other accessories are fitted to the moving and growing assembly. Presently the radiator, bumpers, fairings, and running-

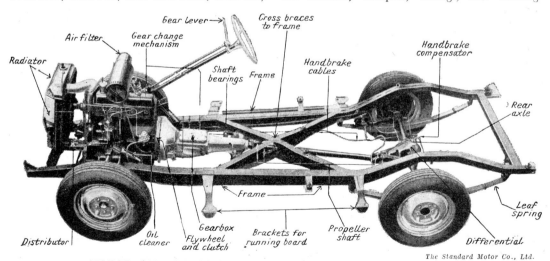

**MOTOR-CAR CHASSIS, SHOWING ITS MAIN COMPONENTS**

*The Standard Motor Co., Ltd.*

**Fig. 2.** Stripped of its bodywork, we see the 'Vanguard' chassis. On the left is the radiator, which helps to keep the engine cool; behind the engine, surmounted by a large air filter (which cleans the air before it reaches the carburetter) are the clutch and gearbox. From the gearbox power is transmitted to the rear wheels through the propeller shaft, differential gear, and twin halves of the rear axle. These half-axles are connected on either side of the differential.

making the se
than the first
twice as many
make only one
twice. This i
crankshaft to
transmission s

So, in the c
that while th
stant speed, w
by large-to-sn
speed for the i
engine shaft b
wish to go mo
which means

**Fig. 6. This i
Left, both axles
both are driven.
crum aro**

shaft and a b
the effort of
and with mo
arrangement

In our sect
(Fig. 3), the
Some of the g
to those shaft
but still will

CHOKE

STARTER

BONNET
LOCK

2  R  LI
3  1

**In addition to p
of some of ther
the gear-chan**

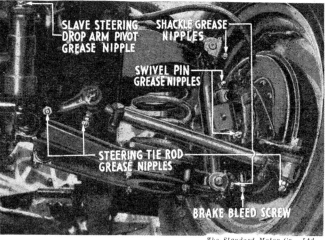

*The Standard Motor Co., Ltd.*

**FRONT WHEEL SPRINGING AND BRAKE DETAILS**
On this car the front wheel suspension consists of a strong spiral spring
beside each wheel, which permits either wheel to move up or down
independently of the other. The lettering refers to lubrication points
for the steering and brake system.

boards are all in place, and the job is complete
except the body. When the unit reaches this
stage it is called a chassis. Finally, the body,
with the instrument panel, swings down from
above and is fastened to the frame. The necessary connexions are made to the instruments—
and instead of the bare frame of a short time ago,
there is a complete car.

### How the Modern Motor-Car Works

The man who drives a car must think of nothing
else. He has enough to do. His hands and feet
are instantly ready and alert, and his whole attention must be divided between the road and the
controls used in operating the car. He has before
him (Fig. 1 in the preceding page) the steering
wheel, the gear lever, the brake pedal and the clutch
pedal, the hand brake lever, and the accelerator
pedal for controlling the intake of petrol-air
mixture, and thus the speed of the vehicle.

Ready to his hand are the starter switch, which
sets the starter motor working to give the engine
an initial movement, the choke control, for lessen-
ing the air intake and so furnishing a richer mixture
of fuel at the start, when the engine is " cold ";
the horn button; the lamp switches and that for
the direction indicator; and the switch for the
windscreen wiper. An ignition switch, with a
warning light, can be operated only by inserting
and turning a special key, and until this is done the
current to the sparking plugs, which fires the fuel
mixture in the cylinders, is " off."

There are other things upon which the driver
must keep his eye, such as the speedometer, the
oil pressure gauge, petrol gauge, and water temperature gauge (for the water in the cooling
system). An ammeter shows if the dynamo is
properly charging the car batteries, which supply
current for the starter, horn, lamps, etc. A radio
set and a car warming apparatus are also often
fitted to cars of today.

The brake pedal operates the " service " brakes,
used in ordinary driving. These brake all four

wheels by means of hydraulic action;
oil is forced along pipes to cylinders of
which the pistons push out metal shoes
lined with friction material. These
shoes thus expand against the surfaces
of the brake drums. The hand brake
usually operates only the rear wheels.

The gear lever is moved into any one
of four, or sometimes five, positions to
select the proper gear ratio for the
varying conditions met in driving. If
it is in " neutral " position the engine
is disconnected from the drive shaft.
When in this position the engine may
be left running and the car will not
move, even if the clutch is left in. The
clutch is used to transfer the power of
the engine gradually to the transmission
and thence to the drive shaft.

THE CHASSIS AND ITS PARTS.—In
Fig. 2 we look down from above on the
chassis of a car with all the essential
parts in place. At the front is the
radiator, which helps to keep the engine
cool. Water circulating in the cylinder
jackets becomes warmed, rises, and flows
to the radiator; here it is cooled by the flow of
air over the radiator tubes, and goes then again
to the jackets. From the engine itself we can
trace the path of the power to the rear wheels
through the clutch, transmission, propeller shaft,
differential, and rear axle. Near the front is
the dynamo which charges the storage battery.
Alongside are the starting motor, the ignition
distributor, and the pump which supplies petrol
to the carburetter. The distributor sends electric
current to the sparking plugs in each cylinder,
timing each spark so that the explosions take
place in proper order. Supported by the frame
is the battery.

At one side of the chassis runs the exhaust pipe
through which the spent gas from the cylinders is
ejected. On it is the silencer, which usually
consists of a chamber or series of chambers in which
the exhaust gases are allowed to expand slowly
through baffle plates. A tail-pipe carries them
out at the rear.

STEERING MECHANISM. The steering column, at
the top of which is the steering wheel, operates
a drop arm by means of worm gearing or other
suitable mechanism. The drop arm is connected
to the steering head by (1) a drag link and (2)
another lever projecting from the head. Thus,
when the steering wheel is turned, a proportional
pull is given to the connecting levers, and so to
the steering head (which is attached to the road
wheel on one side of the vehicle). Tie-rods
connect the steering head of the opposite road wheel
to the mechanism already described, so that both
road wheels are pulled round together. Great
care is taken in designing, manufacturing and
assembling all these parts, so that there is no undue
slackness, and that the road wheels answer immediately to any turning of the steering wheel. Some
steering connexions are seen in the photo above.

THE ENGINE. Fig. 3 shows a four-cylinder
engine seen from the left side. Beginning at the
left we see the fan, driven by a belt from a pulley
on the front end of the crankshaft; then the timing

arrangement is here shown for clearness. The crown wheel A is driven by the bevel pinion B, the crown wheel being bolted to a flange on the differential box or cage C, which rotates on the same axis as the axles D and E, but quite independently of them. The differential box carries two or more bearing pins F, on which the two small bevel pinions G are mounted. These pinions are capable of independent rotation on the pins F, but are both in mesh with the larger bevel wheels secured on the ends of the axles D and E. The pins F are usually integral with a central spider H.

As long as the axles D and E rotate at the same speed, owing to the car travelling in a straight line, there will be no rotation of the pinions G on their pins F, the whole being rotated as if solid by means of the crown wheel A, bolted to the differential box C. The drive is, however, transmitted through the pinions G to the differential wheels all the time, the two wheels being balanced by their engagement with opposite sides of the pinions. For this reason the term balance gear is often used.

When the car turns to the right or to the left, one of the axles D, E will have to turn more quickly than the other. This is because the road wheel which it drives is running on the outside of the curve, and has a curve of greater radius—longer length—to traverse than the opposite road wheel. When this takes place the two small bevel pinions G will have to rotate on their pins F,

while one of the bevel wheels is turning faster than the other. One of the axles then rotates faster than the differential cage, and the other more slowly.

THE DYNAMO AND STARTER.—Motor cars had at first to be started by hand, the driver fitting a cranked handle to the flywheel shaft and swinging it to get a first movement of the engine—as he does now in emergency. The first successful electrical starting, lighting and ignition system was developed about 1913. This method, much simplified, is still in general use. The heart of the system is the accumulator or storage battery. The dynamo is used to charge the battery and so furnish current to the ignition circuit, the lights, and similar units. When the engine is running at ten miles or more per hour, current is drawn from the dynamo, and the current is sent to the battery, there to recharge it.

When the starter switch is closed, current from the battery passes to the starter motor, which

immediately revolves, and a pinion on its shaft engages the flywheel gear. An over-running clutch releases the starting mechanism as soon as the engine gets under way.

THE IGNITION CIRCUIT.—In order to fire the explosive mixture in the engine cylinders, a high voltage current is led to the sparking plug which juts into each cylinder head. There, jumping across a tiny gap at the plug end, it makes a spark at the proper time. Either an induction coil or a magneto-electric generator ("magneto" for short) provides this current (see Dynamo). The distributor—a kind of rotating switch—passes current to the plugs in a certain squence.

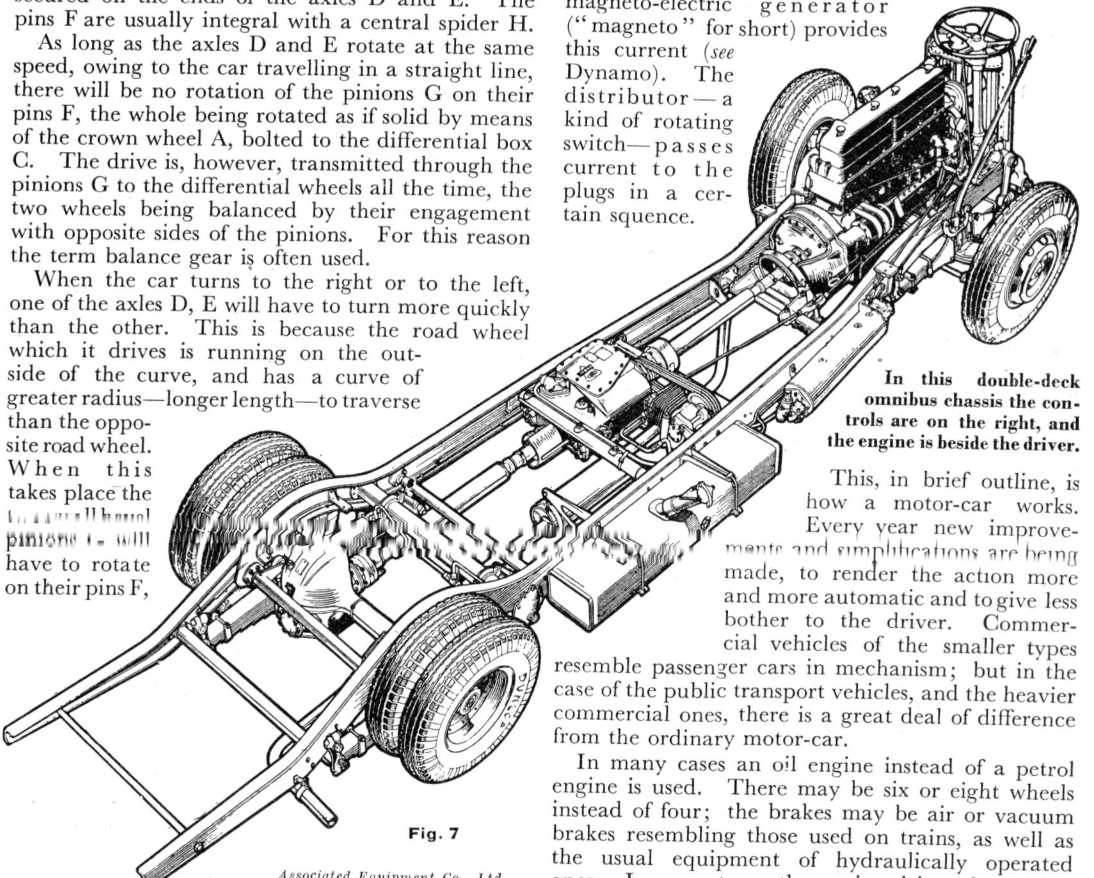

In this double-deck omnibus chassis the controls are on the right, and the engine is beside the driver.

This, in brief outline, is how a motor-car works. Every year new improvements and simplifications are being made, to render the action more and more automatic and to give less bother to the driver. Commercial vehicles of the smaller types resemble passenger cars in mechanism; but in the case of the public transport vehicles, and the heavier commercial ones, there is a great deal of difference from the ordinary motor-car.

In many cases an oil engine instead of a petrol engine is used. There may be six or eight wheels instead of four; the brakes may be air or vacuum brakes resembling those used on trains, as well as the usual equipment of hydraulically operated ones. In some types the engine drives the vehicle indirectly by way of an electric generator, and this generator supplies current to electric motors which actually turn the road wheels.

The chassis of a motor bus, as built for the vehicles run by the London Transport Executive, is illustrated in Fig. 7. The power plant is an oil engine of 125 horse-power, having six cylinders. The principle is similar to that of the Diesel engine (q.v.). There are four speeds and a reverse. The main brakes are operated by compressed air (all four wheels); the hand brake (mechanically operated) acts on the rear wheels only. An air compressor driven by belts from the front of the gearbox charges a reservoir with air at 100 lb. per sq. inch. When the driver depresses the brake pedal, air at about 45 lb. pressure drives out the pistons of the brake cylinders; if he pushes the pedal beyond about three-quarters of its total travel, pressure in the air line then rises to about 80 lb. per sq. inch, giving extra braking force for use in an emergency stop.

Fig. 7

Associated Equipment Co., Ltd.

**Mountaineering.** Given a good "head," reasonable strength and, above all, physical fitness, one may take to mountaineering. It is not a very old sport, dating, in an organized way, from the 16th century, when a club was formed in Zürich, but it was little practised till two centuries later. Of the famous mountains, Mont Blanc was first conquered in 1786 ; after that other Alpine peaks were climbed one by one. In 1857 the Alpine Club was founded, and mountaineering as a real sport came into being. It extended to Norway, Corsica, the Caucasus, then to the greater mountains of America and Asia, and, in 1921, to Mount Everest (*q.v.*). The highest peak yet climbed is Nanda Devi in the Himalayas (25,645 feet). The Swiss, born mountaineers, were joined by the English and Germans, and these nations have probably done more than any others to forward the sport.

From the practical point of view, mountaineering has two quite definite branches: rock-climbing, and snow and ice work. It is possible to be an expert in one of these without having done more than a little of the other. In England, especially, there are far more opportunities for rock-climbing than for snow and ice work; indeed, some of the world's finest rock-climbs are to be found in Great Britain. In England the Lake District, in Wales the region round Snowdon, are the best climbing centres; in Scotland there are many fine centres throughout the Highlands. The most difficult rock-climb in Great Britain is generally supposed to be the Crowberry Ridge on Buchaille Etive, near Glencoe; but in the Isle of Arran, in the Firth of Clyde, there is a climb on Ben Nuis that has been done only once, in 1901. It was not until 1873 that the highest peak in the island of Skye was climbed.

One essential in climbing is to have some knowledge of geology, for while some types of rocks, like the granite and basaltic rocks of the Lake District, will take a great strain and are not likely to break away, others are treacherous ; some, *e.g.* in limestone districts, are too soft to permit of real climbing at all.

Rock-climbing is generally carried out by men roped together, special knots being used, and three being the usual number of climbers on a rope. The system followed in all climbing is for the leader to go ahead, then to take the middle person up to him. He then goes on again, and the man in the middle waits while the third person comes up. The middle then goes on, then the first, then the third again, and so on. The least experienced member of the party is usually put in the middle, the most experienced leading, the strongest—if all things are otherwise equal—coming

at the end. The rope (which is specially made, and can be distinguished by a red thread running through it), though strong enough to bear the weight of a man in normal circumstances is not used to haul persons up, but merely to steady them so that they can devote their whole attention to climbing, and to save them from falling should they slip. For climbing on certain kinds of rock, such as the gritty sandstone of the Tirol, rope-soled shoes are used, but usually proper climbing boots, with nails which grip the edges of the soles and give a hold on the rock, are worn.

The ice-axe is essential for snow and ice work. It is used for cutting steps in the ice—a long and difficult job on which depends the whole safety of the party—for testing the depth of snow, the strength of snow-bridges, and for finding out where crevasses (or cracks) are, and where the snow is likely to be treacherous. The leader of a party on snow or ice must be able to do all these things, and he must, too, be able to tell what sort of conditions are likely to lie ahead: whether the snow is safe, and will still be safe when a descent is being made; whether it is likely to slide away, or to freeze up; and, also, what the weather is likely to do, for on this a great deal depends. Long and difficult climbs on snow or ice are often started at night, to ensure good conditions on the way back; and it is not unusual for the party to reach its goal in the early hours, returning before the sun has begun to melt the snow. Many a life has been lost through neglecting this precaution, and through a party being forced to spend the night on the mountain, and freezing to death. Crampons, which are sets of steel spikes for fitting to the sole of the boots, are sometimes used for snow and ice work, but some mountaineers do not like them.

A heavy rucksack is carried only when the party is actually making a tour, going from place to place along a range ; for excursions to be completed in one day, the minimum of weight is carried, consisting of food, emergency supplies, and the rope, which is carefully coiled when not in use. In winter, mountaineering may sometimes be combined with ski-ing, but this is an occupation for the expert at both types of sport.

There is much literature about mountaineering, and some books on the subject have won the standing of classics. Edward Whymper's book, Scrambles Among the Alps (1871), which is perhaps the greatest of them, tells how the author, after many attempts, was the first to reach the summit of the Matterhorn in 1865, and how his companions lost their lives on the descent. Sir Leslie Stephen's The Playground of Europe (1871), J. Tyndall's Hours of Exercise in the Alps

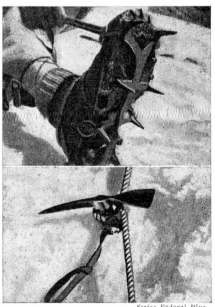

*Swiss Federal Rlys*
**NECESSARY FOR SAFETY**
At the top is shown the correct way to fasten the ' crampons '—spikes by means of which the mountaineer can walk on the steepest ice ; and below, the haft of an ice-axe is stuck deeply into the snow as a support for a rope.

**EAST INDIAN MUD-SKIPPER**
With front fins developed rather like the flippers of a seal, the mud-skipper of East Indian rivers often climbs up on a log and hops about hunting for insects. Other species of mud-skipper are found on the Great Barrier Reef of Australia.

the financial recompense to Mozart was comparatively small. The emperor appointed him to a position at the Austrian court, but the salary was low. His wife was extravagant and a poor business manager, and Mozart found it demanded all his powers to keep his growing family from want. To make ends meet he took pupils, and produced a stream of brilliant compositions.

Under the strain his health began to fail. During the year 1791 he was engaged on three of his greatest compositions. Besides two operas, he had received a commission to compose a Requiem for funeral service, the purpose of which was kept very secret. The mystery surrounding this order made a strange impression on Mozart, for in his weakened condition he became convinced that it was his own requiem that he was composing. Such it proved to be, for just before it was finished the busy, brilliant life of Mozart ended, apparently from typhus fever. There were debts, and there was no money. His wife was ill, and no friends came to help. So his body was buried in a pauper's grave in Vienna.

Of Mozart's operas The Magic Flute is perhaps his best, though The Marriage of Figaro and Don Giovanni rival it in popularity. Of his many symphonies, over 40 in all, the one known as the Jupiter symphony is by many considered the finest, and is so masterly that it is difficult to believe that it was composed in 15 days. His piano concertos are still favourites, and his quartets are equalled only by those of Haydn and Beethoven. His sacred music is beautiful. No one branch of his art surpasses another. In the 600 or more works composed during his short life, there was no form of musical expression that he did not develop.

**Mud-skipper.** A strange contradiction to the everyday rule that fishes cannot live out of water is the " mud-skipper " (*Periophthalmus*) of East Indian rivers. A tiny creature with front fins developed like the flippers of a seal, it comes out on the shore and hops about, hunting for small insects. Other sorts of mud-skippers are found on the Great Barrier Reef of Australia. One such is so adapted to air-breathing that it will drown if kept *under* water.

There is also the four-eyed fish (*Anableps anableps*) of tropical America, so-called because its eyes are divided into two parts—the upper lens suitable for sight in the air, the lower for use in the water. It swims half in and half out of water, and is able to see insects above or below the surface. When alarmed it will skip like a grasshopper, two feet or more at a jump.

Another strange fish of this group is the little Alaskan black-fish (*Dallia pectoralis*). It dwells in the swamps, and its vitality is great. It is said that after being frozen for weeks and then thawed out it is as lively as ever. (*See* also Lung-fish).

**Mulberry.** Found in the temperate regions of both the Old and New World, mulberry trees are cultivated for the feeding of silkworms (for the production of silk) and for the delicious fruit. There are red, black, and white-fruited species. The white mulberry (*Morus alba*), the silkworm mulberry, is a native of China and was introduced to America when the early colonists attempted to raise silkworms. Though they failed to establish silkworm culture as an industry, the white mulberry trees they imported developed into some of the leading fruit varieties of North America. This species was introduced into Britain in 1596. The chief centres of mulberry cultivation and of silk growing are China, Japan, India, France, Persia, and Turkey.

The black mulberry (*M. nigra*) was introduced to Britain, it is believed, from Persia in 1548. Its large, dark purple, almost black, fruit, which looks like a long blackberry, is very juicy and delicious. The red mulberry (*M. rubra*), a native of North America, has fruit of a pleasing tartness, which relieves the sweetness characteristic of the fruits of all mulberry trees. In some parts of Europe this tree is chosen for cultivation because of its hardiness. Other varieties are cultivated for their ornamental forms.

A member of a closely allied genus is the paper mulberry, the bark of which is used for making paper in Japan. The islanders of the Pacific also make a fabric called " tapa cloth " from it by soaking the bark, removing the outer layer, and then laying the remainder on a table and beating it until it has the required thinness.

**DELICIOUS MULBERRIES**　　*J. E. Tyler*
These are the fruits of the black mulberry ; deep blackish purple in colour, they are larger than blackberries, to which they have a superficial resemblance. They make excellent eating.

# Mulberry Harbours.

In 1942 Mr. Winston Churchill, Britain's war-time Prime Minister, gave orders for the planning of portable "piers for use on flat beaches," which must float up and down on the tide. Later the code name "Mulberry" was adopted for the concrete breakwaters and jetties built as a result.

Military and naval advisers had come to the view that a direct assault on existing ports or harbours along the French side of the English Channel was unlikely to be successful, so strongly had the Germans fortified and manned any likely ports. The only alternative was, then, to land the Allied armies of liberation on the flat beaches; and those of Normandy (q.v.) were chosen, eventually, for the landings, which began on June 6, 1944.

Two artificial harbours were constructed, known as Mulberry "A", to be used for the American sector of the invasion; and Mulberry "B", for the British sector. Each harbour was of a size to enclose an area of water roughly of the same dimensions as that of Dover harbour—an immense undertaking when we remember that all the enclosing piers and the protective breakwaters had to be built in secrecy in Britain long beforehand, and be towed to the site over a distance of 100 miles. Together the various structures weighed about a million tons.

A breakwater was made mainly of blockships sunk in such a way as to form a protective wall 24,000 feet long off the invasion beaches, in five sections. Concrete caissons (q.v.) extended this breakwater and filled up gaps. Next, imagining we are at the breakwater, looking towards the beaches, there was the main pierhead, at which coasters and medium sized ships could tie up for unloading. Like the actual piers which connected the pierhead with the shore, the pierhead had to float, since the rise and fall of the tide made a difference of about 20 feet between high and low water levels. The pierways were made up of 80-feet spans linked together, and were supported on pontoons. At the shore end, where there was a shelving beach, the pier ended in a floating ramp. In all, seven miles of pierways were built for the two harbours, "A" and "B". The pierways for Mulberry "B" extended nearly three-quarters of a mile from the pierhead to the beach. The lay-out of the "B" harbour is shown in page 2252.

In the greatest secrecy, the piers, pierheads and caissons were built—in places as far apart as the Thames-side and certain Scottish ports. The prototypes were constructed early in 1943, and after approval, the task of pre-fabricating the many structures was begun. The pierheads were 200 feet long and 60 feet wide. Each was supported on a steel pontoon which rode up and down with the tide between four steel legs or "spuds." These spuds were driven into the sea bed to form guides, on which the actual pierhead slid up and down. The pierway sections, 80 feet long, were linked

British Official

## A PIERHEAD OF MULBERRY HARBOUR 'B'

To overcome the problem of landing supplies for the Allied armies which poured into Normandy in June 1944 two artificial harbours were constructed, the code name for them being Mulberry. That known as Mulberry 'B,' at Arromanches, served the British sector, and in the above photograph one of its pierheads is seen in use: ambulances are carrying wounded to a waiting hospital ship, while lorries laden with supplies (lower right) are moving shoreward.

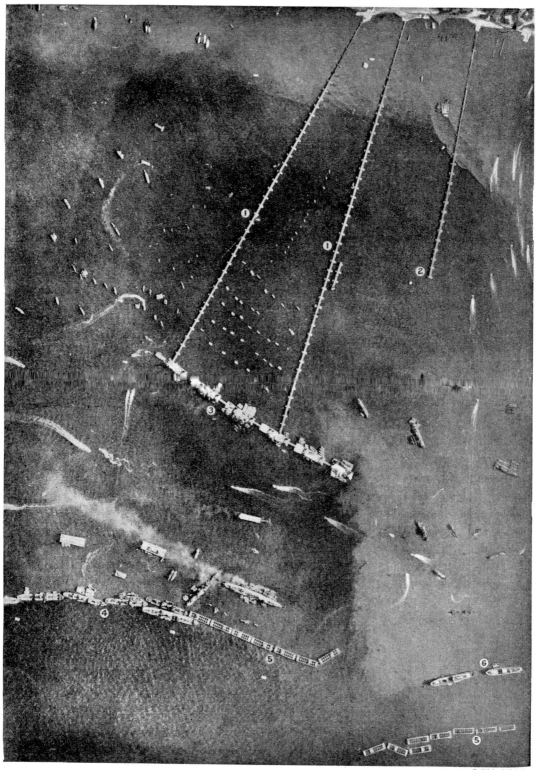

*British Official*

The floating pierways (1) at Mulberry 'B' were three-quarters of a mile in length; running parallel with them was another pier (2) at which barges were unloaded. Coasters and medium-sized craft moored at the main pier-head (3), protected by sunken blockships (4) and a breakwater of concrete caissons (5); similar caissons lay to seaward of the anchorage for larger vessels (6). The comet-like streaks on the water are the wakes of small vessels.

together sideways so that they could slew in winds without interrupting the flow of traffic over them. The roadway itself was flexible, being made of concrete panels loosely bolted to the framing.

The blockships for the breakwater crossed the Channel behind the assault forces, and were sunk by explosives during the five days after June 6, 1944. Meanwhile the caissons, breakwaters and piers were being towed to position, assembled and fixed. By June 18 a large part of the structures was ready for use; then a gale blew for three days, and Mulberry "A" suffered much damage. However, the American forces captured the port of Cherbourg on June 30, and were able to abandon their Mulberry. Another result of the gale and the rough weather which followed it was that the towing of pier equipment to the Mulberry was delayed, and it was not until mid-July that the harbour came into full use. During 100 days after June 6. 2,200,000 men were landed on the Normandy beaches, with 4,000,000 tons of stores and 500,000 vehicles.

**Mule.** The offspring of a male ass and a mare is called a mule; and as almost all these hybrids are sterile, mules are unable to breed. Usually a mule resembles the father in appearance and the mother in size, a good specimen standing 16 hands (a hand equals four inches) at the shoulder and being almost equal in strength to a horse of the same size. The long ears, tufted tail and small hoofs distinguish the mule from the horse.

Proverbially obstinate, mules are exceedingly useful as pack-animals in mountainous country. They are much hardier than the horse, less liable to disease, less particular in the matter of food, of greater endurance and very sure-footed. A mule is fit for work when four years old, is at its prime from eight to 12, and will continue to work well till the age of 14 or 15.

# SIMPLE WAYS *in* MULTIPLICATION

*O*ne of the four branches of arithmetic, multiplication often seems more difficult than addition or subtraction, yet it is only an extension of the same idea as addition. Its application is explained here.

**Multiplication.** When a grocer counts eggs three at a time, he says to himself, " 3, 6, 9, 12, 15, 18, 21, 24," etc. Each of these numbers is called a *multiple* of 3. He is adding three at a time, and the total is made up of threes.

Finding the total of a number of equal numbers is called *multiplication.*

When we think " 4 weeks = 28 days," we are multiplying. To multiply 7 by 4, we must remember the total, or sum of 4 sevens $(7+7+7+7)$. The number multiplied or repeated is called the *multiplicand* ; 7 is the multiplicand in this example. The number of times that the multiplicand is repeated is the number called the *multiplier;* 4 is the multiplier in this example.

We count 10 rows of soldiers marching 4 abreast. Knowing the multiplication table (Fig. 1), we can shorten the process by saying $10 \times 4 = 40$. If we should forget what $10 \times 4$ equals, what are the multiples that we must say to find the sum of 10 fours ?   $4+4+4+4+4+4+4+4+4+4 =$ what number? What number is the *multiplicand* in this simple problem?

The number resulting from multiplying is called the *product;* 40 is the product of 4 and 10.

| | |
|---|---:|
| multiplicand | 6 |
| multiplier | 5 |
| product | 30 |

Products of large numbers are found by calculating. To calculate readily the learner must commit to memory the elementary products shown in Fig. 1. Do without the combinations in lighter type because $2 \times 3 = 3 \times 2$, $2 \times 4 = 4 \times 2$, etc., and so the combinations in black type give all the variations necessary. Repeat oftenest the last four lines as they are the most difficult, viz:

$$6 \times 6 \quad 6 \times 7 \quad 6 \times 8 \quad 6 \times 9$$
$$7 \times 7 \quad 7 \times 8 \quad 7 \times 9$$
$$8 \times 8 \quad 8 \times 9$$
$$9 \times 9$$

This table is usually known as the multiplication table. The facts it summarizes may be more easily

| 1 | 2 | 3 | 4 | 5 | 6 | 7 | 8 | 9 |
|---|---|---|---|---|---|---|---|---|
| 1 | 1 | 1 | 1 | 1 | 1 | 1 | 1 | 1 |
| 1 | 2 | 3 | 4 | 5 | 6 | 7 | 8 | 9 |
| 1 | 2 | 3 | 4 | 5 | 6 | 7 | 8 | 9 |
| 2 | 2 | 2 | 2 | 2 | 2 | 2 | 2 | 2 |
| 2 | 4 | 6 | 8 | 10 | 12 | 14 | 16 | 18 |
| 1 | 2 | 3 | 4 | 5 | 6 | 7 | 8 | 9 |
| 3 | 3 | 3 | 3 | 3 | 3 | 3 | 3 | 3 |
| 3 | 6 | 9 | 12 | 15 | 18 | 21 | 24 | 27 |
| 1 | 2 | 3 | 4 | 5 | 6 | 7 | 8 | 9 |
| 4 | 4 | 4 | 4 | 4 | 4 | 4 | 4 | 4 |
| 4 | 8 | 12 | 16 | 20 | 24 | 28 | 32 | 36 |
| 1 | 2 | 3 | 4 | 5 | 6 | 7 | 8 | 9 |
| 5 | 5 | 5 | 5 | 5 | 5 | 5 | 5 | 5 |
| 5 | 10 | 15 | 20 | 25 | 30 | 35 | 40 | 45 |
| 1 | 2 | 3 | 4 | 5 | 6 | 7 | 8 | 9 |
| 6 | 6 | 6 | 6 | 6 | 6 | 6 | 6 | 6 |
| 6 | 12 | 18 | 24 | 30 | 36 | 42 | 48 | 54 |
| 1 | 2 | 3 | 4 | 5 | 6 | 7 | 8 | 9 |
| 7 | 7 | 7 | 7 | 7 | 7 | 7 | 7 | 7 |
| 7 | 14 | 21 | 28 | 35 | 42 | 49 | 56 | 63 |
| 1 | 2 | 3 | 4 | 5 | 6 | 7 | 8 | 9 |
| 8 | 8 | 8 | 8 | 8 | 8 | 8 | 8 | 8 |
| 8 | 16 | 24 | 32 | 40 | 48 | 56 | 64 | 72 |
| 1 | 2 | 3 | 4 | 5 | 6 | 7 | 8 | 9 |
| 9 | 9 | 9 | 9 | 9 | 9 | 9 | 9 | 9 |
| 9 | 18 | 27 | 36 | 45 | 54 | 63 | 72 | 81 |

Fig. 1

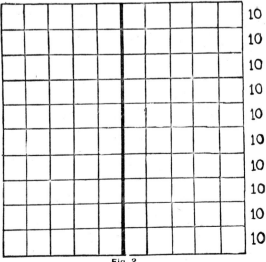

Fig. 2

remembered if studied in connexion with drawings or other constructive work.

Cut 100 one-inch squares of paper. Lay them in rows as shown in Fig. 2 (page 2253).

1. Count the squares by rows—10 at a time—thus: 10, 20, 30, etc.

2. How many squares in 3 rows? 7 rows? 5 rows? 9 rows? 4 rows?

3. Copy this table and fill the blanks:

| | |
|---|---|
| 1 × 10 = | 6 × 10 = |
| 2 × 10 = | 7 × 10 = |
| 3 × 10 = | 8 × 10 = |
| 4 × 10 = | 9 × 10 = |
| 5 × 10 = | 10 × 10 = |

4. Lay squares in rows of 5; count them by fives.

5. Lay 5 rows of 10 squares each. Lay 10 rows of 5 squares each. How many squares in each group?

6. Compare 10 × 5 with 5 × 10. Fill the blanks: 50 = —— × 5 = 5 × ——.

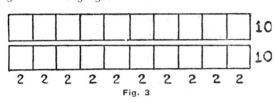

Fig. 3

7. Cut two strips of paper each 10 inches long and 1 inch wide (Fig. 3). 2 × 10 = what number? Cover these strips with inch squares by placing 2, then 2 more, etc. How many twos = 20? Finish the table by filling the blanks:

| | | | | |
|---|---|---|---|---|
| 1 × 2 = | 3 × 2 = | 5 × 2 = | 7 × 2 = | 9 × 2 = |
| 2 × 2 = | 4 × 2 = | 6 × 2 = | 8 × 2 = | 10 × 2 = |

8. Lay 2 rows of 9 squares each. 2 × 9 = what number? Find this number by counting the squares by twos.

9. Add:

| 1 | 2 | 3 | 4 | 5 | 6 | 7 | 8 | 9 | 10 |
|---|---|---|---|---|---|---|---|---|---|
| 1 | 2 | 3 | 4 | 5 | 6 | 7 | 8 | 9 | 10 |

Complete:

| | | | | |
|---|---|---|---|---|
| 2 × 1 = | 2 × 3 = | 2 × 5 = | 2 × 7 = | 2 × 9 = |
| 2 × 2 = | 2 × 4 = | 2 × 6 = | 2 × 8 = | 2 × 10 = |

10. Lay squares to show 10 threes. Count 30 by threes. Complete the following table of threes to 10 × 3:

| | |
|---|---|
| 1 × 3 = 3 | 3 × 3 = 9 |
| 2 × 3 = 6 | 4 × 3 = 12 |

11. Show with squares that 3 × 6 = 6 × 3; 3 × 7 = 7 × 3; 3 × 8 = 8 × 3; and 3 × 9 = 9 × 3:

12. Complete the following statements by filling the blanks:

3 × 6 =     3 × 7 =     3 × 8 =     3 × 9 =

13. Add:

| 1 | 2 | 3 | 4 | 5 | 6 | 7 | 8 | 9 | 10 |
|---|---|---|---|---|---|---|---|---|---|
| 1 | 2 | 3 | 4 | 5 | 6 | 7 | 8 | 9 | 10 |
| 1 | 2 | 3 | 4 | 5 | 6 | 7 | 8 | 9 | 10 |

14. Lay squares and develop the tables of 4 thus:

| | |
|---|---|
| 1 × 4 = 4 | 4 × 1 = 4 |
| 2 × 4 = 8 | 4 × 2 = 8 |
| 3 × 4 = 12 | 4 × 3 = 12 |
| 4 × 4 = 16, etc. | 4 × 4 = 16, etc. |

15. In the same way make tables of 5; 6; 7.

16. How many squares on a draught-board

Fig. 4

(Fig. 4)? Count one row. Count the number of rows. Count the black squares by fours. Count the white squares by fours. Add 32 and 32. Show that 8 × 8 = 64.

17. Count 32 by eights. Show that 5 × 8 = 8 × 5. Count 48 by eights. Count 64 by fours.

Complete table below:

1 × 9 = 9     2 × 9 = 18     3 × 9 = 27     4 × 9 = 36

18. Show that 3 + 3 + 3 + 3 + 3 = 5 + 5 + 5.

19. Show that 5 × 9 = 9 × 5; that 8 × 3 = 3 × 8.

*Principle.* The multiplicand and multiplier can exchange places without changing the product.

### Multiplying Numbers Greater than Ten

*Examples:*

1. Find 2 × 12 (Fig. 5).

*Solution:*

First Form:
$$\begin{array}{r} 12 \\ 12 \\ \hline 24 \ Sum \end{array}$$

Second Form:
$$\begin{array}{ll} 12 & 2 \times 2 = 4 \\ 2 & 2 \times 1 \ ten = 2 \ tens \\ \hline 24 \ Product \end{array}$$

*Answer:* 2 × 12 = 24.

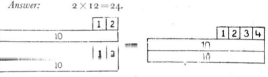

Fig. 5

2. Find 2 × 20. 2 × 30.

*Solutions:* 2 × 2 tens = 4 tens. 2 times 3 tens = 6 tens.

3. Find 2 × 27 (Fig. 6).

*Solution:*

$$\begin{array}{r} 27 \\ 2 \\ \hline 54 \end{array}$$

2 × 7 = 14 = 1 ten and 4 ones.
2 × 2 tens + 1 ten = 5 tens.
2 × 27 = 54.

or;

2 × 7 = 14
2 × 20 = 40

2 × 27 = 54

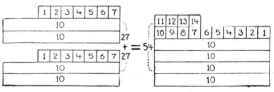

Fig. 6

Accuracy and speed in multiplication are acquired in these ways: (1) By mastering the "fundamental facts" in tables; (2) by counting with as few words as possible in mind; (3) by writing numbers in straight rows and columns; (4) by forming the habit of testing the correctness of all answers.

As an illustration of how few words it is necessary to have in mind, the following problem may be used. In multiplying 9 by 4, think

279
4
—
1116

713
402
—
1420
2852
—
286626

"36." In multiplying 7 by 4 and adding 3, think "28," "31." In multiplying 2 by 4 and adding 3, think "8," "11."

In writing the partial products be careful to keep units under units, tens under tens, and so on. This is particularly important in multiplying by a number in which one or more noughts occur, as in the lower of the two examples on the left.

The tests used commonly to determine the correctness of a product are

(1) Repeating the operation; (2) changing position of multiplicand and multiplier and multiplying again; (3) dividing the product by either the multiplicand or multiplier. The quotient result of the division should be the other factor.

To save time in multiplication it is convenient to know the following short cuts:

To multiply by 10, add a nought to the multiplicand.

To multiply by 100, add 2 noughts to the multiplicand.

To multiply by 1000, add 3 noughts to the multiplicand.

To multiply by 25, add 2 noughts and divide by 4.

To multiply by 50, add 2 noughts and divide by 2.

To multiply by $12\frac{1}{2}$, add 2 noughts and divide by 8.

To multiply by $16\frac{2}{3}$, add 2 noughts and divide by 6.

To multiply by $33\frac{1}{3}$, add 2 noughts and divide by 3.

Can you invent a short way of multiplying a number by 11? By 99, using subtraction?

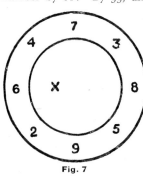

Fig. 7

The accompanying drill chart (Fig. 7) will help to fix in your mind the facts of the multiplication table. Draw it upon a blackboard, or upon a large sheet of paper, place a number in the centre for the multiplicand, and give quickly the product as someone points now to one multiplier and now to another. Change the multiplicand from time to time.

Many strangely symmetrical tables have been developed by students of mathematics. One of the most interesting is that which results from the multiplication of numbers consisting entirely of 1's.

| | | |
|---|---|---|
| $1 \times 1$ | = | 1 |
| $11 \times 11$ | = | 121 |
| $111 \times 111$ | = | 12321 |
| $1111 \times 1111$ | = | 1234321 |
| $11111 \times 11111$ | = | 123454321 |
| $111111 \times 111111$ | = | 12345654321 |
| $1111111 \times 1111111$ | = | 1234567654321 |
| $11111111 \times 11111111$ | = | 123456787654321 |
| $111111111 \times 111111111$ | = | 12345678987654321 |

From this we can form a mechanical rule for the formation of such products: To multiply a number composed entirely of 1's by itself, write the number which represents the sum of the digits in one factor (which, in order that the rule shall hold, must be less than 10), and, symmetrically to the left and right of it, write the digits less than that one, in natural decreasing order. For example, to multiply

11111 by 11111, write, 5, the number of digits in either factor, and, symmetrically to the right and left of it, the natural decreasing order of digits less than 5, i.e., 4, 3, 2, and 1, which give the product 123454321.

Other interesting tables are these:

| | | |
|---|---|---|
| $7 \times 7$ | = | 49 |
| $67 \times 67$ | = | 4489 |
| $667 \times 667$ | = | 444889 |
| $6667 \times 6667$ | = | 44448889 etc. |
| $9 \times 9$ | = | 81 |
| $99 \times 99$ | = | 9801 |
| $999 \times 999$ | = | 998001 |
| $9999 \times 9999$ | = | 99980001 etc. |

**Mummy.** In the Egyptian rooms of the British Museum in London throngs of curious sightseers look into the very faces of the pharaohs and nobles of Egypt who ruled several thousand years ago. Thousands of such mummies or embalmed bodies have been taken from the sands and tombs of Egypt, and thousands more may lie hidden; for the Egyptians practised the art of mummifying their dead for 3,000 years or more, believing that the soul would continue to exist in the world beyond the grave so long as the mummified body was preserved. Some of the mummies discovered date as far back as 3,000 B.C.

The bodies were preserved by the use of bitumen, spices, gums, etc., or sometimes by immersion in honey, and after a 70-day process were wrapped

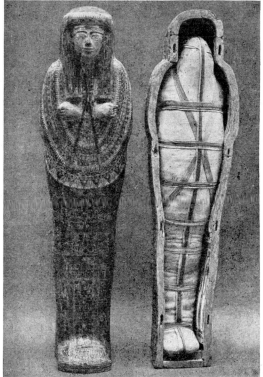

British Museum

**A MUMMY IN ITS CASE**
When the lid of a mummy case is removed, the mummified body (right), swathed in linen kept in place by bandages, is revealed. The corpse is that of an unknown Egyptian princess, whose image is modelled on the lid (left). Some of the mummies discovered date back about 5,000 years.

carefully in linen. Some of the linen bandages are 17 feet long. Then the shrouded mummy was usually placed in two cases of cedar, or of a sort of papier-mâché, made to fit the corpse. The inner case was plain, but the outer one was often covered with elaborate paintings telling of the life and various deeds of the deceased. A moulded mask of the dead, or his portrait on linen or wood, sometimes decorated the head-end of the case. This double case was placed in an oblong coffin and deposited in a sarcophagus. The bodies of the poor were merely dried with salt and wrapped with coarse cloths.

Sacred animals—lions, dogs, crocodiles, birds, fishes, and even insects—were also mummified, and now and then whole shelves are found filled with embalmed cats who centuries ago probably caught mice round the temples of Egypt, where the cat was held sacred. Mummy-making was practised also in Peru and Mexico.

**Munich.** (Pron. mū′-nik). The "Athens on the Isar" was the name by which Munich, capital of the German State of Bavaria, was known before its destruction in the Second World War (1939–45). The city was the target for many raids by the Allied air forces, and almost all the famous buildings were destroyed. It was captured by United States troops on April 29–30, 1945.

Standing on the River Isar, it was one of the best-built capitals in Europe. Its rich art collections were its chief glory. Most great cities owe their fame to advantage of position, but the greatness of Munich (German, *München*) was largely the result of one man's deliberate policy. Early in the 19th century King Ludwig I of Bavaria, at enormous cost, made his capital one of the leading art centres of the world. The broad streets of the city were lined with buildings copied from the world's most famous

structures. And in those buildings might be studied the art and industry of mankind from ancient times up to the present century.

On the walls of one famous gallery (in the Old Pinakothek) hung paintings of the old masters, and just opposite, in the New Pinakothek, were exhibited more modern works. Weapons, household utensils, and other articles from the Stone Age to recent times, were arranged in chronological order, in the Bavarian National Museum; the German Museum, designed to illustrate the growth of natural and technical science, was perhaps the finest science museum in the world. At the Bavarian National Theatre and the Residenz Theatre annual festival performances of Wagner and Mozart were given. The National Library contained 30,000 rare manuscripts and 1,300,000 printed volumes. The university, the academy of science, and the schools of music and painting attracted students from all parts. After 1934, Munich, under the National-Socialists, became the official headquarters of Nazi Art—a perverted and debased form.

The city was celebrated for artistic handicrafts, such as bronze-founding, glass-staining, silversmith's work, wood-carving and lithography, the last having been invented in Bavaria in the 18th century. Among industrial products were railway rolling-stock, wallpaper, gloves, and artificial flowers. The most important industry was the brewing of beer, which still continues but on a lesser scale.

In the course of the revolution of 1918–19, which drove the Bavarian king from his throne and established the Bavarian Republic, Munich was the scene of violent Communist risings, which were suppressed after heavy fighting. The headquarters of the Nazi movement was later at the Brown House in Munich, and there Adolf Hitler (*q.v.*) made his first attempt to seize power in 1923.

At Munich was signed in September 1938 the Munich Agreement between Great Britain, France, Germany and Italy by which Czechoslovakia had to give up to Germany certain border territory peopled mainly by Germans. The population before the Second World War was about 828,000.

**Murdock,** WILLIAM (1754–1839). In the year 1777 Matthew Boulton, James Watt's partner in the engine works at Soho, near Birmingham, was approached by a young Scotsman, who had walked all the way from Ayrshire in search of work. When Boulton said there was no work to be had the lad was so disappointed that he dropped his hat. Boulton was puzzled by the noise that the hat made, and, on questioning the young man, found that it was made of wood, which he had turned on a lathe of his own making. Impressed, Boulton gave the young man employment.

The young man was William Murdock. He was born near Old Cumnock, in Ayrshire. The chief business of the Boulton & Watt firm was to supply pumping-engines to Cornish tin mines, and Murdock was sent to Cornwall to look after them. He lived at Redruth, and there he made a model "steam carriage." He

**MURDOCK'S STEAM CARRIAGE**
Probably made between 1784–86, Murdock's model steam carriage had two driving wheels 9¼ inches in diameter. The piston rod moved the horizontal beam, a connecting rod from the beam turning the axle of the driving wheels. The engine is preserved in Birmingham Art Galley.

tried it out one night on the road leading to the church, and, according to an old story, the puffing apparition nearly scared the vicar of Redruth out of his wits. But James Watt, Murdock's employer, did not want to be bothered with steam carriages. Murdock was his leading " outside man," who spied out the land and discovered what Boulton & Watt's competitors were doing. Murdock saw to the installation of difficult engines, and was too valuable to be encouraged to fritter away time on wild-cat ventures, such as that of a steam carriage must have appeared. So, at his employers' request, after building three such engines, Murdock gave up experimenting.

Murdock was more successful in another direction, namely, in gas-lighting. His house in Redruth was the first to be lit by gas, and from 1803 part of the Soho foundry at Birmingham was regularly illuminated in this way. When we think of the great benefits that gas-lighting and gas-cooking have given to the world we must all be grateful to William Murdock.

For over 50 years Murdock served Boulton & Watt's faithfully, and he was satisfied to let them have the credit for many of his inventions, so that it is difficult to determine exactly how much he did invent. But in 1799 he patented a slide valve for steam engines, which did away at one stroke with the need for three separate valves to let in and let out steam from the cylinders. This invention was the father of later slide valves which were used for many years in locomotives (q.v.) and other engines. On one occasion Murdock was fitting a steam-engine in the brewery of Messrs. Barclay Perkins in Southwark, London. He was asked if he could compare the power of the engine and of the horse it replaced, and after some consideration he worked out a formula for horse-power. On the same occasion the brewers explained to him the difficulty they had in clearing beer, and, after a visit to Billingsgate, he discovered that fish scales could be used for the purpose.

Murdock was a great man in many ways, but without personal ambition, always more anxious to get things done than to receive reward or praise. He died on November 15, 1839, at the house he had built, within sight of the Soho foundry where he had worked so long.

**Murillo,** Bartolomé Estéban (1617–82). A young man of about 25, exhausted from his 250-mile journey afoot across the Sierra Morena Mountains from Seville, arrived in Madrid one evening about 300 years ago. He was penniless, friendless, and very lonely.

" Will you tell me where I can find Diego Velazquez, the court painter ? " he asked a passer-by. The other eyed him with indifference as he gave the directions—not knowing that he was speaking to the man who was destined to be Spain's most beloved painter and one of her few artists who achieved world-wide fame.

*Wallace Collection, London*

**BY THE SPANISH ARTIST MURILLO**
Chiefly religious works, such as The Annunciation here seen, Murillo's later paintings were characterised by splendid colouring, wonderful technical skill and intense feeling. He died on April 3, 1682, and was buried in the church of Santa Cruz in Seville, Spain.

This was a red-letter day in the life of Murillo (pron. mū-ril'-ō; Spanish moo-rēl'-vō), the poor Seville mechanic's son, who, after a promising training, had for two years been earning a scanty living painting crude bright-coloured pictures, which he sold in the market-place at Seville, and who had pluckily set out to seek his fortune in the capital of Spain. For on this same evening the great Velazquez, recognizing the talent of his ambitious young fellow-townsman, took Murillo into his own home, and got permission for him to copy the pictures in the royal galleries.

Murillo worked so well that in less than three years Velazquez exhibited some of his paintings to the king and court. The young man might have looked forward to fame and prosperity in Madrid, but he preferred to return to his native Seville. Soon he painted 11 large pictures for a Franciscan convent, which brought him immediate fame. Then he married a rich woman of rank, became the head of the Academy of Seville, which he helped to found in 1660, and lived happily, painting almost continuously, principally religious works for the churches and convents of Seville, until a fall from a scaffold in 1681 brought injuries from which he died on April 3, 1682.

His body was buried in the church of Santa Cruz at Seville, and the people of Spain mourned over the passing of their lovable, pious, popular, but unspoiled idol, their " angel painter born to paint the sky."

Among Murillo's most attractive pictures are many sympathetic and realistic studies of the ragged urchins and flower-girls whom he saw in the streets of his native city. His later works were chiefly religious compositions, characterized by splendid colouring, great technical skill and intense feeling; the few portraits he painted are of great beauty. So realistic was his style that a spaniel in one of his pictures has been known to make a living dog snarl, and birds have been said to peck at the lilies in his wonderful Saint Anthony of Padua—a picture of the kneeling saint stretching forth his arms to the Christ child.

Thought by many to be Murillo's finest works are his paintings of the Immaculate Conception, of which he made several versions. One of these, which hangs in the Louvre, was brought from Spain by Napoleon's Marshal Soult, and later sold to the French government for more than £24,000— at that time the greatest sum ever paid for one picture. Murillo painted many other masterpieces, and although Saint Anthony, the Immaculate Conception, and the Assumption of the Virgin were his favourite subjects, many admire most his paintings for the Charity Hospital of Seville, among which are Moses Striking the Rock, St. Elizabeth of Hungary Tending the Sick, and the well known St. Peter

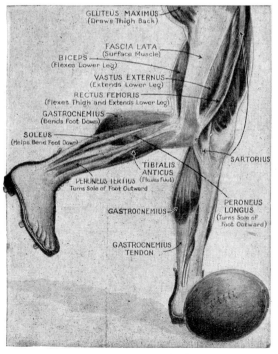

GLUTEUS MAXIMUS
(Draws Thigh Back)

FASCIA LATA
(Surface Muscle)
BICEPS
(Flexes Lower Leg)

VASTUS EXTERNUS
(Extends Lower Leg)
RECTUS FEMORIS
(Flexes Thigh and Extends Lower Leg)
GASTROCNEMIUS
(Bends Foot Down)

SOLEUS
(Helps Bend Foot Down)

TIBIALIS
ANTICUS
PERONEUS TERTIUS (Flexes Foot)
Turns Sole of Foot Outward

SARTORIUS

GASTROCNEMIUS

PERONEUS
LONGUS
(Turns Sole of
Foot Outward)

GASTROCNEMIUS
TENDON

**MUSCLES THAT WORK THE LEGS**
Most of the muscles used in walking, running and kicking are shown in the above illustration. The Sartorius is the longest muscle in the body and enables one leg to be crossed over the other. Muscles make up about half of the body weight.

Released from Prison. Though Murillo's work at times lacks force and originality, his love of colour and his serenity and charm have made him one of the best loved of the world's painters.

**Muscles.** Movement, in the higher animals, is brought about by the muscles—tissues which are able to contract and relax in response to a stimulus. This type of action (contracting and then relaxing) may be compared to that of an elastic rubber strip. Nerves, blood-vessels and lymph channels traverse the muscle tissue.

" Voluntary " muscles are under the control of the will: we walk, or sit, or lift weights by sending commands to the muscle fibres through nerves which, connected to centres in the brain, ramify throughout the muscle bulk. " Involuntary " muscles, such as those of the heart or intestine or lung, keep at work independently of the will. They are controlled by special vital centres at the back of the brain (q.v.), which keep the organism running regardless of what the intellectual centres (at the front part of the brain) may be concerned with at the time. This is obviously a convenient adjustment. No one could decide wisely a knotty point in politics or conduct, while at the same time giving continuous directions to a heart to beat, or to a lung to breathe; and yet without such direction the organ would cease to function, and the person would die.

Many muscles are both voluntary and involuntary in nature. Geared to carry on their work without the interference of the will, they are none the less subject to modifications originating from nerve stimuli. Thus, at will, one can breath more quickly or more slowly; but when the will is distracted by other matters the function of breathing takes on its own normal rhythm, equally well during sleeping or waking moments.

The unit of muscle is the fibre, each enclosed in its own elastic sheath which allows of its lengthening or shortening. These fibres build up into bundles which, running into tough, non-elastic tendons, attach themselves to bones in a system of leverage (see Mechanics). Thus the biceps, on the front part of the upper arm, is fastened by one end to the shoulder; the other end of the muscle is attached to the main bone of the forearm below the elbow. At the same time the biceps is crossed at the elbow by the top muscle of the forearm. Such muscle-bone arrangements, working in unison, enable us to lift, pull or chop. Similar muscle-bone combinations in the leg enable us to walk, run or kick.

There are some 500 muscles in the human body, and together they make up about half of the entire body weight. They become strong and hard in use; or get flabby and weak in disuse. Wise exercise, therefore is the means of muscle health and strength. Cramp is caused by sudden involuntary contraction of a muscle—most often due to " toxic " (poisonous) causes in the arteries which feed the fibres with blood. Deprived of blood, the muscles are robbed of oxygen, and this is the origin of the intense cramping pain.

Fatigue of muscles comes on when a muscle is made to act for some long time, and is due to the circulation of waste products which the blood stream cannot carry away quickly enough. These waste substances affect the end-plates of the nerves which control the muscle, and so prevent destructive over-action of the muscle. Rest restores the muscles to normal function. We can understand why long-continued use of any particular muscular group can make it " tired."

What makes the muscles contract and relax when they receive the appropriate message by way of the nerves? In the long run the action of a muscle is dependent on the release of certain complicated chemical substances at the point where the nerve ending meets the muscle fibre. Many cases of paralysis result from a failure of the body mechanism to elaborate these substances. This mechanism is a relic and a reminder of the conditions of animal life in primordial times, when the nervous system was very simple, and all reactions of the animal were in response to chemical secretions manufactured and released by the body.

**Muses.** Sometimes we say that " we have an inspiration." It seems almost as though some power outside ourselves made it possible for us to think or speak or write or do something better than usual. The ancient Greeks believed that this inspiration came from the Muses, goddesses who presided over the arts and sciences. So poets and musicians began their important works with a prayer to one or more of the Muses.

*Courtesy of the British Museum (Natural History)*
**IN THE NATURAL HISTORY MUSEUM, LONDON**
In Cromwell Road, South Kensington, London, is the Natural History branch of the British Museum, It was opened in 1881. This photograph shows the entrance hall in which there are many interesting exhibits. There are departments of zoology, entomology, botany, geology and mineralogy.

Though the number varies in different accounts, these divinities were generally pictured as nine maidens, the daughters of Zeus, king of the gods, and Mnemosyne (Memory). When the gods gathered together in festive assembly on Mount Olympus, the Muses were always present to furnish inspiration and entertainment. Led by Apollo, they sang of the origin of the world, of gods and heroes. In Greece many places were sacred to them, especially on Mounts Parnassus and Helicon. The word " museum " in its Greek form originally meant a temple sacred to the Muses.

Calliope, the most honoured of the Muses, presided over epic or heroic poetry. Clio was the Muse of history, Euterpe of lyric poetry, Thalia of comedy and pastoral poetry, Melpomene of tragedy, Terpsichore of choral song and dance, Erato of love poetry, Polyhymnia of sacred songs, and Urania, the Muse of astronomy. (*See* illus. page 187).

**Museums.** Again and again, in the pages of this or any other book of reference, you will find mention of museums of various kinds, not merely local museums mentioned in the descriptions of towns and cities but also the more important national museums in which most countries house many of their treasures. The scope of these museums is as wide as it can be. Some include every conceivable type of object that may be found in a country, or outside it, from natural history to relics of great men and works of art; others are more or less confined to one type of object, or even within narrower limits; others, again, show only materials gathered from one definite district; and some may be confined to works of one man or one period.

Museums of art are in general known as galleries (*see* National Gallery), especially where pictures make up the bulk of their objects. There are many art galleries of this type in London, which also has one great museum of art, taking the word in its widest sense, in the Victoria and Albert Museum, at South Kensington, London. This is probably the finest general collection of art treasures. Besides a number of pictures—especially water-colours of the British school—it contains furniture and wood-work, ironwork, pottery, dresses and costume, sculpture, carpets, goldsmiths' and silversmiths' work, and indeed everything of this type that one can think of. It has, like most large museums, an important library.

Britain's greatest museum is the British Museum, whose huge building is in Bloomsbury, London. This is mainly a museum of antiquity, and its contents cover an enormous period ; its collections of Greek and Egyptian material are specially fam-ous. It was founded in 1753. Besides the galleries in which the museum's treasures are shown to the public, there is at Bloomsbury the largest and most comprehensive library in the world, to which copies of every book published in Great Britain are presented, and a magnificent collection of prints and drawings.

London's museums of science are numerous. The chief are those grouped at South Kensington, comprising the Natural History Museum, the Science Museum, and the Museum of Practical Geology. Each of these represents a series of superb collections, and all of them are continually receiving additions. The Natural History Museum in particular shows only a small proportion of its treasures in its galleries, and indeed it is famous abroad as a storehouse rather than as a museum for display. In the Science Museum you may see many of the original in-ventions that have gone to make up our modern world, from the early steam-engines of James Watt to modern aero-planes ; there is also a fine collection of ship models.

In London, too, there are innumerable special museums. The London Museum, for instance, contains collections illustrating the city's history. In the Geffrye Museum is housed a fine collection illustrating the history of the furniture trade; the Horniman Museum in South London deals with anthropology and natural history. At Greenwich is a notable Maritime Museum. The Imperial War Museum is at Lambeth. Less well-known is the Soane Museum, in Lincoln's Inn Fields, London. It is contained in the former house of Sir John Soane (1753–1837), an architect. The collection includes architecture, sculpture and painting.

Most counties have their own museums, situated in the county town and dealing in a general way with the history, natural history, and antiqui-ties of the county. There are, too, museums dealing with famous men, most of them situated in their former homes and containing collections of their relics. An example of this is Down House, at Downe, in Kent, where Charles Darwin lived, and where rooms are arranged just as they were in his lifetime. (See page 977).

On the Continent, Paris has the Louvre, the world's largest collection of art treasures (see page 2033) ; Germany has many fine museums, though some of them were badly damaged during the Second World War (1939–1945); and Italy, Austria, and Spain have famous art museums. On the whole, however, these contain mainly art, and it is necessary to go to the United States to find general museums comparable with those of Britain. There, the New York Metropolitan Museum of Art has a fine collection, somewhat similar to that of the Victoria and Albert Museum. World-famous is the American Museum of Natural History, also in New York, in which are displayed groups of animals in their natural surroundings. (See plates between pages 72–73).

**Mushroom.** One of the best-known of the edible fungi (q.v.), the mushroom (*Agaricus campestris*) is a delicious vegetable when properly cooked. People lucky enough to have access to fields where mushrooms grow wild may gather them in late summer and autumn. But the de-mand far exceeds the supply, so mushrooms are cultivated commercially on a large scale, and for cropping all the year round. They may be grown in a heated green-house or a specially con-structed mushroom-house, in a hotbed garden frame, in a shed or cellar or cave, or (for planting May–July) in outdoor beds. Heat and moisture are both essential.

**COMMON FIELD MUSHROOMS**
Growing ' wild ' in open grassy meadows in late summer and autumn, the common edible mushroom, *Agaricus campestris*, is also cultivated on specially prepared beds as described in the text. See coloured plate facing page 1408.

E. Step

An outdoor bed is com-posed of stable manure, about 14 inches deep after being made quite firm. This material will develop considerable heat, and then its temperature will begin to fall. When it has fallen to about 80° F. the time has come for planting, with specially prepared "spawn" culti-vated from the mush-room's spores (the " dust " produced in vast quan-tities on the gills on the lower side of a mushroom's " cap "). This is generally sold in the form of bricks.

Each brick has to be broken into about eight pieces, and the pieces planted nine inches apart and two inches deep all over the stable manure bed. The surface is then covered two inches deep with sifted soil made firm, and the whole is topped with straw or dry bracken to the depth of a foot (to ensure complete darkness and to help maintain the temperature). To maintain moisture, slight waterings are given occasionally ; tepid water is used for this purpose. The mushrooms begin to push through the soil six to nine weeks after the planting of the spawn. They are best gathered in the unexpanded or "button" stage.

# The ANCIENT ART of Fabled ORPHEUS

*From the earliest times music has been one of the best-loved arts practised by Man ; and today, when so much music is broadcast by wireless, it is more widely appreciated than ever.*

**Music.** It has well been said that " Music washes away from the soul the dust of everyday life." The story of music begins with the story of the human family. Some of the very oldest fables that we have tell us of the power of music. We know that before ever musical instruments were made there must have been chants or songs. And yet, from the days when men heard answering voices in the hills and caverns, there are legends that tell of instruments so sweet that their music beguiled both men and the beasts.

**Pictures from old English books show that the eleven-stringed harp, and horns, were in use in the 9th century.**

One story is that the ancient Greek hero Orpheus charmed not only the beasts but the very trees and stones with the music of his lyre ; and a Chinese musician, reputed to have lived a thousand years before Orpheus, said : "When I play upon my *kin* (a stringed instrument) the animals range themselves before me spell-bound with melody."

Music is what we call an " abstract " art. It is seldom " about " anything. You cannot really describe things in music, or explain music in a definite way. But music can make a listener *feel* ; and so the earliest music was undoubtedly singing— words and shouting jumbled together—the spontaneous expression of emotion. Rhythm was the first element to develop, as you can tell from its connexion with dancing.

We read in the Bible (Genesis iv, 21) that Jubal was the " father of all such as handle the harp and the organ." In the temple of King Solomon, which was built almost a thousand years before the birth of Christ, we are told that there were thousands of priests, with trumpets and harps and psalteries, and singers who sang beside the altar to the harps and other instruments.

The Psalms of the Bible are the words of Hebrew songs. When you have been reading a Psalm, have you ever wondered what was meant by the word *selah* ? According to historians the Psalms were sung by two great choirs, one on either side of the temple. One choir sang the first line, and then the other choir answered with the next line :

*First Choir:* The earth is the Lord's and the fullness thereof.

*Second Choir:* The world and they that dwell therein.

*First Choir:* For he hath founded it upon the seas.

*Second Choir:* And established it upon the floods.

And so they continued through the Psalm until the word *selah* (pause) occurred ; then the singers paused and the instruments played an interlude alone, after which the singing was resumed. Where there was only one choir the opening and alternating lines were given by the priest, and the choir responded. This method is still used occasionally, and is known as " antiphonal " singing.

The Greeks were the first people to leave any sort of written music, and what they left was very crude. They used the letters of their alphabet to represent musical tones. These they placed above the words of the poems which they sang. But this only served to give, in a limited way, the pitch of the tone, and in no manner expressed the length of time during which it was sounded. The Greeks had music in their theatres, just as the Hebrews had in their temples. But naturally the music was different. They used both wind and stringed instruments, and pictures show the chorus dancing and playing their instruments as they sang.

Music as we know it began with the Christian era, though we really have very little knowledge of it during the first 400 years of this period. It was about the year A.D. 350 that the first singing schools were established, for the purpose of training singers for the Church services. In ancient times the congregation sang with the choirs, but the singing came to be so badly done that the ecclesiastical council of Laodicea, which controlled Church discipline in general, in the year A.D. 367 decided to allow only trained singers to take part. The songs they sang would sound strange to our ears, for all sang the same melody in unison. There was no alto, or bass, or tenor. More than this, the songs were mostly chants, which means that several words were sung, half spoken, to one tone. An advance was made by Pope Gregory the Great (c. 540–604), who revised the music of the Church services and introduced what is still called the " Gregorian Chant." All chants or songs had to be learnt by heart, because even then no satisfactory way of writing music had been devised.

### First Attempt at Musical Notation

A young monk named Guido, of Arezzo, Italy, became dissatisfied with this slow process. In a letter written in A.D. 1020 he complained: " When little boys have finally learned to read the psalter, they can read all other books. Whoever has once trimmed a vine or tree will be able to do it again as well or even better. These wonderful singing teachers, however, and their scholars may sing every day for a hundred years, and yet not be able to sing the response without instruction. In the Church service it often sounds not as if we were praising God but rather as if we were engaged in quarrelling among ourselves."

This young monk not only complained; he set out to remedy the trouble, with such success that he has been called the " father of music." He used the musical staff, much as we have it now, and also our system of singing by syllables. The idea came to Guido in this way. A certain Latin hymn, whose first six lines began respectively in the first six tones of the scale, suggested to him that if the pupils learned this song and remembered how to pitch the first tone of each line, they would then know the pitch of that tone wherever they saw it. The lines began with Latin words, the first syllables of which were: *Ut* (afterwards changed to *Do*), *Re, Mi, Fa, Sol, La.* The fact that *sol-fa* singing, with these same syllables, is still in use today proves the soundness of his theory. This idea would have failed had the staff not already been invented on which to write the syllables. The next step was to invent some way of showing the relative length of the tones. Gradually, block notes of different shapes were worked out with a dot or a hook to mark the accented note.

At first all music was sung in triple or three-pulse time, with one strong and two weak beats to each group. Later, double time, with one strong and one weak beat to each group, was used. Then bar lines were drawn across the staff before each strong or accented note. The notes were also made round instead of square, and written music began to look as we see it now.

Two staves were used, one for higher voices and another for lower voices, with a note for a short cross line (now called " middle C ") in the position where one line normally would stand between the two staves. This made the remaining notes of the octaves, written up and down, come in different places on their respective staves. The treble clef is used to mark the upper staff, and the *bass clef* marks the lower one. Notes above or below these staves are placed on or between short lines called "leger lines" prolonging the staff.

The scale resulting from playing all the notes on a staff so constructed is the scale of C major. Since two of the intervals in any scale are half steps or semi-tones, if one desires to write the scale for any other key there must be some device for raising or lowering the pitch indicated by any given note. Such devices are called chromatic symbols. These are the sharp (♯), indicating the half-tone above the written note, the flat (♭), marking the half-tone below the one written, the double sharp (x), meaning one *whole* tone above, and the double flat (♭♭), meaning one whole tone below the one written.

To avoid having to use these symbols before all such marked notes on the staff, it is customary to place the symbols just before the beginning of the passage on the staff. Every note so marked is then to be raised or lowered whenever it occurs. Since certain effects require that this be *not* done, this is indicated by placing a " cancel " mark (♮) before a note to show that it has its " natural " or unmarked staff value.

Sometimes the composer wants to have a gap, or blank spot, in his march of accents. To make this unmistakable, the composer marks it with a rest, of a shape signifying its duration.

To indicate the accent-pattern intended, a " time-signature " is given at the beginning of the music. The signature for waltz time, for example, is $\frac{3}{4}$. The 3 indicates three accents to the measure, while the 4 in the denominator means that one quarter-note is used for each accent. In foxtrot ($\frac{4}{4}$) time, the numerator 4 indicates four accents to the measure, each one a quarter-note in duration.

Although the music of the Church was now set down in writing, there was still much valuable music of which we have no written record. The common folk had their own songs and dances, and bards and minstrels wandered from court to court, always welcome because of their music.

Even during war the bards were welcome in enemy camps, so esteemed was the art of minstrelsy. There is a well-known story telling how King Alfred the Great disguised himself as a minstrel and entered the camp of the Danes as a spy on the eve of a great battle. What, we wonder, did he sing ? Very few of the old folk songs of this far-off time have come to us, and these are so changed, from having been passed down for generations, that we can hardly consider them representative in their present form.

About the 12th century secular music—that is, music that is not religious—began to be very popular. In southern France, the troubadours composed and sang songs of their lady-loves ; in Germany, the minnesingers composed similar songs as well as songs of chivalry, patriotism, and Nature, which they sang to the accompaniment of the harp. Other German singers in the 14th century formed themselves into a guild called the " master singers " (*die Meistersinger*). In this guild, rewards were given

**LEARNING TO WRITE MUSIC**

As early as the 6th century musicians had begun to indicate musical sounds by a complicated system of dashes, curves, hooks, and dots (top). By the 12th century they had introduced a four-line staff with square notes, thus indicating the intervals between the sounds. From the 15th to the 17th century square and lozenge-shaped notes with or without ' tails ' to indicate time values were used, with a five-line staff and key signatures, as in the third and fourth examples. From this it was a short step to the present system (last line above), with time divisions shown by bars at right angles to the staff.

for excellence in musical composition submitted at an annual contest. In Wales, an organization of singers known as the Eisteddfod (*q.v.*), or congress of bards, dating back long before the Christian era, assumed its present form during the 4th century, and continues to the present day. In these ways both vocal and instrumental music were stimulated. Many new instruments were used, and old ones improved.

Music is made up of three elements—melody, rhythm, and harmony. Up to this time only two elements, melody and rhythm, had been developed. Another hundred years were to elapse before the third element, harmony, was added.

For many centuries all singing had been in unison or in octaves, and an important step was made when two or more independent parts, or "voices," were used at the same time. We do not know when this began, but there exist specimens of part-writing which date from the 9th century. This music sounds strange to us, for it used successions of "fourths," such as C–F (sounded together) followed by D–G, or "fifths," such as C–G followed by D–A; whereas today our ears are accustomed to "thirds," such as C–E followed by D–F. In time part-writing developed.

The third element in music was at first called "counterpoint," so called because the notes of the melody written on the staff were called "points"; and now, in addition to these points, a second melody of points was written, point for point, for the two melodies were to be sung at the same time. As the choirs learned to master the two-voiced songs, third, fourth, and fifth melodies were added, giving rise to what is called the polyphonic ("many-voiced") form.

The earliest surviving example of secular part-writing, entitled Sumer is icumen in (Summer has come in), is believed to have been written as early as 1240 by an English monk, John of Fornsete. This is called a "canon" or "round," a type of composition in which each part has exactly the same tune, but enters separately, delayed perhaps by one phrase or two, as in the French children's song Frère Jacques. It also has a definite "ground bass," that is, a set part or figure, which is repeated all through the piece and not a real tune in itself. Presently the methods of polyphonic writing developed for Church use were employed for secular music in what were called "madrigals." These are part-songs with lively dancing rhythms and emphatically developed individual melodies for each voice. In Henry VIII's and Queen Elizabeth's reigns England was full of madrigals. If you went out to dinner, you were expected to sing your part at sight in a madrigal by Morley or Weelkes.

Every gentleman was supposed to be able to play the lute (a mandolin-like instrument) or the cittern, a stringed instrument resembling the lute whose modern descendant is the guitar. The favourite instrument for ladies was the virginal, or small harpsichord, on which Queen Elizabeth herself was a skilled performer. Several other instruments of the keyboard type also came into

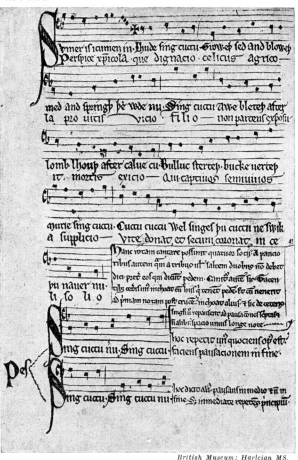

*British Museum; Harleian MS.*

## EARLIEST ENGLISH MUSIC

The first recorded specimen of early English music is the famous catch ' Sumer is icumen in,' a perfect example of a part song for four voices. The manuscript reproduced above was written not later than 1240, and, as a concession to religious feeling, had the words of a hymn in Latin written beneath the English verse.

popular use. These were used at first, singly or in combination, to accompany singers. Composers then saw their possibilities and began to write for them alone.

In the so-called Flemish school of composers (1400 to 1600) music abroad reached a higher point than it had ever before attained. The "Venetian School" of musicians (1527–1612) saw that the different voices in "counterpoint" really combined to form a succession of chords, and launched the idea we find running through modern music—that of chords enriching the principal melody and also carrying subordinate melodies.

With these new developments, musicians of the Catholic Church began to create really beautiful music for their formal services. The mass was a favourite form of composition. One outstanding name in this connexion is that of the Italian composer Palestrina (c. 1525–94). A peasant by birth, he was educated at Rome under a teacher from the famous Flemish school of music. He not only became the greatest organist of his time, but wrote masses which are as yet unsurpassed. Of one of his masses Pope Marcellus II said: " These are the harmonies of the ' new song ' which the

Debussy (1862–1918), whose compositions were as revolutionary as Wagner's. The last great exponent of French impressionistic music was Ravel (1875–1937), a pupil of Fauré (1830–1914).

In Russia a nationalistic school led by Borodin (1834–87) and Moussorgsky (1835–81) influenced such composers as Rimsky-Korsakov (1844–1908) and Tschaikovsky (1840–93). The Russian Revolution gave rise to a young and vigorous group, the chief of whom were Shostakovitch (b. 1906) and Prokofiev (b. 1891), whose aims appeared academic in comparison with those of Stravinsky (b. 1882), whose ballet Petroushka, produced in 1911, made him world famous.

Important developments in 20th century music may be traced to Honegger (b. 1892), who worked in France; Schönberg (b. 1874) in Austria before the Second World War (1939–45); and to Béla Bartók (1881–1945) in Hungary. The Finnish composer Sibelius (b. 1865) wrote symphonies and tone-poems which rank with those of the great masters.

Parry (1848–1918) and Stanford (1852–1924) began a revival in English music towards the end of the 19th century. Elgar (1857–1934), whose symphonies, and oratorio The Dream of Gerontius were famous throughout Europe, was one of the best-known composers of his time, and helped to restore English music to the position it enjoyed at the time of Purcell. Holst (1874–1934) was known chiefly for his suite The Planets. Delius (1862–1934), a solitary genius and profound recorder of Nature was in many respects one of the most sensitive composers. Sir Arnold Bax (b. 1883), appointed Master of the King's Musick in 1942, showed imaginative genius in his tone-poems and chamber music. Younger British composers include William Walton (b. 1902), Michael Tippett (b. 1905) and Benjamin Britten (b. 1913).

In recent years the gramophone and broadcasting have popularized all music to an extent never before achieved and have created a vast new music-loving public. The brilliant performances by the B.B.C. Symphony Orchestra, the playing of new works and the rescuing of pieces from oblivion, have had a remarkable effect upon musical appreciation. Yet, despite these inventions, far more people go to concerts. The Queen's Hall Promenade Concerts were a feature of London's musical life (the Hall was destroyed in an air raid in 1941), and after the Second Great War the " Proms " attracted even greater audiences to the Royal Albert Hall.

Professional musicians may be divided into three main sections: performers, teachers, and composers. To the first of these belong solo artists, whether pianists, violinists, vocalists, etc. ; conductors ; singers in the opera and the choirs of churches and cathedrals ; and, most numerous of all, members of orchestras and bands for restaurants and dance-halls. The second group includes professors of music at universities and colleges and teachers of music, who are employed now in most large schools. The third class includes composers of various types of music, and writers on music, including the critics.

## Musical Instruments.

If you stretch a string or wire tightly and pluck it, the string vibrates and makes a pleasing sound. If you close one end of a hollow tube and blow into (or across the top of) the other, the air in the tube is set vibrating and makes a different sort of sound. Again, if you strike a thin piece of leather stretched over a box, or a piece of metal suspended by a string, you get another kind of sound caused by the vibration of the leather or the metal.

From these three modes of causing sounds come all the various kinds of musical instruments. When you first look at the piano, the organ, and the many instruments used in bands or orchestras, they seem very different from each other. But a little observation will show that they all fall into these three great groups or families, according to the way they produce their sounds. Those in which the sound comes from vibrating strings are known as *stringed* instruments ; those in which a column of air is set in motion are called *wind* instruments; those which themselves are set vibrating by being sharply struck are called *percussion* instruments.

Of these families the string group is the largest. The piano (*q.v.*) is its best-known member. Open the case and you find the strings. They are of wire and are stretched across a great sounding board of fine strong wood that will not crack or warp. Now, with a quick touch press one of the keys in the centre of the keyboard. You will see that you cause a felt hammer to lift away from the string, and at the same time a metal hammer to strike the string. When this happens you hear a tone.

Now take your finger from the key, and you will see the felt hammer fall back against the string; at once the tone is hushed. This is because the felt pressing against the string stops the vibrations. Sound a key well down towards the left-hand end of the keyboard; the tone you will hear is much lower. This is because the bass strings are so much heavier and longer that they vibrate more slowly and the tone that reaches your ear is deeper.

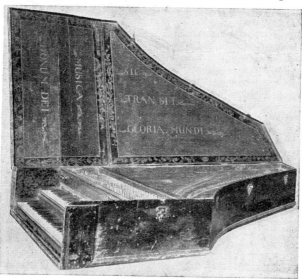

**HARPSICHORD USED BY HANDEL**
Before the invention of the pianoforte the most important of stringed instruments with a keyboard was the harpsichord. This photograph shows the one on which Handel played. It is now in the Victoria and Albert Museum, London.

*British Broadcasting Corporation*

## STRINGS, WIND AND PERCUSSION

Orchestral instruments are of three main types : strings, of which the largest kind, the double bass, is shown above ; wind, exemplified by clarinets (top right), with French horns behind ; percussion (lower right), with, in foreground, a xylophone, then tambourine, side drum and cymbals.

The harp (*q.v.*) has almost as many strings as the piano, but all except those in the bass are made of catgut, and, instead of being struck, they are plucked with the fingers. Most of the harp tones are thus made without vibrations of any metal, and are therefore sweeter and richer than the tones of the piano. When you hear a harp, you will recall the story about the boy David, who, thousands of years ago, played upon his harp to soothe the king. It is one of the oldest of all instruments.

Other less important stringed instruments, also plucked, but held across the body, are the guitar, the mandolin, and the banjo. The zither has a horizontal " table " of strings.

The violin (*q.v.*), the most important member of the string family, is played in a different manner. Instead of being plucked or struck, its strings are usually set vibrating by drawing a horse-hair bow across them, though occasionally harp-like effects are obtained from it by plucking (called *pizzicato*). Closely related to the violin are the viola, violoncello, and double bass, which are larger forms of the same type, producing deeper sounds.

Now we come to the great family of wind instruments. The flute, probably the most ancient of all musical instruments, is the typical member. This is simply a closed tube in which the air is set in vibration by blowing into it through a hole in the side. A smaller form of the flute with a shriller sound is called the piccolo. The recorder, forerunner of the modern flute, was played extensively in the 17th and 18th centuries. In recent times it has been revived for amateur performances, especially in England and Germany.

After the invention of the flute men discovered that they could get different and more varied effects by using a longer tube with a mouthpiece against which their lips would vibrate. Thus originated the wind instruments of the horn and trumpet type. Very long tubes are required to produce a deep tone, and so in most instruments of this kind the long tube is curved into an oval or circular form.

In one type, the trombone, the tube is made in two parts, one fitting into the other, so that it can be drawn in or out and thus made shorter or longer. The familiar cornet and the great bass tuba are also members of this group, which is known to musicians as the " brasses."

There is another group of wind instruments known as the " reeds," because they have reeds in their mouthpieces. These reeds are set in rapid vibration by the breath, and they in turn start the air vibrating in the tube, thus producing the sound. Among the common reed instruments are the oboe, cor anglais or English horn, bassoon, clarinet, and saxophone.

Next are the percussion instruments, those that themselves vibrate when struck. They are of two kinds, drums and bells. Everyone knows the big bass drum and the smaller drum, which are so much used in bands to mark the time and to produce rumbling martial effects. These drums produce indefinite sounds of no fixed pitch, but there is another kind, the kettle-drum, which can be tuned to a definite pitch and is much used in orchestras (see Drum). In the bell group are such instruments as the triangle, the glockenspiel, the xylophone, the celesta, and the cymbals.

The great pipe organ and the smaller cabinet or reed organ are improved wind instruments. In these the air supply is fed by means of bellows instead of the player's breath, and a number of pipes or freely ventilating reeds is brought under control by means of one or more keyboards (see Organ). In addition to these more important musical instruments, there are a great many minor ones. Since each musical instrument has its characteristic "timbre" (quality of tone) and strength of note, composers have a tremendous variety of musical effects which they can use in expressing their ideas. Even the existing variety, however, is not enough, and many composers have invented special instruments to produce particular effects for certain compositions.

## Musk-deer (Moschus moschiferus). From early times this animal has been hunted and trapped for the sweet-smelling musk which it yields. Neither male nor female has antlers, but the male has sharp tusks projecting about 3 inches downward from the upper jaw. These are used in fighting.

Musk-deer inhabit thickets on the slopes of the Himalayas in Central Asia, usually live in pairs, never in herds. A full-grown specimen is about three feet long and 20 inches high at the shoulders. They vary in colour, but are commonly greyish or yellowish-brown, and whitish below.

The musk is found in the male only, in a sac the size of a very small orange, situated on the under surface of the abdomen. The sac contains an ounce or more of the crude musk, which, when fresh, is said to resemble moist gingerbread in colour and consistency. Because of its powerful and enduring odour this substance is used in making perfumery, and is an important article of commerce.

## Musk-ox. In size and shape the musk-ox, Ovibos moschatus, resembles the ox, but in habit it is like the sheep, and hence it is sometimes called the musk-sheep. It is very agile, swift, and sure of foot. It is now restricted to Arctic America, but formerly it was more widely distributed; its bones have been found in Great Britain.

The musk-ox is a strange-looking creature, covered with long hair tangled at the shoulders. The legs are short and erect, the head massive, the tail very short; the horns meet in the middle of the

*Canadian Official News Bureau*
### MASSIVE MUSK-OX
With its long, shaggy coat of hair, its heavy build, and its long horns meeting across the top of its head, the musk-ox is a strange-looking beast ; yet it is agile and quick in its movements. One can see from its appearance that it is well-equipped for existence in the icy wastes of America's Far North.

forehead and curve downward and outward, with the tips pointing up. The coat close to the body is fine and soft, of a light brown colour; the outer hairs are coarser, darker, and sometimes a foot long. The hairy coat is shed during hot weather. A full-grown male reaches a weight of 450 lb. The animal gets its name from its peculiar musky odour, which is not due to a gland as in the musk-deer.

Musk-oxen live in herds and feed on grasses, lichens, moss, willow and pine shoots. The flesh and milk, although slightly flavoured with musk, provide food for the Eskimos, who can domesticate these creatures.

## Musk-rat. Perhaps no animal shows so well the dangers of interference with the "balance of Nature" as the musk-rat, Ondatra zibethicus. This rodent is a native of North America, where it is trapped and farmed for its fur, known as musquash, which is sometimes also used as a name for the animal itself. In 1907, in the hope of making it a valuable fur-producer in Europe, a pair were turned loose in Austria. Free from their natural enemies, these beasts quickly spread all over Central Europe, so that they became a permanent and ineradicable pest, costing many thousands of pounds annually to the governments of countries in which they were established. Wherever they settle, these creatures undermine the banks of rivers, canals, and lakes, make swamps of the fields surrounding the stretches of water, and ruin the drainage system of the land.

In 1927 a few musk-rats were introduced to England for fur-farming ; but, realizing the danger—for some of them always escape—the Ministry of Agriculture forbade any further importations. Some of the musk-rats had already escaped, and were doing damage, but these were soon killed off. Yet it was 10 years before the Ministry could really claim that the "musk-rat menace" was over.

A full-grown musk-rat is over a foot long, very heavily built, with a tail of nearly another 12 inches. The fur is red-brown, and the hind-feet are partially webbed to assist swimming. The creatures live in burrows in the banks of stretches of shallow or stagnant water, and in the middle of lake, stream, or swamp they construct "lodges," huge mounds of bitten-off reeds and vegetable refuse. These provide winter food for their inhabitants, and are eaten from the centre outwards. Reeds, floating on the surface and sharply bitten off at the ends, are a sure sign of musk-rat presence.

## Mussolini, BENITO (1883–1945). The son of a blacksmith, Mussolini was born in the Italian province of Forli on July 29, 1883. He became successively school teacher, bricklayer's helper, journalist, teacher of French, editor, soldier,

member of parliament, revolutionary leader, and then dictator of Italy—all before he was 40.

Though he was educated for the profession of teaching his chief interest was in politics, and he became an extreme Socialist. His fiery utterances led to his expulsion, first from Switzerland (where he had gone to continue his studies, in poverty-stricken circumstances, at Lausanne) and later from the Trentino, then under Austrian rule. Continuing his revolutionary propaganda in Italy, he was sent to prison: on his release he became editor of the official Socialist paper Avanti.

During those years his ardour for Socialism had been waning, and when the First World War broke out in 1914 he left the Socialist party and founded a new paper (Popolo d'Italia), through which he urged Italy to join the Allies, which she did on May 23, 1915. He himself fought in the ranks and was wounded when on bombing practice. Then he returned to his work of firing the national spirit for victory and founded groups of ex-soldiers, known as Fascisti, to combat defeatism.

After the Armistice of November 1918 Mussolini turned the Fascists into a political party, and between them, on the one hand, and the Socialists and Communists on the other, violent clashes became frequent all over the country.

In October 1922 Mussolini denounced the Government, demanding a new Parliament. Later in the same month (October 27) he ordered a general Fascist rising and staged a march on Rome, he himself following later by train when on October 30 King Victor Emmanuel III, fearing civil war, invited him to form a Government. The change of government he effected was profound. The king remained, but all actual power was centred in the hands of Mussolini as Prime Minister. He did away with Parliament, its place being taken by the Fascist Grand Council, dominated by himself. The industrial life of the country was controlled by a series of Corporations, who received their orders from Mussolini. He assumed the title of *Duce* (pron. dōō-'chā), meaning leader. (*See* Fascism: Italy).

His suppression of the free press and of all criticism and his brutal treatment of all anti-Fascists, combined with his love of military display and his vainglorious speeches, gave Mussolini the semblance of unlimited power. But he later became subservient to his imitator Hitler, in the Alliance called the Rome-Berlin Axis, created in 1936.

**BENITO MUSSOLINI**
Dictator of Italy from 1922 to 1943, Mussolini strove to make her a great military power and to gain control of the Mediterranean. He was killed by Italian patriots in 1945.

*Keystone*

Throughout the troubled years between Hitler's rearming of Germany and the outbreak of the Second World War in 1939, Mussolini gambled with the destiny of his country, and in the end lost both his own life and the African empire he had aimed at building up on the model of ancient Rome.

His aggressive foreign policy, which resulted in the annexation of Abyssinia in 1936, his militarization of all Italy, and his successful defiance of the League of Nations, from which he withdrew in 1936, were all part of his plan to give Italy new power and authority in international affairs. His intervention in the Spanish Civil war (1936–39), his anti-British propaganda and his expressed intention to dominate the Mediterranean greatly increased tension in Europe and led to his own dependence upon Hitler. On April 7, 1939, he invaded and quickly conquered Albania, with a view to obtaining a base from which later to attempt the conquest of Greece. On May 22 of the same year he concluded a formal military alliance with Germany.

At the outbreak of the Second World War (1939–45) he declared Italy a non-belligerent, but his cupidity and ambition led him to declare war on June 10, 1940, against France, already apparently overwhelmed by the German army: and against the United Kingdom, too, which he thought would soon yield to Hitler. Next, in October 1940, Italy under Mussolini attacked Greece, but the Greeks resisted so fiercely that Italy had to be rescued from that adventure by German troops, who overran Greece in April 1941. In the years 1941 to 1943 Italy lost the whole of her African empire. British forces speedily conquered Italian East Africa in 1941, and the campaign in North Africa terminated in May 1943 with the surrender of the German and Italian armies in Tunisia. In July 1943 the Fascist Grand Council turned against Mussolini and he was compelled to resign. Held prisoner by the provisional Government, which was suing for peace with the Allies, he was rescued by German parachutists and he then established a Fascist Republic in Northern Italy behind the German lines.

On September 3, 1943, Italy capitulated to the Allies, but German forces continued to resist in Central and Northern Italy until May 1945. When the German surrender in Italy was near, Mussolini tried to escape to Switzerland, was captured by Italian patriots on April 26, 1945, and shot: his body was ignominiously displayed in the Piazza Loreto, Milan.

**Mustard.** Physicians knew the medicinal value of mustard over 2,000 years ago, and it was early used as a condiment. Mrs. Clements, of Durham, England, in 1720, is said to have been the first to grind the seeds into flour for table use. Commercial mustard is prepared from two species of the mustard plant—one having white seed (*Brassica alba*), the other black (*B. nigra*). Most of the black seed comes from California and Kentucky. The best grades of white seed are cultivated in England and the Netherlands, but the plant will grow almost anywhere. The seeds, which are extremely tiny, weigh from one-fiftieth to three-fiftieths of a grain.

Dry mustard is prepared by cleaning the seeds, extracting their oil in presses, grinding them, and sifting the flour through silk cloth. Usually the two varieties are blended, the black for aroma, the white for pungency. Wet or prepared mustard is made by adding vinegar, salt, and spices to the crushed seeds.

Mustard is a counter-irritant, used as a plaster, in liniment, or in foot baths. It is also used as an emetic, taken in warm water. White mustard is also grown as a salad plant, for eating in the seedling stage.

In addition to the two foregoing, British species include the charlock (*B. arvensis*), commonly seen flaunting its yellow flowers from May to August, as a weed infesting cornfields; and the Jersey mustard (*B. adpressa*), which in some respects closely resembles the black-seeded mustard plant.

**Mysore.** An Indian State forming part of the republic of India. Mysore is on the south-west or Malabar coast of the sub-continent of India, with Bombay on the north, Madras on the east and south, and Coorg on the south-west. The surface of the State, which has an area of 29,458 square miles, is mainly flat, but here and there isolated hills rise from the plain.

Much land is irrigated from the Cauvery river, but as the country receives both the north-east and south-west monsoons there is an ample rainfall. Most of the people are engaged in agriculture; millet, cotton, sugar cane and rice are grown. Gold is mined at Kolar, and manganese at Shimoga.

Mysore city, the capital, has a population of 150,000, the largest town being Bangalore (248,300). Efficient government has gained for Mysore the reputation of being a model State.

In the latter part of the 18th century Mysore was ruled by a Mahomedan adventurer Haider Ali and his son Tippoo, who besieged the British in Madras until Sir Eyre Coote relieved the city in 1784. Tippoo was finally defeated by the Duke of Wellington (then Colonel Wellesley) at the battle of Seringapatam in 1799—and was killed in the fight. The British assumed control of the State in 1831, but in 1881 self-government was restored under a Hindu Maharaja. When British rule in India ceased in August 1947, Mysore joined the new Dominion of India. The population is 7,329,100.

**Mythology.** When primitive Man first sought to understand how the world had come to be as it is, and how the sun, moon and stars followed their regular courses, he invented stories of beings like himself but immeasurably greater and immensely more powerful. According to some of these stories, or myths as they are called, one such being

had originally created Man, and taught him what to eat and other useful things.

Myths of these kinds have been traced among the ancient civilizations of Babylonia and Egypt, and many are still current among backward tribes. It is to the Greeks, who were a nation of poets, that we owe the most beautiful stories of gods and heroes, and it is their mythology that has made the deepest impression in literature.

It is interesting that some of the myths found in lands far apart are remarkably alike. Many of the Greek myths are like not only those of the sub-continent of India and of Egypt, but also those of the Scandinavian countries, and even, in some cases, the myths of the American Indians. Both Nature and men are much the same all the world over, and it is natural that the first attempts to find answers to the riddles of day and night, earth and sky, sun, moon and stars, should have resulted in similar stories.

It is, perhaps, even more interesting to discover how each race has stamped its own character upon its mythology. That of the Greeks reflects their joy in life and love of beauty. Scandinavian (Norse) mythology reveals a warlike spirit, and shows the conflict with stern and rugged forces of Nature. That of the Hindus is full of awe at the mysterious and sublime powers of Nature. The mythologies of savages are almost unbelievably childish and absurd. Their gods are often represented as beasts. The Bushmen of South Africa regard an insect, the mantis, as the highest of their supernatural beings. The Zulus worshipped their ancestors, which appear to men as snakes.

Besides the beliefs still held by savages and formerly by the less educated classes in such countries as Russia, Japan, the sub-continent of India, and China, and besides the nursery stories— myths of Jack the Giant Killer type—there is a constant tendency for myths to spring up in connexion with men and events which appeal to our sense of the marvellous. However, the spread of science and the preservation of records, together with the love of accuracy fostered by our historians, tend to prevent the formation of new myths and to break down the belief in old ones. Mythology, nevertheless, is an important part of history, for the light it throws on early ideas.

It is also a part of literature, and we cannot understand the literature of the early peoples without knowing something about their mythology. Especially is this true of Greek and Roman literature, and as this literature has had a profound influence upon that of today, so has the old mythology become interwoven with the very fabric of our literature.

**Mytilene** (LESBOS). In this beautiful island of the Aegean Sea, now again called by its early name Lesbos, Greek lyric poetry flourished. It was the birthplace of the musician Terpander (*c.* 700 B.C.), and of the poet Alcaeus (*c.* 600 B.C.), and the poetess Sappho (*c.* 580 B.C.).

With an area of 675 square miles, it is mountainous and very fertile. Olives are the principal product and are largely exported. The population of the island is 165,000.

In 1462 it came under Turkish control, and so remained until the close of the Balkan Wars (1913), when, with other Aegean islands, it passed to Greece. The chief town is Mytilene (population 28,000).

# N

**Nagoya.** Third largest of the cities of Japan, Nagoya is on the island of Honshu, midway between Tokyo and Osaka. The city is famous for its enamel work; the first cloisonné products were made there. About 12 miles from Nagoya is Seto, where glazed pottery was manufactured after the secret process involved had been learned in China in 1229. A centre for the manufacture of textiles, Nagoya had aircraft factories and locomotive works. During the Second World War (1939-45) it was frequently bombed by the United States air force, and nearly one-third of the city was destroyed. The population is 483,000.

**Nails.** Not all nails are made of metal, for when the carpenter has to fix oak timbers together he may use a hardwood pin called a " trenail," the reason being that the juices of oak and certain other woods corrode iron or steel nails, especially when the work (as in an oak-paled fence) is exposed to the weather. The Old English word for both tree and timber is *treo;* hence the name trenail.

The main kinds of nail are wire nails, cut nails and wrought nails. The first are stamped out from mild steel plate of the proper thickness for the body of the nail, some receiving no other treatment—for example, floor brads, used to nail down floorboards to joists. Clasp nails have the body tapered in thickness as well as in width, and have a head which projects on two sides; the floor brad has

merely an L-shaped projection on one side and is the same thickness throughout. Wrought nails today are mainly those with fancy or extra large heads, which are made by hammering, or by a similar operation done by machine. Cut nails are not fine-pointed, and some skill is needed in their use if the wood is not to be split in the process. The brad-awl got its name from its use in boring a starting hole for the cut brad.

Wire nails, sometimes called " French " nails, have taken the place of the older kinds except for heavy or rough work, and certain special operations —for example, nailing down flooring. The points are sharp, and the heads are a better shape. Round wire nails are used for general work ; oval nails can be employed where the nail-head is not to be very conspicuous ; the head is merely an enlargement of the oval-section body. But, of course, the oval head has not the same holding power as the bigger one of the round-bodied nail. Some nails, known as " lost-heads," have a round shank and a tiny head rather like that of the oval type. Clout nails, again, have an extra broad head.

Wire nails are made continuously by an automatic machine which works off a reel of wire of the proper thickness for the nail shank. Vice-like jaws grip a portion of the wire and hold it firm; before this, the wire has travelled through straightening rolls to take out the bend. Simultaneously, a

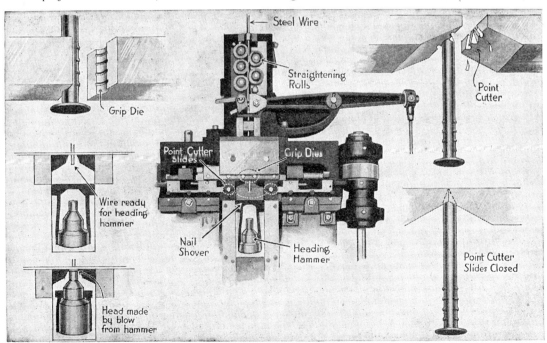

## MAKING A THOUSAND NAILS A MINUTE

This group of pictures shows how steel wire is made into nails. After entering the machine and passing through the straightening rolls, the wire is caught by the grip die, which forms the barbed or roughened portion, to give more holding power. Then the point cutter closes upon the wire, forms the point and almost severs the nail. Simultaneously the heading hammer comes up against the lower end and flattens out the head. As soon as made, the nails are knocked off from the parent wire by the ' nail shover,' and fall into a basket at the rate of a hundred to a thousand a minute !

heading hammer, working in conjunction with a die, forms the nail-head, and a point cutter shapes the point and at the same time partly severs the complete nail from the rest of the wire. More wire is fed into the machine, and the process is repeated for the next nail. For small and fine nails the speed is very rapid; stouter nails take longer, and the rate at which they are turned out varies from a hundred to a thousand a minute accordingly.

Most wire nails have smooth shanks, but in some types the top of the shank, under the head, is roughened or barbed to afford a firmer grip in the wood. Our pictures show such a nail in process of manufacture. It must be remembered that it is friction which keeps a nail in place ; and the same force which we use in hammering it into the timber must be used to pull it out. Have you ever tried to use a steel gramophone needle as a nail ? You will find that, owing to the smooth, highly polished surface, it can hardly be persuaded to stay in the wood at all !

Cabinet makers and others use steel " points "—headless nails—for certain work where a head must not show, but these are far from being as smooth as the gramophone needle. The holding power of a nail depends roughly upon the depth to which it enters the wood. As an example, a six-inch wire nail with a smooth shank was driven into a piece of Australian hardwood ; in order to pull it out again, a force amounting to about 1,000 lb. per inch of depth was required. When a nail is hammered into timber, the point forces the fibres aside, and they close in on the shank again with considerable force. The nail is thus a kind of wedge, and it is interesting to note that the old-fashioned cut nail, with its rougher surface and its tapering shank, has greater holding power than our modern wire nail !

Ezekiel Reed, an American, took out a patent for a nail-making machine in 1786. In an improved form this machine is still used for making cut nails. In 1780 a nail-making machine was invented by T. Clifford in England. About a century afterwards the wire nail came into general use, almost driving out the cut nail.

**Nairnshire.** With a coastline of about 10 miles on the Moray Firth, this Scottish county is bounded on the east by Moray, on the south and west by Inverness. Four-fifths of Nairnshire, which has an area of 163 square miles, is hilly, the highest peak being Cairn Glas (2,162 feet). The chief rivers are the Findhorn and the Nairn.

Much of the land is only suitable for sheep-farming, though the coastal plain is fertile. Industries include distilling, tanning, and sandstone and granite quarrying. The county town is Nairn (population 4,200). Also in the shire are Cawdor and Kilravock, with their castles. The population of Nairnshire is 8,700.

**Names.** Why should there be so many persons bearing the surnames of Smith and Brown ? Let us find out by going far back into the history of names—one of the most fascinating of studies, because every name, both of persons and of places, has a meaning and a story of its own.

In very early times each person had only one name—his " given " name—which he might receive at birth or later. Where men lived in small tribal groups this single name was enough.

But in larger communities there would be many of the same name, and so it became necessary to add some qualification—perhaps the name of the father—as a distinction. Thus you could distinguish between two men of the same name by calling one Demosthenes " the son of Clinias," and the other Demosthenes " the son of Socrates."

Sometimes the name of the birthplace was added, and in many cases a nickname denoting some personal peculiarity would be used to make a distinction between people with the same name. Thus one Demosthenes might be called " of Athens," and another " The Lame." With the Romans this practice developed into the use of genuine " family names " (cognomina), which descended to all members of the same house, in addition to the " personal name " borne by the individual. In the name Gaius Julius Caesar, Gaius is the *praenomen* (first or given name), Julius the *nomen* (name of the gens or clan), and Caesar the *cognomen* or family name.

### How Family Names Arose

Family names did not come into general use in England until after the Norman Conquest (1066). There were so many Johns and Samuels and Williams that it became convenient to refer to a man as John the *smith*, John the *miller*, or John the *carpenter*, and so in the course of time these designations became accepted as surnames or family names. The names Taylor, Wright, Turner, Clark (clerk), Cook, Carter, and Gardiner are a few of the many derived in this way from occupations. The reason there are so many Smiths today is that in medieval times the name was applied to all smiths or workers in metal—blacksmiths, goldsmiths, silversmiths, and locksmiths.

Another common way of forming surnames was from the Christian name of the father. Such names are called *patronymics*, meaning father-names. Johnson is simply " John's son," and Jones and Jennings are modified forms of the same surname.

The name of Brown was first given to a man as a nickname because of his complexion, or possibly because of the colour of his dress. In like manner such names as Long, Short, White, Little, Longfellow, and Cruikshank were originally derived from personal characteristics. Other names were derived from the place where a man lived or from which he had come, as Hill, Cliff, Field, Dale, Ford, Lake, Wood.

Biblical characters and saints have furnished many surnames. Adam has given the familiar names Adams, Adamson, Ade, Atkins, and Atkinson, all of which mean " the son of Adam." From Elijah come Ellis and Eliot, and so on.

In most other languages surnames are formed in much the same way as in English. Corresponding to the English suffix *son*, we find the Scots prefix *Mac*, the Irish *O'*, the Norman-French *Fitz*, and the Welsh *ap*, which give us the names Macdonald, O'Brien, Fitzherbert, and Bowen (originally ap Owen). The Russian suffix -*ovitch* likewise means " son," hence the Russian name Ivanovitch, son of Ivan, the Russian equivalent of John, corresponds to the English Johnson.

Place-names are a particularly interesting subject of study. In Britain, almost the only relic of the Celtic peoples are words like *dun* (a fortified hill), *aber* (a meeting-place of two rivers), and *ben* (a mountain). The Danish invasion of East Anglia has left its mark in terminations like *by* (a village). Saxon suffixes include the very common *ton* (a town) and *ham* (a hamlet). Other names often show the military nature of the Roman occupation. *Castra* (a camp), for example, gives us names like Chester, Doncaster and Winchester.

**Nanking.** On the Yangtze river in the Chinese province of Kiangsu some 200 miles west of Shanghai, Nanking is a walled city that has been capital of China several times. The city is said to have given its name to Nankeen cloth, which is manufactured locally; other products are satin crêpe, paper, porcelain, and Indian ink. Government establishments include an arsenal, a powder factory and a mint. There are a university, a naval college, and an agricultural experimental station, with a school of forestry.

After Nanking became the Chinese capital in 1928 airports were constructed, new wide roads built, harbour improvements carried out, and buildings to house Government departments were erected. Outside the city, on Purple Mountain, is the tomb of Dr. Sun Yat Sen (1866–1925), the first President of the Chinese Republic.

Dating from the 5th or 6th centuries B.C., Nanking (meaning Southern Capital) was the capital of China for several periods between A.D. 222 and 501, and again from 1368 to 1403, when Peking (*q.v.*) became the northern capital (capital

*Daily Mirror*

**FRIDTJOF NANSEN**

First becoming famous for his adventurous crossing of Greenland in 1888, Nansen is seen here during that expedition. He received the Nobel peace prize in 1922, and died on May 13, 1930.

of all China in 1421). In 1912 China was proclaimed a Republic, and in 1928 the Government moved to Nanking. In 1937, when Japan invaded China, the city was all but destroyed by the Japanese, who captured it in the December of the same year. During the occupation it was for a time the capital of the Japanese-sponsored Government. On August 25, 1945, Chinese troops entered the city, where the formal surrender of the Japanese forces in China took place on the following September 9. On May 1, 1946, Nanking was capital again for a while. The population is 1,100,000.

**Nansen,** FRIDTJOF (1861–1930). In the story of Arctic exploration Nansen's achievements will always be remembered. He was born near Christiania (Oslo) in Norway on October 10, 1861, was educated at Christiania University, and was appointed assistant curator at the Natural History Museum at Bergen, Norway.

In 1888–89 he crossed Greenland from east to west, studying the people and natural history; a description of his journey appeared in his books The First Crossing of Greenland, and Eskimo Life. With a view to testing his theory of the existence of a current flowing across the Arctic regions towards the east coast of Greenland, he sailed in 1893 from Christiania in a specially built ship named the Fram, which he allowed to drift with an ice floe. Satisfied that his theory was correct, Nansen left the vessel and travelled across the ice until he

**NANKING'S MEMORIAL TO A NATIONAL HERO**

*Central Press*

Just outside the city of Nanking is the tomb of Sun Yat Sen, the Chinese Republican leader who died in 1925 and whose memory is still held in reverence in China. His body was interred in the mausoleum seen on the left of the photograph, in 1929. The approach to the tomb is a magnificent tree-lined avenue, cut through the old city and extending to the banks of the Yangtze river. The mausoleum and the arch in front of it show modern Chinese architecture at its best.

reached latitude 86 degrees 14 minutes, the most northerly point attained at that time. His account of this expedition is entitled Farthest North.

After the separation of Norway from Sweden in 1905 Nansen was appointed the first Norwegian ambassador to Great Britain; he resigned in 1908 to carry out more research work in the Arctic. In 1919 he became the Norwegian delegate to the League of Nations, and in 1920 was appointed Director of an international organization for the repatriation of ex-prisoners of war from Russia. During 1921–23 he was in charge of famine relief in Russia. He received the Nobel (*q.v.*) peace prize in 1922, and died at Oslo on May 13, 1930.

**Nantes.** (Pron. nahnt). Capital of the department of Loire-Inférieure, this city of France is built on several islands in the Loire river, and, although 35 miles from the sea, is a busy port. Besides shipbuilding the main industries are engineering, paper-making, food preserving and the manufacture of chemicals. The Cathedral of St. Pierre was founded in the 6th century, but was extensively rebuilt at later dates.

Nantes was the capital of the Gallic tribe of the Namnetes, and for long was ruled by the Dukes of Brittany, coming into the possession of the King of France in 1491. It was there in 1598 that Henry IV of France issued the famous Edict of Nantes, by which religious toleration and civil rights were granted to the Huguenots or French Protestants.

Occupied by German troops on June 20, 1940, during the Second World War (1939–45), the dock area of Nantes was bombed several times by Allied aircraft. The city was liberated by United States forces on August 9, 1944, the Germans offering little opposition, though they destroyed the old Pont de la Vendée before withdrawing. The population is 200,300.

**Naples,** ITALY. To catch the spirit of Naples the visitor should see it first as he sails between the islands of Ischia and Capri and enters the celebrated Bay of Naples, some 22 miles wide. There, at the bay's northern apex, lies perhaps the most picturesque and most fascinating of Italy's historic cities. As the ship steams forward, the sloping city appears, flanked seven miles to the east by Mount Vesuvius, with its smoking crater, and on the west by the graceful heights of Posilipo. During the last century the population increased at a rate far more rapid than did the dwelling-places, and for many decades the poorer people were crowded together so thickly that disease and crime flourished unchecked in filthy tenements. In 1884 an epidemic of cholera carried off thousands of victims. Shortly afterwards the centre of the old district was demolished. Modern buildings and broad streets were built, and an excellent water supply and drainage system introduced.

Naples is an industrial centre, producing ships, cars, locomotives, glass, cotton, wool, perfumes,

*E.N.I.T.*

NAPLES, LARGEST CITY OF SOUTHERN ITALY

One of the finest open spaces in Naples is the Piazza del Plebiscito, seen in this photograph taken before the Second World War (1939–45), during which it suffered little damage. The domed building in the foreground is the Church of San Francisco de Paola, built between 1815 and 1818. Opposite it (to the left) can be seen part of the Royal Palace, once the home of the Kings of Naples and Sicily, with a façade of 554 feet; it contained the National Library. Between the two, on the far side of the Piazza, is the palace which formerly belonged to the Prince of Salerno

linen and silk. The chief exports are wine, brandy, fruit, paper and hemp. The city has a number of museums, theatres and opera houses. The cathedral dates back to 1272; the university was founded in 1224. The National Museum of Naples is one of the most important in the world. In it are housed objects dug up at near-by Pompeii and Herculaneum—cities utterly destroyed by an eruption in A.D. 79—and unequalled Greek and Roman relics, the Farnese (old Italian family) group of paintings and sculpture, and 600,000 books, pamphlets, and manuscripts containing many rare historical writings. A big marine aquarium contains one of the largest collection of living sea animals in the world.

Naples originated in an old Greek settlement (called *Neapolis*, the New City), founded about 450 B.C. and conquered by the Romans in 326 B.C. The Normans captured the city about 1130, and it became the capital of the " Kingdom of the Two

Sicilies." In the Middle Ages it was continually changing hands, until in 1504 the King of Spain became the ruler of the Two Sicilies. In 1713 it passed to the Hapsburgs of Austria, and then in 1743 to a branch of the Bourbons of France. While Napoleon Bonaparte was conquering Europe, his elder brother Joseph sat for a time on the throne of the Two Sicilies, to be followed by Joachim Murat, Napoleon's brother-in-law. After Napoleon's fall Naples was again under the Bourbons until it became part of the new kingdom of Italy in 1860.

As one of Italy's chief industrial centres, Naples was repeatedly bombed and shelled by the Allies during the Second World War (1939–45). Allied forces entered the city on October 1, 1943, after the Germans had withdrawn. The harbour facilities had been demolished and many of the factories and public buildings destroyed. The Germans also burnt the contents of the university library. The population is 967,700.

# *The* RISE *and* FALL *of* NAPOLEON

*B*oundless *ambition proved the downfall of Napoleon, for it seemed he could never be satisfied with his achievements. Though his military successes have attracted most notice, he was also a great statesman and law-giver.*

**Napoleon I.** (1769–1821). Not a drop of French blood flowed through the veins of Napoleon Bonaparte, who for 16 years was the absolute master of France. He was barely a Frenchman by birth, for the island of Corsica, in which his native town of Ajaccio was situated, was handed over to France by the republic of Genoa in 1768, only a year before Napoleon was born on August 15, 1769.

Napoleone Buonaparte—such was the Italian name under which he was christened—was a typical Corsican, " moody and exacting but withal keen, brave, and constant." For years his most intense emotion was hatred of France, which he regarded as an oppressor of his native land. He carried this feeling with him to the French military school at Brienne, to which he was admitted at the age of nine. At 16 he began his service in the French army as second lieutenant of artillery, but the stirring events of the French Revolution, which broke out in 1789, aroused little interest in him. He passed much of his time on leave in Corsica during the early period of the Revolution, and his studies of the works of the French philosopher Rousseau disposed him to accept the new political doctrines. He came into conflict with the monarchist faction on the island and, with the rest of his family, was forced to escape to France in June 1793.

In the same year, at Toulon, Napoleon first gave evidence of his energy and genius in directing the artillery at the siege of that rebellious French city. But for a time fate was against him. Robespierre and the Jacobins (*q.v.*) with whom he had established friendly relations, fell from power;

and in 1795 Napoleon was back once more in Paris, deprived of his command, without money or friends, and under suspicion by reason of his Jacobin connexions.

That year was the last year of misfortune for a time. In September, with what Carlyle called a " whiff of grape-shot," he defended the Republican Government against a serious royalist rising in Paris. The Directory (government) rewarded the young man by making him commander of the French army of Italy, against the Austrians and their allies. In the meantime Napoleon had fallen in love with and married a young widow, Josephine de Beauharnais. (*See* Josephine).

The Italian campaign showed General Bonaparte's great military genius, and stirred to life again great ambition. In 1796 he defeated the Sardinian troops five times in 11 days, threatened Turin, and compelled peace. Then Bonaparte turned eastwards against the Austrians and had advanced to within 80 miles of Vienna when the enemy offered peace, in 1797. By the treaty of Campo Formio. France was given Belgium (the Austrian Netherlands), and accepted the Rhine as the frontier between the republic and the Cisalpine Republic which Napoleon had established in northern Italy. By way of compensation he gave to Austria most of the territories of the old Venetian Republic, which he had destroyed.

Napoleon next persuaded the French Government to send him with a large army to Egypt. There on the banks of the Nile he hoped to strike a blow at France's most powerful enemy, England, by opening a route to India. He seized Alexandria, and at the Battle of the Pyramids, fought near Cairo

**NAPOLEON I**
Master of most of Europe early in the 19th century, Napoleon died on May 5, 1821. This picture is after the painting by H. Delaroche.

(July 1798), the Egyptian army was defeated: but Napoleon's fleet was destroyed by the British in the Battle of the Nile at Aboukir Bay (*see* Nelson, Horatio), and he was cut off from reinforcements. He succeeded in evading the British frigates and landed in France on October 9, 1799.

There he found the Government discredited, and joined in a plot which in November 1799 overthrew the old regime and set up in its place a government called the Consulate, with Bonaparte as the first of three consuls. In 1802 he became First Consul for life. (*See* illustration in page 1367).

Napoleon had now grasped political power and become master of France. His old ambition was realized, but already new ones were forming. He had failed to build up an eastern empire, but now aspired to restore the western one of Charlemagne. At the battle of Marengo (1800) he defeated the Austrians, and by the treaty of Amiens, in 1802, France obtained peace with Britain. But even in peace the First Consul continued to carry out his ambitious plans. In the 14 months before the conflict began anew he became president of the Italian Republic, annexed Piedmont, Parma, and the island of Elba to France, planned the partition of Turkey and the foundation of a colonial empire to include America, Egypt, India and Australia.

The other European Powers felt compelled to renew the conflict : but still victory smiled on

*From the painting by H. Lefevre, Musée de Versailles; photo, Neurdein.*
**NAPOLEON IN HIS CORONATION ROBES**
**On December 2, 1804, Napoleon was crowned Emperor of the French in the cathedral of Notre Dame, Paris, and in this portrait he is seen in his Coronation robes, with the orb on his right. The Pope was present to perform the ceremony, but Napoleon seized the crown and himself placed it on his head.**

Napoleon. By his complete defeat of the Austrians and Russians at Austerlitz (December 2, 1805), by his crushing blow to the Prussians at Jena (October 14, 1806), and by the battle of Friedland against the Russians (June 14, 1807) Napoleon brought most of Europe to his feet.

Only one obstacle apparently barred his way to the complete mastery of western Europe: that was Great Britain. In 1805 he had planned to invade Great Britain and reduce it to submission. But the favourable moment never came, and after England's Navy under Nelson had destroyed the French and Spanish fleets in the battle of Trafalgar (October 1805), Napoleon had no chance to conquer Britain, for without command of the sea he could not transport his armies.

Napoleon's fame rests not only on his military genius but also on his work as a statesman. A sound currency was established in France, the Bank of France created, roads and canals improved, and agriculture and industry fostered.

The Roman Catholic Church, which had been suppressed in the Revolution, was re-established by an agreement with the Pope, known as the Concordat of 1801. The old confused legal system was swept away, and Napoleon founded a new system— the Code Napoléon.

Step by step now Napoleon was building up his own position. In 1804 he secured a popular vote sanctioning a change from the Consulate to an Empire, with the title Emperor of the French and the right to hand down the throne to his descendants. In 1809 he divorced Josephine and married Marie Louise (1791–1847), the 18-year-old daughter of the Austrian emperor, thus allying himself with one of the oldest royal families of Europe. He set himself, also, to the work of reorganizing Europe. The Cisalpine Republic was now changed to a monarchy, Napoleon himself being crowned king of Italy.

" Roll up that map of Europe: there will be no need for it for 10 years to come ! " the English Prime Minister Pitt had said after the battle of Austerlitz. And for almost that period Napoleon changed the map at his will. His stepson Eugène was made viceroy of Italy. Napoleon's brother Louis received the kingdom of Holland: and Joseph became king first of Naples and then of Spain— General Murat, who had married Napoleon's sister, succeeding to the vacant Neapolitan throne. The shadowy Holy Roman Empire was dissolved in 1806.

The high point in Napoleon's career was reached in the years which followed the peace of Tilsit (1807). There, on board a raft in the River Niemen, the Tsar Alexander of Russia was won over to Napoleon's plans. Napoleon and he were to divide Europe between them. In return Alexander was to aid Napoleon in his " Continental system." The object of this was to close Europe to British goods and so destroy Britain's trade. At one time or another every State of

*Guildhall Art Gallery, London*

## NAPOLEON AFTER HIS DEFEAT AT WATERLOO

The battle of Waterloo was fought on June 18, 1815, and when Napoleon realized that he was hopelessly defeated he hastened back to Paris. He was two days on the journey, which was broken only by brief rests at private houses. In this picture by Marcus Stone, R.A. (1840–1921), he is seen crouching before the fire in the cottage of a peasant ex-serviceman, who, with his wife and children, regards the fallen Emperor with mingled pity and awe.

continental Europe, except Turkey and Portugal, was forced into this commercial system. But all in vain.

Napoleon had aroused a force which was to bring about his ultimate downfall —the spirit of nationalism. In Spain the patriotic fire first blazed forth in 1808. The British sent troops to help the Spaniards, thereby starting the Peninsular War (1808–14), and little by little the French forces were pushed back beyond the Pyrenees.

Austria plucked up courage to renew the struggle, but was crushed at the battle of Wagram (July 1809). Then Napoleon struck at Russia for deserting his unworkable Continental system. Invading Russia, he reached Moscow. Suddenly, the day after his arrival (September 14, 1812), flames burst out, and nine-tenths of the city was

## NAPOLEON IN EXILE

The last years of Napoleon's life were spent in exile on the island of St. Helena in the South Atlantic. This sketch of him was drawn from life there and shows him as he was in 1820, about a year before his death. It is now in the British Museum.

reduced to ashes. It was impossible to winter in Moscow, and on October 19 began the disastrous retreat which soon became a disorderly flight, in which Napoleon lost his army.

Napoleon's career of conquest was over. The flames of national patriotism burst forth in an uprising of Europe; Austria, Russia and Prussia joined with Great Britain in the War of Liberation. Napoleon raised new armies and won a few unimportant victories; but in the three days' battle of Leipzig (1813) the French were outnumbered and outfought. Slowly but surely the allies then closed in upon Paris.

On March 31, 1814, they entered the French capital, and Napoleon was forced to abdicate (April 11, 1814). He was allowed to retain the title of Emperor, together with the little island of

*Musée de Versailles; photo Neuerdein*

**EMPEROR NAPOLEON III**

Napoleon I fell when his nephew, who afterwards became Napoleon III, was only seven years of age. Switzerland, Germany, England and America sheltered him for a time before he became Emperor in 1852. This painting by Flandrin (1809–64) shows him at the height of his power.

Elba. In the person of Louis XVIII the Bourbons returned to occupy the throne of France.

But to remain quietly so near France without trying to regain his lost power was impossible for Napoleon. In March 1815 he slipped quietly away from Elba and landed in France. As by magic an army rallied to his support, and for the brief " Hundred Days " he enjoyed a return of his former glory. But the allies again united against him, and at Waterloo (*q.v.*) on June 18, 1815, he was decisively and finally defeated.

To avoid falling into the hands of Blücher, the commander of the Prussian army, who had sworn to shoot him as an outlaw, Napoleon, who had fled from the battlefield, surrendered to the British Government, and was sent to the lonely British island of St. Helena, in the South Atlantic, 1,200 miles west of Africa. There Napoleon lived in exile, until his death on May 5, 1821.

**Napoleon III.** (1808–73). Son of Louis Bonaparte, younger brother of Napoleon Bonaparte, his father was King of Holland when Louis Napoleon was born on April 20, 1808. But within two years Louis Bonaparte had lost his throne, and the child was taken to live in France. After the battle of Waterloo (June 18, 1815), he went with his parents to live in Germany, where he attended school, and he finished his education in Switzerland.

An ambitious man, he was always planning for the restoration of the Bonaparte family to the French throne, and his opportunity came in 1848 when a revolution had driven Louis Philippe from

the throne and a French Republic was established. Elected President, Louis Napoleon soon began to follow in the footsteps of his illustrious uncle, proclaiming himself Emperor of the French in 1852 and taking the title of Napoleon III.

His power was now absolute and, though he curtailed the liberty of his subjects, he organized banks, built railways, constructed canals and established hospitals. He joined England in the costly and ill-managed Crimean War (1854–56) against Russia. He longed to win military glory as Napoleon I had done, though he himself was no military genius. The Franco-Austrian War of 1859 gave him Savoy and Nice ; but his disastrous attempt to establish the Austrian Emperor's brother Maximilian as Emperor of Mexico discredited him at home. In fact, his whole foreign policy in his later days was a failure.

In an attempt to reduce the opposition to his rule he began granting reforms. But when France was crushingly defeated in the Franco-Prussian War (1870–71) and he surrendered with an army at Sedan on September 2, 1870, the Empire came to an end, France once again becoming a Republic. Napoleon III died in exile in England on January 9, 1873, and was buried at Farnborough.

**Narcissus.** Nothing makes gardens more lovely in springtime than the white and yellow narcissi. The blossoms, drooping from the end of a tall slender stalk, have an exquisite grace and beauty, and some species have a delightful fragrance.

The plant takes its name from a Greek myth. Narcissus was a beautiful youth, who, because he had spurned the love of the nymph Echo, was condemned by the gods to lose his heart to his own

*R. A. Malby*

**PHEASANT'S-EYE NARCISSUS**

A lovely flower of springtime—attractive in colour, shape and scent—is the narcissus. The species shown here, the pheasant's-eye, is among the most beautiful of the many kinds. It is also known as the poet's narcissus.

image reflected in a clear pool. Fascinated, he gazed day and night at the beautiful apparition, becoming weaker and weaker from lack of food, until he pined away and died. The gods in pity changed him into the flower bearing his name.

There are several species of the botanical genus *Narcissus*, including the daffodils and jonquils. One is the pheasant's-eye narcissus (*Narcissus poeticus*), so called from the red-rimmed corona or crown of its white flowers. The trumpet narcissus (*Narcissus pseudo-narcissus*) is the common English daffodil; it grows wild in many woodland districts, being then a smaller and more delicate plant than the cultivated forms. *Narcissus tazetta* is the species from which the cultivated varieties have been developed.

**Nasturtium.** The plants which are familiar in British gardens as nasturtiums should properly be called *Tropaeolum*, the name nasturtium being botanically correct only for the watercress plant (*N. officinale*). But the former name has become commonly accepted for the garden *Tropaeolums* and so we continue to call them nasturtiums. The

*J. E. Tuler*

**NASTURTIUM BLOOMS**
The name nasturtium really belongs to the watercress plant, but it has become accepted for the garden *Tropaeolums*, some of whose orange, red, and yellow flowers are here seen.

shield-shaped leaves and helmet-like blossoms suggested the scientific name of *Tropaeolum*, from a Greek word meaning "trophy."

The yellow, orange or red flowers are carried on climbing or creeping or dwarf stems, from early summer until the first frost. The plant is a native of South Africa, and was introduced into Spain, France and England in the 16th century. One species (*T. tuberosum*) produces underground tubers, which South Americans boil and eat like potatoes. Seed-pods of the common nasturtium are sometimes pickled and used for seasoning; and the leaves are added to salads. Included among the *Tropaeolums* is the climbing yellow-flowered canary creeper (*T. adunium*).

**Natal.** One of the four provinces of the Union of South Africa, Natal lies in the extreme south-east of Africa, and is bounded by the Cape Province and Basutoland on the south-west and west; by the Orange Free State on the north-west; by the Transvaal and Portuguese Mozambique on the north; by the Indian Ocean on the east. The province, including Zululand, has an area of 35,284 square miles and is generally hilly; bordering the Orange Free State and Basutoland is the Drakensberg range, the highest peak being Mont aux Sources (11,000 feet). The chief river is the Tugela; others are the Umkomanzi, and the Umzimkulu.

The soil of Natal is not very fertile, but various kinds of tropical fruits are plentiful in the warm regions near the coast, where also tea, sugar, coffee and cotton are grown. Coal is the most important mineral, but iron is also found in large quantities and in close proximity to the coal. Gold is mined, and there are marble quarries at the mouth of the Umzimkulu.

The largest town is Durban (*q.v.*), but Pietermaritzburg (European population 29,000) is the seat of the provincial Government; other centres are Ladysmith, Dundee and Newcastle. There are railway connexions with the Cape Province, the Orange Free State and the Transvaal. Natal was discovered by the Portuguese explorer Vasco da Gama on Christmas Day 1497, and received its name in honour of Christ's birth (or natal) day. A few attempts were made to establish settlements; but the native tribes were left almost to themselves until 1835, when a British colony was formed at Durban. In 1837 the first Boer settlers entered the country, and came into conflict with the Zulus. Though the Zulus were overcome the British were driven out of Durban, the Boers remaining more or less independent until 1843 when Natal became a British Colony. In 1893 it was granted responsible government, and in 1910 joined the newly-formed Union of South Africa. The population is 2,182,700.

*South African Railways*

**IN NATAL'S NATIONAL PARK**
Containing some of the finest scenery in the world, Natal's National Park covers an area of 20,000 acres and includes a section of the Drakensberg Mountains (above), in which some of the peaks reach 5,000 feet.

## National Gallery.

Under many of the pictures reproduced in this work you will see the words "National Gallery." This means that the original paintings are in the National Gallery, London, and are therefore national property. The gallery stands on the north side of Trafalgar Square, occupying what has been called "the finest site in Europe." It is not, however, a very impressive building from the outside. Its somewhat insignificant dome and cupolas have caused it to be called, in fun, "the National Cruet-stand." But its contents are beyond all price, the chief glory of the gallery being its collection of Italian paintings of the 15th and 16th centuries. The earlier Florentine altarpieces are better represented there than anywhere else in the world, but every one of the other great historic "schools" of painting—Dutch, Flemish, Spanish, French, German, and British—is represented by

*National Gallery*

**A FIFTEENTH-CENTURY MASTERPIECE**
Among the many precious art treasures which adorn the walls of the National Gallery in Trafalgar Square, London, is the original of this charming, poetic conception of The Nativity, painted by the early Italian artist Piero della Francesca (1416–92).

more than one world-famous masterpiece.

The National Gallery was founded in 1824, when the State, at the suggestion of King George IV, purchased 38 pictures from a private collection. Originally housed in Pall Mall, it moved to the present building in 1838. Since then the collection has been enriched by many generous bequests. From time to time various governments have also purchased valuable pictures as they came into the market ; and many others (including Holbein's portrait of the Duchess of Milan, reproduced on the opposite page) have been acquired for the gallery by the National Art Collections Fund.

During the Second World War (1939–45) many of the pictures were removed for safety to the University of Wales at Bangor, the National Library of Wales at Aberystwyth, and Mentmore House, Buckinghamshire. Later a repository was

*Topical*

**NATIONAL GALLERY, FACING LONDON'S TRAFALGAR SQUARE**
Occupying the north side of Trafalgar Square, London, the National Gallery was moved to there from Pall Mall in 1838. The pictures are arranged according to schools of painting, and the Gallery is particularly rich in Flemish and Dutch works. Italian artists are equally well represented, the collection showing some of their finest masterpieces. The spired building seen at the right is the famous church of St. Martin-in-the-Fields. *See also illus. in page 2012.*

built in a slate quarry near Blaenau Festiniog in Merionethshire, N. Wales. The building in Trafalgar Square was badly damaged by bombs, and many of the rooms remained unopened for some years after the war. But at no time was the gallery entirely closed. Indeed, it achieved a new popularity as a temporary centre for public midday musical concerts.

The Tate Gallery (*q.v.*) is sometimes called the National Gallery of British Art, but is now under separate administration.

## National Portrait Gallery.

In St. Martin's Place, London, is this impressive building in the Italian style, containing a collection of portraits of personalities famous in Britain's history. It is a rule that no portrait of any living person, except of the reigning sovereign and of his or her consort, shall be displayed, and no modern copy of an original portrait.

There were few native portrait painters in England before the 18th century, and this period is covered by the works of distinguished foreign artists who were painting in this country at that time. Among the 3,500 paintings, sculptures and drawings in the collection are portraits by Holbein, Van Dyck, Gainsborough, Romney, Raeburn, Watts and Sargent, the Anglo-American painter.

Founded in 1856, the Gallery was first opened in 1859 at 29 Great George Street, Westminster. It was housed at South Kensington during 1869–85, and at Bethnal Green Museum during 1885–95. The existing structure was completed in 1895, the west wing being added in 1933.

## National-Socialist Party.

When Adolf Hitler joined the " German Labour Party " of Munich it was a small group which held meetings at an inn. The party had been founded by a workman named Drexel in 1919, as an offshoot of the German Fatherland Front originated by Admiral Tirpitz. Drexel lost control after Hitler, in 1921, became the leader or " Fuehrer " of the group, which had been renamed the National-sozialistiche Deutsche Arbeiterpartei (National-Socialist German Workers Party) in 1920. The Party came to be better known in most countries under the abbreviation " Nazi Party."

The programme of the Party, as proclaimed on February 24, 1920, had many aims to which little exception could be taken. Profit-sharing in the great industries; better provision for old age among the workers; the creation of a healthy middle class; land reform ; a raising of the standard of health. Then there were aims which appealed to the Germans' patriotism: equality of rights in dealing with other nations; revision of the peace treaties of Versailles and St. Germain (which not only Germans thought to be harsh and unjust); the union of all Germans on the basis of the right to self-determination of peoples to form a Great Germany; the return of German colonies taken away by the war settlement of 1919.

Among certain ugly features of the Nazi plan, which showed themselves even at that early date, were the declaration that no Jew, or any person of non-German blood, could be a member of the nation. A totalitarian plan of government was outlined, with the State supreme in all walks of life and exercising stern control of the Press, religion, art and

**A NATIONAL GALLERY TREASURE**
One of the most beautiful portraits in the world, this painting by Holbein, done in 1538, of Christina of Denmark, Duchess of Milan, shows her as a girl-widow. It was purchased for the National Gallery, London, in 1909.

literature. Ruthless war was to be waged upon those whose activities—in the view of the Party leaders—were injurious to the common interests. The death penalty was demanded for such offences. The leaders swore to proceed regardless of consequences towards the fulfilment of the programme—if necessary at the sacrifice of their lives.

This, then, was the foundation upon which was built the Party which, under Hitler's leadership, came to dominate Germany and eventually to spread its tenacles over all aspects of government.

Nazi leaders had bodyguards of storm-troopers—Sturmabteilungen, or S.A., as the name was abbreviated. Later came the fanatical and cruel

S.S. (Schutzstaffeln)—"protective squadrons"—formed in 1925; the security police or S.D. (Sicherheitsdienst); and the Gestapo or secret State police (Geheime Staatspolizei), formed in 1934 directly after Hitler came to power.

At the top was Adolf Hitler. Then came Hermann Goering, designated Hitler's successor; and Rudolf Hess, deputy-Fuehrer and successor to Hitler after Goering. Martin Bormann was Hitler's secretary, and the chief of the Party Chancellery. Innumerable officials extended the chain of control downwards, so that every State office had its duplicate Party control. Most of the leading members of the Party also held important posts in the State machine. After Hitler came to power he thus found it easy to impose his will upon the country, and to organize it for aggressive war upon others.

The Nazi Party came to an end after Hitler, on April 30, 1945 (just before the end of the Second World War), killed himself in his concrete refuge in the grounds of the Berlin chancellery. Joseph Goebbels, the Party propaganda minister, also committed suicide. Goering and Hess, with other leaders, were arrested and brought to trial after Germany's surrender. Goering defeated justice by killing himself while awaiting execution. Hess was sentenced to life imprisonment. Bormann was never found, and was presumed to have died. Other leaders and commanders hanged after trial were Joachim Ribbentrop, foreign minister; Field-Marshal Wilhelm Keitel; Ernst Kaltenbrunner; Alfred Rosenberg; Hans Frank, governor of occupied Polish territories; Wilhelm Frick, minister of the interior and "protector" of Bohemia and Moravia; Julius Streicher, leading anti-Semite organizer; General Alfred Jodl, chief of army staff; Fritz Sauckel, labour chief; and Arthur Seyss-Inquart, one-time chancellor of Austria, and later Nazi commissar for the occupied Netherlands.

The trials, by an international tribunal of the Allies, took place at Nuremberg, and lasted almost a year. Judgement was pronounced on September 30 and November 1, 1946. The indictment charged the defendants with war crimes, crimes against peace, and crimes against humanity. Besides those sentenced to death, seven others were given terms of imprisonment; three were acquitted.

**National Songs.** There is scarcely a country but has its national hymn or song, and this in a number of instances is an old folksong that expresses in melody and words the soul of the people.

The air of God Save the King, the national anthem of Great Britain, has been used, perhaps more widely than any other. It is variously attributed to Dr. John Bull (1563–1628) and to Henry Carey (died 1743); it first became popular in 1745 at the time of the Jacobite rising. The melody is said to have inspired Haydn to compose his Emperor's Hymn, which was the national anthem of Austria until that country became a Republic in 1918. This tune was in turn appropriated for the song entitled Deutschland über Alles, written in 1848, which was made the anthem of the German Republic in 1919.

Another famous British national song is Rule Britannia, other outstanding songs of the British Isles being the Wearing of the Green (of Eire), Scots wha Hae (Scotland), and the Men of Harlech and Land of my Fathers (Wales). Among the songs of the Dominions of the British Commonwealth are The Maple Leaf for Ever, of Canada, with words and music

**REGIMENTED HUMANITY AT THE NAZI SHRINE**
*Associated Press*
Before the outbreak of the Second World War in 1939 there were annual displays of military might by the National-Socialists in the Luitpold Arena at Nuremberg, Germany. Massed ranks of uniformed Nazis and huge crowds of spectators were addressed by the German leader Adolf Hitler, who was greeted with hysterical demonstrations of loyalty.

by A. Muir; and The Song of Australia, words by Mrs. Carleton, music by Singer.

The Marseillaise of France dates from 1792 at the time of the French Revolution (*see* Lisle, Rouget de). The words of the American Star-Spangled Banner were written by Francis Scott Key in 1812, and the song was adopted as the national anthem of the United States in 1931. Belgium has the stirring Brabançonne; the music was written by François van Campenhout, in 1830. The "workers' song" of the Soviet Union was the Internationale, until 1944, when a new anthem, the "hymn of the Soviet Union," was introduced.

*Courtesy of National Trust*

**BEAUTIFUL VALLEY OWNED BY THE NATIONAL TRUST**
Founded in order to save the lovely countryside of England and Wales from exploitation by the builder and roadmaker and also to throw open to the people regions which, while in private hands, might never be visited, the National Trust now owns many buildings and tracts of land. This is part of picturesque Dovedale in Derbyshire, 30 acres of which belongs to the Trust.

**National Trust.** With the object of preserving places of historic interest or natural beauty a British society with the title of National Trust for Places of Historic Interest or Natural Beauty was founded in 1895; since when it has been steadily purchasing, or has received as gifts, ancient buildings and tracts of land in England and Wales, so that these may be preserved as a heritage.

Beauty spots owned by the Trust include Stonehenge, Wiltshire; Leith Hill, Surrey; Bolt Head, Devon; Longshaw Moor, near Sheffield; and tracts in the Lake District and the New Forest. Among private estates presented or acquired are Bateman's, Rudyard Kipling's 17th-century manor house at Burwash, Sussex; Lord Astor's estate of Cliveden at Cookham-on-Thames; and Sir Charles Trevelyan's property at Wallington, Northumberland. Buildings of interest include the 16th-century George Inn in Southwark, London, and Flatford Mill, Suffolk, made famous by Constable's painting.

The National Trust for Scotland for Places of Historic Interest or Natural Beauty is an independent body, and was founded in 1931. Among other property it owns the Pass of Glencoe.

# TURNING *the* PAGES *of* NATURE'S BOOK

*F̃or town dwellers especially Nature study is a passport to a new and enchanted world, the fascination of which increases as more is learnt about it. Nature is, indeed, full of lovely pictures and wonderful stories.*

**Nature Study.** If you were lost in the woods in the daytime could you find the north? Which birds in your neighbourhood stay throughout the winter and which go south? Do you know when each winter absentee gets back in the spring? When do the first house-flies appear, and where do they come from? When do the horses and other farm animals begin to shed their winter coats? Are potato roots above or below the tubers? What does a clover leaf do every night? Does a wood sorrel, which has a similar leaf, do the same thing? Why are the pebbles in the bed of the brook all rounded? Have you seen rounded pebbles anywhere else? What do they tell you?

One misses a tremendous amount of the joy of living in this remarkably interesting world if one goes through it blind to the curious and beautiful sights spread out before one's eyes, and deaf to the fascinating stories told by every leaf and pebble and feather. Too many of us look at things just enough to make sure that we fasten the right names to them—that we do not call a cat a dog—and there we are liable to stop.

How many of us show intelligent curiosity in regard to " common things "? We take a day off to go to the zoo or the menagerie and stare at the lion and the hippopotamus, without realizing that we have at home in the pet kitten a specimen of the genus *Felis* which is just as interesting as a lion or a tiger; and that on any August day we can pick up from the field a more grotesque creature than the hippopotamus—a grasshopper!

Perhaps we think we know all about cats, grasshoppers and grass. Do you know how many toes a cat has on each foot, or how a newly hatched grasshopper differs from a full-grown one? Nature

sun shines and the temperature rises. There are, too, all the winter visitors among the birds, and you may observe your own residents by feeding them in positions where they may be watched.

April, May, and June conspire to furnish almost too much material, and after a bit you must try to decide just which subjects you now want to study most—flowers, insects, trees, birds, etc. July and August will provide many experiences, especially if this is your one chance of visiting the seaside.

If you are lucky enough to possess a camera you will find " camera hunting " one of the most fascinating of pursuits. This use of the camera has proved of distinct value in aid of Nature study, providing the means of gaining a clear and intimate knowledge of wild animals, birds, and reptiles, their appearance, their haunts, their habits, and all the phases and conditions of their life.

Other branches of Nature study are described under Biology, Botany, Ecology, etc.

# *How* SHIPS & AIRCRAFT FIND THEIR WAY

*Here is the story, in brief, of the development of navigation. With the coming of aircraft, new calls were made upon inventors and scientists to provide methods of finding a way over thousands of miles from point to point.*

**Navigation.** Men have been sailing in ships since the dawn of civilization, many centuries before the Christian Era. But the science of navigation, as opposed to pilotage in coastal waters, is of unknown origin. Its introduction is now generally attributed to the Cretans, who are believed to have ventured into the open sea for 20 centuries before the catastrophe which destroyed them about 1400 B.C.

The Egyptians, who were their contemporaries, preferred coasting, as did the Greeks; but their successors the Phoenicians certainly struck into the open sea, although their voyages were too long for them ever to have been for many days out of touch with the land to replenish their water supply. They are believed to have navigated largely by the stars, as did the Arab seamen who shared with them the trade from the Indian Ocean and who pushed their way through to China seas at a very early age.

There they encountered the primitive Chinese junks which may have already been using a form of magnetic compass; it was the Arabs who brought it to Europe. The Crusaders learned about it from them and it attracted interest in the West; although it was regarded for many years as a scientific toy, whose use was dangerous as being liable to be regarded as witchcraft.

In Northern Europe the Norsemen must have had some means of discovering and keeping to their latitude, or they could never have made their regular voyages to Iceland and Greenland and back again. Although their single square sail was used principally for running before the wind, they could adjust it to drive the ships through quite a large arc of the compass. When the wind was too far ahead for that they resorted to their oars. Longitude was quite unknown to them; and if they did not make their landfall as intended they carried on until they did reach land, which was the way Leif Ericsson reached America in A.D. 1000.

At a later date we find that more scientific means of finding latitude are now well known. The astrolabe was invented for observing and mapping the stars about A.D. 150, but it was not used at sea for many centuries afterwards. Before that the cross-staff was used—a square-section graduated rod which had two wooden cross-pieces sliding on it; when the bearing of the sun had been taken the observer held his eye to one end while an assistant moved the cross pieces until one centred on the sun and the other coincided with the horizon.

The marine astrolabe of the 15th century was far more reliable. A circular metal plate had pivoted to its centre a pointer. One man held the instrument so that an engraved line was as nearly vertical as could be contrived in a rolling ship; when the pointer was directed to the sun or to an identified star, the angle shown on the engraved plate was far more accurate than one obtained with a cross-staff. The quadrant was used about the same time. The Polynesians in their long voyages picked up tiny islands without fail, using half a coconut shell in a way now unknown.

Columbus, Vasco da Gama and other 15th century navigators, therefore had the service of improved instruments for finding latitude and understood something of the compass's variation from true North. At the same time the improved rig and hull of ships made them capable of sailing very much closer to the wind than the earlier types. Improvements continued all through the 17th century, when ships were able to make a good landfall in North or South America and work round the Cape to Eastern seas. The quadrant was improved early in the 18th century, and almost simultaneously the sextant was devised by three scientists working entirely independently. Even today, with so many scientific improvements, the sextant is still the mainstay of the navigator, permitting him to take observations of sun, moon or stars which will " place " a ship in the open sea within about a mile of its actual position when carefully worked out.

That still left the problem of finding longitude with reasonable accuracy instead of having to rely on " dead reckoning " which was little more than guesswork. To get a reliable observation it was necessary to have an absolutely accurate timekeeper. The King of Spain in 1598 offered a reward to anybody who could make one; Holland, France and Venice did the same. In 1714 the British Government offered £10,000 for a clock which would permit longitude to be reckoned within one degree, and £20,000 to half a degree. This reward was finally won by John Harrison, a carpenter, who completed five remarkably accurate chronometers between 1735 and 1770, but had great difficulty in getting the money. (*See* Chronometer).

With the sextant, the chronometer, the improved compass and the log towed astern (*see* Log), which gave the speed tolerably accurately, the navigator managed until the early days of the 19th century.

Then ships built of iron, and with a great deal of iron even in wooden ones, interfered with the compass until measures were taken to compensate for the magnetism in the ship. The latest development is to do without " polar magnetism " altogether and to have a compass worked with a gyroscope whose centrifugal force will keep it pointed to true North once it has been set. Its disadvantage is that it will only work while it is kept spinning rapidly by an electric motor. If anything interferes with the ship's current the gyro-compass is useless, so that magnetic compasses are always installed and kept in good order as a reserve. Similarly, every ship keeps two or more chronometers going while getting time signals by wireless. (See Gyroscope).

As the direction from which a wireless message is sent can be ascertained precisely, Directional Wireless is also used to check the ship's position well out to sea. She can send out a signal which is picked up by two shore stations; they each get an accurate bearing, and where the two bearing lines intersect on the chart is her position. Alternatively, wireless beacons on shore emit a continuous distinctive signal; the ship gets bearings on two of

these with her own direction-finding gear, and the navigating officer marks the point of intersection.

Electric devices can also give the depth of water far beyond the power of any sounding lead. The speed at which sound waves travel through water is very accurately known; a signal emitted from the ship will bounce off the bottom of the sea, and can be picked up by a delicate receiving instrument— the " echo gear." The time taken is automatically reckoned, and gives the exact depth—from hundreds of fathoms to one or two under the ship's keel; in shallow water the hand lead is preferred. In deep water which is accurately surveyed, and the depths marked on the chart at frequent intervals, a line of soundings obtained with the echo gear, compared with a similar line of depths on the chart, gives a good idea of the position, although the possibility of coincidence of depth in another locality makes navigators check it by other means.

Safe navigation naturally demands different methods in shallow water approaching the coast, particularly where the channels are tortuous, and also for avoiding collisions. Charts and sailing directions, and the international regulations for

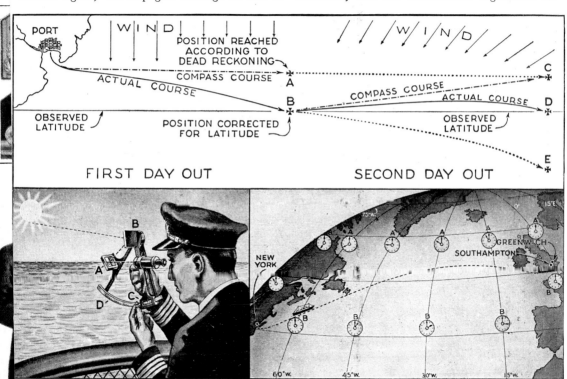

## HOW SHIPS FIND THEIR WAY ACROSS THE OCEAN

The upper diagram illustrates a part of a ship's course in practical navigation. The ship leaves port, sailing east toward point C. The captain's first latitude observation shows, however, that instead of reaching A, on the true compass course, the ship has been blown off course to B. The captain now lays a new course to reach C, but next day finds himself at D instead. The error, however, is comparatively small ; whereas if he had not altered his course the day before, the ship would have reached E. By such repeated corrections a ship is kept on the desired course. At the lower left we see how the sextant is used to determine latitude. First, the officer sights on the horizon through the unsilvered half of the mirror (transparent glass). Second, he moves

arm C until the upper mirror, B, which is attached to C, throws an image of the sun upon the silvered half of A (which mirror is set at the requisite angle). Third, he reads the altitude of the sun above the horizon as indicated on scale D by the pointer on C. From this, the officer computes the latitude. At the lower right we see two examples of how a ship's local time, when compared to Greenwich time, establishes the longitude of a ship's position. The row of clocks marked A show the local time every 15 degrees westward when it is noon at Greenwich. The row of clocks marked B show an identical comparison when it is 4 o'clock at Greenwich. If, for example, it is noon by the sun when the Greenwich chronometer says 4 o'clock, then the ship has reached the 60th meridian west.

# CONTRASTS IN TYPES OF WARSHIPS OF LONG AGO

The two illustrations show types of warships of the 16th and 17th centuries. The lower is from the painting by the Italian artist Vicentino of the battle of Lepanto, fought between the Holy League of Western European powers and the Turks on October 7, 1571. It was the last sea fight in which oared galleys rowed by slaves took part. Under Don John of Austria a combined fleet of 202 vessels attacked a Turkish fleet estimated at 275 galleys, and inflicted upon it a signal defeat from which Turkish naval power never recovered. The upper painting by Van de Velde, is of the battle of Texel, in which the English fleet under Monk defeated the Dutch under Van Tromp on July 31, 1653. The ships differed little from those of later date except that they carried square sails instead of jibs on the bowsprit.

*Central Press Photos*

## H.M.S. VANGUARD WITH DESTROYER ESCORT

With displacement of 42,500 tons, length of 814 feet, width of 107 feet, engines of 130,000 h.p. and speed of 30 knots, H.M.S. Vanguard is armed with eight 15-inch, sixteen 5·25-inch and more than 70 anti-aircraft guns.  The cost of this battleship (which was completed in 1944) exclusive of 15-inch guns and mountings, was £9,000,000.  (*See* also illustration page 2302.)

armed liners, but their whole line could have been rolled up without difficulty by a single German man-of-war had she dared to pass our warships whose crews were fretting in apparent idleness in the Orkneys or in Scottish harbours.  The surrender of the German fleet in November 1918 was the most spectacular ending to any naval war.

In the Second World War it was the Royal Navy which saved Britain from being invaded after the fall of France, just as the Royal Air Force ruined the German plan to bomb Britain and so to break the spirit of the people.  Allied ships, with British ones predominant, were mainly responsible for the defeat of Italy on both sides of the Mediterranean.  British, Dominion and American ships, with the full co-operation of aircraft, beat the U-boats in the Atlantic which threatened to starve the British people; and, again with aircraft, made possible the invasion of the Continent which led to its liberation from the Germans.

In the Indian Ocean the Navy, with the infant Indian Service taking a gallant part, checked the westward advance of Japan.  In the Pacific the United States played the major part, but the British and Dominion fleets gave very great help.  The soldiers who did the land fighting freely admitted that they could not have reached their battlefields without the Navy, while the Royal Air Force could not have made such a name for itself had the Navy not secured its supplies of petrol, oil and personnel.  Modern warfare is almost always a matter of combined operations.

Each naval war teaches its own lessons, generally at a great cost to victors and vanquished, for the lessons of the most recent always lead to great improvements in attack and defence which present new problems.  Each new weapon demands its antidote, and each defensive or offensive measure not only means additional weapons or gear which demand space on deck and below, but also additional personnel who have to be given sufficiently well-ventilated living space to keep them healthy in the great strain of modern naval warfare.

The numerous forms of Radar gear—and a big man-of-war carries a lot—must be given a clear field.  So must the various types of anti-aircraft guns: the medium quick-firers to reach an attacking plane at great height and the numerous pom-poms and machine-guns to deal with dive-bombers.  Air attack has added to the tactical value of speed at the cost of other features in the ship, and the possibility of gas shells being used has to be guarded against.  Modern shells, torpedoes and mines are far more powerful than they were in the First World War, and their antidote, in the form of armour and subdivision, presents many problems.  Against air bombs the armoured decks of ships have to be made thicker than ever, introducing serious problems of stability, and measures have to be taken against a greater danger of fire than ever before. Each new feature, or new type of ship, is bound to influence others.

While everything in sea warfare and naval architecture is constantly changing there are many principles which remain constant and others which, abandoned for a time, are revived to meet new conditions. The battleship, whose existence has been threatened by small-craft and air enthusiasts ever since the 1870s, remains the heavyweight of the fleets. Three German battleships, which seldom came out of their Norwegian refuge during the Second World War, upset the whole distribution of the British heavy squadrons until they were sunk in succession by British capital ships. In the Pacific the American Navy, which had retained battleships against the views of a big body of public opinion, found that they were the only ships that could deal adequately with the Japanese fortified positions, and they bombarded most effectively in the Normandy operations. The battle-cruisers (battleships in which protection had been sacrificed for speed) were already out of fashion owing to the casualties at Jutland, and their vulnerability was confirmed during the Second World War. Only one remains afloat, in the Turkish Navy, but they may one day be revived with a different rôle.

### Functions of Cruisers and Destroyers

The cruiser classes cover a wide range of design but act as the cavalry or tanks of the fleet. They work in co-operation with the battle squadrons, screening them from destroyer attack and being ready to deliver the *coup de grâce* to a stricken enemy battleship, carry out detached operations of all sorts, destroy enemy commerce and protect the most important convoys of their own side.

Similarly, the destroyers fulfil any number of functions, earning them the nickname of " the Navy's Maids-of-all-Work." Originally designed to run down and destroy torpedo boats, they are now used for delivering torpedo attacks themselves, rushing forces to threatened points at high speed, convoying, hunting submarines, bombarding shore positions, and scores of other jobs. The modern destroyer is so expensive to build that it is necessary to design smaller vessels, called sub-destroyers, to relieve the bigger vessels of any jobs which are within their power. That work is largely concerned with convoying and anti-submarine operations, for which they are combined with other escort vessels—sloops, frigates, corvettes, etc.

The submarines are in a class by themselves, relying almost entirely on their torpedoes as weapons; and finally the modern Fleet has an enormous number of small craft of all kinds, auxiliaries which make the " Naval Train " and supply ships. Most of them are manned from the reserves and some by Merchant Navy ratings.

The latest major type to be introduced into the world's navies is the aircraft carrier, which did magnificent work in the Second World War. She is the most expensive type of man-of-war afloat and in spite of recent improvements she is still so vulnerable that she has to be given a strong escort. Improved flying technique has recently reduced the demands that the aircraft make on their carrier;

they can take off very much more quickly, so do not require the former great length; while they can also land safely in much smaller space. Naturally the flying branch has taken advantage of that to put bigger planes into the carriers.

The British fleet aircraft carriers are therefore divided into heavy and light, the former up to about 37,000 tons and the latter about 18,000 tons. The Americans are to build one of 65,000 tons. In addition a number of merchant ships have proved valuable when converted into carriers for limited duties. Officially they are escort carriers; the U.S. Navy calls them " baby flat-tops," and the British Navy nicknamed them "Woolworth carriers." It is generally considered that the carrier is the class of ship whose design will be altered most radically when the lessons of the Second World War, and of the experiments which followed it, have been fully digested.

What the future trend of naval warfare and naval construction will be nobody can foretell. After the First World War, President Harding of the United States called the naval powers to a conference at Washington which, after a good deal of discussion, established a limit to the size of capital ships (35,000 tons) and cruisers (10,000 tons) in a light condition without fuel, etc., on board. They also limited the gun calibre, and established a " yardstick " which fixed the proportions of the British, American, Japanese, French and Italian fleets with regard to battleships.

Later conferences enlarged the scope of the scheme but each one proved more difficult to arrange, and in 1938 Japan ended the whole scheme by refusing to disclose the size of her new ships. The Second World War proved that both Germany and Japan had cheated outrageously; the Bismarck and Tirpitz were 45,000 tons instead of the 35,000 that Hitler's government had declared, and the Japanese battleships were as much as 64,000 tons. That naturally made more people distrust the whole idea of international agreement.

### Development of Naval Design

We can trace the history of naval design and fighting back for well over 3,000 years, with a good many gaps in the early days as a matter of course. During that period there has nearly always been steady development with few revolutionary changes. The first recorded naval action, which had a very big influence for centuries, was in 1194 B.C. when the Egyptians under Rameses III, working in conjunction with an army on land, met the huge fleet of the Greek peoples and their allies who were migrating from the north towards Egypt by sea and land. Both fleets consisted of galleys with a single mast and sail, but they differed greatly. The Greek ships had no rams but were stoutly built, designed to be laid alongside an enemy to fight it out hand-to-hand. The Egyptian ships were not nearly so well built; for they were confined to acacia wood, which was in short lengths.

The concussion of a ship driving alongside it would probably sink one of their ships almost immediately, crushing her like a matchbox; but on the other hand their ingenious construction gave them great strength longitudinally and they were fitted with rams, although high above the waterline. Their handiness permitted them to use

# THE ROYAL NAVY: SHIPS AND GUNS

*Admiralty Official*

The British battleship Duke of York displaces 44,650 tons when fully laden. Length is 745 feet and width 103 feet. Her engines develop 110,000 h.p. to give her a speed of 27 knots, and she is armed with ten 14-inch, sixteen 5·25-inch, eight 40-mm., thirty-eight 20-mm., and eighty-eight 2-pdr. guns. She has a crew of 1,900 officers and men. Top, the Duke of York leaving Portland Harbour, Dorset. Lower, she is steaming at speed. Completed in 1941, she took Mr. Winston Churchill to the United States that year for the first Washington Conference. (*See also* page 2304).

**BATTLESHIP THAT GAVE ITS NAME TO THE KING GEORGE V CLASS**

H.M.S. King George V (above) is one of five magnificent warships commissioned in 1940, some months after the outbreak of the Second World War (1939–45). She became the flagship of the Home Fleet. Her displacement is 35,000 tons and the speed 30 knots. Ten 14-inch guns are carried, in two quadruple turrets and one double turret; the secondary armament includes sixteen 5·25-inch and a battery of 4·5-inch guns. The battleships each cost about £8,000,000. Another ship of this class, the Prince of Wales, carried Mr. Churchill to his meeting with President Roosevelt in August 1941, when the Atlantic Charter was drawn up, stating the war and peace aims of the United States and Great Britain. The Prince of Wales went to Singapore towards the end of 1941, and was sunk by Japanese aircraft on December 10 of that year.

# SWIFTER AND LIGHTER UNITS OF THE FLEET

*Graphic Photo Union*

The cruiser H.M.S. Sheffield (upper) has a displacement of 9,100 tons, is 558 feet long and 61 feet wide, and her 75,000-h.p. engines give her a speed of 32 knots. She is armed with nine 6-inch and eight 4-inch guns. The destroyer Finisterre (lower) displaces 2,315 tons and has a speed of 34 knots; her armament includes four 4·5-inch and fourteen 40-mm. guns, and ten 21-inch torpedo tubes. The Armada, another Battle class destroyer, was finished in 1948.

# TWO OF BRITAIN'S LARGEST AIRCRAFT CARRIERS

*Admiralty Official*

H.M.S. Indomitable (upper), photographed from one of her own aircraft as she ploughs through the Indian Ocean with an aeroplane on the flight deck ready to take off, displaces 29,730 tons in war trim, is 766 feet 6 inches long and 95 feet 9 inches wide, and is armed with sixteen 4·5-inch guns and 79 smaller weapons and carries more than 60 aircraft. Her engines develop 148,000 h.p. to give her a speed of 32 knots. She was completed in 1944. H.M.S. Implacable (lower) is of the same class as the Indomitable but slightly larger, having a war tonnage of 32,000 tons.

# CATAPULTED TARGET PLANE AND MINESWEEPERS

*Admiralty Official*

In the top photograph an unmanned and radio-controlled seaplane is being catapulted from the deck of a cruiser to act as target for anti-aircraft gunners. Below are the minesweepers H.M.S. Bramble and H.M.S. Foam, with an aircraft carrier in the distance. The Bramble (nearest) is one of the fastest minesweepers in the British Navy, with a speed of 16·5 knots; she displaces 1,040 tons and is armed with one 4-inch and four 40-mm. guns. She was completed in 1945. In the immediate foreground is seen a signalling searchlight on the bridge of another minesweeper.

# INSIDE AND OUTSIDE A GUN TURRET

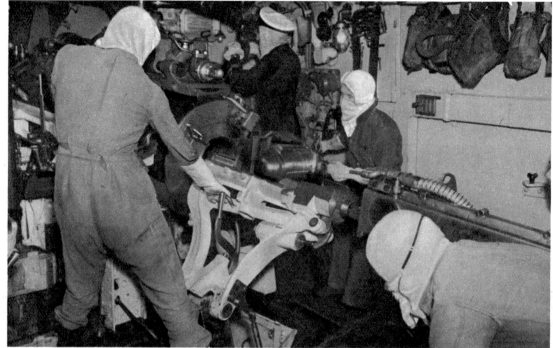

Admiralty Official; Central Press

Inside the six-inch gun turret of a British cruiser (upper photograph) the gun is at the final stage of loading. Members of its crew, wearing protective flash-helmets and gauntlets, are (from left to right) operating the shell tray ; waiting to close the breech when the shell is in position ; and the captain of the gun at the rammer. The officer in charge (background) is looking through the periscope. In the lower photograph ratings are scrubbing deck beneath the 15-inch guns of H.M.S. Vanguard, the ship in which the Royal Family went to South Africa in 1946.

# PREPARING A TORPEDO FOR ITS DISCHARGE

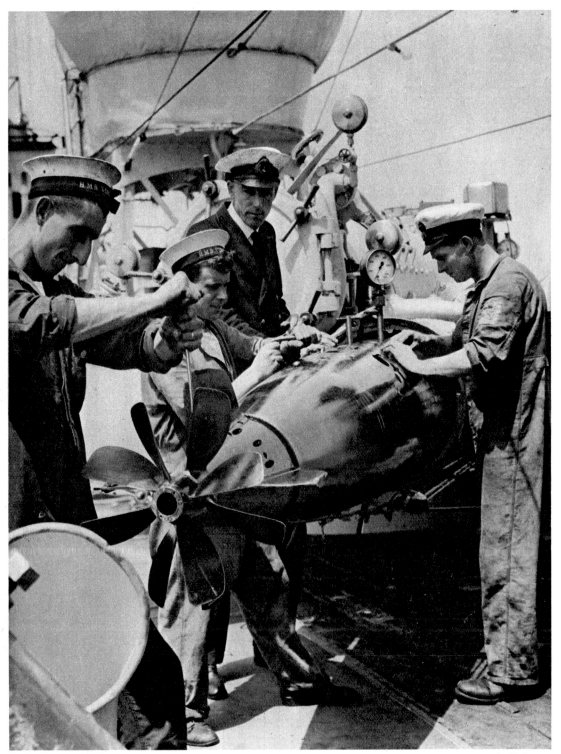

*Charles E. Brown*

Torpedo practice is in progress on board a destroyer, and here adjustments are being made before the weapon is launched through the tube—the breech of which can be seen behind the warrant officer in the centre. The propellers at the stern of the torpedo are driven by com-pressed air. In use for practice it has no explosive 'war-head,' and after it has been fired it is recovered by men in a boat and used again. Other types of torpedo, developed in secret during the Second World War (1939–45), are driven by electricity and leave no wake to betray their presence.

# MAIN RADAR AERIALS OF H.M.S. DUKE OF YORK

*The Times*

Here is a close-up of the fore-funnel and signal mast of H.M.S. Duke of York. Projecting from the mast platform and yards are different kinds of aerials for the radar receivers which enable the ship to navigate in fog and to range her guns against unseen air and surface targets. The box-like structure at the left is the main ranging aerial. A 40-mm. Bofors anti-aircraft gun is mounted on the lower platform at the left; its ammunition is stored in the lockers on the right. At lower left, wearing dark blue berets, is a group of Royal Marines. (*See also* page 2297).

these rams, and their men were trained to pour in arrows from a range at which the Greek spears were useless. In the battle, off the Palestinian or Syrian coast, these new tactics were completely successful; the Greek fleet was annihilated, and Egypt was free from invasion for many years.

That action naturally started a craze for the ram in Mediterranean waters, where the low free-board galley, lightly built, could survive in the average weather to be expected. (The freeboard is that part of the side between the deck level and the flotation line.) There was plenty of slave labour available for rowing, and the fighting galley developed to a high pitch within its limitations. From the single row of oars in the small Egyptian galleys they developed until before the beginning of the Christian Era there were quinqueremes with five banks of oars. How these were arranged is still unknown, but it was certainly not on five decks for the galley was always a low freeboard vessel. As a result of the Battle of Actium in 31 B.C. the heavy and cumbersome galley went out of fashion and the handier "Ligurian" galley took its place, although the size of that type immediately began to increase.

## Ships of the Viking Age

In the north we have far less information until the days of the Vikings, but the earliest boats dug up show that they were better prepared for heavy weather than the Southerners. By the Viking Age, beginning about the 8th century, the science of design and construction had reached a high level; the Norsemen were all free men, pulling the oars with their shields and weapons beside them, and they also believed in hand-to-hand fighting at close quarters.

The principles of the Viking design persisted in the north for centuries, although the ships naturally developed in size and strength. The open boat was decked over and made far more seaworthy; the beautiful lines of the "long ship" were marred by the desire for better carrying, and for a long time the warship and the merchantman were normally built on the same lines, although some kings maintained a few galleys and tried to make the Mediterranean design suit northern conditions. These galleys fell out of favour, and gradually the various governments relied on their merchant ships for their fleets, converting them into men-of-war by the addition of temporary fighting castles at either end and at the top of the mast. Later, these castles were made much stronger, and the fore and after castles were permanently built into the ship to provide accommodation in fore-castle and poop.

In due course guns were carried on shipboard, but to begin with they were only "murdering pieces"—light breech-loaders designed to sweep the enemy's deck of her crew or to annihilate boarders who had got on board. Henry VIII bought some of the newly-invented muzzle-loaders for his ships; they would stand a much heavier charge without bursting, and would damage or even sink a ship at considerable range. But their weight, and the concussion of their discharge, would shake any of the earlier ships to pieces, so that new systems of construction had to be worked out to give greater strength. The warship began to be quite distinct from the merchantman, although the latter was still used as an auxiliary.

Progress was greatly accelerated by the Elizabethan "gentlemen adventurers" who took their ships on long voyages and were willing to "pull and haul with the men." In the Mediterranean the Battle of Lepanto (October 7, 1571) had proved the superiority of the broadside sailing ship over the galley, but Englishmen brought more original minds to the question and many of them saw the objections to the towering sterns which had been introduced in Henry VII's reign in imitation of the Spaniards and which were designed for close fighting. After great argument the school which believed in the lower and handier vessel, more seaworthy and able to sail much closer to the wind, had its way.

The defeat of the Spanish Armada justified that type. Its handiness permitted it to keep out of range of the Spaniards' smaller guns and to pound them into submission, or put them out of action through damage, with heavy muzzle-loaders. The English seamen-gunners never gave the Spaniards the chance of boarding the English ships when, with their huge companies of soldiers-at-sea, they must inevitably have conquered. It was the lessons of Rameses's victory and the Battle of Actium (September 2, 31 B.C.) over again.

Another point which was to have a great influence was the success of Drake's fireships in demoralising the Spaniards. Before then fighting at sea had been simply a *mêlée*, each ship tackling the nearest enemy; but with this new weapon it was obviously necessary for the admiral to have proper control of his fleet, and the line-of-battle came into being with the ships divided into classes, or rates as they later came to be called, for each to undertake its particular work. The fireships never scored another considerable success, but the ordered handling of the fleet which they introduced has been recognized as essential ever since.

## Progress in the 17th and 18th Centuries

Early in the 17th century there was a tendency to return to the towering stern-works; but the longer voyages that were undertaken demanded seaworthiness, and before the end of the century the line-of-battleship had taken to the form familiar in all pictures of the Battle of Trafalgar. She carried her guns in two or three continuous decks. During the 18th century she was further developed for efficiency and seaworthiness. The majority of the line-of-battleships were 74- or 80-gun two-deckers, being as strongly built and carrying the same size of gun as the less handy three-deckers, which were usually admirals' flagships. After several unhappy experiments the cruiser—frigate she was called in those days—became a fast, handy and highly efficient vessel with one gun deck. Below her came the sloops, ship or brig-rigged, the gun-brigs, cutters and other small craft.

When steam was introduced into the British Navy it was efficient only with paddle wheels. The paddles were vulnerable to gunfire and also made it impossible to mount a full broadside; instead, heavier guns than had ever been carried before were mounted on deck. When the screw propeller was introduced the broadside ship was revived, and the first ironclads, starting in 1860, were built on that principle. But the iron armour, inefficient as it seems to us today, demanded much bigger guns. A ship's fire-power would be so reduced if a single gun were put out of action by enemy shot that the guns had to be gathered together behind the thickest protection.

Guns on the broadside are bound to have a small arc of training, so the fashion began of mounting them on deck at the ends of the ship and cutting away the midship superstructure so that they could turn through the greater part of a circle. That system is now used for even comparatively small guns, placing them in an armoured gunhouse or turret which revolves on top of a barbette (a fixed armoured tower going deep into the ship and protecting the ammunition hoists, and preventing the turret being immobilised by a shell below it).

To increase the gun power, modern turrets fire over one another with practically no damage to the lower turret from blast when the upper guns are fired. Little quick-firing guns and machine-guns were first carried as a defence against torpedo boats; the modern destroyer demands quite a big shell to stop her, but air attack gives the light guns plenty to do.

The material, good as it has to be, is only regarded as the less important side of a navy; in the final tests it is the men who count for most in making the ship a good fighting weapon. This applies both to the officers and the ratings and, by no means the least, to mutual good relations.

Before Tudor days, when naval officers were first trained to make the Service their profession, the good relations factor was woefully lacking. Knights or barons were in command of a ship without knowing anything about her handling, and they took their archers and men-at-arms on board with them to do the fighting. The master and crew of the ship were there only to take her where the knight ordered; and as he often ordered her to be taken into the eye of the wind, or something equally impossible, quarrels were frequent. The only fighting that the sailors were allowed to do was to man the topcastle at the masthead when there was a sea running and the motion made the soldiers seasick. Things are different now and the Royal Marines—"soldiers and sailors too"—are a highly respected part of the ship's company.

There are three ways now of becoming an officer in the Royal Navy. In the first, the cadet must enter the Royal Naval College at Dartmouth while quite a boy; and his training there will be a mixture of professional subjects and general education. In the old days it was always very expensive for his parents, but in 1941 great reforms were started and nearly one-third of the vacancies were to be filled by scholarships. Half of these scholarships were to be reserved for boys from

*Charles E. Brown*

### WHEN THE DAY BEGINS ON BOARD A MAN-OF-WAR

On a man-of-war the sailors sleep in canvas hammocks. They are roused in the morning at 5.30 by the boatswain's-mates' piping and loud shouts of 'Heave Out! Show a leg! Lash up and stow!' In the photograph a man is showing a leg by 'heaving out' of his hammock. Later the men will roll up their hammocks, lash them into a bundle, and then throw them down to the lower deck where others, detailed as hammock-men, stow them away. The hammocks are slung from hooks on the mess deck, and in fact almost everywhere that space is available in the vessel.

# CADETS IN THE FIRST STAGE OF SEA TRAINING

*Central Press*

Some of the boys who are to be future officers of the Royal Navy begin their training with a course at the Royal Naval College, Dartmouth, at the age of about 12 or 13. The course lasts for just under four years, and the boys then go to sea in a training-ship carrying about 250 cadets and a small crew of trained seamen. During the cruise the cadets perform the ordinary duties of a ship's crew. Here boys on board a training-ship are stowing the after-deck awning.

grant-aided secondary schools, and an extra scholarship each term was reserved to the son of a naval rating.

The cadet had to pass the traditional interview, where he was brought before a board of very senior naval officers who chatted with him on all sorts of subjects to discover, as far as they could in the time, whether the lad had the qualities which would make him a good officer and leader of men. The 1941 plan is still the basis, although alterations are constantly being made in matters of detail. If he passes both examination and interview, his three and a half years at Dartmouth are either free of all cost or at fees graduated according to the income of his parents.

The second method is the " Special Entry " scheme, wherein the candidate has to sit for the Civil Service examination alongside candidates for the Army and Royal Air Force at between 17 and 18 years of age. He then goes through an intensive course of training and joins his future shipmates from Dartmouth as a midshipman. Both systems produce first-class officers. The third method is promotion from the ranks, which has produced some conspicuously fine men but also others who were, unfortunately, unpopular with the " bluejackets." Constant efforts are being made to find a satisfactory means of increasing the number of officers from the lower deck.

Engineering, Secretarial and Royal Marine officers go through quite a different training to prepare them for their particular duties, and Medical officers are not admitted to the Service until they are fully qualified professionally. The Royal Naval Reserve, which consists of professional seamen, and the Royal Naval Volunteer Reserve, which consists of amateur seamen who undergo training in their spare time, are only mobilised in war or serious emergency.

The ranks in the Navy, the branches being distinguished by the initial letters of the branch in brackets, are Cadet, Midshipman, Sub-Lieutenant, Lieutenant, Lieutenant-Commander, Commander, Captain (who sometimes holds the appointment of Commodore), Rear-Admiral, Vice-Admiral, Admiral and Admiral of the Fleet. The Royal Marines have the same ranks as Army officers. In both Navy and Royal Marines there are warrant officers with rank midway between the commissioned and non-commissioned grades, but who are always given the respect due to an officer.

### Periods of Lower Deck Service

The lower deck consists of so many branches that it is impossible to give details of the methods of entry and the ladder of promotion for all of them. The grades are Boy 2nd Class, Boy 1st Class, Ordinary Seaman, Leading Seaman, Petty Officer and Chief Petty Officer. Until quite recently ratings could enter the Service as boys, in the Seaman and Artificer Branches only, between the ages of 15 and 16, or as men from $17\frac{1}{2}$ upwards. That left a gap between 16 and $17\frac{1}{2}$, during which period many who were anxious to join the Navy got settled in shore jobs and were persuaded to give up the idea. In 1948, therefore, the Admiralty opened a new class to enter between $16\frac{1}{4}$ and $17\frac{1}{2}$ years of age for nearly all branches of the Service, to be called junior ratings.

Those who enter the Seaman Branch at between 15 and 16 years of age start as Seaman Boy Second Class and must engage for Continuous Service, that is to say for 12 years from the age of 18 when they start their " Man's Time "; but they may, in certain circumstances, apply just before their 18th birthday for transfer to the Special Service engagement, in which only seven years are spent on active service in the Fleet and the remaining five in the Royal Fleet Reserve, getting civilian employment but keeping abreast of naval development and being called up for service in war. The seaman who is near the completion of his 12 years' man's time may volunteer to serve a total of 22 years man's time, which makes him about 40 years of age when he becomes eligible for a pension for life.

### Training in a Royal Dockyard

Boys are also taken as artificer apprentices and " serve their time " much as they would as an apprentice in a private shipyard, while they are being given a very thorough technical and practical training in one of the Royal Dockyards, doing a good deal of work on board warships which come in for refit. They also are required to sign a Continuous Service agreement, for the country spends a lot of money on their training; but their pay is excellent and their standing in the ship's company is a considerable one.

The new junior ratings will enter under a Special Service engagement, but instead of seven and five years it is for eight years with the Fleet and four in the Royal Fleet Reserve. Between 17 and 23 years of age volunteering is permitted in practically all the branches, either for Special Service or Continuous Service, the latter being compulsory only in the case of Rating Air Pilots. At whatever age he may volunteer, the embryo bluejacket must remember that the standards of character and physique demanded by the Navy are very high indeed, although some relaxation is made in the latter for boys entering at an early age, because naval life will almost invariably make up the deficiency in a very short time.

In addition to the apprenticeship avenue to the Artificer Branch a certain number may enter as Engine-Room, Electrical or Ordnance Artificers or Shipwrights from the age of 19 upwards; if over 21 years of age they have petty officers' rate at once. They must, however, be very highly qualified for their particular jobs when they apply and must pass a strict trade test. It is the same for the men who enter as Artisans.

It must be realized that practically all the 11 branches of the lower deck cover many jobs. A man in the Seaman's Branch, for instance, may take up gunnery, torpedoes and submarine work, detection, Radar plotting, Radar control, quartermaster, surveying, boom defence, physical and recreational training or sailmaking. These various jobs formerly carried additional pay, but the new scheme is to have a basic pay for each grade, with an extra allowance in certain specially skilled jobs; and added to that an increment for length of time in the Service and extra pay for each good conduct badge won and retained. In addition there is an allowance for the upkeep of kit and a marriage allowance. Little wonder that the Royal Navy is regarded as a grand life for the right type of man.

# The BOYHOOD HOME of JESUS CHRIST

*O*ne of the most sacred places in the Holy Land, Nazareth is still the little town
*that it was when within its bounds Our Lord, as St. Luke says, 'increased
in wisdom and stature, and in favour with God and Man.'*

**Nazareth.** In the Holy Land of Palestine, pleasantly situated among fig-trees, olive-trees, and cypresses on the southern slope of a hill midway between the Sea of Galilee and the Mediterranean, stands the little town of Nazareth—sacred to Christians because it was there that Jesus Christ spent His years of boyhood and later, as a young man, worked in the carpenter's shop and taught in the synagogue.

Few objects remain to remind us of the actual surroundings wherein He passed those 30 years of preparation for His mission. At one time the synagogue there possessed a book from which Jesus was said to have learned His alphabet, as well as the bench upon which He sat ; and nowadays visitors are sometimes shown Joseph's workshop and Christ's table, and many sites are identified with incidents in His career.

There is little doubt, however, that most of these identifications are quite without foundation, though the Virgin's Well was probably visited times without number by His Mother, Mary, as it is the only well in the neighbourhood. Then, too, not far away are some steep slopes, one of which may well have been " the brow of the hill whereon their city was built," over which His incensed fellow townsmen threatened to " cast Him down headlong " when He told them " Verily I say unto you, no prophet is accepted in his own country" (Luke iv, 24).

There is no mention of Nazareth in the Old Testament; it became important simply because of its connexion with Jesus Christ, who is often called Jesus of Nazareth or Jesus the Nazarene.

For some hundreds of years after Jesus had left Nazareth for the last time, the little town continued its obscure and uneventful life. The first Christian pilgrims came to it in the 6th century, and in course of time large and imposing churches were built.

In 1100 Nazareth was captured by the Crusaders, and 87 years later it fell to Saladin, the Saracen leader. After many further vicissitudes it was captured by the Turks in 1517, and it remained in their hands for just over 400 years, until, late in 1918, during the First World War (1914–18), it was taken by British cavalry. After the First World War Great Britain controlled Palestine under a mandate from the League of Nations, and Nazareth again became a centre of Christian pilgrimage. In May 1948 the British withdrew from Palestine, and fighting broke out between the Arab and Jewish inhabitants for possession of the country, Nazareth being situated within the territory occupied by the Jews. Its principal industries are lace-making and the manufacture of souvenirs for tourists. The fertile surrounding district is not fully exploited by the inhabitants of the town, who are content merely to satisfy their own requirements of wheat, olives, and figs. The population is about 15,000.

W. F. Taylor

**NAZARETH'S WELL THAT JESUS MAY HAVE KNOWN**
The Fountain of the Virgin or the Virgin's Well is probably the only relic left of the old Nazareth of the time of Jesus Christ. To this well—still the only supply of water for the town—or at least to this spot, the Boy Jesus may often have accompanied His Mother when she went to draw water for the family.

**Nazi.** (German pronunciation, nah-tsi). This is an abbreviation of the first word in the name of the German political party called the *National-sozialistische Deutsche Arbeiterpartei* (National Socialist German Workers' Party). Founded in 1919, the Nazi party came under the leadership of Adolph Hitler (*q.v.*) in 1921. It had the avowed intention of restoring to Germany the territory she lost under the terms of the Treaty of Versailles, which ended the First World War (1914–18). The spirit and organization of the party were militaristic, and at the termination of the Second World War (1939–45) the Allies proclaimed it an illegal body. (*See* National-Socialist Party).

**Nebraska.** One of the most important farming centres of the United States of America, Nebraska is situated to the west of the River Missouri and to the east of the Rocky Mountains, with Kansas in the south, Colorado and Wyoming in the west, South Dakota in the north, and Lower Missouri on the east. Across the State flows the Platte, a tributary of the Missouri. Nebraska is a vast plain (area 77,237 square miles) on which huge herds of cattle are grazed, and thousands of acres of maize, sugar-beet, and other cereals are grown. It is sometimes known as the " tree-planters' State," from the extensive forests planted by early settlers. The largest city is Omaha (population 223,000), where meat-packing, smelting and butter-making are the chief industries. The capital is Lincoln (80,000). The population of the State is 1,315,000.

**Nebulae.** Some celestial objects, when examined carefully with a telescope (only a few are bright enough to be seen by the naked eye), are found to have a hazy look instead of the sharp pinpoint appearance of a star. These are the nebulae. The name *nebula* is the Latin word for " mist " or " small cloud."

There are two quite different sorts of nebula. One kind, the galactic nebulae, so called because they are found in or near the Galaxy or Milky Way, are clouds of gaseous matter, often mixed with dust, which have an infinite variety of shapes. The other kind, the extragalactic nebulae, seem to avoid the neighbourhood of the Milky Way. They consist of millions of stars like our own sun ; but as they are very much farther away than the galactic nebulae, the separate stars can rarely be distinguished and they look to the eye like mist or cloud. They are usually much more regular in outline than the galactic nebulae, sometimes being globular or oval in shape and sometimes showing a spiral structure, like that in Andromeda.

Two nebulae are clearly visible to the naked eye ; the great nebula which forms the middle "star" of Orion's sword, and the spiral nebula in Andromeda. The first of these is a typical galactic nebula; the second is an extragalactic nebula, spiral in shape, which probably resembles quite closely our own galaxy of stars.

The galactic nebulae may be bright or dark. If they are illuminated by near-by stars they are bright. If not, they make their presence known by obscuring the background of Milky Way stars, and so look like dark patches empty or nearly empty of stars. They are often named because of fancied resemblances to terrestrial things, e.g. the Dumbbell Nebula, the Crab Nebula, the Keyhole Nebula or the North America Nebula. These are all bright nebulae. The Horse's Head Nebula in Orion (*see* illus. in facing page) and the Coal Sack near the Southern Cross are dark nebulae.

The bright nebulae are not self-luminous, but shine by reflected light from neighbouring stars. Sometimes, if the star close by is very hot, its ultra-violet light is absorbed by the gaseous cloud, which then emits a greenish glow. This green light, a puzzle for many years, was found in 1927 to be due to oxygen and nitrogen in a state difficult to produce in the laboratory. This is because the gas in a galactic nebula is extremely rarefied : it is probably at a pressure lower than that of the highest vacuum our best pumps can reach.

The galactic nebulae are enormous in size : if the sun were put in the middle of the Orion nebula its boundaries would extend far beyond all the planets to include several of the nearest stars. But these sizes are completely dwarfed by the extra-

*Yerkes Observatory*
**THE GREAT NEBULA IN ANDROMEDA**
Just visible to the naked eye as a fuzzy star, or nebula, in the girdle of Andromeda (a constellation of the northern hemisphere) this mass of glowing gas is millions of miles across. Here we see how it appears when viewed through a powerful telescope.

**NEBULAE LIGHT AND DARK**
This photograph, taken at the Mount Wilson Observatory, California, shows part of the great 'light' nebula just south of the star Zeta in Orion's belt. The black patch in it is the famous Horse's Head, one of the 'dark' nebulae, probably composed of opaque gas. The bright rim round the fantastically-shaped head probably indicates that its other side is luminous.

as if the whole visible universe is expanding—blowing up like a gigantic balloon. This process has probably been going on since the Earth was born.

The first catalogue of nebulae (1784) was made to enable these bodies to be distinguished from comets ; another, compiled by Sir William Herschel (1738–1822) and his son John Frederick Herschel (1792–1871), listed 5,000 nebulae, but included many subsequently found to be star-clusters. John Louis Dreyer (1852–1926), Danish astronomer, catalogued some 13,000, nearly all of which are true nebulae.

**Needles.** Needles of fish-bone, stone, iron and bronze have been found that were used by peoples of Stone Age and later times. Some of these old needles have the eye for carrying the thread at the point, as in the modern shoemaker's awl ; some have it halfway between the head and the point ; some have no eye at all, having been used like an awl to punch holes, through which the plant fibres or thongs of leather could be drawn.

Many different processes go to the making of a steel sewing needle today. We must begin with an account of the steel wire and how it is fashioned. The steel is one containing about eight parts of carbon in a hundred. The steel bar while white-hot is rolled to reduce thickness and increase length. Further rollings turn it out as a cylindrical-sectioned rod about a quarter-inch in diameter. Now it is ready to be made into wire by drawing through steel dies with smaller and yet smaller holes until it becomes of the proper diameter for the required needle.

Next the wire, after being annealed and softened, is cut into pieces the length of two needles end to end. As the wire has been wound on spools, these little pieces of wire are slightly curved. To make them straight they are gathered into

galactic nebulae. These objects are themselves galaxies like our own ; they have been happily named " island universes." Hundreds of thousands are known, yet each one probably contains some hundreds of millions of stars and measures so far across that light travelling 186,000 miles in a second would take about 30,000 *years* to go from one side to the other. They occur everywhere in the sky except close to the Milky Way, where they are obscured from view by absorbing matter like that which is concentrated into the dark galactic nebulae.

The more powerful the telescope the more numerous the visible extragalactic nebulae are seen to be. There seems to be no limit to the extent of space filled by these enormous collections of stars. But perhaps the most wonderful thing about them is that the farther away they are, the faster they are moving away from us. It looks

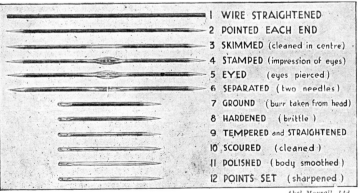

| | |
|---|---|
| 1 | WIRE STRAIGHTENED |
| 2 | POINTED EACH END |
| 3 | SKIMMED (cleaned in centre) |
| 4 | STAMPED (impression of eyes) |
| 5 | EYED (eyes pierced) |
| 6 | SEPARATED (two needles) |
| 7 | GROUND (burr taken from head) |
| 8 | HARDENED (brittle) |
| 9 | TEMPERED and STRAIGHTENED |
| 10 | SCOURED (cleaned) |
| 11 | POLISHED (body smoothed) |
| 12 | POINTS SET (sharpened) |

*Abel Morrall, Ltd.*

**FASHIONING A STEEL NEEDLE**
Modern machinery produces millions of needles of faultless quality for a variety of uses. This picture shows some of the various stages through which an ordinary sewing needle passes during manufacture.

*Professor D. K. Absolon*

**NEEDLES OF THE STONE AGE**
In the far-distant Stone Age housewives did their mending with eyed needles carved from reindeer horn, and with bodkins of ivory and bone. The implements here shown were found in Moravia, a province of Czechoslovakia.

bundles and heated until they glow dull red; as they cool they are rolled to and fro over an iron plate and pressed with a curved bar.

Now the wires are carried along to a grindstone and held against its face till a sharp point is put on each end. A rapidly revolving pulley draws these wires from the wheel and feeds them into a machine which marks the place for the eyes. The eyes are punched, and the double needles are then divided between the two eyes. (*See* illustration on page 2311).

Then the needles are hardened by heating red-hot, followed by quenching in liquid. This leaves them too hard, and brittle ; so they must be tempered, by reducing the hardness just enough to allow them to keep sharp without breaking easily. Then comes the polishing and sharpening ; thousands of needles are rolled up in a canvas sheet spread with emery powder and soft soap; the rolled sheet goes through heavy rollers backwards and forwards for a long time until the friction of the emery has made them bright and has shaped the points. If the needles are to be plated (nickel for the body and, perhaps, gilt for the eye), the points will then need a last sharpening before packing by automatic machinery in anti-rust paper.

**Negro.** In the broad sense, this term includes the woolly-haired, thick-lipped, broad-nosed, black or dark-brown inhabitants, or former inhabitants, of Africa. From central Africa, where the pure Negro is found (darkest of all in Northern Nigeria), the type shades off by gradual and imperceptible steps into the Semitic (Arab) and Hamitic (Egyptian and Libyan) types in the north, and into the Bushmen and Hottentots in the south.

Outside Africa, types resembling the Negro, called " Negroids " and " Negritos," exist on some of the larger islands and coasts of the western Pacific Ocean, notably in certain parts of the Philippines, in Malaya, and in New Guinea.

Through importation as slaves, true Negro types are found in almost all parts of the two American continents, in many places mixed with white and native Indian blood, the mixture of Negroes and Indians occurring chiefly in Central and South America. In Brazil, where the slave trade with Africa continued until 1854, the Negro elements form a large proportion of the population (*see* Brazil). In most parts of the West Indies, except Cuba and Puerto Rico, the black race predominates.

In the United States an exceptional situation exists, for the races have not blended together to the same extent as elsewhere. A sharp line of distinction is drawn between whites and blacks; and all who have Negro blood, even in a small proportion, are classed generally as Negroes.

Until after the American Civil War (1861–65) little effort was made to educate the Negro. In fact, slaves were often forbidden by law to learn to read and write. As soon as they gained their freedom, Church societies in the northern States sent large numbers of men and women teachers to teach them to read and write. Today, through the efforts of educated Negroes, much is being done to supply cultural facilities, and each year sees more teachers, physicians, lawyers, and business men among the Negroes, though in the south there are still many difficulties in the way of their development.

It is estimated that the African Negro population is about 125 million. The racial groups and their widely differing habits and customs, languages and religious beliefs, will be found described under the heading Africa.

**Nehru,** JAWAHARLAL (born 1889). In the early years of the 20th century there was studying at Harrow School, Middlesex, an Indian boy who was so brilliant that his teachers forecast for him a highly successful future, though few would have anticipated that, some 40 years later, he would be chosen as the first Prime Minister of the newly created Dominion of India.

Jawaharlal Nehru (pron. nā-roo̅′) was born at Allahabad, in the United Provinces, on November 14, 1889, the son of a rich lawyer, and was sent to England to be educated. From Harrow he went to Trinity College, Cambridge, and he became a barrister in London in 1912. Later he returned to India, and practised in the High Court there. In 1918, having become interested in politics, he joined the All-India Congress Committee, a Hindu organization which was trying to attain self-government for the country. (*See* India).

He took part in Gandhi's Non-Co-operation Movement, which advocated a policy of refusing to work with the British authorities ; and he was several times imprisoned for taking part in what were then illegal activities against British rule. He was very popular with his own people, and when, in 1947, the two sister dominions of India and Pakistan were created to take over self-government of the former Indian empire, Nehru was chosen as Premier of the Dominion of India. (*See* illustration on page 1717).

# The IMMORTAL VICTOR of TRAFALGAR

*H*istory's most brilliant sea-captain, a man of immense courage, the real saviour
*of England from Napoleon—no wonder Nelson was admired by his country-
men in his lifetime, and has been a national hero ever since.*

**Nelson,** HORATIO (1758–1805). The most famous naval commander of the greatest maritime power in history was so frail that, at his birth on September 29, 1758, he was not expected to live to maturity. His father's small income as rector of Burnham Thorpe in Norfolk forced the boy to leave his quiet home at 12 years of age and enter the Navy as "captain's servant." His uncle, on whose vessel Horatio made his first voyage, thought that the idea of trying to make a sailor out of the delicate, undersized boy was a piece of folly, and that the most merciful course would be to discourage him. So the first day at sea he ordered the boy aloft, saying, "Are you afraid, lad?" "Yes, sir," replied the shivering child. "I'm afraid, but I'm going to the top of the mast, sir!" He never forgot that sickening experience, and when at the age of 21 he was captain of a frigate he used to race the new boys up the mast and salute them at the top, by way of encouragement. He abolished some of the punishments then customary, declaring that cruelty made cowards.

Nelson's rise to fame began in 1793, during the war with the French Republic, when he was placed in command of the 64-gun ship Agamemnon. Repeatedly during the next three years he distinguished himself by bravery, coolness and sound judgement. During one of the famous engagements of this period—the battle of Calvi, in Corsica —he lost his right eye; and not long after, in an assault on Santa Cruz, in the Canary Islands, he received a wound which cost him his right arm.

His heroism was rewarded by a pension, knighthood of the Order of the Bath, and promotion to the rank of rear-admiral. Now came Nelson's great chance. He was assigned to hunt out and destroy the fleet with which Napoleon hoped to invade Egypt and strike British commerce at its most vulnerable point—the overland route to India between Port Said and Suez.

On August 1, 1798, with a fleet consisting of 14 ships of the line, Nelson attacked the French ships in Aboukir Bay, one of the mouths of the River Nile. "Where there is room for a French ship to swing an anchor," he said, "there is room for an English ship to sail." So he boldly sent half his fleet into the narrow space between the French ships and the shore, while the rest attacked from seaward, thus raking the enemy from both sides. This crushing victory of the Battle of the Nile, as it was called, made the one-eyed and one-armed admiral the idol of England. He was raised to the peerage as Baron Nelson of the Nile, and honours were heaped upon him.

Three years later (1801), when he had become vice-admiral, Nelson won a notable victory over the Danish fleet at Copenhagen. In the midst of the battle Nelson's superior, Sir Hyde Parker, from a distance imperilled success by hoisting signal of recall. Putting the telescope to his blind eye, Nelson murmured: "I really do not see the signal!" and turned what might have been disaster into triumph. As a reward for this victory he was created a viscount.

In May 1803 Nelson was called from retirement to defend England once more from the menace of Napoleonic invasion, and he was put in sole command of the Mediterranean fleet. For weary months he lay off the port of Toulon, and when the French fleet slipped out, he chased it to the West Indies and back, finally bringing it and the allied Spanish fleet to action off Cape Trafalgar on the south-west coast of Spain (October 21, 1805). When going into battle, Nelson flew from the mast-head of his flagship, the Victory, the signal that ever since has been Great Britain's watchword: "England expects that every man will do his duty.."

Nelson went into battle wearing his decorations, and when Captain Hardy, commander of the Victory, remonstrated, pointing out that they would make him an obvious mark, Nelson replied, "In honour I won them, and in honour I wear them!"

In arranging the order of battle, Nelson appointed his own ship, the Victory, to a place of great importance and danger. In the course of the engagement the Victory became entangled with a large French ship, the Redoubtable, and a fierce fight ensued. A broadside from the Victory drove the French gunners from their posts; but they continued to fight with muskets. Then the Frenchmen tried to board the English ship to capture her in a hand-to-hand fight, but a storm of grapeshot put an end to the attempt.

At this moment Nelson, walking the quarter-deck with Hardy, was wounded by a musket-shot from the Redoubtable—his medals, as Hardy

ENGLAND EXPECTS THAT EVERY

MAN WILL DO HIS

D U T Y

**NELSON'S SIGNAL**

No fewer than 31 flags were needed by the signalling code in use in 1805 to send Nelson's famous message to the fleet before Trafalgar.

*National Portrait Gallery*

**The greatest figure in British naval history, Horatio Nelson (above) saved England from invasion by Napoleon.**

**NELSON MORTALLY WOUNDED IN THE HOUR OF VICTORY**
This illustration from the picture by Sir Benjamin West, R.A., shows the scene on the quarter-deck of the Victory when Nelson fell mortally wounded by a shot fired by a marksman from the mizzen top of the French ship Redoubtable. The bullet penetrated the spine, and Nelson was carried below to the cockpit where he lived for three hours, dying at half-past four on the afternoon of October 21, 1805. In the picture, Hardy, the captain of the Victory, is seen holding Nelson's hand, and he was present when Nelson died.

was unhappy. In 1798 he fell passionately in love with Emma, Lady Hamilton, whom he had met at Naples, when she was the wife of the British Ambassador there. On his death Lady Nelson was given a pension of £2,000 a year, and his brother, the Rev. William Nelson, was created Earl Nelson of Trafalgar with a pension of £5,000 a year. This pension continued to be paid for over 100 years, until in 1946 an Act of Parliament was passed ending the payment on the deaths of the 4th Earl (who died in 1947) and his brother. Up to 1946 about £70,000 had been paid to the holders of the title of Earl Nelson. The 5th Earl then decided that Trafalgar House, near Salisbury, which was given to the Nelson family, would have to be sold, though the relics of Horatio Nelson were to be presented to the National Maritime Museum.

had feared, had made him conspicuous. He fell to the deck, and when Hardy attempted to raise him he said, " They've done for me at last, Hardy ! "

While Nelson lay dying in his cabin his men had gained a decisive victory over the French, and before he died Hardy brought him word that 14 or 15 of the enemy's ships had surrendered. " That is well," Nelson said, " but I bargained for twenty." And with the words " Thank God, I have done my duty ! " he passed away, at about half-past four on October 21, 1805, in the very hour of victory.

His flagship (*see* page 2297) brought the news home, and England learned with pride of her greatest naval victory since the defeat of the Armada, and with sorrow of the death of her valiant commander, England's " greatest seaman since our world began," as Tennyson aptly called him. He was buried in the crypt of St. Paul's Cathedral, London, on January 9, 1806, and is commemorated by the Nelson Column and its site, Trafalgar Square, in the heart of London.

As a young officer on the West India station Nelson, in 1787, had married M's. Nisbet, a doctor's widow with a little boy; but the marriage

**LADY HAMILTON**
In 1798 Nelson fell in love with Emma, Lady Hamilton, one of whose portraits by George Romney (1734–1802) is seen here.

Lady Hamilton died (in reduced and rather sad circumstances) at Calais in 1815. She was one of the most beautiful women of her time, a fact to which more than 20 portraits by Romney bear witness ; one of these is reproduced below.

**Nemesis.** (Pron. nem'-ē-sis). The personification of divine justice, Nemesis was represented in early Greek mythology as a goddess, the daughter of Night. The name meant originally the one who measures out ; hence she was regarded as the one who distributes good or bad fortune to each man according to his deserts, and punishes any violation of justice or any arrogance or presumption on the part of men. Later she was thought of largely as the angry avenger of crime, pursuing the evil-doer relentlessly like the Furies or Erinyes. She was sometimes represented as carrying a measuring-rod, a bridle, a sword, and a whip—emblems of her functions.

**Neon.** When you see an illuminated sign which gives a brilliant crimson glow, and which is made of glass tubing bent so as to form the words and other parts of the sign, you are looking at the glow which the rare gas neon gives when it is enclosed in a tube under low gaseous pressure and exposed to an electrical potential at a high voltage.

Scientists often investigate things just for the sake of doing so; applications of their work useful to Man often come later. Neon, and later neon lights, were discovered because Lord Rayleigh, about 1893, found that nitrogen obtained from our atmosphere was slightly heavier than nitrogen prepared by chemical methods. This observation led to an investigation by Sir William Ramsay and Morris Travers. These two chemists, assisted by others, found, after a great deal of painstaking work, that the earth's atmosphere contains not only common gases like oxygen and nitrogen, but also small percentages of several rare and chemically inert gases, which were named helium, neon, argon, krypton and xenon.

Although our atmosphere contains only about one part in 55,000 of neon, yet we obtain all the neon we need by distilling liquefied air.

Like the other rare gases named, neon does not react chemically with other elements. As already explained, neon is used in advertising signs; it is also used in beacons for airways, and in other forms of illumination like the neon bulbs sometimes used as night lights. Only a trace of neon is needed to give the crimson glow; by adding a little mercury vapour, the colour of the glow may be changed to blue or green. (*See* Air).

**Nepal.** (Pron. ne-pawl'). Among the mighty Himalaya Mountains, between the sub-continent of India and Tibet, lies the independent kingdom of Nepal. Since 1867 the sovereign of Nepal has delegated all power to his Prime Minister, who holds a hereditary rank by special rules of succession.

Nepal is by no means small; the area is about 54,000 square miles. The population consists largely of the famous Gurkha tribes, from whom were recruited some of the pick of the Indian and the British armies. Though Nepal is friendly with Britain few Europeans travel the road that leads to Khatmandu (pop. 108,000), the capital.

The visitor must first cross a long, narrow region of downland called the Terai; north of this is forest abounding in wild game. Along the boundary with India are some of the highest mountain peaks on earth; Everest (*q.v.*), Kinchinjunga (28,146 feet), and Dhaulagiri (26,795 feet) are among them. The soil is extremely fertile, and a thriving export trade is carried on in hides, tobacco, and cereals.

**Neptune.** In Roman mythology the name Neptune is given to the Greek sea-god Poseidon (*q.v.*). He is usually shown as a bearded man standing in a shell drawn over the sea, and holding a three-pronged spear, or trident.

In astronomy Neptune is the outermost planet but one of the solar system. It is 30 times as far from the sun as the earth. Its discovery in 1846 came as the result of certain investigations in the movements of Uranus, which led two astronomers, J. C. Adams (Cambridge) and U. J. J. Leverrier (France) to predict the presence of an unknown planet at almost the exact place where the telescope of J. G. Galle (Berlin) revealed Neptune. This planet is over four times the diameter of the earth, and takes 165 years to go round the sun. It has a "moon," called Triton. (*See* Astronomy; Planets).

**Neptunium.** Until fairly recent times chemists believed that all the substances in the world were made up of elements that could be fitted into the 92 spaces of Mendeléev's Periodic Table (*see* Chemistry ; Mendeléev). Even the discovery of isotopes (*q.v.*) did not upset the idea that there were only 92 elements, because isotopes of any particular element are chemically the same, have the same atomic number, and are indeed chemically the same element.

But when scientists began to bombard elements with neutrons (*see* Atom), they not only found that the nucleus of the atom of the element known as uranium 235 could be split by a process known as " nuclear fission " (a process which forms the basis of the atomic bomb); but also that the atom of ordinary uranium (element 92), uranium 238, could " capture " neutrons (without undergoing nuclear fission) to form the isotope, uranium 239.

Uranium 239 is radio-active, and soon changes into an element called neptunium (element 93), which in turn undergoes a radio-active change to form plutonium (element 94), another element suitable for making atomic bombs. So the chemist must now add new elements to his list.

The uranium atomic " pile " may supply Man with heat and power, but it also produces neptunium, and hence plutonium. Chemists have assigned the symbol Np to neptunium, and the symbol Pu to plutonium.

**Nero,** EMPEROR OF ROME (A.D. 37-68). Lucius Domitius Ahenobarbus Nero began his reign at the age of 17, a handsome, talented, and by no means bad-hearted youth. Although Nero owed his throne to a crime, the blame for this rested on his wicked mother Agrippina, whose ambition for her son knew no bounds. She married as her second husband the Emperor Claudius, and influenced him to put aside his own son, Britannicus, in favour of Nero, whom he adopted. Then, becoming impatient to see her own son seated upon the throne, she caused Claudius to be poisoned.

**NERO**

He was one of the worst of the Roman Emperors, the last nine years of his reign being an orgy of tyranny. He committed suicide in A.D. 68.

The Romans looked with favour upon Nero, since he was descended on both sides from Augustus, the first Roman emperor. Under the influence of his tutor, Seneca—a wise philosopher and brilliant writer (*c.* 4 B.C.–A.D. 65)—all went well for a year. Then Nero's evil traits began to develop. He was cowardly, and committed one crime to cover up another. He caused Britannicus to be poisoned, in A.D. 55, and four years later had his own mother murdered. He divorced and later put to death his wife Octavia. He killed his second wife Poppaea Sabina in a fit of rage. A third woman, who refused to marry him, was slain, and he killed the husband of a fourth so that she might become his wife. He was insanely suspicious of all his associates, and upon discovering a plot against him he had Seneca put to death, together with many other famous men.

In A.D. 64 fires broke out in Rome which burned for a week and destroyed more than half the city. It was rumoured that Nero himself had started the fires, and that, as he watched the conflagration, he played upon his "fiddle" (lyre) and recited verses about the burning of Troy.

Historians are generally agreed that there was probably no foundation for this charge, but at the

**NERO VIEWS THE RUINS OF ROME**
Though it was whispered at the time that the fires which destroyed half of Rome in the year A.D. 64 were planned by the Emperor Nero himself, historians are now inclined to believe that there is no truth in the assertion. This imaginative painting by Carl Peloty depicts Nero, wearing a wreath, viewing the ruins after the destruction of the city.

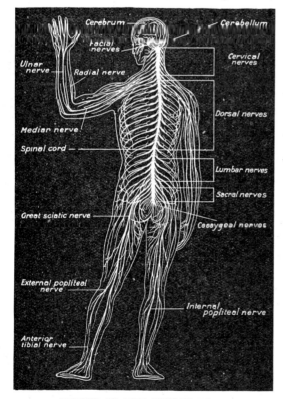

**NERVES OF THE HUMAN BODY**
From the spinal cord issue, in all, 31 pairs of spinal nerves, each pair coming from between two vertebrae through an opening called the intervertebral foramen. There are eight pairs of cervical, 12 pairs of dorsal, five pairs of lumbar and sacral, and one pair of coccygeal nerves.

time many believed it. In order to free himself from suspicion Nero fastened the blame upon the Christians, and caused numbers of them to be put to death with the most cruel tortures. This is reckoned as the first of the 10 great persecutions of the Christians under the Roman Empire.

After the fire Nero set about rebuilding the city, and erected for himself a magnificent palace called the Golden House. But heavy taxation, misgovernment, and cruelty caused first discontent and then revolt in the provinces. Galba, the Roman governor of Spain, marched with his troops upon Rome, and was joined by the emperor's own bodyguard. Nero fled, news reaching him in his hiding-place that the Senate had sentenced him to death and proclaimed Galba emperor. At the approach of the horsemen who came to drag him to execution Nero commanded an attendant to stab him to death, exclaiming, "What an artist dies in me!"

Thus passed away the last of the Augustan line of Caesars. His enthusiasm for art, and any other good qualities he may have had—he was always a generous donor to the poor—were soon forgotten and his name is black in history.

**Nerves.** The nerves form the "telephone system" of the human body. Although the comparison is over-obvious, and somewhat overworked, no other analogy is so good. The nerves put every individual part of the body into direct communication with the "exchange" in the brain, and thus with one another. Anything which interferes with this communication leaves some part of the organ so cut off that its nutrition may be endangered, its wastes may accumulate, and it may become a prey to disease. In any case it is out of control, and its usefulness is impaired until nerve communication is again established.

The nervous system consists partly of cells and partly of fibres; each of the latter is a long " process " extending from a nerve cell. The brain and the spinal cord form the " central nervous system." Each of the nerve "wires" or fibres carries messages only in one direction. Oftentimes there is a special line which takes care of a particular affair, and of that only. For example, the optic nerve takes care of " sight " messages only; the auditory nerve of " sound," and so on.

Those nerves which carry incoming messages, i.e., towards the brain, are called "afferent" nerves, and it is they that bring all information about heat cr cold, or pain, and so on from the outside world. Those which carry outgoing messages are known as " efferent " nerves, and they are concerned with the various activities of the body. (Afferent is from the Latin *ef*, " to," and *ferre*, " carry " ; efferent is from Latin *ef*, " out," and *ferre*.) Some efferent nerves are " motor " ones— that is, they cause muscles to contract and allow of movement by their attachment to bones in a leverage system; others are " secretory " nerves—that is, they cause glands to secrete.

Ths nerves can be seen as the whitish cords that run between the muscles of the body, branches going into each muscle and to every part of the skin. Usually the nerve fibres for any part of the body are bound together into one bundle, and they do not separate until just before they reach the spinal cord. There they divide into two roots, and each root contains only one kind of fibre. One root, containing efferent fibres, enters the spinal cord towards the front. The other root enters the spinal cord at the back and is composed of afferent fibres.

These afferent and efferent fibres connect with collections of nerve-cells in the cord. Such collections we know are composed of " grey matter," and they both receive and originate messages. They are the " branch exchanges " of the telephone system, and are connected with the chief exchange in the brain. Those efferent nerves which deal wholly with the involuntary or unconscious life (such as heart action, secretion, stomach and intestinal movements and the like) are called the " sympathetic" nerves ; while those nerves which deal with conscious movements, directing voluntary acts, are known as the " cerebro-spinal " nerves, and are attached to the spinal cord. The sympathetic system has its own connecting fibres running outside the vertebrae, and has three great centres—known as the cardiac, solar, and hypogastric " plexuses,"

In the human body there are twelve pairs of nerves connected with the brain, called the cranial nerves; and thirty-one pairs connected with the spinal cord, called the spinal nerves.

It is interesting to note that the nerves develop in the same direction that the message is to travel. For example, the optic nerve (which carries an ingoing message) begins to grow at the retina and grows in towards the brain ; while the motor nerves (which carry outgoing messages) begin at the nerve centres and grow towards the outside of the body.

In the embryo animal the development of the central nervous system is continuous with that of the skin, which turns inwards to form that system. Thus, looking at an individual one is indeed looking at the " essential person "; the external features are not only a reflection of his nervous characteristics, but are one and the same with them.

Some nerve cells can " regenerate," as when a nerve is cut in a wound. The nerve cells can leap quite a distance to join up with their colleagues, even when a severed nerve is not sewn end to end by the surgeon. But some types of " master cells " never grow again when destroyed, so that paralysis or loss of function follows any disaster to them.

**Netball.** Like basketball (*q.v.*), netball is an exceedingly fast game. Played in Britain mainly in girls' schools, it requires speed, ability to dodge with extreme quickness, and a keen eye.

The game may be played either indoors or outdoors on any level space on which a rectangular court, usually 100 feet by 50 feet, can be marked out. At each end of the court, which is divided into three equal parts, a shooting semi-circle is marked 16 feet round the goal post, which is placed in the centre of the goal line. In the centre of the ground a circle four feet in radius is drawn. The ball used is an ordinary Association football. The goals consist of an iron ring 15 inches in diameter, placed horizontally 10 feet above the ground, projecting six inches from the support, and bearing a net open at the bottom, through which the ball must pass.

**TUSSLE AT NETBALL**
The player in the centre is jumping to intercept a shot made by the girl behind her. The goal is a single upright post, fitted with a ring 10 feet above the ground ; attached to the ring is a net through which the ball must pass to score a goal.

*Fox*

There are usually seven players in a team— centre, attacking centre, goal scorer, defending centre, attack, defence, and goalkeeper. At the start of the game one of the two umpires bounces the ball in the centre circle. The game is played by throwing the ball to one of your own side until it reaches the goal scorer. The opponents try to prevent this happening by catching the ball in mid-air and passing it to one of their side. The ball may not be carried, kicked, or punched.

# LAND *of* BULBS *and* WINDMILLS

*Though it is a small country Holland is full of interest to the visitor. Its canals,*
*windmills and extensive bulb-fields provide beauty. Its reclaimed land is*
*evidence of Dutch industry and courage.*

**Netherlands.** The kingdom of the Netherlands is popularly called Holland (*q.v.*) because of the historical, economic and political importance of the two provinces, North and South Holland. It consists of the delta land of three rivers: the Rhine, the Meuse (or Maas, as the Dutch themselves call it), and the Scheldt, with an area of 13,550 square miles, excluding water. Almost one-half of the land, including the three largest cities—Amsterdam, Rotterdam, and The Hague—lies below sea-level. The highest spot —in Limburg—is at 966 feet. The shores of sea and of rivers alike are dyked and thousands of windmills and electric pumps help to keep the sea from submerging the land.

> **Extent.**—North to south, 210 miles; east to west, 120 miles. Area about 13,550 sq. miles, exclusive of gulfs and bays. Population over 10 million.
> **Natural Features.**—Level surface, with almost all the coastal portion below sea-level and protected by dykes and extensive drainage systems; mouths of Rhine, Maas (Meuse), and Scheldt rivers; and numerous canals.
> **Products.**—Butter, cheese and milk; flower bulbs, rye, oats, potatoes, sugar-beet and wheat; herring and oysters; coal; cut diamonds, ships, textiles, flour, shoes, margarine, bricks, tiles, machinery, electrical and radio apparatus, printed matter, cocoa and chocolate.
> **Cities.**—Amsterdam (capital, 814,000), Rotterdam (653,000), The Hague (seat of the Government, 542,000), Utrecht (187,000), Haarlem (159,000), Groningen (133,000), Eindhoven (136,000).
> **Overseas Territories.**—The Netherlands West Indies include Surinam or Netherlands Guiana, and the Netherlands Antilles (formerly Curaçao), and are part of the Kingdom of the Netherlands. Surinam: area 55,143 square miles; population 191,628. Netherlands Antilles: area 384 square miles; population 133,800.
> In 1949 the Netherlands East Indies, exclusive of Dutch New Guinea, became the Republic of the United States of Indonesia, linked with the Netherlands by a Netherlands-Indonesian Union. Population of the Republic about 68 million; area 736,268 square miles.

North Sea swept into the very heart of the country and covered hundreds of towns and villages and formed the Zuider Zee. During 1920–24 work was begun on draining a large area of the Zuider Zee, and when, in 1933, the last gap of a nearly-20-miles-long dyke was closed the Zuider Zee was finally cut off from the North Sea and was named the Ijssel Lake. Further reclamations were started in other areas before the Second World War (1939–45).

A Dutch saying goes, "God made the world, but the Dutch made Holland." Those dykes are among the world's finest engineering achievements. The sea itself has tossed up a natural barrier in the sand dunes which line the coastal area. The Dutch reinforce these

The dykes are carefully guarded, for Holland had its warning more than 500 years ago when the dunes with dykes built of stone, clay, and earth on foundations of concrete posts or long wooden piles.

*J. G. van Agtmaal*

**WHERE WINDMILLS KEEP THE SEA AT BAY**

Through many centuries the people of the Netherlands have waged a hard fight to keep the sea from inundating their low-lying country. Dykes and dams are not sufficient, and pumps are always at work to clear away the surplus water. Many are electrically driven, but a large number of them are still worked by windmills, and rows of these, such as those seen in the photograph, are so familiar a feature of the landscape that Holland has been called 'the land of windmills.'

## HOLLAND'S NEVER-ENDING STRUGGLE AGAINST THE SEA

One of the most difficult feats carried out by Dutch engineers was the damming of the Zuider Zee, a vast tract in the north of the Netherlands which was flooded when the North Sea swept inland more than 500 years ago. Work was begun in 1920 and completed in 1933, when the last gap in the huge dam 18½ miles long was closed (above). Most of the bed of the inland sea was drained, and the remaining water was renamed the Ijssel Lake. The Germans reflooded part of the area during the Second World War (1939–45), but by 1946 the Dutch had repaired the dykes and recommenced draining.

The stork is popular in Holland because the bird eats the teredo, a worm which bores into the piles. Some of the larger sea dykes, 200 or 300 feet wide, are as tall as three-storey houses, with a highway or railway running on top. The rich farm lands, wrested from the waters and protected by the dykes, are called polders. Water is pumped off them into the canals. Much of Holland has been reclaimed in this way to support a rapidly growing population, nearly 700 people to the square mile. Although small farms are still numerous, the movement of the population towards the cities has been increasing rapidly in recent years, and only about 20 per cent of the people now work on the land.

In Holland, many of the cottages are brightly coloured—some with blue walls and yellow roof, others lavender and rose, made brighter by gay-coloured window blinds. And usually there is a neat garden in front, often enclosed by a hedge clipped in bird and animal shapes. Dutch homes are usually of brick, because wood and stone are scarce, and their roofs are tiled or thatched. Barn and house are frequently under one roof to save space —the family at the back, the cattle in front in quarters almost as clean as the house. Stoves and open fires are kept going all the year round, for the climate is damp and cool, with severe cold in winter and but few hot days in summer. Boats are tied in front of houses along the canals as commonly as motor-cars are parked in other countries.

If you visit the Netherlands you may think that it looks like no other country in the world, with its flat meadows; its canals and their barge population, living their whole lives in those queer craft with bright red cabins and miniature gardens ; its storks; its windmills, and its red-roofed villages. Holland's pleasant land has an attractive people. The Dutch were known to tourists at one time for their quaint costumes, varying with the district—wooden shoes and baggy trousers of the farmers and fishermen, and the queer, neat caps worn by the women in many provinces. But these are seldom seen today.

Almost everywhere in Holland the past is as much in evidence as the present. There are Gothic or Renaissance cathedrals, generally whitewashed inside. There are many old town-halls, and weigh-houses where for hundreds of years cheeses have been weighed. Everywhere are reminders of the Spanish domination of the Netherlands, of Prince William the Silent, who in 1572 led the revolt against the Spaniards, and of Holland's struggle to establish a republic. Then there are the houses of Holland's saints, philosophers, and scholars—among which are Thomas à Kempis, Erasmus, Spinoza and Hugo Grotius.

In art as well as in architecture the past is represented. The art galleries of even some of the smaller cities are the envy of other countries, not only for their collections of the Dutch school—Rembrandt, Gerard Dou, Frans Hals, Jan Vermeer, Ruysdael, Hobbema and others—but of the schools of France and other lands.

No matter how long you may stay in the Netherlands, and in spite of knowing that it is a small

*Netherlands Travel Bureau*

**IN THE OLD UNIVERSITY TOWN OF LEIDEN**
A very ancient Dutch city and at one time the centre of the weaving industry, Leiden is now chiefly noted for its university (above). It was founded in 1575 as a reward for the city's stout resistance against the Spaniards in 1573–74, and is the most important in the Netherlands. The town is nine miles north-east of The Hague.

quaint old university town of Leiden (or Leyden).

If you are at Leiden in April it is worth while to make the short rail journey to Haarlem, in the heart of the bulb-growing country. For mile after mile the train passes fields carpeted with red, yellow, white and purple tulips and hyacinths. Great heaps of the bright flowers are piled in the corners of the fields waiting to be ploughed in to enrich the soil, for the bulbs and not the flowers are sold, immense quantities being exported to Britain and elsewhere.

Haarlem is 10 miles by train west of Amsterdam, which is the commercial capital of the Netherlands. From Amsterdam there are the short excursions to be made—to the picturesque village of Marken, where there was a flourishing fishing community until the draining of the Zuider Zee took the sea away; to Edam, the home of cheeses with bright red rind, and which was once the port of Amsterdam before that city was connected with the North Sea by a canal; to Alkmaar, where peasants from neighbouring farms unload cargoes of cheeses from boats to be sold at the Friday cheese market.

About 42 minutes by train from Amsterdam and 35 minutes from Rotterdam lies Utrecht, "the city of spires" and also of bridges. It was there that the northern provinces organized their resistance to Spanish

country, as a visitor you will continue to be surprised that its cities are so close together. From Rotterdam a ride of an hour and a half on a river steamboat will take you past fisheries and shipyards to the city of Dordrecht, the four rivers and the connecting canals giving it a resemblance to Venice. Dordrecht was once the richest town in the Netherlands and is still one of the most beautiful, being a favourite with painters.

A steam barge will take you by canal from Rotterdam to Delft, once famous for its potteries, now for its quiet picturesqueness and for the fact that it contains the tombs of William the Silent and of Grotius. Not far north of Delft lies The Hague, the political capital of the Netherlands. From there it is only a short distance to Scheveningen, once a fishing-village with an attractive old-world air, now a fashionable watering-place; and to the

sovereignty in 1579; and there that a peace treaty between France, England and Austria was concluded in 1714. From Utrecht an hour's ride will take you to Arnhem, lying in a district of wooded hills. It was near there, on September 17, 1944, during the Second World War, that British and Polish parachute and glider-borne troops landed in an attempt to seize the bridge over the Rhine at Arnhem towards which the British 2nd Army was advancing from the south. Heavily outnumbered by the Germans, they fought for nine days and eight nights to keep a footing in the town until reinforcements could reach them; but all efforts to relieve them failed, and the survivors had to be withdrawn across the river during the night of September 25–26. Out of a strength of some 11,000 the British and Polish parachute and glider-borne troops suffered more than 7,000 casualties.

D. McLeish

## SAILS OVER THE NETHERLANDS

Windmills, like this one near Flushing, are to be seen all over the Netherlands, for
the sails work the pumps that help to keep the sea from overflowing on to the land.
There are not so many as there were, however, for electric pumps are being
increasingly used in their stead.

*Nicholls and D. McLeish*

The traditional costume of the Dutch fisherfolk, seen in the upper photograph, is one of the most delightful survivals in this picturesque land. The harbour of the tiny island of Urk (lower), on the edge of the Ijssel Lake, still provides anchorage for sturdy smacks, though not so many as when they fished the Zuider Zee, of which only the lake now remains.

Chief among Holland's imports are iron and steel, textiles, coal and coke, timber, machinery, wheat, corn and linseed. Among its exports in normal times are meat, butter, cheese, eggs, coal and coke, wireless equipment, coffee, chocolate, cocoa, spices, vegetables and, of course, those famous bulbs. No other part of the world has a bigger harvest per acre of wheat, but still the Dutch are unable to grow sufficient to supply their own needs. Rye and oats, potatoes, sugar-beet, flax and barley are other important crops. The farms are small, some no larger than two acres, so that little machinery is used on them; instead, they are intensively cultivated by hand. Wood and stone are so scarce

to about 5,000 miles of reasonably good roads—narrow and usually of brick—and some 2,300 miles of railway. Air services are maintained with the countries of western Europe, with North America and the East.

The early history of this country is one of unrest. In the Middle Ages the present kingdoms of Belgium and the Netherlands were a group of disconnected provinces and duchies, some forming part of France and some part of the Holy Roman Empire. Gradually these passed into the hands of the Dukes of Burgundy, and Charles the Bold (*q.v.*) sought unsuccessfully to weld them together and create a border kingdom between

*K.L.M., Netherlands*

### MIDDELBURG BEFORE THE GERMAN BOMBING

On the island of Walcheren, Middelburg contains many old buildings, including the 17th century Stadthuis or Town Hall in the Groote Markt (Great Market), here seen—in the centre of the photograph—as it was before May 1940, when it was severely damaged by German bombers. When the Royal Air Force breached the dykes on the coast of Walcheren in October 1944, to flood the German positions, the town was inundated, but was restored after repairs to the dykes in 1945.

that farmers divide their fields with ditches or hedges. The seaside fishermen catch herring, flounders, eels, oysters and mussels.

Coal is mined in the southern province of Limburg. The country has few other minerals, except salt. Though handicapped by lack of iron and coal the Netherlands is one of the foremost shipbuilding nations. Cotton weaving, diamond cutting, flour milling, and printing are leading industries; machinery, especially electrical equipment, woollen goods and condensed milk are also important products.

Canals and rivers provide the chief means of transport for both passengers and freight. In winter the people skate frequently, even making long trips on the frozen canals between the towns. Besides the coastline of about 200 miles, there are over 4,800 miles of navigable waterways, as compared

France and Germany. The marriage of his daughter Mary to Emperor Maximilian of Austria in 1477 brought the Low Countries (Netherlands), as this whole group of territories was then called, under the rule of Austria. On the abdication of Charles V, King of Spain and Holy Roman Emperor, in 1556, they passed to Philip II of Spain.

Against the political and religious tyranny of Spain, culminating in the infamous rule of the Duke of Alva, the Dutch revolted in 1568. But the 10 southern provinces were Catholic in religion, while the seven northern ones were Protestant, so dissension crept in. In 1579 the Protestant provinces formed the separate Union of Utrecht, and thenceforth were usually called the United Provinces, sometimes the Dutch Netherlands. In 1581 they issued their formal declaration of independence. In 1609 Spain signed a truce virtually acknowledging

# TRADITIONAL DRESS IN THE LAND OF THE DUTCH

The first three pictures illustrate the traditional costumes still worn on special occasions by peasants in different parts of the Netherlands. The two women with the shoulder 'wings' (1) are from Axel, a city 20 miles west of Antwerp. The man and his wife (2), both in their best clothes, are fisher-folk from Scheveningen, a fashionable watering-place. The two girls in the centre (3), with typical caps, are from the city of Volendam. The lower picture (4) shows the interior of a typical Dutch home on the island of Marken, where a local style of dress still persists. The houses of the Dutch people, no matter how poor the occupants, are always clean and attractive.

**THE INAUGURATION OF QUEEN JULIANA**

On the abdication of her mother Queen Wilhelmina in 1948, Princess Juliana succeeded to the throne of the Netherlands and was inaugurated as Queen on September 6 of that year. She is seen at the ceremony in the Nieuwe Kerk (New Church), Amsterdam. On her left is her husband, Prince Bernhard, who took the title of Prince of the Netherlands.

*Keystone*

provinces (Belgium). This connexion ended when Belgium revolted in 1830, and proclaimed itself a separate kingdom. In 1890 the death of King William III, without sons, brought to the throne his daughter, who became Queen Wilhelmina, and who abdicated in 1948 in favour of her daughter, now Queen Juliana. The government is a constitutional monarchy.

In the tremendous upheaval of the Second World War (1939–45) the Netherlands hoped to maintain neutrality, which had been respected by both sides in the First World War, 20 years earlier. The Germans, however, invaded the country on May 10, 1940, did tremendous damage in the cities which were bombed (especially Rotterdam), and conquered the whole country in five days. The Royal family and the Cabinet moved to London, and a resistance movement organized by the Dutch occupying German troops. The R.A.F. dropped food in stricken areas early in 1945. The country was not entirely freed until the general German surrender on May 8, 1945. (*See also* Indonesia.)

the Provinces as independent, but formal peace did not come until the Treaty of Westphalia (1648).

Until the Dutch wars with Great Britain (1652–54 and 1664–67), the United Provinces were the greatest commercial and maritime State in the world. The attempt of Louis XIV of France (in 1672–78) to conquer the Netherlands inflicted another serious blow on the Provinces. The republic ended when members of the House of Orange became hereditary rulers of the Netherlands in 1747. When the wars of the French Revolution broke out, the French revolutionaries overthrew the rule of the House of Orange and made the Netherlands again a republic (1795). Napoleon set his brother Louis over it as king (1806–10), but later annexed the land directly to France. The Congress of Vienna (1814–15) restored the Netherlands as a kingdom under the House of Orange, and added to it the southern

**PROCLAIMING THE BIRTH OF PRINCESS BEATRIX**

About the Court of the Netherlands much of the pageantry of old days still persists on State occasions, though the ordinary life of the Royal Family is devoid of unnecessary ceremony. This photograph shows heralds in quaint medieval costumes, blowing a fanfare as they passed through the streets of Amsterdam on January 31, 1938, to proclaim the birth of their first daughter to Princess Juliana, as she then was, and her husband, Prince Bernhard.

*Keystone*

# FAMOUS DUTCH *and* FLEMISH PAINTERS

*Though less notable for its achievements in the other arts, Holland has given
birth to some of the world's greatest painters, members of the renowned Flemish
and Dutch schools. Their names are chronicled here.*

**Netherlands:** ITS ART. The art of the
Netherlands falls into two periods, so distinct as
to be virtually separate phases in the history of art
—the Flemish and the Dutch. The northern Gothic
architecture did not lend itself to mural decoration
as did that of Italy, and painting was therefore done
on wooden panels, such works being used largely for
decorating the town halls and guildhalls as well as
the churches of Flanders. During that period, the
preparation of colours and panels was done by
apprentices in the painters' workshops. The advent
of Flemish painting as we know it was delayed until
the second half of the 14th century, when in Italy
the new birth of art was already accomplished.

Then, suddenly, there appear the brothers Van
Eyck, Hubert (*c.* 1366–1426) and Jan (*c.* 1380–
1441), founders of Flemish panel painting. The
former, inspired apparently by Italian works, began
a famous altar-piece at Ghent which was completed by his younger
brother. The Van
Eycks were not, as was
long believed, the in-
ventors of oil painting.
This method was al-
ready known in the
10th century, but
nothing remained of
the work of the artists
who used it. The Van
Eycks renewed the
method. Jan's master-
piece depicts Arnolfini
and his wife (National
Gallery, London).

Contemporary with
the Ghent school was
that of Brussels, led by
Roger van der Wey-
den (*c.* 1400–64) and
Hans Memling (*c.*
1430–94), in many
ways the greatest of
these early Flemings.
Ranked by some with
the famous Italians
whom he preceded,
Memling possesses a
tender mysticism and
unaffected graceful-
ness. His most famous
work is the shrine of
St. Ursula, exhibiting
eight panels and six
medallions. Yet
whereas the great
period of Italian art
from Cimabue to Fra
Angelico evolved over
a century, the rise and
development of the

Flemish school occupied but a short period. Other
artists who reached a very high standard were
Hugo van der Goes (*c.* 1435–82) ; Dierick Bouts
(*c.* 1410–75), and Gerard David (*c.* 1450–1523),
all of whom were actually Dutchmen ; and Petrus
Cristus (*c.* 1400–73), originator of Netherlandish
*genre* (household and family) pictures.

In the 16th century Flemish painting suffered
to a considerable extent through the work of a
group of painters who have been termed "Italianizers," because they overwhelmed their native
art with the lusciousness and richness of the
Italians. Their work is seen in the paintings of
Mabuse (*c.* 1472–1532) and Van Orley (*c.* 1490–
1540). Alongside of them, however, flourished
several fine schools of native Flemish painters. At
Antwerp, Quentin Matsys (1466–1530) initiated a
new *genre* school whose colour was also far more
brilliant than that of earlier Flemings.

Patinir (*c.* 1475–
1524) and Hendrik
Bles (*c.* 1480– *c.* 1550)
were perhaps the first
of genuine landscape
painters, in whose pic-
tures Nature is for the
first time more im-
portant than Man.
Patinir and his pupils
especially delighted in
strange rocky shapes
and broad rivers, with
sky and distance alike
done in a brilliantly
cold, hard blue. Into
these pictures (which
you may see in the
National Gallery,
London) are intro-
duced figures of the
Holy Family or of
early saints.

At Antwerp, again,
worked the Brueghels,
a family of *genre*
painters who followed
Bosch (*c.* 1460–1516)
and are famous for the
fantastic detail of their
paintings, in many of
which the back-
grounds are crammed
with scores of little
figures. Pieter Brue-
ghel the elder (died *c.*
1570) was nicknamed
"the Peasant" because
he was best known for
his robust and humor-
ous scenes of peasant
life (*see* Brueghel).

**A MASTERPIECE OF DUTCH ART**
In this painting by Jan van Eyck, dated 1434, are depicted an
Italian merchant Jan Arnolfini, his wife and their dog. It was
found in Brussels after the battle of Waterloo (June 18, 1815) and
brought to London, later being placed in the National Gallery.

# GLORIOUS ART OF THE NETHERLANDS

*Photo, Alinari*

Jan Vermeer of Delft, who painted this lovely Girl Reading at a Window, is one of the three finest artists of the Dutch School, and his pictures are extremely rare. In this one all the qualities for which he is deservedly famous are visible : simplicity of design ; a setting in the interior of a house ; warm, almost glowing light ; and, above all, a gentle grading of tones, with no strong, direct contrasts, and yet a truth to life that is almost startling.

2325

2 1E5

Church of St. Bavon, Ghent; photo, Mansell

## SUPREME EXAMPLE OF THE ART OF THE TWO FLEMISH BROTHERS VAN EYCK

The paintings of the brothers Van Eyck of Ghent show the full flowering of the glorious Flemish School. Here is a part of what is often considered to be their greatest masterpiece, a huge altar piece done for the burgomaster of Ghent. This consisted of some 20 panels, of which that shown here, The Adoration of the Lamb, is the lower central and by far its name to the whole work. The realism of these early Flemish painters is here seen to advantage, while we cannot fail to notice their truth to Nature, and the care with which every flower and every leaf are depicted. The picture as a whole is an allegory—one of a class of paintings by which the teachings of the Church were brought home to the humbler people. This work, begun by Hubert van Eyck, who died in 1426, before its completion, was finished by his brother, Jan, who died in 1440.

MOVEMENT AND GRACE IN AN UNUSUAL WORK BY RUBENS

Rubens (1577–1640) was famous for his figure-studies and religious paintings, but everything he did was imbued with the same amazing life and movement. In few of his works, however, are these features so evident as in this Dance of Peasants. Notice the skill with which the artist has interwoven the pattern of his dancers, using the horizontal lines of the outstretched arms of the left-hand quartet to give the impression of speed and movement; to the right of the picture, where the action is slowing up, there is less movement, but one outstretched arm is used in an attempt to link the ends of the broken circle together.

Prado Gallery, Madrid; photo. Anderson

# ONE OF REMBRANDT'S MANY MASTERPIECES

A Man in a Golden Helmet is the title of this painting, considered one of Rembrandt's best works. Dimly-lit portraits such as this, characteristic of the greatest of all the Dutch artists, would seem to offer small scope for the expression of tremendous gifts; but one has only to look at it to see the character which the artist finds in his sitter's face, and the skill with which he transfers it to the canvas for the pleasure of future generations

# HOMELY STUDY BY A GENIUS OF PORTRAITURE

Frans Hals is best known for grand portraits such as the famous Laughing Cavalier (*see* page 1569), in which the detail is subservient to the general effect; but in this delightful Nurse and Child you see with what care and skill he could reproduce in paint the complicated lacework and embroidery of a small child's dress, ruffles and headgear. There is much charm, too, in the attitude of the nurse who is keeping the child amused.

# OUTDOORS AND INDOORS IN 18th-CENTURY HOLLAND

*Lower, from the painting in the possession of Viscountess Swinton;  top, National Gallery, London*

Perhaps no Dutch landscape is so well known as The Avenue, Middelharnis (upper), Meyndert Hobbema's most popular painting. In design alone it is an outstanding work, for there are few painters who would so courageously tackle a subject of this type. David Teniers (the younger), artist of the Corps de Garde (The Watch) seen below the landscape, provides a link between the Flemish and Dutch schools, for while he himself belonged to the former, he was followed in manner by many members of the latter school. He died on April 25, 1690.

# DUTCH LIFE AS DEPICTED IN ITS ART

*Top, The Hague; photo, Mansell. Lower, from the painting in the possession of Sir W. Hyde Parker*

The Dutch marine painters form a group apart, unapproached in their special type of painting by those of any other nation. The upper picture is by J. van de Velde, member of a famous family of artists, and is entitled Quiet Sea with Shipping. In winter the Dutch of yesterday (like those of today) betook themselves to the ice which covered their innumerable canals and waterways and provided subjects for paintings of another type. Catwyck in Winter, by Abraham Beerstraaten, is a typical example of this form of painting.

## REALISM AND DETAIL EXPRESSED IN DUTCH STILL LIFE

An important school of Dutch art included the painters of flower-pieces, many of whom displayed wonderful skill. In this Vase with Flowers, by Jan van Huysum (1682–1749), you see not only flowers, but fruits, insects, and even a bird's nest, all displayed with the same astonishing realism which sought to portray even the drops of dew on individual blossoms and the blemishes on the wings of the insects. For beauty of colour and skill of composition, too, these pictures have seldom been rivalled in the world of still life.

Other followers of the various groups included Paul Bril (1554–1626), who carried on the landscape tradition, and the portraitist Antonis Mor (1512–76), who worked also in Spain and in England, where he was known as Sir Anthony Mor. (*See* English Art).

Peter Paul Rubens (1577–1640) studied under various masters and, having spent some years in Italy, settled in Antwerp in 1608. There and elsewhere he executed an enormous number of paintings, remarkable for their size and their general excellence as well as for their actual number; even allowing for the fact that he was assisted by his best pupils, his achievement is colossal. He brought the full radiance of Italy—and especially of Venice—to the less emotional outlook of the Fleming, and united these with his own superb powers of draughtsmanship and design. If he lacked the "soul" that makes painters of the very highest rank, he outdid every painter the North had produced in almost everything else. In religious paintings, in portraits, and in landscapes he was alike excellent. His influence was naturally tremendous, yet he had only one great pupil, Anthony van Dyck (1599–1641), who began his career as an assistant in Rubens's studio. Van Dyck, who, like Mor and Rubens, was knighted in England, was above all a portrait painter, and his finest works in the grand manner, in which he excelled, rank among the world's great portraits. Of his followers the most important were Philippe de Champaigne and Sir Peter Lely. (*See* French Art and English Art respectively).

Rubens failed to influence all the Flemish painters with his Italian ideas. The native tradition was stressed by Jordaens (1593–1678), who did robust portraits and peasant *genre*, and Snyders (1579–1657), who painted fine scenes of animals and still-life of flowers and fruit.

Flemish painting was dying by the end of the 17th century, but links between it and the Dutch school are found by following the *genre* of Adriaen Brouwer (*c.* 1606–38) and David Teniers the younger (1610–90), both of whom painted the "low life" of the Low Countries. But Teniers raised this art to a pleasing and almost delicate one, such as was followed by the Dutch *genre* painters. An example appears in page 2330.

Before dealing with Dutch *genre*, we must note the two great portrait painters who brought the

St. John's Hospital, Bruges; photo, Mansell

**SUPERB PORTRAIT BY HANS MEMLING**
Perhaps the best of the early Flemish painters was Hans Memling (*c.* 1430–94), whose easy and graceful style is seen to advantage in his portraits. This one is of Martin van Nieuwenhove, and it occupies the right hand panel of a pair painted for him by Memling in 1487, the other showing the Virgin and Child.

whole school into prominence. Although there had been a number of good painters before him, Frans Hals (*c.* 1580–1666) was the first master of the Dutch school. His Laughing Cavalier (*see* page 1569) is one of the world's best-known pictures, and gives a good impression of his work at its finest. His paintings reflect closely the life and prosperity of his country. Contemporary with Hals was Holland's greatest master, Rembrandt.

Dutch painting was naturalistic; with Rembrandt van Rijn (1606–69) naturalism develops into great poetry. He tried to express the hidden soul; he brought forth the humanity as well as the divinity of the Scriptures. As portraitist he excelled; he painted profoundly religious pictures; as a landscape artist he was almost equally good; and as an etcher he has never been approached. (*See* illus., page 2328).

One Dutch painter, Honthorst (1590–56), who painted candlelight scenes, was strongly influenced by Caravaggio, but few showed any influence other than that of their own school. There were portrait and *genre* painters, followers of Teniers, such as Ter Borch (1617–81) and Adriaen van Ostade (1619–85), whose scenes of peasants outside inns have a great reputation. Ostade, too, was an etcher in almost the same class as Rembrandt himself. Isaac van Ostade (1621–49) did similar themes with rather more of a landscape background. Interiors provided the setting for the very neat and detailed work of Gerard Dou (1613–75) and Metsu (*c.* 1630–67), and their numerous followers.

On a slightly higher level stands Nicholas Maes (1632–93), whose figures have considerably more character than those appearing in earlier works, and from him branch off the works of Jan Steen (*c.* 1626–79), Pieter de Hooch, and Vermeer. Steen painted rather larger pictures than most of these "little Dutch masters," and there is a strong realism in his carousing peasants and jolly, greedy

little boys. De Hooch (1629–*c.* 1683) excelled in the simple scenes of the Dutch houses, with their tiled floors and neat, perfectly arranged furnishings. With Jan Vermeer of Delft (1632–75) this art reaches its highest pitch. Vermeer's paintings are of great value and rarity. His greatest point is perhaps a warm, glowing sunlight which illumines the beautiful rooms in which sit his young ladies, often engaged in some musical occupation. In technique, as in design and feeling, he was a master, while his solitary landscape—the View of Delft—attains equal greatness in its own way.

It should be remembered that the Dutch school of the 17th century forms a separate phase in the artistic history of Europe. Political events had separated the painters of this period from Italy ; religion and politics hemmed in Protestant artists in their own cities, with the result that they were compelled to concentrate their attention on the smallest details of their own immediate surroundings.

Considered the first of the Dutch landscape school, Jan van Goyen (1596–1656) produced work with a somewhat browner, more mellow tone than that of later members of this school. Among these were artists who specialized in cattle, such as Albert Cuyp (1600–91) and Paul Potter (1608–54), or in horses, such as Wouwerman (1619–68), whose paintings have a great appeal for children. Philip de Koninck (1619–88) did broader, greener landscapes, often with a fine effect of sunlight, and these lead on to the landscapes of Jakob van Ruysdael (*c.* 1628–82), perhaps the finest Dutch painter in this manner. Ruysdael and Hobbema (1638–1709) both interested themselves in trees to a greater extent than their contemporaries, while Hobbema excelled as a painter of skies. His notable Avenue at Middelharnis (*see* illus., page 2330) is in the National Gallery.

The Dutch marine painters are deservedly even more famous than the landscape artists. Of them, Adriaen van de Velde (1636–72), who chose mainly

*Mansell*

**CHARMING EXAMPLE OF A DUTCH INTERIOR**
By Pieter de Hooch, a 17th-century Dutch artist, this painting shows the fine draughtsmanship and the clever use of lighting which make his pictures so attractive. Interiors were favourite subjects of the Dutch painters of this period, and De Hooch was one of the greatest of the ' genre ' painters—those who favour scenes drawn from rustic or peasant life. His pictures were almost always small. This example is now in the National Gallery, London.

shore landscapes, and his brother Willem (1633–1707) are perhaps the finest. Their father was another Willem, who is more renowned as an accurate marine draughtsman than as an artist ; numerous drawings executed for Charles II and James II are almost reports of the sea-fights of the Restoration period, although at one time the members of this family were fighting against Britain. A follower of the Van de Veldes who excelled at sky effects was Jan van de Cappelle (*c*. 1624–*c*. 1675), while ships in more lively seas occupied the attention of Backhuysen (1631–1708). Besides these marine painters there were the still-life painters and especially the masters of the truly marvellous "flowerpieces," in which great masses of richly-coloured blossoms are grouped together in a jar, while over and among them flutter butterflies and other insects. Supreme among flower painters is Jan van Huysum (1682–1749). Others are the De Heem family, and Hondecoeter (1636–95), who painted dead game.

Since the early 18th century Holland has produced few painters of note. In the 19th century many artists appeared, of whom Josef Israels (1824–1911), Jacob Maris (1837–99), and Anton Mauve (1838–88) deserve mention. Of more importance is Jongkind (1819–91), a forerunner of the Impressionists; but it is hard to realize when one looks at his paintings that even he lived at the same time as one of the most important of all modern masters, Van Gogh (1853–90). Like Jongkind, Van Gogh belongs, artistically, to the French rather than to the Dutch school. (*See also* French Art; Impressionism ; and articles on Hals, Rembrandt, Rubens, Van Dyck, etc.).

## Netherlands East Indies.
This was the name given to former Dutch possessions in the East Indies (*q.v.*). After the Second World War (1939–45) the native inhabitants demanded the right of self-government from the Dutch, and in late 1949 the islands (with the exception of Dutch New Guinea) became an independent republic with the title of the United States of Indonesia. (*See* Indonesia).

## Nettle.
In full flower, with the sun shining upon them, massed stinging nettles are by no means unattractive, even though the flowers (produced from June to September) are green and, individually, very small. It is when one makes too close personal contact with the plants that the unattractive side becomes apparent. The stinging hairs with which they are so plentifully covered

*A. W. Dennis*
**NETTLE IN FLOWER**
Included among Britain's stinging nettles is the so-called Roman nettle, *Urtica pilulifera*. The female flowers of this species are borne in showy, rounded clusters, each ' ball ' being about half an inch across. The male and female flowers are separate.

are sharp-pointed little tubes containing formic acid (the same poison which makes the bite of an ant so unpleasant), and when these break off in the skin intense irritation results.

Two species native to Britain are common in gardens and fields. They are the great stinging nettle, *Urtica dioica*, and its smaller relative *U. urens*. The former grows as high as four feet and, being a perennial, comes up year after year from a creeping rootstock. The smaller stinging nettle grows about two feet in height and is an annual—that is, it dies after it has flowered and borne seed. Less common in Britain is *U. pilulifera*.

Though they are troublesome weeds they are not altogether "bad." In the spring, when the young tops are still tender, they can be boiled and eaten as "greens." Before they start to flower the plants can be cut and dried for use as hay. And the great stinging nettle especially is the source of a vegetable dye (extracted from the dried leaves) used in medicinal, food and toilet preparations.

The so-called "dead" (stingless) nettles belong to an entirely unrelated genus, *Lamium*. The commonest British species are the red dead nettle, *L. purpureum*, the yellow archangel, *L. galeobdolon*, and the white archangel, *L. album*, with flowers of those colours, large and graceful in shape, and quite unlike those of the stinging nettles.

## Nevada.
Sixth largest State of the United States, Nevada has an area of 110,540 square miles. A western State, it is bounded on the north by Oregon and Idaho, on the East by Utah and Arizona, on the west and south by California. Most of Nevada lies in the Great Basin of western United States, which is a mountain-ribbed depression whose rivers have no outlet to the sea. The Sierra Nevada range flanks the western border, the snow-covered peaks giving the State its name, which in Spanish means " snowy." The climate is dry, the average annual rainfall about nine inches.

Cattle and sheep breeding are important industries, and dairy-farming is carried on by means of irrigation. Forage, fruit and vegetables are principal crops. The State is rich in minerals ; the Comstock Lode is a rich source of gold and silver. Other minerals include copper, manganese, lead, zinc, gypsum and mercury ; metal refining is a leading industry.

On the Colorado river, at the State boundary between Nevada and Arizona, is the Boulder Dam, completed in 1936. The dam irrigates more than a million acres of land and generates hydro-electric power, supplying half the requirements of southern California. (*See* plate facing page 960).

The capital of the State is Carson City (population 2,500). The largest town is Reno (population 21,000). Nevada was part of the territory taken from Mexico by the United States in 1848 ; it became a State of the Union in 1864. The population is 110,000, including about 5,000 Red Indians.

## New Brunswick.
A maritime province of the Dominion of Canada, New Brunswick is bounded on the north-west by the province of

---

**Area.**—27,895 sq. m., of which only 74 are water. Population 457,400.
**Physical Features.**—A fertile plain, with a large area of dense forest in the centre, and a spur of the Appalachians in the north. Rivers include the St. John and the Miramichi. Grand Lake, and a few other lakes.
**Products.**—Lumber, wood-pulp ; iron, coal, and other minerals ; fish.
**Principal Towns.**—St. John (51,700), Fredericton (capital; 10,000).

---

Quebec, on the east by the Atlantic Ocean (except where the Chignecto isthmus connects it with the province of Nova Scotia), on the south by the Bay of Fundy, on the west by the United States. The area is just under 28,000 square miles, and its surface is for the most part rolling plain, the centre being one vast forest. The longest river is the St. John (400 miles) ; others are the Miramichi, Restigouche and St. Croix.

The soil is fertile, wheat, oats, barley, apples and potatoes are the chief crops. Cattle are bred, and there is some dairy-farming. Iron, coal, gypsum and oil are among the minerals. Lumbering, the making of wood-pulp, and fishing are important industries. The province is one of the favourite resorts of the hunter and the angler, for in the forests are plenty of game, including moose, caribou and wolves. Salmon and other fish are plentiful in the streams.

*Courtesy of the High Commissioner for Canada*
**ST. JOHN, NEW BRUNSWICK**
One of Canada's chief winter ports, St. John, at the mouth of the St. John river, has a good natural harbour and its docks can accommodate the largest vessels. Industries include the manufacture of boots and shoes and textiles.

The railways in New Brunswick are the Canadian Pacific and the Canadian National systems. St. John (population 51,700) is the principal port, open all the year round. Other important centres are Fredericton (the capital, population 10,000) and Moncton.

The first settlement was established by the French in 1604, and the territory was given up to Britain by France in 1713 at the end of the War of the Spanish Succession. It was combined with Nova Scotia until 1784, when it was formed into a separate province. The population is 457,400.

## Newcastle-upon-Tyne.
"Carrying coals to Newcastle" is an old ironic saying. We could appreciate its meaning if we sailed up the narrow, crowded waters of the River Tyne to this bustling city, at whose docks in normal times steamers and barges are endlessly engaged in loading coal for export ; for Newcastle lies between the coal regions of Durham and Northumberland (it is in Northumberland), and before the Second World War (1939–45) was one of the most important coal-shipping centres of Europe.

The city's shipbuilding yards and locomotive, engineering, and ordnance works are among the largest in Britain. George Stephenson (1781–1848) was born near Newcastle, and the city was associated with many of the first steps in the development of railways. From its factories come soda, vitriol, bleaching-powder, salt, and other chemicals, also earthenware, cement, grindstones, fire-brick,

*Topical*
**FROM NEWCASTLE TO GATESHEAD**
The newest of the seven bridges crossing the Tyne at the industrial city and seaport of Newcastle is that shown above. Opened in 1928, it resembles the Sydney Harbour Bridge (*see* page 567), and was built by the same engineers. On the extreme right is part of the Swing Bridge, also for road traffic.

and refined lead. There are large engineering and electrical works. Newcastle has markets for wheat, hay, straw, cattle, fish and vegetables.

The cathedral of St. Nicholas, of which the principal feature is a very fine lantern tower, was completed in 1350, the tower being a later addition. Other churches are St. Andrew's and St. John's, dating from the 12th century ; the church of St. George at Jesmond, and St. Mary's Roman Catholic cathedral. Remains of the Norman castle, built in the 11th century and after which the town was named, include the Great Tower, or Keep, and the Black Gate—now a museum of the city's history and antiquities. Newcastle is well provided with educational facilities. These include

King's College of the University of Durham and the Royal Grammar School.

Neighbouring industrial ports on the Tyne include, on the Northumberland bank, Tynemouth, North Shields, Wallsend, Walker, and Elswick; and, in Durham, South Shields, Jarrow, Hebburn, and Gateshead, to which Newcastle is joined by several bridges. Newcastle was not of any importance until the fort known from 1080 as the New Castle was built there. In 1320 the town was the northern port of the wool trade, becoming a county in itself in 1400. The shipbuilding industry added greatly to Newcastle's prosperity ; as also, from the 17th century to the late 19th century, did glass-making. Population is 291,000.

# GREAT BRITAIN'S FIRST COLONY

*Almost the first land of the New World to be discovered by navigators from England, and the first country to be colonized by the English, Newfoundland has a proud history. In 1949 it became a Province of Canada.*

**Newfoundland.** At the mouth of the Gulf of St. Lawrence, the gateway to Canada, this rugged island was one of the lands discovered in the New World by John Cabot in 1497. The most northerly point is at the Strait of Belle Isle, which is about seven miles wide and divides Newfoundland from Canada. The area is 42,734 square miles, and much of the surface is covered with lakes and rivers ; there are also large marshes. The longest rivers are Exploits, Humber and Gander ; the largest lake is Grand Lake, on the west side of the island, 56 miles long.

> **Extent.**—North to south, about 330 miles ; greatest width, east to west, 316 miles. Area 42,734 square miles. Population (including Labrador) 321,170.
> **Physical Features.**—Coast broken by fiords and island-dotted bays ; Anguille Range and Long Range mountains in the west, and isolated peaks (highest point 2,673 feet). Principal rivers : Humber, Exploits and Gander. Grand, Red Indian and Gander lakes.
> **Products.**—Fish (chiefly cod) ; lumber and timber products (paper) ; ships ; iron and copper, and coal ; hay, potatoes, cabbage, turnips, oats.
> **Principal City.**—St. John's (capital ; population 56,000).

The climate on the whole is temperate, with an abundant rainfall, and the coastal fogs seldom penetrate inland. The island has little good agricultural soil, and much of the land under cultivation is in small garden plots. Potatoes, cabbages and turnips are the main crops ; wheat, cucumbers, tomatoes, beans and peas grow well in sheltered places.

There are large deposits of coal and petroleum, and copper and iron ore mines are worked. Extensive forests provide timber for paper and pulp mills and for shipbuilding. The fisheries, however, have for centuries formed

*Newfoundland Government*

**TIMBER FOR THE PULP MILLS GOING DOWN THE EXPLOITS RIVER**

The longest river in Newfoundland, the Exploits drains 4,000 square miles and flows through the extensive wooded districts which supply the bulk of the timber for the wood-pulp mills. During the winter months the trees, chiefly spruce and other soft woods, are felled, cut into logs and hauled to the banks. There they remain until the spring floods, when they are pushed into the river (above) to be carried down to the mills at Grand Falls and elsewhere.

the chief industry of Newfoundland, the richest grounds being the Newfoundland Banks—a submarine plateau extending about 200 miles offshore and reaching to within 100 or 200 feet of the surface. Here accumulates a seemingly inexhaustible supply of plankton (minute marine organisms upon which cod and other fish feed) ; and while this food drifts down from the Arctic and up from the tropics on the Gulf Stream there is little danger that catches from the Banks will decrease.

There are some 800 miles of railway. Steamers provide communication between various points on the coast and between the island and the mainland of North America. There are trans-Atlantic airports at Botwood and Gander. At Heart's Content the first Atlantic cable was brought ashore in 1867, and within a few miles of the same point the first successful Atlantic flight (by Sir John Alcock and A. Whitten Brown) started on June 14, 1919. The capital and chief port is St. John's, with a population of 56,000.

The discovery of Newfoundland (together with Cape Breton Island and Nova Scotia) earned for John Cabot from King Henry VII of England the sum of £10. From 1521 English, French, Portuguese, Spanish and Basque fishermen regularly visited the island to fish for cod. In 1583 Sir Humphrey Gilbert formally annexed Newfoundland to England, the first permanent settlement being founded shortly afterwards. Other British colonists established themselves there in the 17th century. A French station also existed on the island, and there were constant disputes between

England and France as to fishing rights. Although France agreed to recognize exclusive British sovereignty in 1713, the disputes were not finally settled until 1904.

In 1933 the country had run heavily into debt, and the government and financial responsibilities were taken over by the British Government, this form of administration being continued throughout the Second World War (1939–45). In 1948 the people of Newfoundland voted for union with Canada, and the Canadian Government agreed that Newfoundland, with its dependent territory of Labrador (q.v.) should form a province of the Dominion, that status being assumed in March 1949. The population of Newfoundland and Labrador is 321,170.

**New Guinea.** Much of this vast island in the South-West Pacific was unexplored until the Second World War (1939–45), when military operations opened up hitherto unknown regions. By far the larger part of New Guinea is still occupied by savages, and head-hunting raids and cannibal feasts continue in the interior.

New Guinea, which has an estimated area of 311,000 square miles, lies north across the Torres Strait from Australia, just south of the Equator (for map, see East Indies). It stretches east and west about 1,500 miles and is about 450 miles across at its widest. Greenland and Australia are the only larger islands. The western half of New Guinea belongs to the Netherlands ; the eastern half, to the British Commonwealth as a dependency of Australia

### HARBOUR OF ST. JOHN'S, THE CAPITAL OF NEWFOUNDLAND

On the east coast of Newfoundland, St. John's has one of the most remarkable natural harbours in the world. It is approached through the Narrows, a channel about half a mile long running between sandstone cliffs which in places rise to a height of 500 feet. At the narrowest point it is only 400 feet wide, but ocean-going vessels can pass through it at all states of the tide. St. John's, with a population of 56,000, is the business and commercial centre of the island.

A backbone of mountains, with snow-clad peaks, runs nearly the entire length of the island. Rugged spurs extend from this backbone, dividing the land into deep valleys and isolated plateaux. Numerous rivers flow down from the mountains, passing through broad belts of forest and swamplands to the sea. The most important river is the Fly, which is 800 miles long and flows into the Gulf of Papua; next are the Sepik and the Mamberamo, which empty into the Pacific Ocean on the north. Lakes lie in hills and valleys, or form chains in the lowlands along the rivers. Where mountain spurs reach the sea, the coast is high and rocky; elsewhere it consists mostly of tidal swamps.

In the rainy season terrific storms sweep the island. In the lowlands even the dry season is damp enough for the giant grasses and trees to continue growing. Acacias, eucalyptus, cypress and palms grow here, with trees that have no English names; among their branches flourish many varieties of orchids. Creepers and climbing vines form a tangle so dense that explorers who leave the rivers to cut their way through the forests count two or three miles a day a fair rate of travel. The air is filled with the hum of millions of insects;

**NEW GUINEA NATIVES' NEST-LIKE HOMES**
Some of the New Guinea natives have such troublesome neighbours that they are obliged to live in houses perched up in trees like those shown above, so arranged that whenever they go 'upstairs' they can pull the stairs up after them. The houses consist of a framework of sticks covered with long grass. These tree dwellings are found in the hilly interior.

clouds of mosquitoes hover above water teeming with crocodiles and huge leeches. Brightly-coloured butterflies abound in the lowland forests.

The wild life of New Guinea resembles that of Australia, including egg-laying mammals called spiny ant-eaters, and several marsupials such as the wallaby (a miniature kangaroo), the ring-tailed opossum and the bandicoot. The wild pig is the island's largest known mammal. Huge fruit eating bats abound. Conspicuous among the birds are the ostrich-like cassowary, so powerful that it can kill a dog with a blow of its foot, the egret, the bower-bird, and birds of paradise.

Lizards, some of great size, and snakes, exist nearly everywhere. In the coastal waters live sea-mammals called sea-cows or dugongs, and turtles.

From district to district the natives of New Guinea differ considerably in appearance, customs and language. Some are black as Negroes; others are no darker than a well-tanned white man. Some are six feet in height; others are pygmies. A tribe with broad noses and thick lips may have long-nosed and thin-lipped neighbours. There are small groups that live without settled homes, carrying their possessions on their backs. There are, on the other hand, large tribes with an elaborate social organization and remarkable skill in architecture, boat-building, sculpture, painting, weaving and pottery-making. The culture of the New Guinea natives ranges from that of the " dawn men " of Europe to that of the lake dwellers of Neolithic times. (*See* Man).

The best-known of the natives belong to the so-called " Papuan " types. They are sooty brown to deep black, with long frizzy hair. Many have oval faces with prominent noses, high cheek-bones, and lofty foreheads. The men go nearly naked; their bodies are decorated with knife scars in intricate patterns, made at the ceremonies initiating them into the status of warrior. They wear necklaces of teeth and shells, ear-rings, feathered headdresses, and cassowary bones thrust crosswise through the cartilage of the nose. The women generally wear grass skirts and much simpler ornaments than the men.

The typical Papuan village lies near a river bank, hidden behind a screen of trees. The buildings are well made of log frames, with thatched walls and roofs. Near the river are concealed the war canoes, hollowed out of tree trunks with axes and adzes made of stone or shell. Gardens fringe the village, where the women raise yams, taro, bananas and sugar-cane.

The family houses surround a long club-house and armoury, called a *dubu*, strictly reserved for men. In front of it is an open space where tribal song-dances are held to the intricate rhythm of drums. Inside the dubu hang carved and painted canoe paddles, bows and arrows, spears, and daggers. Most prized of all, in the remoter regions, are the trophies of human skulls and smoked heads,

each representing a victim killed and perhaps eaten. Cannibalism and head-hunting have ceased near the coast. The oldest product of New Guinea is copra, the dried " meat " of the coconut. Rubber and sisal hemp are raised on plantations under European direction. The forests teem with valuable timber. Indications of petroleum have been found. The mountains yield some gold, copper, silver and osmiridium; but lack of communications hinders the exploitation of the mines. Aeroplanes are used to carry stores and machinery to the mines and to transport gold back to the coast for shipment. Missionaries and government officials are slowly penetrating the interior, and airmen are mapping regions hitherto uncharted.

Dutch New Guinea has its capital at Merauke on the southern coast and is ruled by the Netherlands Government. The Territory of New Guinea, which is under the Government of Australia, includes, to the east, a part of the Solomon Islands and all the Bismarck Archipelago, comprising New Britain, New Ireland, and the Admiralty Islands. Kikopo on the island of New Britain is the capital of the Territory. Papua, which is also controlled by Australia, has its capital at Port Moresby on New Guinea's south-east coast and includes, to the east, the Louisiade Archipelago, the D'Entrecasteaux Islands and the Trobriand Islands.

Portuguese and Spanish adventurers of the early 16th century were probably the first white men to sight the coast of New Guinea. In 1606 a Spaniard, Luis de Torres, sailed through the strait between New Guinea and Australia which bears his name. The Dutch annexed the western half of the island in 1793, and Germany and Great Britain

declared protectorates in the eastern half in 1884. British New Guinea came under Australian control as the Territory of Papua in 1906, and German New Guinea went to Australia as the Mandated Territory of New Guinea by decision of the League of Nations in 1920, after the First World War (1914–18).

New Guinea was a main objective of the Japanese in the Second World War (1939–45) as a base from which to invade Australia. Japanese troops landed on New Britain and New Ireland on January 23, 1942, and at Lae and Salamaua, on New Guinea, on March 8; but an advance on Port Moresby was halted in September, and by January 23, 1943, Australian forces had cleared the enemy from Papua.

**SHOOTING FISH IN NEW GUINEA**

E.N.A.

In the south-eastern part of the island of New Guinea, known as the territory of Papua, the natives have a peculiar method of catching fish by shooting them with small bows and arrows. Above, boys of Mailu Island are seen busily engaged in shooting in this manner fish which have been left by the receding tide in the pools of a coral reef.

Aided by reinforcements of United States units, the Australians recaptured Lae and Salamaua in September 1943, and advanced along the coast towards Netherlands New Guinea, where Allied landings were made in the Hollandia district in April 1944. Fighting continued until the Japanese in New Guinea ceased fire on August 22, 1945, the official surrender taking place at Wewak, on the coast of the Territory of New Guinea, on September 13 of that year. The native population of the whole of the island of New Guinea is estimated at 1,178,500.

# New Hampshire.

One of the 13 original States of the American Union, New Hampshire is bounded on the north by Quebec, Canada; on the east by Maine and the Atlantic Ocean; on the south by Massachusetts; on the west by Vermont. It has an area of 9,304 square miles. Most of the State is hilly, and Mount Washington, one of the peaks of the White Mountains, is the highest point (6,288 feet). The Merrimac, Androscoggin, Connecticut, Piscataqua and the Saco are the main rivers and provide abundant water-power. There are 1,300 lakes, the largest being Winnipesaukee.

Chief industries are the manufacture of boots and shoes, textiles, paper and wood-pulp. Granite is quarried, and there are deposits of clay, mica and feldspar. Hay, maize, potatoes, oats and fruit are cultivated in the valleys of the Connecticut and Merrimac. Though the State has only a 19-mile stretch of coast and only one port (Portsmouth, on the Piscataqua river), it has lobster and haddock fisheries and considerable shipping.

The capital, Concord, has a population of 27,100. Manchester (population 77,700) is the largest town. Among the educational institutions is St. Paul's School at Concord, which is one of the most famous schools for boys in the United States. Higher education is offered by the University of New Hampshire at Durham, and Dartmouth College at Hanover.

The first settlement was established by English colonists in 1623 at the mouth of the Piscataqua river, the district being part of a grant of land made by King James I to his friend John Mason and named after Mason's home county of Hampshire. At one time part of Massachusetts, it became a province in 1741, and in 1776, at the outbreak of the American War of Independence, it was the first colony to establish a government independent of Great Britain. The population is 491,500.

*F. O. Hoppé*

**NEW GUINEA WOMAN**
To leave her hands free for work, this Papuan woman has slung her baby over her back in a net-work bag. The women wear a short grass skirt, and do not decorate themselves with clumsy necklaces of bones and shells as do the men.

**New Jersey.** Only three States of the United States—Rhode Island, Delaware and Connecticut—are smaller than New Jersey, which has an area of 7,836 square miles. On its east is the Atlantic Ocean, on the south Delaware Bay, on the west Pennsylvania, on the north New York.

There are five distinctly marked sections of New Jersey, running in almost parallel strips across the State from north-east to south-west. Paralleling the Delaware river in the north-west are the heavily wooded Kittatinny Mountains, rising to 1,800 feet, and a favourite resort for visitors in summer. South of these mountains lies a wide valley with excellent farming land. The third division is the Highlands, a hilly region with superb scenery. Still farther south is the Piedmont Plain, noted for its crops of maize, fruit and vegetables. At the extreme south is a coastal plain covering half the entire State. A wooded area, with sandy soil, much of this plain is undeveloped.

Notable for the variety of its industries, New Jersey produces textiles, clothing, chemicals, refined petroleum, smelted copper, machinery, leather and rubber goods, pottery and glass. Situated as it is in the most populated part of the United States, market-gardening and dairy-farming are highly important industries.

The capital is Trenton (population 123,000), but Newark (population 429,700) is the largest city and has one of the world's biggest airports. Hoboken, Newark, Jersey City and Elizabeth are residential suburbs for New Yorkers—New York being on the opposite bank of the Hudson river—and the cities farther south house thousands of Philadelphia's workers. Educational institutions include Princeton (founded in 1746), Rutgers, Newark and Drew universities.

New Jersey was first settled by the Dutch in about 1620, but in 1664 England took possession of the region, the name New Jersey being given to it because the land was granted to Sir George Carteret, who had been Governor of Jersey in the Channel Islands. During the American War of Independence (1776–82) the State was the scene of some 100 battles and skirmishes between the colonists and British troops. It witnessed some of the most dramatic events of the whole conflict— the retreat of George Washington from Long Island through the British lines, the defeat of the British at Trenton, and the battles at Princeton and Monmouth. The population is 4,160,200.

**Newman,** JOHN HENRY, CARDINAL (1801–1890). When all else that Newman wrote has been for the most part forgotten, his name will still be kept alive by his well-known hymn:

Lead, Kindly Light, amid the encircling gloom,
Lead Thou me on;
The night is dark, and I am far from home;
Lead Thou me on.
Keep Thou my feet; I do not ask to see
The distant scene—one step enough for me.

These beautiful lines have found their way into almost every heart and hymn-book. Newman composed them in 1833, while on shipboard returning to England from a voyage to the Mediterranean, before there had arisen those religious doubts which led him from the Church of England to the Church of Rome.

He was born in London on February 21, 1801. Two years after taking his degree at Trinity College, Oxford, he obtained a fellowship at Oriel. Always of a religious temperament, he became a clergyman of the Church of England as well as an Oxford tutor. He was a leading spirit in the famous Oxford Movement, its aim being to secure for the Church of England a definite basis of doctrine and discipline in case it should ever cease to be recognized as the State Church. His romantic vision of the medieval Church restored in its power and grandeur gradually led this simple, sincere man, with grave kind eyes and thoughtful smile, to join the Roman Catholic Church, which he called " a home after many storms." He was ordained a priest at Rome in 1845, and was appointed a cardinal in 1879. He died at Birmingham on August 11, 1890.

It was by his many sermons, lectures and writings that Newman became one of the religious forces of his day. The spiritual fervour and the charm of his personality were supplemented by a fine prose style which for ease, clearness and beauty has seldom been surpassed. Among Newman's many important writings are his Apologia pro Vita Sua (1864), considered one of the classics of English prose; Verses on Various Occasions (1868), in which is included the beautiful Dream of Gerontius; An Essay in Aid of a Grammar of Assent (1870); and Letter to the Duke of Norfolk (1875).

**New Mexico.** In the south-west of the United States, New Mexico is fascinating on account of its strange beauty and its relics of Indian civilizations. With an area of 121,666 square miles, it ranks fourth in size among the States, and it is a plateau broken by many mountain ranges, except in the south-east. The Rocky Mountains enter New Mexico in the north and extend south-east

**CARDINAL NEWMAN**
Besides being a master of English prose Newman was a preacher who, without any mere rhetorical flourishes, carried his congregations with him by his spiritual fervour and deep sincerity.

for about 120 miles, the highest point being Truchas Peak (13,306 feet), in the north central part.

A characteristic feature is the flat-topped hills that rise straight up from the surrounding country. On the summit of Acoma is an Indian village believed to be the oldest continuously inhabited place in the United States. The Carlsbad caverns, in a National Park of 70 square miles in the Guadalupe Mountains, are among the deepest and most extensive in the world, with an area of 16 square miles.

The principal industries are stock-breeding and farming. Maize, wheat, alfalfa (lucerne) and cotton are chief crops. Agriculture is carried on largely by the aid of irrigation, one of the biggest dams being at Elephant Butte in the Rio Grande valley. Mineral resources include copper, coal, zinc, silver, gold and oil.

The capital of the State is Santa Fé (population 20,300). At Albuquerque, the largest town (population 35,400), is the State university. In the desert of Los Alamos, northwest of Santa Fé, was a centre of atomic energy research; Alamogordo air base, 125 miles south-east of Albuquerque, was the site of the first atomic bomb explosion on July 16, 1945.

The peaceful Pueblo Indians, who were living in New Mexico when the Spaniards arrived in the 16th century, still retain their colourful costumes, their remarkable communal village organization, and their ancient tribal customs. Their one-time troublesome neighbours the Navajos, now settled on a reservation extending from Arizona to New Mexico, till the soil and practise simple industries, notably the weaving of blankets. The fierce Apaches, to escape whom the Pueblo Indians built their dwellings in almost inaccessible cliffs, were finally subdued in 1886, and two Apache tribes settled on reservations in New Mexico.

Explored by the Spaniards early in the 16th century, New Mexico was made a Mexican province in the 17th century. The State came into the possession of the United States in 1848 at the end of the Mexican War, entering the American Union as the 47th State in 1912. Population, 531,000.

**New Orleans.** The outlet for the State of Louisiana and for the whole of the Mississippi basin, this seaport of the United States has two distinct sections. The older part is picturesque in character, with a large Creole (American-born French or Spanish) population, who cling to the customs and speech of their ancestors. Modern New Orleans, on the other hand, is a typical North American metropolis, making anything and everything, and the largest cotton market of America.

One of the biggest manu-
facturing cities in the
South, its products in-
clude clothing, furniture;
paints, sugar and cotton
goods. Among the lead-
ing industries are rice-
milling, oil-refining, and
coffee-roasting.

Along the Mississippi
the erection of several
embankments or levees
has been necessary, for the
land in the delta is very
marshy and below the
level of the river at high
tide. Another curious re-
sult of this marshiness is
that ordinary cemeteries
cannot be used, and so
coffins are stored in tiers
in vaults. A famous fea-
ture of New Orleans is the
Mardi Gras (Shrove Tues-
day) carnival. It is also
worth noting that it was
in the Negro quarter of the
city that jazz music was
developed in the first

**MAIN STREET OF NEW ORLEANS**

Canal Street, the chief shopping centre of New Orleans, runs north and south, and divides
the city into two parts : the old, or French, portion on the east, and the modern portion on
the west. The width of the street can be judged from the fact that even with four tramway
tracks in the centre it has ample room for several lines of other traffic.

years of this century. Settled in 1717 by the
French, who named it after the Duke of Orleans,
then Regent of France, New Orleans was later de-
serted, and then resettled in 1722. Coming into the
possession of Spain in 1763, it was retaken by the
French in 1800, and purchased from them by the
United States, together with the remainder of
Louisiana, in 1803. The population is 494,500.

**New South Wales.** This oldest
State in the Australian Commonwealth lies on the
east coast between Queensland and Victoria and
has an area of 309,433 square miles. New South

Wales shares the characteristic geographical feature
of eastern Australia—a narrow coastal plain,
backed by a range of mountains about 80 miles
inland. This range, in which is Mount Kosciusko
(7,328 feet), Australia's highest peak, is known by
various names—Snowy Range, Blue Mountains,
and New England Range ; and to the east of it is
a plateau carved by rivers into valleys and gorges.
To the west another plateau descends more gently
to vast plains which are almost level.

The main rivers of the east are the Shoalhaven,
Hunter, Manning and Clarence; on the west are

*Courtesy of Director of Australian Trade Publicity*

**WINTER SPORTS IN NEW SOUTH WALES**

Australia is not usually associated with cold weather, for
though most of the Continent experiences ground frosts at
night the average temperature in winter is about that of an
English spring. In New South Wales the winter temperature averages between 53° and 46° Fahrenheit ; but in the
extreme south the Muniong Range, a group of the Australian
Alps, is snow clad, and here the people of New South Wales
can enjoy winter sports, including ski-ing. This photograph
was taken from Mount Kosciusko (7,328 feet), the culminating point of the range and the highest peak in Australia.

the Murrumbidgee, Lachlan and Darling. Rainfall is distributed uniformly throughout the year, but varies from an annual fall of 64 inches in the east to 10 inches in the west.

Much of the land is devoted to sheep and cattle-raising. In the east, lumbering and dairy-farming are the main industries. Sugar-cane and tropical fruits are cultivated near the north-east coast, and vines in the south. Gold, silver, copper, tin, lead, coal and zinc are the chief minerals. Exports include wool, butter, wheat, flour, timber, meat, hides, tin, copper, coal and gold.

The chief towns are the capital Sydney (q.v.), Newcastle (population 127,660), Broken Hill and

---

**Area.**—309,432 square miles (excluding Federal Capital Territory of Canberra). Population 2,912,800 (excluding aborigines).

**Physical Features.**—Dividing Range, including Blue Mts. and a region of high table-lands : coastal lowlands, and western plains extending over two-thirds of the State. Rivers include the Murray, Darling, and Murrumbidgee.

**Principal Products.**—Wheat ; sugar ; wool ; oranges and other fruit ; dairy products ; coal, lead, and gold.

**Chief Cities.**—Sydney (capital, 1,398,200) ; Newcastle (127,660).

---

Lithgow. Canberra, the Federal capital, lies geographically within New South Wales. Higher education is provided by the University of Sydney, which is attended by more than 3,000 students.

New South Wales was discovered and named by Captain Cook (q.v.) in 1770. In 1788 the first convict settlement was established at Port Jackson, near the present site of Sydney, but the shipment of convicts from Great Britain ceased in 1850. The Colony formed its own Government in 1856, and joined with the other Australian States to found the Commonwealth of Australia in 1901. The population of the State is 2,912,800, of whom one-half live in Sydney.

# How NEWS comes to the BREAKFAST-TABLE

*The production and distribution of a newspaper is a daily achievement at which it is worth while to pause and marvel. Some light is thrown here on the workings of a great organization.*

**Newspapers.** There are few things which we take more for granted than newspapers.

Normally, every morning, except Christmas Day, Boxing Day, and Good Friday, when we come down to breakfast, there on the table lies our paper. If it did not arrive we should think that the news-agent had forgotten to deliver it—never that the staff of the paper had failed in their task or that the printing machines had failed to turn out their multitudes of copies recording the happenings of the previous day. And yet the production of a newspaper is one of the most complex affairs in the world, requiring a large staff of men and women possessing highly specialized knowledge. Let us take a tour through a modern newspaper office.

For our purpose we will choose a London illustrated morning paper, which records the events of the world not only in print but by the aid of pictures of universal interest. One of the first men to arrive at the office is the news editor. He has in front of him a diary of events that are due to take place that day, and as he glances through it he decides which are of sufficient value to be reported. At the same time the art editor, who deals with pictures, is looking through his diary, making notes of events important enough to require photographs to be taken. Then they both go to the office of the editor-in-chief, who is responsible for the whole policy of the paper, for the customary " editorial conference."

This is usually attended by other members of the staff, and its object is to submit ideas for news-stories to the editor and to arrange that representatives of the paper shall be present at events which it is known are to take place that day, so that they may be recorded.

The news editor, for instance, may raise the matter of a fashionable wedding that is to take place in the afternoon. The art editor has the event on his list, too, and it is decided to send a reporter and with him a photographer to take

pictures, or the securing of the pictures may be left to a photographic news agency. A great number of pictures come through the agencies. And the transmission of photographs by wireless enables British papers to print a picture of an event shortly after it has happened at the other side of the earth.

As soon as necessary after the editorial conference a number of reporters will be on their way to various scenes, their tasks ranging, maybe, from the description of a film star's arrival from across the Atlantic to the summing-up by the judge at an Old Bailey trial.

Telephone bells start to ring as one reporter after another phones his story to the office. With the receiver clamped to his ear a man takes it down in shorthand and then dashes it off on a typewriter. Three or four lines are all that go on a sheet of paper, each of which, as it is finished, is taken by a copy-boy to the sub-editors' room.

There, at a long table, sit the men who check the facts and add to or cut down the copy so that it shall fit the space on the page it is intended for. Titles to the news stories are written and hurried along to the composing room, where they are given to linotype operators. Almost as fast as the words come from the typewriter the linotype machines cast them in lines of type. (*See* Linotype).

In the Second World War (1939–45) many newspapers and news agencies had their representatives accredited to the Royal Navy, the Royal Air Force and the Army. These reporters and photographers were given officer's uniform, but without badges of rank, and were placed in the charge of a conducting or liaison officer, who arranged their itineraries. Reporters and photographers had to submit all material to a Service censor before sending it to their papers. In some theatres of war reporters used the various Signals services for transmitting purposes. In certain cases courier planes were used as well as civil

# HOW WE GET OUR PRINTED NEWS DAY BY DAY

From the editorial room (1), where the 'stories' are prepared, the copy goes to the Linotype machines (2) to be set in lines. When the text and headlines are assembled (3) they are 'made up' in page formes (4). Papier-mâché moulds taken from the formes are sent to the stereotyping room (5), where metal plates are cast. As soon as the plates are put in place the huge presses (6) are started and newspapers begin pouring out, to be despatched to all quarters (lower). Other pictures show illustration blocks being made. Transmission of photographs by wireless enables newspapers to print a picture of an event shortly after it has happened—perhaps thousands of miles away.

cables, telephones and radio-telephones. The Press correspondents not only sent their papers stories of battles but also told the public how the men were living from day to day—what they ate, the songs they sang, the catch phrases they used.

Not by any means does all the news comes from the newspaper's own reporters. Amidst the general din will be heard the clicking of tape-machines : various news-gathering agencies supply the information that appears, letter by letter, on the thin paper ribbon. In every part of the world are the reporters of these agencies, and they send in reports by telephone, telegraph and radio-telephone. Thus a speech by the President of the United States in Washington appears word for word on the tape-machines in scores of newspaper offices within a few minutes of its being spoken. The result of a football match in Scotland is known in London before the crowd has left the ground, and the evening papers insert it immediately in their space reserved for " stop press " news.

In the meantime the art editor is busy with his pictures, selecting the most interesting with expert eye. He has to " lay out " his pages so that each picture fits exactly and he tries to make the final result pleasing to the eye.

When a photograph has been chosen, it may have to be enlarged or reduced in size in order to fit into place. It will probably want retouching, or slight alteration to make it come out well in the paper. After being " squared up "—the portion of the print which is to be used marked, as also the size to which it is to be enlarged or reduced—it passes to an artist who with a few deft touches " lines " the figures so that they stand out more prominently. From him the print is hurried to the engravers in order that a block may be made from it. (*See* Process Engraving).

Now let us watch a newspaper going to press. The first edition has to be ready in a few minutes, for it has to catch a train or aeroplane which will take it as far away as the north of Scotland in time to be delivered at the breakfast table the following morning.

By the " stone "—a large flat table—stands a man in his shirt sleeves. He is the " make-up " man. In front of him lies the " chase "—a metal frame the size of a page.

From the compositors comes the metal type, which, after having a rough proof taken from it, is passed to the make-up man. Into the chase it goes—headline, text, picture block and wording —until the forme, as it is called, is full and fits the chase exactly. He is just about to lock up the forme (secure it with wedges) when the telephone bell rings. Can he hold up the page for a few minutes? One of the reporters has got a " scoop " —a story which no other paper has got—and the editor wants it to be in the first edition at all costs.

The make-up man glances anxiously at the clock, and looks over his page. Along comes the " scoop," three or four lines of which have been given to different compositors in order that the whole shall be done as quickly as possible. Something has to come out of the page to make room for the new matter. It is only the work of a second for the make-up man to decide what is to be cancelled or transferred to another page.

Hurriedly the forme is locked up and speeded on a truck to a table, where a sheet of papier-mâché is pressed on to the page of type so that it takes the impression of every letter. These moulds pass to the stereotyping room, and are put into the " casting-box," and within three minutes metal plates are cast from them. They reproduce the original forme of type exactly, but with one difference —the plates are curved instead of flat, so that they may fit the revolving, or rotary, presses on which the newspaper is printed.

Now we shall see the last and, from the mechanical point of view, the most wonderful part of the whole process. We follow the curved plates down to the press-room and watch them being placed on the cylinders of a complicated piece of machinery.

At one end is a mighty roll of white paper (called newsprint) some five miles in length. A signal is given, and the

**RECEIVING THE FIRST NEWS**
An important part in every newspaper office is played by the tape machines, operated by the news agencies, which print the latest news on strips of paper. These machines are installed also in many big business houses and in clubs. In front of the tape machine in this picture is a teleprinter, which types out the news.

*Fox*

*Fox*

## MORNING PAPERS LEAVING PADDINGTON FOR PENZANCE

At 12.50 a.m. every morning the ' newspaper special ' slides out of Paddington bound for Plymouth and all stations beyond to Penzance, carrying to the people of Devon and Cornwall their morning papers, with the news of the world's doings of the day before. Readers in London and the Home Counties receive a later edition. This photograph shows bundles of newspapers being loaded on to the West of England newspaper train at London's Paddington station.

paper is fed into the press at high speed. Operation after operation goes on faster than the eye can follow—printing, cutting, folding—until at the other end of the machine we see rushing out 1,000 finished copies a minute, separated into quires of 26.

Endless belts send them to another room, where they are packed up into bundles and hurried to the waiting motor-vans which take them to the station just in time to catch the train. Then the whole process starts all over again, for another edition has to get to press within minutes.

Certain newspapers print special editions for particular parts of the country. The main news items and special feature articles will be provided by the London office, but all other material will come from the local sources. Pages of a paper are sometimes transmitted over a telephoto system, the original page being photographed and sent by radio or telephone. At the receiving end the page is re-photographed and from it a block is made, from which the page can be printed in the same way as an ordinary newspaper illustration.

Such is life on a daily newspaper. There are, however, other people connected with the paper of whom no mention has yet been made. There is the advertisement manager, with his staff—and very important to the paper he is, for the majority of newspapers are only able to bear the tremendous expense of production by the revenue which comes from advertisements.

There are various editors—the literary editor, the sporting editor, the City editor—who have each a portion of the paper for which they are responsible. There is the printing manager, who looks after everything and everybody connected with the printing of the paper; and there is the publisher, who concerns himself with the distribution and sales. Then there are specialist journalists writing the " features," the book reviews, the topical articles, the dramatic and film criticisms, and so on; and artists drawing their " comic strip." Each is a cog necessary to keep the mighty mechanism running smoothly.

Just as there are many kinds of news, so there are many kinds of newspapers. There are newspapers devoted to finance and the Stock Exchange, and others to sport. There are weekly newspapers, which review the more important of the week's events, in addition to giving the latest information on happenings of the workaday world in every department of activity.

Nearly all the great strides in newspaper-making have come in the last hundred years. It was not such a far cry from the *Acta Diurna* (Daily Events) of ancient Rome—short bulletins of battles, fires, elections, etc., compiled by government officials and posted up in public places—to the official *Notizie Scritte* which the government of Venice issued in the 16th century. This was a hand-written bulletin; and the written journal persisted long after the use of printing began, largely because government censors kept a close watch on printed newspapers. About the same time private presses in other cities of Europe began issuing news-letters from time to time reporting the most remarkable events of the time. In 1615 the news-letter developed into the first regular weekly newspaper, the German Frankfurter Journal. The first regular newspaper in England was the Weekly Newes, which was started in London in 1622. The freedom of the press from censorship before printing was first established in England in 1695.

There was no compulsory censorship of the British Press during the Second World War, but it was an offence for anyone to publish anything that might give useful information to the enemy. Editors were asked to withold publication of certain items, such as the sinking of a vessel or the return of an army division to Great Britain. Anything that an editor considered to be questionable was voluntarily submitted to the censor.

The big British dailies, evening papers, and Sunday papers, nearly all of them published in or near Fleet Street in London, are now grouped as follows: the Kemsley group, consisting of the Sunday Times, Daily Graphic, and Sunday Graphic (the last two are " picture " papers); The Times, founded in 1785 as the Daily Universal Register, and long famed the world over for its sober and unsensational style and for the ripe wisdom of its leading articles; the group founded by Lord Northcliffe, including the Daily Mail—first creation of the " new " popular journalism—Evening News, Sunday Dispatch, and formerly two picture papers, the Daily Mirror and Sunday Pictorial, which are now independent; the Beaverbrook group, owning the Daily Express, Evening Standard, and Sunday Express; the group consisting of the Liberal News Chronicle and Star (evening), and Odhams, controlling the Daily Herald (the official Labour paper) and the People, published on Sundays. The Observer, News of the World, Reynolds's, and

Sunday Referee are all weeklies. The Daily Telegraph, owned by Lord Camrose (Lord Kemsley's brother), was at one time part of the Kemsley group, but is now independent. The most important of provincial newspapers include the Manchester Guardian and the Yorkshire Post.

Most of the London " national " papers have enormous circulations, despite the rivalry of broadcast news bulletins and news reels in the cinemas.

The efforts of innumerable men and women working at high pressure in every corner of the globe—many of them sent out as special correspondents to report at first-hand events of importance and interest to those at home—combine to give us our daily newspaper. For a penny or threehalfpence or three pence each day we glean something of what is taking place in every civilized land. And yet, as we glance over its pages at breakfast, we often remark: "Nothing in the paper today!" little realizing the romance that lies behind its production.

In the European countries occupied by German forces during the Second World War patriots, who organized various movements to harass the invaders and aid the Allies in every way that lay within their power, printed and distributed secret newspapers. These were usually single sheets, printed on hand-operated presses, the news being obtained by listening to the foreign-language broadcasts of the British Broadcasting Corporation. Passed from hand to hand these " underground " newspapers, which did so much to maintain the morale of the people, included the Belgian Le Soir; the Boj (Struggle) of Czechoslovakia; Glos Polski (The Voice of Poland); Liberté, Peuple de France, and La Voix de Paris of France.

# He EXPLAINED the LAW of GRAVITY

*One of the world's greatest scientific discoverers—yet he wrote just before he died : " I seem to have been only a boy playing on the seashore and diverting myself in now and then finding a smoother pebble or prettier shell than ordinary, whilst the Great Ocean of Truth lay all undiscovered before me."*

**Newton,** SIR ISAAC (1642–1727). " Nature and Nature's laws lay hid in night " for ages, but light slowly broke in during the 17th century. Last of a line of forerunners of that dawn, Galileo died in January 1642. That same year saw the birth of one greater than he, destined to shed the full light of day on the work of his predecessors—Isaac Newton, who was born on December 25, 1642, in the village of Woolsthorpe, Lincolnshire.

To compare the 17th century with the 20th is like comparing a stage-coach with an aeroplane, or a wax candle with an electric light. In ideas the two centuries are even farther apart than in inventions, and the difference is largely due to the wonderful series of discoveries begun by Newton. To realize what those discoveries mean to us, therefore, we must try to look a little way into the minds of men of two or three centuries ago.

In the first place, the iron clutch of *authority* on beliefs was only gradually being loosened by observation and experiment. " Authority "—do you know what that means? It means that when one asked a question about any scientific matter, one

was answered, not by "Watch and find out," or " Try it and see," but " Here is what Aristotle, or St. Augustine, or some other writer dead a thousand years says about it."

Again, the bare idea of *natural law which did not change* was vague and unformed. Of course, men had always recognized a certain order underneath Nature's apparent confusion. The sun always rises in the east and sets in the west; summer and winter, day and night, always follow each other; heavy objects dropped in mid-air always fall to the ground. But to most people, amid all the seeming incalculable waywardness of wind and weather and life and death, this seemed merely like the queer streak of reasonableness one sometimes finds in otherwise capricious persons.

The wonderland of science was at hand in the commonest everyday things, but its truths could not be understood except by thinking of natural laws. What passed for natural science in most people's minds before Newton's time was a mere hash of childish curiosities and far-fetched fables. What today are known as the " natural sciences " had

*National Portrait Gallery*

### SIR ISAAC NEWTON

**As a physicist Newton was a brilliant genius and, like most geniuses, lived a very simple life, even after his incomparable gifts of intellect had won him high honour and place. This portrait by John Vanderbank shows the distinguished scientist at work among his books and apparatus.**

then no place in education, for the very good reason that they scarcely existed. The nature of light, of heat, of sound, and of electricity were unknown; chemistry was still befogged with alchemy, and astronomy with astrology. Scientific instruments were still crude and unreliable.

Such was the intellectual world into which Newton was born. He was the son of a gentleman farmer, who, dying before his only son's birth, left his widow in very moderate circumstances. At Grantham School young Isaac, according to his own later accounts, was rather an idler. The classical Greek and Latin education of the times must, indeed, have been deadly dull to a mind like his, all alive with curiosity about the nature of the universe. Not being able to find out what he wanted to know in school, the boy made now a windmill, now a water-clock, and now a carriage to be propelled by the occupant—as well as sun-dials, and even doll's furniture for little girl friends.

One science, to be sure—mathematics—did form a part of "every gentleman's education," and in

*British Museum*

### NEWTON'S PRISM

**Isaac Newton's greatest achievement in optics was the analysis of white light into the primary colours. The prism above, presented by a descendant of Newton to the British Museum, is the one he used in his optical studies.**

this Newton was a discoverer almost as soon as he had finished his first studies at Cambridge. He developed the new method of the calculus (or, as he called it, "fluxions,") in the year in which he took his degree at Trinity College, Cambridge—in 1665. The method is of great importance, not only in itself but as a means later used in proving the theory of gravitation, the germ of which seems to have lodged in Newton's mind about the same time.

The story that an apple fell in an orchard and gave Newton the first idea of gravity is probably a fable. The calculations of the moon's orbit, which he made to test the gravitation theory, agreed "pretty nearly" with the known facts, but "to a mind like Newton's 'pretty nearly' is as bad as 'not at all,'" and so the study of gravitation was laid aside for the time being.

Now began a series of careful, logically conducted experiments on light and colour, which were to lead to the first of his marvellous discoveries in natural science. By 1669, the year in which he was appointed professor of mathematics at Cambridge University, Newton had demonstrated the compound character of light, and the fact that colour resides not in the object but in the light itself. These discoveries were not made public, however, until 1672, when Newton reported them to the Royal Society. His studies of light also led him to the invention of the reflecting telescope.

Newton explained light by the corpuscular theory—that is, that it was a stream of minute particles or corpuscles given off at a high velocity by a luminous body. Scientists later adopted the wave theory (*see* Light). But since then the discovery of radium and the manifestations of radio-activity have proved the existence of minute particles moving with the high speeds needed for Newton's corpuscular theory, and now scientists are not so sure that Newton was wholly wrong on this point. (*See* Atom; Radium).

Just when Newton resumed his study of the problems of gravitation is not known, but in

*Science Museum*

**The telescope made by Newton in 1671 is now the property of the Royal Society. Here is a copy, exhibited at the Science Museum, London.**

1684 the astronomer Edmund Halley (1656–1742) stumbled upon the fact that the quiet Cambridge scholar had worked out in solitude the principles of the theory. At Halley's request Newton set them forth in the work generally called the Principia (*Philosophiae Naturalis Principia Mathematica*, or Mathematical Principles of Natural Philosophy), probably the most important single contribution to science ever made by any one man. It established the ideas of "mass" and "force," the principles of the mechanics of the heavenly bodies, and the science of theoretical mechanics as it exists today. (*See* Gravitation ; Mechanics ; Physics).

Newton shrank from publicity to a degree nowadays almost unknown. He kept secret for a time many of his greatest discoveries, for fear of the notoriety they might bring him. When he communicated to the Royal Society's magazine, Philosophical Transactions, his solution of the moon's rotation round the earth, he forbade the publication of his name. " It would, perhaps, increase my acquaintance—the thing which I chiefly study to decline." Controversy was distasteful to him, and a dispute with the German scientist G. W. Leibniz (1646–1716) over the calculus (which the two seem to have invented independently) was the exception to a rule deliberately adopted and closely kept. But when James II interfered illegally with the universities, Newton took an active part in defending the University of Cambridge. Later, he was elected to a seat in the Convention Parliament which seated William and Mary on the throne in place of James II. His friend Charles Montague, Chancellor of the Exchequer, then appointed him to a position in the Mint in 1696, and in 1699 he was made its head.

In 1703 he was elected president of the Royal Society, a position which he held for a period of over 20 years. Knighthood at the hand of Queen Anne followed in 1705. So peace and prosperity were Newton's lot until his death at Kensington, London, on March 20, 1727. He was buried in Westminster Abbey, and a statue of him stands at Trinity College, Cambridge.

# New Year's Day.
When the first day of the New Year is celebrated, a custom is followed that dates back to the very dawn of civiliza-tion. For nearly all peoples have observed a New Year celebration, though the time has varied widely —sometimes as early as the autumnal equinox (about September 21), and sometimes as late as Midsummer Day (June 24). If we could travel round the world and observe the New Year celebrations in the various countries, what a wonderful variety of customs we should find!

If you were in China, where New Year's Day coincides with that of the western world, you might think that the people were celebrating all their holidays for the year at once, for they close their shops for several days while they make merry with feasts and fireworks and a general exchange of gifts and good wishes. In preparation, every debt must have been paid before New Year's Day, every house swept and cleaned, and each person provided with holiday clothes and a supply of preserved fruits, sweets and ornamental packages of tea to give away.

The traditional Japanese New Year festival is perhaps even gayer. No matter how poor he may be, everyone endeavours to provide himself with new clothes, and takes three days off from work to visit his friends or entertain them at his home. Every gate-post is adorned with dark-green pines and feathery, light-green bamboos, while over the doorways hang vivid red lobsters and crabs, and scarlet, tangerine-like fruits, symbolical of long life and happiness; the streets are thronged with children playing battledore and shuttlecock.

Throughout the rest of the Orient, too, the opening of the New Year is celebrated with elaborate festivals that correspond to the Christmas celebrations of western countries. In some European countries, especially France and Scotland, New Year's Day is almost more important a holiday than Christmas. If you were a French peasant boy or girl you might put your *sabot* (wooden shoe) on the hearth for a gift to be deposited in it at Christmas; but grown-ups in France exchange gifts at the New Year festival, when there are also family parties.

Scotland celebrates New Year's Eve with a heartiness nowhere surpassed. In Scotland and in parts of England the old tradition of " first-footing " still survives, the belief being that the first person who enters a house on New Year's Day brings good luck according as, in different localities, he is light or dark haired.

Some cities have their special local customs. Formerly in Leningrad (Russia) the New Year was ushered in by a cannonade of 100 shots fired at midnight. In some Scandinavian cities, also, the New Year is welcomed with a noise of firearms, while the Yuletide celebration continues until Twelfth Night.

March 25 was the usual date for beginning the new year in most Christian countries in the Middle Ages, and England retained that date until 1752. In those few countries which still use the Julian calendar New Year now comes on January 13 of our reckoning (*see* Calendar). The Jewish New Year, which opens with Tishri, our September, is called the Feast of the Trumpets, and the celebrations last for 48 hours.

*L.N.A.*

**GREETING THE NEW YEAR**
Dancing has always been one of the chief means of expressing jubilation, and so we find that people herald the arrival of the New Year in this way. Above we see a merry throng dancing in the Royal Albert Hall, London, on the occasion of a New Year's Eve Ball.

# GREATEST CITY *of the* NEW WORLD

*We have been made familiar with many of the sights and sounds of
New York by the cinema. The short tour taken in these pages will show
us still more of America's greatest city.*

**New York.** In size, in wealth, in financial operations, in manufacturing, in foreign commerce, and in its motley racial elements, New York is one of the two greatest cities of the world. Its population of nearly eight million exceeds that of Sweden, Norway, and many another nation, and is exceeded only by that of London among the world's great cities.

It is the most important manufacturing and business centre of the United States, and is one of the leading financial centres of the world. It is a very rich city, with many luxurious buildings; yet a walk of 10 minutes from its financial and shopping centres will take you to haunts of extreme poverty on East Side; though Mayor Fiorello LaGuardia, who held office in New York from 1934 to 1945, did much to help the poorer people.

*Aerofilms*
**The Statue of Liberty, on Bedloe's Island, in New York's Upper Bay, was given by France to the United States.**

In the middle of the Upper Bay of New York, which lies south of the city, is Bedloe's or Liberty Island. On this stands Bartholdi's far-famed statue of Liberty Enlightening the World, given by the people of France to the United States in 1884.

Looking north-east, you see the tip of the tongue-shaped island of Manhattan, the heart of New York, crowded with skyscrapers. On each side of Manhattan are wide rivers swarming with ships, ferry-boats, and launches. The river that skirts it on the west is Hudson river, still called in its lower course North river by New Yorkers to distinguish it from the Delaware, the South river of old colonial days. On its western shore lies the State of New Jersey.

The winding East river, on the other side of Manhattan, is crossed by great bridges—the Brooklyn, Manhattan, Williamsburg, Queensborough, and Triborough structures. In East river are three large islands—Welfare, Ward's, and Randall's—that are occupied chiefly by prisons and other municipal institutions of Greater New York. On the other side of East river is Long Island, whose populous boroughs of Brooklyn and Queens are part of New York City.

Now look south towards the neck of the pear-shaped bay, the mile-wide channel called the Narrows, which connects the Upper Bay and the Lower Bay. East of it is Long Island, and on the west are the beautiful wooded slopes of Staten Island (Richmond Borough), a densely populated but still pretty suburb of New York. Between it and Manhattan Island ferries are constantly plying.

Returning in the ferry from Bedloe's Island to Manhattan you will pass Ellis Island, where in former years thousands of people might be given entrance to the United States. There immigrants were medically examined and underwent educational tests; now all this is done at United States Consulates abroad, and most immigrants do not pass through the island. To serve those detained for any reason there are a hospital, a cinema, and a nursery for children. At the entrance to East river you will also get a glimpse of Governor's Island, formerly the residence of the British governor when New York was a colony, and now the headquarters of the First Army; and then in a few minutes you arrive at the Battery, the southern tip of Manhattan. Battery Park (21 acres) occupies the site of old Dutch fortifications. The famous aquarium formerly occupying the round fort is to be housed in a new building at Coney Island.

Manhattan Island is only one to two and a half miles wide and 13¼ miles long. Until 1874 the city did not extend beyond its limits. A good walker could cross the island in 30 minutes, and he could walk its length, from the Battery up Broadway to the Harlem river, in a few hours; today more than one-third of New York's total population is crowded in this small space. On the average square mile there are more than 85,000 people.

To accommodate this immense working population the business quarters have been covered with towering structures, many of which house as many people as a small town would do. By the invention of the steel skeleton type of construction (*see* Building Construction) it was made possible to carry these buildings 20, 40, 50, and even 100 storeys into the air; while their enormous weight is sustained on piers sunk to bedrock, far below the surface.

The tallest structure constructed here by Man is the Empire State Building, mammoth of mid-town Manhattan. It is 102 storeys high, and rises to 1,250 feet. There are 35 other skyscrapers in Manhattan more than 500 ft. high.

The streets of Manhattan are indeed wonderful. There is Wall Street, the financial centre of the United States; an extremely narrow thoroughfare, hardly half a mile long, it has an importance altogether disproportionate to its size. At the head of Wall Street, in the midst of the banks and great office buildings and just beyond the roar of the kerb market in Broadway, stands Trinity Church, built in 1846 on the site of two earlier buildings. Half a mile to the north another tiny but famous street runs east from Broadway, the historic Park Row, once the home of several great newspapers.

The shape and street " layout " of Manhattan make it easy for us to make a survey of the island. The present street plan was devised in 1811, to provide orderly growth beyond the " crazy quilt " area of the old town. East-west *streets*, numbered northward, connected the two rivers; while about a dozen *avenues*, numbered from First Avenue on the

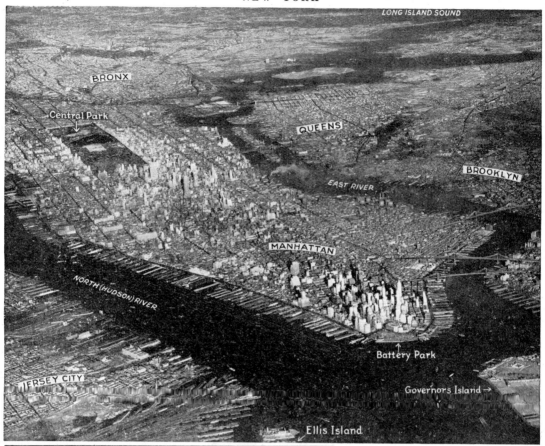

LONG ISLAND SOUND
BRONX
Central Park
QUEENS
BROOKLYN
EAST RIVER
MANHATTAN
NORTH (HUDSON) RIVER
Battery Park
Governors Island →
JERSEY CITY
Ellis Island

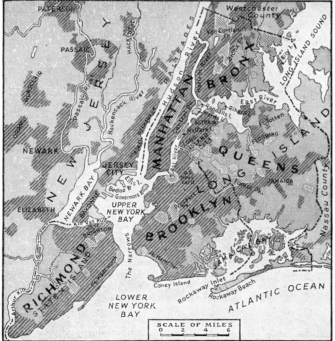

In the map above, which shows the same area as is seen in the photograph at the top of the page, heavy shading indicates the densely-populated areas. The dotted lines serve to mark the outer boundaries of New York City.

### ABOVE THE SKYSCRAPERS
This aerial photograph shows the main features of New York, with Manhattan Island in the centre. 'Midtown' is south of Central Park.

east, ran north and south. This idea in city planning seemed sound at the time, when everyone thought that industry would hug the river banks and people would move east or west in going to and from work. Actually, the tremendous growth of New York has thrown most of the traffic burden on the few north-and-south avenues.

The most important of these is Broadway itself, which runs in a zig-zag fashion north-eastward through the island from the Battery to the Harlem river and beyond. In the lower part of the city the thoroughfare is strangely narrow, but contains some of the most famous buildings in New York. Besides Trinity Church, St. Paul's Chapel is in this street, a cherished relic of colonial days. Office buildings in Broadway include the Singer Building and the Woolworth Building, two of the older but still outstanding skyscrapers of New York.

Near the six-cornered crossing of Broadway with Sixth Avenue and Thirty-third Street is one of the

*Wide World*

hat a wonderful expanse of New York is spread before us om the upper windows of one of its skyscrapers! In this view om the City Bank Building, the tall majestic structure on the t is the headquarters of the Bank of Manhattan (838 feet) on Wall Street. The skyscraper of somewhat similar appearance which rises in the distance, on its right, is the Woolworth Building, 792 feet high, situated on Broadway. When we are up as high as this we almost feel that our heads are 'scraping the sky.'

The Gothic tower (top left) of New York's Riverside Church rises high above Riverside Drive and the Hudson River; in the background at the left is the tomb of President Grant. In contrast is the East Side slum in the top centre, with its washing hung over the street. Luxurious skyscraper hotels (top right) overlook Central Park at Fifth Avenue and 59th Street. In the lower photograph Broadway at the left and Seventh Avenue at the right run north from Times Square in all their night-time glitter. The theatre district centering here extends a considerable distance.

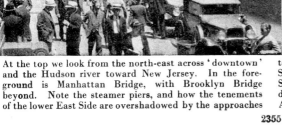

At the top we look from the north-east across 'downtown' and the Hudson river toward New Jersey. In the foreground is Manhattan Bridge, with Brooklyn Bridge beyond. Note the steamer piers, and how the tenements of the lower East Side are overshadowed by the approaches to the mighty bridges. In the ferry picture we see the Staten Islanders coming to work, and below we look at the Subtreasury Building in the heart of the Wall Street district. Lower right, a glimpse of fashionable Park Avenue where it tunnels through a big office building.

# A TRIP INTO NEW YORK'S LOVELY COUNTRYSIDE

Lake George

Wilmington Notch, Ausable River

The Palisades

Hudson River

Delaware River

Long Lake

Though the State of New York is chiefly notable for its wealth and industries it also possesses beautiful scenery, with lakes, mountains, rivers and quiet streams flowing through fertile valleys. Lake George, in the eastern part of the State, is a well-known and attractive holiday resort. Wilmington Notch is one of the many lovely spots in the Adirondack Mountains. The Palisades loom above the Hudson river within sight of New York City. In striking contrast are the upper valleys of the Hudson and the Delaware with their restful scenes. Long Lake, 14 miles long and one mile wide, is in the Adirondacks, which are much frequented as health resorts and contain the headwaters of the Hudson. There are extensive forests of pine, beech and birch in these mountains, about 4,000 square miles of which form a State park, a summer and winter holiday resort.

(population 127,000) is now the capital. Larger cities are New York, Buffalo (575,000), Rochester (325,000) and Syracuse (206,000). Other towns include Schenectady, a great electrical and broadcasting centre, and West Point, home of the U.S. Naval Academy.

The State has a magnificent harbour, and an inland highway to the west through the valleys of the Mohawk and Hudson rivers, abundance of waterpower, and coal-beds near at hand. Among the rivers are the St. Lawrence (forming the Canadian boundary), the Hudson, the Mohawk and its tributaries, and the Niagara. Long Island is one of the greatest island possessions of the U.S.A., and the picturesque " Thousand Islands " in the St. Lawrence are favourite summer resorts. The Adirondack and Catskill Mountains are much frequented.

Among important industries are the manufacture of clothing, the publishing of newspapers, periodicals and books, the making of paper and wood-pulp, electrical machinery, photographic materials, dairy products, foundry and machine-shop products, textiles, and packed and dressed meats.

The first European to enter New York harbour was Giovanni Verrazano, who arrived in 1524. In 1609 the Englishman Henry Hudson, acting on behalf of a Dutch company, explored the Hudson river, and Champlain entered the State from Canada. The first trading-posts, made by the Dutch at Fort Nassau (Albany) and on Manhattan Island, started in 1614. For all Manhattan Island the Dutch in 1626 (it is said) paid the Indians roughly £5 in beads, brass ornaments, and bright cloths! In 1664 an English fleet sent by the Duke of York (afterwards James II) captured the district, including New Amsterdam, and its name was changed to New York in the duke's honour. New York was the last portion of the Old Thirteen Colonies to be evacuated by the British. The population of the State is nearly 13½ million.

# The OTHER BRITAIN of the FAR SOUTH

*Almost exactly on the other side of the world from the Mother Country lies Britain's farthest Dominion—a beautiful land of fertile plains and snow-clad Alps, and of plentiful natural resources.*

**New Zealand.** The islands which constitute the Dominion of New Zealand are situated in the South Pacific, about 1,200 miles to the south-east of Australia, and they are regions of strange and beautiful contrasts. The area of the Dominion is 103,935 square miles. The North Island and the South Island have an area of 102,000 square miles and contain the bulk of the population.

The North Island, of 44,281 square miles, is warmer and has land more suitable for farming than the South Island, though it is somewhat smaller. The northern portion is a semi-tropical region, with some amazing geological features. Cone-shaped volcanoes rise from its central plateau, and around Rotorua is a region of geysers, hot springs, and vast crevices where boiling mud bubbles up from the depths of the earth.

The interior of the North Island is mountainous, and for this reason the large cities have grown up on the coast. Auckland, the largest city in New Zealand, has a population of 281,900 and is the chief port for foreign trade, serving the rich farm lands of the Waikato district and Northland. The capital, Wellington, is situated on Cook Strait, and has 183,100 inhabitants.

The South Island is more rugged than the North Island, and in the south-west the coast is broken by picturesque fiords. Lofty mountains, the main range of which is called the Southern Alps, stretch from end to end of the long narrow island, which has an area of 58,093 square miles. On their western slopes these mountains are covered with forests, on the east with scrub and tussock grass. The highest peak is Mount Cook (12,349 feet), others exceeding 10,000 feet. The largest city of the South Island is Christchurch (population 159,400), an important manufacturing city and the commercial centre for the lamb, wool, and grain-growing district of Canterbury; its port is Lyttelton. Dunedin (population 87,700), is on Otago Harbour and resembles Scotland's Edinburgh in appearance and climate. The frozen mutton export industry was started there in 1881.

Dense forests originally covered about half of New Zealand. But settlers, in establishing millions of acres of pasture-lands, burnt off huge areas, the remaining forest totalling about a fifth of the Dominion's area. Sub-tropical forest predominates in the North Island, and sub-antarctic forest in the South Island. Among the trees of the sub-tropical forests are the kauris (with trunks often 12 feet thick), rimu, kahikatea and totara, all yielding excellent timber. The sub-antarctic forests are mainly of beech. Large areas are planted with exotics. principally *Pinus insignis*. Their care has for many years been in the hands of the State Forest Service.

New Zealand has no land animals of her own. The only wild animals have been introduced into the country and have run free, most of them becoming pests—pigs, goats, deer, rabbits, weasels and opossums. The native birds include the kiwi, which cannot fly, the musical bell-bird, the kea parrot, the wood pigeon, and the recently rediscovered Takahe (*Notornis hochstetteri*). Imported birds which have established themselves include the sparrow, thrush, skylark, blackbird and magpie. There is an amazing

---

**Extent.**—Area (including annexed islands) 103,935 square miles. Population 1,823,074.

**Physical Features.**—In the South Island are the Southern Alps, reaching 12,349 feet in Mt. Cook; to the east are the Canterbury Plains. There is also mountainous country in the North Island, with many volcanic peaks; several lakes, including Taupo (22 miles long) and many short rivers.

**Principal Products.**—Sheep, wool ; butter, cheese, wheat, oats, barley ; coal, gold.

**Chief Cities.**—Auckland (281,900), Wellington (capital, 183,100), Christchurch (159,400), Dunedin (87,700).

variety of seabirds. There are no snakes, and only a few species of annoying insects.

From the sea come many kinds of fish, among the edible species being schnapper, blue cod and flounder. The rivers and lakes provide a wide range of edible fish, including eels, lampreys, and brown and rainbow trout.

Two-thirds of New Zealand is occupied by farmers. The soil is fertile, and the climate allows live-stock to be kept out of doors all the year. Cattle, sheep, pigs and horses are raised. Wheat, oats, barley, maize, potatoes and onions are the chief crops. Fruit trees thrive in certain areas. Chief exports are butter, cheese, frozen meat, hides, wool and apples. The processing of meat and dairy products is the chief industry, most of the manufactures supplying only domestic needs, such as vehicles, timber, clothing, shoes and hosiery. Gold has been mined since 1860 ; coal, iron, silver and tungsten also are worked.

The Dominion has a highly developed transport system. The State operates 3,500 miles of railway, and there are 76,000 miles of roads. The State also controls civil aviation which serves the main towns ; there are air links with Australia, the United States, Great Britain, and several of the Pacific Islands.

Education is free and compulsory; every child must be at school by the age of seven and may not leave until he or she is 15. About half the students attending the four university colleges and two agricultural colleges are receiving free education.

New Zealand has been a pioneer in Social Legislation. For instance, it was the first country to introduce Old Age Pensions (1898). The State provides a minimum income (usually £4 a week for a man and his wife) for the aged, the unemployed, widows and invalids, as well as free medical care, free medicines, certain dental treatment, and other " social " benefits. All are required to contribute to a Government Fund from which these payments are made, and all may benefit in one way or another.

Labour laws include compulsory membership in a Union, and, in most cases, a 40-hour, 5-day week. Labour disputes are subject to settlement by an Arbitration Court which fixes wages and conditions of work.

After the Second World War (1939–45) there was an acute housing shortage, which was tackled partly by private building schemes and partly by a State housing plan. The building of large suburbs of State houses involved the provision of sites for schools, sports grounds, parks and commercial centres. Both town and country folk live mostly in neat wood, brick or concrete houses, usually of the one-storey bungalow type and each having a garden.

New Zealanders have the leisure and excellent facilities for recreation. The main sports have national organizations and many of these are affiliated to the National Council of Sport, which encourages and assists sports generally. The national game is Rugby football; other popular sports include cricket, hockey, ski-ing, tennis, baseball, swimming and yachting.

Over 100,000 New Zealanders are Maoris, a friendly, hospitable and intelligent people who migrated across the Pacific from Polynesia in the 14th century. When the first Europeans landed, in the 18th century, the Maoris were a race of gardeners, fishermen and warriors. They welcomed the newcomers for the knowledge and tools they brought; but, as the number of white settlers grew, Maori animosity over land ownership was aroused, and this led to regular warfare in the 1860s. For a time after that, the Maori population declined. It has, however, doubled in the last 50 years, probably owing to the general respect for the Maori which has become a feature of New Zealand life.

Maori children go to the same schools as other New Zealand children, though in many centres of Maori population there are special Maori schools. Maoris are free and equal citizens of New Zealand and work at the same sort of jobs as other New Zealanders and take part in the same recreations. Some of them have risen to important governmental positions or distinguished themselves in other ways. The revival of Maori arts and community interests is one of the most significant cultural events to take place in the Dominion.

It was a hardy Dutch seafarer, Abel Janszoon Tasman, who discovered these islands in 1642 and gave the land the name it bears today. But no white man seems to have visited New Zealand from that

**THE DOMINION OF NEW ZEALAND**

# CITY AND COUNTRYSIDE VIEWS OF NEW ZEALAND

*By courtesy of the High Commissioner for New Zealand*

The photograph at the top left shows two of the chief buildings in Dunedin, the second largest city of the South Island : the Town Hall (left), and the Cathedral. Scottish settlers gave Dunedin the old Gaelic name for Edinburgh, which it is thought to resemble in climate and appearance. Luxuriant foliage is characteristic of northern New Zealand, and in the photograph at the top right tree ferns are seen growing beside the lake in Pukekura Park, New Plymouth, North Island. The lower photograph was taken on a sheep farm in pastoral country typical of the eastern half of the South Island, where the Canterbury Plains, which lie east of the Southern Alps, are widely noted for their sheep.

during the French Revolution. In 1804 Napoleon made him Marshal, and Ney distinguished himself at the battles of Jena, Eylau and Friedland.

Sent to Spain in 1808, Ney returned to France in 1812, having quarrelled with Marshal Masséna, under whom he had been called upon to serve in the invasion of Portugal to oppose the British under Sir Arthur Wellesley (later Duke of Wellington). He accompanied Napoleon in his campaign against Russia, and his victory at Borodino (1812), during the retreat from Moscow, saved the remnants of the French army from the pursuing Russians. This

time until 1769, when Captain James Cook, the famous English navigator, visited the islands and explored the coasts and the dividing strait which bears his name. He also visited them in 1773, 1774, and again in 1777 on his last voyage. During the next 60 years whaling vessels and trading schooners seeking timber reached New Zealand. The first settlement, by missionaries, was made in 1815.

In 1840 New Zealand became a British colony, achieving the status of a self-governing Dominion in 1907. It includes, besides the North and South Islands and Stewart Island, various remote groups, the chief of which are the Cook Islands to the north, the Chatham Islands to the east, and the Auckland and Campbell Islands to the south. The former German colony of West Samoa was ruled by New Zealand under a League of Nations mandate, and in 1947 it was proposed that the Dominion accept a trusteeship under the United Nations. The population of the country is 1,823,074.

*High Commissioner for New Zealand; Keystone*

**MAORI CITIZENS OF NEW ZEALAND**
Inhabitants of New Zealand before the coming of the white man, the Maoris enjoy equal rights with the rest of the Dominion's population. The young carvers (top) are pupils at a school near Rotorua, in the North Island; (lower left) student at a theological college. Above, Maori chief in traditional costume of his ancestors. Today Maoris wear European clothing.

**Ney,** MICHEL (1769–1815). "The bravest of the brave" was the title given by Napoleon Bonaparte to Michel Ney, one of his famous Marshals. Ney (pron. nā) was born on January 10, 1769, at Saarlouis, France, the son of a cooper, and joined the army in the ranks in 1788. Promotion was rapid

achievement brought him the title of Prince of Moskova (Moscow). In 1813 he was present at the battles of Lützen and Leipzig, and on the abdication of Napoleon in April 1814 he joined the Royalists.

When Napoleon returned from exile on the isle of Elba, Ney was sent to oppose him; but he deserted with his army to his old master. He fought a drawn battle with Wellington at Quatre Bras, Belgium, on June 16, 1815; and he commanded the centre of the French army at Waterloo. After Napoleon's final defeat, Ney was tried for his desertion of King Louis XVIII, whom the Allies had placed on the French throne in 1814, and was sentenced to death; he was shot in Paris on December 7, 1815.

# The WORLD'S most FAMOUS WATERFALL

*Everyone who is able to do so visits the Niagara Falls, one of the greatest natural spectacles the world can provide for the tourist. It is valuable, too, as a source of almost unlimited electric power.*

**Niagara Falls.** Anthony Trollope (1815–83), the English novelist, once wrote that " of all the sights on earth which tourists travel to see " he knew of none " so beautiful, so glorious, and so powerful " as the falls on the Niagara river, between Canada and the United States, and about 22 miles north-west of the city of Buffalo, New York State. Some people differ from him, and since the discovery of Victoria Falls in Southern Rhodesia, of Iguassu Falls, on the Argentine-Brazilian frontier, and of Kaieteur in British Guiana, Niagara Falls can no longer claim the distinction of being the highest falls in the world. But certainly in point of scenic splendour they are not only the most sublime of all cascades but are among the foremost of " all beauties of Nature prepared by the Creator for the delight of His creatures."

Every minute of the day and night about 15 million cubic feet, or nearly 417,000 tons, of water sweep over the falls. The torrents shoot with such force over the ledge that they land some 50 feet in front of it, where they churn themselves into a seething, swirling cauldron. The ceaseless roar explains the name Niagara, meaning Thunder of Waters, given by the Iroquois Indians.

In the centre of the river, Goat Island splits the cataract into two falls—the Canadian on the left or west side, and the American on the right side. The Canadian Fall, also called Horseshoe Fall because of its shape, measures 3,000 feet round the curve and is 158 feet high. The American Fall, which is almost straight across, is about 1,000 feet in length. Though its descent is 167 feet, its volume of water is only one-twentieth to one-tenth of the total flow.

Caves have been formed in the wall of rock behind the majestic curved sheets of water of both falls, from which sightseers, clad in waterproofs, obtain a magnificent view. The Canadian Fall has excavated a basin as deep as the height of the fall, which temporarily retards the waters and enables a small steamer to poke its nose up into the spray. Scenic railway lines skirt the river.

Scarcely less marvellous than the falls are the river rapids above and below them. The Niagara

*Canadian Pacific*

**NIAGARA FALLS SEEN FROM THE CANADIAN SIDE**

The Horseshoe Falls (right) are in Canada. The American Falls are in the United States. They are separated by Goat Island, which is in the centre of the river, and together are known as the Niagara Falls. The tremendous rush of water is gradually eating away the ' lips,' the edge of the American Falls receding from two to seven inches a year, that of the Horseshoe Falls from two to five feet annually. A seven-mile gorge has been worn away by the process.

# TILTED LAND THAT CREATED THE NIAGARA FALLS

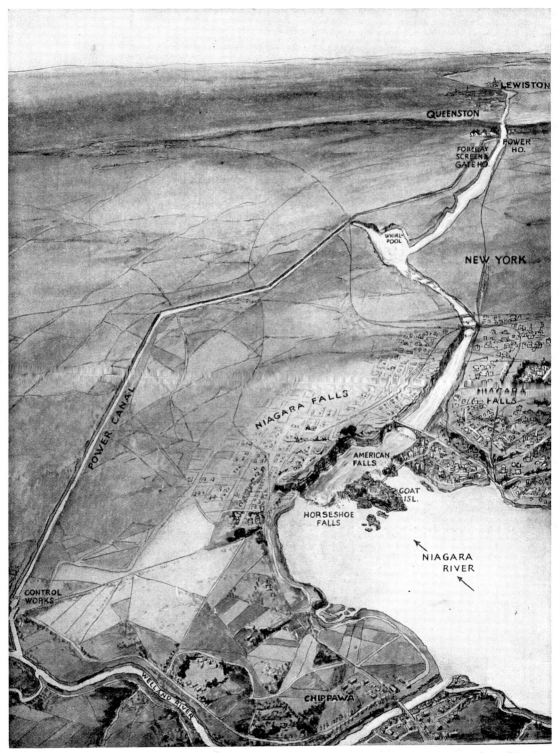

Looking northward you see here the 15 miles of the Niagara river's course between Chippawa and Queenston. Near Queenston the land drops suddenly and it is this Niagara Escarpment, as it is called, that created the Falls at the end of the Ice Age. Through the centuries the river has been wearing down its bed and carving out a gorge, until the Falls are now about seven miles nearer Lake Erie than they were originally. The Canadian Power Canal (left) carries water to a power-house near Queenston. The electricity generated along the river banks serves chemical and aluminium industries near by and also supplies light and power to towns within a radius of more than 200 miles.

river, part of the boundary between New York State and Ontario, Canada, is Lake Erie's outlet into Lake Ontario, 33 miles northward. The level of the latter lake is about 330 feet lower than that of Lake Erie, but for about 20 miles the river makes only a small portion of the descent. Then it narrows from about three miles in width to less than a mile, and in the remaining mile or so above the falls it descends 52 feet, gaining such velocity that it forms the foaming Upper Rapids.

Making about half its total descent at the falls, the river enters the picturesque Niagara Gorge—flanked by perpendicular walls of rock 200 to 300 feet high—flows two miles farther, and then forms the famous Whirlpool Rapids, extending for a mile and descending about 100 feet. Just below these rapids, the river, making a sharp turn to the left, has worn a large circular basin in the rock. This is the celebrated Whirlpool.

Fed by the mighty reservoirs of the Great Lakes, Niagara pours over its precipice a volume of water great enough to develop over 3,975,000 horse-power. If the full drop from lake to lake were used, over six million horse-power could be attained. At present well over one million horse-power is generated.

Although little was done towards the "harnessing" of Niagara until the invention of the dynamo and the transmission of electric power by cable, the building of power-houses and factories soon after threatened to destroy the falls as a spectacle by diminishing the flow of water. To guard against this, in 1910 the governments of the United States and Canada made provision for restricting the water used for industrial purposes to 20,000 cubic feet a second on the American side, and 36,000 cubic feet a second on the Canadian side. In 1949, because of a serious shortage of power in Ontario, the U.S. government agreed to divert some of Niagara's water to the Canadian flow.

Niagara has inspired many feats of reckless courage and skill. In 1859, a tight-rope walker named Blondin not only crossed on a rope but took a passenger in a wheelbarrow (*see* illus., page 473). Others have perished in trying to go over the falls in barrels, or to swim the rapids, which were first swum by Lord Desborough (1855–1945).

**Nibelungs,** SONG OF THE. (Pron. nē′-be-loongz). In the Middle Ages, when castles crowned the hill-tops of the Rhineland, wandering minstrels roamed from stronghold to stronghold entertaining the people with song and story. Tales of a mythical German race called the Nibelungs were a favourite theme for song, and glorious were the deeds of the gods and warriors of whom the minstrels sang. Later on these lays were written out and collected into a book called the Nibelungenlied or Song of the Nibelungs, and on it have been founded many famous works. Four of Richard Wagner's stirring operas, comprised in the cycle which is known as the Ring of the Nibelungs, were taken from this medieval source.

Once upon a time, one of the older versions states, three gods, Odin, Loki and Hoenir, visited the earth, and while wandering near a stream saw an otter devouring a salmon. They killed and skinned the otter and, bearing the pelt with them, sought shelter for the night in the abode of Rodmar, a heartless miser. Rodmar recognized the pelt as being that of one of his sons, who had the power of changing his shape. He demanded as recompense for the slaying of his son as much gold as would completely cover the otter pelt.

To get the gold the gods hastened to the river and seized a priceless treasure which was guarded by a giant fish, but when all was heaped upon the fur one hair remained uncovered. Yielding to Rodmar's demand, Loki placed on this a ring which bore a curse : " Evil shall come to him who wears it ! " This treasure passed after a time into the hands of the Nibelung kings, and played a tragic part in the Nibelungenlied.

In the Song of the Nibelungs all this wealth is found in the possession of Siegfried, a daring warrior, who has slain the two kings of the Nibelungs to obtain it. Little mention is made of the curse; the story deals chiefly with the adventures and loves of humans, the gods having altogether disappeared from the scene. The plot centres around Kriemhild, the beautiful sister of Gunther, king of the Burgundians, who holds his court at Worms, on the Rhine. Siegfried comes to Worms to woo Kriemhild, and in due course they are wedded.

Many characters are introduced into the story, one being Brunhild, an Icelandic princess of wonderful beauty and enormous strength. Only he who could overcome her in deeds of skill and strength might win her love and hand. King Gunther, attracted by the fame of her beauty, goes to woo her, Siegfried accompanying him as his friend and ally. Wearing a cloak of darkness to make himself invisible, Siegfried helps Gunther in defeating Brunhild in three tests of prowess—hurling the spear, putting the weight, and jumping with Gunther in his arms far beyond the limit that Brunhild could reach. So Gunther weds Brunhild, and she comes to dwell in the court at Worms. Later on she learns of the deception practised upon her, and that Siegfried and not Gunther was the warrior worthy of her hand.

Not long after, Siegfried is treacherously slain by one of Gunther's followers, and Brunhild slays herself with his sword. Kriemhild vows vengeance on her brother, for she knows that he is really responsible for her lord Siegfried's death. She marries Etzel (Attila), king of the Huns, and after many years invites Gunther to visit the kingdom. He comes, bringing his followers, but is taken prisoner by Kriemhild. Gunther is put to death, and Siegfried is thus avenged.

The treasure again enters the story at this point, Kriemhild demanding from Hagen, a vassal of Gunther and the slayer of Siegfried, the secret of the hiding-place of the hoard. He refuses to impart it, saying :

None knoweth of the treasure save God and me alone : And unto thee, she-devil, it never shall be known.

Enraged, Kriemhild grasps Siegfried's sword and decapitates Hagen, but is herself slain by a follower of Etzel.

**Nicaragua.** The largest of the Central American republics, Nicaragua stretches across the isthmus from the Caribbean on the east to the Pacific coast. Its area is 57,143 square miles. Honduras and Salvador form the northern boundary, and Costa Rica lies to the south. Though it possesses wonderful natural resources, Nicaragua is

**PALACE OF THE PRESIDENT OF NICARAGUA**

Since its destruction by earthquake in 1931, much of the city of Managua, Nicaragua's capital, has been rebuilt. Among the new buildings is the president's palace, which stands on the fortified hill called 'La Loma.' The city has a population of 124,300.

*E.N.A*

still one of the least developed of the seven countries of Central America.

The eastern portion of the Republic produces bananas, coconuts and pineapples; the western coffee, sugar-cane and cocoa. Gold and silver are mined, and there are deposits of copper, tin and zinc. The forests yield mahogany, cedar and medicinal plants.

As in most countries of Central America, the majority of the people live along the volcanic Pacific slope. The principal port is Corinto, in the north, from which nearly two-thirds of the country's shipping is done. Leon, 25 miles to the south-east, with a population of 50,000, has public buildings considered among the finest in Central America. Still farther south is the capital, Managua (population 124,300), lying near the foot of a mile-high pyramidal cone, Momotombo, on the south shore of Lake Managua, which is surrounded by volcanoes; the town was almost destroyed by an earthquake in 1931. Granada, a city of 35,000 people, stands on beautiful Lake Nicaragua, which is also set about with giant volcanoes, their sides covered with coffee plantations. Lake Nicaragua, 110 miles long and 3,000 square miles in area, is the largest lake in Central America. A canal right across Nicaragua, to include the lake, has long been projected.

There are 367 miles of railway; most of the roads are mere tracks over which ox-carts alone can travel in the wet season. Air services communicate with the Central and South American Republics and the United States. The population is 1,389,000.

**Nice.** (Pron. nēs). At the extreme eastern end of the French Riviera is the famous pleasure city of Nice. There people go in normal times to bask in the sun, to throw flowers and confetti at one another in the famous carnival, to watch the

fireworks from the gardens on the front, to stroll along the fashionable Promenade des Anglais, and to gamble at the Casino.

The town, which stands on the Baie des Anges, an opening of the Mediterranean Sea, itself is divided into three parts—the New Town, the Old Town, and the Port. Nice has a cathedral, museums, an observatory, and libraries. Its main product is olive oil, others being perfume, soap, leather and furniture.

Greek colonists from Marseilles first settled in Nice over 2,000 years ago, its name (Latin *Nicaea*, from Greek *nike*, victory) being derived from a victory over neighbouring tribes. It became subject to Rome in the 2nd century B.C., and since then has suffered in many wars and at the hands of many races. In 1860 it was given to France as the price of aid rendered in creating the former kingdom of Italy. Its most famous son was Garibaldi, the Italian patriot (1807–82), who helped to unite Italy under a central government. Nice, like all the Riviera, has at times slight earthquakes; in the last century there were four, the most serious being in 1887. The population is 211,200.

*Fox*

**CARNIVAL AT NICE**

Famous pleasure city of the French Riviera, Nice is renowned for its carnival festivities. Above is seen the annual procession of 'King Carnival,' with its accompaniment of triumphal cars, grotesque giant figures and false faces.

**Nicholas.** Tsars of Russia. An attempted revolution when, in 1825, he succeeded his brother Alexander I, made Tsar Nicholas I (1796–1855) a ruler who believed in keeping power in his own hands and was opposed to all reforms. Though he fought against Turkey in 1828–29 to enable the Greeks to win their independence, he used his armies to crush the Hungarian rising against Austria in 1849.

The chief event of his reign was the Crimean War (1854–56), which he began with a view to securing Constantinople (now Istanbul) and those parts of Turkey in Europe on the Black Sea. Disappointment at the failure of these plans owing to the aid given to Turkey by Great Britain, France and Piedmont, may have caused his death, which occurred on March 2, 1855, a year before the end of the war.

Nicholas II (1868–1918), the last of the Tsars, reigned from 1894 to 1917. Great-grandson of Nicholas I, he succeeded his father Alexander III on October 24, 1894. A weak but well-meaning ruler, he was influenced largely by his wife (a German princess). The first Hague Conference, called by the Tsar in 1899 to consider disarmament, showed a sincere desire to remedy the evils caused by countries having to keep large navies and armies. The disastrous Russo-Japanese War (1904–05), in which Russia was defeated, showed clearly the inefficiency and corruption of the Government.

Widespread revolutionary movements which followed that war forced the Tsar to call together the Duma (legislative assembly), which was expected to introduce a parliamentary form of government, but under the autocratic rule of Nicholas the Duma had no real power, and the suggested reforms were dismissed. When war threatened in 1914 Nicholas II was torn between his desire to protect Serbia against Austria and his fear of a general European war.

When the First World War (1914–18) came, the corruption, negligence and lack of ability of the Tsar's officials brought about Russia's defeat in the first two years. The inefficiency of the Government, the suspicion that the court party meditated making a separate peace with Germany, and the forfeiture of public respect through the influence of the " holy man " Rasputin over the Tsarina and the feeble Tsar, made a revolution inevitable.

The storm broke in March 1917, and Nicholas was forced to abdicate the Russian throne. Immediately he became virtually a prisoner, and he and his family (the Tsarina and their four daughters and one son) were eventually taken to Ekaterinburg (now Sverdlovsk) in the Ural Mountains. There they lived until, on July 17, 1918, the Tsar and his entire family were murdered by Bolsheviks.

**NICHOLAS II IN CAPTIVITY**
The last Tsar of Russia, Nicholas II is here seen in captivity at Tsarskoe Selo (now Detskoe Selo), shortly after the Bolshevik Revolution of 1917. Later, he and his family were sent to Ekaterinburg (now Sverdlovsk) in the Urals, where they were murdered on July 17, 1918.

**Nickel.** This is a metallic element with the chemical symbol Ni. Its atomic weight is 58·7; atomic number, 28; density, 8·9. It is white in colour, with a faint yellow tinge; hard, ductile, malleable; slightly magnetic, and capable of taking a high polish. This last property, coupled with the fact that it rusts very slowly, makes it useful as a coating for other metals. The nickel coat is applied by the process of electro-plating (q.v.). Alloyed with two parts of copper and one of zinc, nickel forms a bright silvery alloy known as " German silver " or " nickel-silver," largely used for making cutlery, tableware, and as a basis for silver-plated ware. Alloys of copper, tin, or zinc and nickel are extensively used for coins. The American " nickel " coin (value 5 cents) contains one-fourth nickel, the rest being copper.

About 60 per cent of the world's nickel production is used for the manufacture of nickel steels, alloys which are useful for a great variety of purposes. Alloyed in steel, sometimes with other metals such as chromium, nickel plays an important role in, for example, armour plate and guns, aircraft and motor-cars, railway equipment, machine tools, mining and milling machinery, and the stainless steel used to make our cutlery, door knockers, water taps, etc., as well as things like steam turbine blades.

All alloy called " nichrome," containing about 60 per cent of nickel with about 11 to 25 per cent of chromium and some iron, resists corrosion even at high temperatures, and is used for the coiled heating elements of electric fires.

" Monel Metal," a silvery white alloy of nickel with copper and a little manganese and iron, resists corrosion better than brass, is stronger, and is used in making things like bathroom fittings and laundry machinery.

One nickel-steel known as " invar," containing about 36 per cent of nickel, expands very little with rise of temperature, and is therefore often used to make things that must not change in size appreciably with day-to-day changes of temperature, such as measuring instruments, clock pendulum rods, and watch parts. Another nickel-steel has almost the same rate of expansion under heat as glass, and so may be used as a substitute for platinum for the wires sealed into incandescent electric bulbs.

Finely divided nickel is used as a catalyst (*q.v.*) during the hardening of oils to make margarine. (*See* Margarine ; Hydrogen).

Nickel combines with the gas carbon monoxide to form a gaseous compound, a property of nickel of great importance during the preparation of the pure metal, and the basis of a process called the Mond nickel process.

Nickel is dissolved with difficulty by most acids except nitric acid, which readily attacks it and forms a green solution. The green liquid sometimes seen in glass vessels in chemists' windows is often a nickel salt dissolved in water.

The sulphide ores of Sudbury, Ontario, Canada, supply Man with more than 86 per cent of his total requirements of nickel. Nickel ore deposits are also found in Finland, Norway, Russia, and New Caledonia Island.

## Nicknames.
"Nicknames and whippings," said Walter Savage Landor, "when they are once laid on, no one has discovered how to take off." Nations, like persons, have nicknames which grow up in curious ways. "John Bull," the personification of the English nation, is repre-

**JOHN BULL**
After a drawing by Sir John Tenniel ; reproduced by permission of the proprietors of Punch.

sented as a stout, ruddy-faced, matter-of-fact, blunt fellow attired in leather breeches and top-boots, generally with a cudgel in his hand and a bulldog at his heels. The name 'John Bull" was first used in a political satire published by Dr. John Arbuthnot at the time of the War of the Spanish Succession, in Queen Anne's reign (1702–14). In his History of John Bull the nations of Europe were given the names of various animals.

The nickname "Uncle Sam," applied to the United States, is known the world over. This is the way in which it originated. During the War of 1812 with Great Britain someone inquired as to the meaning of the letters "U.S." stamped on government goods. He was told that they stood for "Uncle Sam," the local nickname for Samuel Wilson, the government inspector. This jest ran through the country; the name stuck, and "Uncle Sam" came to personify the United States government and the American people. Uncle Sam is portrayed as a tall thin man with long narrow beard, long-tailed coat, high hat, and a shrewd but humorous countenance—attributes which marked the typical American of the

*Dorien Leigh*

## THE BROAD WATERS OF THE MIGHTY NIGER RIVER

Africa's third longest river (exceeded in length only by the Nile and the Congo) and the main waterway for the western equatorial region, the Niger (see article, p. 2367) is seen above flowing past Jebba in western Nigeria. Here the river is crossed by the railway which runs from the port of Lagos to Kano in the north. One of the native craft in the foreground has a framework of bamboos, which is covered with grass mats in the rainy season to protect the occupants.

early days. Citizens of the United States are often called Yankees, a name of uncertain origin.

Not very complimentary nicknames include "Froggies" for Frenchmen (because they sometimes eat frogs), and the American slang names, "Wops," of doubtful origin, for immigrants from the south of Europe, and "Dagoes," from the Spanish Diego (James), a contemptuous term for Spaniards or Italians.

Places, too, have nicknames, of which perhaps the most famous is "Pompey," the name given by sailors to Portsmouth. Regiments and ships, too, may have them. The 17/21st Lancers are called from their badge (skull and crossbones) and motto the "Death or Glory Boys"; and the Yorkshire Regiment is known as "The Green Howards," having been raised by a Colonel Howard and wearing green facings on their uniforms.

Some people have thought that the word nickname came from "nick," to cut, since a nickname is often a shortened form of the full name; but a nickname was originally an "eke name," meaning an added name.

**Niger** (Pron. nī'-jer), RIVER. There is no better way of seeing tropical Africa than by a voyage down the River Niger, next to the Congo and the Nile the largest river in the continent. Its course of 2,500 miles leads through mountainous uplands, traverses broad prairies, skirts the vast wastes of the Sahara Desert, plunges through forests, and feels its way to the ocean through a score of mouths bordered with mangrove swamps.

Rising only 150 miles from the sea in French Guinea, north of Sierra Leone, it sweeps first north-eastward, then south-eastward, finally flowing south into the Gulf of Guinea. Its course forms a huge arc which encloses one of the richest African territories—a region chiefly divided between France and Great Britain.

The Niger is of immense importance as an artery of trade. Steamers of light draught can make their way over most of its length; and with its largest tributary, the Benue, it provides a highway for 900 miles eastward into Central Africa. A railway, one of several, connects the upper reaches of the Niger with the River Senegal, which flows into the Atlantic near St. Louis, in the French colony of Senegal. Travellers can reach the markets of Sansanding, Segu, Timbuktu, and other river stations far in the interior towards the Sahara.

Shipping on the Niger is chiefly engaged in transporting palm-oil, oil seeds, copal (a resin used for varnishes), gum, rubber, coffee, and ivory.

The Niger delta is one of the most remarkable in the world, consisting, from 40 to 70 miles from the coast, of a network of intersecting creeks and broader channels, in which it is impossible to trace the main river. The chief entrances for large ships are the Nun Mouth, the Forcados, the Brass Mouth and the Bonny river. In 1795 the African explorer Mungo Park tried unsuccessfully to locate the headwaters of the Niger, but it was not until 1885 that the Timbi source in French Guinea was discovered. (*See* illustration in facing page).

**Nightingale.** No bird has been more celebrated in literature than the nightingale, from Greek times up to our own. Homer wrote

E. J. Hosking

**SWEET-VOICED NIGHTINGALE**
Though the song of the nightingale is heard mostly at night, in spring and early summer in England, the male also sings by day. Here is a male bird, spruce and alert, taking a beakful of food to its nestlings.

of the "sweet, tawny nightingale." Milton called it the "most sweet, most melancholy bird." And Keats is writing of the nightingale when he refers to the

> . . . . song that found a path
> Through the sad heart of Ruth, when, sick for home
> She stood in tears amid the alien corn;
> The same that ofttimes hath
> Charm'd magic casements, opening on the foam
> Of perilous seas, in faery lands forlorn.

This bird (*Luscinia megarhyncha*) is found throughout Europe, most abundantly in southern France, Spain and Portugal. In England its song is heard most frequently in spring and early summer for a few weeks after its return from the south whither it migrates in the autumn. The Persian *bulbul* (*L. hafizi*) and another species of night-singing bird found in Asia, are probably the nightingales of the Persian poets.

During the mating and nesting season—from the middle of April to the middle of June—the male sings both day and night. He is heard, however, chiefly at night, because then most other birds are silent; and during the last two weeks of May and the first of June his song is at its best: a melodious outpouring of glorious tone, and although there are several very distinct phrases, these may be repeated in varying order, the song following no set plan. Nightingales are bold singers, too, giving their performance often within a few feet of the noise and lights of a main road at night.

The bird is about six inches long, with rusty-brown and grey plumage. The nest, loosely built of grass-stalks and dry leaves, is usually hidden among brambles or nettles. The eggs are olive-brown.

# STORY of 'The LADY with the LAMP'

*One might say that the lamp which Florence Nightingale carried round the wards of her hospital shed a light throughout the world, for it was she who raised nursing from drudgery to a noble profession.*

**Nightingale,** FLORENCE (1820–1910). This Englishwoman, the first and greatest of women war-nurses, who revolutionized the methods of caring for sick and wounded soldiers, was born in the city of Florence, Italy, on May 12, 1820; but she grew up on her father's estates at Lea Hurst, Derbyshire and Embley Park, Hampshire. As a girl she made patients of all the sick and aged in the neighbouring villages, and, much against her parent's wishes, would visit them with invalid food she had herself prepared, and with bandages and other dressings she had made at home. Her treatments were so successful that she vowed to devote herself to nursing the sick—though this was laughed to scorn by her relations and friends, so despised was the nursing profession in those days.

At 18 she was presented to Queen Victoria; and as a young girl in Court circles she could have had a gay time and perhaps made a brilliant marriage. But caring nothing for society, she spent her time in studying the work of the great hospitals. In a year or so she left her home and her friends for the hard training of a nurse in convent hospitals at Kaiserswerth on the Rhine and in Paris. At that time it was an unheard-of thing for a gentlewoman to become a professional nurse.

Returning to England, Miss Nightingale attracted attention by reorganizing the Harley Street Home for Sick Governesses. She was 34 years old and already widely known in the medical world when the Crimean War (1854–56) broke out and a British army was sent overseas to help Turkey against Russia. Reports came of the terrible sufferings and high death-rate of the sick and wounded British soldiers and sailors, and she offered her services to the Government on October 14, 1854. Within a week she enlisted 37 nurses, filled a ship with supplies, and embarked for Scutari on the Bosporus in Asia Minor, where she arrived in time to receive the wounded from the battle of Balaclava.

The story of Miss Nightingale's heroic labours in hot and unhealthy camps, and in barracks which served for hospitals, is one of the finest chapters in British military annals, for men were dying like flies when she took charge. She soon changed over unwilling, dirt and neglect into space, order, cleanliness and prompt attention. The death-rate fell from 42 to two per cent. When stricken with fever herself, she refused to leave her post; no matter how long and hard the day's work had been, she always made the night round of the wards, lamp in hand, to see that the attendants were on duty, and to speak cheering words to her charges. Ever afterwards she was known to her fellow-countrymen with grateful affection as "The Lady with the Lamp."

She remained in the Crimea until August 1856, and returned to England to find herself a popular heroine. The fund of £50,000 that was raised for her by public subscription she used in founding

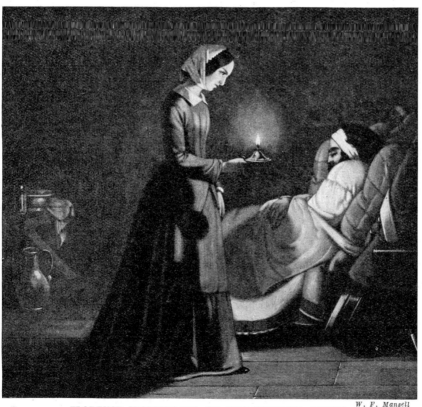

W. F. Mansell

**FLORENCE NIGHTINGALE ON HER HOSPITAL ROUND**
During the Crimean War (1854–56) Florence Nightingale established a military hospital at Scutari on the Bosporus in Asia Minor ; in this engraving she is depicted visiting the sick and wounded. Her habit of going round the wards at night, lamp in hand, won for her the affectionate title of ' The Lady with the Lamp.'

the Nightingale school and home for nurses at St. Thomas's Hospital, London. Queen Victoria's comment after Florence Nightingale visited her at Balmoral was: " Such a head! I wish we had her at the War Office! "

Miss Nightingale's health had been so undermined by her war-work that, although she lived to the age of 90, she became a semi-invalid. Nevertheless, her life continued to be one of the widest usefulness. She wrote standard books on nursing, the most famous being Notes on Nursing (1860), and advised a number of countries on the building and managing of public, private and military hospitals. No one did so much as she to raise the profession of nursing to a place of honour.

Apart from her work and writings in connexion with military and civil hospitals and nursing, Miss Nightingale was very keenly interested in hygiene and sanitation generally. While a nurse, she had always laid great stress on the importance of fresh air, cleanliness, light, diet, and so on, and this principle she was very anxious to see extended to ordinary everyday life. When she was 72 years of age she did not consider herself too old to take part in organizing an elaborate health campaign in Buckinghamshire. Competent instructors were secured, and these were sent on a tour round the county, giving advice to the villagers on ventilation, drainage and other points.

S. G. Payne & Son, Aylesbury

**FLORENCE NIGHTINGALE AT HOME**
In addition to her work in connexion with hospitals, Florence Nightingale founded several schools and institutions for nurses and did much to promote rural hygiene. In 1907 she was awarded the Order of Merit by King Edward VII. The above is one of the last photographs taken of her.

F. Vear

**MRS. NIGHTJAR AND HER FAMILY**
In their babyhood nightjars have no warm nest and have to huddle together on the bare ground, like those shown here under the eye of their mother. That eye is so placed that it can see forwards or backwards.

The bird builds no nest but lays its mottled eggs—usually two in number—on the bare ground. So well do both eggs and mother bird resemble their surroundings that they need no further protection. Nightjars, which are migrants so far as the British Isles are concerned, arriving in May and departing in September, are widely distributed in the northern temperate regions. A well-known North American species is called, from the notes of its song, whip-poor-will. In South America there is a group with very long, forked tails.

**Nightshade.** Growing in various parts of the world is an annual weed, a plant which is related to the potato, whose slender, erect stem about two feet high, pointed oval leaves, drooping clusters of

In 1907 Miss Nightingale was awarded the Order of Merit, an honour which had never before been given to a woman. She died in London on August 13, 1910.

**Nightjar.** Probably no bird has so many nicknames as this. Night-hawk, dor-hawk, fern-owl, moth-owl, lich-fowl, puckeridge, goat-sucker, and flying-toad—these are some of the names it goes by in various parts of England. The name goat-sucker refers to a belief that these birds take the milk from goats; while other names refer to the nightjar's food—large moths and beetles. It is called a nightjar from its peculiar, jarring cry.

About 10 inches long, the nightjar (*Caprimulgus europaeus*) is a bird of nocturnal habits, grey-and-brown mottled, with long wings and tail like those of a hawk. The plumage is as soft as that of an owl, so that it is absolutely silent in flight. It has a flat head and wide gaping mouth.

Dennis; Bedford

**NIGHTSHADES**
Berried spray (left) of the deadly nightshade or dwale, and (above) berries of less poisonous black nightshade.

2369

white flowers, and small, round, black berries are often regarded with suspicion. However, it is only when animals chew the fresh leaves of this common or black nightshade (*Solanum nigrum*), or when people eat too many of its berries, that injury results. The leaves are boiled in some warm climates where the plant makes vigorous growth, and are eaten as a sort of green vegetable.

Another plant of this nightshade group is the bittersweet or woody nightshade (*S. dulcamara*), whose somewhat poisonous scarlet or orange berries taste both bitter and sweet. This species is easily recognized by its flowers, which are purple with a yellow centre. The trailing stems sometimes

scramble up a hedge to the height of five or six feet. It is often called " deadly nightshade," but that plant belongs to another genus.

The true deadly nightshade or dwale (*Atropa belladonna*) is found in Europe, Africa and Asia, and its leaves and roots are used in medicine. This is a disagreeably smelling shrub with dull green leaves, purple bell-shaped flowers, and black cherry-like fruit. Because it can dilate the pupil of the eye, atropine, obtained from this plant, is used by oculists. The deadly nightshade is found in various parts of England, especially on soil containing chalk or limestone. It is easy to distinguish because the leaves grow in pairs, of which one is large and one small; and that, together with the smell, the form of the flowers, and the berries, will help you to know and to shun this highly poisonous plant. It grows to a height of three or four feet.

**Nile.** For thousands of years there was a question as to where the Nile, the longest river of Africa, might be said to begin. In one sense it begins at Khartum. There the Blue Nile, flowing clear and blue from the Abyssinian mountains, or reddish-brown in flood-time, meets the greyish-green White Nile, which comes from the lake region of Central Africa. The sources of the Blue Nile were known in ancient times, but of the White Nile the geographers told legends of the Mountains of the Moon and of underground channels.

It is only in fairly recent times that explorers have followed it back through the swampy *sudd* region, with its dense floating vegetation and its mosquitoes, past the rapids and waterfalls in which it descends from Lake Albert or Albert Nyanza (*nyanza* means lake) to the lake itself, and thence through the beautiful gorges of the Victoria or Somerset Nile, which feeds Lake Albert, to Lake Victoria, and afterwards to the Kagera and other streams which are discharged into this lake.

*Dorien Leigh*

**THE NILE SEEN FROM ONE OF CAIRO'S BRIDGES**

Longest river of Africa, the Nile is of vital importance to Egypt and the northern part of the Sudan, since the fertility and prosperity of those countries are entirely dependent on the irrigation of the land by its waters. A remarkable journey by the English explorers J. H. Speke and J. A. Grant, in 1860–63, gave us our first real knowledge of the sources and extent of this river. The photograph was taken from the Kasr-en-Nil, or Great Nile bridge, which spans the river between Cairo, the capital of Egypt, and the island of Gezira.

**NINEVEH, CAPITAL CITY OF ASSYRIA, IN ITS ANCIENT GLORY**

The ancient capital of the Assyrian empire lay on the left bank of the upper reaches of the River Tigris, opposite where today is the town of Mosul in Iraq. In the 7th century B.C., when the men of Nineveh were defeated by the Medes and Chaldeans, the city was almost entirely destroyed. Numerous excavations have been carried out on the site of Nineveh, and from the knowledge so acquired the above sketch was made, showing how the city may have looked.

From Khartum to Assuan the Nile descends in six cataracts. After passing Khartum it receives only one tributary, the Atbara, another Abyssinian stream, which is 600 yards wide in flood-time and at other times almost dries up so that fish, turtles, crocodiles, and hippopotami remain imprisoned in the deep pools of its upper reaches until released by the next flood.

After watering huge areas of Egypt and passing through the capital, Cairo, the Nile finally reaches the Mediterranean through two channels. These are called the Rosetta and the Damietta mouths, and the general region is known as the Delta. Having received no new tributaries and having lost much through oozing and evaporation, the Nile ends as a smaller river than it was higher up.

The yearly flood of the Nile has for centuries been the secret of Egypt's fertility. Heavy April rains in the basin of the White Nile start the first flood, and the May rains in Abyssinia give the real flood of rich muddy water that fertilizes as well as irrigates. The great dam at Assuan (built in 1902 and extended during 1907–12), together with the dam at Sennar on the Blue Nile (built in 1921–25) and several barrages, store up the surplus flood, and release it later on so that the Nile valley may be watered all the year round. The length of the Nile from Lake Victoria to the Mediterranean is about 3,500 miles. The Blue Nile is about 840 miles long. It was near the Nile Delta that Nelson won his first notable victory over the French forces under Napoleon in 1798. (See Dam).

**Nineveh.** (Pron. nin′-i-ve). When the people of Israel were groaning under the yoke of the proud and ruthless Assyrian kings, the Old Testament prophets called down the vengeance of Heaven on Nineveh, the splendid capital of the Assyrian Empire: "The Lord will make Nineveh a desolation and dry like a wilderness."

The prophecy was fulfilled when the hordes of the conquering Medes and Chaldeans more than 25 centuries ago (612 B.C.) swept over the doomed city and made it a desolate waste. As the centuries passed, the sun-dried bricks of which most of the houses were built crumbled to dust, and the drifting sands covered the ruins, mounting higher and higher, until every trace was lost of this mighty city, whose walls were 100 feet high and so broad that three chariots could be driven abreast.

It was not until the middle of the 19th century that scholars set to work on the vast flat-topped mounds with pick and shovel, and uncovered evidence that the mounds did indeed mark the site of one of the most magnificent capitals of antiquity. More than that, the walls and sculptures and libraries they brought to light have enabled men to re-write the lost chapters of history that tell of the empire of the Assyrians. Nearly every important fact we know today about Assyria has been discovered in the past 100 years, as the result of excavations at Nineveh and other sites in the ancient valleys of the Tigris and the Euphrates.

One of the earliest and most successful of these investigators was Sir Austen Layard (1817–94), who unearthed the palaces of Sennacherib and Ashurbanipal during 1845–51, finding alabaster bas-reliefs of hunts and sieges and battles, and colossal winged man-headed statues of bulls and lions. Most important of all, he found many thousands of engraved clay tablets of Ashurbanipal's library, which have been deciphered and tell us the story of science, history, religion, and literature in those days in Assyria and Babylonia. These tablets are now in the British Museum.

The mounds, which extend at intervals for 15 miles along the Tigris opposite the modern city of Mosul, represent not only the city of Nineveh proper but also Dur-Sargon, the city of Sargon II (c. 750 B.C.), and Kalah. Nineveh, though it existed at least as early as 2000 B.C., was chiefly the creation of Sennacherib (705–681 B.C.), who built walls with 15 gates and many towers. The city stretched for two and a half miles along the Tigris. Here Sennacherib built a great new palace and laid out extensive gardens. He also improved the supply of drinking-water by canals from the hills. It was the destruction of these canals which made a wilderness of Nineveh.

**Niobe.** (From myth-ogy) One of the saddest stories in Greek mythology is that which tells how the proud Niobe, daughter of Tantalus and wife of Amphion, king of Thebes, was punished for her presumption. She boasted of her 12 child-

Alinari
**NIOBE AND HER YOUNGEST CHILD**
In Greek and Roman mythology we read the sad story of Niobe, the wife of Amphion, King of Thebes in Greece, whose 12 children were killed by Apollo and Diana. This statue shows the tragic mother trying to shield her youngest child from the vengeful deities.

ren, and despised the goddess Leto (Latona) who had only two children. But the children of Leto were the great Apollo, god of the sun, and Artemis (Diana), goddess of the moon, and for this arrogance they slew all the children of Niobe with their arrows. Niobe's grief was so great that Zeus out of pity changed her into a rock on Mount Sipylus, from which tears continued to flow.

**Nitric Acid.** When sodium nitrate is heated with sulphuric acid in a retort the sulphuric acid displaces the more volatile nitric acid from its sodium salt, and the nitric acid distils over, leaving behind sodium sulphate and bisulphate (the mixture of these two is called nitre cake). John Rudolph Glauber (1604–70) first used this method 300 years ago, and until recently all the nitric acid used in industry was made in this way. Now most nitric acid is manufactured by the oxidation of synthetic ammonia, which is passed with air over a heated platinum catalyst (q.v.), and the oxides of nitrogen are absorbed in water, thus giving nitric acid.

Nitric acid is a very strong acid often called "aqua fortis." It destroys many organic materials, and if it gets on the skin it stains it yellow and burns it badly. It dissolves nearly all metals—including some, such as copper, which are not easily dissolved by other acids. When metals dissolve in it gases

are produced, including poisonous brown fumes of nitrogen peroxide.

Nitric acid is used in making explosives, celluloid and plastics. It is also employed in the manufacture of synthetic dyes, drugs (such as phenacetin and "M. and B."), and of chemicals used in the laboratory and in industry. Artificial musk and a compound eight times as sweet as saccharin are among the many things made with the aid of this acid.

**Nitrogen.** Four-fifths of the great sea of air that rolls over the earth is free nitrogen. Most of the remainder is oxygen. If burning or respiration takes place in a closed space, the oxygen is used up and the nitrogen is left. Fire cannot burn in this nitrogen, and plants and animals would be suffocated in it.

Nitrogen gas is only a little heavier than the lightest of all gases, hydrogen. It is slightly lighter than oxygen and so it is very slightly lighter than air, since the latter is a mixture of the two. It is given the chemical symbol N, although the gas is usually written $N_2$, as each particle contains two atoms. It is colourless, odourless and tasteless as we know for ourselves, remembering that we cannot smell or taste it in the air.

Although nitrogen forms such a large part of the air it is present only to a minor extent in the compounds of the earth's crust. It is, as it were, wary of the company of other elements and enters into direct combination with only a few of them. We say it is " inert "—without active properties; to get it to combine chemically with other elements, drastic measures such as high temperatures and high pressures are usually required. The simplest compound of nitrogen is the pungent smelling ammonia, which is composed of nitrogen and hydrogen (formula $NH_3$). Nitrogen also forms several oxides or compounds with oxygen. One of these is the anaesthetic nitrous oxide or " laughing gas." Another dissolves in water to give nitric acid, which is one of the most powerful acids we know. Other compounds of nitrogen will be mentioned as we go on. Some of them are very complicated.

Curiously enough although nitrogen is itself inert, compounds which contain fixed nitrogen are often very active chemically. They break up easily, as if nitrogen hated to be tied down. Numerous explosives contain nitrogen compounds, e.g.

gunpowder, dynamite, T.N.T. and the recently discovered "blockbuster" explosive "R.D.X." This chemical reactivity of nitrogen compounds is probably the cause of their being so varied and so

interesting. Many of the most important dyes and drugs contain nitrogen. Indigo dye, cocaine, the deadly poisonous strychnine, the nicotine in tobacco, and the caffeine which makes tea so refreshing to drink—these are all nitrogen compounds. A large part of the tissues of plants and animals is made up of stuff called protein, of which nitrogen forms a very important part. Muscle, skin, hair and horn are largely made of this protein. Some of the new plastics now used so much are made from nitrogen compounds, and nylon also contains it.

Nitrogen gas can be obtained from certain chemical compounds which contain it. For example, a solution of ammonium nitrate when heated gives off the gas in a fairly pure state. Then nitrogen can be obtained from air by removing the other gases as completely as possible. The carbon dioxide which is always present in small amounts is absorbed by caustic potash, and then the oxygen can be removed by passing the air, now free of carbon dioxide, over red-hot copper, when oxide of copper is formed. The remaining gas is nearly pure nitrogen, but it does contain a small amount of the gas argon which is difficult to remove.

In industry nitrogen is obtained from the air by making it liquid, which requires very strong cooling of the air under pressure. The liquid air is then boiled in a special apparatus; the nitrogen now boils off first, while the other gases come off later and can be collected separately. Nitrogen is sold in steel cylinders under pressure.

Although life could not exist without nitrogen, very few live beings can take in and use the free nitrogen from the air. Most of them need to have it prepared in some way before they can use it. We are faced with the sober thought that the higher and more specialised the forms of life, the more they depend on less advanced organisms for their nitrogen. Human beings and animals depend on plants for their nitrogen, and even

carnivorous animals which feed on other animals depend on plants in the end.

Most plants depend on nitrates in the soil (i.e salts of nitric acid) for their nitrogen. Some plants (mentioned later) can get it direct from the air. Nitrates are produced in the soil by the decomposition of the bodies of previous generations of plants and animals. This decomposition is brought about by means of bacteria (which are minute forms of life related to plants). Some nitrates are produced by the action of lightning, which burns the air in its path. The high temperature of the discharge of lightning causes the nitrogen and oxygen to combine, forming oxide of nitrogen. These oxides dissolve in rain, and so get washed into the soil to form nitrates.

A number of plants belonging to the *Leguminosae* family (which includes peas and beans, vetches, clovers, and the ground-nuts of hot countries) have nodules on their roots containing colonies of bac-

*Imperial Chemical Industries, Ltd.*

**THE 'NITROGEN CYCLE' AND MAN-MADE AMMONIA**
The natural circulation of nitrogen, as we have been able to trace it, is shown in the diagram at top of page. Animal proteins decay, forming amino-acids, which bacteria break down into ammonia ; then nitrifying bacteria turn this into nitrates, from which plants re-make proteins. The other half of this cycle is described in the text. The complex apparatus in the photograph above synthesises (builds up) ammonia for fertilizers from nitrogen and hydrogen.

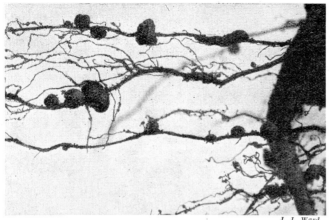

**UNDERGROUND NITROGEN 'FACTORY'**

*J. J. Ward*

Here are the nodules containing nitrogen-fixing bacteria on the rootlets of a scarlet runner bean. The bacteria obtain their food from the plant's own supply, and pass into the plant the nitrogenous compounds which they build up. Leguminous crops, such as vetches, restore the nitrogen content of the soil when their roots are dug or ploughed in.

teria which have the power of fixing atmospheric nitrogen, so forming compounds which can be used directly by the plant. When the plant dies and decays the soil has become richer in nitrogen. When two organisms act in co-operation—in this case the leguminous plant and the bacteria in its root nodules—so that each assists the other, the combination is described as symbiosis. The roots of some other plants and trees are believed to be able to fix nitrogen with the aid of moulds (*see* Mildews) attached to them.

Besides these bacteria attached to the roots of leguminous plants there are other kinds of bacteria living free in the soil which convert atmospheric nitrogen which, of course, is always present in the porous soil, into compounds useful to plants. There is probably a great deal we do not know about the ways of bacteria in fixing nitrogen. There are some bacteria, known as denitrifying bacteria, which change the nitrates in the soil back into free nitrogen. We can call these harmful bacteria.

All these changes of nitrogen from free nitrogen in the air to protein, and thence by decomposition to ammonia, and then to nitrates and back to protein, are known as the "nitrogen cycle." The nitrogen goes round and round much as water does when it evaporates from the sea, forms clouds, comes down as rain, and goes back to the sea again down the rivers and streams.

Farmers and planters know that growing certain crops, such as wheat, tobacco and cotton, too long on the same ground "wears out the land." This is because they take from the soil more of the things necessary for plant life than they give back.

In order to keep the soil in good condition while growing nitrogen-consuming crops, the farmer must either make use of nitrogen-containing fertilizers, or he must "rotate his crops" so that a nitrogen-using crop is followed by a nitrogen-restoring crop.

The fixed nitrogen of the earth is like a fortune which has been slowly accumulated by the painful toil of generations of owners, but which one spend-thrift heir can scatter in a few short years. The

human race has played the part of spendthrift heir. Untold amounts of nitrogen-rich animal wastes have been allowed to escape into the sea as sewage; the use of explosives in war is very wasteful of nitrogen; intensive agriculture tends to deplete the soil of fixed nitrogen. Therefore, it is most important that these wastes should be checked before the world begins to starve for lack of nitrogen compounds.

Fortunately Man has to some extent started to re-balance the nitrogen budget. (1) Deposits of nitrogen compounds such as the nitrate deposits of Chile, and guano formed by sea-birds, have been returned to the soil as fertilizers. These sources are limited in extent and will eventually be used up.

(2) Ammonia is now made by combination of nitrogen and hydrogen in the presence of a catalyst and at a high temperature and pressure. In another process, free nitrogen is made to combine with calcium carbide (the greyish lumps used to produce acetylene in cycle lamps) at a high temperature to give calcium cyanamide, which can be used as a fertilizer or can be reacted with steam to give ammonia. Many thousands of tons of ammonia for fertilizers are made every year by these methods.

(3) Imitating the action of lightning, nitrogen and oxygen have been made to combine by passing them through an electric arc furnace. The oxides of nitrogen formed at these very high temperatures form nitric acid on dissolving in water, and this acid can be converted into nitrates. This process was used where there was plenty of water-power to give cheap electricity, such as in Norway, but it has now been replaced entirely by the ammonia-making processes mentioned in (2).

(4). The fixing of nitrogen by leguminous plants has been found to be assisted by inoculating the soil on which they are to be grown with cultures of the particular kinds of bacteria which produce the nodules in the plant roots.

**Noah** AND NOAH'S ARK. In the early days of human history, according to what we read in the Book of Genesis, God was so displeased with the people He had created that He decided to destroy them. One man only, Noah, the son of Lamech, found grace in His eyes. So God told Noah to build an ark, and how he was to construct it. When it was ready Noah and his wife, and their three sons, Shem, Ham, and Japhet, with their wives, went into the ark, taking two of each kind of animal.

Then God made it rain for 40 days, until the face of the earth was flooded and all living things were drowned except Noah and the other passengers in the ark. "And the waters prevailed upon the earth an hundred and fifty days."

When the waters showed signs of subsiding, Noah sent out first a raven, and then a dove; and when the dove returned with an olive leaf "Noah knew that the waters were abated from off the earth."

When the ark came to rest—upon Mount Ararat, as tradition has it—Noah and his family and the animals of all kinds landed. "And God blessed

Noah and his sons, and said unto them, Be fruitful and multiply, and replenish the earth." And as a token that He would never again drown the earth in a deluge God set the rainbow in the sky.

Recent archaeological discoveries in Mesopotamia have proved that a great flood occurred about the time Noah is said to have lived. Thus at Kish, Sir Leonard Woolley (born 1880), digging down through the debris of thousands of years, came upon a layer, 18 inches thick, of clean river sand or clay, and below this traces of an earlier civilization which had apparently been submerged by the waters.

**Nobel Prizes.** It is a curious fact that Alfred Bernhard Nobel, a Swede who died in 1896 at the age of 63, invented one of the most deadly explosives—dynamite—and yet left £1,750,000 for five annual prizes, one of them for the greatest contribution to world peace. These prizes, worth about £8,000 each, have been given since 1901. Apart from the Peace Prize (decided upon by a committee elected by the Norwegian Parliament) they are awarded by the appropriate learned Swedish Academies. The other four are for literature, medicine or physiology, chemistry, and physics.

Famous British names figure in the list of those who have received Nobel Prizes. These include

*Vatican, Rome; photo, Anderson*

**NOAH AND HIS SONS BUILD THE ARK**
The story of Noah and his Ark, by which he saved creation from God's anger, is familiar to everyone. In this picture by the Italian painter Raphael we are shown Noah directing the labours of Ham, Shem and Japhet in the building of the Ark.

Rudyard Kipling, W. B. Yeats, George Bernard Shaw, John Galsworthy and T. S. Eliot, for literature; Sir Austen Chamberlain, Sir Norman Angell, Arthur Henderson, and Lord (Robert) Cecil for work in the cause of peace; Sir Ronald Ross, Sir Frederick Banting, Sir F. Gowland Hopkins, and Sir Charles Sherrington for medicine; Sir William Ramsay, Lord Rutherford, and Sir Robert Robinson for chemistry; Lord Rayleigh, Sir J. J. Thomson, Sir William Bragg, and Sir Edward Appleton for physics. Madame Curie is the only individual of either sex to win prizes in two of the prescribed sections—in her case in physics (1903) and chemistry (1911). The physics prize, however, was shared with her husband.

**Norfolk.** Bounded on the north and east by the North Sea and the estuary of the Wash, the county of Norfolk is 2,054 square miles in area, thus being the fourth largest county in England.

The surface for the most part is flat, especially the Fen country. The western part of the county is drained by the Great Ouse and its tributaries. On the eastern side the chief river is the Yare, with its tributaries the Waveney, Wensum, and Bure, which flows

*The Times*

**SAILING ON THE NORFOLK BROADS**
The village of Wroxham, seven miles north-east of Norwich, is one of the yachting centres of the Norfolk Broads. Wroxham Broad (above) covers an area of 120 acres. The Broads, a region of shallow lakes in Norfolk and Suffolk, provide some 200 miles of navigable waterway, which in summer are crowded with pleasure craft.

into the sea at Yarmouth. The tract of shallow freshwater lakes known as The Broads is much frequented for yachting, under both sail and power, fishing, and shooting.

Agriculture is the chief industry. Barley, wheat, and oats are important crops, and much mustard is grown. Some land is given up to fruit-growing. Norfolk is famous for cattle, sheep, and pigs, and large numbers of poultry are raised. The fisheries, both inshore and deep-sea, are valuable.

Barrows and old entrenchments occur in many places, traces of lake-dwellings have been met with, and Roman remains have been found. When the Roman power decayed, the county was colonized by the Angles and formed part of the kingdom of East Anglia. In the 12th century the manufacture of worsted was introduced by the Flemings, and later wool was a great industrial product.

Norwich (q.v.) is the county town. Other important towns are Great Yarmouth (population 56,000), a centre of the English herring industry, where Charles Dickens placed notable scenes in his book, David Copperfield, and King's Lynn. Hunstanton and Cromer are favourite watering-places, and Sandringham House is a royal residence. There are interesting ruined castles at Castle Rising and Castle Acre. Population of the county, 504,000.

**Normandy.** A country of streams, of orchards of cider apple trees, of wide straight roads, lined on either side with trees behind which hide trim farmhouses with neat thatched roofs—such is the ancient French province of Normandy, whose curving shores form the middle section of France's northern coast, between Picardy and Brittany.

It was into this region that the Northmen (q.v.) poured in the 9th and 10th centuries, steering their dragon-prowed ships up the wide mouth of the Seine. It was here in 911 that King Charles the Simple of France signed a treaty with their chief Rollo, which gave the Northmen a permanent home on French soil. Indeed, the name Normandy means Home of the Northmen.

In the century and a half that followed, the Northmen leaders became Norman dukes—Christians, French-speaking and among the most progressive of French rulers. From one Norman family five sons found their way to southern Italy, founding the Norman kingdom of Naples and Sicily there late in the 11th century. The Dukes of Normandy meanwhile became more and more powerful until one of them, William, crossed the Channel and took possession of England in 1066.

William (called the Conqueror) brought over the germs of many institutions that were later to develop into England's most precious contributions to law and government. But the seat of government was soon transferred across the water, so that it was England that owned

ROUEN : CHIEF CITY OF NORMANDY

*Aerofilms, Ltd.*

On the River Seine, between Paris and the English Channel, Rouen is both a port and an important manufacturing centre. Many of its buildings suffered severely from Allied air raids and German demolitions during the Second World War (1939–45). The 13th-century Cathedral, seen in the centre of this view, was partially gutted and its lovely rose windows were destroyed. The bridge in the distance was blown up by the Germans in 1944.

Normandy instead of Normandy that owned England. Norman leaders then rebelled against the king of England and asked for help from the French kings. Disorder and confusion followed until the French king Philip Augustus conquered Normandy during 1202–04 from King John of England. The struggle was renewed in the Hundred Years' War (1337–1453), which ended in the expulsion of the English not only from Normandy but from all France, except Calais, which remained in English hands for another century.

The centuries of its stirring early history have left their marks on this fair land. In the ancient city of Caen on the River Orne, about 10 miles from the Seine Bay, stand two famous abbeys, the Abbey for Men and the Abbey for Women, built by William the Conqueror and his wife Matilda. In common with many historic towns of Normandy, Caen suffered devastation during the Second World War (1939–45). Near Caen is Bayeux (q.v.), another of the Conqueror's towns, where is kept the famous Bayeux Tapestry

But most famous of all Norman towns is Rouen, the ancient stronghold of the Northmen, and the place where Joan of Arc was burned at the stake. Here was built a Gothic cathedral, in which was entombed the heart of the English king Richard I, nicknamed Coeur de Lion.

Normandy has some of the finest harbours in France, among them Le Havre at the mouth of the Seine; Cherbourg, at the tip of the peninsula of Cotentin; and Dieppe, in the north-east.

Many of the people of this province are tall, blue-eyed, and fair-haired, showing their descent from the Northmen. They are among the most industrious inhabitants of France, proud of their ancestry and of their beautiful fertile country. The Normans cling to their old habits and customs; in some parts you may still see the peasants in their old-world dress, and the " butterfly " caps of the women of Avranches are famous.

The Channel Islands at one time formed part of the duchy of Normandy, but they remained in the possession of England when Normandy itself was incorporated in France.

The story of the Allied landings on the shores of Normandy on June 6, 1944, during the Second World War, is given in the following article.

# Allied D-DAY LANDINGS in NORMANDY

*The greatest land-sea-and-air operation in the history of warfare was put into effect on June 6, 1944, when the Allies launched their mighty assault for the liberation of North-West Europe.*

**Normandy Invasion.** "On the eve of this great adventure I send my best wishes to every soldier in the Allied team. To us is given the honour of striking a blow for freedom which will live in history; and in the better days that lie ahead men will speak with pride of our doings. We have a great and a righteous cause.

" Let us pray that the Lord Mighty in Battle will go forth with our armies and that His special providence will aid us in the struggle.

" I want every soldier to know that I have complete confidence in the successful outcome of the operations that we are now about to begin.

" With stout hearts, and with enthusiasm for the contest, let us go forward to victory !"

With these inspiring words Britain's Lord Montgomery (q.v.)—then General Sir Bernard Montgomery—launched the greatest land-sea-and-air operation in the history of warfare—Operation Overlord, the Allied invasion of the continent of Europe on June 6, 1944, the historic D-Day. (During the Second World War " D-Day " was the name given to the first day of an important operation.)

The Germans had had four years in which to fortify the coasts of Europe. All along the Atlantic shore were concrete and armoured gun emplacements, minefields, wire entanglements, steel and concrete obstacles and tank traps. The " West Wall " (the coastal defences) was thought impregnable; and behind it stood 60 German divisions under well-tried commanders, Field-Marshals von Rundstedt and Rommel.

Against this army the Allies pitted a force totalling 130,000 men and 20,000 vehicles. Strange and terrifying weapons had been forged for the assault —flail tanks to set off the enemy mines, tanks that carried bridges, tanks that laid mats on soft ground, tanks with ramps over which other tanks could climb walls, and amphibious assault tanks which could swim ashore from two miles out at sea, spitting fire and steel at the German defenders.

But this was no operation of armies alone. It was as Lord Montgomery himself wrote, " essentially the concern not of one Service but of all three working in close co-operation "—of the navies, armies, and air forces of the British Commonwealth and the United States.

In supreme command was the United States soldier, General Eisenhower (q.v.). Commanding the assault force—21st Army Group, as it was called— was General Montgomery; he had at his disposal one United States and one British Army, the latter including a Canadian Corps. A tremendous fleet of naval craft, more than half of which were British, had been assembled under Admiral Sir Bertram Ramsay, R.N., to transport and give support to the land force; while Air Chief Marshal Sir Trafford Leigh-Mallory, R.A.F., commanded the largest air armada ever beheld in history.

The strip of coast chosen for the assault was in Normandy, between Valognes and Cabourg, In the plans it was referred to as " Neptune," and the beaches all had their code-names—" Utah " and " Omaha," where the Americans were to land; and " Gold," " Juno," and " Sword " in the sector of the British and Canadians. The secret of the chosen area was guarded up to the last, and to ensure that the Germans should have as little warning as possible allied naval craft and aeroplanes " demonstrated " farther along the coast just before the landings.

The date originally fixed was June 5, 1944. But so rough was the sea, so low the cloud, on the preceding day, that at the last moment General

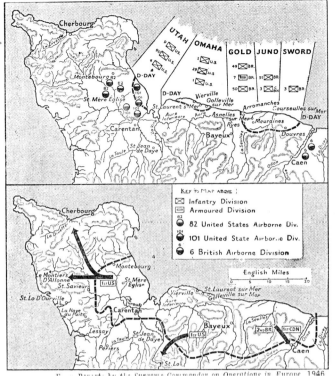

## ALLIED OPERATIONS IN NORMANDY

The assault beaches on D-Day (June 6, 1944), with their code names and the formations that landed on them, are shown in the upper map. The lower map shows the area captured by the Allies up to June 19.

ships began to assemble ready to assault at dawn on the 6th. Operation Overlord had begun.

The actual assault force consisted of 12 divisions, six British or Canadian and six United States. But the landings on the beaches were presaged by airborne attacks, the Royal Air Force alone using over 700 aircraft and 355 gliders to transport the parachute and glider-borne troops which were to seize and occupy key points behind the German defences.

The airborne landings began at 1.30 in the morning, a British parachute company being the first to alight on French soil. Two United States airborne divisions dropped on the Carentan peninsula, south of Cherbourg, and the British 6th Airborne Division took up positions to the east of the River Orne. At the same time more than 1,100 night bombers opened the air offensive, 6,000 tons of bombs falling on the coastal batteries before dawn.

Then 1,300 heavy day-bombers, with medium and fighter-bombers, roared over the Normandy coast, and warships opened fire on the German defences. The assault craft ran on to the flat, sandy beaches; the infantry swarmed out. The first landing was made by United States troops on Utah beach; supported by amphibious tanks, they got ashore without serious loss and during the day penetrated more than five miles inland, making contact with the airborne troops.

Eisenhower countermanded his order for the operation to commence on June 5. Next day the forecast was better, though conditions were still far from favourable; and on the night of June 5 the

At "Omaha" rough seas and dense obstacles caused heavy casualties among the Americans. The United States infantry had unluckily attacked where a German division was deployed for action,

*Associated Press*

## LANDING BRITISH EQUIPMENT ON THE NORMANDY BEACHES

Shepherded across the English Channel by the Allied navies, steamers and landing craft carried tanks, guns, vehicles and general supplies to the Normandy beaches in the summer of 1944, the work of unloading proceeding in broad daylight (above). Barrage balloons above and anti-aircraft guns on the beaches gave protection against low-level attacks by German aircraft. Waterproofed tanks and vehicles drove ashore in three or four feet of water.

yet by nightfall they had won themselves a bridge-head about a mile deep—a bridgehead being the first ground gained.

The British 50th Division attacking at " Gold " beach reached its objectives on the road between Caen and Bayeux, and was five miles inland when darkness fell. On their left the Canadians, after trouble with the beach defences, encountered stiff resistance but made steady progress. On " Sword " beach the British 3rd Division lost half its am-phibious tanks in the sea ; but the landing, assisted by Commando operations, was successful, and they linked up with the 6th Airborne Division before dusk. When night fell the assaulting troops had a firm foothold on the French coast. Losses were, in

Lord Montgomery's words, "much lower than had seemed possible." The enemy's defence was strong in patches, and it was clear that surprise had been achieved, and that the bombing of the previous night had disorganized his communications. Throughout the day Allied aircraft attacked behind the German lines—171 fighter squadrons were used. Allied aircraft flew 11,000 sorties in the first 24 hours of the landings.

A week later the Normandy bridgehead was 50 miles long and 12 miles deep. The " fortress of Europe " had been successfully invaded. Though much stern resistance had still to be overcome, the end of the Second World War was at last in sight. (*See also* Mulberry Harbours).

# The VAST NEW CONTINENT of the WEST

*When Columbus discovered the West Indies off the coast of North America in 1492, no one realized what a land had been brought to light—a continent that was to become the richest of the Earth.*

**North America.** When we consider the history of North America we cannot but wonder what qualities this continent possessed that caused it so quickly to surpass the other " new " worlds in the race for people and wealth and power. In the space of some 400 years it has emerged from barbarism, outstripped the centuries-old civiliza-tion of Asia and northern Africa, and taken its place alongside Europe as a leader in the world's progress. South America, Africa, and Australia shared with North America in Europe's explorations and civilizing influence; but none of these has experienced such a complete transformation as that seen in North America.

Of all the continents North America was the most hospitable to European influence. It alone opened wide its rivers and harbours to immigration, making it easy for newcomers to reach a friendly interior. Except Europe, it has the longest coast-line in proportion to its size of any of the continents; and it has many excellent harbours on the east coast. It lies largely in the middle latitudes—the region that is pre-eminently " white man's country," since climatic conditions are, on the whole, not too extreme. There are no high mountains on the east barring entrance to the interior; the vast central plain stretches unbroken from the Arctic Ocean to the Gulf of Mexico, with an unequalled sys-tem of waterways.

It was fortunate that the discoverers of America did not come first to the Pacific shore, for there they would have found a more uniform coast and high mountains facing the Pacific in an almost

unbroken wall. Except in the north there are few good harbours; and on the whole coast there are only two rivers valuable for navigation—the Yukon, which opens into the heart of Alaska, and the Columbia, which leads to great mountain systems and an inhospitable country. The only other westward-flowing river of any size—the Colorado—drains a large but arid region, its chief interest being the scenery of its majestic canyon.

Alaska on the west balances Labrador on the east, as Lower California balances Florida; but such great gulfs as Hudson Bay and the Gulf of Mexico are lacking on the Pacific side. If, however, Asiatic nations had been the explorers of the 15th century they could have reached the continent without a long sea voyage, either by the stepping-stones of the Aleutian Islands or by the Bering Strait, which at one point is only 40 miles wide.

Fortunately, in the temperate zone North America is much closer to Europe than to Asia, and its discovery and settlement fell to the lot of Europeans. Columbus came and found the tropical West Indies, the threshold of the New World, smiling a ready welcome. Other Europeans followed, and to them the Gulf of Mexico and the Caribbean Sea gave entrance as the Mediter-ranean does to Europe, and the rich mines of Mexico led rapidly to Spanish occupation.

Settlers from the more northerly European countries were no less fortunate in their land-ing-places. Except where the Arctic islands stretch into an icy sea, all the many indenta-tions of the American coast were friendly to them. As early as 1500 a

**Extent.**—North to south about 4,500 miles ; east to west 3,000 miles. Area about 9,400,000 square miles. Peninsulas ; Alaska, Labrador, Nova Scotia, Florida, Yucatan, Lower California. Pop. about 185,000,000.

**Mountains.**—On the east the Appalachian System—White and Green Mountains, Adirondacks, Blue Ridge (highest peak, Mt. Mitchell, 6,684 feet). On the west the Cor-dilleran System—Rocky Mountains (highest peak, Mt. Logan, 19,850 feet) ; Alaskan Mountains (highest peak, Mt. McKinley, 20,300 feet, the highest on the continent) ; Cascade Range (highest peak, Mt. Rainier, 14,408 feet) ; Sierra Nevada (highest peak, Mt. Whitney, 14,495 feet) ; Sierre Madre (highest peak, Mt. Orizaba, 18,700 feet) ; Coast Range.

**Rivers and Lakes.**—Rivers : Mississippi-Missouri (3,988 miles), Mackenzie (2,400), Yukon (2,100), St. Lawrence (1,900), Rio Grande (1,650), Nelson (1,600), Columbia (1,270). Lakes : Great Lakes (Superior, Michigan, Huron, Erie, Ontario), Great Bear, Winnipeg, Great Slave, Nicaragua, Great Salt.

**Political Divisions.**—United States (including Alaska, Panama Canal Zone, and Puerto Rico), 3,612,000 square miles ; Canada 3,800,000 square miles ; Mexico 767,000 square miles ; Central American States (Guatemala, Honduras, Nicaragua, Salvador, Costa Rica, and Panama) ; Cuba ; Haiti ; Dominican Republic. British possessions (excluding Canada), Bahamas, Bermudas, Jamaica, British Honduras ; Danish colony, Greenland.

*Dorien Leigh*

## TWO OF THE HIGHEST MOUNTAINS IN NORTH AMERICA

The cloud-encircled peaks of Mt. McKinley (20,300 feet) and Mt. Foraker (17,000 feet) are here viewed from Wonder Lake. Mt. McKinley is the highest in North America, and is situated in the Mt. McKinley National Park, Alaska.

These mountains form part of the Alaska Range. Mt. McKinley is locally known by the native name of Denali. Note the glacial moraine (accumulation of rock waste, brought down by ice) in the foreground of the picture.

fishing colony was established on the island of Newfoundland at the mouth of the St. Lawrence; and by that river Cartier and Champlain carried the flag of France far into the heart of the continent.

The Dutch sailed up the Hudson, which is still the chief doorway of the U.S.A.; and the English found the rivers flowing into Chesapeake Bay in the south and the harbours of New England excellent gates to permanent colonisation. All along the fertile coastal plain, from the St. John river to the Gulf of Mexico, colonies were established and prospered, gradually spreading inland.

The first check encountered by American expansion was the Appalachian Mountains, which extend in a long and practically unbroken chain from the Gulf of St. Lawrence almost to the present States of Florida and Alabama. Nowadays we are not accustomed to think of these moderately high wooded ridges as barriers but to regard them rather as storehouses of vast wealth in timber, coal and iron, and other natural resources. In colonial days, however, highways were lacking and this country was inhabited by hostile Indians.

For 150 years the English colonists were thus hemmed in on the seaboard. Nevertheless, the nation owes much to the Appalachian barrier. It held together the 13 original colonies (*see* United States) when they might have scattered, and thus promoted the sound growth in strength and population which made possible the winning of the War of Independence, and, after that, the organization of the United States.

French explorers found that the wide St. Lawrence led to the largest bodies of fresh water in the world, the chain of the Great Lakes. Their size makes them resemble inland seas, and they have a similar effect upon the climate of the region about them. Not only are they invaluable for transport, they also lend charm to the surrounding country, and give to eastern America its greatest natural wonder—the Niagara Falls. A short journey from the southern shore of Lake Michigan brought the French explorers to the Illinois river; this carried them down to the mighty Mississippi, which the Indians called the Father of Waters.

This name was certainly justified, for the Missouri and Mississippi with their tributaries form an enormous river system affording inland navigation for more than 14,000 miles, and draining an area of 1,240,000 square miles.

Nowhere else does a single river give access to such valuable agricultural territory. From the Arctic Ocean to the Gulf of Mexico one may travel without passing any elevation of more than 1,000 feet above sea-level. In the middle of the continent the river valley merges with the Great Lakes plain, which, farther north, blends with the valley of the Mackenzie river, flowing to the Arctic Ocean.

After sweeping over the central plain the pioneers found themselves confronted by broad table-lands, crested by the many high ranges which are known collectively as the Cordilleras. These chains enter the continent in Alaska, broadening as they pass through Canada, and attaining their greatest width in the United States, where the table-land is in some places 1,000 miles in breadth. All of Mexico except a narrow coastal plain is a part of this vast plateau, but there the mountains are

# JOURNEY THAT LED TO THE FOUNDING OF QUEBEC

The most important expedition made by the French explorer Samuel de Champlain (1567–1635) had for its object the exploration of the then unknown region of Canada. He ascended the St. Lawrence river in the canoes of friendly Red Indians (above), and on July 3, 1608, disembarked on the site of what is now Quebec. There he established a settlement, building a fort and a number of houses, and laying out fields and gardens after much hard work in clearing the ground of trees and undergrowth. The discoverer of Lake Champlain, which lies between Vermont and New York in the United States, he remained in Canada as Governor of Quebec for the French king, and died there on Christmas Day, 1635. Champlain also explored the West Indies.

# THE VARIED ANIMAL LIFE OF NORTH AMERICA

*Daily Mirror; H. J. Shepstone; L. Matthews*

This selection from the wild animals found in the continent of North America shows: 1, puma or mountain lion; 2, wapiti; 3, common black bear; 4, pair of quaint racoons; 5, beaver, one of Nature's most wonderful 'wild' builders. Although, as in other countries that have been invaded by Man, these creatures are not so common as they used to be, some of them are now preserved in the National Parks of Canada and the United States.

# GLIMPSES OF CANADA AND THE UNITED STATES

*Canadian Official; Keystone; Dorien Leigh*

Some of the ways in which the natural wealth
of North America is produced are seen here:
1, stooked wheat on a farm in Alberta, Canada;
2, coal products plant at Pittsburgh, United
States; 3, oil field in Texas; 4, mechanical
cotton picker in Louisiana.

generally lower and the rainfall is greater. In southern Mexico occurs a break in the long system, known as the Isthmus of Tehuantepec; but in Central America the mountains rise again, fringing the western coast.

The region of the Cordilleras is the scenic wonderland of America. In Alaska are glaciers more marvellous than those of the Alps; and Mount McKinley, the highest peak on the continent, raises its head almost 5,000 feet higher than Mont Blanc, which is the highest peak in western Europe.

The Cascades and Sierra Nevadas, which lie near the coast of Canada and the United States, present some of the most magnificent mountain scenery in the world; and in the Rocky Mountains is a region of geysers and hot springs, part of which is preserved for visitors in Yellowstone National Park. Farther south lies the so-called Dead Sea of America—the Great Salt Lake; and still farther southward, the Grand Canyon of the Colorado river.

### Mineral Wealth of the Pacific Slopes

From Alaska down to the Isthmus of Panama the Cordilleras contain rich veins of gold, silver, lead, and copper. No navigable streams lead to the region except the Missouri, and even it will not take the traveller nearer than several hundred miles from the mountain wall. Moreover, the plain country which leads to the mountains is so dry that it did not tempt farmers from the well-watered central valley; and at several places in the central basin are extensive cactus-covered deserts. The whole region was in early days the hunting ground of tribes of warlike Indians.

But as gold had lured men into the mountains of Mexico, so it has lured them to the Pacific shore of the United States and Canada, and later to Alaska; and in less than half the time it took to conquer the Appalachians, men had crossed deserts and mountains and established their settlements on the far-distant Pacific slope.

When Man had finally penetrated every corner of this continent, he found few places which could not contribute something to his needs. The only considerable exception is the extreme north, where the icy islands of the Arctic Archipelago stretch away to a point only 450 miles from the North Pole. In these low regions there is little vegetation, and hardly any animal life except in the sea, from which the Eskimos who live there derive their sole support. On the whole, it has been estimated that the barren lands of North America, including the few desert regions, comprise only two per cent of its entire area.

Large areas in northern Canada and Alaska, in addition to the vast Rocky Mountain and Appalachian regions (in all, about one-fifth of the continent), are covered with valuable forests. The semi-arid regions of the west (comprising one-fourth of the entire continent) are at least suitable for grazing. Approximately half of North America is excellent for agriculture, and this proportion is steadily being increased by dry farming and the irrigation of lands which formerly were thought useful only for grazing.

Although North America contains less than one-tenth of the earth's people, it is a land of enormous wealth. It furnishes about one-fifth of the entire world's supply of wheat, half of its cotton crop, and half of its maize. Of the precious metals it contributes about one-fourth of the gold and almost two-thirds of the silver of the world; and in the so-called " baser "—though really more valuable—metals, its supply is unexcelled.

Of iron, North America produces more than one-fourth of the world's supply. Its coal deposits are richer than those of any other continent, with the possible exception of Asia; and they furnish almost a third of the world's coal production. North America also contributes two-thirds of the petroleum and nearly half the copper.

Like other continents, North America consists of a broad fold of the earth's crust, only a part of which rises above the level of the sea. In very ancient times, when this uprising fold first emerged above the surface of the waters, it did not appear as a single united land. The tops of the mountains arrived first, making groups of islands of varied size, like the West Indies. We do not know just where the first peaks were; but it seems clear that they included the Appalachian Mountains in the U.S.A. and the Laurentian Mountains in Canada, and that these first upheavals were followed much later by the Cordilleras. Until comparatively recent geological times the Mississippi valley was entirely under water, forming a sea that extended from what is now the Gulf of Mexico all the way to the Arctic Ocean. We know this because fossil remains of fish have been found in the rocks there.

Gradually, because of the rising of the original islands or the receding of the ocean, the Mississippi basin became more shallow. Wind and rain cut down the mountains, and the sediment which the rivers carried from them filled up the inner sea, forming the deltas and flood plains which are now among the most fertile lands of the country. Finally, the various archipelagos were united into one great land.

### How the Coal Period was Established

Ages after the first emergence, when the climate was warmer and wetter than it is now, occurred what is called the Coal Period. Extensive swamps filled with tall tree-ferns covered much of the continent like a tropical jungle, extending as far north as the Arctic Circle. The land was still unstable, and after these forests had grown for a few hundred years the plains sank beneath the sea, and layers of mud, sand, and gravel collected over them. In time these layers became solid rock and the vegetation beneath was changed to coal as a result of pressure. Then the land rose again and new forests grew, causing one layer of coal to be formed over another. All this time, and at other periods, deposits of iron, copper, gold, and silver were also being laid down. Minerals, melted in the fierce heat below the surface, surged up through cracks, and then cooled and hardened into veins of valuable ore.

In more recent geological times the climate became much colder, just as in the Coal Period it was much warmer. A vast sheet of ice appeared in the north, and crept slowly southward, covering a large part of Alaska and Canada, and about one-third of what is now the United States. Thousands of years were required for its slow advance, and thousands more for its disappearance; some of the

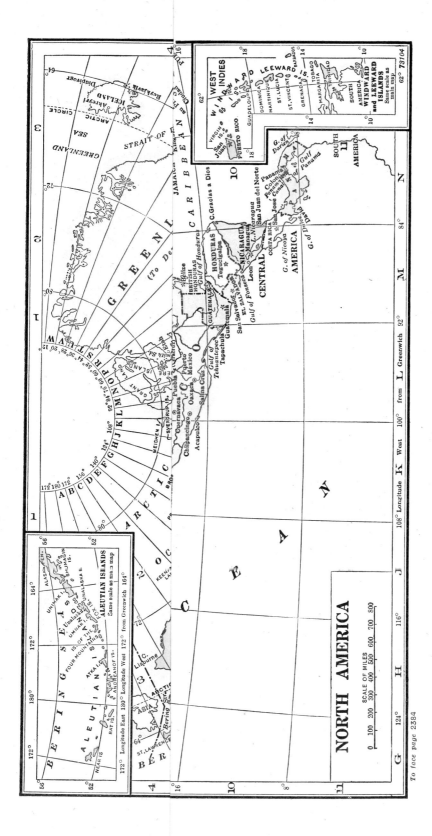

# NORTH AMERICA

SCALE OF MILES

0   100  200  300  400  500  600  700  800

ALEUTIAN ISLANDS
Same scale as main map

172° Longitude East 180° Longitude West 172° from Greenwich 164°

WEST INDIES

LEEWARD IS.

WINDWARD and LEEWARD ISLANDS
Same scale as main map

62° 73104

# FACTS YOU SHOULD KNOW ABOUT NORTH AMERICA

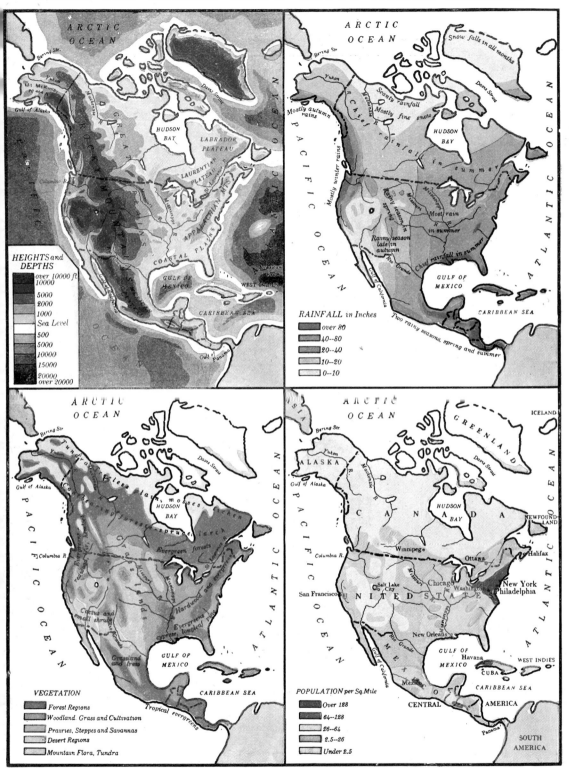

As if the very mountains themselves had anticipated the spirit of the pioneers, we find the old worn-down ranges in the east and the young lofty mountains in the west (top, left). In the upper map on the right you can pick out the well-watered regions and those which are shut off by mountain barriers from the moisture-laden sea winds. The maps below strikingly show how the typical vegetation of the different regions and the relative density of population are in large part determined by these natural conditions. The greatest concentration of population is, as you see, about the coasts, especially the eastern seaboard of the United States, and the Great Lakes and Mississippi valley regions.

To face page 2385

continent is still really in the Ice Age, since remnants of the ice-cap still cover the greater part of Greenland and parts of Arctic North America. (*See* Ice Age).

Ice scoured the rocks over which it passed, and swept away the soil that covered the land. It deposited bits of ground-up rock called " drift," which produced a fertile soil in many places; but sometimes it failed to grind up the rock, and thus left boulders and pebbles, which still trouble the farmer. Moreover, it blocked up the courses of former rivers, and it dug out and left great hollows, which are now the lakes and ponds of north-eastern North America. Even the Great Lakes, which vary in depth from 200 to over 1,000 feet, are largely the result of this glacial action.

But the most important work of these millions of years—that which was to have most influence on the climate, and, therefore, on the crops—was the forming of the mountain systems. The Laurentian and Appalachian mountains, as stated, rose in very early ages; and since then they have been slowly worn away by weather and water. Being low, they allow winds to carry much moisture over them.

The Cordilleras are younger than the more eastern mountains, and considerably higher. They are, in fact, still growing, as is seen by the earthquakes caused now and again when they crack under the enormous strain. When winds from the west reach these lofty mountain ranges they are forced to drop much of their moisture as rain; and when they reach the eastern side they have little left. This causes the plains and plateaux of the western regions to be dry or arid.

Of great importance in its effect on commerce is the fact that the coast of North America is slowly sinking in the north and rising in the south. A sinking coast allows the ocean to enter the lowlands, leaving the higher land to form peninsulas and islands, while the valleys make bays and inlets. Thus on the Pacific coast, north of Seattle, we find a very ragged outline; in the Arctic north are big islands and peninsulas; and on the Atlantic seaboard is a very irregular coast as far south as New York. These indentations have given rise to many important cities on the Atlantic coast, because of the excellent harbours which the submerged river valleys have made.

South of New York and Seattle the dominating movement of recent times has been upward. A large part of the Southern states, bordering on the Atlantic and the Gulf of Mexico, was once part of the ocean bottom or " continental shelf." This shelf is still rising, with the result that there are few good natural harbours on the Atlantic coast below New York, and, with the exception of San Diego, none below San Francisco on the Pacific. (*See* Canada ; Mexico ; United States; etc.).

## Northamptonshire.

This English inland county (called Northants for short) is situated to the north of Oxfordshire. It is 998 square miles in area, with a population of about 361,000. The north-eastern part is low and flat, being fen country, but elsewhere the land is undulating. Formerly there were several forests, as is shown by the names of some of the districts—Rockingham Forest and Yardley Chase. The Welland, the Nene, and the Avon are the chief rivers; other

waterways include the Grand Union Canal. Wheat, barley, and oats are grown, and stock-raising and dairying are important.

Roman remains have been found at Castor, Irchester, and elsewhere, and the two Roman roads, Watling Street and Ermine Street, traverse the county. The cathedral at Peterborough (population, 51,800) is a magnificent building. The chief industries of this city are the manufacture of railway rolling stock and agricultural implements.

The district around Peterborough is known as the Soke cf Peterborough, and is a separate county for administrative purposes. " Soke " is an old word which meant the right to hold a court of law, and then came to be applied to a district which possessed such a right.

Northampton (population, 104,000), the county town, on the Nene, is the chief centre of the English boot and shoe industry. Other places of interest are Kettering (population, 35,000); Daventry, where an important broadcasting station is situated; Naseby, where King Charles I was defeated in battle by the Parliamentarians in 1645; Oundle, famous for its public school; and Pytchley, home of Northamptonshire's best-known hunt.

## Northcliffe,

ALFRED CHARLES WILLIAM HARMSWORTH, VISCOUNT (1865-1922). The newspaper which is pushed through your letterbox in the morning or which you buy in the evening, is largely the creation of one man. But for Lord Northcliffe, it would have been far less bright in appearance and without many of the features which nowadays we have come to expect.

Alfred Harmsworth was born at Chapelizod, Dublin, on July 15, 1865, the eldest of the seven sons of a barrister. His first venture into journalism was in 1878, when as a boy of 13 he started a school magazine at Henley House School, Hampstead, London. Two years later he received his first paid appointment as a journalist, and when 17 was made assistant-editor of the magazine, Youth. From 1885 to 1887 he was on the staff of the publishing house of Iliffe & Sons at Coventry. Then, returning to London, he started his first paper, the weekly journal Answers.

Harmsworth realized that the Education Act of 1870 had created a vast new reading public. Millions of people whose fathers and grandfathers had never had any education—perhaps could not even read—were now being turned out by the board schools into a world where most of the reading matter was what would now be called highbrow. Nearly all the books were written by educated men for educated men; the newspapers were dull in style and concerned almost entirely with questions of politics and literature. Harmsworth, having had a very limited schooling himself, knew just what the new reading public was waiting for. Here, he said to himself, is an army of men, women, and young people who want something to read—something interesting, something lively, something which will give them information without any suggestion of dullness or the school text-book. He set out to meet this demand—and succeeded in full measure, as the success of his newspapers showed.

The weekly Answers—its original name, Answers to Correspondents, helps to explain its popularity in the light of what has just been said—was followed by many other journals that appealed to the man in the street, to the woman in the home, and to the schoolboy and schoolgirl. The appeal was very wide.

But Harmsworth's greatest achievement was the launching of the Daily Mail, the first number of which appeared on May 4, 1896. It was the first popular morning paper published at a halfpenny, and made it possible for hundreds of thousands of those who had hitherto felt that a daily newspaper was beyond their means to have one on their breakfast-tables. The Daily Mail gave the day's news almost as completely as the penny newspapers, but in a much more interesting fashion, and one of its novelties was a serial story. The paper reflected Alfred Harmsworth's own vigorous and independent views. In conducting it Northcliffe put his strong political convictions before every other consideration, and expressed views that often aroused hostility, but were always read with interest.

After the success of the Daily Mail Lord Northcliffe became the predominating power in British journalism. In planning the Daily Mail he had been guided to a great extent by his experience with the London Evening News, which he and his brother Harold, afterwards Lord Rothermere, bought in 1894 when it was almost bankrupt and soon raised to a high level of prosperity.

In the meantime Lord Northcliffe had joined his weekly and monthly publications together in the gigantic business of the present Amalgamated Press, which was later bought by Lord Camrose. In 1904 he brought out the Daily Mirror—the first picture-paper, originally founded in 1903 as a daily paper for women—and at the outbreak of the First World War in 1914, he controlled The Times, the Daily Mail, the Evening News, the Weekly Dispatch, the Overseas Daily Mail, and the Continental Daily Mail, among other papers. Their vast circulation gave him great influence, and he showed characteristic courage and independence in his attitude towards the events of the war, criticizing when he felt criticism was deserved, but using his power to hearten public opinion and to discourage a defeatist spirit.

In 1918 Lord Northcliffe—he had been made a baron in 1905 and a viscount in 1917—was appointed Director of Propaganda in Enemy Countries. With an astounding insight into German psychology and with equally remarkable ingenuity in distributing to the enemy countries information about the true state of affairs, he did much to contribute to the collapse of the Central Powers. General Ludendorff, indeed, described him as "a master of mass suggestion," and after the Armistice (November 11, 1918) Lloyd George, then Prime Minister, in expressing his thanks, stated that he had "many direct evidences of the success of your invaluable work."

Lord Northcliffe was always deeply interested in the great adventures of mankind. In the early years of his success he financed the Jackson-Harmsworth Polar Expedition (1894), and when he first saw Wilbur Wright fly in France in 1908 he recognized that there was a great future in the aeroplane, and by the offer, through the Daily Mail, of large money prizes for big flights did much to encourage aviation. After the First World War, Lord Northcliffe's health began to fail, and he died on August 14, 1922. In 1887 he had married Mary Elizabeth Milner, but left no children.

*E. O. Hoppé*

## NORTHCLIFFE AND CHURCHILL
The launching of the Daily Mail, the first popular morning newspaper to be published at a halfpenny, was perhaps the most notable achievement of Lord Northcliffe (upper). A firm believer in the future of aviation, he is seen in the lower photograph (right) talking with Mr. Winston Churchill at a flying meeting in 1911.

# WHEN THE VIKINGS WENT A-ROVING

*F ew countries in Europe were free from the onslaughts of the 'hurricane of the north,' for the Norse warriors swept over the Continent as far south as Sicily and as far east as Russia.*

**Northmen.** In their long, shallow, black boats, the sides hung with round shields, yellow and black, with striped sails and with high-curved prows carved in the form of a snake or dragon, the Vikings of the north once scoured the sea in pursuit of adventure, plunder, commerce and conquest.

The Northmen, who are also called Vikings, were the ancestors of the modern Swedes, Norwegians and Danes. The long coastline and many fiords of the Scandinavian peninsula on which they mainly dwelt made it natural for them to become sailors. They took to the sea to catch fish and to make long trading and raiding expeditions to the lands of their richer and more highly civilized neighbours to the south, east and west.

For nearly three centuries—the 9th, 10th, and 11th—they ravaged the coasts of Europe from the British Isles and France in the north to Italy in the south. They even rowed up rivers into the heart of France and Germany. Their invasions were the last wave of the Teutonic conquests which began with the Goths and the Vandals five centuries earlier and overran all Europe.

Wherever they went they spread destruction and terror. So feared were their raids that a prayer was offered in churches against them: "From the fury of the Northmen, good Lord, deliver us."

How those Viking chieftains must have loved their roving life on the stormy sea! They even chose their ships as their tombs. Sometimes they were cast adrift, but at other times the ship was buried in a "barrow" or long grave mound, as shown in the illustration in page 2388. At Gokstad, in southern Norway, a Viking ship was found containing the body of the captain, with his horses, his dogs and even a peacock, around him. Only weapons remained of the treasure that had been placed in the ship. Arabian coins of the 9th and 10th centuries, money from England and Germany, weapons and gold ornaments, saddles and silks from Oriental countries, have been found in the barrows around Birka and Visby in Sweden, telling us of the Northmen's ways of living.

Stones with pictures and runic (old Scandinavian script) writing also have preserved for us descriptions of the life and wanderings of the Vikings. One such stone in Sweden tells how a woman named Sirid raised it to her husband Sven, who, "often sailed with costly ships to Semgallen (Russia)." Five other runic stones remain to tell us that Jarlabanki, a rich farmer, owned the whole of Täby, a parish still existing in Sweden. One Viking left the story of his life in an inscription on a marble lion at Athens, which now stands in Venice. In this

## NORTHMEN WARRING AMONG THEMSELVES

In their long, shallow, black boats, with high curved prows carved in the form of snakes and dragons, the Vikings of Denmark and Scandinavia scoured the known and unknown seas in search of adventure, conquest and booty. At times, also, they fell out among themselves, as in the scene pictured here. War was one of the delights of life to the Northmen. The thing they dreaded was that they might die at home of sickness instead of in the excitement of battle,

Norse language the alphabet had only 16 letters, resembling the early Gothic of the Germanic tribes.

Skalds, or minstrels, sang of the exploits of Viking leaders and kings during the long winter evenings before the guests and retainers of the chieftains. Sagas based on the songs of the skalds were written in the 12th and 13th centuries, thus preserving for us still more knowledge of Viking life. The Eddas tell the stories of the gods of the Northland. (See Odin; Scandinavia; Thor).

At the beginning of the Viking period, late in the 8th century, a number of walled trading towns were already flourishing: Upsala, Birka, and Sigtuna in Sweden; Visby on the island of Gotland in the Baltic Sea; Skiringssal in Norway; Schleswig or Hedeby in Jutland, Denmark; and Dorstadt in Friesland, the Netherlands.

The oaken boats of the Vikings swarmed in the many harbours. Their great joy was to seek out new lands, from which they could take booty and tribute. Their religion taught them that only by death in combat could a warrior hope to enter Valhalla, the fighting man's paradise.

As early as A.D. 800, numbers of Norsemen and Danes were migrating to the Orkneys, the Shetlands,

Towards the end of the 10th century Eric the Red, a Norseman of Iceland, established a colony in Greenland. Not many years later, according to the sagas, his son Leif Ericsson was driven from his course on the way to Greenland, reaching a land of maple trees, wild oats, and wild grapes. This land, discovered in 1000, he called Vinland; it is thought it was the coast of Nova Scotia or New England. Two years later Thorfinn Karlsefni with three ships and 160 men and women attempted to found a colony there, but were driven off by the Indians.

In 862 a Viking from Sweden, named Rurik, with his oarsmen (rusmen), invaded what is now North Russia, settling at Ladoga on the Volkhov river and giving the country the name Russia.

Christianity everywhere prevailed over the heathen gods by 1050, and the Vikings, as Norman knights, became Crusaders. Under Robert Guiscard, they founded the kingdom of Sicily.

Just when the Scandinavian peninsula became populated we do not know, but graves of people living in a stone age and in a bronze age prove that civilizations much earlier than that of the Vikings had existed there. First cousins of the Anglo-Saxons, who came from the region just south of the Jutland peninsula in Denmark, the Scandinavians were one of the Low German tribes of north-west Germany.

Forests covered the homeland of the Vikings; but by the many rivers and lakes, and along the coast, were clearings burnt in the timber, where strips of barley, rye, oats and wheat were cultivated. In the centre of the small fields stood the village of 10 to 15 houses. Around the houses were barns, granaries, separate kitchens, and houses in which wool was spun. Just beyond the village was the common meadow which furn-

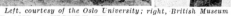

Left, courtesy of the Oslo University; right, British Museum

**VIKING SHIP AND A FIGURE-HEAD**

**Above is an old Viking ship, as found in 1903 at Oseberg, Norway, and now (restored) in Oslo Museum. In it some Norse warrior was buried, the whole being covered over with a mound of earth. On the right is what is believed to be the only survivor of the animal-headed carvings which adorned such ships, either as figure-heads or stern-posts.**

the Hebrides and the more distant Faroes. In the second half of the 9th century Danes established trading posts which became the first cities in Ireland; and Danish armies in England made themselves masters of the district known as the Danelaw (most of eastern and south-east England), though King Alfred drove them out of Wessex in 878. However, in the next century they were forced to acknowledge the overlordship of the King of England. (See Alfred the Great; Canute.)

In France the Vikings met with a check when they unsuccessfully laid siege to Paris in 885; and in 911 Charles the Simple, King of France, concluded a peace with Rolf, or Rollo, the leader of the Northmen. Under the terms of the treaty the Northmen were allowed to settle in a rich section of northern France on both sides of the Seine, Rolf becoming a vassal of the French king. The name Normandy (q.v.) was given to this district, and the Northmen who lived there were called Normans.

ished hay for the winter. On the slopes of neighbouring mountains were meadows where dairymaids herded the cows in the summer and made butter and cheese. Horses also grazed in these meadows; and swine grew fat on the acorns of the forest.

Some farms have remained in the possession of the same family down to the present day. Family pride demanded that land should never go out of the family; it usually descended to the eldest son, the other sons seeking their fortunes elsewhere.

In the Icelandic story Rigsthula we find a description of a freeholder during the Viking age. His beard was trimmed, his hair lay on his forehead, and he wore a tight shirt. There was a treasure chest on the floor. His wife was winding wool on a distaff; she wore a headdress, a smock, a kerchief round her neck, and pin-brooches on her shoulders. She called her child Karl (meaning man), and wrapped him in linen. When he grew up, he would train oxen, make ploughs, build

# NORTHMAN WHO FOUNDED AN EMPIRE IN RUSSIA

From the painting by H. N. Koekkoek

According to tradition, when the Russian tribes of the 9th century found themselves involved in constant quarrels amongst themselves they called upon the Northmen to restore order. In response came Rurik the Oarsman, and his brothers Sineus and Truvor, with a large band of followers—all bold sea-rovers. They put an end to Russian disputes by conquering the land from what is now Finland to the Volga. In 864 Sineus and Truvor died, and Rurik established his capital at Novgorod on the River Volkhov. Under his successors the kingdom of Novgorod was united with a second, established at Kiev by other Swedish Vikings, or Varangians. Rurik's descendants ruled in Russia until the end of the 16th century, when the dynasty died out.

timbered houses, barns and carts, and plough the land. His parents would choose his bride for him, and drive home with " the maiden with the hanging keys and with the goatskin kirtle (blouse-like coat)." Viking women always carried a bunch of keys, a symbol of their rule over the house.

Slaves, called thralls, were captured in battle or bought at slave markets. Most freemen had several thralls, and rich jarls and chieftains had many. Jarls, or king's men, were warriors or retainers who attended the chieftains of the tribes. As reward for special service in battle they were given land and became wealthy.

But the jarls stood no higher than the karls (ordinary men) in the village councils; nor was there much difference between them when it came to farming, for even kings personally managed their fields. Thus in 1014 we find King Sigurd Syr of Ringerike in Norway out in the fields, when his famous stepson, Olaf Haraldsson (St. Olaf), arrived on an unexpected visit. King Sigurd had " a blue kirtle and blue hose, high boots bound about the legs, a grey cloak and a grey hat, a shade about the face, and in his hand a staff, which had at the top a silver knob overlaid with gold, and in it a ring of silver."

In honour of his noted stepson, King Sigurd put on his best clothes. He had " his boots taken off and set on his feet hose of cordwain (fine leather), and bound upon them gilded spurs; then he took off his coat and kirtle, and clad him in gala clothes, and over all a scarlet cloak, and girt about him a decorated sword, and set upon his head a gilded helmet and mounted his horse."

Meals were simple even in the homes of chieftains. King Sigurd gave his guests fish and milk every other day, and alternated it with meat and ale. Mead, an intoxicating drink made of honey, was served on festive occasions. All ate with their fingers, and cut their food with the hunting knives that hung at their belts. Before and after meals women passed basins of water and linen towels to wash and dry their hands. Spoons were of wood, horn or bone, and sometimes of silver.

### Primitive Dwellings of the Northmen

The houses of poor and rich alike were built of logs, differing only in size. A long room with a high-pitched roof was the most important part of the house. In the middle of the hard-beaten clay floor was an open fire, above it being a hole in the roof to let out the smoke. Windows were cut in the roof and covered with thin semi-transparent skin.

Shields and weapons, and tapestries woven by the women of the household adorned the walls. A place of honour was reserved for the father of the home on the " high-seat " (wooden chair on a dais) in the middle of one of the long walls, between the benches that lined them. In front of the " high-seat " stood the two " high-seat posts," dedicated to the gods. At night the benches were used for beds. In better-class homes beds were built into the walls and covered with rugs and cushions of down. At meals, long narrow tables were set before the benches.

The village council or *thing*, composed of the freemen, tried cases according to the village law or *byalag*. If anyone committed murder he had to pay *wergeld*, or a fine, to the family of the murdered man, or be outlawed. Gradually, governing bodies were developed for all the Scandinavian kingdoms. The Norwegian parliament is still called the Storting (derived from *thing*). In Sweden, the county councils are named Landsting.

What contributions did the Northmen make to European civilization? First, their merchant vessels and trading towns stimulated commerce between all the regions of Europe which they touched, and helped to break down the isolation of the early Middle Ages. Second, they gave England and France their first fleets, and introduced armour better than any that had been known before. Third, their adventurous and seafaring tendencies quickened the life of the rest of Europe. Fourth, with their genius for government, they influenced the formation of the established forms of government of England and other countries, and they formed the first government of Russia. The thousand-year-old parliament of Iceland, the Althing, is the oldest existing parliament in the world; and the Isle of Man has a parliament of Norse origin almost as old.

**North Pole.** The northern extremity of the earth's axis is the North Geographical Pole, and is the central point in that artificial boundary we call the Arctic Circle, which is drawn on the globe at 66 degrees 30 minutes N. The South Geographical Pole is similarly the central point in the Antarctic Circle (which means *opposite* Arctic), drawn at 66 degrees 30 minutes S. Equidistant between the N. and S. Poles is the Equator, the name being derived from the Latin word *æquus*, " equal." Of the thrilling story of Man's attempt to reach first the North and then the South Pole you may read in our account of Polar Exploration. The climax to this tale of adventurous striving came when a party of Russian scientists camped on an ice floe at the N. Pole in 1937, and remained nine months on the floe until it had drifted some 1,500 miles towards Greenland (*see* illus. in page 224).

The North Magnetic Pole does not coincide with the geographical pole (*see* illus. in page 223). The angle which a compass needle makes with the terrestrial meridian (imaginary line joining the N. and S. geographical poles) is called the magnetic declination, and varies in different places (*see* Magnetism); moreover, the declination, which denotes the amount by which the compass needle points away from the geographical North, changes from year to year, and even alters slightly during the course of 24 hours. So we cannot say that the Magnetic North resides at any fixed place on the earth. For British Admiralty charts the position is taken at Latitude 70 degrees 40 minutes N.; Longitude 96½ degrees W. A Royal Air Force meteorological flight in 1945 determined that the Magnetic North was in Bathurst Island, about 300 miles N.N.W. of its previously determined position in the Boothia Peninsula. A new observation made in 1947 gave the position as in the vicinity of Prince of Wales and Somerset Islands.

Sir Douglas Mawson in 1914 established the position of the South Magnetic Pole as Latitude 71 degrees 10 minutes S.; Longitude 150 degrees 41 minutes E. (*See* Arctic; Antarctic; Compass).

**North Sea.** An area of the Atlantic Ocean, the North Sea (once known alternatively as the German Ocean), is one of the roughest seas in the world. The average depth of the southern portion is only about 100 feet; towards the middle it reaches 250 feet, and in the north 400 feet. In places it is shallower still. Indeed, we should have to go back only a few thousand years to find this region dry land, for it was in comparatively late geological times that this sea was formed, when the Atlantic swept over the plains which had joined the British Isles to the mainland of Europe.

The Dogger Bank, a sandbank 170 miles long by 60 wide in the centre of the sea between England and Norway, is but 50 to 100 feet under water. The only really deep place is in the Scandinavian Deep, where the depth is 1,000 feet 20 miles from shore, and over 2,400 feet at the entrance to the Skagerrak. This arm, the most notable of the many fiord, bay, and estuary formations that indent the shores of the North Sea, separates Norway from Denmark, and connects, through the Kattegat, with the Baltic Sea.

You could lose 180 North Seas and more in the Atlantic Ocean, for its area is only a little over 190,000 square miles, not much more than that of the Caspian Sea. Its greatest length from the Shetlands and the southern coast of Norway to the Strait of Dover is only 600 miles, its maximum width, between East Lothian (in Scotland) and Denmark, is 420 miles, and the distance from Calais to Dover is only 21 miles. In the North Sea, particularly on the Dogger Bank, lie some of the richest fishing-grounds in the world.

## Northumberland.

Separated on the north from Scotland by the river Tweed and the Cheviot Hills (which rise to 2,676 feet), this county, with an area of 2,018 square miles, forms the most northerly part of England. To the east, it has a long coastline on the North Sea.

Watered by the Tyne and its tributaries, and the Tweed, Blyth and several other streams, Northumberland is famed for its cattle and sheep. And an intensive trade in coal, mined in many parts of the county, is carried on. The salmon fisheries of the Tyne and Tweed have long been celebrated. Agriculture is a leading industry.

Alnwick, on the River Aln, is the county town and has a population of 6,800 ; Newcastle-on-Tyne (q.v.) is the largest city. Other centres away from the Tyne are Berwick-upon-Tweed (q.v.), Blyth (population 32,000), and Morpeth (7,000).

Opposite Bamburgh, a coastal village with an historic castle founded in the 6th century, are the Farne Islands, famous as a haunt of sea-birds. To the north of the Farne Islands, two miles from the coast, is Holy Island, or Lindisfarne. There St. Aidan founded a monastery in the year 635. There are remains of a Benedictine priory church (1093), St. Mary's church (1130), and a 16th-century castle on the island. Another ancient relic in Northumberland is a long stretch of Hadrian's Wall, which was built by the Romans about A.D. 122 and ends at the town of Wallsend.

Several battles have been fought in Northumberland, notably Otterburn, a Scottish victory over the English in 1388, and Flodden where the English under the Earl of Surrey crushed King James IV of Scotland in 1513.

The literature of Northumberland is largely contained in the stirring Border ballads. The population is 756,800.

*Gibson*

### NORTHUMBERLAND'S PROTECTION AGAINST THE BARBARIANS

Two immense defensive works were built on England's frontiers in early times, the Welsh border having Offa's Dyke—a deep ditch and earthwork—and the Scottish border being protected by Hadrian's Wall. Running through Northumberland from the Tyne westward to the Solway Firth, the Wall was built about A.D. 122 by the Romans. Part of it is seen above looking westward toward Housesteads 'mile-castle,' the ruins of which are on the south (left) of the Wall. The Wall was eight feet broad and 12 to 14 feet high, with a castle at intervals of a mile.

**North-West Territories.** About one-third of all Canada is included in the huge region—1,309,680 square miles in extent—known as the North-West Territories. This consists of a plain stretching north from the prairie provinces to the Arctic Ocean, and includes a large group of islands, the northernmost of which extends to within 475 miles of the North Pole.

The chief rivers are the Mackenzie, Slave, Great Fish and Coppermine; there are a number of lakes, Great Bear and Great Slave being the largest. The Barren Lands, a vast treeless plain, occupy about half the territory. Fur-bearing animals abound, and in parts the musk ox and caribou are found.

The only important industries are mining and the fur trade. Gold and silver are worked in the Yellowknife region, on the north shore of Great Bear Slave Lake; radium and uranium are produced at Great Bear Lake. Oil is obtained at Norman Wells in the Lower Mackenzie basin. Wheat, oats and barley are cultivated on some of the better land in the west. Elsewhere only small trees, mosses, lichens, etc., are found. There are no towns.

The territories are the remains of the area purchased from the Hudson's Bay Company by the Dominion of Canada in 1869. Various parts were subsequently taken away to form the new provinces of Alberta and Saskatchewan and to increase the size of older ones, chiefly Ontario and Quebec. The Territories are divided into three districts—Mackenzie, Keewatin and Franklin—and are governed from Ottawa. The population is 12,000.

# RUGGED LAND *of the* MIDNIGHT SUN

*Ocean-girded Norway is a place of great natural beauty, and a romantic land with a long and fascinating history. This article gives us the opportunity to tour the country without moving from our own firesides.*

**Norway.** Land of summer twilights that last until dawn, of snow-capped mountains, glaciers descending to the sea, and mountain lakes as clear as crystal; of waterfalls and rushing rivers, of high pastures with cow-bells tinkling, and deep valleys edged with sombre pines and glistening birches; of fiords, placid and smiling, or dark and threatening, whose beauty defies description—such is Norway, land of the Vikings of old.

Norway (in the Norwegian language, *Norge*) is the north-western part of Scandinavia, that peninsula which juts out from the mainland of Europe into the North Atlantic and Arctic oceans. The peninsula is split in the south, where the Skagerrak, an arm of the North Sea, cuts into the land to form two projections, the southernmost parts of Norway on the one hand, and of Sweden on the other.

Extending northward and eastward from here, a ridge of mountains, chief of which is the Kjölen or Keel range, forms a barrier between these two countries and covers most of the surface of Norway, making it one of the most distinctly mountainous regions in Europe. These highlands, however, are not so much a system of mountain chains as a group of elevated plateaux, grooved by deep valleys cut during the Ice Age by glaciers.

Even more rugged and irregular than the surface of the land is its coastline—its cliffs broken by innumerable fiords, and bordered by a fringe of rocky islands. If we were to measure all round these indentations and islands we should find the coastline to be about 12,000 miles, long enough to extend nearly half-way round the earth. We might expect to encounter violent storms along such a rough coast, but within the skargård or "island-fence" the waters are comparatively smooth.

Although Norway extends almost 300 miles into the Arctic zone, and nearly a third of the entire country is in the domain of the Midnight Sun (the sun shines day and night during part of the summer) and the winter darkness, the climate on the west, tempered by the warm winds from the Atlantic, is far milder than one might suspect. Only on the east coast and among the central mountains is the cold severe. The winters, however, are longer than those of the British Isles.

Though Norway is in the same latitude in which lie the almost uninhabitable Arctic regions of America and of Siberia, the waters of the western fiords, warmed by the Gulf Stream drift, never freeze except at their inland ends.

If we arrive at Oslo (*q.v.*), formerly Christiania, the capital and largest city, in February, we shall find the national winter sport of ski-ing at its height. The hills and mountains about the city, now covered with snow, are the pleasure-ground for the populace, who with their skis or toboggans make their way to the top of Holmenkollen Mountain, to come shooting back at speed over the five-mile course from the very top of the peak down to the foothills.

With the approach of summer we may strap our knapsack on our back and start out on a walking tour through one of the many lovely valleys in central or southern Norway. The roads are excellent, the scenery is ever-changing, and good accommodation is easily obtained.

The valleys are the chief agricultural regions, but these

**Extent.**—South-west to north-east, about 1.100 miles ; east to west, 60 to 250 miles. Area, about 125,000 square miles; coastline, including fiords and islands, about 12,000 miles. Population 3,123,900.

**Physical Features.**—Surface a rugged table-land, with numerous isolated mountain masses, snow-fields, and glaciers. Chief ranges : Kjölen (Keel), on border between Norway and Sweden (the highest point, Sulitelma, 6,158 feet); Dovre Fjeld (Snehaetta, 7,615 feet); Rjondane Fjeld (Högronden, 6,929 feet); Jötun Fjeld or Jötunheim (Galdhöppigen, highest mountain in Scandinavia, 8,399 feet). Largest glacier in Europe, Jostedalsbreen (area, 580 square miles). Principal fiords: Oslo, Halse, Bukken, Hardanger, Sogne, Nord, Trondheim, Geiranger, Vest (West), Lyngen, Varanger. Chief rivers: Glemma, Drammen. Numerous lakes.

**Products.**—Oats, barley, rye, wheat, and potatoes; cattle, sheep, and dairy products; cod, herring, mackerel, and other fish; whale oil ; iron, copper, nickel, silver ; lumber and timber products ; chemical paper, and food products.

**Principal Cities.**—Oslo, capital (population about 427,000); Bergen (population 109,000) ; Trondheim (population 56,000) ; Stavanger (population 49,000).

Wilse

## READY FOR SKI-JÖRING'S THRILLS

So popular is ski-ing amongst the Norwegians, and so proficient are they at this
sport, that they have been described as being born with skis on their feet. The
young Norwegian girl above is about to go ski-jöring, a variation of the sport in
which the skier is drawn along by a horse.

To face page 2392

*Underwood*

# THE GLACIER'S PATH IN NORWAY

The grandeur of Norway's mountains has become familiar to many tourists. Among these peaks of the wild Horunger mountains, which overshadow the hamlet of Turtegrö, huge glaciers run across the valley heads. More than 2,000 square miles of Norway are covered with perpetual snow and ice.

*To face page* 2393

comprise less than four per cent of the total area of the country. The Saetersdal, in the extreme north, is particularly interesting because, owing to its being far removed from a railway, it is one of the few places in Norway where the inhabitants still cling to their old habits and peasant costumes.

The farmsteads all over Norway are built of timber, and consist of four or more separate buildings surrounding an open space. Of these buildings the *stabbur*, or storehouse for food, is picturesque, with a bell-tower, wide overhanging eaves, and with piles at each corner which raise it several feet off the ground. Frequently they are roofed with birch-bark or with turf, on which grass, flowers and even small trees grow. In addition to their lowland farms, most of the farmers possess *saeters*, or mountain pastures often one or two days' journey distant, where the cattle are sent to graze during the summer months, and where the winter supply of cheese is made, principally from goats' milk.

The Kjölen mountains, which separate Norway from Sweden, extend from north to south in a series of peaks and high plateaux. From the central valley, called the Gudbrandsdal, Dovre mountains can be seen to the north, and the peaks of the Jötunheim to the south. Skirting the valleys are forests of pine and fir, one of the chief natural source of Norway's wealth. The lovely Hardanger plateau in the south-west is the largest in Europe.

As we mount higher the evergreens are replaced by birches, dwarf willows, and reindeer moss, and finally we reach the vast regions of perpetual snow and ice. Norway has the most gigantic glaciers in all Europe; one of them, the Jostedalsbreen. covers

580 square miles, is 1,400 to 1,600 feet thick, and thrusts scores of branches into the neighbouring valleys, and in some cases even into the sea itself.

But of all the wonders and the charms of Norway none can compare with the majesty and the sublimity of her fiords, those long arms of the sea extending far inland, sometimes for more than 100 miles—twisting and turning between cliffs of towering mountains.

If we were to take a summer cruise we should find the splendid harbours filled with ships. Doubtless we should visit Stavanger, at the head of the Bukken fiord; quaint old Bergen, second largest city in Norway and one of the chief trading-stations of the old Hanseatic League (*q.v.*); and Trondheim, third city of Norway, the ancient spiritual and intellectual centre of the north, famous for its Gothic cathedral, the grandest church in all Scandinavia, where the kings of Norway are crowned.

One hundred miles north of the Arctic Circle are the Lofoten or Lofoden Islands, with steep, jagged snow-capped peaks 4,000 feet above the sea, their lower levels inhabited by millions of eider ducks, whose down is so valuable. Between two of the islands the tide forms the famous Maelstrom whirlpool. The Lofoten islands are the centre of the Norwegian cod fisheries, and are annually visited during the first three months of the year by a large fleet of fishing vessels.

Near by is Narvik, terminus of a railway which cuts across the Scandinavian peninsula from the Swedish port of Lulea on the Gulf of Bothnia, and one of the most northerly railways stations in the world. Narvik, noted for its export of iron ore, was

*Interstate Press Pictures, Ltd*

### MOUNTAIN GIRT WATERS OF A NORWEGIAN FIORD

A very popular method of spending the summer holidays in normal times was a cruise along the coast of Norway. Steamers ventured far up the fiords, giving passengers an opportunity to admire some of the finest scenery in the world. Above is a cruising vessel in the Nordfiord between Bergen and Christiansund. Some of the fiords are surrounded by mountainous cliffs from 3,000 to 5,000 feet high, these sheltered waterways forming excellent harbours.

the scene of crucial episodes in the Second World War (1939–45). On April 10, 1940, British destroyers steamed up Narvik Fiord and sank six German supply ships and one destroyer. Three days later the British battleship Warspite, with escorting destroyers, sank seven enemy destroyers in the harbour. These actions crippled German sea power in Norwegian waters, greatly facilitating the Allied landings in Norway. On May 26, Allied forces attacked the Germans entrenched outside the town and two days later captured it after heavy fighting. The fall of Narvik and the subsequent Allied advance along the railway to the Swedish frontier promised to be the turning point in the Norwegian campaign ; but German successes in France made imperative the withdrawal of the Allied troops in June. (*See* end of this article for story of Norway in the Second World War.)

Two hundred and fifty miles north of the Arctic Circle is Tromsö, a seaport of 10,000 inhabitants and a busy trading-post for fur and fish. During the long winter "night," from the middle of November to the end of January, the city is lighted by electricity—as are all buoys and lighthouses along Norway's coast.

Eventually we reach Hammerfest, the northernmost town in the world, built on an island off the Finmark coast and in normal times visited by tourists who come to view the splendours of the Midnight Sun. For, as seen from Hammerfest, the sun does not set from the middle of May to the end of July.

Fifty miles north of Hammerfest the coast of Norway and of Europe reaches its farthest point north in the grey cliffs of the North Cape. Spitsbergen (Svalbard), a valuable group of islands placed under the sovereignty of Norway in 1919, lies 360 miles north in the Arctic. This archipelago of five large islands and many small ones has immense coal deposits; other mineral resources, still undeveloped, include iron, copper and zinc.

Oats is the chief grain produced in Norway; rye and barley are the bread cereals. Wheat, being less hardy than the other grains, is grown in smaller quantities, and only in the southern parts of the country. Potatoes grow well almost everywhere and are one of the chief foods. Cattle and sheep are kept in large numbers; and quantities of butter and cheese are made for export as well as for domestic use. The nomadic Lapps in the far north keep herds of reindeer, which supply them with meat, milk, and hides, and which they also employ as draught animals.

The forests and fisheries are Norway's chief natural sources of wealth. Fishing is the oldest of Norwegian industries, and still remains one of the most important. Norwegian cod, either salted or dried, and cod-liver oil, are shipped to European countries and to America. Whales are hunted in the Arctic seas. Every year whaling factory-ships, each accompanied by six or more small steamers, which actually catch the whales, visit the Antarctic whaling grounds, returning with cargoes of oil, whale meat and bone meal. Whaling is one of Norway's most profitable industries, and whale oil is exported in considerable quantities. More than 20 per cent of the area of the country is timber-land, and about three-fourths of this is pine. Lumber, wood-pulp and other timber products are among the principal exports.

The mining industry is relatively unimportant. Copper, nickel and silver are found, and considerable quantities of iron, but coal is entirely lacking on the mainland. In spite of this, Norway has been able to develop manufactures to a considerable extent, owing to its splendid water-power resources. Chemicals, machinery, wooden ware, silk, cotton and woollen goods, and paper are leading products.

Steamers are the most important means of communication between Norwegian ports, although railways also are well developed. There are air services between the principal towns and to Sweden, Denmark, the Netherlands, France and Great Britain. Telegraphs and telephones are found in the remotest places, and the mail service is prompt. Education is compulsory, and there are excellent schools. The Royal Frederick University at Oslo is the chief institution for higher education.

S. J. Beckett

### YOUTH AND AGE IN NORWAY

**Weather-beaten indeed is the face of this old Norwegian farmworker, holding his grand-daughter on his knee while he enjoys a respite from his labours. Hard-working and thrifty, the Norwegians are a long-lived race.**

The government of Norway is a constitutional monarchy. The king exercises his authority through a Council of State composed of the Prime Minister and at least seven other ministers. The Parliament (called Storting) is divided into two houses. Since 1913 women have voted on an equal footing with men. The State Church is Lutheran.

From the fiords of Norway in the early Middle Ages set forth some of the most famous of the

# NORWAY AND HER SCANDINAVIAN NEIGHBOURS

he Scandinavian peninsula comprises Norway and
weden and forms the northern tip of Europe, extending
r into the Arctic Circle. A fringe of thousands of rocky
lands protects the greater part of the west coast, which
the most broken stretch of seaboard in the world. The
map shows where enormous shoals of cod, mackerel and
herring are to be found in the cold waters that wash the
coast, and also some of the natural resources and products
of the peninsula. Most of the surface of Norway is mountainous, almost three-quarters of it being unproductive.

# DOWN ON THE QUIET FARMS IN NORWAY

Goats are kept on most Norwegian farms and cheese is made from their milk. At the top left three are on the rocky side of a mountain road, out for their daily exercise. At centre right is a farmer's storehouse. Farm buildings are often built of logs (lower right), timber being plentiful ; the farms are small, generally with an area of less than five acres. Bread is made by the daughters of the house (lower left), in many farms which are remote from shops.

# THE OLD AND THE NEW ENRICH NORWAY'S LIFE

Modern and smart is the Grand Hotel, the building with the many awnings seen below in the photograph of the Eidsvolds Plads in Oslo, capital of Norway. To the right is the Parliament House, with its circular central section and long wings.

Lacking coal, the Norwegians use their swift-flowing streams. Below, huge pipes bring water to the hydro-electric plant at Rjunkan. There Norway's mightiest waterfall provides power for a nitrate factory.

Girls of the Geiranger Fiord region (above) in local dress.

Many old sagas may have been recited in the room below, which dates from the 15th century. The substantial furniture, with its fine strong lines and simple carving, belongs to the same period.

Second largest town in Norway, Bergen is a centre of the fishing industry (oval photograph). The old sailing vessels have been largely replaced by motor-boats or steam trawlers.

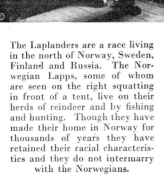

The Laplanders are a race living in the north of Norway, Sweden, Finland and Russia. The Norwegian Lapps, some of whom are seen on the right squatting in front of a tent, live on their herds of reindeer and by fishing and hunting. Though they have made their home in Norway for thousands of years they have retained their racial characteristics and they do not intermarry with the Norwegians.

The kings of Norway are crowned at Trondheim in the Gothic Cathedral (above), founded in the 11th century and later restored.

Vikings whose raids long troubled Europe (*see* Northmen). The land was united into a single kingdom and Christianized early in the 11th century. In 1397 it was united with Denmark and Sweden in the Union of Kalmar. Sweden seceded from this union 125 years later, but for more than 400 years Norway continued as a dependency of Denmark.

At the close of the Napoleonic wars, in 1815, Norway was taken from Denmark and given to the Swedish king to recompense him for the loss of Finland to Russia; but Norway retained its own government. In 1905 long-standing disputes led the Norwegian Storting to declare this union dissolved. The Swedish Government reluctantly agreed to this, and the Norwegians chose Prince Charles of Denmark as their king. He was crowned in 1906, as Haakon VII.

Norway endeavoured to remain neutral during the Second World War (1939–45); but on April 9, 1940, German airborne troops landed at Oslo, gaining possession of the city in a few hours. On the same day other German forces seized all the principal Norwegian ports, aided by pro-German Norwegians led by a Major Quisling (*q.v.*). Except around the port of Narvik there was no organized front line, and resistance was mainly of a guerrilla character. The Allies promised support, and British, French and Polish troops were landed. Lacking suitable equipment and without air support they achieved success only in the far north, where Narvik was recaptured on May 28, 1940.

A few days later, owing to the German victories in France, the Allied forces were withdrawn, the Norwegians themselves surrendering on June 9. In the meantime King Haakon had gone to England, where he headed a Norwegian Government in exile.

All free Norwegian vessels entered Allied service; and within the country patriots carried on an underground war against the German occupation forces, sabotaging mines, factories and railways. On October 25, 1944, Russian troops, pursuing the Germans retreating from Finland, entered the Norwegian port of Kirkenes and advanced as far as the Tana river. No more Norwegian territory was liberated until the general German surrender on May 8, 1945. On May 31, 1945, the exiled Government returned amidst great public rejoicing. The population is 3,123,900.

**Norwich.** (Pron. nor'-ij). The ancient county town of Norfolk, Norwich stands on the River Wensum near its junction with the Yare. Its chief glory is the beautiful cathedral, begun in Norman times but not finished until about 1500. Little remains of the castle, which also dates back to Norman times; part of it is now used as a county museum and art gallery. Other notable buildings are St. Andrew's Hall and the Guildhall, both dating from the 15th century. The house of Norwich's most famous literary son, George Borrow (*q.v.*) is preserved.

Norwich is the business centre of a large district and the headquarters of important insurance companies and the central market for the agricultural products and cattle of East Anglia. Among its industries are light engineering, and the manufacture of boots and shoes, beer, starch and mustard. In the Middle Ages the city was important for its wool trade. The population is 114,700.

**Nottinghamshire.** Wholly inland, this English county of lace-making fame has an area of 844 square miles. The surface is mainly flat, except in the south-west where there are some rolling moorlands and hills. The Trent is the chief river, forming in part the eastern boundary with Lincolnshire.

The county is well wooded; although many trees have been cut down, there are still some magnificent specimens left in Sherwood Forest, especially in the part known as the Dukeries, which once contained the residences of four dukes. Sherwood Forest was originally a royal forest, and is remembered as

*J. Dixon-Scott*

**SPLENDID CATHEDRAL OF NORWICH**
From the cricket ground at Norwich one gets this view of the beautiful cathedral, standing between the River Wensum and the castle. Founded in 1096, it was not finished until about 1500 ; the Perpendicular spire and the roof of the nave date from the 15th century.

the haunt of the legendary Robin Hood and his merry men. Besides the making of lace and hosiery, engineering is an important industry. Coal is mined, and clay, sandstone and limestone are quarried.

There are several notable mansions in the county. In the part called the Dukeries are Clumber House, Thoresby House, Worksop Manor, and Welbeck Abbey with its underground passages and vaults made by the eccentric 5th Duke of Portland. Wollaton Hall, near Nottingham, is a splendid late 16th-century building. About eight miles from Nottingham is Newstead Abbey, where Lord Byron (1788–1824) lived. It was formerly an Augustinian priory, and parts of the old monastic buildings remain.

Nottingham (population, 290,300), famous for its lace, drugs and cycles and its Goose Fair, is the county town; it stands on the Trent. Other important towns are Newark (23,000) and Mansfield (49,000). In the ruined castle at Newark King John died in 1216. Coal seems to have been worked as far back as 1259, when Queen Eleanor complained of the smoke. The population of Nottinghamshire is 712,700.

*Fox*

OPENING NOTTINGHAM'S GOOSE FAIR

For nearly 800 years a great occasion at Nottingham has been the Goose Fair, held every October. Originally mainly for the sale of geese, it has now become largely a pleasure fair with roundabouts and other amusements. Above, the Lord Mayor of the city, attended by other dignitaries, declares the Fair open.

**Noun.** A noun is a word that *names*. It may name anything of which anybody may think or speak—as *school, London, kindness, justice, children.* If it is the name of one particular person or object or place, it is called a proper noun. In this sense " proper " means " belonging exclusively to." Your name, *Frank* or *Mary*, is a proper noun, because it belongs to you and distinguishes you from other persons. *London, Saturday, Scotland, January, Piccadilly*, are proper nouns.

Any noun that is not a special individual name is a " common " noun—as *cloth, man, book.* Such nouns are called " common " because they belong to more than one person or thing. A special kind of common noun is the " collective " noun, for a group of things or persons, as *class, flock.*

Most nouns in English have two forms, according to whether they indicate one object or more than one. The form which denotes one is called the singular, and the form which denotes more than one is called the plural—

as *bird, birds.* The plural is generally formed by adding *s* to the singular. When adding *s*, nouns ending in *y* after a consonant change the *y* to *ie*, as *city, cities.* Several nouns ending in *f* or *fe* change the *f* to *v*, as *self, selves ; knife, knives.*

Some nouns ending in *o* add *es*, others add *s* only —as *cargo, cargoes ; piano, pianos.* Nouns that end in a sound difficult to pronounce with a final *s* add *es*—as *church, churches.* A few form their plurals by adding *en* or by changing the internal vowel—as *ox, oxen ; tooth, teeth.* The adding of *en* was the common way of forming plurals in Old English. There are also some foreign plurals in common use —as *stratum, strata ; crisis, crises.* A few nouns make no change.

Many nouns, especially those denoting persons or animals, have another form called the possessive case, because it is chiefly used to denote possession, like the genitive case in Latin. Singular nouns, and all plurals not ending in *s*, add the apostrophe and *s* to form the possessive—as *lady's, children's.* Plurals ending in *s* add the apostrophe only—as *ladies', boys'.*

In ordinary use, most names of things are not used in the possessive; instead of *the book's cover, the chair's back*, the usual

| HOW NOUNS MAY BE USED |
|---|
| Subject and predicate noun : A *shilling* saved is a *shilling* gained. |
| Direct object : He saved a *shilling* a week. |
| Object of a preposition : He kept account of every *shilling* that he spent. |
| Indirect object : The occasion gave that *shilling* a value. |
| Secondary or complementary object : I will make your wages a *shilling* a day. |
| Possessive modifier : Give me a *shilling's* worth of sugar. |
| Adnominal use (exactly like an adjective) : This is a *shilling* toy. |
| Appositional : His reward—a *shilling*—seemed enormous. |

form is *the cover of the book, the back of the chair*. But nouns denoting time are often found in the possessive—as *a day's work, a seven days' journey*.

Besides the possessive case, nouns, like pronouns, have two other cases, according to the construction in which they are used. Nouns do not change their form to distinguish these cases, though most pronouns do. Nouns and pronouns used as the subject substantive of a verb are said to be in the nominative ("naming") case. Nouns and pronouns used as either the direct or indirect objects of verbs or verbal nouns, and as the objects of prepositions, are said to be in the objective case. A noun or pronoun in apposition to another (that is, used to modify or explain the meaning of another noun or pronoun meaning the same person or thing —as "Caesar, the *conqueror*") is put in the same case as the word it modifies.

To give in order the various forms which a noun or pronoun may take to indicate different meanings or uses in the sentence is called "declining" it, or giving its "declension." Thus the declension of *child* is: singular, nominative and objective, *child ;* possessive, *child's*. Plural, *children, children's*.

In addition to number and case, nouns, like pronouns, have two other properties: gender and person. (For a discussion of grammatical person, *see* Pronoun). Nouns, except those in direct address, are always in the third person.

In English gender denotes merely whether the noun distinguishes male or female, or the absence of sex—as *prince, princess, table*. Those denoting males are masculine; those denoting females, feminine; those denoting things without sex, neuter. Nouns which refer to both sexes are said to be of common gender—as *people, birds*, etc.

In foreign languages the division into the three genders is often quite different from the English system. For instance, in Latin, river (*fluvius*), table (*mensa*), and town (*oppidum*) are respectively masculine, feminine, and neuter, while in English all three are neuter. In German, the word for girl, *Mädchen*, is neuter, and so is *Fräulein*, young lady.

**Nova Scotia.** Geographers have aptly called the Canadian maritime province of Nova Scotia " the door-step of the continent," for it lies at the entrance to the St. Lawrence river, the passage-way to the interior. It occupies the southeastern peninsula of Canada and the adjoining island of Cape Breton, being connected with the mainland by a slender neck of land called the Isthmus of Chignecto.

Nova Scotia has an extensive coastline, and since the 17th century, when it was settled by the French and called Acadia, fishing has been one of the principal industries. The Nova Scotians are among the finest seamen in the world; it is said that they can handle a small boat in rough seas better than any other race.

Considerable stretches of forest furnish another source of wealth, quantities of lumber being shipped each year from Halifax. In the northern part of

*Department of the Interior, Canada*

**A FISHING PORT OF NOVA SCOTIA**

The Canadian province of Nova Scotia was a French settlement early in the 17th century, and was known as Acadia until it was ceded to the British by the Treaty of Utrecht in 1713. Though it is largely an agricultural province, its fisheries are among the most valuable in Canada. Lunenburg, seen above, is a fishing port on the southeast coast of the province, where many boats are fitted out for the fishing fleets which operate off the Grand Banks of Newfoundland. The produce of these fisheries is one of the main sources of Nova Scotia's prosperity.

the peninsula and in Cape Breton Island are rich coal-mines, which produce about half of Canada's coal. In the southern part are small gold-mines and rich deposits of iron ore.

Agriculture is very important. Dairy produce, poultry and fruit are the chief products, the apples of the fertile Annapolis valley being famous. Oats and potatoes are widely cultivated. The capital and chief port is Halifax (q.v.), one of Nova Scotia's 12 spacious harbours. Nova Scotia is a favourite summer resort with the people of the eastern United States because of its delightfully mild summer climate and the picturesqueness of its coasts, meadows and orchards.

One of the smallest provinces of Canada, it is thickly populated, and the majority of the inhabitants are of British stock. Another considerable group is descended from the original settlers, the

> **Area.**—21,068 square miles, of which 325 are water.
> **Population.**—612,000.
> **Physical Features.**—Peninsula of Nova Scotia and Cape Breton Island to the east form a Province of uplands, with areas of forest. Several islands off the coast, and lakes (including Rossignol and Bras d'Or).
> **Products.**—Fruit ; dairying ; coal ; lumber ; fish.
> **Principal Towns.**—Halifax (70,500), Sydney, Glace Bay.

French Canadians or Acadians, who went there early in the 17th century.

Almost from the time of the founding of Port Royal (now Annapolis) by the French, in 1604, Nova Scotia was a focal point in the struggle between the French and the British for the New World, and changed hands several times. Fighting between the two nations was nearly continuous until the final blow to French aspirations was delivered, in 1759, by the capture of Quebec. The previous year had seen the capture of the fortress of Louisburg, which the French had built on the Atlantic coast of Cape Breton Island to serve as their main naval base in North America. Although the peninsula was won by the British in 1713, the island was not formally handed over until the peace of 1763. In 1867 Nova Scotia became part of Canada. The population is 612,000.

# *A* READER'S GUIDE *to* GOOD FICTION

*The novel is, of course, the most popular form of literature ; indeed, numbers of people read no other form. But we should be careful how we choose our fiction ; this article will act as a guide.*

**Novel.** Many of the characters in fiction are more real to us than those in history. We feel as well acquainted with them as with the people we meet in real life and often understand them better.

What makes a good novel? There are three essentials—characters, plot and setting. A good novel represents life-like characters talking and acting under interesting circumstances, and through their acts becoming involved in a complication of events which is brought to a satisfactory conclusion. But many excellent novelists show no such harmonious development of these three elements. Dickens, for instance, often pays little attention to plot, while with Scott the portrayal of character is subordinate. They used a large rambling structure on which to build and develop their themes. It is impossible to lay down hard and fast rules, for it is the privilege of genius to break all rules of art. But one thing we can demand of a novel and that is that it must ring true. Even a romance must not violate the fundamental truths of human nature.

The novel as we know it today was unknown in ancient times, though the Greeks and Romans had their prose tales and romances, such as the Golden Ass of Apuleius, which contains the story of Cupid and Psyche.

The immediate ancestor of the modern novelist was the minstrel of the Middle Ages who travelled from place to place telling or singing his tales. Troubadour romances, long-drawn-out and full of high adventure, were popular with the upper classes, because they found in them an idealized picture of their own lives. The common people liked tales that satirized the valiant knights and pious churchmen, stories of rogues and rascals seeking adventure, or of life as they themselves lived it.

So alongside of the metrical romances we find the *fabliaux*, telling lightly in verse stories of ordinary life; and similar stories in prose, called by the Italians *novelle*, meaning "new stories," from which the English term "novel" is derived. A little later there appeared in Spain another type of story dealing with low life, the "picaresque" novel, which told at considerable length the adventures of a *picaro*, or rogue, as the romance sang the noble deeds of the knight-errant. Somewhat akin to these picaresque novels and yet different from anything that had appeared before was Cervantes' famous burlesque romance Don Quixote. (*See* Cervantes).

The two classes of stories—the romance on the one hand, and the *fabliau*, novella, and picaresque novel on the other—grew up side by side and were the forerunners of the two main types of modern prose fiction, the "romance" and the "novel." The term novel is now usually applied to a narrative of considerable length with a more or less intricate plot, which pictures life as it is, dealing with characters and events that have been or might be real. The romance frees the imagination, deals with more unusual aspects of life, and is usually more concerned with telling an exciting story than with the study of character. Thus Scott's Ivanhoe may be styled a romance, while George Eliot's Mill on the Floss is a novel. In common usage, however, any work of prose fiction is called a novel, the two kinds being called "realistic" and "romantic" novels, a definition which no longer holds good since the development of the novel by writers such as James Joyce and Virginia Woolf in the 1920s.

Many prose romances were written in England in the Elizabethan period, the age of Shakespeare, though they are quite overshadowed by the epic dramas of that time. Lyly's Euphues is remarkable for its elaborate artificial style, its involved and nicely balanced phrases.

Bunyan's Pilgrim's Progress, the great Puritan prose epic designed to teach the people, still holds its popularity because of its truth to human nature. Although it is an allegory, it is, strange to say, in some ways very much like the old picaresque or rogue novel ; only here the adventures of the hero are symbolic and spiritual.

Robinson Crusoe is often called the first English novel, yet it is hardly a novel in the modern sense. It is a " documentary " tale of adventure in a far-away place rather than of life as we know it; it lacks plot, being a series of happenings loosely strung together, and there is no character analysis. The novel of ordinary domestic life and manners in England owes its beginning, in the middle of the 18th century, to an accident. Samuel Richardson, a London printer, was invited by a publisher to prepare a volume of letters which might serve as models to letter writers. It occurred to Richardson that the letters would be more instructive and interesting if they were made to tell a connected love story and point a moral. The result was Pamela, or Virtue Rewarded (1740).

So great was its vogue, especially among women, that it was followed by another novel, Clarissa, or the History of a Young Lady, usually considered Richardson's masterpiece, and then by one with an ideal man as its hero, Sir Charles Grandison. Richardson's fault was his pretentious moralizing. Henry Fielding was moved to burlesque Pamela in his first novel Joseph Andrews (1742), but he became so interested in his characters that the result was a realistic novel rather than a burlesque. Here, and most of all in his masterpiece Tom Jones, we feel that his characters are real flesh and blood.

**DAVID COPPERFIELD**
One of the best-known of Dickens's novels, David Copperfield was illustrated by the artist Hablot Knight Browne, better known by his pseudonym of ' Phiz.' The etching shows David's meeting with his aunt Betsy Trotwood, in the garden of her house above the cliffs of Dover.

Richardson, Fielding, and most of their contemporaries are not read to any great extent today. Except for his Sentimental Journey, neither Sterne nor Smollett (the author of Humphrey Clinker), important as their work was in the history of the novel, have a wide appeal. But one novel written a little later still remains a favourite of young and old. That is Goldsmith's Vicar of Wakefield, a sentimental story of simple home life.

In the early part of the 19th century there was a revived interest in the Middle Ages, and the historical novels of Sir Walter Scott were a natural outcome; the Waverley Novels were copied all over Europe. During the same period lived a writer who was not interested in depicting the world of history or even the stirring events of her own day. Jane Austen wrote novels which gave a universe in miniature—the life of country society. She wrote about the people that she knew, and with sly humour showed character so skilfully that Sir Walter Scott compared her with Shakespeare. Pride and Prejudice and Emma sparkle at the third reading as much as at the first.

During the 19th century the field of the novel immensely widened, to keep pace with the growing complexity of life. Old laws no longer fitted new customs, and a new race of writers grew up to combat them. Unlike the ironic, well-mannered novels of Jane Austen, the writings of Charlotte Brontë were a passionate avowal of the individual. Her Jane Eyre and Villette are moving and intensely human documents. Emily Brontë, a poet of genius, wrote Wuthering Heights, one of the strangest and most imaginative of English novels.

Charles Kingsley, Mrs. Gaskell, Charles Reade, and, above all, Charles Dickens, were writers of the humanitarian novel. Perhaps the first two writers felt just as keenly as did Dickens, but they did not possess in so great a degree the humour, pathos, power of dramatic description, and vitality that made Dickens's work endure. His own life-story, with some modifications, forms the basis of his novel David Copperfield.

Dickens was of the people; Thackeray belonged to the upper classes. History became the background of some of his finest novels, as in Esmond and The Virginians among others. In his best-known novel, Vanity Fair, Thackeray exposes the shams and meanness of fashionable society.

George Eliot (Mary Ann Evans), who wrote a little later, did not depict the world as a dramatic spectacle, as did Dickens and Thackeray. She was more interested in the minds and souls of her characters. She knew how to make the struggle in a girl's mind as interesting as a battle. When one remembers that Maggie in The Mill on the Floss is really George Eliot herself, it is easier to see why the author has such an uncanny insight.

Later writers included R. L. Stevenson, the disciple of Scott, and of the French romancer Dumas; George Meredith, carrying the novel of the mind and manners to extreme complexity; Anthony Trollope engaged in depicting life in English cathedral cities ; and Thomas Hardy, writing realistic stories of the English countryside which have all the elements of inexorable fate found in a Greek tragedy. The French realistic school founded by Flaubert influenced George Moore, one of the greatest masters of English prose.

Still later came Barrie, Bennett, Wells, Galsworthy, Conrad and a host of others. H. G. Wells, who began with scientific romances, was mainly concerned with social reform. Arnold Bennett, who wrote books that recall the old Flemish painters in their careful detail and their faithful description of ordinary experiences, learned much from the French masters of fiction, especially De Maupassant. His most characteristic work centres about the "Five Towns" of the pottery industry of England, and his masterpiece The Old Wives' Tale ensured him a permanent place in English literature. Galsworthy drew sombre pictures of the injustices of modern society. Joseph Conrad, born a Pole but living the greater part of his life as an officer in the English Merchant Marine, wrote of the sea and of strange lands in novels that are masterpieces of style and of insight into character. (*See further* English Literature).

*W. F. Mansell*

**BEATRIX DUBS ESMOND HER KNIGHT**

In Henry Esmond, Thackeray wrote what many consider to be the finest historical novel in the English language. The scene above shows Beatrix dubbing Henry Esmond her knight for his gallant conduct in Marlborough's campaigns. Behind Esmond stands Beatrix's mother, Lady Castlewood, and on the left is Esmond's step-mother, the Dowager Viscountess Castlewood. This painting, by A. L. Egg, is in the Tate Gallery, London.

After the First World War (1914–18) the English novel was strongly influenced by the psycho-analytical discoveries of Freud. Writers depicted the workings of the subconsciousness, the hidden motives and suppressed desires of human beings. James Joyce's book Ulysses was of great significance in the development of the psychological novel, and influenced important writers during the 1920s and 30s, an influence which contended with that of the French Marcel Proust. This school practised what was known as " the stream of consciousness " method—a term implying the presentation of the thoughts and emotions of the various characters independently of " plot " or story.

But the main stream of novel writing flowed along a more traditional course, and the full effect of writers such as Virginia Woolf and Dorothy Richardson was not felt until the 1940s. In the inter-war years there were many fine examples of the art of story-telling, one of the most notable being J. B. Priestley's story The Good Companions.

The novel in America showed for many years much the same tendencies as in England. James Fenimore Cooper in the first half of the 19th century " laid the foundations of American romance " and won the title of " the American Scott." Hawthorne probed deep into the recesses of the human mind and soul. In the later 19th century and reaching well into the still more complex 20th century, we find Henry James, writer of psychological novels, concerned mainly with depicting Americans set against a European background; Henry James's approach to novel writing was in advance of his time. Other outstanding American novelists of this period included William Dean Howells, distinctly a realist of everyday American life; Edith Wharton, influenced by Henry James; Ernest Hemingway, a writer of great power and vitality; William Faulkner, an experimentalist of outstanding ability; Upton Sinclair, a vigorous exposer of social evils; Sinclair Lewis, a satirist of the front rank. There were many popular writers who appealed to a wide public. Of these the most prominent included Edna Ferber, Margaret Mitchell, Willa Cather, and John Dos Passos. (See United States Literature).

We can only glance at the novel in other lands. It is to Italy, in a sense, that we owe the novel form, but the Italian " novella " resembled our short story rather than our novel. Alessandro Manzoni in the 19th century is the first modern Italian novelist of international importance. Matilde Serao, Grazia Deledda, Giovanni Verga and Gabriele D'Annunzio (the latter better known as a poet and dramatist) were his greatest successors.

In Spain there has been no name as great as that of Cervantes, but since the middle of the 19th century the novel has been a popular form. The best-known names are Fernan Caballero, Pedro Antonio de Alarcon, Pereda, Galdos, and Blasco Ibañez, the last probably more widely read in England and America than in his own country.

In the Scandinavian countries Björnson, the greatest novelist of Norway, was followed by Selma Lagerlöf, who wove the folklore of Sweden into sagas, and by Johan Bojer and Knut Hamsun, who have produced powerful, realistic works. Henryk Sienkiewicz, author of With Fire and Sword and

*From Könnecke's Bilderatlas zur Geschichte der Deutschen Nationalliteratur*

**HEROINE OF GOETHE'S FIRST NOVEL**

This vignette by Daniel Chodowiecki (1726-1801) is an illustration from Goethe's first novel, The Sorrows of Young Werther, published in 1774. Werther, calling to take Lotte to a ball, surprises her in the act of cutting bread and butter for her brothers and sisters. The sentimental story is a tragedy of unrequited love, and was suggested to the author by the actual experience of a young friend.

other historical romances dealing with the struggle of the Poles, is the chief representative of Poland.

In Germany in the 18th century Goethe wrote the most famous of sentimental novels, The Sorrows of Young Werther, and the great autobiographical novel Wilhelm Meister. Then came the picturesque, humorous stories of Jean Paul Richter; and the romances of Tieck, Fouqué, Von Kleist, and others. Paul Heyse, Gottfried Keller, Hermann Sudermann, Éric M. Remarque, Heinrich and Thomas Mann, and Franz Werfel, are among the most important German novelists of later times. The Czech-born Franz Kafka is usually included among German writers. His three great novels The Castle, The Trial, and America (all unfinished) were published posthumously.

In France it was not until the 19th century that the novel became one of the chief forms of imaginative writing. Victor Hugo and Alexandre Dumas were inspired by Scott to enter the realms of history and romance. Flaubert in his Madame Bovary combined romanticism and realism. Balzac insisted that fiction must be based on observation and experience. He enriched literature with an extensive gallery of memorable characters. Zola went further, attempting to dissect human nature and to remedy existing social evils. The early 20th century gave rise to a number of brilliant satirists, chief of whom was Anatole France.

One of the most important writers, whose long series of novels was published under the title In Pursuit of Lost Time, was Marcel Proust, a novelist of great influence. Other novelists included André Gide, André Malraux, and François Mauriac.

Perhaps no other country has given so great an impetus to the novel as has Russia. The powerful novels of Gogol, founder of the realistic Russian school, of the imaginative and poetical Turgenev, of Dostoievski with his subtle psychology, and of Leo Tolstoy came as a challenge to the rest of the world. (*See* Literature, Children's ; and articles on the literatures of the chief countries mentioned).

**Nuffield,** WILLIAM RICHARD MORRIS, 1ST VISCOUNT (born 1877). Born at Cowley, near Oxford, on October 10, 1877, young Morris was educated at the village school there, and began his career as an apprentice to the cycle trade in a small repair shop in 1894. Nine months later he set up in business as a bicycle maker, racing with machines of his own construction and winning seven county championships in 1900. Having gained some engineering knowledge he began shortly after 1900 to build motor bicycles,

*Morris Motors, Ltd.*

**LORD NUFFIELD'S FIRST CAR**

Beginning as a motor-cycle maker in 1900, Viscount Nuffield, then Mr. William Morris, constructed his first light car in 1912, and he is here seen at the wheel of the original model. Since then his business has developed into one of the largest in the world. Noted for his donations to Oxford University and other institutions, Lord Nuffield was made a Baronet in 1929, a Baron in 1934 and a Viscount in 1938.

followed in 1912 by light cars of robust construction, but economical to run, the need for which he had clearly perceived.

The business throve during the First World War (1914–18), and after it was over Morris embarked on mass-production of family cars on an enormous scale. His great organizing abilities, coupled with his policy of catering for a vast market, rapidly established his firm as one of the largest car makers in the world. The creation and the continued success of the Morris combine, employing thousands of workmen all over the world, are thus largely due to the industrial and commercial genius of one man. For his services to industry and his philanthropic work Morris was made a baronet in 1929, raised to the peerage as Baron Nuffield in 1934, and became a viscount in 1938.

To his gifts to various institutions such as the universities and hospitals there seemed to be no end. During 1936 he gave a total of £2,000,000 to Oxford University and another £2,000,000 to areas where there was much poverty and unemployment. At the end of 1937 it was estimated that his gifts amounted to more than £11,000,000, and in 1943 he set up a trust fund, The Nuffield Foundation, to which he gave £10,000,000, to be used for various educational and other purposes, especially medical research.

**Numerals.** From the earliest times men have counted on their fingers, and the system of making straight marks or " tallies " as a record of numbers probably grew out of this practice. When the habit arose of " scoring " tallies with cross strokes into groups of five, each group obviously represented the fingers of one hand. After a time this was found to be too small a unit, and men came to adopt the decimal system of counting by tens, representing the fingers of both hands.

Of all the older systems of number notation, the Roman system is the best known. Indeed, we still use it for certain purposes, such as marking the hours on clock dials, numbering the volumes and chapters of books, and sometimes for dates. In this system seven letters are used to represent numbers, with the value given below:

| *I* | *V* | *X* | *L* | *C* | *D* | *M* |
|----|----|----|----|----|----|----|
| 1 | 5 | 10 | 50 | 100 | 500 | 1,000 |

The letter *C* is the initial letter of the Latin word *centum*, meaning hundred, and *M* that of *mille*, thousand. It is generally thought that V represents the top half of X, and L the lower half of C. When a letter of less value is written *before* one of the greater value, the numeral represents the *difference* between the two values. Thus IV equals 4; XL equals 40; XC equals 90. When the letter is written after one of greater value, the sum of the two is represented. When a bar is placed over a letter its value is multiplied by 1,000. Thus V̄ equals 5,000 ; X̄IV equals 14,000. (*See* table).

In part the greater simplicity of the so-called Arabic system is due to the fact that each of the

Arabic digits is a single character (1, 2, 3, and so on, up to 9), instead of being composed, as are all of the corresponding Roman numerals except I and V, of several characters or letters. It is also due to the fact that the Arabic system is based on an improved principle, that of place value. In the number 555, for example, the 5 at the right stands for 5 units or ones, the middle 5 for 5 tens or 50, and the one at the left for 5 hundreds. This makes possible a *decimal* system, the place value of the numbers increasing tenfold to the left of the units figure and decreasing similarly to the right.

The Arabic system of numbers is a convenient one, but before the nought or zero was invented, for several hundreds of years after the system came into use, men found it difficult to write such a number as 1,030, or 3,042,050. The invention of the nought made possible the simplified arithmetical processes in use today in place of the older ones which required the abacus or counting frame (*see* Arithmetic). The use of the nought gave the world a system of numbers which has proved a great help in advancing both science and trade. The nought is for this reason considered one of the great inventions of the world of mathematics.

In their earliest form the Arabic numerals were not really Arabic at all, but came from India. The first trace that we have of them (without the nought, however) is in some rock-cut inscriptions in Central India, which go back over 2,000 years. In Europe we find some examples of the nine digits (again no nought) in manuscripts dating from early in the Middle Ages, probably derived from contact with the Saracens, who then ruled Spain.

The real introduction of the Arabic system into Europe came with the rise of commerce which followed the Crusades. Then for the first time West and East were brought into continual contact, and we may consider the new system of notation as one of the many gains of Europe from the activities of the Italian merchants. The nought was now an established part of the system. The old and cumbersome Roman system, however, was used to some extent in business until the 16th century.

In most everyday problems we calculate in pounds, shillings, and pence, feet, or other definite units (*see* Weights and Measures). Numbers carrying this meaning as to kind are called *denominate* numbers. To make such everyday calculations we must have rules and methods. To learn the rules and to develop new methods we must study numbers by themselves, regardless of the object which they represent. Such numbers are called *abstract*. Digits, by themselves, are abstract. The next simplest class of numbers are the *integers*, or numbers made up of one or more digits, such as 33, 4,000, and 2,950. These are termed " whole " numbers, as opposed to the various fractions and other classes of numbers.

One of the most useful of these additional classes of numbers is the " negative number." Suppose, instead of thinking of addition as placing

| TABLE OF ROMAN NUMERALS SHOWING THEIR ARABIC EQUIVALENTS | | | |
|---|---|---|---|
| I . . 1 | XI . . 11 | XXI . . 21 | D . . 500 |
| II . . 2 | XII . . 12 | XXX . . 30 | DC . . 600 |
| III . . 3 | XIII . . 13 | XL . . 40 | DCC . . 700 |
| IV . . 4 | XIV . . 14 | L . . 50 | DCCC . . 800 |
| V . . 5 | XV . . 15 | LX . . 60 | CM . . 900 |
| VI . . 6 | XVI . . 16 | LXX . . 70 | M . . 1,000 |
| VII . . 7 | XVII . . 17 | LXXX . . 80 | MM . . 2,000 |
| VIII . . 8 | XVIII . . 18 | XC . . 90 | ĪV . . 4,000 |
| IX . . 9 | XIX . . 19 | C . . 100 | V̄ . . 5,000 |
| X . . 10 | XX . . 20 | CC . . 200 | ĪX . . 9,000 |

more objects on a heap, and subtraction as taking objects away, we work our problems with a button sliding on a wire, marked as below, with o for the middle, thus :

etc.   $-5-4-3-2-1$   $0+1+2+3+4+5$   etc.

Numbers to the right are marked $+$ and those to the left are marked $-$. To start, the button would stand at o. Now suppose we are given the addition, $3+2=$? First we set the button at $+3$. Then, since the next number is $+2$, we move the button two more places to the right (always to the right when the sign is $+$). The button stops on $+5$, which is the answer.

Now take the problem $5-2=$? The symbol " 5 " without a sign means $+5$, and that is where the button is; " $-2$ " means " move two places to the left " (always to the left when the sign is $-$). The button stops at $+3$, which is the answer.

So far we have accomplished nothing that we have not done in simple addition and subtraction. But now take the problem $3-5=$? (This might arise if a boy having three shillings wanted to buy a book costing five shillings and wished to know how much more money he would need.) If we used only positive or plus $(+)$ numbers, and the idea of addition and subtraction as merely adding to or taking from a heap, we could not solve the problem; for we cannot take a greater quantity from a less. But with our button and wire, the problem is easy. We move the button three places to the right, and then five places to the left, and it stops on $-2$. (In the case of our boy buying the book, this would mean he got the book, paid his three shillings, and instead of having three shillings he is two shillings in debt.) Minus 2 $(-2)$ is a *negative* number—that is, it is a number less than 0; so the minus $(-)$ sign now means not only an operation (" subtract," or, on our wire, " move to the left "), but, affixed to a number, it means a number which is less than zero or nought.

Another type of number is one which has a definite value, though this value is not known. A good example would be if we are given some facts indicating the number of pupils in a schoolroom, and are asked to find how many there are. To do this we say, " Let $x$ stand for the number," then proceed with our calculations to find what integral number it is that $x$ represents. Such a number as $x$ is called an *algebraic* number, and methods of calculating with such numbers form the subdivision of mathematics called algebra (q.v.). Only the integral and fractional numbers of definite known value (called *arithmetic* or *natural* numbers), such as 0, 27, $\frac{1}{2}$, $1 \cdot 25$, and another class called *transcendental*, are used in arithmetic. The transcendental numbers are constant quantities such as the one denoted by the Greek letter $\pi$ or $pi$, the ratio of the circumference of a circle to its radius, having the value about $3 \cdot 1416$.

**Nuremberg.** In this city of Bavaria, Germany, the old walls and turrets, the great gateways flanked by massive towers, the irregular streets and quaint gable-faced houses, all dated back hundreds of years to the time when Nuremberg (German *Nürnberg*) was the gateway through which passed many of the rich goods of the East on their way from Venice to northern Germany.

An old house that was one of Nuremberg's most treasured relics was that in which Albrecht Dürer, the great artist, lived. It was Dürer and his companion artists of the Nuremberg school who made the city " the home of German art." At St. Sebald's Church were the Twelve Apostles, the masterpiece of Peter Vischer, Germany's famous worker in bronze.

High above the ancient section of the city towered the old castle with its underground passages and its medieval chamber of horrors.

The city was one of the most important Nazi centres, and the annual Congress of the National Socialist Party was held there. An enormous stadium was built in 1938, where Adolf Hitler (q.v.) made a speech every year until 1944. As a result of repeated Allied air-raids, and heavy shelling and bombing in the final attack by United States forces in April 1945, the old city was practically obliterated and the stadium damaged; the city was captured on April 20. St. Sebald's Church was gutted and other ancient buildings, including the Rathaus, were left in ruins.

The trials of civil and military leaders of Nazi Germany, together with certain Nazi organizations, were held at Nuremberg from November 20, 1945, to October 1, 1946. An Allied Military Tribunal was established for the purpose, its members representing the United Kingdom, the United States, France and the Soviet Union. The accused who had been arrested (with the exception of Bormann who had disappeared and Hitler and others who had committed suicide) after the surrender of Germany on May 8, 1945, were charged with crimes against humanity, war crimes, committing crimes against peace and of planning and waging wars of aggression. The population of Nuremberg at the outbreak of the Second World War was 430,800. (*See* National Socialist Party; Nazi).

**Nursing.** It is only within the past 100 years that trained nursing has become a recognized profession. During the Middle Ages religious organizations cared for the sick, and today the Sisters of Mercy are one of several such bodies animated by the same motive. It was not until the great and noble work of Florence Nightingale (q.v.) that the impetus was given to the movement that lifted nursing to importance and dignity as a profession for lay members of the community.

There is probably no occupation for women which presents a wider field than does nursing. While the term originally meant little besides taking care of the sick, it now includes a large number of public and social duties. Public health work, school health supervision under a doctor, inspection of housing conditions, the direction of medical gymnastics, manual and electrical massage are only a few of the avenues of service open to the trained nurse, and the list is constantly growing.

The larger general hospitals conduct training-schools for nurses. Application for entrance is made to the superintendent, and after a medical examination the applicant is received for a term of probation. The age minimum is between 18 and 19 years. If, in the few months of probation, the applicant proves physically and mentally able to meet the demands of the profession, she signs an agreement to remain for the rest of the required term. Student nurses receive board, lodging, and laundry free, and a small salary sufficient to buy the uniforms and a few simple necessities. Lectures covering anatomy, physiology, and all departments of medicine are given by the physicians and surgeons, and the sister tutor teaches bandaging and dressing of wounds, etc. Some hours each day are spent on duty in the wards.

Nurses have to pass two examinations, the preliminary and final, before they can be registered as qualified nurses by the General Nursing Council. District nursing is a branch of the profession often attractive to those who desire a more independent form of work. It was started in an organized form in 1859. The most comprehensive district nursing organization is the Queen's Institute for Nurses. A recent development in nursing is the industrial nurse, attached to a large factory and looking after the health of the workers.

**Nuthatches** AND CREEPERS. The nuthatch (*Sitta caesia*) is an expert bird gymnast. He can hop head-first down a tree trunk, or sideways round it, quite as easily as he can hop up it, for he is furnished with sharp claws well adapted for holding to rough bark, and his feet spread wide to aid his grip. He is also an expert at cracking nuts, as his name—in its older form, " nuthack "—implies. First, he fixes the nut firmly in a crevice of the bark of a tree, and then, swinging his body well forward, delivers tremendous blows with his long beak on exactly the right spot of the shell.

Nuthatches are small birds related to the creepers, and, like them, they feed on insects as well as on nuts, and make their nests in the holes of trees or in crevices of rocks, usually plastering up the opening with clay or mud to the required size.

The European nuthatch, *Sitta europaea*, is a common woodland bird in England. It is about

*Eric J. Hosking*

**A NUTHATCH COMES HOME**

When the nuthatch has found a nesting-hole in a tree, as here, the bird sometimes reduces the size of the opening by plastering the edges with mud or clay until the entrance is small enough to make a tight squeeze. The nest itself is little more than a layer of dry leaves.

five inches long, is bluish-grey above, buff-white below, has a slate-blue and white tail, and the sides are chestnut-red. In summer it feeds chiefly on insects, and in the autumn on nuts, beech mast, hard seeds, and the stones of berries. Often you can hear the nuthatch's strong clear whistle even when you cannot see the bird itself. In winter it comes close to the house for food.

Creepers are found in temperate regions. They are small birds with long slender bills, and get their name from their habit of creeping up tree trunks, where they find the small insects on which they feed. The British tree creeper, *Certhia familiaris*, is somewhat smaller than a sparrow, brown above and brilliant white below. It creeps and darts about the tree trunks, sometimes uttering a soft, squeaky little song. It makes a nest of leaves and chips behind broken bark or in crevices.

**Nutmeg** AND MACE. The fragrant spice we call nutmeg is the seed of the nutmeg tree, *Myristica fragrans*, a bushy evergreen, with straight trunk about 25 feet high, the branches extending nearly to the base of the tree. The flowers are small and yellow, and have a fragrance resembling that of the lily of the valley. From the fruit of this tree is also obtained mace, another popular spice, which has an unmistakable and characteristic flavour of its own, quite unlike that of nutmeg. " The nutmegs must be able to smell the sea " is a common saying, referring to the fact that there have been few successful plantations of nutmegs at any distance inland. Indeed, most of them are on tropical islands, chiefly the Banda Islands of the Netherlands East Indies, which are almost covered with nutmeg plantations.

The nutmeg tree blooms and bears fruit continuously. The fruit, which is pale orange in colour and about the size and shape of a pear, splits open, revealing the crimson fibre—the mace—which covers the seed.

When the fruit is collected, the fleshy husk is removed, and the mace is stripped off, dried, and prepared. Then the seed shell is broken off, revealing the hard kernel, the nutmeg of trade. The latter is elliptical in shape, about an inch long, and irregularly ridged. From the smaller nutmegs " oil of mace " is prepared by crushing. The fleshy part of the fruit preserved in syrup is a favourite sweetmeat in its native place.

**Nuts.** Many primitive peoples who had not yet learned to catch fish, hunt game, or till the soil subsisted chiefly on roots, berries, and nuts. Of these, nuts were the most concentrated and nourishing, for they are especially rich in oil and protein. Furthermore, the nut " meats " were preserved inside airtight shells and could be kept to be eaten through the long cold winters when other foods were unavailable.

Today only a few nuts are of much importance as food, but a constantly growing number provide materials useful in industry. A true nut has a hard shell; it does not split open when ripe; and the kernel or " meat " is in one piece. Walnuts, pecans, butternuts, hazelnuts or filberts, hickory nuts, beechnuts, acorns and chestnuts are among the true nuts in the botanical sense. But in the popular sense many other fruits and seeds are called nuts, including the peanut ,(*see* Ground-nut) ; and the almond and the coconut, which are drupes or stone fruits.

One of the most delicious is the Brazil nut which grows in Brazil and other parts of tropical South America and in French Guiana. These three-sided nuts grow in clusters of from 14 to 28, tightly packed inside a hard round shell, the colour of a coconut and as big as a man's head. When the nut is ripe it crashes to the ground, and since the trees are 100 or more feet high it is best to stay out of range. Oil from the Brazil nut has medicinal properties, and is also used for lubrication and lighting; the husk provides a kind of oakum for caulking ships.

Pistachio nuts are oily and have a distinctive aromatic flavour. Their pale green kernels are enclosed in a thin-parted shell. They are seeds of a tree native to Asia Minor.

The queer kidney-shaped cashews have long been popular. Cashew trees flourish on land unfit for farming and where other trees could not exist. India is the chief producer. The shell of the cashew is a valuable source of oil used in swift-spinning engine mechanisms, such as magneto armatures.

Tung nuts of China, now raised extensively in Florida, contain an oil used in paint and varnish manufacture. From the meat of West Africa's palm nuts is expressed an oil used in soap-making; the endosperm is a source of oil for colouring imitation butter. The edible cohune nut, from a palm of Honduras, also supplies a lather-producing oil. When the soap oil shortage occurred during the Second World War (1939–45), Brazil's rich-lathering babassu nut, hardest nut in the world, became extremely important in soap manufacture. Another source of oil is the dika nut, which is the seed of a West African mango tree.

The candlenut, found throughout the tropics, is one of the most versatile of all nuts. It can be lighted and used like a candle. A purgative oil can be squeezed from its raw meat. If roasted, it is a good food for man and cattle. Gru-gru nuts

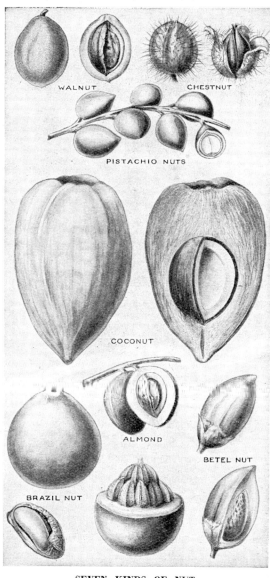

**SEVEN KINDS OF NUT**
There is often considerable difference between the appearance of nuts when growing on the tree and when displayed in the fruiterer's shop. Here some are shown whole and also cut open. Notice how Brazil nuts are packed closely together in a big outer shell.

of South America and the West Indies yield a violet-scented oil used in soap-making. Necklaces made of them keep their fragrance for many years. Brazil's cumara nut supplies an oily perfume.

Buttons are made from the "vegetable ivory" obtained by drying the kernels of the tagua or corozo nut and of the coquilla nut, both of South America. This vegetable ivory is exceedingly hard and can be sawed, carved, turned on a lathe, coloured, and polished. Oil from the fresh kernels is a good substitute for coconut oil in soap-making.

The Chinese litchi nut has inside its brittle shell a "meat" that resembles a strawberry when fresh and a raisin when dried. Betel nuts are chewed as a narcotic. Cola or kola nuts, native to Africa and cultivated elsewhere in the tropics, contain much caffeine and are used as a basic ingredient in making cola drinks.

**Nymphs.** To the imaginative Greeks of ancient times all the seas, streams, fountains, caves, hills, and woods seemed to be peopled with divinities. The fair young goddesses who presided over various parts of the world of Nature were called nymphs. In the springs, fountains, brooks, rivers, and lakes dwelt the Naiads, beautiful water nymphs. The Oceanids (daughters of Oceanus) were nymphs of the great sea which was believed to surround the whole earth. The Nereids were the nymphs of the Mediterranean, clad in flowing green robes; of their number was Thetis, the mother of Achilles. The Oreads, or mountain nymphs, were the constant companions of Artemis, the huntress goddess. The unfortunate Echo (q.v.) was an Oread. Every tree was believed to have its own nymph, called a Dryad or Hamadryad, who was born when the tree began to grow, dwelt in it, suffered if it was mutilated, and sickened and died when the tree withered and perished. Although Dryads were subject to death, they remained young while they lived. The word nymph is sometimes used to describe a stage in the development of certain insects.

# O

**Oak.** Long ago forests of oak covered large areas of England and central Europe, and although they have been gradually cleared with the spread of farming, the oak remains among the most important trees of France, Germany, and southern Russia, supplying quantities of valuable timber. There are more than 200 species distributed over the temperate parts of Europe, Asia, North America, and northern Africa, a few species extending into the tropical Andes, the Himalayas, the Philippine Islands and Borneo.

All oaks bear acorns, a fruit peculiar to these trees. The acorn, borne in a "cup," consists of a tough skin enclosing two cotyledons, equivalent to the two first leaves of most seedling trees, and the germ, the real seed. These cotyledons supply the early food for the root and shoot of the seedling.

In former times pigs were driven out under the oaks in autumn, for they delight in acorns. Squirrels store them for food; some which they forget to eat may germinate and so we find isolated oaks cropping up in strange places; also, acorns are dropped here and there by birds, especially pigeons and jays, both of which are very fond of them.

The English oak, *Quercus robur*, is the biggest and most valuable of all. It is Britain's largest native tree, sometimes as high as 120 feet, with a girth of anything up to 60 or 70 feet. It lives to a great age, and some fine specimens still standing probably date back to the Anglo-Saxon period; one near Wetherby, Yorkshire, is considered to be 1,800 years old. This species, liberally scattered over most of the continent of Europe, is often sub-divided into two: the sessile oak (*Q. sessiliflora*), in which the acorns grow almost direct on the twigs and the leaves have longish stalks; and the pedunculate oak (*Q. pedunculata*), whose leaves have very short stalks while the acorns are on long ones, called peduncles. The sessile sort is also called the durmast oak, and the timber of this tree may sometimes be mistaken for that of the sweet chestnut.

The next most important European oak is the Turkey oak (*Q. cerris*), which was introduced into England about the middle of the 18th century. It grows very quickly in the southern counties, but its wood does not stand weather like the English oak. You can know it by the leaves, which are deeply cut with pointed lobes and are mealy beneath; and by the acorn-cups, covered with curled scales, which give it a mossy appearance. It is a semi-evergreen.

The ilex or holm oak (*Q. ilex*), so called from its resemblance to holly (Middle English, *holin*, *holm*), is evergreen, and is useful as an ornamental tree and for affording shelter from the wind.

About 50 species of the genus are native to America. Among the best-known is the white oak (*Q. alba*), reaching a height of 70 to 100 feet. Its trunk is covered with whitish, furrowed bark, and this gives the tree its name. The bur or pin oak (*Q. macrocarpa*) is another well-known and valuable American species. The American red oak (*Q. rubra*) is perhaps the most striking. Its large, lobed leaves are pink and furry in spring, green in summer, and deep purple-red in autumn. The bark

*J. Dixon-Scott*

### TYPICAL OAK OF OLD ENGLAND

**The largest and most valuable of all the oak trees, the English *Quercus robur* sometimes reaches 120 feet in height, and it may have a girth of 70 feet. Its timber was once in great demand for building ships for the Navy, for it is among the most durable of woods.**

H. Bastin

**FRUIT OF THE OAK**

The acorn, held in its ' cup,' consists of a casing enclosing two cotyledons from which the seedling gets its first food. As these acorns are on longish stalks this is a ' pedunculate ' oak ; the leaves have very short stems.

is dark brown, thick and furrowed. This species of American oak is often grown in England.

The wood obtained from the oaks varies greatly from one species to another. English oak is of superior commercial value, the heartwood being tough, hard and close-grained. It excels most wood in durability, defying drought and moisture, and is almost indestructible when under cover. The sapwood, though highly valued, is less durable. Though English oak is usually too gnarled and difficult to work well for ornamental purposes, for structural work—beams and roof-timbers—the wood excels.

Eric J. Hosking

**OAK-APPLES OR GALL-NUTS**

Produced on oak trees by insect parasites known as gallwasps or gall-flies, which lay their eggs in the tissues of the twigs, oak-apples are hard brown excrescences in which the young insects develop.

The hard galls, or gall-nuts, sometimes called oak-apples, found on oaks are produced by gallflies or gall-wasps which lay their eggs in the tissues of the twigs. The tissues swell up at the point of puncture and form firm nut-like structures, inside which the young insects develop. Each kind of gall-fly or gall-wasp produces a different kind of gall. Oak-galls contain much tannic acid, a substance once much used in the manufacture of ink and the preparation of leather. At one time oak-bark was largely used for tanning.

**Oats.** "A grain which in England is generally given to horses, but in Scotland supports the people." This is the definition of oats given in the dictionary written in the 18th century by Dr. Samuel Johnson. "True enough," was a Scotsman's ready reply to this gibe, " and where will you find such fine horses as in England, or such fine men as in Scotland? " Oats indeed are valuable as muscle builders. The oat grain contains more crude protein than does maize, and exceeds wheat and nearly equals maize in fat content.

The world's production of oats approaches that of maize and is about equal to the wheat crop. Oats will thrive on poorer soil and in wetter, colder climates than other grains, hardy varieties being grown almost up to the Arctic Circle. In the bleak climate of northern Scotland, Alaska, Russia, and Siberia, oats are a staple food crop. Common northern oats cannot be successfully raised in warm regions such as the countries bordering the Mediterranean, which grow red oats instead, this kind requiring less moisture.

The wild oat, considered by some to be the ancestor of common oats, is distinguished by long reddish-brown hairs at the base of the glume or scale protecting the kernel, the long twisted and bent " awns," or spikes at the tip of the grain, the closely covered and distinctly articulated kernels, and delayed germination. The cultivated variety originated apparently in central Europe, and probably was not known to the ancient Egyptians, Hebrews, Greeks, and Romans. Oats were first known as "pillcorn" in England.

Man consumes large quantities of oats in the form of rolled oats or oatmeal, and oats are used as food for live stock, particularly horses. Oats are grown also for pasture or for hay. Oat straw is fed to stock, used for stock bedding and returned to the land, or used to make paper, for packing, and for stuffing mattresses.

Many varieties are cultivated. They differ principally in the form, colour, or

H. Bastin

**OATS**

The feathery appearance of oats makes it easily distinguishable from wheat or barley. It thrives on poorer soil than other grains.

thickness of the grain, in the length of the straw, and in the time needed for ripening. All varieties of oats are hardy, and are practically free from insect pests or plant diseases except rust and smuts; but plant breeders have developed varieties which are highly resistant to or immune from rust or smut, besides being productive early.

The oat is a cereal grass of the genus *Avena.* Wheat, rye, and barley are members of one subdivision of the grass family which bear their seeds in spikes; oats, however, stand alone, the grain being borne in a panicle, a branching head. There are two main classes of common oats—the spreading oats with a panicle branching in all directions, and the side, horse-mane, or banner oats, with branches extending from only one side of the stem. An interesting kind is the so-called "animated" oat (*Avena sterilis*) with a twisted awn which absorbs moisture in wet weather and untwists, moving the grain.

THE OLD OBSERVATORY AT GREENWICH, LONDON

Greenwich Observatory, headquarters of the Astronomer Royal, was founded by Charles II in 1675, on a hill in Greenwich Park. Through there runs the zero meridian of longitude used in charts and maps, and from here, too, is still reckoned what is known as Greenwich Mean Time. In 1946 it was decided to move the Observatory to Hurstmonceux Castle, Sussex, owing to the impurity of the London atmosphere and the lightness of the sky at night.

*Fox*

## Observatory.

The first observatories were the ancient temple towers on the banks of the Rivers Tigris and Euphrates, where the early Chaldean priests sought to penetrate the mysteries of the heavens to fix the dates of their religious ceremonies. A modern observatory, with its mosque-like domes, reminds us of those earliest temple-observatories, but the dome is simply a roof for the huge telescope—with its mirror sometimes as much as 200 inches in diameter—with which the astronomer studies the heavenly bodies.

Setting the telescope for a night's work is an interesting operation. First, the astronomer touches a button or lever which, by means of electric motors, wheels the big instrument round to the part of the sky which he wishes to study. Another lever shifts into position the dome itself, which rests on rollers, and the shutter is thrown back, opening up the slit through which we see the heavens. In some observatories ladders are employed to bring the observer to the eye-piece; in others motors move the floor itself up or down; at Mount Palomar, California, the observer actually rides on the 200-inch telescope.

To keep the instrument pointed to the star we are studying, we must constantly move the telescope. This is owing to the rotation of the earth, which makes the stars appear to rise and set in the same way as the sun does. Today we move our telescope by clockwork which causes it to follow the star.

The combined stand and mechanism by which this is made possible is known as an equatorial mounting. The telescope is fastened to a graduated circle, called the declination circle. The axis of this circle is attached at right angles to the axis of another graduated circle called the hour circle. The hour-circle axis is pointed to the pole in the heavens, and the hour circle is parallel to the celestial equator. The result of this combination of axes is a universal joint, making it possible to point the telescope at any part of the sky.

We know that a watchmaker has a difficult task to make an instrument that will keep accurate time to small fractions of a second. And now consider that the clockwork of the telescope must be strong enough to move an instrument weighing 20 or more tons, and delicate enough to permit the astronomer to adjust it by hand so as to keep a spider thread $\frac{1}{6000}$ of an inch in diameter constantly cutting in two a star image that is $\frac{1}{8000}$ of an inch in diameter.

If we visit a great modern observatory we find that besides the telescopes there are other complex and interesting instruments. One of the most important of these is the spectroscope (*q.v.*) by which we learn the elemental composition of the sun and stars. Another is the spectroheliograph, by which astronomers can photograph parts of the sun that could formerly be seen only at the time of an eclipse. In many observatories special telescopes which move only in a north and south plane are used for making time-fixing observations of stars crossing the meridian. Telescopes mounted in this way are known as transit instruments.

In our visit to the observatory we are sure to find the astronomers spending more time at their desks than in the operation of their instruments. That is because a majority of the actual observations are now made with photographic attachments. With a photographic plate it is often possible to get results in a few minutes that would require hours to work out with observations made by the eye. The camera is attached at the eye end of the instrument, and the

# STAR-WATCHING AT MOUNT WILSON OBSERVATORY

H. J. Shepstone

An observer is seen at the eye-piece of the huge telescope at Mount Wilson Observatory in south California, United States. The reflecting mirror measures 100 inches in diameter, weighing about five tons, and the instrument was the largest of its kind until surpassed by the 200-inch reflector built for the Hale Observatory on Mount Palomar, also in south California, and installed in 1947. The Mount Wilson Observatory is 6,000 feet above sea level, and materials for its construction had to be brought nine miles up steep mountain tracks from Pasadena.

delicate clockwork keeps the great tube pointed at the star as long as necessary to get a full exposure.

For several years the great observatories of the world have been engaged in a co-operative project of photographing the whole heavens. This chart of the sky will comprise more than 44,000 separate photographs. A study of such photographs is of the greatest importance in astronomical work; many new stars have been found by this means.

The Royal Observatory at Greenwich was founded by Charles II in 1675. In 1946 it was decided to move it to Hurstmonceux Castle, Sussex. The impurity of the London atmosphere and the brightness of the sky at night due to street lights made this necessary. The meridian of Greenwich will still be used as a basis for longitudes, and Greenwich Mean Time will still be reckoned from the old observatory. All ships' chronometers are set by, and regulated to keep, Greenwich time, thus affording navigators a

certain method of determining longitude east or west of the Greenwich meridian. The observatory at Edinburgh is also a royal observatory. Oxford, Cambridge, and London Universities have important astronomical observatories.

The Yerkes Observatory of the University of Chicago is notable for its 40-inch telescope, the largest *refracting* telescope in actual operation. The 100-inch *reflecting* telescope in the Mount Wilson Observatory, California, was the largest of its kind but is now surpassed by the 200-inch reflector built for the new Hale observatory belonging to the California Institute of Technology, on Mount Palomar.

In Great Britain there are also meteorological observatories: that is, observatories for studying the weather. The most important of them are at Kew, the central meteorological observatory of Great Britain, and at Eskdalemuir in Scotland. (*See also* Astronomy; Telescope).

# EXPLORING *the* VASTNESS *of the* SEAS

*Fascinated by the mysteries of the great ocean depths, scientists are adding to our knowledge of life in the sunless underworld of salt water that covers so much of our earth's surface.*

**Ocean.** The oceans fill five huge basins, and together they cover about 70 per cent of the earth's surface. If the sea were 2,000 feet deeper, and the land 2,000 feet lower, there would be nothing left on earth but a few hill-tops in a wilderness of water.

Of the five oceans, the Pacific is the largest. It has an area of more than 60 million square miles, and covers a larger surface of the globe than all the continents. Off Mindanao, Philippine Islands, it is over 35,000 feet deep. The Atlantic covers some 30 million square miles, and the Indian Ocean 28 million square miles. Both the Arctic and Antarctic Oceans are much smaller, but the figures for these are uncertain, as large areas of them are frozen.

The waters of these oceans cover at least 140 million square miles ; and their volume is 14 times that of all the land above sea-level. Their average depth is about 12,000 feet. The whole volume of water in the oceans, if it were frozen into one ball, would form a globe 850 miles in diameter. There are oceanic areas as large as Canada where no satisfactory soundings have been taken; but we know that the beds of the oceans are not so varied as the surface of the continents. Though they have mountain ranges, plateaux, and vast lowland plains, they are mostly without the hills and valleys which characterize the land.

For sounding the ocean's depths the old-fashioned lead and line has been largely discarded for electrical devices such as the sonic depth-finder and the fathometer, by which the depth can be quickly ascertained. These measure the speed of sound waves through sea-water, and the depth is estimated by the time required for a sound sent from the ship's bottom to echo back from the ocean floor. A series of such soundings taken from the shore out to sea shows that the sea bottom slopes gently downwards out to distances of from 10 to 150 miles. This slope is called the continental shelf. From the edge of it the sea-bottom drops very much more steeply to the floor of the oceans. A sounding line may some-

times be combined with a grab to obtain specimens of the deposits on the ocean floor.

All the water in all the seas contains salt, the same salt as that which we use in our food. Mixed with it are many other minerals. In a gallon of sea-water there is, on the average, a little more than a quarter of a pound of salt. The saltest water is found where, owing to the heat, evaporation is greatest—for example, in the Red Sea. The waters of the Great Salt Lake in Utah, U.S.A., and the Dead Sea of Palestine, contain a great proportion of salt, as the rivers there bring down an abnormal amount of salt.

In every cubic mile of ordinary sea-water there is about 100 million tons of salt—washed out of the land by the streams and rivers that flow to the sea. The rivers, indeed, are dumping salt into the ocean at the rate of over 150 million tons a year, so that the water is becoming more salt all the time. If the salt could be extracted from the sea and dried, there would be enough to make a layer more than 100 feet deep over the whole earth.

The water of the oceans contains many of the mineral substances found on land. Even when we cannot extract them directly, we find them in sea-weeds and sea creatures. Such an unlikely substance as silver has been found deposited on the copper-sheathed bottoms of ships, and it has been estimated that there must be tons of silver in the sea. Companies have been formed to try to get gold from sea-water, but none of them has succeeded.

Even the depths of the sea have not been too dark and inaccessible for scientific research, and we know a lot about the life of the ocean bottom. There are men who have spent their lives exploring, though indirectly, the deepest parts of the oceans.

The ocean deeps present a challenge to Man. He has risen high into the air, has cut out vast cities in the coal under the surface of the earth, but the deep sea checks him; the pressure of the waters is greater than the human frame can bear. Even with Dr.

W. Beebe's metal globe, called the bathysphere, which is stout enough to withstand the crushing pressure, we are limited to a depth of a few hundred fathoms; his book entitled Beneath Tropic Seas, published in 1928, gave a fascinating story. The boldest diver in the ordinary diving suit dare not descend more than about 100 yards out of 10,000, and even this journey into the water-world is full of peril. The first man to go down 90 yards into the sea was protected by a metal helmet and a metal breast-plate, and air was pumped down to him by six sailors; he had a terrible struggle to get back alive. The undercurrent at the bottom of the sea swung his lifeline about and entangled it, so that he could not reach the surface, and for 20 minutes he fought for his life in the ooze and darkness. Then, after 90 minutes of struggle, they raised him to the top.

Imagine the weight of the Atlantic Ocean at the depth of a mile or two! With $2\frac{1}{2}$ miles of water over their heads human beings would be crushed, if let down suddenly. On each square inch of their bodies there would be a pressure of about $2\frac{3}{4}$ tons.

Even with scientific instruments our knowledge of ocean depths has been built up slowly and in curious ways. One of the first ocean explorers filled a glass tube with air, sealed it, wrapped it in thick flannel, and put it in a copper tube, making tiny holes at the top and bottom of the tube so that water might enter. Then he sent the tube, filled with air, down 12,000 feet. When it came up the thick copper tube was pressed flat, and the glass was reduced to powder. That was the experiment which revealed the fact that the pressure on every square inch of the body of a creature at that depth is more than 20 times greater than the pressure in the average locomotive boiler.

From all this experience men for a long time believed that there could be no life down in the black ocean depths. No sunlight ever reaches more than a few hundred feet below the surface, and where there was no sunlight, it was once thought, there could be no plant life. Where there was no plant life there could be no animal life, and so the great floor of the ocean, it was reasoned, must be a desolate region of emptiness and death. Then a strange thing happened. A telegraph cable in the Mediterranean broke at a depth of more than 7,000 feet, and when the broken ends were raised it was found that the cable was overgrown with an astounding variety of living

LIGHT ENDS.
EXPOSED PLATE
SHOWS NO IMAGE

500 FATHOMS

1 MILE

1000

PRESSURE INCREASES AT RATE OF 1.18 TONS TO THE MILE

1500

2 MILES

AVERAGE DEPTH OF OCEAN

2000

2500

3 MILES

3000

4 MILES

3500

4000

5 MILES

4500

5000

6 MILES

DEEPEST POINT SO FAR DISCOVERED, OFF MINDANAO, P.I., 35,400 FEET. PRESSURE ABOUT 15,800 POUNDS, NEARLY 8 TONS PER SQUARE INCH

5500

6.7 MILES    5900

**OCEAN DEPTHS**

If you could drop Mt. Everest into the deepest part of the ocean it would not reach within a mile of the surface.

creatures. It was certain that they had been alive in the dark and icy cold of the sea bottom (always near the freezing point of fresh water), with tons of water bearing down upon them.

Now men have devised new means of exploring the ocean depths. They let down nets and iron hooks; instruments for measuring the temperature of the water; and bottles which open when they touch the bottom, fill with water there, and then close so that water at higher levels cannot enter. They make great nets which touch the bottom of the sea and close up tightly as soon as they are raised above the floor; in these nets it is possible to bring up from the bottom living creatures from a realm that no man has seen. They let down weighted plummets with a sticky substance on the base, which brings up a sample of the ocean bed.

And what men find is that in this kingdom of the deep sea—a kingdom of darkness and almost freezing cold —is a great variety of life. The floor of the sea, it may be said, is a mena-gerie of animal life; for there are no plants at the great depths, where the light essential to such life is com-pletely absent. Most deep-sea creatures are more or less blind, or have enormously enlarged eyes, and many are more or less phosphorescent, or glowing.

Explorers declare that on some parts of the floor of the sea there are millions of little creatures shining like glow-lamps, and the discoveries that have been made in this direction are among the most interesting of all. The phosphorescent light of deep-sea creatures—like the light of the glow-worm—is made without waste of heat. Even some sharks are able to light up their paths through the deep sea with a white and heatless radi-ance. Certain glands in their skin give out a sticky substance, and it is this substance that makes them shapes of living light. It is doubtful, however, if the shark ever penetrates to the deepest ocean beds, and it is the deep-sea animals which are most phosphorescent.

Animals can live under the great pressure of the deep sea because the pressure inside their bodies equals the pressure on the outside. A tin-can could never be crushed by pressure from without if the pressure outward on the inside was equal to the pres-sure inward from the outside.

Though the inhabitants of the ocean abysses are able to live under a vast load of water, they are liable to strange accidents. If, in searching

# HOW THE DEEP OCEAN WATER IS EXPLORED

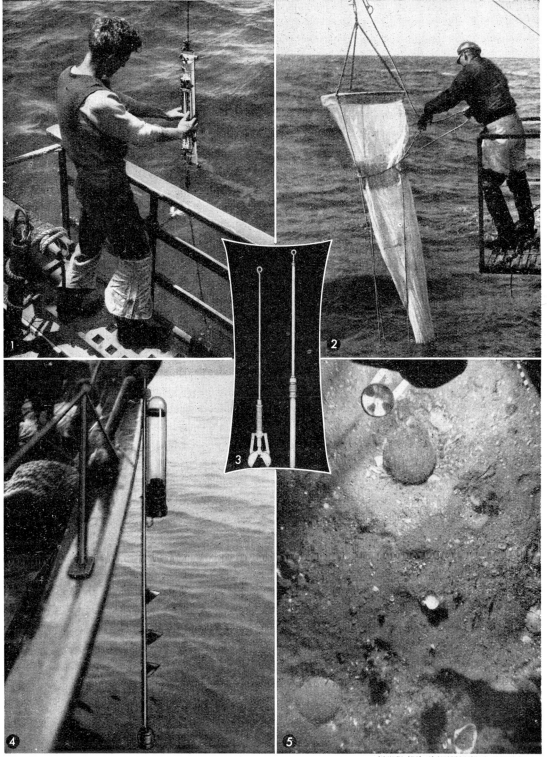

Scripps Inst. of Oceanography, Woods Hole

Since men cannot yet descend to the lower depths of the ocean they send exploring instruments down instead. 1. To determine the temperature at various levels a deep-sea thermometer is lowered. 2. This net with its opening and closing device will gather samples of the life at any desired depth. 3. These instruments bring up samples that show the composition of the ocean bottom. 4. An underwater camera is lowered in a glass tube; the lamps on the rod provide light for the picture. 5. A photograph taken with such a camera 400 feet down.

**OCEAN LIFE OBSERVED IN SAFETY**

Seated in a submerged metal chamber connected to a boat by a flexible, telescopic metal tube, a mother and her baby gaze at the wonders of the ocean, while a leopard shark investigates the thick glass window through which this photograph was taken. The 'studio' was used for photographing sea-life off the Bahamas, West Indies.

animal life must have plant life to feed on. This is as true of the animals of the deep as of the cattle of our pastures. But we have seen that no ordinary plants can grow in the sunless underworld of water. How, then, is animal life maintained there? A few years ago no man was able to answer this question properly, and it was not until much progress had been made in the study of the microscopic forms of life that the secret of the ocean abyss was fully revealed.

We now know that in addition to the conspicuous inhabitants of the ocean which can be seen with the naked eye, the waters teem with swarms of microscopic creatures. According to their general habits, all organisms in the seas can be placed in three groups. The *benthos* comprises plants and animals which live on or are attached to the sea bottom. Such, for instance, are the rockweeds and corals, and many of the worms and molluscs. Organisms which live in the water itself, like the fishes, whales and seals, and move about actively from place to place, are the *nekton*. Still other forms—most of them so small that they can be seen only with the aid of a microscope—which float about passively, drifting here and there at the mercy of the tides and currents, are known as *plankton*. This last group of plants and animals was almost unknown until the middle of the 19th century, but we now know that it is the primary and all-important group upon which all other ocean life depends.

A traveller over the sea may think he is sailing through an almost barren waste of waters because no life may be visible. But let him draw a fine net through the water and examine the catch of "scum" under a powerful microscope and he will be astonished at the wealth of living creatures revealed. He would see diatoms, which are single-celled creatures called algae encased in a glasslike box, so graceful and varied in shape and so delicately ornamented that no artistic jewelry of the finest manufacture could surpass them in beauty. He would see protozoa, too, with elegant shells of mineral material, strange larvae of all sorts, tiny crustacea, and other forms of life which only an expert could recognize and name. Minute as are these organisms, many others yet smaller he could not see because they escape through the meshes of even the finest net.

It is these diatoms and other green plants of the plankton which make the sea a pasture. They are to the fishes and other animals of the ocean what grass is to the cattle in the fields. They live in the surface waters, and especially in the shallow water zone where they can use the sunlight in building up

for food, they rise some distance above the floor of the sea, the gases of bladders by means of which they swim expand under the reduced pressure, and they become lighter. Up to a certain point the muscles of their bodies can resist this tendency to go floating upwards, and the deep-sea fish that has not completely lost control of itself can win its way back to its home in the dark, cold water.

If, however, it travels too far towards the world of sunlight its muscles are not strong enough to drive the body down. The fish continues to swell, and is gradually killed in its long voyage to the surface. Thus the deep-sea fishes are exposed to a danger that comes to no other animal in the world—the danger of tumbling upwards! That such accidents do occur is shown by the fact that some unknown kinds of fish were found floating dead on the level of the ocean long before men dreamed that life could exist at such depths. When brought up suddenly from the depths, fish sometimes explode because of the expansion of gases within their bodies when pressure from the outside is greatly reduced; and this adds to the difficulty of finding out what these creatures of the great deeps are really like.

The problem which has for many years perplexed the explorers of the deep sea is the question of how life is maintained so far below the surface. What do the creatures of the abyss feed upon? It is clear that they cannot keep alive merely by eating one another, although all but the smaller forms of really deep-sea fish are carnivorous. Yet, basically, all

# OCEAN MARVELS SEEN THROUGH THE MICROSCOPE

Resembling a landscape in some world of fantasy, this illustration shows what the microscope revealed in a rocky pool, in a spot less in area than the nail on one's little finger. Most of these creatures are so small that the naked eye could not perceive them, but a powerful microscope reveals them in all their fascination. With the aid of modern instruments we are gradually learning more and more about all the strange types of animal and plant life in the seas, and to read the story of evolution—a story which began hundreds of millions of years ago in ocean waters. It is from creatures such as these that scientists are slowly putting together the story of how higher forms came into existence, for many of them are the present-day descendants, practically unaltered in appearance and habits, of the first forms in which organized animal and plant life appeared on our planet. Truly the ocean is a fascinating book of life, when even little drops of water hold such wonders as these.

# THEY CARRY THEIR SEARCHLIGHTS WITH THEM

Scientists have thus far, in spite of all their knowledge, been unable to produce light without at the same time wasting much energy in creating heat. Man could save vast sums if the secret of the phosphorescence of these fish which dwell in the ocean depths could be discovered. It seems strange that numbers of deep-water fish thus always carry a light with them, when others have not even eyes. Some of these fish are also remarkable for their formidable array of teeth. The angler fish (bottom right) has a kind of rod and line, with an illuminated bait, which it can dangle in front of its mouth to attract its prey. This is an artist's impression of life in the ocean depths.

the top of thi⋯
stood the city⋯

Chief amor⋯
called Woden⋯
centre of the ⋯
and the seaso⋯
in his hand h⋯
of the ash Yg⋯

Though Oc⋯
and the unde⋯
could not con⋯
of the frost g⋯
lay to the ne⋯
waged unceas⋯
and Odin lon⋯
him greater t⋯
gods to trium⋯

The only ⋯
acquired was⋯
knowledge. ⋯
beard, guarde⋯
drink of its v⋯
saw Odin ap⋯

" What do⋯
from sunny /⋯

## HO⋯

**Odysse**⋯
most famous⋯
against the ⋯
called Ulysse⋯
rugged little⋯
Greece, and,⋯
chieftains, w⋯
Penelope an⋯
went to battl⋯
joining the ⋯

When the⋯
found Odyss⋯
which he h⋯
took the bab⋯
of the furrov⋯
him. Odyss⋯
showing tha⋯

When Oc⋯
refuse to go⋯

**A** DVERSE⋯
wander⋯
to the south⋯
days land v⋯
them shorev⋯

The men⋯
found an en⋯
gave them t⋯
had such m⋯
forget their⋯
Forgetting, ⋯
land, they v⋯
food, and li⋯

their bodies. They are like little chemical factories, employing the heat and light of the sun in making food from the minerals dissolved in sea-water. They multiply at an astonishingly rapid rate and form the basic food for all other ocean animal life. Even when they die their bodies fall into the depths of the ocean and provide food for the animals there; that, indeed, is partly the answer to the question of how the smaller deep-sea creatures get anything to eat.

The value of the diatom does not end with death. Its crystalline case endures for millions of years. Through ages past diatom shells have accumulated on the ocean floor in immense deposits. Great geological convulsions have frequently raised these ocean beds and they have become dry land. And the land thus produced provides valuable soil for farming and a variety of purposes.

The life of the oceans is most abundant in the surface waters down to about 600 feet, is less abundant in the intermediate depths, and becomes more plentiful again, at and near the bottom. A whitish or greyish ooze covers about one-third of the ocean bottom, and there are vast areas of red clay formed by the decomposition of shells and by pumice and other volcanic matters, and wind-blown dust, which has landed on the surface of the sea and gradually sunk. These and other types of clay and ooze are distributed according to the depth of the ocean floor, and definite types may be expected in particular districts and at certain depths.

If we consider merely the quantity of living matter in the oceans the imagination reels before it, but a few figures help us to realize it. It has been estimated that in the North Sea there are 10,000 million fishes; and there is a record of a fishing fleet that once ran into a school of mackerel that was 50 miles around.

What helps us to form some notion of the number of fish in the sea is the number of eggs which various fishes lay. Even a little sprat deposits about 5,000 eggs, and in the roe of a cod are found some eight million. A common herring lays about 25,000 eggs, a big halibut as many as three and a half million, and the turbot is calculated to lay 14 million eggs. Imagine the number of fishes laying eggs at these rates, and one might think that the products of the sea are inexhaustible. But even so, proper methods of conservation are needed. (See Marine Life).

The circulation of the ocean waters is caused by three types of current: (1) those caused by differences in density of sea-water, due to changes in temperature and salt-content ; (2) those caused by winds ; (3) tidal currents and currents associated with internal waves. The first type is the most important, and the great ocean currents such as the Gulf Stream and the equatorial currents belong to it. As a moving mass of surface water strikes the continents—such as, for example, South America— it is divided, part of it being turned northward and part southward. The northward part of such a current is the Gulf Stream of the North Atlantic. The corresponding current in the Pacific Ocean is

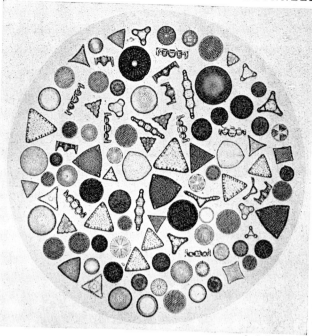

## DIATOMS OF THE OCEAN

These minute forms of vegetable life, here magnified 65 times, are present both in the sea and in ponds. Oozes are formed from their skeletons, which have contributed to many of the flinty oozes of the past that are now become beds of flint. (See colour plate facing page 2620.)

*J. G. Bradbury*

the Japan Current. These warm currents of ocean water moving northward warm the air over them, and in middle latitudes this warmed air is carried over to the continents on the east sides of these oceans, because the prevailing winds there blow from the west. This is one of the reasons why Scandinavia and Alaska are so much warmer than the same latitudes on the east side of the continents.

From the bodies of ice in the polar regions large volumes of ice-cold water are poured into the oceans and move southward along the east side of continents but presently sink beneath the surface. These plentiful supplies of cold water from the polar ice keep the temperature of the ocean low. The warm currents in the oceans give rise to fogs, which may prove extremely troublesome to navigation. The warm air over the Gulf Stream, for example, is heavily charged with moisture, and when it is carried by the winds beyond the Gulf Stream over colder waters the moisture in the air condenses into fog.

The water evaporated from the sea is borne to the land, and some of it is condensed and falls as rain or snow. More than 6,500 cubic miles of water falling on the land is yearly sent back to the sea by rivers, carrying with it salts and earthy matters.

**O'Connell,** DANIEL (1775–1847). Throughout the 18th century Ireland was in a very unhappy state. Roman Catholics, the overwhelming majority of the nation, were forbidden to take any part in politics; Protestant landlords, most of them residing in England, lived on rents paid by the poor Irish peasantry; and there were laws preventing Irish manufactures from competing with English ones. In 1782 the Irish Parliament had been

granted re
but after
rebellion
accepted
Union w
Britain
the prov
which lei
only with
ant repre
in the Bi
liament
minster,
Daniel
nell was
Cahir
county F
land, on
1775, an
cated at
and Dou
He stu
and in i
practisir
he set a
Catholi
cluded
Parliam
exclude
gained
organiz
Catholi
powerfu
In 18
the Bri
tinued i
Membe
in 1828
more fo
the nat
Rather
Parliar
pation
Cathol
at We
Irela
O'Con
agitati
that is
Parliai
later c
He als
which
tenant
Catho
ing tit
last
O'Coi
○ d c
mile
wheat
of th
River
lookir
Odes:
Socia
Sovie
Sit
of th

sailors to destruction on the rocks. Odysseus well knew his peril, for he had been forewarned by Circe.

The winds abated; the sea fell quiet; the air was so still that it seemed as though the gods in heaven listened for that celestial harmony. Odysseus stuffed the ears of his men with wax; but, wishing to hear the Sirens himself, and yet to escape with his life, he had himself bound to the mast. Then he ordered his men to row quickly past the island where the Sirens sat and sang.

He knew that if he was lured to their land he would die there. Yet such was the charm of their voices that when their clear-toned song reached his ears he begged and commanded his men to set him loose. But, strictly obeying his first orders, they bound him yet more securely, and continued rowing until that fatal shore was left behind.

### The Perils of Scylla and Charybdis

Odysseus had not gone another 100 leagues before he faced another peril against which Circe had warned him. When he saw smoke above a mountain peak, heard a yelping as of dogs, and the rushing of waters in a whirlpool, he knew that his galleys were nearing that part of the Mediterranean now known as the Strait of Messina, between Sicily and Italy. There the sea foamed and roared between rocky walls. On one side the sea monster Scylla dwelt in a cliff whose top was shrouded in storm clouds ; when a vessel passed she stretched out six hideous heads from her cave and snatched six sailors from the deck. On the other side rose the dread cliff of Charybdis, and from under a fig tree dwelt a still more fearful monster with a huge mouth. Thrice every day she sucked in the sea, and then poured it forth seething like a huge cauldron on a fire. Any passing ship was hurled to destruction ; there was no escape.

Choosing the lesser peril, Odysseus steered closer to Scylla. With her terrible long-necked heads, she seized six of the rowers, bore them writhing to the cliff, and devoured them. " And this was the most pitiful thing that mine eyes have seen of all my travail in searching out the paths of the sea ! " said Odysseus when he recounted the many adventures he had met with.

Further woe awaited them, for Odysseus's men devoured the sacred cattle of Helios, the sun god, on the Isle of Thrinacia, and for this offence Zeus (Jupiter) destroyed their ship by a thunderbolt. All were lost save Odysseus himself, who floated for nine days on a raft, and on the tenth day was cast ashore on the Isle of Ogygia, far off in the western sea.

Here in this far land dwelt the sea nymph Calypso in a lovely grotto-palace. Around the cave was a wood of alder and poplar and sweet-smelling cypress, and purple grapes hung over the entrance. Sparkling fountains mingled their plashing with the songs of birds, and violets carpeted the ground.

But Odysseus had no mind for these pleasant sights nor yet for the sweet singing of the nymph. Eight years he dwelt there with her, sorely against his will, but she loved him and would not let him depart. She would have made him immortal if he would have remained with her. But he refused the boon and besought the gods to let him return to his island of Ithaca, where dwelt the wife and child he had not seen for so many weary years.

At last the goddess Athene (Minerva) interceded with her father Zeus on behalf of the hero, and the father of gods, acceding to her request, sent a messenger to Calypso bidding her send him thence. The nymph dared not disobey. She gave Odysseus an axe and tools to build a raft, and with her own hands wove him sails, and showed him the star by which he should steer. So the great-hearted Odysseus embarked once more.

But Poseidon, ruler of the deep, was not yet minded to give Odysseus rest from his troubles. Seeing him near the end of his journey, Poseidon roused all the winds of heaven against him, so that he was buffeted about for many days. At length, when his raft had been dashed to pieces, Odysseus stripped off his clothing and swam for two days and two nights, Athene helping him, until a wave cast him up on the island of Scheria, the country of the Phaeacians, a people like to the gods. Overcome with weariness Odysseus crept into a thicket of olive trees and, lying down on a pile of leaves, fell asleep.

It happened that same night that Nausicaa, daughter of Alcinous, king of this land, had a dream in which Athene appeared to her, telling the maiden that her wedding day was near, and bidding her arise at daybreak to wash the garments of the family that all might have seemly raiment. Early the next morning the clothes were heaped on a wagon, and Nausicaa with her attendants drove out of the city to the bank of a clear-flowing stream to do their work.

### Princess Nausicaa Meets the Hero

When all the linen had been washed and spread in the sun to dry, Nausicaa and her maidens bathed and dressed their hair. Then they ate and played games. In a mischievous mood she threw a ball so that it bounded from the rocks and splashed into the river. The girls screamed, so that Odysseus awoke. When he appeared, they fled in terror, for he was covered with salt and matted seaweeds, and for clothing he had only a leafy bough which he held before him. But Nausicaa stood firm, because she was the daughter of a king.

" Oh, maiden," the stranger said, " I know not if thou art a princess or a goddess, for never did I see so fair a flower as thou. Have pity and give me a garment to cast about me ! "

When he had bathed himself, and donned one of her brother's tunics that she had brought to be washed, the stranger glowed with such beauty and grace that all marvelled at him. After the maidens had given him food and drink Nausicaa bade him follow to her father's palace.

A feast was spread for him in the great hall. When a blind bard began to sing of the Greek heroes of the Trojan war, the illustrious stranger was overcome with emotion. At last he announced himself as Odysseus, king of Ithaca, and companion in arms of Achilles, Agamemnon, Menelaus and other heroes of that war. There was much excitement, for everyone had heard of the brave, wise and clever Odysseus, who by the artful trick of the wooden horse had captured the city of Troy.

While a ship was being made ready to carry him home, Odysseus told of the dangers he had survived. Here was the hero of Nausicaa's dreams, but he was not for her. With her heart swelling

**NAUSICAA AND HER MAIDENS AT PLAY**
This princess of the mythical island of Scheria dreamed that she was to prepare for her wedding by washing the garments of the household, and she went with her attendants to a stream to do this. While they were at play they woke Odysseus, who had been sleeping in a wood near by.

*From the painting by Abel Boué*

she stood, tall and pale and lovely, by a silver pillar, listening to his tales.

"Farewell, stranger," she said, with a touch of sadness at the thought that she would never see him again. "Remember me for a time, because thou owest thy life to me!"

"All my days for evermore shall I do thee worship as a goddess," Odysseus warmly returned, "for thou, lady, hast given me my life."

The next evening king Alcinous put the hero on board a ship and gave him many gifts. Then the vessel departed.

Twenty years had now passed since Odysseus had set out for Troy. His son Telemachus had grown to manhood. His wife Penelope still awaited him, never ceasing to pray the gods for his return. No wandering beggar came to Ithaca but she questioned him for tidings of her husband.

When Odysseus had been away 17 years, suitors for Penelope's hand had appeared. Five score and more of the nobles of Ithaca and of the neighbouring islands came with their minstrels and servants, and took up their abode in the palace of Odysseus. Each one hoped to wed Penelope, so that he might rule over Ithaca and possess the flocks and herds, fields and vineyards of Odysseus. Telemachus was his father's heir; he was but a youth, without powerful kindred to defend him. So these intruders wasted the wealth of the absent king, plotted against his son, and persecuted his unhappy queen.

The wise Penelope devised a plan to delude her suitors. She must weave a winding-sheet for Odysseus's age-stricken father Laertes before she could wed again, she said, and so she retired to her chamber and sat at her loom. But the cloth grew not in length, for what she wove by day she unravelled by night. For three years this

stratagem stood her in good stead, and then her wooers discovered it. More insolent than ever after they learned the trick she had played upon them, they pressed Penelope with increased persistence to make her choice of a new husband.

But the day of reckoning was at hand, for at last the gods had brought Odysseus safely to his homeland. That he might not be known, the goddess Athene changed him into the form of an old beggar in rags, and in this guise he was received and made welcome in the hut of Eumaeus, a swineherd, who had been his faithful servant. Thither came Telemachus, who had just returned from a fruitless quest for news of his father. Revealing himself, Odysseus embraced his son, and then the two took counsel together how they might kill the hated suitors.

In his beggar's disguise, Odysseus went boldly to the palace. No man knew him. But his faithful dog, Argus, worn out by age and neglect, recognized his master, and wagged his tail in joyful greeting just as he was breathing his last.

The unsuspecting revellers received the returned king with insults, ridicule and violence. When they had departed for the night Odysseus and Telemachus collected all their weapons so that the suitors might have no means of defence when the hour of vengeance came.

Then Telemachus departed to his chamber, leaving his father alone in the hall, devising plans for the morrow. Presently the wise Penelope came down to sit by the fire. Long she questioned the beggar, hoping for news of her absent lord. He told her that he had recently seen Odysseus, who was now at last almost home.

Overjoyed, Penelope returned to her chamber. She called the old servant who had nursed the hero in his infancy and bade her attend to the wants of the beggar. As the aged nurse was washing his feet she recognized a scar on his instep, and she cried out with joy. But the king bade her keep his secret.

The next day the wooers returned to their revelry. After the banquet Penelope took down the large bow of Odysseus from its place on the wall and declared she would wed the man who could bend the bow and send an arrow through 12 rings suspended in a row.

One after another the suitors attempted the feat, and failed. Only the despised beggar was able

**FAITHFUL ARGUS WELCOMES HIS MASTER HOME AGAIN**
In his beggar's disguise, Odysseus went boldly to the palace. No man knew him. But his faithful dog Argus, worn out by age and neglect, recognized his master and wagged his tail in joyful greeting, just as he was breathing his last.

to bend the bow and send the arrow to its mark. Then, suddenly stripping off his rags, Odysseus leaped to the threshold and sent arrow after arrow whizzing among the panic-stricken suitors. The doomed men fell one upon another, and when his arrows were spent Telemachus brought him shield and spear. With fury the king and his son renewed the slaughter, and ceased not until the last man of the suitors was slain.

The bodies were carried out, the air was made sweet with incense, and Odysseus was clad in his royal robes. Then the old nurse was sent to Penelope with the joyful news of her husband's return.—*Retold from Homer.*

**Oedipus.** (Pron. ē'-di-p*us*). Perhaps the most tragic hero in Greek legend is Oedipus, king of Thebes in ancient Greece. His father Laius, king of Thebes, learned from an oracle that his own son should kill him; and he therefore pierced and bound the feet of the new-born babe and caused him to be exposed on a mountain, in order that he might perish. But a shepherd found the child, and named him "Oedipus," meaning "swollen foot." The child was taken to the king of Corinth, who, having no heir, reared him as his own son. When Oedipus was grown to manhood he learned from an oracle that he would kill his father and marry his own mother. To escape so dire a fate he decided to leave home, for he believed that the king and queen of Corinth were his parents.

On the way to Thebes he met a chariot in which sat an aged man. An attendant who preceded it ordered Oedipus out of the way and a combat followed, in which Oedipus slew both master and servant. So the first part of the oracle was fulfilled, for the aged stranger was Oedipus's real father, King Laius.

About this time the terrible Sphinx appeared in the neighbourhood of Thebes (*see* Sphinx). This monster put to all who passed her a riddle, killing and eating those who failed to answer it. Many were devoured, for no one was able to give the correct answer. To rid themselves of this scourge the Thebans offered the vacant throne and the hand of Queen Jocasta (widow of Laius) to whoever should succeed in overcoming the monster.

" What animal," asked the Sphinx when Oedipus confronted it, " walks on four legs in the morning, on two at noon, and on three at night ? " Oedipus replied, " Man, for in the morning, the infancy of his life, he creeps on all fours; at noon, in his prime, he walks on two feet; and when the darkness of old age comes over him he uses a stick for better support as a third foot." Thereupon the Sphinx dashed herself over a precipice and perished.

Oedipus then became king and was married to Jocasta, but soon the country was devastated by a plague. An oracle promised relief when the murderer of Laius should be banished. Oedipus then learned from a seer that he himself had killed his father and married his mother. In horror he put out his eyes, while his mother hanged herself. Blind and helpless, Oedipus wandered away with his daughter Antigone.

After the abdication of Oedipus, his two sons, Eteocles and Polynices, became joint rulers of Thebes, but Eteocles, desiring to rule alone, seized the reins of government and expelled Polynices from Thebes. Thereupon Polynices went to the city of Argos, where he married the daughter of Adrastus the king, and enlisted the latter's help against Eteocles.

Adrastus and the army of Adrastus attacked Thebes with great valour. Finally Eteocles, grieved to think that all this bloodshed was on his account, offered to decide the issue by single combat with his brother. The duel took place just outside the city walls, both Eteocles and Polynices being mortally wounded and dying on the field.

Creon, brother of Queen Jocasta, now became king of Thebes. He gave Eteocles burial with royal honours, but decreed that the body of the younger brother should lie unburied. Antigone dared to defy the royal edict, and performed the funeral rites necessary to give his soul rest.

The Greek dramatist Sophocles tells the story of Oedipus and his children in the trilogy of Oedipus the King, Oedipus at Colonus, and Antigone. In this last play he gives a beautiful picture of the noble character of the maiden. When Creon asks: " And thou didst dare to disobey these laws ? " Antigone replies:

Yes, for it was not Zeus who gave them forth,
Nor Justice dwelling with the Gods below,
Who traced these laws for all the sons of men:
Nor did I deem thy edicts strong enough,
That thou, a mortal man, should'st over-pass
The unwritten laws of God that know not change.
They are not of today nor yesterday,
But live for ever, nor can man assign
When first they sprang to being.

But Creon was unmoved. Even the pleas of his son Haemon, who loved Antigone, were of no avail, and she was condemned to die by being buried alive in a cave. Haemon succeeded in entering the vault, but too late, for Antigone was already dead ; whereupon he threw himself on his own sword and expired beside the body of his beloved Antigone. His mother, Eurydice, in her grief, killed herself. Thus Creon was doomed to a widowed and childless old age.

**Offaly.** Formerly known as King's County, the name given it in 1556 in honour of Philip II of Spain, the husband of Queen Mary, this county of Eire is in the province of Leinster, covering some 772 square miles. It lies almost wholly in the central plain of Ireland, except a small part in the south-east where the beautiful Slieve Bloom mountains form the boundary between it and County Laix. The River Shannon skirts the county on the west.

The soil consists largely of bogland and light loam, but there are rich pastures on which cattle, sheep and pigs are reared. The main crops are oats, barley and potatoes. There is a dairying industry, but there are no manufactures.

The county town is Tullamore (population, 5,000). Other centres are Birr, Clara and Edenderry. In the county are the ruins of Clonmacnoise. The population of the county is 52,000.

**Ohio.** Of the two mighty tributaries that flow into the Mississippi, the River Ohio, though shorter in length, is vastly more important than the Missouri, for its navigable waters traverse more than 1,000 miles of the greatest industrial and farming district in the United States, furnishing means of transportation for many of the raw materials and

*The Louvre, Paris; photo, Alinari*
**OEDIPUS ANSWERS THE SPHINX'S RIDDLE**
This painting, by the French artist Ingres (1780-1867) shows Oedipus solving the riddle propounded to him by the Sphinx. According to the story, those who could not answer her riddle paid with their lives.

manufactured products of the region. It serves such industrial centres as Pittsburgh, Cincinnati and Louisville.

This river is formed by the junction of the Allegheny and Monongahela rivers at Pittsburgh in Pennsylvania. It flows thence in a south-westerly direction, until it reaches Cairo, where it joins the Mississippi. The Ohio forms the north-western boundary of West Virginia, the northern boundary of Kentucky, and the southern boundaries of Ohio, Indiana and Illinois. Its waters are gathered from numerous tributaries which drain the neighbouring country.

Formerly the course of the river was impeded by falls and sand-bars and by trees growing up from the river bed ; from June to November the waters were too low to accommodate craft of any size. These conditions have been gradually overcome. Canals and locks have been built around the falls, the largest of which are at Louisville, Kentucky, the river being virtually one long canal, with a channel nine feet deep.

The State of Ohio, with an area of 41,222 square miles, is bounded on the north by Michigan and Lake Erie, by Pennsylvania and West Virginia on the east and south-east respectively, by Kentucky on the south, by Indiana on the west. Except in the south-east, where it is hilly, the surface is mainly rolling plain. The Maumee, flowing into Lake Erie, is the chief northern river; the southern part is watered by many tributaries of the Ohio.

Although Ohio is essentially a manufacturing State it produces large quantities of maize, wheat, hay, oats, tobacco, fruit and vegetables ; stock-breeding and dairy-farming are important industries. The coalfields comprise an area of 12,000 square miles. Natural gas, oil, limestone and china clay are among the minerals obtained. Leading manufactures include iron and steel products, flour, rubber goods and chinaware.

The capital of the State is Columbus (population 306,000). The largest city is Cleveland (population 878,300). Cincinnati, Toledo, Akron and Dayton all have a population of more than 200,000. The State, Ohio, Cincinnati and Miami universities are among the higher educational institutions.

The first settlement was made in Ohio in 1788, and by the end of the 18th century 15 towns had sprung up. The State was admitted to the Union in 1803. The population is 6,907,600.

# LIQUID FUELS *from* MOTHER EARTH

*The introduction of mineral oil for lamps was the first great boon the oilfield gave us. Since then we have seen petroleum in many forms harnessed to our needs ; and Man has learnt to ' make ' oils from coal and coke.*

**Oil.** The development of the petroleum industry in just under a hundred years has been most spectacular. It has grown from nothing into an industry which lubricates and provides power for our motor-cars, tractors, ships and aircraft. During this time the world output of petroleum has about doubled every eight years. Yet " rock oil," as petroleum was once called, has been known for thousands of years.

The flaming wells and springs of Baku, Russia, have been known since time immemorial. Seep-ages of oil from the ground were known in various parts of the world before recorded history. The solid form, asphalt, was used as a cement in Babylon and Ur of the Chaldees, and the Egyptians used it in preserving their dead. The use of oil as fuel was known to the Greeks and Romans.

The crude oil was not, however, suitable for household use as it smoked and had an unpleasant odour; but in 1847 Dr. James Young made illuminating and lubricating oils from Derbyshire coal. He patented the process in 1850. Later he used the paraffin wax he obtained as a by-product to make candles.

In the early 1850s petroleum from Burma was distilled in England, and at the same time coal oil was distilled from coal and crude petroleum in North America. This oil displaced the whale-oil used hitherto. In 1859 Edwin L. Drake " struck oil " in Pennsylvania. The first well was 69 feet deep. After this, development was rapid in North and South America and in Mexico, Russia, Iran, Iraq, Netherlands East Indies, Rumania, Japan, Burma and other parts of the world.

Crude petroleum belongs to the group of substances known as bitumens, and these include natural gas and solid asphalt and mineral wax (ozocerite), as well as liquid petroleum oil. The colour of petroleum varies from pale yellow through greenish brown to black. In consistency it varies from a thin liquid like petrol to a semi-fluid state like that of tar.

Several suggestions have been made to account for the way in which oil was formed. It is generally considered today as being the result of decomposition of animal and vegetable remains, probably in the absence of air. Recently small amounts of derivatives of chlorophyll (green matter in plants) and haemin (occurs in red colouring matter of blood) have been found in oil; this supports the idea of its formation from living matter. Such decay of matter probably took place in conjunction with types of sedimentary rocks such as clays and limestones—the " source " rocks. These source rocks are too compact to make it possible to exploit them for oil, but fortunately the oil has often migrated into other kinds of rocks—e.g. sandstones and dolomites, known as " reservoir " rocks.

This migration may continue a considerable distance from the source rocks. The oil and gas tend to rise to the highest level in the reservoir rocks, and so pools are formed provided that the reservoir rocks are bounded by impervious rocks such as shales, which are known as " capping " rocks.

Oil formation has been quite common on the earth; but it becomes available to Man only when the conditions are just right, and where there are source rocks, reservoir rocks and the right geological formation (e.g. capping rocks). Only then are oil pools formed so that the oil can be recovered and used. The formation of oil pools *in* the earth is rather like the collection of water into ponds and

# MODEL IN MINIATURE OF A MIGHTY OIL WELL

GLACIAL CLAY

1440 FT. OF ROCK OMITTED

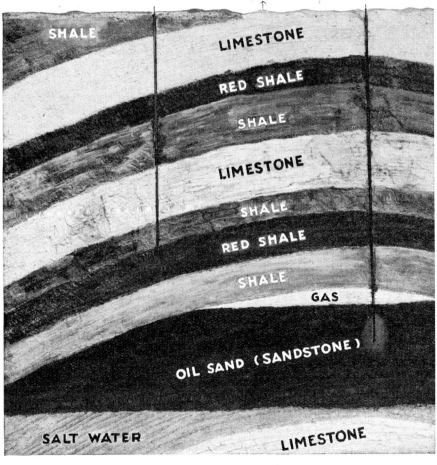

SHALE

LIMESTONE

RED SHALE

SHALE

LIMESTONE

SHALE

RED SHALE

SHALE

GAS

OIL SAND (SANDSTONE)

SALT WATER      LIMESTONE

YOU can see how an oil well works by looking at this picture of an oil well model from the Field Museum of Natural History, Chicago, shown at the left.

The model has two borings going down through the rock layers. The boring at the right is completed. It has reached the oil in the porous Kirkwood oil sand at the bottom, a cavity has been made at the foot of the bore by blasting, and the oil is being pumped out by the small triangular pump jack at the top of the shaft. These pump jacks are commonly used in Illinois and some other states instead of derricks. This model shows a well in the Lawrenceville oil field, Illinois.

The power to run this pump jack and others not shown comes from the power house in the centre. In it is a horizontal wheel, 18 feet wide, and an eccentric operating rods running to the jacks.

The boring at the left represents a new well being drilled. Above it is a derrick operating a simple "churn drill." A steam engine drives a large "walking beam," from one end of which the heavy steel drill and drill rod is suspended. The motion of the beam causes the drill to move up and down in the well. In the derrick are tools to clean the shaft and pipes for casing it.

Notice how the layers of rock have an upward bend, or "anticline," which forms an inverted basin in which the oil has been caught. It is held there by the upward pressure of the salt water on which it floats. The hard shale above it will not let it escape.

variety of chemical processes. By "cracking" kerosene or gas oil (which is done by heating with catalysts), the molecules can be split up into smaller ones, and "cracked" petrol results. The importance of this process can be seen if we remember that the yield of petrol obtained by distillation ("straight-run" petrol) is about 25 per cent to 30 per cent of the crude oil; but, by obtaining further petrol by cracking, the yield can be increased to 60 per cent of the crude oil.

Besides giving more petrol the cracking process produces gases (including ethylene) which can be separated into their individual components and used to produce a large variety of substances. These substances include plastics such as "polythene," used in the electrical industry as an insulator; solvents, including acetone and alcohol, and glycol (used in "anti-freeze" for motor-cars), and many other substances. During the Second World War (1939–45) these gases were used in the U.S.A. and in Germany to produce synthetic rubber (Buna rubbers).

This making of chemicals from petroleum is an important new industry and has grown up mainly in the last 20 years. Hydrogen (q.v.) can also be produced from cracked gases and used for many commercial purposes, such as making synthetic ammonia and for hydrogenation.

The cracked gases as well as the natural gases from the oil wells can be made to polymerise (a process in which small molecules join up to form larger ones), and the result is motor spirit. Polymerisation is brought about by heating the gas under pressure with catalysts.

This short account of the chemical treatment of petroleum may help to show how, by manipulation of the crude oil, any fraction can be increased or decreased in amount. If petrol is short it can be made from other fractions. If, later on, heavier fuels such as kerosene or gas oil are required for jet engines, they could be increased in amount at the expense of the petrol yield.

Besides these materials, made from gases, lubricating oils can be cracked to give smaller molecules which can be treated with sulphuric acid to give synthetic soaps and detergents (q.v.). These have many important uses both in the home and in such industries as the textile industry.

Petrol is now produced from coal by hydrogenation. The Billingham plant for this process (see illustration in page 2429) was in operation before the war of 1939–45. Later it was changed over to make petrol from creosote. Coal from (A) is taken by a conveyer (B) to storage at (C). The mills (D) grind it with heavy oil (S) from the bottom of the "converter" (G), forming a fine paste. Injectors (E) pump this at a pressure of 3,700 lb. per square inch through the heater (F), where it mixes with the hydrogen from (P) and goes into (G), where the actual hydrogenation occurs at a temperature of 842° F. The products and gases go through the cooler (H) to the "catch-pot" (I), which separates the gases and liquids, distributing them to (P) and (J) respectively. The pump (K) forces the liquid through the furnace (L) into the fractionating column (M). Petrol is here distilled off and condensed at (N) before being stored in the tanks (O) ready for shipment.

This plant was used throughout the Second World War mainly for production of aviation spirit (about 100,000 tons per annum). Another plant was built at Heysham in the early years of the war, but instead of coal heavy petroleum oils were hydrogenated to produce aviation spirit. During the war the Germans produced nearly all their aviation spirit (3 to 4 million tons a year) by the hydrogenation of coal.

In 1925 two Germans, Fischer and Tropsch, discovered a process by which carbon monoxide (CO) and hydrogen would react at a temperature of about 200° C., and in the presence of iron, cobalt or nickel catalysts, to give hydrocarbons ranging from methane to waxes. By suitably adjusting the process the right size molecules of hydrocarbons could be made, so that petrol resulted. By 1939, Fischer-Tropsch plants capable of producing 750,000 tons per annum from coke had been built in Germany. Although this figure was not reached during the war period, as priority was given to the hydrogenation of coal, the Fischer-Tropsch process was varied to make many useful "petroleum" products such as lubricants, synthetic soaps (ordinary soap made from fats was very short in Germany) and waxes. The German plants were destroyed by aerial bombing in 1944. Although the Fischer-Tropsch process has still to be developed in Great Britain, large scale use of it is contemplated in the United States for the manufacture of motor spirit.

The carbon monoxide and hydrogen mixture (called water gas) used in the Fischer-Tropsch process is made by passing steam over red hot coke. The chemical equation is so simple (although the details of the process are not) that it is worth noting:

$$H_2O + C = CO + H_2$$
steam    coke    carbon    hydrogen
monoxide

Oil is obtained from deposits of shale, and there is a shale oil industry in Scotland. But, compared with the large quantities of petroleum oil produced, only tiny amounts are made by distillation of shale. The home industry started with Young's manufacture of coal oil in 1850 (already mentioned). It was largely eclipsed by the American petroleum industry and is kept going by a customs duty on imported petrol. In the last few years (since 1941) oil wells have begun to be operated in England and Scotland.

Vast reserves of oil shale exist in the Rocky Mountains in the U.S.A. and elsewhere, and when the oil-fields of the world become exhausted this shale oil may come into its own.

At a typical oil-field the oil goes first to the operator's "field tank"; next it is pumped to the "tank farm." Thence it passes into the pipes by which it is transported to the refineries. These pipes are from two to eight inches in diameter in the field lines where the oil starts, and from six to twelve inches in the main trunk lines. Gravity and pumps are both used. Pumping stations are ordinarily from 25 to 40 miles apart. The pipe line is much cheaper and more satisfactory than tank cars, and it has almost entirely superseded other methods of land transport in all parts of the world where oil is being produced.

Refined oil is generally distributed by tank railway cars and tank motor trucks. It is shipped in great steel tank steamers, built for the trade and owned by the oil companies. Not only does it save space and labour to use the vessel itself as an oil-container, but the risks of fire are diminished because of the decrease in waste spaces where vapours can accumulate and in surfaces from which leakage and evaporation can take place. A large modern tanker may be more than 500 feet long and carry more than 4,500,000 gallons.

The fact that transport in peace and war is so dependent on oil, and that world resources are limited, is an important feature of world politics. An oil area such as that of the Middle East is likely to be coveted by all nations, and their foreign policy is directly affected by these considerations. In ancient and medieval times many wars were fought for the possession of grain-growing regions or good pasture lands ; today the possession or control of an oil-bearing region is a more likely " bone of contention."

**Oklahoma.** The Land of the Red Man —which is the meaning of the Choctaw Indian word Oklahoma—was until 1889 a country reserved by the United States Government as a last home for the remnants of various tribes of Red Indians, so that its development is comparatively recent.

The State lies between Kansas on the north, Texas on the south and west, Arkansas and Missouri on the east, and the area is 69,919 square miles. Part of the basin of the Mississippi, it is mostly plain, with the Ozark Mountains in the north-east and the Ouachita range in the south. Much of the State is arid, and the rivers, of which the chief are the Arkansas, Cimarron, Canadian and Red, are frequently waterless in summer.

Two-thirds of the area is farm land, the main crops being cotton, wheat and maize. Cattle, pigs and poultry are raised extensively throughout the State. It is, however, the development of the oil industry which has in a few years transformed little villages into fine cities, for the eastern part of Oklahoma is one of the world's richest oil regions ; the mineral was discovered in 1890. Oil-refining is the chief industry. Coal, zinc, clay, natural gas, marble, salt and gypsum are also found.

The State capital is Oklahoma City (population 204,400). Other large towns are Tulsa, Muskogee, Enid and Shawnee. The population of the State is 2,336,400.

**Olive.** Probably the earliest tree to be cultivated by Man, the olive is also one of the longest-lived. In ancient olive groves there are to be found specimens 20 feet around and from 700 to 1,000 years old. The tree does not come into full bearing until it is about 30 years old, but from that time it continues to produce fruit for the rest of its life. The fruit, known as olives, which follow the white, funnel-shaped, fragrant flowers, resemble small dark-green plums.

Today, as in ancient times, the products of the olive are greatly valued for food and other purposes. Ripe and dried, olives are eaten raw in Greece ; in most countries they are eaten after pickling, either ripe or green. Pickled olives and olive oil come from a variety of the olive, *Olea sativa*. When green olives are picked from the tree they

*American Colony, Jerusalem*
**PICKING OLIVES IN THE HOLY LAND**
A woman of Palestine is here seen gathering olives, often termed the 'meat and butter' of the Palestine peasant. The tree grows in several other countries ; it is common all along the shores of the Mediterranean and is found in South Africa and New Zealand.

have a very bitter flavour, and to remove this they are soaked in lye (a solution of lime and wood ashes), and, after rinsing, are put in a strong solution of salt.

The fruit contains 60 to 70 per cent of oil, which gives it considerable value as food. In countries where olive trees are grown extensively many people extract the oil for their own use by crushing the fruit in a press similar to that used in England for making cider from apples. For the commercial production large mills are used. Before the discovery of soap, anointing the body with olive oil was a widespread habit among wealthy Greeks and Romans and among Greek athletes before exercise.

In countries around the Mediterranean, olive oil is used for cooking much as butter and other fats are elsewhere. It is highly prized in most parts of the world as a salad oil ; inferior grades provide fuel for lamps, and it is among the ingredients for making hair oil and shampoos.

Native to Southern Europe and Asiatic Turkey, the olive tree has been cultivated for thousands of years; one of its peculiarities is that it does best in soil composed chiefly of volcanic ash. The strength and fruitfulness of the tree are proverbial, and the olive branch has long been taken as a symbol of peace. The tree is mentioned in the Bible, and Palestine still has its Mount of Olives near Jerusalem. In ancient Greece it was sacred to the goddess Athene; a crown of olive leaves was part of the prize given to victors in the original Olympic Games.

The tree (*Olea europaea*) reaches a height of about 20 feet, and is covered with grey bark. Its evergreen leaves are smooth, thick, greyish-white on top and white underneath. The wood, which is very hard and has a beautiful grain, is used for ornamental cabinet work.

## Olympic Games.

The world's most important international athletic contests are the Olympic Games, in which the representatives of nearly every nation take part. Though in their modern form they date only from 1896, they may be regarded as the counterpart of the Olympic Games of the ancient Greeks.

For more than 1,000 years these Games were held in July of every fourth year in honour of Zeus, the supreme god of the Greeks. A traditional list of the victors compiled in later times went back to the Games of 776 Before Christ, and this date was later taken as a convenient basis from which to reckon time, using as units the "olympiad," or four-year period between the celebrations.

The Games were held in the valley of Olympia in Southern Greece, in which stood temples and statues designed by the finest artists of the land. Most magnificent of all the shrines was that of the father of gods himself, in which stood a colossal statue of Zeus wrought of ivory and gold by the sculptor Pheidias (c. 490–432 B.C.), and reckoned as one of the Seven Wonders of the World.

Across the sacred grove, after due sacrifice had been made to the gods, the athletes marched to the stadium, where the contests took place. At first the only event was a 200-yard race. Later this was supplemented by the *pentathlon*, a five-fold match consisting of running, wrestling, jumping, throwing the discus, and hurling the javelin. Other trials of strength, skill and endurance were added still later, including boxing and chariot races.

The prizes were simple wreaths from a sacred olive tree planted, according to tradition, by Heracles (Hercules), the founder of the Games. Thus crowned, the winners marched in procession around the sacred grove, while their admirers chanted triumphal songs written for the occasion by a famous poet. In their native cities the victors were received with extraordinary honours.

As previously mentioned, the Games were revived in 1896, to foster the ideal of "a sound mind in a sound body," and to promote international friendship, as the former Olympic Games had done in the ancient Greek world. Since that year, with the exception of the periods of the two World Wars, the events have been held at four-year intervals. More than 30 different branches of sport are represented, including track and field athletics, rowing, sailing, swimming, shooting, figure-skating, hockey and other games.

It is a remarkable fact that the victorious countries in the revived series of Games have always been found among the Northern races. Thus British, Finnish, German and U.S. athletes have all done extremely well at various times.

Many countries start training their teams for the next series as soon as the last one has finished, and they have a highly paid and fully qualified permanent coach from one series of Games to the next, who is in fact more or less a "dictator," in the sport which he is controlling. He will see to it that the right men train for the right sports, that they do not get stale, and that they do not waste time on

*After a reconstruction by Bühlmann*

**RUNNING CONTEST AT THE FIRST OLYMPIC GAMES**

In this reconstruction of the Great Stadium in the sacred plain of Olympia, Greece, we see the culminating moment of the famous foot race. On the right are the Hellanodikai, the umpires or 'Judges of the Hellenes.' The Stadium, which was just over 200 yards long, was used mainly for foot races, while chariot and horse races took place in the Hippodrome.

# OLYMPIC GAMES TORCH IN THE LONDON ARENA

*Graphic Photo Union; Olympic Photo Association*

The ceremony to mark the commencement of the 1948 Olympic Games took place in Wembley Stadium, London, on July 29, when the competing teams lined up in the centre of the arena (upper) to await the arrival of the Olympic torch which had been lit at Olympia, Greece, and then borne by warships and runners to England. In the lower photograph the last bearer of the torch is running round the arena before setting light to the Olympic Flame, which burns while the Games are in progress. On the results board at the back is set out the Olympic motto.

unprofitable methods. In this way, and by concentrating on events in which they are weakest, those countries have gradually come to the fore. Most British athletes who take part in the Games are business men and can therefore train only in their spare time.

Some countries excel in certain events. Thus, the British have produced some of the finest middle-distance runners ; the Americans are magnificent sprinters and high-jumpers ; the Swedes excel at throwing the discus and javelin ; and the Finns are among the world's finest long-distance runners.

The scene at an Olympic meeting is a great spectacle. Normally it is the practice to build a whole Olympic village where all the athletes live, the representatives of each country in their own quarter. Most of the competitors strive to arrive several weeks before the opening of the festival, in order to become accustomed to the strange air and the water. Each group, living under the management usually of one man, with also probably a non-competing captain, usually takes with it a supply of the type of food it is used to at home, as well as a cook.

There are also winter Olympic Games, held usually in the winter just previous to the other Games, in some country which provides suitable conditions. In these the contests include bob-sleighing, various ski-ing and skating races, and figure-skating for men and women.

The Olympic Games of 1948 were held in the London area in July–August; the corresponding winter sports were concluded in the preceding January and February at St. Moritz, Switzerland. Competitors from 54 countries took part, and representatives of the United States were outstandingly successful in athletics and swimming. Mme. Fanny Blankers-Koen, of the Netherlands, won three of the women's athletic events, a feat never before equalled by a woman. At the end of the 1948 Games the order of the leading nations was United States first, Sweden second, while France and Hungary tied for third place.

**Onion.** From the fragrant Easter lily to the humble onion with its pungent odour may seem a far cry; but the gap is not so great for both belong to the lily family. The odour and flavour of the onion come from a sulphurous oil, allyl.

The mildest and biggest onions are those of the white Spanish variety, which often weigh a pound or more. The potato-onion is a form that has several small irregular bulbs instead of one single bulb.

Onions have been grown for their edible bulbous roots from time immemorial ; their original home is supposed to have been in Central Asia. They belong to the same genus, *Allium*, as the milder leek, and the more pungent garlic, both of which are extensively cultivated in Britain. Chives are smaller members of the same genus; they have very attractive flowers, and the leaves are used for seasoning. Shallots have a flavour somewhat milder than garlic.

Some of the onions propagate themselves, like other members of the lily group, by bulbils, small bodies borne on the stems or among the flowers and taking the place of the seeds which often fail to ripen.

**Ontario.** The industrial heart of the Dominion of Canada, Ontario may also be regarded as the centre of Canada geographically and politically. Lying between the Provinces of Quebec and Manitoba, it connects the old part of Canada with the prairie regions of the west, and at Ottawa —an Ontario city and capital of Canada—is centred the political life of the Dominion.

The province is abundantly supplied with water-power, the chief sources being Niagara Falls, the rapids of the St. Lawrence, and the falls of the River Ottawa and its tributaries. This cheap power, with plentiful raw materials and ample transport, have made it the chief manufacturing province of the Dominion.

The southern portion is dotted with towns and cities, the most important being Toronto (*q.v.*), the capital of the province, Ottawa (*q.v.*), London, Kingston and Hamilton. Numerous railways, steam and electric, form a

**ONTARIO'S GORE PARK**

Typical of the fine layout of the modern cities of Ontario is the district around Gore Park, in the heart of Hamilton, the port at the western end of Lake Ontario. In the centre of the photograph is the Cenotaph commemorating the Canadian dead of both World Wars.

network over the region. A system of canals, chief of which are the Sault Sainte Marie, the Welland and the Upper St. Lawrence, gives additional transport facilities.

On the tongue of land between Lake Huron, Lake Erie and Lake Ontario quantities of grapes, pears, peaches, plums and apples are grown, and the region is famous for its dairy and meat products, making an enormous quantity of cheese.

North of Lakes Superior and Huron towns and cities are fewer. Formerly, people thought that this land was useful only to the fur-trader and the lumberman, but it has been discovered that hardy grains can be grown, despite the long cold winter, and the district is being settled by farmers. A more valuable source of wealth in this northern region has been found in the rich mineral deposits from which come nearly half of all Canada's mineral production. In the Sudbury district north of Lake Huron large quantities of nickel are mined. From the Cobalt region comes silver, Canada being one

> **Extent.**—Greatest length east to west, about 1,000 miles; north to south, 885 miles. Area, 412,582 square miles, including about 49,300 square miles of water surface. Population, about 4,107,000.
> **Physical Features.**—Great Lakes (Superior, Huron, Erie, Ontario) and St. Lawrence on the southern boundary; James Bay (an arm of Hudson Bay) on the north. Lakes: Nipissing, Nipigon, Lake of the Woods, and numerous smaller lakes. Principal rivers: Ottawa (tributary of the St. Lawrence), Albany, Moose, Attawapiskat and Severn (flowing into Hudson Bay).
> **Products.**—Hay, oats, wheat, maize, flax, apples, grapes and small fruit; cattle, sheep, pigs and horses; fur; butter and cheese; nickel, silver, copper, gold, iron and natural gas; lumber and timber products; iron and steel products, machinery, electrical apparatus, paper and pulp, textiles and clothing, meat products, flour and meal, leather goods and shoes.
> **Chief Cities.**—Toronto (capital, about 667,500), Hamilton (166,300), Ottawa (Dominion capital, 155,000), Windsor (105,000), London (78,000).

of the leading silver-producing countries. Copper, iron, zinc, gold —in fact, almost every useful mineral, including coal—are all found in Ontario.

North of the Height of Land, which divides the water systems of Hudson Bay and the St. Lawrence, towns disappear entirely; forests extend over most of the northern districts. Here in winter is cut spruce from which paper-pulp is made, pine for timber, and white cedar for shingles (wooden tiles for roofs) and laths. And through this region roams the fur-trader seeking the otter, the beaver and the marten.

After the close of the American War of Independence (1776–82) many British loyalists settled in Ontario, because they wished to continue to live under the British flag. In 1791 England organized the territory as the Province of Upper Canada but in 1841 it was reunited with Lower Canada or Quebec. In 1867 it was again established as a separate province, under its present name. The population of Ontario is 4,107,000.

# World-famous STORIES told in MUSIC

*You will be able to appreciate the musical beauty of an opera more fully if you are well acquainted with the story. And this chapter contains the stories of many of the most famous operas of all.*

**Opera.** Like many beautiful things in our modern world, grand opera had its beginnings in ancient Greece. The great tragedians combined music, poetry and dance to tell their dramatic tale; the actors would recite their dialogue with special intonations, while with their voices moved the music of lyre or flute, in harmony with the theme of the drama. This was not, of course, grand opera, but from it came opera, centuries later. (*See* Drama; Greek Language and Literature).

The old Greek entertainment was forgotten during the Middle Ages, but then came the Renaissance, and Europe turned back to the splendid, lost, pagan world. A group of cultivated men in Florence, called the *Camerata*, revived some of the old Greek plays, with musical accompaniment, at the aristocratic house of Bardi in 1584. Music, finding new wings in those stirring days, suggested fresh harmonies for this new-old entertainment, and poets supplied new plays. In 1600 the first opera was given in public, Jacopo Peri's musical setting of the poet Ottavio Rinuccini's Euridice; in this the ancient myth of Orpheus and Euridice was arranged so that the various characters sang the story, accompanied by a small orchestra. The opera had an enormous success.

It is sometimes erroneously stated that the first opera was Le Jeu de Robin et Marion, by Adam de la Halle, produced in Naples in 1285. This production, however, was nothing more than a

pastoral in dramatic form, with the dialogue broken by extraneous ballads; nor was any part of the drama enhanced, interpreted, or accompanied by music. Opera did not begin with this pastoral, but with the efforts of the *Camerata*.

Claudio Monteverde, one of the pioneering spirits of the period, at once recognized the possibilities of the Camerata's new plaything, and made a living work of art out of their previous wooden imitations of the Greeks. His pupil, Pietro Francesco Caletti-Bruni, better known as Cavalli, permitted the actors to delay the action and sing a song—the first operatic aria.

In so doing he nearly destroyed opera, for his successors allowed the aria to hold up the drama. For instance, a character, in a moment of great danger, might be made to sing a long and elaborate solo about his impending peril.

Even Alessandro Scarlatti, who founded the Neapolitan school in the late 17th century, was unable to give drama its proper dominance. He produced the first operas in which all the words were sung, with no recitative.

All forms of Italian art were rapidly spreading to other countries. Opera entered France with the red cloak of Cardinal Mazarin, who brought in his wake a kitchen scullion, Giovanni Battista Lulli, who became known as Jean Baptiste Lully. By a rapid rise he became head of the Royal Academy of Music, fostered the ballet in opera,

*A. Console*

A SCENE FROM MOZART'S YOUTHFUL OPERATIC MASTERPIECE

When only 26, the Austrian composer Mozart (1756–91) wrote the delightful *singspiel*, or comic opera with spoken dialogue, called Die Entführung aus dem Serail, better known today by its Italian title of Il Seraglio (The Harem). It has been produced successfully at the Glyndebourne Opera House, Sussex, where this photograph of the scene in the garden of Selim's harem was taken. A magnificent humorous character is that of Osmin, guardian of the palace.

and originated the overture. France was always inclined to emphasize the ballet and the pageantry of opera, Italy the music and the aria, while in Germany it was the drama that was the most important feature.

The downfall of the ranting and oppressive aria came only with the German, Gluck, in the 18th century. Thoroughly disgusted with the Italian operas, in which composers showed off their learning and singers their voices, he wrote operas in which choruses and solos were not allowed to bring the drama up short at an awkward moment, or interrupt its continuity.

French opera, as we have seen, emphasized pageantry and the ballet, so much so that these incidental features in many cases overbalance the development of the story. In the 20th century, however, such French composers as Debussy and his followers have given the opera, not only in France but in all Europe, the same tendency to "impressionism" that marked most work in other musical forms until the death of Ravel in 1937.

Side by side with the development of the grand opera proper, a lighter form of music drama has grown up. The humorous Neapolitans, who had never taken the heroics of opera too seriously, introduced between acts lively musical farces, often parodies of grand opera, which they called *opera buffa* (funny opera). In this type of opera the stiff setting adopted in the old classical opera is replaced by an effort to represent more closely scenes of actual everyday life, and the stilted set "recitative" and "aria" are largely replaced by swiftly moving dialogue. In England during the 18th century the ballad-opera became popular, the most notable example being John Gay's The Beggar's Opera.

A more recent development along this line is represented by the "comic opera," or "light opera" in which liveliness and bright humour are the chief aims. The work of Gilbert and Sullivan in England, and of Franz Lehar (The Merry Widow), Johann Strauss (Die Fledermaus, and The Gipsy Baron, for example), and others abroad, has made this the most popular form of opera.

In France opera buffa became the ancestor of both *opéra comique* and *opéra bouffe*. Opéra comique was not always comic but differed from grand opera only in having some of its dialogue spoken, not sung. Opéra bouffe was farcical, satirical, and light. The work of Offenbach served to crystallize the distinction between them. In Germany, opera buffa developed, in the hands of the genius Mozart, into fine productions such as The Marriage of Figaro and The Magic Flute. The German opéra comique, called a *singspiel*, includes Beethoven's Fidelio and Weber's Der Freischütz.

Great as were the improvements made by Mozart in opera proper, they had no lasting effect. The Italians slipped back under the tuneful spell of the interfering aria, though Rossini in the realm of light opera and Donizetti and Bellini in the more serious vein endeavoured to raise the level of operatic standards. Meyerbeer cleverly catered for the romantic taste of the early 19th century.

The next great upheaval came from Richard Wagner, whom many regard as the greatest operatic composer of all time. True to German preferences, he thundered with all his strength against the feebly tinkling tune, wrote his own librettos on heroic themes, made the music fit the mood and the drama dominate the entire production. All the possibilities of the instruments and singers (whose voices Wagner often used as if they were instruments) were employed to express the story. To him we owe the *leit-motif*, a recurring brief air to symbolize the return to the scene of a certain mood or a certain character. When Lohengrin comes on the stage we hear the Lohengrin theme running in the music.

Wagner's influence was felt in all countries. He had refused to call his later operas by the old name and termed them " music dramas," in order to emphasise the important part which was played by the libretto. Since his time grand opera has been more sincerely a drama set to music, and less of a musical " grand uproar " as the facetious have sometimes called it.

*A. McBean*

**IN A MODERN ENGLISH OPERA**
This scene from Peter Grimes, an opera by Benjamin Britten, which was first staged at Sadler's Wells Theatre, London, in 1945, shows Grimes, the fisherman, and Ellen Orford, the village schoolmistress, discussing the fate of Grimes's young apprentice.

In so brief a space it is possible only to mention a few of the other outstanding names on the long roll of celebrated composers of opera. These include, in France, Charpentier, Gounod, Bizet, Massenet,

*Start Walter*

**A  MASTERPIECE  BY  THE  ITALIAN  COMPOSER  VERDI**
Simone Boccanegra, composed in 1857 by Verdi, was not produced in England until 1948, when it was performed at Sadler's Wells. An account of political intrigue in Italy in the Middle Ages, its complicated story for long made it unpopular outside the composer's own country. But its music is as good as anything that Verdi wrote and, as this scene from the Sadler's Wells production demonstrates, it gives the producer an opportunity for striking stage effects.

Saint-Saëns, and Debussy; in Italy, Verdi, Boito, Mascagni, Ruggiero Leoncavallo, Puccini, Wolf-Ferrari, and Italo Montemezzi; in Russia, Glinka, Borodin, Moussorgsky, Rimsky-Korsakov, and Tchaikovsky; in Germany, Christoph Gluck, Friedrich von Flotow, and Richard Strauss. Nowadays, for various reasons, little serious opera is written. Benjamin Britten's work Peter Grimes (1945) marked an important development in English opera within recent years.

The "musical comedy" of today, which sprang from light opera, has for the most part become a mere series of farcical and spectacular scenes with songs and incidental music interspersed, and can claim no relationship with genuine opera.

The expenses of producing opera are so enormous that only the largest and most wealthy cities are able to maintain a grand opera company. However, favourite selections from grand opera are frequently broadcast, and often heard from the concert platform, and are also reproduced with great fidelity by gramophone records. Large companies also sometimes visit smaller cities after finishing their home seasons. In London, the opera seasons at Covent Garden and Sadler's Wells are ever popular. The D'Oyly Carte company keeps the comic operas of Gilbert and Sullivan alive. Two agencies—Sir Thomas Beecham and the Carl Rosa Opera Company—have done work of special importance to encourage opera in England during recent years.

To help the music-lover to follow the performance of an unfamiliar work with more understanding, synopses of the plots of many of the most important operas are given below.

# THE STORIES OF SOME WELL-KNOWN OPERAS

**Aïda.** (Pron. ah-ē'-dah). Rhadames, an Egyptian general, loves the captive princess Aïda. Through his love he unwittingly betrays his country and is sentenced to death. The Egyptian princess Amneris also loves Rhadames, and offers to save his life if he will marry her. He refuses and is placed in a subterranean vault. Aïda joins him, and there the lovers die.

Music by Verdi. Written for opening of Italian Theatre, Cairo, Egypt, 1871.

**Barber of Seville.** Count Almaviva tries to win the beautiful and wealthy Rosina whose guardian Bartolo watches her carefully, trying to keep her and her money for himself. With the aid of Figaro the barber, the Count wins Rosina, making great fun of Basilio, a music master and marriage agent.

Music by Rossini. Produced Rome, 1816.

**La Bohème.** (Pron. bō-ām'). In an attic in the Paris Latin Quarter, four friends live gaily but precariously. Rudolph, a poet, is in love with Mimi, a frail little embroiderer, and Marcel, a painter, with Musetta. The lovers quarrel and part, but are reunited when Mimi, dying of consumption, is brought back to Rudolph.

Music by Puccini. Produced Turin, 1896.

**Carmen.** The fiery Spanish gipsy, Carmen, is arrested for stabbing a companion, but so fascinates Don José that he allows her to escape. He deserts his old sweetheart Micaela and follows Carmen, who however, transfers her love to Escamillo, a toreador. Don José, madly jealous, kills her.

Music by Bizet. Produced Paris, 1875.

**Cavalleria Rusticana.** (Pron. kav-al-er-ē'-a rōōs-ti-kah'-na) RUSTIC CHIVALRY. Action takes place in one act in a square outside a church in a Sicilian town on a glorious Easter morning. Turiddu, a soldier, has just returned from war to find his sweetheart Lola married to Alfio. Turiddu then takes Santuzza, a village maiden, as his beloved; but Lola wins him back. This leads to a duel with Alfio in which Turiddu is killed.

Music by Mascagni. Produced Rome, 1890.

**Don Giovanni.** At Seville the licentious Don Juan or Giovanni, attempts to seduce Donna Anna. Her screams alarm her father, Don Pedro, the Commandant. Giovanni crosses swords with the old man and kills him. Assisted by his servant Leporello he escapes. Donna Anna, betrothed to Don Octavio, implores her lover to aid her in bringing vengeance upon her father's murderer. Meanwhile Giovanni amuses himself with Zerlina, a village girl. Donna Anna and her lover enlist the aid of Donna Elvira, whom Giovanni has abandoned, and together they plan to bring retribution upon Giovanni at a masked ball at his palace.

Donna Anna has commemorated her father by a lifelike statue erected over his grave, and Giovanni in a moment of bravado invites the statue to supper. Elvira, who still loves Giovanni, vainly attempts to warn him of approaching danger, but as she turns to leave him the guests are appalled at the sudden appearance of the statue in the banqueting hall. Giovanni is reminded of the supper invitation, but the statue explains that it has no need of earthly food. The Commandant then invites Giovanni to a banquet, and as the latter recklessly accepts he is bidden to repent. He refuses, and despite his efforts to free himself he is carried off by demons.

Music by Mozart. Produced Prague, 1787.

**Falstaff.** Libretto adapted by Boito from Shakespeare's Merry Wives of Windsor, with a little material from Henry IV, featuring the comic, boastful drunkard, Sir John Falstaff.

Verdi's last opera. Produced Milan, 1893.

**Faust.** Weary of life, Faust, an aged philosopher, is offered youth and power by Mephistopheles in exchange for his soul. Shown a vision of the lovely Marguerite, Faust signs the compact. He wins Marguerite's love, but betrays her. She finally dies in prison, her soul ascending to heaven, and Faust is carried off to the underworld.

Music by Gounod. Libretto based on Goethe's "Faust." First production Paris, 1859.

**Hänsel and Gretel.** Children of a poor broommaker, Hänsel and Gretel go out one afternoon to gather strawberries in the forest near their home. They get lost, and their father, Peter, fears that they have been ensnared by an old witch who entices children into her den and then bakes them into gingerbreads in her oven. When darkness comes on they are frightened and fall fast asleep in each other's arms. At daybreak they see before them a delightful little house made of cakes and sweets. Hungrily they nibble at the good things, until the old witch—for it is the witch's home—comes out and takes them both captive.

Hänsel is put in a cage to "fatten," as the ogress says, but Gretel helps with the preparations; she remembers the incantations used by the witch to overcome her brother. As soon as the witch's back is turned, Gretel disenchants Hänsel, who is thus freed from the cage; and together, after pushing the witch into the oven, they disenchant and bring back to life all the boys and girls who had been made into gingerbread. The parents of Hänsel and Gretel arrive to find that the old witch herself has been baked into a gingerbread cake.

Music by Humperdinck. Produced 1893.

**Lohengrin.** (Pron. lō'-en-grin). The young Duke Godfrey has disappeared and his sister Elsa has been accused of his murder. When her champion is called for, a handsome knight in a swan-drawn boat appears. He makes one important demand of Elsa: she must never ask his name or rank. On her wedding day, driven wild with curiosity by Ortrud, Elsa asks the fateful question. Before everyone, the knight announces he is Lohengrin, and departs immediately in his swan-drawn boat. In glee, Ortrud shrieks that the swan is Godfrey whom she herself has bewitched. Lohengrin is lost to view, and Elsa sinks lifeless to the ground.

Music and text by Wagner. Produced Weimar, 1850.

**Louise.** A seamstress, Louise leaves home to live with her lover Julien, an artist, in Montmartre, Paris. Hearing her father is ill, she returns home, but her parents reject her.

Libretto and music by Charpentier. Produced Paris, 1900.

**Lucia di Lammermoor.** (Pron. lōō-chē 'ah dē lam-er-mōōr'). By forgery, Sir Henry Ashton forces his sister Lucia to marry Sir Arthur Bucklaw for financial reasons. At the wedding feast her lover Edgar appears. Lucia goes mad and kills Sir Arthur, later dying herself.

From Sir Walter Scott's novel. Music by Donizetti. Produced Naples, 1835.

**Madame Butterfly.** Sojourning in Japan, Pinkerton, an American naval officer, "purchases," in Japanese fashion, a Japanese wife, Butterfly (Cho-sho-san). He sails away for three years, not knowing how seriously she has taken his love. When he returns with a wife, Butterfly stabs herself.

Music by Puccini. Produced Milan, 1904.

**Manon.** The lovely young Manon elopes with Des Grieux; but, tempted by a nobleman's wealth, she leaves him. Des Grieux enters a monastery; Manon is finally deported, as a loose woman. Des Grieux follows her, and she dies in his arms.

Music by Massenet. Produced Paris, 1884.

**Manon Lescaut.** (Pron. les-kō'). The same story as above. Music by Puccini. Produced Turin, 1893.

**Marriage of Figaro.** (Pron. fē'-gah-rō). From the second of Beaumarchais' Figaro comedies, containing similar characters as Barber of Seville (q.v.); this time it is Figaro himself who marries, amid many amusing complications.

Music by Mozart. Produced Vienna, 1786.

**The Mastersingers of Nuremberg.** (Die Meistersinger von Nürnberg). The young knight Walter von Stolzing becomes enamoured of Eva. He determines to win the Mastersingers' song contest the following day in order to obtain her as a bride, although he knows nothing of the rules. Beckmesser, town clerk, a pedantic stickler for rules and himself in love with Eva, opposes him. But Hans Sachs, a cobbler and a genuine musician, sees real inspiration in Walter's singing and favours him. At the contest Walter wins with his glorious Preislied (Prize Song).

Text and music by Wagner. Produced Munich, 1868.

**Mignon.** (Pron. mēn-yon'). A little dancing girl, Mignon is saved from her gipsy master by Wilhelm Meister, a travelling student. He allows her to follow him as his page. She is in love with him, but he is enamoured of Filina, an actress. Mignon is injured in a burning castle and is brought to Italy by Lothario, an old minstrel, who in reality is an Italian nobleman who has lost his memory. In the last act he recognizes in Mignon his daughter, stolen as a child by gipsies. Wilhelm realizes his true love for Mignon, and all ends happily.

Music by Ambrose Thomas. Produced Paris, 1866.

**Othello.** Libretto is based upon Shakespeare's tragedy of same name (see Othello). Music by Verdi. Produced Milan, 1887.

**I Pagliacci.** (Pron. pal-yah'-chē). THE PLAYERS. Opens with a prologue sung by clown Tonio. Canio, leader of a troupe of strolling players, is furiously jealous of his beautiful wife, Nedda, who is planning to run off with Silvio, a villager. In their little play a similar tragedy of a jealous husband and erring wife is enacted. In the play Canio stabs his wife, forcing her to call upon her lover, Silvio, who rushes upon the stage and is killed by Canio, who then surrenders.

Music and libretto by Leoncavallo. Produced Milan, 1892.

**Pelléas and Mélisande.** Golaud finds the mysterious Mélisande in the wood and brings her back to the king's castle as his wife. There she and Pelléas, half-brother of Golaud, fall in love. Wildly jealous, Golaud slays Pelléas. Mélisande dies, maintaining the innocence of their love.

Music by Debussy. Produced Paris, 1902.

**Peter Grimes.** The story, based by Montagu Slater on an episode in George Crabbe's narrative poem The Borough, concerns a fishing community on the Suffolk coast at the beginning of the 19th century. The fisherman Peter Grimes has become a social outcast. Half madman, half-visionary, he is suspected of having caused the death of his boy assistant. He is brought before the magistrate, but released since nothing can be proved against him. He then takes another boy from an orphanage. Ellen Orford, the village schoolmistress, whom Grimes loves, not only befriends him against malicious gossip but seeks to protect the boy. Terrified by Grimes's brutal manner the boy falls to his death over a cliff. Grimes, a hunted man, takes his boat to sea and sinks it, never to return.

Music by Benjamin Britten. Produced at Sadler's Wells, London, 1945.

**Rigoletto.** (Pron. rē-gō-let'-tō). The dissolute Duke of Mantua has won the love of Gilda, daughter of the hunchback, Rigoletto. Rigoletto conspires to have the Duke killed, but Gilda sacrifices herself to save him, and Rigoletto is given the assassin's sack containing his own dying daughter.

Music by Verdi. Produced Venice, 1851.

**Der Ring des Nibelungen.** The Ring of the Nibelungs; a vast musical work by Richard Wagner based on the old legends of the Nibelungs (see

Nibelungs, Song of the). The whole work consists of Das Rheingold, an introduction to the dramas, Die Walküre, Siegfried, and Götterdämmerung, which are outlined under the next four headings.

**Das Rheingold.** (Pron. dahs rin'-gōlt). The hideous dwarf Alberich learns from the Rhine maidens that he who would renounce love for ever might steal their treasure, the Rhine gold, and that a ring made from it would render the possessor master of the world. Alberich seizes the gold and has the ring made, also a magic helmet, Tarnhelm. Wotan, father of the gods, takes the gold ring and helmet from Alberich and gives it to two giants to repay them for building the new castle of the gods, Valhalla. Alberich puts a curse on the ring. The giants quarrel, and one is slain. The gods proceed to Valhalla.

Produced Munich, 1869.

**Die Walküre.** (Pron. dē vahl-kē'-re). THE VALKYRIES. The Valkyries are nine daughters of Wotan whose mission it is to ride forth each day on flying horses and bring to Valhalla the bravest of the slain. Brunhild, their leader, is Wotan's favourite. However, in a fight between Wotan's earthly son Siegmund and Hunding, Brunhild protects Siegmund against orders. Wotan intervenes, causes Siegmund to be slain, and then slays Hunding himself. Brunhild carries to safety Siegmund's sister-wife, Sieglinde, to whom she gives the fragments of Siegmund's sword. Brunhild is made a mortal woman for her disobedience, and is put to sleep surrounded by a wall of magic fire and destined to become the wife of the first man to break through the fire and awaken her.

Produced Munich, 1870.

**Siegfried.** (Pron. sēg'-frēd). His mother, Sieglinde, dying at his birth, Siegfried is brought up by the dwarf Mime. He becomes a magnificent hero. From the fragments of his father's sword he forges a mighty weapon. With it he kills Fafner the giant who has made himself into a fierce dragon to protect the magic ring and Rhine gold. Licking a drop of the dragon's blood, he is suddenly able to understand the birds, and one leads him to Brunhild, whom he wakens. In the meantime, he has met Wotan and fearlessly broken Wotan's spear.

Produced Bayreuth, 1876.

**Götterdammerung.** (Pron. gê-ter-dem'-er-oong). THE TWILIGHT OF THE GODS. Siegfried gives his magic ring to Brunhild, lovingly bids her farewell, and goes into the world. There Hagen, son of the dwarf Alberich, gives him a magic drink, which causes him to forget Brunhild and fall in love with Gutrune, sister of King Gunther. He agrees to bring Brunhild to the king for wife. Another drink causes him to remember, just before he is killed by Hagen. Brunhild learns of the drinks and forgives Siegfried. She has a huge pyre built for his body and, with the ring on her finger, rides into the flames. The Rhine overflows, and the Rhine maidens seize the ring triumphantly. Valhalla is shown in flames, and through the sacrifice of Brunhild the finer era of love begins.

Presented Bayreuth, 1876.

**Der Rosenkavalier.** (Pron. dār rōz'-en-kaval-ēr). The story, depicting the loose morals typical of 18th-century Vienna, concerns the successful efforts of the young Count Octavian (the Rose-bearer) to win Sophie, daughter of the newly rich Faninal. He exposes the vulgar old Baron Ochs to whom Faninal was trying to marry Sophie.

Music by Richard Strauss. Produced Dresden, 1911.

**Samson and Delilah.** Samson, Hebrew leader of gigantic strength, is ensnared by Delilah. She delivers him into the hands of the Philistines. In Act III he appears shorn, blinded, and chained, treading a mill, praying God for mercy. He is led in shame before the feasting Philistines, but, praying for strength, seizes the marble pillars and overthrows the whole temple.

Music by Saint-Saëns. First produced in Weimar, Germany, 1877.

**Tales of Hoffmann.** Opens with a prologue, the poet Hoffmann agreeing to tell a group of tavern companions of his three great loves. Story of loves forms the next three acts. All are frustrated by an evil genius that follows him. The first girl is an automaton, the second a mocking coquette, the third a dying consumptive. In the epilogue he is left alone, only the poetic Muse remaining faithful.

Music by Offenbach. Produced Paris, 1881.

**Tannhäuser.** (Pron. tahn'-hoi-zer). The minstrel knight, Tannhäuser, has been enticed into the Venusberg, but he wearies of the pleasures of Venus and returns home. There he is reunited with his old sweetheart Elizabeth and his old friend and rival Wolfram. But after singing the praises of sensuous love he is banished, and goes on a pilgrimage to Rome. In the end his soul is saved by the prayers of Elizabeth, and he falls dying on her bier. Libretto and music by Wagner. Produced Dresden, 1845.

**La Tosca.** Tosca, a singer, and Mario, a painter, are lovers. Mario, by hiding a revolutionist friend, is in the power of the malicious Scarpia, chief of police. Scarpia promises to make Mario's execution only a sham affair if Tosca will give him her love. She agrees, but stabs him. Mario's execution is real. Tosca commits suicide. Music by Puccini. Produced Rome, 1900.

**La Traviata.** (Pron. trah-vē-ah'-tah). At a gay party in her Paris salon, Violetta, a beautiful woman of bad reputation, meets Alfredo. They fall in love. Alfredo's father, Giorgio, intervenes, imploring Violetta to give up Alfredo for the sake of his family's reputation. She does so, but Alfredo misunderstands, believing her to be fickle. She dies of consumption in the presence of father and son. (Same story as Dumas's Dame aux Camélias.)

Music by Verdi. Produced Venice, 1853.

**Tristan und Isolde.** Tristan is escorting the Irish princess Isolde to Cornwall, to be the wife of his uncle, King Mark. Isolde, imagining Tristan does not care for her, prepares a cup of poison and invites him to drink. They both drink; Isolde's maid Brangäne has substituted a love potion for the poison, and the couple fall under its spell. King Mark discovers them. One of his soldiers wounds Tristan fatally, and Tristan and Isolde die together.

Libretto and music by Wagner. Produced Munich, 1865.

**Il Trovatore.** (Pron. ēl-trō-vah-taw'-rā). THE TROUBADOUR. Manrico the troubadour has been brought up as the son of Azucena, a gipsy. He is really a brother of the Count di Luna, for Azucena stole him as a child to avenge her mother's death. Both the Count and Manrico are in love with

# TENSE MOMENTS IN FRENCH AND GERMAN OPERAS

*A. McBean; A. Console*

Composers of all civilized countries have written memorable operas. These two scenes come, respectively, from the work of a Frenchman and a German. At the top is seen a dramatic moment in Gounod's Faust, which was first produced in Paris in 1859. Lower, Act II of Der Rosen-kavalier, probably the most popular work of Richard Strauss, first staged in Dresden in 1911. Both these operas have been enthusiastically received all over the world.

Leonora. The Count has Manrico imprisoned. Leonora offers to marry the Count if he will free Manrico. The Count agrees, but Leonora takes poison and dies in Manrico's arms. The Count has Manrico put to death while Azucena, avenged at last, cries : " You have killed your brother ! "

Music by Verdi. Produced Rome, 1853.

**Opium.** Chief of the narcotic drugs which have both helped and harmed mankind is opium, the dried juice from the seed pod of the opium poppy, *Papaver somniferum.* Used as medicine, opium deadens pain. But when it is taken for its pleasurable effects it saps energy and mental strength and forms a habit which can be broken only with the greatest difficulty.

Opium poppies, with their fragile flowers of red or white or purple, thrive in a hot climate, but cannot endure heavy rain. Since each plant yields but little juice and since the fields must be weeded often, the poppies can be grown profitably only where land and labour are cheap. Opium is produced chiefly in China, the Dominion of India, Iran, Turkey, and Soviet Russia. Much is sent to Europe and the United States, where it is manufactured into opiates for medicinal use—morphine, laudanum, and codeine. Japan, once a large manufacturer, was forbidden after the Second World War (1939–45) to produce opiates.

Opium smoking and eating have long been grave problems in the Orient. The governments of the Dominions of India and Pakistan permit the moderate use of it, but prohibit exports except for medical use. Japan has long banned use of the drug, but produced it in the puppet state of Manchukuo (now Manchuria) as a government monopoly. China has often tried to abolish opium smoking by banning the growing of the opium poppy. It fought the so-called " Opium War " with Great Britain (1839–42) to stop British imports of the drug from India into China. In 1935 the Chinese government took over the control of opium and established cure centres.

Ancient peoples used opium medicinally as early as the days of the Assyrians. In the Middle Ages Arabs introduced it into India and China, and its use spread into Europe. In the 18th and 19th centuries, almost all " pain killer " medicines contained opiates. Physicians now prescribe opiates only to relieve pain and to bring needed sleep.

The first international opium conference met at Shanghai in 1909 at the suggestion of President Theodore Roosevelt.

Later conferences at The Hague in 1912 and at Geneva in 1925 and 1931 resulted in treaties designed to regulate the opium trade. Three permanent international organizations watch the traffic and suggest measures for controlling it. Despite these efforts, enormous quantities are smuggled into large countries.

**Opossum.** The peculiar way in which the opossum (*Didelphus*) rears its young sets it apart from all other American animals. As many as a dozen may be born at a time, each about half an inch long. At once they crawl into a pouch on the mother's abdomen. There they fasten themselves to the milk glands and remain helpless for about six weeks. When they first come out of the pouch they are the size of mice. For some time after that they ride around on their mother's back, clinging to her fur and crawling back into her pouch to sleep.

This way of rearing the young is peculiar to the group of mammals called *marsupials* (from the Latin word *marsupium*, " pouch "), including kangaroos. The opossums of North America and their relatives in South and Central America are the only marsupials now found outside the Australian region.

When full grown, the common opossum is about the size of a house cat (33 inches to the tip of the tail). The head is small, but has long narrow jaws set with 50 teeth. The feet are five-toed. Each toe on the forefoot has a long sharp nail that helps in climbing trees. Four toes on the hindfoot also have nails. The nailless first toe is used like a thumb to grasp branches. The tail, long and ratlike, helps in climbing. There are two coats of fur; the inner coat is soft and short, and the outer is coarse, long, and a grizzled grey in colour.

During the day the opossum sleeps in a burrow or hollow log or tree. At night it hunts in trees or on the ground. It grows fat from eating birds, frogs, fish, eggs, insects and fruit.

Hunting the opossum with dogs is a favourite sport in parts of America. When surprised by a hunter, the opossum pretends to be dead. From this trick has come the expression " playing 'possum." The flesh is enjoyed by some, and the fur is prized for making women's coats.

*F. W. Bond*

**OPOSSUM AND FAMILY**
When the young opossums are old enough to leave the pouch in which the mother carries them from birth they frequently ride about on their parent's back. These animals are found only in North, Central and South America.

**Orange.** A member of the citrus fruit group, which includes the citron, lemon, lime and grape-fruit, the orange (*Citrus aurantium*) is the most important. In normal times oranges are available in Britain for the greater part of the year, cargoes from the West Indies being followed after

# ORANGES FROM THE TREE TO THE MARKET

To the base of the foothills stretch the orange groves of southern California in the United States. 1. All year long they offer a golden crop. 2. Pickers wear gloves, for a bruise will start decay in the fruit. 3. The oranges have a warm bath with soft brushes. 4. They are rinsed in cold water and conveyed on rollers to the drying room, 5, where a current of warm air dries them. 6. The sizing machine, a roller runway narrow at one end, drops them according to size into bins. 7. Before being packed each fruit is wrapped in tissue paper by a girl wearing gloves.

Christmas-time by supplies from Spain, Palestine, California and South Africa.

The wild orange was cultivated in early times, and has been carried westward with the march of civilization. Originally a native of eastern Asia, it became a valuable crop in Asia Minor and the Mediterranean regions, establishing itself in the sunny mild climate of Italy, Spain and southern France. The Spaniards carried it to the West Indies, Brazil, and to the southern parts of what is now the United States. Now South Africa and Australia also produce large quantities of oranges.

The trees begin to bear when they are about six years old. Fruit is produced more or less continuously, and flowers and fruits in all stages of development can be found on the same tree at almost every season throughout the year.

The golden fruit and the white blossoms—the bride's favourite flower—and the dark leaves make an orange grove very beautiful. The trees are planted in rows, and stand from 25 to 30 feet apart. They require regular pruning, and must be sprayed often to destroy the various insect pests that feed upon them. If there is any danger of frost, everything must be in readiness to light fires throughout the groves. These, usually of crude petroleum, produce a dense smoke-blanket which keeps the temperature above freezing-point.

The battle is not over when the crop is ready to harvest. Every precaution is taken against injury to the fruit. The oranges are cut from the bough with scissors, and only very short stems are left so that they will not injure other fruit. The pickers wear canvas gloves, for bruised or scratched orange skins may open the way for the germs of decay. At the packing-house the oranges are sorted and graded, wrapped in tissue paper stamped with the name of the firm, and packed in boxes. A certain number of oranges of each grade fill a box, about 96 of the largest grade and about 200 of the smallest.

The largest orange of commerce is the seedless, fine-flavoured navel, which has a queer little miniature orange tucked into the blossom end. It grows in the United States. Other well-known varieties of the sweet orange are the Maltese or Blood (so called from the deep red tint of the pulp), the St. Michael, the Jaffa, and the mandarin and tangerine. Tangerine and mandarin oranges are small, fragrant, and somewhat flattened, with loose skin easily separated from the pulp. The bitter Seville orange (*C. aurantium*, variety *amara*), an Arabian variety brought into Spain by the Moors, is used to make marmalade. Kumquats are a fruit related to the orange. They are an inch or so long, and make a delicious conserve.

**Orange** RIVER AND FREE STATE. When in 1486 the Portuguese navigator Bartholomew Diaz sailed down the west coast of Africa on the famous voyage in which eventually he doubled the Cape of Good Hope, he came to a part of the ocean in which his two small ships sailed through water of a strange greenish colour and on which floated vegetation from the distant shore. Though he did not know it, he was off the mouth of South Africa's largest river—the Orange river, also called the Gariep or Groote river, which has its rise in the Drakensberg mountains, 800 miles away from its outlet into the Atlantic Ocean 45 miles north-west of Port Nolloth in Cape Province.

Its name has no reference to its colour, but was given it in 1779 by Colonel Gordon, a Dutch officer, who hoisted the Dutch flag in the middle of the stream and named it after the ruling family of Holland. In those days the Dutch were the only white settlers in South Africa, having established a colony at Cape Town in 1652.

The basin of the Orange comprises 40,000 square miles of plateau country; its upper tributaries flow amongst magnificent mountain scenery in Basutoland. Between the Orange and its tributary the Vaal lies the territory of the Orange Free State, which is one of the original provinces of the Union of South Africa. An almost treeless tableland with an average altitude of about 5,000 feet, it has an area of 49,647 square miles, and is bounded on the north by the Transvaal, on the east by Natal, on the south and west by Cape Province.

The climate is temperate, and the rainfall is moderate—chiefly in the form of thunderstorms in late summer. Cattle, sheep and ostriches are reared. Maize is the chief crop ; others are wheat, oats, potatoes, tobacco

*South African Railways and Harbours*
**CAPITAL OF THE ORANGE FREE STATE**
On the Modder river, Bloemfontein, the capital of the Orange Free State, is 4,518 feet above sea level. Here is seen Maitland Street, one of the main thoroughfares. Founded in 1846, the city is the seat of the Supreme Court of South Africa.

and fruit. Diamond and coal mines are worked. Gold and iron are found; one of the richest gold-fields was discovered in 1946 at Odendaalsrust. Bloemfontein (population 64,000) is the capital and largest town; other centres are Harrismith, Smithfield and Kroonstad.

The first settlers in the region were Dutch, who arrived about 1824. Some six years later a steady stream of Boers (Dutch farmers), who had left their farms at the Cape because of the decree of the British Government abolishing Negro slavery, began to flow into the land. In their huge wagons the farmers trekked with their slaves and cattle for hundreds of miles. But there were already many natives in possession of the land—Hottentots, Bushmen, Griquas and Basutos—and it was some time before the Boers were able to settle down. For a few years, indeed, the British had to intervene to keep order, and there was some fighting between the Boers on the one hand and the Griquas and their British protectors on the other.

In 1854 a Boer republic was established, and this lasted, under the name of the Orange Free State, until the South African War (1899–1902) when the State was annexed by the British and renamed the Orange River Colony. In 1910 the colony entered the newly formed South African Union under its former title. The population of the Orange Free State is estimated to be 772,000, of whom 570,000 are natives.

**Orang-utan.** (Pron. or-ang'-oo-tan'). The name of this member of the ape family, found in the swampy forests of Borneo and Sumatra, comes from the Malay language and signifies " man of the woods." It is well named, for like the chimpanzee and the gorilla it approaches closely to Man in appearance and structure. A full-grown male orang-utan (*Simia satyrus*) occasionally reaches a height of four and a half feet, but the outstretched arms cover more than seven feet. The body is bulky and covered with long, reddish-brown hair. The legs are short, but the arms are so long as to reach the ankles when the animal is erect, and in walking the knuckles are placed on the ground. Orang-utans, however, are awkward on the ground and prefer the trees, where they can travel at the rate of five or six miles an

*W. S. Berridge*

**ORANG-UTAN, A FOREST-DWELLER**

Native to Borneo and Sumatra, the orang-utan approaches closely to Man in appearance. It is more at home in trees than on the ground and, as can be seen above, its feet are as well adapted as the hands for grasping. The long hair is reddish-brown.

hour, without special effort, by swinging along on the branches, which they grasp mainly with their hands.

They feed on fruits and succulent shoots, being strictly vegetarian in their diet. They live in pairs, and as a rule are peaceable, but when disturbed they are fierce fighters. They retire to rest at sunset in nests of broken boughs 20 or 30 feet above ground. In captivity they are teachable and affectionate, and the changing expression of the face makes them most interesting, though they are not so active and intelligent as the chimpanzee.

**Orchestra.** The difference between an orchestra and a band is this—when we listen to an orchestra we really hear four " bands " in one. There is the *string* " band," made up of various members of the violin family; the *wood-wind* " band," made up of all the wind instruments that are made of wood; the *brass* " band," with its various kinds of " horns "; and the noisy group of big and little drums, and all the other *percussion* instruments that are struck or beaten.

In Queen Elizabeth's time, before the modern full orchestra was thought of, these sections of instruments were called " consorts " (not to be confused with *concerts*) and often played separately. Thus Shakespeare's plays refer to a " consort " of viols or of hautboys (oboes). All large orchestras also have one or more harps. The usual so-called " brass " or " military " band includes wood-wind instruments as well as those of brass.

The " strings " form the foundation of the modern orchestra. They are capable of the greatest variety of expression in revealing the depths and heights of human emotion. The violins sing the soprano, the second violins the alto, the violas the tenor, the violoncellos (or " cellos ") the baritone, and the double-basses (or bass viols) the bass.

Next in importance is the wood-wind group, which is divided into three families. The first consists of the flute, which with its clear, sweet, liquid notes is the most agile and flexible of the woods; and the piccolo, a shriller flute, which has been called " the imp of the orchestra." The second includes the oboe, with its plaintive pastoral tone, and the deeper English horn and bassoon, which may be regarded as alto and bass oboes. The third comprises the clarinets, which are known by their full, rich, mellow tones. There are usually three of these of different pitch. Oboes and clarinets, as distinguished from flutes, are reed instruments; the oboe has a double reed, the clarinet a single one.

The " brasses " consist of the French horn, which is the old hunting-horn adapted to orchestral purposes; the trumpet, with its full, round, brilliant tone (often replaced by the cornet); the majestic trombone, an instrument of great range and power, and the deep-toned tuba, the bass of the brass band.

Of the percussion instruments, often called " the battery," some produce " noises " rather than definite musical notes. Such are the bass and side drums, triangle, cymbals, etc., whose purpose is to accentuate the rhythm or add to the volume of sound, or help to produce various descriptive effects. The kettle-drums, or *tympani*, however, which are among the most interesting instruments in the orchestra, can be tuned to sound certain notes. The bells, " glockenspiel " or " carillon," and the steel plates of the celesta, likewise have a definite pitch. A large orchestra today contains usually up to about 100 players, although the composers Berlioz and Wagner envisaged orchestras of some 400 performers.

The name " orchestra " derives from the Greek, in which language the word meant " dancing place," and the name came to be given to the players of instruments, because in the old Greek theatre those players used to be placed in the circular space in front of the spectators, where the chorus danced and sang.

With so many instruments playing together it is obviously very important to have a conductor to indicate the time and to preserve the proper balance between the groups. As recently as two centuries ago, when orchestras were still very small, it was the custom for the harpsichord player to lead the musicians without a special conductor. Handel used to do this frequently. How complicated the modern conductor's task is you realize when you look at the many lines of notes on each page of a conductor's score. The *leader* of an orchestra is the first violin, seated on the conductor's left hand.

There are numerous fine orchestras in the world today. The names of combinations like the Philadelphia Symphony, Vienna Philharmonic, Chicago Symphony, Berlin Philharmonic, Amsterdam Concertgebouw, and Boston Symphony Orchestras are known everywhere, and the music-loving public will go to any lengths to watch them " in action " under famous conductors such as Arturo Toscanini, Wilhelm Furtwängler, Bruno Walter, Victor de Sabata, or Sergei Koussevitsky.

British orchestras include the B.B.C. Symphony Orchestra, Royal Philharmonic, London Philharmonic, London Symphony ; the Hallé Sym_

*British Broadcasting Corporation*

**BROADCAST PERFORMANCE OF A SYMPHONY ORCHESTRA**

Assembled in a studio at Broadcasting House, London, is the British Broadcasting Corporation's Symphony Orchestra. The instruments are usually grouped as above ; the strings in front, with the first violin, who is the leader of the orchestra, on the left of the conductor (standing on the dais, baton in hand, left foreground); next the wood wind, with the brass behind them ; at the back, the percussion instruments. Some conductors vary the arrangement slightly.

Cross, for commissioned officers of captain's rank or below and warrant officers; the Military Medal, for warrant officers, non-commissioned officers and men of the army; the Distinguished Service Cross and the Distinguished Service Medal, naval decorations; the Distinguished Flying Cross and the Distinguished Flying Medal, Air Force decorations. During the Second World War (1939–45) King George VI instituted the George Cross and George Medal, primarily for civilians performing acts of great heroism in circumstances of extreme danger.

Membership of the French Legion of Honour is awarded for meritorious service to France. The award is made in both military and civil life. A scientist may receive the decoration for some valuable discovery, as well as a soldier for conspicuous bravery. The order was founded by Napoleon Bonaparte in 1802, and includes the following ranks: Grand Master (the President of the Republic), Grand Cross, Grand Officers, Commanders, Officers and Chevaliers. Membership of the order may be conferred upon foreigners and women. The Croix de Guerre, established during the First World War, and the Médaille Militaire, founded by Napoleon III, are France's chief military decorations.

Germany's highest military decoration was the Order for Merit (Ordre pour le Mérite), dating back to 1740. The grades of the Iron Cross, which was founded in 1813, were bestowed very freely in the course of both World Wars.

The chief Italian decoration is the Medal of Honour. In Belgium the Order of Leopold and the Military Cross are the most highly prized. In the United States the most coveted decoration is the Medal of Honour, or Congressional Medal, established in 1861, awarded to members of both Army and Navy for acts of extreme heroism in war.

The British orders of knighthood confer upon the holder a rank of precedence. Those who are "knights" use the prefix "Sir" before their Christian names, unless they have some higher title. Simple knighthood, that is, the knighting of anyone not belonging to an order, by the King or Queen, still exists in Britain. This method of bestowing knighthood is the oldest of all, and recipients are known as knights bachelor. Among the most important of the British orders are the following: The Order of the Garter, established by Edward III about 1348. Its motto is *Honi soit qui mal y pense* (Evil be to him who evil thinks); membership is indicated by the letters K.G. The Order of the Thistle is an ancient Scottish order founded by James II in 1687; initials K.T. The Order of St. Patrick, for Ireland, was created in 1783; initials, K.P.

The Order of the Bath, founded in 1399, consists of three classes—Knights Grand Cross (G.C.B.), Knights Commanders (K.C.B.), and Companions (C.B.). The Order of St. Michael and St. George was created in 1818, and is similarly divided into three classes (G.C.M.G., K.C.M.G., and C.M.G.). There are two further orders of knighthood to be mentioned, the Royal Victorian Order (G.C.V.O., K.C.V.O., C.V.O., and M.V.O.), founded in 1896 (the statutes of which were amended in May 1936 by King Edward VIII so that women might receive the order, Queen Mary becoming the first Dame Grand Cross), and the Order of the British Empire (G.B.E., K.B.E., D.B.E., C.B.E., O.B.E., and M.B.E.), founded in 1917. The letters D.B.E. are

used
recip
name

As
two
Star
found
Emp
in 18

A
order
with
(O.M
The
and i
armec
artists
emine
kind,
of the
orders

**Or**
Unite
miles,
ton, o
and C
The S
region

In
separa
Willia
on the
is a pr
tains.
northe
part of
sive tr

The
and he
rain ar
In the
crops i
and fru
farming
excelle
and cec
curv, p
manufa

The
but Po
mercial
Eugene.
The po

**Orga**
organ i
itself, fo
Above t
of pipes
organ is
room, ar
are hidc

In an
sands, o
trees; th
than a lc
pipes are
trolled b
the orga
group, h

Allegro.

**A PAGE OF AN ORCHESTRAL SCORE**
Great conductors retain many long scores in their memory. You may get some idea of what this means from the page (above) showing eight bars of Beethoven's Fifth Symphony; each staff represents the music for only one group of instruments.

phony (Manchester); and orchestras in Liverpool, Birmingham and other cities. Famous conductors include Sir Thomas Beecham, Sir Adrian Boult, John Barbirolli and Sir Malcolm Sargent.

The B.B.C. Symphony Orchestra of 119 players is composed as follows: 20 first violins, 16 second violins, 14 violas, 12 cellos, 10 double-basses, five flutes, five oboes, five clarinets, five bassoons, eight horns, five trumpets, six trombones, one tuba, two tympani, three percussion, and two harps.

The smaller municipal

orchestras maintained by certain towns—particularly coastal resorts such as Bournemouth or Hastings—reach a high standard of playing and aim at providing good music for all tastes. (*See also* Music; Musical Instruments).

**Orchid.** (Pron. ŏr′-kid). Fabulous prices have been paid for a single specimen of some of the rare members of this remarkable family of plants. And many an eager collector has climbed precipices, waded through malarial swamps, endured the dangers of tropical forests and braved even the head-hunters of Borneo to get these treasured flowers.

There are hundreds of genera of the orchid family (*Orchidaceae*), and the number of species is variously estimated at 6,000 to 12,000 species. They thrive in all parts of the world where it is not too hot or too cold, and are the most highly organized flowers among the monocotyledons.

Some orchids grow upon the ground; others grow in marshy places and live on dead organic matter. The most valuable group are the air plants or epiphytes. These grow on trees in tropical and sub-tropical regions, obtaining their nourishment not from the support that some of their roots cling to but from their long, spongy, aerial roots, which absorb water from the moisture-laden atmosphere, storing it in bulbils (small bulbs) which grow on the stems.

To botanists orchids are especially interesting on account of their methods of ensuring fertilization. Instead of the ordinary arrangement of pollen on two anthers, there are two pollen-bearing bodies, called *pollinia*, which are so arranged that when an insect visits the orchid it removes these pollinia on its antennae or forehead; so that when another orchid is visited, the pollinia come into contact with the stigmas, to which they adhere. (*See* Flowers).

The typical orchid flower has three sepals and three petals, all of which are coloured, sometimes with brilliant hues on a white or green background. The central, lowest petal, called the *lip*, is often strangely shaped.

Often, too, there is a long spur at the back which contains the nectar, and such species as have this

**ORCHIDS OF GREAT CHARM AND BEAUTY**
In a greenhouse maintained at a suitable temperature some striking orchids may be grown and flowered in Britain. The blossoms illustrated are *Laelio-cattleya* (left), *Coelogyne cristata* (centre), and the quaintly shaped *Oncidium papilio* (right).

**BRITISH ORCHID**

Known as lady's tresses, this orchid is to be found growing on the English South Downs.

*E. J. Bedford*

have a most beautiful scent; an English example of this type is the butterfly orchid (*Habenaria*), whose lovely white flowers are to be found in beech woods. Of insect-mimicking forms, there are several in Britain, including the bee and fly orchids. The spider orchis and lizard orchis look strangely like those creatures. Also native to Britain is the curious man orchis, which looks like a tiny green man on a stalk. The commoner British species include the early purple, spotted, and marsh orchids. Others are the pale brown bird's-nest orchis, which is a saprophyte (plant that grows on decaying vegetable matter) found in beech woods; and the lady's tresses, whose stem is twisted into a spiral; the flowers of the latter are very small and are green.

The seeds of one species of orchid furnish the vanilla of commercial use, and the roots of another the medicinal salep of oriental countries.

it with the keyboard. The air which causes the pipes to sound is forced into them from an air chamber into which it has been directed by bellows or by an electric fan.

Some organs have as many as five rows or banks of keys. Each row is called a manual, because it is played by the hands (from the Latin word *manus*, hand), and each manual is connected with a particular set of pipes. When a key is pressed down, a valve is moved which admits air to a certain pipe. The most important manual is called the great organ; the other keyboards control the choir, swell, and solo organs. If the organ has a fifth manual, it is for the echo organ; if a sixth manual, for powerful trumpet stops. In the largest instruments, which have seven or eight organs, one or more of the manuals may control two organs. In addition to manipulating the stops and the different manuals the organist operates with his feet another keyboard, called the pedal organ. These keys are made of wood and are very large.

The organs of early days were very different from modern ones. The first instrument of this type was the Pan's pipes of the ancient Greeks, which consisted of a set of pipes sounded by the player's breath. About 200 B.C. a device was invented for forcing air into the pipes by water-power, and keys were added to open and close the pipes.

Centuries later bellows came into use, instead of water-power, to furnish air. An organ built in the 10th century for Winchester Cathedral, Hampshire, had bellows so powerful that 70 men were needed to pump it. In modern organs the motor that pumps the bellows may be of 25 or even 40 horsepower; yet so improved is the mechanism of the keyboard that the touch of a finger is all that is required to open the pipe-valve.

The greatest changes are due to the use of electricity. So much of the machinery is now electrically operated, that the inside of an organ looks like a telephone exchange. By means of electricity one person can control the 18,000 pipes found in some of the largest organs. A number of the finest organs are used in cinemas.

Much like the pipe organ is the harmonium, sometimes called the reed or cabinet organ, often found in rural schools and churches. Instead of pipes it has a number of freely vibrating "reeds," or thin strips of wood or metal of varying length and thickness, which produce the various tones. Air is provided by a bellows worked by the feet. Famous organs in England include the concert organ in the Royal Albert Hall (reconstructed in 1934 at a cost of £26,000), the B.B.C. concert and theatre organs, and the instrument installed in Westminster Abbey for the Coronation in 1937.

**HOW THE ORDER OF THE GARTER**

The traditional incident at the court of King Edward III from which, it is said, the institution of the Order of the Garter originated is depicted in this painting by A. Chevallier Taylor. The story goes that the King picked up a garter accidentally dropped by a Court lady

2448

*Fox*

**AMONG THE PIPES OF A NOTED LONDON ORGAN**

The organ at the Royal Albert Hall, London, is said to be one of the largest and finest in the world. It weighs 175 tons, and has no fewer than 10,491 pipes. In the 1930s this organ was changed from mechanical to electropneumatic action, and the reconstruction, which took six years to complete, cost £26,000. The solo and bombarde complement to the organ are seen in the photograph. The solo is sometimes called the orchestral organ because many of the stops resemble orchestral instruments. The bombarde, or echo organ, supplies the deep-toned loud passages.

2450

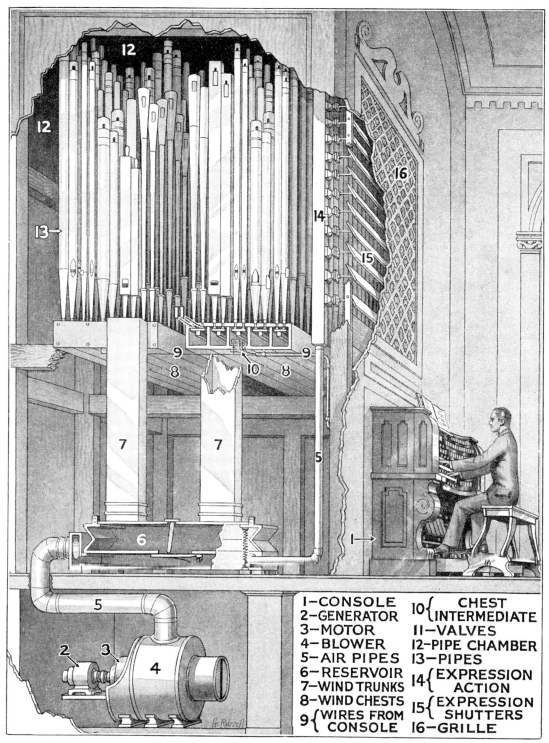

| 1—CONSOLE | 10 { CHEST INTERMEDIATE |
| 2—GENERATOR | 11—VALVES |
| 3—MOTOR | 12—PIPE CHAMBER |
| 4—BLOWER | 13—PIPES |
| 5—AIR PIPES | 14 { EXPRESSION ACTION |
| 6—RESERVOIR | |
| 7—WIND TRUNKS | 15 { EXPRESSION SHUTTERS |
| 8—WIND CHESTS | |
| 9 { WIRES FROM CONSOLE | 16—GRILLE |

When the organist touches the keys of his console (1) an electric contact sends a current along a wire (9) to an electro-magnet called the chest intermediate (10). Magnetized by the current, the chest intermediate lifts a metal disk, releasing some of the air pressure which holds a little valve (11) against the pipe base. As the valve drops, air from the wind chest (8) rushes up through the pipe, sounding the note. A blower (4) driven by a motor (3), with a generator (2) if direct current is not available, forces compressed air through the air pipes (5), reservoir (6), and wind trunks (7) to the wind chests. Pedals on the console control bellows of the expression action (14). They open or close shutters (15) outside the pipe chamber (12), to increase or reduce the sound. A grille (16) hides the mechanism.

**Orinoco,** River. " I know all the earth doth not yield the like confluence of streams and branches, the one crossing the other as many times, and all as fair and large and so like one to another as no man can tell which to take." Thus Sir Walter Raleigh described the huge delta of the Orinoco, which he visited on his search for El Dorado (legendary city of gold) in 1595. His description is not at all exaggerated, for this fan-shaped delta, nearly as large as the island of Sicily, is traversed by more than 50 channels. The soil is even more fertile than that of the Nile valley, and produces fine tropical fruits; but much of the river's valley is covered by dense forests.

Above the delta, 120 miles from the sea, even in the dry season the river is no less than 12 miles in width. Ciudad Bolivar, 200 miles from the sea, is the metropolis of the Orinoco basin and can be reached by ocean-going steamers. The land immediately above the delta is mostly a vast, grassy plain—the *llanos*—where large numbers of cattle, sheep, and horses graze.

British Museum; Natural History
**GOLDEN ORIOLES**
Ranging from northern Russia to South Africa, the golden oriole is a regular annual visitor to south-west England and the Scilly Isles. About the size of a thrush, the cock bird is golden yellow, with black wings and tail.

One of the largest rivers in South America, the Orinoco rises in the Sierra Parima range on the Brazil-Venezuela boundary (the source was discovered in 1931) and flows through central Venezuela to the Atlantic. It is about 1,600 miles long, and is navigable for large steamers for 700 miles.

**Oriole.** Some members of this family of birds are hatched from eggs laid in a cup-shaped nest hanging from the tip of a branch of a high tree; their hammock is very strongly woven of shreds of bark and most skilfully slung. Orioles are found in the temperate and tropical parts of the Old World. About the size of a thrush, they are usually brilliantly coloured. Their food consists chiefly of insects; they also eat berries in the autumn.

The golden oriole (*Oriolus galbula*) often visits Great Britain, but very rarely nests there. It is not uncommon on the Continent, but it is more at home in Africa and southern Asia. The male is rich golden-yellow and black; the upper parts of the hen bird are yellow-olive. The eggs, of which

E.N.A.
**LIFE ON THE BANKS OF THE GREAT ORINOCO RIVER**
At Ciudad Bolivar in Venezuela the Orinoco sweeps past this rocky headland with such force that it has scoured out a channel 262 feet deep. The white patches on the rocks are washing put out to bleach in the tropical sun. The town of Ciudad Bolivar, 200 miles from the Atlantic Ocean, can be reached by ocean-going steamers. The Orinoco, which is 1,600 miles long, rises in southern Venezuela, near the Brazilian frontier. Its source was discovered in 1931.

---

there are usually four or five, are white, blotched with reddish purple.

The birds called orioles in the United States belong to a different family, the *Icteridae*.

**Orion.** (Pron. or-ī'-on). A mighty hunter famed in Greek legend, Orion was noted for his beauty, gigantic size and strength. According to the best-known story about him, Orion was loved

About 30 of the islands are inhabited; on the largest, Pomona or Mainland, is Kirkwall, the capital of the Orkneys, with about 4,000 inhabitants. Also on Pomona is Stromness, the next largest town and a favourite summer resort. Other islands are Westray, Sanday, Stronsay and Hoy. Oats, barley, turnips and potatoes are the main crops. Cattle, sheep and pigs are reared. Fishing is a leading industry. There are regular passenger and mail steamer and air services with the mainland.

The Orkneys were known as the Orcades in early times. In the 9th century they were conquered by the Northmen (*q.v.*) and made dependencies of the united kingdom of Norway and Denmark. In 1468 King Christian I of Denmark handed over the islands to Scotland as security for a loan, which was never repaid; and the Orkneys were formally transferred to Scotland in 1590.

Scapa Flow, an anchorage protected by three of the islands, was a British naval base in both World Wars; here the German fleet was interned after its surrender in 1918. The population of the islands is 21,400.

by the goddess Artemis (Diana), whose hunter he became. Her brother Apollo was angered at this, and one day, seeing Orion swimming, he pointed out to Artemis a black object in the water and challenged her to hit it with her arrow. She shot at it, discovering when too late that it was the head of her lover. After his death he was placed among the stars—the constellation of Orion being one of the brightest in the northern heavens. The three bright stars—Rigel, Betelgeux and Bellatrix—across its centre are called "Orion's Belt."

**Orissa.** A state of the republic of India, Orissa is situated between Bengal and Madras. Its area is 32,198 square miles, and it contains the southern part of the Chota Nagpur plateau and includes the lower valley and the delta of the Mahanadi. The coast lies between Bengal on the north and Madras on the south.

Rice is the main crop; rice-milling and the production of silver filigree work are important industries. Cuttack, an ancient city on the delta of the Mahanadi, is the capital, with a population of 65,000. On the coast is the town of Puri, where is the famous temple of Jagannath (Juggernaut). The population is 8,728,500, mostly Hindus.

**Orkney Islands.** Like a fleet of ships sailing from Scotland up into the Arctic Ocean lie the 90 islands and islets of the Orkneys. Windy and treeless, they are noted for their wild, rocky scenery. The group lies off the north coast of Scotland, separated from the mainland by the Pentland Firth, from 6 to 8 miles in breadth.

*F. W. Hardie; Valentine*
**COAST AND TOWER OF THE ORKNEYS**
Typical of the Orkney coast are stacks or rock pillars (upper) which have been separated from the mainland by the action of the sea. The lower photograph shows the Mass Tower, built in 1540 and forming part of the Bishop's palace at Kirkwall, the capital of the Orkneys.

**Orléans.** (Pron. or-lā-ahn). Many historic memories cling to this old French city, situated at the northernmost point of the River Loire, about 200 miles from the river's mouth and 75 miles south-west of Paris. The capital of the department of Loiret, it has broad boulevards, pleasant squares, and extensive quays along the river and Loire canal.

The outstanding building is the Cathedral of the Holy Cross, which was reconstructed in 1562; the north tower was damaged by shell-fire in the Second World War (1939–45). The 15th century church of St. Aignan has a 9th century crypt. The former Town Hall, dating from 1442, is now a museum. The Joan of Arc Museum was among the notable buildings destroyed in the Second World War.

Orléans has textile, engineering, shoemaking, glass and electrical industries, and factories for preparing foodstuffs and preserves. It is an important railway centre. The University, founded in 1309, became renowned as a centre of learning in the Middle Ages.

The city occupies the site of the ancient town of Genabum, which Julius Caesar laid in ruins when the Gauls rose against him in 52 B.C. The Roman city which succeeded it was named Aurelianum, from which " Orléans " is derived. Besieged by the English in 1429, during the Hundred Years' War, it was relieved by Joan of Arc (q.v.). Her memory is preserved by an equestrian statue and a cross on the left bank of the Loire. In the Franco-Prussian War, Orléans fell to the Prussians on October 11, 1870. During the Second World War the Germans captured it again, on June 17, 1940. It was liberated by United States troops on August 17, 1944. The population is 70,200.

**Orpheus.** (Pron. or'-fūs). " The father of song," as he was called, was a legendary poet and musician of ancient Greece. Presented with a lyre by the god Apollo and instructed by the Muses, Orpheus by his divine music not only enchanted men and beasts but even trees and rocks. On his travels with the Argonauts (q.v.) in search of the Golden Fleece his music put monsters to sleep and arrested falling cliffs.

When his wife Eurydice (pron. ūr-id'-is-ē) died, Orpheus followed her to Hades, and his music so pleased iron-hearted Pluto that the latter allowed her to follow him back to earth, provided he did not look around while they ascended. But Orpheus, in his anxiety, forgot this condition, looked back at Eurydice, and lost her for ever.

His grief led him to treat with contempt the women of Thrace, where he dwelt; and in revenge, according to one story, they tore him to pieces. The Muses gathered up the fragments of his body and buried them at the foot of Mount Olympus, and they set his lyre among the stars.

**Osaka.** (Pron. ō'-sah-kah). Spread out on both banks of the River Yodo and along Osaka Bay, Osaka, the largest city of Japan after Tokyo, is cut by hundreds of canals, rivulets, and arms of the sea, and is spanned by numerous bridges. Harbour improvements enable Osaka to receive large ships and handle much of the foreign trade that formerly went to Kobe, 20 miles distant. In normal times the principal products are cotton

*W. F. Mansell*

**ORPHEUS LOSES EURYDICE**
**Depicting the loss of his wife by Orpheus, as recounted in the Greek myth of Orpheus and Eurydice, this is a reproduction of a picture painted by George Frederick Watts (1817–1904) and now in the Tate Gallery, London.**

goods, refined metals, leather, glass-ware, confectionery, metal goods and patent medicines.

Osaka Castle, about three miles distant, dates from 1584 ; but the superstructure was almost entirely destroyed by fire in 1868. About A.D. 300 an imperial palace was built at Osaka ; but the city's commercial importance dates from 1583–98, when it was the national capital. In 1945, during the Second World War, many of the city's industrial plants were wrecked by United States bombers. The population in 1940 was 3,252,300.

**Osiris.** (Pron. ō-sīr′-is). The most popular of the gods in Egyptian mythology was Osiris, the son of Seb (the earth) and Nut (the sky). According to tradition, he was a wise and just king, who conquered all Egypt, introduced culture to the ignorant and barbarous people, and established good laws and institutions. He was slain by his brother Set, who having induced him to lie down in a coffin, cast it into the Nile. Isis, the wife of Osiris, after a long search discovered the body. Set then seized it and cut it into pieces, which he scattered far and wide. These Isis gathered, and buried with due honour.

According to another version of the story, Isis joined the parts of the body together by her magic power, and Osiris became ruler of the dead in the lower world. His son Horus

*Cairo Museum*
**OSIRIS**
Although he had several aspects, Osiris is, perhaps, best known as Egyptian god of the future life and king of the lower world.

when he grew up, avenged his father's murder by conquering Set. On earth Osiris became incarnate in the sacred bull Apis. From the combination of the two came the name Osiris-Apis, and from this Serapis, later regarded as a separate diety. Osiris is usually represented in human form, though sometimes with the head of an ox, ibis, or other animal. (*See* Isis.)

**Oslo.** The capital, largest city and chief seaport of Norway, Oslo stands at the head of Oslofiord, which cuts deep into the south-eastern part of the country. As we approach it by sea, we see on a high promontory on the right the old fortress of Akershus (built about 1390), now used as an arsenal and prison. On a hill to the north-west, overlooking the city and its chief street, Karl Johans Gate, is the royal palace. Farther back and encircling Oslo are mountains which offer superb views of the capital and the fiord.

In the city are buildings which house the Parliament or Storting, the National Theatre, and the University. Near the University are the Museum of Art and a historical museum. At Bygdöy, south-west of the capital, are exhibited three very ancient Viking ships. The modern Oslo has an underground railway, good schools and beautiful suburbs.

The old city was founded by King Harold Sigurdsson in 1048, but

**IN THE HEART OF MODERN OSLO**

*Norwegian State Railways*

During the last 100 years the growth of Oslo has been singularly rapid, and today Norway's capital has a number of handsome streets lined with modern buildings. Here we see Storting (Parliament) Street, with the imposing National Theatre, partially hidden by trees. In the left foreground is the stone parapet round an entrance to Oslo's underground railway, which five miles away comes to the surface as a suburban line to Holmenkollen, a winter sports centre.

Iago has practised on him. He is seized with terrible remorse and in agony slays himself, while Iago is led off to well-merited prison and torture.

The play is one of Shakespeare's four supreme masterpieces in tragedy. It is Iago, hinting that Desdemona's good name stands endangered, who says—

Good name, in man or woman, dear my lord,
Is the immediate jewel of their souls:
Who steals my purse, steals trash; 'tis something,
    nothing:
'Twas mine, 'tis his, and has been slave to thousands;
But he that filches from me my good name
Robs me of that, which not enriches him,
And makes me poor indeed.

Poor Othello in his final speech asks only—

Speak of me as I am; nothing extenuate,
Nor set down aught in malice: then, must you speak
Of one that loved not wisely but too well;
Of one not easily jealous but, being wrought,
Perplexed in the extreme; of one whose hand,
Like the base Indian, threw a pearl away
Richer than all his tribe; of one whose subdu'd eyes
Albeit unused to the melting mood,
Drop tears as fast as the Arabian trees
Their medicinal gum.

**Ottawa.** A magnificent sweep of hills, fringed in green and crowned with lofty and dignified towers—such is one's first impression of the city of Ottawa. The capital of the Dominion of Canada, it is situated on the right bank of the River Ottawa, near the eastern corner of the rich province of Ontario. It has picturesque tree-lined streets, parks, and several fine bridges over the River Rideau, which flows into the Ottawa from the south, skirting the city to the south and east.

Over all towers the group of impressive Gothic style buildings on the summit of Parliament Hill, rising 150 feet above the river. Here the Canadian parliament sits, and near by are the executive offices of the Dominion Government, where are administered the affairs of a country nearly as vast as all Europe. Besides the group of government buildings, which includes the Parliamentary Library, Ottawa has two cathedrals—one Church of England and the other Roman Catholic— the University of Ottawa (Roman Catholic), and several colleges and technical schools.

Within a radius of 10 miles Ottawa has available a rush of waters capable of producing more than a million horse-power. Much of this is already harnessed to the city's thriving industries. Below the city the Ottawa becomes navigable, forming a highway through the St. Lawrence to the sea. The Rideau Canal running southward connects Ottawa with the Great Lakes at Kingston, and the valleys of the upper Ottawa and the Gatineau

*Canadian News Bureau*

OTTAWA : THE THRIVING CAPITAL OF CANADA

Dominating the River Ottawa in the centre of this view is the lofty towered Parliament building. The structure was burned down in 1916, but was soon rebuilt. Immediately behind it is the Royal Alexandra railway bridge over the river. Founded in 1829 by Colonel By as a residence for engineers and workmen engaged in constructing the Rideau Canal the city was known as Bytown until 1854, when its name was changed to Ottawa; it became the capital in 1858.

**OTTER : CHAMPION SWIMMER OF THE LAND ANIMALS**

Here is an artist's impression of an otter standing guard over a salmon which it has caught. The English otter (*Lutra vulgaris*) grows to a length of about three and a half feet, including the tail, and a full-grown specimen weighs about 25 lb. It is becoming increasingly rare in Great Britain and Ireland on account of the fact that it is so destructive to fish (its natural food) that where trout and salmon streams are preserved otters are shot or trapped.

bring to the city the products of the rich regions stretching away to the west and north.

The timber industry surpasses all others. Millions of feet of logs are floated down the Ottawa and Gatineau rivers every year. Meat packing, leather factories, brick and tile works, machine shops, railway carriage and repair shops, foundries, clothing factories, and cement works add to the list of thriving industries. The Canadian Pacific, the Canadian National and the New York Central railway lines meet here.

Philemon Wright, a New Englander, who settled on the north side of the river in 1800, may be regarded as the founder of Ottawa. In 1826 Colonel John By was sent from England to construct the Rideau Canal, and his engineers and workmen established the settlement of Bytown, which formed the nucleus of the present city. In 1854 its name was changed to Ottawa, meaning " boiler," the name which the Indians gave to the Chaudière Falls on the River Ottawa. Four years later Queen Victoria selected the city for the Canadian capital and it retained its position after the formation of the Dominion in 1867. The population is 163,700.

**Otter.** If the land animals should hold a swimming and diving contest the otter would assuredly be a candidate for championship honours. It is as much at home in water as on land, diving, rising, and turning with lightning quickness; and yet it can move fast enough on land to outpace many dogs.

The English otter, *Lutra vulgaris*, is related to the weasel, but is much larger. Its body is about three and a half feet long, including the tail, which measures 15 or 16 inches, and it has short limbs and webbed feet. It is seal-like in form, and is covered with a thick coat of fine dark-brown fur. Its nest is usually in a hollow in a river bank.

The common otter is widely distributed over Europe and Asia, and allied species are found in North, South and Central America, and parts of Asia. In the sub-continent of India and China tame otters are used to catch fish. In Great Britain and Ireland the otter is becoming scarcer, for it is so destructive to fish, which forms its principal food, that where the rivers are preserved for fishing otters are shot. Otter-hunting also accounts for a good many of these creatures.

The sea-otter (*Latax lutris*), which is a related form that belongs to another genus, is much larger and heavier than the common otter. One of the most valuable of all fur-bearing animals, it was once abundant in the Pacific from California northward, but now is very rare, except about the Aleutian Islands, where it is protected by law.

About four feet long, it has fine, dense, almost black fur, sprinkled with white-tipped hair.

**Otto.** EMPERORS OF THE HOLY ROMAN EMPIRE. Four emperors of the Holy Roman Empire bear the name Otto (Otho). OTTO I (912-73), usually known as Otto the Great, ruled Germany from 936 to 973 and in 962 re-established the empire of Charlemagne (*q.v.*) under the name of the Holy Roman Empire of the German Nation. His deeds show him to have been a man of energy, courage and military skill. He strengthened royal control over the unruly German dukes, and in 955 won a victory over the

Hungarians (Magyars) at the battle of Lechfeld in Bavaria, thus staying the Magyar menace.

His son, OTTO II (955–83), was emperor from 973 to 983, his 10 years' reign being largely spent in warfare, by which he lost Lorraine to the French. He died in Rome on December 7, 983, and was buried there in St. Peter's.

OTTO III (980–1002) succeeded his father Otto II when he was three years old, and was crowned emperor in 996 by the Pope at Rome. His mother was a Byzantine princess, and his tutor Gerbert (later Pope Sylvester II) was one of the most learned men of that day, especially in mathe-

matics. The young emperor himself, however, was dreamy and unpractical, and proved inadequate to his position. He died on January 23, 1002.

OTTO IV (c. 1182–1218) was the second son of Henry the Lion, Duke of Bavaria and Saxony, and was educated at the court of Richard I of England. Elected German king in 1198, he became Emperor in 1208, but was so hostile to the Church that the Pope excommunicated him in favour of Frederick II. Beaten by the French at the battle of Bouvines in 1214, in northern France, with his ally, King John of England, Otto continued a desultory resistance, but died on May 19, 1218.

# The TRUTH about the WISE OLD OWL

*Its solemn face is alone responsible for this bird's reputation for wisdom, for in its actions it shows no more intelligence than other feathered creatures. But if not particularly wise it is beneficial to agriculture.*

**Owl.** Because owls see but poorly in daylight their food-hunting is done mostly at night. In the daytime they sleep—or just sit and blink—and their reputation for wisdom, as in the case of some humans, is probably due to their solemn aspect and their silence.

They are distinguished from all other birds by peculiar radiating ruffs of feathers around the eyes,

these ruffs being bounded by a rim of stiff recurved feathers that give the effect of a mask. The neck is short and thick, and the legs are set so far back on the body that the bird naturally sits in an upright position. The plumage is fluffy, and this makes the body look larger than it really is. The feathers of the wings especially are very soft, and to this the owl owes its complete silence when flying.

Their food consists of rats, mice and other rodents, moles, frogs, worms and insects. Thus they help the farmer in reducing the numbers of pests that interfere with his crops. Owls swallow their food whole, and later eject indigestible portions from their mouth, in the form of pellets, and it is possible to tell from the pellets found near an owl's roosting place just what species of owl is there. Owls build no nests but lay their eggs, as a rule, in cavities in rocks and trees, or in the discarded nests of hawks or magpies or squirrels, or in the burrows of rabbits. The eggs are invariably white.

Owls are found in all parts of the world. Barn owls (*Tyto alba*) are fairly generally distributed in Great Britain, and as their call is a kind of scream they also go by the name of screech-owl. The barn owl is about 12 inches long and the colour of the face and all the underparts is pure white. On the upper parts it is yellowish-buff, with brown, grey and white markings. The eggs are sometimes laid at rather long intervals, so that in one brood one may find nestlings of different ages and also eggs still to be hatched.

The tawny or wood owl (*Strix aluco*) is found in almost every part of the world. It is common in England and its note is the well-known hooting cry " tu-whit, tu-whoo." Its length is 14–16 inches,

*J. T. Roberts*

**FIERCE-LOOKING LITTLE OWL**

Only about eight inches long, and with a wing-span of twelve inches, the Little Owl (*Carine noctua*) is the smallest species in Great Britain. A native of the Continent, it soon established itself in the British Isles when imported into the eastern counties many years ago. It hunts its food by day as well as by night.

# TAWNY OWL, NIGHT-WATCHMAN OF THE WOODS

The largest of Britain's native owls, the tawny owl is known also as the wood owl and brown owl, and it frequents districts where there are plenty of trees. Most specimens have rather less white about them than the one here depicted, but the general build of the bird, whatever its colour, is typical of its group. Notice the way in which there is a real 'face,' with feathers radiating out all round the eyes, and that the feet are covered with soft feathers. The tawny is the true hooting owl.

Stanley Crook

## FLUFFY PAIR OF TAWNY OWLETS

THESE two little owlets have evidently just come out from their nest, situated in a hole in the old tree in whose crutch they are standing. They have not yet lost the coat of down which has covered them since birth, although the right-hand one has begun to get proper feathers on its wings. Caught at this stage, or a little younger, they make excellent pets, although a good deal of time and trouble is often needed to feed them, since their appetites are tremendous. Moreover, if two are kept together in the same cage they are liable to turn cannibal and try to eat each other! These youngsters will grow up into big tawny owls like the one shown in the colour plate overleaf. This bird lays its eggs (it makes no real nest) in trees, in buildings or on the ground. It is most useful to the farmer, killing many rodents, besides insects.

To face page 2461

and it generally sleeps in hollow trees, occasionally in ruins. It is essentially a woodland bird and is seldom seen in open country. Like other owls, if it stirs from its home in the daytime it is usually mobbed by numbers of finches, tits and other small birds ; it makes no attempt to defend itself.

Like the wood owl, the long-eared owl (*Asio otus*) is a forest-dweller. It is called "long-eared" because of its prominent "ear-tufts" of feathers. Unlike most owls, its voice is seldom heard. It is 12–14 inches long, and the bulk of its food consists of rodents. (*See* illustration in page 446).

The short-eared owl (*Asio flammeus*) has a world-wide range, but is much less common in Britain than the long-eared owl, which it resembles in size and plumage. It hunts its

*Fischer; Ray Palmer*

**OWLS OF MOOR AND SNOW**
Above is a short-eared owl (*Asio flammeus*), which has a world-wide range in open country, where its speckled plumage serves as excellent camouflage. Below is a snowy owl (*Nyctea scandiaca*), whose white feathers make it almost invisible amid the ice and snow of the far northern regions of Europe, Asia and America.

food by day, and is not found in woods but in open fields and moors, mainly in the northern countries. It lays its eggs, from six to ten in number, on the ground. It feeds chiefly on voles.

The little owl (*Carine noctua*), which is the one associated in classical literature with Pallas, the goddess of wisdom, was introduced into Britain from continental Europe many years ago. At one time this species was regarded as a pest in that it was supposed to kill many young poultry and game-birds, but that judgement has now been modified, for, like other owls, it eats enormous numbers of mice and noxious vermin generally. It nests in holes, often in rabbit burrows, and frequently also on the bare ground without any protection. The smallest British owl—its length is about eight inches—it hunts by day as well as by night. It may also be observed sitting about in broad daylight, mobbed by other birds, but unperturbed. Its note is a repeated *cu-cu-cu*.

The beautiful snowy owl (*Nyctea scandiaca*), with white plumage, breeds in cold regions, Northern Siberia, Lapland and the northern regions of North America being its favourite haunts. It is occasionally seen in Britain.

# 'TOWN and GOWN' in OXFORD CITY

*F or centuries a centre of learning, this city still plays an important part in the national life as (equally with Cambridge) a great University whence come recruits to government, the professions, commerce and the arts.*

**Oxford.** Cupped in the hollow of gently sloping hills between the Thames (here often known as the Isis) and its lovely tributary the

*A. F. Kersling*
**In Tom Tower (above) at Christ Church, Oxford, is the bell called Great Tom, which weighs more than seven tons.**

Cherwell this famous English city is wrapped in an atmosphere of romance and beauty. To its venerable colleges have come Britain's youthful statesmen, poets, and philosophers to be brought up in the traditions of beauty and wisdom.

The origin of Oxford is lost in the mists of antiquity. It first appears in history about the year 737, when St. Frideswide founded her nunnery on the site of Christ Church. Before long a thriving market-town sprang up, which was raided by the Danes. The oldest known architectural remains are the tower of St. Martin's Church (1034) and the castle tower (1071). In this tower the Empress Matilda, daughter of Henry I (1068–1135) was

besieged by Stephen of Blois in 1142 ; she escaped by fleeing over the frozen snow-covered river—clad in white garments in order to escape detection.

Legend attributes the founding of the University of Oxford to Alfred the Great, but the first discoverable traces of organized teaching in the city are about 200 years later, in the 12th century. By the end of that century it had an academic population numbering about 3,000.

There were as yet no university buildings, no laboratories, no endowments. " Masters " gave instruction—all in Latin—to such students as chose to attend their lectures, and their entire income came from fees collected from their pupils. They were turbulent souls, those early students, and enlivened their scholastic routine by fighting with the townsmen, so that the " town and gown " riots of Oxford became proverbial.

Dominican and Franciscan friars began building monastic establishments in the 13th century, and they came to Oxford in such numbers that they soon aspired to the control of the University. This caused ceaseless strife between the religious orders and the ancient colleges, which ended only when Henry VIII suppressed the monasteries in 1539. During the civil wars of the 17th century Oxford became the seat of Charles I and the Royalist court. Several important battles of the period were fought in the neighbourhood.

*W. F. Taylor*

### LOOKING WESTWARD ALONG HIGH STREET, OXFORD

University College can be seen on the left in this view of the High Street, Oxford. It is the oldest college, for it was founded in 1249 ; one of its most famous sons, the poet Shelley, was expelled in 1811 for writing an atheistic pamphlet. Facing University College is Queen's College, with a cupola over the entrance ; it was established in 1340. Farther up the street, on the right, is the spire of St. Mary's, the University church, between All Souls and Brasenose colleges.

# MAGDALEN'S TOWER BESIDE THE CHERWELL

*J. Dixon-Scott*

Where an old bridge carries the London road across the Cherwell, at the foot of Oxford's High Street, stands the tower of Magdalen College, seen above. Magdalen (pron. maudlin), apart from its beauty, is famed for the music of its chapel, and upon the summit of this tower the choristers greet the dawn with a Latin hymn on May-day morning each year. The College was founded by William of Waynflete, Bishop of Winchester and Lord Chancellor, in 1458.

In organization and method Oxford University is strikingly different from most other universities. It is made up of men's colleges and halls, each with its own history, income, regulations, and organization, and similar establishments for women.

The principal men's colleges and halls, with the dates of their foundation, are :

| | | | |
|---|---|---|---|
| University | 1249 | Corpus Christi | 1520 |
| Balliol | 1263 | Christ Church | 1546 |
| Merton | 1264 | Trinity | 1554 |
| Exeter | 1314 | St. John's | 1555 |
| St. Edmund Hall | 1317 | Jesus | 1571 |
| Oriel | 1326 | Wadham | 1612 |
| Queen's | 1340 | Pembroke | 1624 |
| New | 1379 | Worcester | 1714 |
| Lincoln | 1427 | Hertford | 1740 |
| All Souls | 1438 | Keble | 1870 |
| Magdalen | 1458 | St. Peter's Hall | 1928 |
| Brasenose (B.N.C.) | 1509 | Nuffield College | 1937 |

Founded in October 1937 by Lord Nuffield, whose main motor works are at Oxford, Nuffield College is a centre of scientific and especially medical research. It receives no undergraduates but, like All Souls College, is open only to those who have already been awarded a degree.

The women's colleges are Lady Margaret Hall (1878), Somerville (1879), St. Anne's (1879), St. Hugh's (1886), and St. Hilda's (1893).

The University is an independent self-governing corporation. Its main functions are holding examinations, conferring degrees, and looking after the discipline of students when outside their colleges. Degrees are open to both men and women. Within the massive semi-monastic buildings of the colleges —each grouped around its own quadrangle— the students live a life hedged about by strange, long-established rules. For instance, on all academic occasions, such as lectures, conferences with tutors, chapel, and dinners " in hall " (in college), the undergraduate must wear his quaint short gown and his " mortar-board " cap. If he lives in College, he must be within the walls of his own college before midnight, and he is required to pay a small fine (1d., 2d., or 6d.) if he comes in after the main gates are closed at nine o'clock in certain colleges.

Members of the University are in residence only half the year; there are three terms known as Lent, Trinity, and Michaelmas. Much of the real reading for a degree is done during the six months of vacation. Lectures, essay writing, conferences with tutors, and reading take up from four to six hours of the average man's daily schedule during the term time. The rest of the day is given over to social life and sport. Like Cambridge, Oxford awards " Blues " and " half-Blues" to its representatives in sporting events. Oxford representatives at sports are known as " Dark Blues," and those of Cambridge as " Light Blues." 

Under the will of Cecil Rhodes (1853-1902), the South African statesman, a trust was established to grant Oxford scholarships to students from the United States, the British Dominions, and Germany, the last-named being withdrawn during the two World Wars. The scholars are selected with regard to their literary and scholastic achievements, sport-

*W. F. Taylor*

**RADCLIFFE CAMERA SEEN FROM BRASENOSE**
The library known as the ' Camera ' was built by the bounty of John Radcliffe, physician to William III, who left £40,000 for its erection. Constructed between 1737 and 1749, it was, in 1860, lent to the University as a reading-room for the Bodleian Library, and was at one time known as the Physic Library.

eastern coast of North America (*O. virginica*) With their relatives—cockles, mussels and scallops—oysters belong to the group of molluscs known as *Lamellibranchia* (*see* Molluscs). The pearl oyster belongs to a different family, as do those which live in fresh water.

Spawning occurs in early summer, the eggs hatching out in about 10 days. The young oysters, known as spat, are round in shape, and swim about freely by means of hair-like growths called cilia. They have only a rudimentary shell; though their internal organs, including a heart and a digestive system, are much like those of the adult mollusc. After a short period of freedom the young oysters grow a hard shell and, anchoring themselves to the rough bottom of the shallow sea, settle down to a sedentary life.

The most productive oyster the molluscs when they att for the c

ing qualifications, moral qualities and strength of character. The number of scholarship holders at any one time is about 200, and the annual value of a scholarship is approximately £500.

During the Second World War (1939–45) some of the colleges were taken over by the Government, their buildings being used for war purposes. There were very few students at Oxford during the war years, and two or more colleges often combined temporarily for residential use.

In the centre of the old city of Oxford is Carfax (derived from an old English word *Carfoukes*, which comes from the Latin *Quadrifurcum*, four forks, i.e. cross-roads). To the east runs the High Street, as far as Magdalen Bridge. Half-way along "the High" is the University Church, St. Mary's. This was the first home and centre of the University, where all its business, academical as well as ecclesiastical, was transacted. But the church is and was a parish church, lent by the town to the University for scholastic business. Near by is a group of notable buildings. They include the Bodleian Library—the most important in the country after that at the British Museum—and the Sheldonian Theatre. This splendid building, designed by Sir Christopher Wren (1632–1723), was erected by Archbishop Sheldon (1598–1677) to accommodate the University at the Encaenia, the solemn rite of admitting Masters of Arts to teach—and also to receive the Arundel Marbles (collection of statues, busts, and engraved stones) presented by the Duke of Norfolk. The opening of the theatre is still celebrated as Commemoration. The Ashmolean Museum, adjoining it, was added in 1683 to house the collection of antiquities of Elias Ashmole. Close to the Sheldonian is the University Press. It is in the Clarendon building, erected in 1713 with funds arising from the sale of Lord Clarendon's history.

The chief industries of Oxford are steel pressing, the manufacture of motor-cars, and catering for members of the university. There are also breweries and a big cattle market. The residential population is 103,600.

## Oxford and Asquith, HERBERT HENRY ASQUITH, 1ST EARL OF (1852–1928). Born at Morley, Yorkshire, on September 12, 1852, Asquith was educated at the Moravian School,

Topical

**EARL OF OXFORD AND ASQUITH**
Created an Earl in 1924, the Liberal statesman is here seen making a speech while he was still Mr. Asquith. On his right is his then colleague and later rival, Mr. Lloyd George, who succeeded him as British Prime Minister in 1916, when Asquith resigned owing to criticism of his conduct of the First World War (1914–18).

Pudsey, the City of London School, and Balliol College, Oxford. Called to the Bar in 1876, he soon had a large practice, so that at the end of 10 years he was able to realize another ambition and stand for Parliament. He won a seat in the General Election of 1886 as Liberal member for East Fife, which he represented until 1918. From 1892 to 1895 he was Home Secretary.

In December 1905 he became Chancellor of the Exchequer in Sir Henry Campbell - Bannerman's Government and while in that office he laid the foundations of the Old Age Pensions scheme. On the retirement of Campbell-Bannerman in 1908, Asquith became Prime Minister with Mr. Lloyd George (*q.v.*) as his Chancellor of the Exchequer. He succeeded in compelling the House of Lords to pass the Parliament Act, which greatly curtailed their powers, and his Government also passed many measures of social reform.

On the outbreak of the First World War in 1914 he defended British intervention in speeches remarkable for their lucid statement of fact and logical argument. In the conduct of the war, however, he appeared to lack driving force. He first met criticism by forming a coalition Government with the Conservative and Labour parties, but a revolt of some of his colleagues led him to resign in December 1916, when Mr. Lloyd George became Prime Minister. Asquith was defeated at East Fife in the general election of 1918, but two years later he was elected for Paisley, which he represented until defeated again in 1924. He was then created Earl of Oxford and Asquith. He died on February 15, 1928.

By his first wife Lord Oxford had four sons and a daughter. She died in 1891, and three years later he married Emma Alice Margaret (Margot), daughter of Sir Charles Tennant, Bart., by whom he had a daughter and a son. Lord Oxford's eldest son was killed in the First World War and he was succeeded by his grandson Julian.

## Oxfordshire. Known sometimes as Oxon, this south Midland county of England has an area of 748 square miles and lies mostly in the basin of the Thames, which is its southern boundary. Most of the county is flat, but there are some hills and broad well-wooded valleys in the north and south. Across the south stretch the Chiltern Hills, which rise to 800 feet, and in the north-west are some

## OXFORDSHIRE

spurs of the Cotsw[...]
principal rivers are [...]
Evenlode, Cherwell [...]
Oxford the Thames [...]

Agriculture is the [...]
oats, and beans and [...]
cattle, sheep and pi[...]
factures of gloves at [...]
ments at Banbury, [...]

Besides Oxford it [...]
fine churches, amon[...]
Norman church at [...]
Woodstock is Blen[...]
the Duke of Marlb[...]
heim in 1704. Ther[...]
the Thames, Hen[...]
resort whose annua[...]
county town is Oxf[...]
county is 209,600.

## Oxygen.

abundant substan[...]
widely distributed [...]
as an uncombined [...]
combination with [...]
water, sand, limes[...]
sugar, cloth, paper[...]
up one-fifth of the [...]

In its free state [...]
odour, or taste. [...]
chemically, and [...]
with nearly all [...]
p[...] t[...] [...]
moisture, as in th[...]
wood burns, the [...]
with the carbon [...]
chemically, " fir[...]
of a substance.

When oxygen [...]
gen, water is for[...]
if a piece of cold [...]
flame of any sort ([...]
formed from the [...]
of the air will be [...]

In this glass-wall[...]
air-lock double d[...]
under observation [...]
formed by the pati[...]

---

grows irregularly according to the supply of those small sea creatures which form its food.

The soft body is attached to the shell by a stout muscle, extending from one half of the shell through the body to the other, thus enabling the oyster to close up tightly. A fold called the mantle, growing from each side of the body, completely lines the shell and secretes a material which makes new shell. Two folds conceal the mouth, and other large flaps form the gills.

Throughout its life the oyster is attacked by hordes of enemies. Many young swimming oysters are eaten by the adults and by fishes of various kinds. Starfish sometimes destroy several hundred thousand of marketable oysters in a season, forcing the shells apart and boring in between them. Among other enemies are fish with crushing teeth.

The oyster has been under culture longer than any other water creature. A simple form of

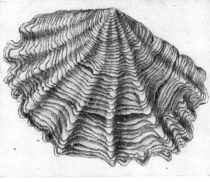

**THE PEARL OYSTER**
While pearls have been found in every variety of oyster, the genuine pearl oyster occurs principally in the East Indies. The shell is often eight to 10 inches in diameter.

cultivation, embodying the formation of artificial beds, flourished in China at a remote period. In Italy oyster culture began about 100 B.C. Perhaps the most elaborate system is that adopted in France. The spat is there usually collected on tiles placed near the spawning bed ; next the young oysters are removed to partly enclosed lakes, which admit the tides through sluices, and when fully grown the oysters are fattened. This process is carried out by enclosing them in small ponds, where their natural enemies, such as the starfish, cannot get at them. The oyster is then able to extract from the currents of water which pass through its body the minute sea creatures of various kinds on which it feeds. Oysters rank high in food value, and are second only to calf's liver as a source of iron and copper. (*See also* Pearls.)

These divers of Ceylon, carrying their day's catch of oysters ashore, work in constant danger from sharks.

The oysters are allowed to decay, and are picked over for even the tiniest pearls. The old man (left) hopes for a rich reward.

In the circle is an oyster shell which formed some hollow ' blister ' pearls while repelling a boring parasite. Perfectly round or pear-shaped pearls (above) are the most valuable.

**HARVESTING PRECIOUS PEARLS FROM THE LOWLY OYSTER**

# P

**Pacific Ocean.** Stretching 9,300 miles from the Arctic Circle at Bering Strait to the frozen seas of the South Polar zone, and nearly half-way round the Earth along the Equator, from the coast of South America to the East Indies, this, the largest of the oceans, contains about half of the water on the Earth.

It is the deepest of oceans, averaging two and a half miles, and reaching its maximum near Mindanao, one of the Philippine Islands, where yawns a chasm measuring 35,400 feet—6,259 feet deeper than Mount Everest is high. It washes the shores of four continents—Asia, North and South America, and Australia—and its waters mingle in the south-east with the Atlantic Ocean and in the south-west with the Indian Ocean.

But it is not on the shores of America or of Asia or of Australia that you will find the Pacific of the films or story books; that lies far out where countless islands, large and small, are scattered over the ocean. There, titanic disturbances at the heart of the Earth have thrust mountains and volcanoes above the waters, and tiny coral creatures have crowned the sea with thousands of ring-shaped atolls.

The air that sweeps these islands is fragrant with flowers and spice. Bright warm days and clear cool nights follow each other in eternal procession, while the rolling swells break in never-ending roar on the dazzling shores, and the slender coconut palms wave slowly in the breeze.

When white men first landed on the Pacific Islands the inhabitants—tall, magnificent men and handsome women, they were for the most part—apparently had not a care in the world. Coconuts and bread-fruit grew at the doors of their huts; the surrounding waters were filled with turtles and fish. For clothing they had little need. Disease was unknown. The first explorers frequently became so fascinated that they forgot their homes and settled down among the natives for the remainder of their days. Now the peoples who used to live in such care-free happiness are rapidly vanishing.

On certain Islands, where 100 years ago thousands lived, a few score perhaps remain. Diseases were implanted among them by the crews of vessels trading with the islands. The bodies of the islanders, from time immemorial free from the attack of disease, had slight power to resist sickness; so they fell, and continued to fall, easy victims to the scourges of civilization.

Scattered through the island groups, from one side of the ocean almost to the other, are found the remains of an ancient race of skilled builders. Ruins have been discovered of altars, tombs and dwellings built of gigantic blocks of stone fitted together without mortar. Traces exist in some places of houses built out over the sea, and of canals and gigantic piers and breakwaters.

On tiny Easter Island (*q.v.*), over 1,000 miles from any other inhabited island, are found great walls and platforms 30 feet high, surmounted by pedestals upon which once stood colossal statues, now lying near by. These statues, crumbling with age, still show resemblance to the human form.

The largest is 37 feet high, and in a quarry on the island is a figure, half cut out of the volcanic rock, which measures 70 feet high. On some of the stones are traced geometrical figures and the shapes of animals. Some of these statues are in the British Museum, London. Who were those builders, whence did they come, and whither did they go? The natives who were living on those islands when the white men first arrived knew no more about the mystery than we do.

The western shores of the Americas are remarkably unbroken, the coastal islands off Southern Chile, the Gulf of California, and the long chain of Aleutian Islands off Alaska being the only important features. Almost the only deep-sea islands are the Galapagos and the Juan Fernandez groups.

To this shore-line the coast of Asia presents a great contrast. It is broken by numerous bays and peninsulas, and is skirted by a series of large islands which almost enclose parts of the Pacific important enough to be named as separate seas. From north to south these are Bering Sea, bounded by the Aleutians; the Sea of Okhotsk, hemmed in by the

**SOUTH SEA ISLAND HAIR STYLE**
The natives of the French-owned Marquesas Islands are physically among the most striking of all the South Sea islanders. They are friendly people, and are fond of extravagant fashions in arranging their hair.

natural harbour. In the lagoon, too, fish abound, but for some reason their meat is frequently poisonous, though the same species caught outside the lagoon will be safe to eat.

The volcanic islands have an altogether different appearance. They rise steeply from the sea, often to considerable altitudes, forming impressive mountains whose outlines are softened by a dense growth of vegetation. Rain is more abundant on these islands, and the rich soil supports the taro (whose roots, ground into paste and allowed to ferment, form the native dish called *poi*) and the banana, yam, sago-palm and the indispensable bread-fruit. Here also grows the paper mulberry, whose inner bark is pounded into *tapa* cloth, so widely used for mats and clothing throughout the islands. Wild pigs and goats, descendants of those set free by early explorers, over-run many of the larger islands, and birds of bright plumage dwell in the forests.

Everywhere, on islands large or small, the coconut palm waves its plumes over the land. This palm is the " fairy godmother " of the native. It gives him food, drink, a roof for his house, and fibre for his baskets, ropes and fishing-nets. And the dried coconut kernel, called *copra*, is the chief article of island trade, and often takes the place of money in business transactions among the natives. Copra is exported for the sake of its oil, which is largely used in Europe in the manufacture of margarine, soap and candles. Another valuable article of commerce is trepang or bêche-de-mer, highly valued as food by the Chinese. It is prepared from the dried bodies of certain large sea slugs, also known as sea cucumbers.

In recent years many of the Western Pacific islands have been found to be composed largely of phosphate of lime, highly prized as a fertilizer, and this has been dug out and exported on a large scale. Several of the bigger islands yield important quantities of metal ores, New Caledonia, for instance, being one of the world's chief sources of nickel.

The climate of the Central Pacific is generally very equable, for the natural heat of the tropics is tempered by the constant ocean winds. But in the west typhoons and hurricanes frequently do great damage, and occasional tidal waves, set in motion by submarine disturbances, sweep over coastal settlements, bringing devastation.

Perhaps the first European to see the eastern Pacific was Vasco Nuñez de Balboa, who in 1513 glimpsed it from a mountain top in the Isthmus of Panama; though as early as 1512 the Portuguese were entering the Pacific from the western side, following Vasco da Gama's voyage round the Cape of Good Hope. Eight years later Ferdinand Magellan (*q.v.*) sailed round South America and crossed the Pacific to the Philippines, where he was killed. He sighted few islands on the way.

Little was accomplished in the way of wider exploration until the 17th century, when the Dutch in the person of Abel Tasman, explored Tasmania (Van Diemen's Land), New Zealand, the Tonga Islands, the Tuamotu group, and the Bismarck Archipelago. In the following century Jacob Roggeveen explored Samoa and the neighbouring islands. Samuel Wallis and Philip Carteret, in 1766, acting for Great Britain, and De Bougainville for France, carried out other important voyages of discovery.

The greatest of all was Captain James Cook (*q.v.*), who between 1769 and 1778 made three long trips, visiting nearly all the important eastern groups, including the Hawaiian Islands, where he was killed. Vancouver and others followed, and before very long the period of actual discovery and exploration of the Pacific Islands was succeeded by one of scientific study.

In the second quarter of the 19th century numerous scientific expeditions were organized to study the formation and the life of the Pacific Islands, the most famous being those of Charles Darwin, in the British warship Beagle, and of Alfred Russel Wallace. On their heels came traders, seeking copra, trepang, pearls, tortoiseshell and sandalwood. Whalers and sealers also visited the islands.

Deserters and shipwrecked sailors often settled down in the more hospitable islands, defrauding the inhabitants in trade and exerting evil influences

E.N.A.

**SETTLED BY MUTINEERS FROM THE BOUNTY**
Pitcairn Island lies about midway between Auckland, New Zealand, and Lima in Peru, and is peopled mostly by descendants of the mutineers of H.M.S. Bounty, who landed there in 1790. The upper photograph gives a general view of the island. The lower one shows the only landing place for boats. Discovered in 1767, the island takes its name from the midshipman who first sighted it.

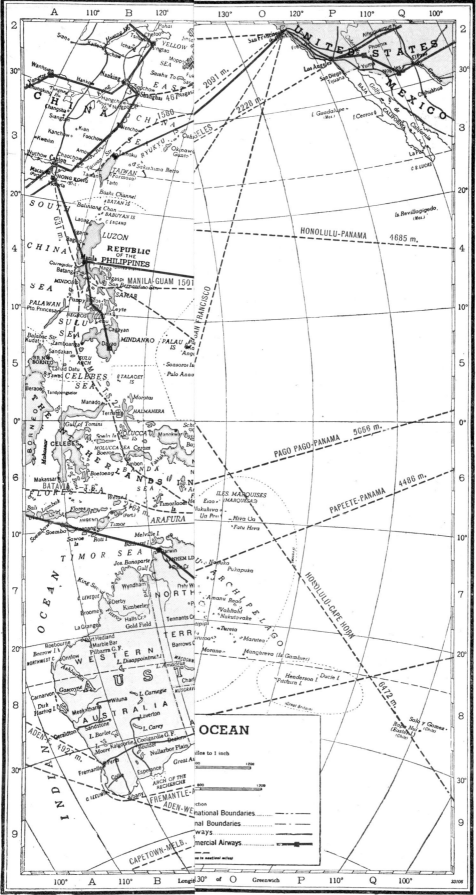

on politics. These thriftless men, who lived from hand to mouth on the bounty of the natives, came to be known as " beachcombers."

The practice of kidnapping natives for the South American and Australian labour markets, which prevailed for many years, led to conflicts with the island tribes. This and the activities of the beachcombers made exceedingly difficult the task of the missionaries, who began their work among the islanders at an early date. To-day virtually all the inhabitants of Polynesia and Micronesia profess Christianity, though many old religious beliefs are secretly kept alive.

One of the most romantic tales of the Pacific centres about Pitcairn Island, a tiny isolated rock

*Wide World Photos*

**END OF A LONG PACIFIC TRAIL**

High adventure, achievement and tragedy have been enacted in the vast expanse of the Pacific Ocean through the centuries. Here is shown the culminating triumph of an endeavour of modern times—the arrival at Auckland Harbour, New Zealand, in 1937 of an American flying-boat after her 7,000-mile flight from her homeland. The aerial link thus welded was the start of a regular service between New Zealand and the United States.

rising some 2,000 feet from the sea, south-east of the Tuamotu Archipelago. There, in 1790, nine mutineers from the British ship Bounty, accompanied by six Polynesian men and 12 Polynesian women, sought refuge from the law. They burned their vessel and started to build homes. Disorder and bloodshed followed, and within 10 years only one Englishman, John Adams, with eight women and a number of children, were left alive. When this strange colony was discovered in 1808, Adams had restored order and Christianized his people. The island was annexed to Great Britain in 1839, and 17 years later its people, numbering about 200, were removed to Norfolk Island, north-west of New Zealand, but several returned to Pitcairn. Today Pitcairn has about 200 inhabitants, mostly descendants of the original settlers. In religion the islanders are Seventh Day Adventists.

### Control of the Pacific Islands

Before the Second World War (1939–45) Japan had several groups of islands in the Pacific ; these are now controlled by the United States under a trusteeship of the United Nations. Great Britain directly administers the British Solomon, Gilbert, Ellice, Phoenix, Fiji, and Tonga groups. Australia has the Bismarck Archipelago and some of the Solomons. New Zealand possesses Western Samoa and the Cook, Chatham, Auckland, Kermadec, and Union (Tokelau) islands. France has New Caledonia and the Loyalty, Wallis, Society, Tuamotu, Marquesas, Leeward, Gambier, Tubuai, Rapa, and Makatea islands. The New Hebrides

are a British and French condominium; that is, they are under joint French and British control. The United States controls the Marianas, Marshall, Caroline, Pelew, Hawaiian and American Samoan islands, also the islets of Guam and Wake.

The air conquest of the Pacific has given new importance to some of the islands, as airports and refuelling bases. There is a regular air service operated by an American company between San Francisco and China. Another service goes to New Zealand. Commercial rivalry among the nations for the vast potential trade of the lands on the west coast of the Pacific has caused international problems of grave importance. Great Britain, Russia, France, and other European nations have vast commercial interests there. The United States, too, is concerned to maintain its commercial rights and ensure the security of its Pacific island possessions and its continental seaboard. Hence developments that menace the peace in any part of this area are of grave concern to the whole world.

The entry of Japan into the Second World War (1939–45) was marked by an attack on the U.S. naval base of Pearl Harbour (*q.v.*) in the Hawaii Islands, on December 7, 1941, which for the time being crippled American naval power in the Pacific. The Philippine Islands, Malaya, Burma, Borneo, Java and Sumatra, all fell into the possession of the Japanese, and by the end of April 1942 the Japanese were making preparations for the invasion of Australia. The battle of the Coral Sea (May 4–9, 1942), in which the Japanese Navy suffered heavy losses from attacks by United States carrier-borne

**THE CLOSE OF WAR IN THE PACIFIC**
The unconditional surrender of Japan (Second World War) was signed on
board the U.S. battleship Missouri in Tokyo Bay on September 2, 1945.
Here the Japanese representative is signing, watched by Admiral Nimitz.
At the microphone (left) is General MacArthur, the American C.-in-C.

*Keys.one*

aircraft, ended the almost unbroken sequence of successes by the Japanese.

The battle of Midway (June 3–6, 1942) restored to the United States Navy the balance of strength it had lost at Pearl Harbour. United States forces landed in the Solomon Islands on August 7, 1942, while American and Australian troops were driving the Japanese from south-east New Guinea. The United States Navy prepared the way for further advances by shattering Japanese naval power in the battle of the Bismarck Sea (March 2–6, 1943), the battle of Kula Gulf (July 5, 1943), and the battle of Vella Gulf (August 6–7, 1943).

The Gilbert Islands were captured by the Americans in November 1943, and the Marshall group in February 1944. Advancing from one island to another, the United States forces under General MacArthur (*q.v.*) moved steadily northwards toward Japan. The Pelew or Palau Islands were taken in October 1944, the struggle for the Philippines beginning on October 20 with an attack on Leyte island. On July 5, 1945, General MacArthur announced the complete liberation of the islands. Meanwhile Iwo Jima in the Volcano Islands, 750 miles from Japan, had been cleared of Japanese troops; and by June 21, 1945, the last Japanese defenders of Okinawa, in the Ryukyu Archipelago, had been eliminated. The Americans were then in a position to invade Japan itself. The first atomic bomb was dropped by a United States aircraft on the Japan-

ese city of Hiroshima on August 6, 1945, and the second on Nagasaki on August 9. On August 10 Japan sued for peace, and surrendered unconditionally on August 15, 1945.

**Paderewski,** IGNAZ JAN (1860–1941). As musician and as statesman, Paderewski (pron. pad-er-ef'-ski) has a unique place in history. His father, an administrator of large estates in Poland, was an accomplished painter and sculptor, and his mother had musical talent. Born at Kwrylowka, in Russian Poland, on November 18, 1860, he was educated in Warsaw, the Polish capital, began to play the piano at the age of three, and when 17 years old he made his first concert tour. Later he became a pupil of Leschetizky, a Polish teacher of the piano in Vienna, and in 1889 he appeared as a soloist at concerts in Vienna and Paris, taking his audiences by storm. A series of triumphs in London and the United States placed him in the front rank of pianists. His compositions include an opera, titled Manru, produced in 1901, a suite for the orchestra, and numerous piano pieces.

During the First World War (1914–18) Paderewski and his wife organized and supervised relief work for war-devastated Poland; and he directed the formation, equipment, and training of an American-Polish legion to fight on the side of the Allies. Largely through his efforts the Allies declared in favour of establishing, after the war, "a united independent Polish state, with access to the sea." Returning to Poland, he was made the first Premier and Minister of Foreign Affairs in January 1919. He presented the case of Poland to the Peace Conference in Paris in the same year, voicing and interpreting the political spirit of his countrymen as he had before interpreted the spirit

**IGNAZ JAN PADEREWSKI**
Regarded as one of the world's finest pianists, Ignaz
Paderewski also made a reputation as a statesman,
being the first Premier and Minister of Foreign
Affairs of Poland, in 1919. In the same year he
gave up his political career in favour of music.

*Donald McLeish*

of Poland in music. He retired from the Premiership before the end of the year. Paderewski received honours from all parts of the world, including the G.B.E. (Knight Grand Cross of the Order of the British Empire) and honorary degrees at Oxford and Cambridge Universities. He died in New York on June 29, 1941.

**Paine,** THOMAS (1737–1809). Born at Thetford, Norfolk, on January 29, 1737, Thomas Paine was a staymaker (like his father before him), sailor, schoolmaster, tax-collector and tobacconist before he emigrated to North America in 1774. There he arrived shortly before the outbreak of the War of American Independence (1775–83) between Britain and her North American colonies. He at once threw himself heart and soul into the cause of the colonists, and helped them by serving for a time in their army, but very much more by his persuasive pen.

" Freedom has been hunted round the globe. Asia and Africa have long expelled her. Europe regards her like a stranger; and England has given her warning to depart. O, receive the fugitive and prepare in time an asylum for mankind ! " That was his clarion call to the American colonists, published in January 1776, in his pamphlet Common Sense. Everybody of importance read it, and, as Washington said, it turned the scale of public opinion towards complete freedom from the Mother Country. When peace came in 1782 and independence had been won the Americans granted Paine money and land.

THOMAS PAINE

A supporter of the French Revolution (1789–95) Thomas Paine himself narrowly escaped execution, because he was opposed to sending King Louis XVI to the guillotine.

*After Romney*

He returned to Europe in 1787 with a model of an iron bridge which he had invented, and which was exhibited in Paris and in London. Then, when the French Revolution broke out in 1789 Paine became one of its English supporters.

He wrote a book called The Rights of Man, in reply to an attack on the Revolution published by Edmund Burke, the author and statesman.

Today the political views expressed in Paine's book seem very moderate, but for publishing it he was indicted for treason and he fled to France. There he was elected to a seat in the Revolutionary Parliament called the Convention. Though he was a Radical, Paine was not an extremist, and he opposed the execution of Louis XVI, proposing that, instead, Louis should be allowed to go to America. This won Paine the ill-will of the Jacobins, only Robespierre's fall saving him from the guillotine.

Paine's attack on President Washington, which was published soon after his release in 1796, and his criticism of revealed religion in his Age of Reason lost him many of his old friends. He returned to America in 1802, but only a few now remembered his services to the cause of the colonies. He wandered from place to place, until his death in New York City on June 8, 1809.

# BRUSH and PALETTE down the AGES

*H̲ere we are given a short history of the ' queen of the arts ' from the simple efforts of the cave-men down to the modern schools that the ' man in the street ' often finds difficult to understand.*

**Painting.** The history of painting begins in the remote ages when Man depended for his existence solely on his skill as a hunter. Among the men of the Old Stone Age, more than 20,000 years ago, there were painters who possessed the adroitness of hand and power of observation that enabled them to paint, with amazing fidelity and spirit, pictures of bison, horses, deer, and other animals which by any standards are recognized as being masterpieces of art.

In the cave of Altamira in northern Spain we can still see their paintings of these animals, in three colours, executed with an assurance of line that would do credit to the highly trained draughtsman of modern times (*see* plate facing page 2084).

When Man had advanced a little farther in culture and learned to domesticate animals and raise crops, these naturalistic drawings disappeared. Perhaps because they belonged to a different race, perhaps because they were no longer dependent entirely upon the skill of hand and of eye as hunters, the men of the New Stone Age seem to have lost their interest and adroitness in drawing. Such primitive attempts as we find representing men and animals in this period were greatly inferior to those of the Old Stone Age. There seems to have been no re-development of the art of painting until the beginnings of the historic period, when men began to erect elaborate tombs and temples and decorate them with pictures.

The paintings of the ancient Egyptians consisted simply of outlines filled in with flat colours.

They knew nothing about the rendering of depth or of light and shade. They tended to conventionalize the human form, drawing it with the shoulders in front view, the head in profile, and the eye full-face. This method is known as the law of frontality, a method practised also by the archaic Greeks of the 7th century B.C. Yet within their limits the artists of ancient Egypt achieved remarkable success. Men and animals were depicted in characteristic attitudes, often with touches of humour, and every phase of life was shown on the walls of their tombs. In many of their paintings the colours—yellow, red, brown, blue, and green, harmoniously combined with black and white—have remained vivid to this day (*see* illustration page 1115).

While the art of painting was thus developing along the banks of the Nile, it made also considerable progress along the Tigris and Euphrates, where the Babylonians and Assyrians were learning to decorate the interior of their stucco-covered mud-brick walls with painted scenes, while they adorned the exterior with artistic glazed tiles. They were inferior to the Egyptians in their attempts to represent human figures, but far surpassed them in the vigour and spirit with which they represented animal figures.

In prehistoric Greece, Crete and other Aegean lands, about 2000 years B.C., artists decorated vases in rich designs and painted the walls of palaces with animated scenes from the life of the time (*see* Aegean Civilization). The people who succeeded them, the Greeks of history, sweeping all this away, built up from primitive beginnings a greater art of their own.

We can trace an ever-growing feeling for design in the black and red vases that have survived from this time, but their great paintings have disappeared. We can, however, form some idea of the genius which runs continuously through Greek into Roman times from the paintings on the buried walls of Herculaneum and Pompeii. (*See* Greek Art ; Pompeii).

Early Christian painting, though influenced by the art of the ancients, shows a marked change in subject and spirit. The followers of the new faith, persecuted by the Roman Empire, sought refuge and a place of worship in the great underground cemeteries known as the catacombs. They decorated the dark walls with religious symbols and with pictures of Christ and the saints, simply and crudely drawn. Later, when they were permitted to worship openly, they built churches and adorned their walls.

Often mosaics took the place of the mural or wall paintings, and many of these more permanent works of art still remain, while the paintings have been destroyed (*see* Italian Art ; Mosaic). Wrought out of tiny bits of marble and glass, they represent the personages who take their parts in the sacred narratives as figures of epic grandeur.

With the barbarian invasions and downfall of the Roman Empire in the West there was a general decline of the arts, including painting. Byzantine art, which reached maturity in the 6th century and flourished in the 10th and the 12th centuries, profoundly affected early Christian art, and gave an imported conventionalised splendour to the paintings and mosaics of Venice and other Italian cities. (*See* Byzantine Empire).

In the Middle Ages northern Europe was carrying on the traditions in its glorious illuminated manuscripts and in wall paintings (*see* English Art; Manuscripts, Illuminated), and by the 13th century painting in Italy and elsewhere in western Europe was taking on a new form, abandoning the stiff conventionalism of the Byzantine for a primitive realism which paved the way for the great period of the Renaissance.

### Art Reaches Maturity in Italy

The story of painting from the 13th to the 15th century is, in fact, almost the story of the art in Italy (*see* Italian Art). The names of Giotto, Masaccio, Uccello, Leonardo da Vinci, Michelangelo, and Titian mark further stages as the great art developed. From its use as a means of showing the people scenes from the Bible and for emphasizing New Testament teachings, painting came to be more of a secular and purely pictorial art. Wall-paintings and " frescoes," in which the paint was applied while the plaster was still wet, were supplemented by easel pictures done in " tempera "— powdered pigments applied on a panel by mixing with yolk of egg or some similar medium.

Meanwhile, a strong and independent art had been developing in Holland and Flanders. Hubert and Jan van Eyck headed the Flemish school of the 14th and early 15th centuries, and the latter of them is regarded as the inventor of oil painting. In the first half of the 16th century Germany could boast of

two artists, Albrecht Dürer and Hans Holbein, who are among the great geniuses in the history of art.

Just as oil technique was taken to Italy from Flanders, so the next generation of Flemish painters studied in Italy and imported the Italian methods. Out of these " Italianizers " came the mighty Rubens, who, without losing his own individuality, brought into his work a good deal of the richness and fullness of Venetian art.

In the 17th century in Holland and Flanders there came a new democratic expression, when the Dutch " Little Masters," as they are sometimes called, raised the painting of common life to a great art. Their vision found beauty in the court of kings, the sordid market-corner, the meadow or the farmyard—wherever, indeed, the magical effects of light or colour were seen. It was Rembrandt (1606–69), the greatest of all the Dutch school, who first proved conclusively this principle of modern painting. He insisted that it was appearance and not reality that was important. He and the Spaniard, Velazquez (1599–1660), are accounted among the greatest of the world's painters who subordinated details to the impression of the whole. The Cretan, El Greco, who worked in Spain, brought an intense and highly individual vision to his deeply religious compositions (*see* Spanish Art). Both Dutch and Flemish painting are described under the heading Netherlands Art.

### The Development of Landscape Painting

Landscape painting became highly developed for the first time in the 17th century. Earlier artists had regarded landscape as incidental to the figure or the story of the picture ; now it became the picture. The Dutch painters Ruysdael and Hobbema were followed in France by Claude Lorrain, and there developed what is known as " classical landscape," in which very beautiful but more artificial effects were produced.

In the 18th century French painting reached tremendous heights, and Watteau in particular simplified the art for all posterity by the cleverness with which he evolved new ways of rendering light and shade, new " tricks of the trade " for simplifying the work of the artist and yet further deceiving the spectator (*see* France, Art). England, too, came to the fore, through Reynolds and Gainsborough as portraitists and, in landscape, through the brilliant work of Constable, who replaced the sombre browns of the Dutch landscapists by the green tints of Nature. He and J. M. W. Turner (1775–1851), " the greatest magician of light who ever wielded a brush," bring us into the 19th century.

The first new school was the Barbizon group, named from a village in the Forest of Fontainebleau, near Paris, of which the leaders were Théodore Rousseau, Millet, Corot, Troyon, and Daubigny.

In England a few years later came the Pre-Raphaelite movement, which owed its inspiration chiefly to Ford Madox Brown, and included the painters Rossetti, Holman Hunt, and Millais. (*See* Pre-Raphaelites).

But there was to come soon a new point of view in the expression of painting. In the early 1860s in France a group of painters were stirred to rebel against classic traditions, and initiate a new movement. The name " Impressionists," which soon attached itself to this school, indicates their funda-

W. F. Taylor

### ONE OF THE FIRST MEETINGS OF THE ROYAL ACADEMY

Founded in 1768 by King George III, the first meetings of the Royal Academy took place in some rooms in Pall Mall, London. Not until 1869 was the Academy housed in its present quarters in Burlington House, Piccadilly, London. On January 2, 1769, the president, Sir Joshua Reynolds, gave the first of his discourses, dealing with the value of academies and the right way in which to study art. This old print shows one of the early exhibitions.

mental purpose, which is to paint the immediate impression the artist receives from objects in Nature.

The leader of this school was Édouard Manet (1832–83), and other chief Impressionists were Claude Monet, Sisley, Degas, Pissarro and Renoir. In England, the American, James McNeill Whistler, was the chief exponent of Impressionism, to be followed by Tonks, Sickert and Wilson Steer.

The Impressionist movement was followed by the short-lived " Post-Impressionism " which represents a reaction against many of the traditional theories and practices of painting. The followers of this school no longer attempt to paint Nature, but seek to express feeling through form and colour.

Roger Fry, one of the important English critics associated with the movement, declared: " The Post-Impressionists do not seek to paint form, but to create form; not to imitate life, but to find an equivalent for life. They wish to make images which, by the clearness of the logical structure and by their closely knit unity of texture, shall appeal to our disinterested and contemplative imagination with the same vividness that the things of actual life appeal to our practical activities."

Of the Post-Impressionists the most famous are the two Frenchmen Cézanne (1839–1906) and Gauguin (1848–1903), and the Dutchman, Van Gogh (1853–90). Cézanne maintained that all shapes could be reduced to cylinders, cubes, pyra-mids, and spheres, and thus inspired the Spaniard Picasso (born 1881), who formulated Cubism. Picasso, perhaps the most important influence in 20th-century painting, at least since the First World War (1914–18), studied abstract ideas with the intention not of imitating form but of creating it. In France, there was another group known as the " Fauves." They were led by Henri Matisse (b. 1869), who invented new qualities in the relation of colour and line.

These movements were followed by others, such as Vorticism, inspired by the Englishman Wyndham Lewis; Italian Futurism; Expressionism, a violent German art; and the many types of abstract painting, with which may be coupled Surrealism (q.v.).

**Paints.** Though it is often lost sight of by people in general, the main purpose of paint is protection. Without its coats of paint the steel ship would be eaten through by rust; the steel bridge would gradually lose its strength by insidious corrosion until the time came when the bridge failed under its load and collapsed—or was swept aside by gale or flood. The outside woodwork of a house or other building, unless its surface was sealed against damp and other climatic variations by several coats of paint, would decay.

Every year you may see gangs of men hammering away at steel bridges and other similar structures to remove the scales of rust—iron oxide—which even the most regular and careful painting cannot prevent. Wire brushes, used by hand, or circular ones driven by an electric motor, scratch away the rust fragments after scaling and leave the surface clean for a coat of red lead, which is the first protective covering. This goes on at all the places where rust and scale have been removed ; it makes strange " crazy " patterns on the metal, at which you may often have wondered in passing.

Red lead is a tetroxide of the metallic element, and has the chemical formula $Pb_3O_4$. Mixed with linseed oil—a common " vehicle " for the pigment which goes to make paints—the red lead is a preservative against rust. After the steel bridge has been cleaned and treated with red lead, there follow the all-over coats of paint (again with lead as the protective ingredient) which give the structure the pleasing appearance we expect. So you see that for outside work the paint has a twofold function, to protect and to beautify.

### Preliminary Work on the Surface

When woodwork is ready for fixing, it is given a " priming " coat to fill the pores, penetrate joints and crevices, and cover nail holes (which should have previously been filled with putty, a plastic substance made of whiting, lead compounds and linseed oil, which hardens in time). Priming paints are made of red lead or white lead, the first-named for outside woodwork, and the second (a basic carbonate in chemical language) for interior woodwork. On wood the priming leaves a good hard surface which prevents the next coat—the undercoat—and the finishing coats from sinking in.

The colour of a painted surface is given mainly by the undercoats. These are of more opaque material—which means that there is more pigment in proportion to the vehicle than is the case with the priming. We must bear in mind that the object is to coat the wood or iron or steelwork with a substance which, when it solidifies, will give a firm continuous layer. The finishing coats give smoothness and gloss to the work. Sometimes a " flat "—non-glossy—finish is preferred ; in other cases there is a coat of varnish applied after the paint coats have dried. Varnish is made from oils and resins, or from some of the newer synthetic resins (sometimes called " lacquers ").

Glossy finish-coat paints are sometimes called enamels, though true enamels (q.v.) are those which are fused by intense heat in an oven, as on bicycle frames, and have a glassy composition.

An oil-paint consists, as we have seen, of a *vehicle*, or containing medium, such as linseed oil; and a *pigment*. The vehicle holds the particles of pigment (ground up to very tiny grains) in suspension. That is, the pigment does not dissolve in the vehicle, and if we let the paint stand for a while, we shall find that the solid particles have sunk to near the bottom; the mixture requires frequent stirring to avoid this. The vehicle must be one which will solidify naturally, and so produce a thin, hard film of paint. In addition, a *drier* is included, this being usually a mixture of metallic compounds—for example, lead, cobalt, manganese—which hastens the drying and hardening of the paint. Then, also, a *thinner* such as turpentine or white spirit (*see* Oil) is added to give the proper consistency to the paint.

Where do the attractive colours come from to beautify our homes ? Many are metallic oxides and other metallic compounds, or are natural earths such as the ochres. Reds are got from lead oxide, iron oxide and vermilion (mercuric sulphide). Yellow pigments include chrome yellows (lead chromates), ochre (limonite); and various compounds of zinc, arsenic or cadmium. For greens there are chromium sesquioxide, malachite, or mixtures of blue and yellow pigments. Among the blues are cobalt aluminate and Prussian blue (ferric ferrocyanide). " Pastel " shades are made from a white body-pigment tinted with dyestuffs. Carbon black or lampblack serves for black paints.

Then there are the metallic paints or " bronzes," such as aluminium, copper and " gold "—the last made from bright yellow alloy resembling brass. Modern advances in the turning of such metals into powdered form has given us lustrous, smooth-flowing metallic paints of great value. Aluminium paint has a high protective power and is commonly used for interior pipes and fittings, sometimes with a coloured transparent medium added, to give a pleasing shade over the glittering metallic body.

Other protective " paints " include coloured cement washes and asphaltic or bitumen coatings applied with a brush.

Water-paints are made from some of the pigments mentioned, ground in a watery vehicle. Usually some glue-like substance such as size or casein is included to bind the pigment and make the paint adhere to walls, etc. These paints are sold in paste form, needing only to have water added. Similar are the " distemper " for the outhouses. Lime-wash, made principally from lime, is a germ and vermin killer, as well as giving a cream-coloured, light-reflecting coating on rough walls not deemed suitable for painting. White-wash is made from whiting, a form of chalk; an improved grade is used to colour ceilings, though here a lightly tinted colour is often preferred instead. While water-paints set hard by drying, oil-paints dry by oxidation of the oily vehicle.

### Painting with a 'Gun'

Oil-paints were for long almost the only ones used for durable work; but advances in synthetic chemical manufacture have given the paint industry some valuable alternatives as vehicles, in the form of resins like those we make into plastics. Very attractive enamels, in colours never before available, have come into use to turn the often drab and dingy cupboards and shelves of the kitchen and scullery into bright and light-reflecting surfaces with a smooth finish upon which dust cannot cling. Workers in factories are happier and more healthy, and turn out more or better work, if their surroundings are painted in hues which are bright but restful, instead of merely being distempered in crude colour, or left rough.

Many such advances would be too expensive were it not for the invention of spray-painting. In this process the paint is contained in a " gun " held in the painter's hand ; a trigger admits compressed air, which forces out the paint in a fine spray which quickly and evenly coats a wall—or applies the paint or lacquer to the body of a motor car, or to the cabinet for a refrigerator. Even if the enamels are vitreous ones, which have to be

" stoved " in order to set the coating, the same spraying process can be used. This is how the durable non-chip coating for gas cookers and stoves is applied. Altogether, in recent years, painting has done much to save labour and bring pleasure to Man.

Artists' colours are made from some of the same type of pigments as those mentioned for commercial paints; but far more care is taken to secure pure substances, which will be little affected by the atmosphere, and will last for years without deterioration. Some other ingredients are scarce and expensive—for example, ultramarine, made by grinding up the mineral lapis lazuli, which is also esteemed as a gem-stone. (*See* Colour; Painting).

**Pakistan.** The Mahomedan State with the largest population in the world, the Dominion of Pakistan (pron. pahk′-is-tahn) is divided into two parts—West Pakistan and East Pakistan—which are separated by territory belonging to the republic of India. The area of Pakistan is 360,935 square miles, West Pakistan being 306,920 square miles in extent and East Pakistan 54,015 square miles.

West Pakistan is divided into four provinces— Baluchistan, Sind, West Punjab and North-West Frontier Province. It adjoins Afghanistan and Persia in the west and north-west, and the republic of India in the east. To the north lies the State of Jammu and Kashmir, to the south and south-west the Arabian Sea. The entire area to the north and west is covered by ranges of the Hindu Kush and Sulaiman Mountains, rising, in places to 14,000 feet. The Salt Range lies slightly to the east of these mountain systems and from it a vast plain extends southward to the Arabian Sea.

> **Extent.**—Total area of Pakistan 360,935 square miles ; West Pakistan 306,920 square miles ; East Pakistan 54,015 square miles. Population of Pakistan estimated (1948) at 80 million.
> **Physical Features.**—West Pakistan ; Hindu Kush and Sulaiman mountains in the north, rising to 14,000 feet ; extensive plain stretching from the Salt Range to the Arabian Sea. Chief rivers : Indus, Jhelum, Chenab, Ravi, and Sutlej. East Pakistan : vast alluvial plain, with low mountain ranges in the south-east. Chief rivers : Ganges, Brahmaputra.
> **Chief Products.**—West Pakistan : wheat, rice, millet, cotton, fruit, cattle and sheep. East Pakistan : rice, jute and tea.
> **Chief Cities.**—West Pakistan : Karachi (population 359,500) capital of the Dominion ; Lahore (950,000) ; Peshawar (275,000) ; Rawalpindi (300,000) ; Quetta (900,000). East Pakistan : capital Dacca (population 550,000) ; Chittagong (36,000).

The five main rivers of West Pakistan are the Indus (*q.v.*) and its tributaries the Jhelum, Chenab, Ravi and Sutlej, all rising in the Himalayas. Though much of the land in Baluchistan and in the western regions of the North-West Frontier Province is either too dry or too mountainous for cultivation, West Pakistan includes some of the finest agricultural land in the world and a magnificent system of irrigation canals.

Apart from wheat, which is the main crop, millet, barley and maize are cultivated. In point of quantity West Pakistan produces only about one-third as much cotton as the republic of India, but the superior qualities are grown entirely in Pakistan. Oil seeds are produced for export ; live-stock-breeding is an industry of West Punjab. Quantities of fruit are grown in West Punjab and to a lesser extent in Baluchistan. West Pakistan is rich in mineral resources, including oil, coal, gypsum, chromite, steatite, and salt, which await development. There are textile and sugar factories, flour-mills, tanneries, and iron and steel foundries.

There are more than 5,000 miles of railway and some 35,000 miles of roads. Air communication exists between East and West Pakistan and with Europe, the Far East and Australia. The capital of the Dominion of Pakistan is Karachi (*q.v.*) which is also the chief port of West Pakistan. Lahore, with a population of nearly a million, is the largest city and the capital of the province of West Punjab. Other large centres are Peshawar, Quetta, Rawalpindi, Multan and Dera Ismail Khan.

The inhabitants of West Pakistan are predominantly Mahomedan, and though such peoples as the Pathans of the North-West Frontier Province, the Punjabis and Baluchis have their own languages or dialects, Urdu is widely understood. The population of West Pakistan is about $32\frac{1}{2}$ million.

Nearly the whole of East Pakistan, which comprises the provinces of East Bengal and Sylhet, is a plain bounded on the west, north, and a part of the east, by territory of the Indian republic. The Bay of Bengal forms the southern boundary, and Burma part of the eastern. The most outstanding feature of East Pakistan is its network of rivers—the Ganges and Brahmaputra with their tributaries. These waterways furnish a cheap means of transport; they contain huge quantities of edible fish, and bring down fertilizing silt which they deposit over the land. The forests of the Sunderbans in the Ganges delta abound in tigers, leopards, bears and wild boars.

With an average rainfall of 60 inches a year irrigation is unnecessary, and the warm damp climate and fertile soil yield two harvests annually. Rice is the main crop and staple food, but jute is more important commercially, East Pakistan being the principal jute-growing area in the world. The Sylhet district is famous for its tea, which forms a valuable export. Besides agriculture there are a few other industries in East Pakistan, the most important being cotton spinning and weaving.

There are 1,600 miles of railway and 20,000 miles of road, but the internal waterways provide the cheapest and most useful means of communication. The principal port of East Pakistan is Chittagong, which has a fine natural harbour; the capital is Dacca. About three-quarters of the inhabitants of East Pakistan are Mahomedans; so though they speak Bengali, religious ties link them with the people of West Pakistan. Throughout Pakistan English is the official language; it is taught as a second language in schools, and is used as the medium of instruction for higher education. The population of East Pakistan is about 47 million.

The Dominion of Pakistan came into being on August 15, 1947, when the British Empire in India was divided between the Dominions of India and Pakistan. The population of the Dominion is about 80 million, of whom nearly 80 per cent are Mahomedans. The first Governor-General of Pakistan was Mahomed Ali Jinnah (*q.v.*), succeeded in 1948 by Khwaja Nazimuddin. In 1947 Liaquat Ali Khan became the first Prime Minister.

# A JOURNEY through the HOLY LAND

*The troubled country of Palestine, a place of pilgrimage alike to Mahomedans, Jews and Christians, the birthplace of the Prince of Peace, has not itself found a lasting peace in 5,000 years.*

**Palestine.** On December 11, 1917, during the First World War, quietly and unostentatiously, General (later Field-Marshal, Lord) Edmund Allenby, commander-in-chief of the Allied armies in the East, entered the city of Jerusalem and delivered Palestine from the age-long tyranny of the Turks.

This mother of Jericho wears on her head a ' halo ' of coins consisting of the dowry given her on marriage.

Under their oppressive rule the people had suffered for centuries, and the once beautiful and fertile land had become barren and desolate. For ages the hearts of half the world had turned with devotion and longing towards this land of Canaan, which was the Promised Land of the Israelites and the birthplace of Christianity. By Jew, Christian, and Mahomedan alike it is reverenced as the Holy Land.

As you stand on the top of Mount Ebal—which, with Mount Gerizim opposite, guards the ancient city of Shechem (now Nablus)—and let your eye sweep over the landscape you can view almost the whole of Palestine. To the west you see the waters of the Mediterranean, bordered by sand-hills; to the east the River Jordan and—far to the north, beyond the boundaries of ancient Israel—snow-crowned Mount Hermon; while to the south you look upon Jerusalem on its height, and beyond to the southernmost hills of Judea skirting the wilderness.

Leaving the Mediterranean port of Jaffa, the traveller passes through beautiful orange groves and then across the flat plains of Sharon. Here in ancient times dwelt the Philistines (*q.v.*), from whom the entire country was named Palestine. In some of the fields Arab farmers may be seen ploughing in much the same primitive fashion as in Biblical times, while on the hillsides shepherds clad in their long robes and turbans still watch their flocks as did the Israelites of old. On many farms, however, ploughs and tractors of the latest design are used by Jewish immigrants.

Camels still plod along the roads, but motor-cars and lorries now run between the chief towns, and there are buses in the streets of Jerusalem. The Holy City has changed, too; splendid modern suburbs have sprung up outside the walls of the Old City. (*See* Jerusalem).

From Jerusalem a winding and precipitous road leads to Jericho, which lies nearly a quarter of a mile below the level of the sea. Jericho was the first city which the Israelites conquered when they entered the Promised Land, many centuries before the birth of Christ, and it was already a city noted for its wealth and luxury. It was rebuilt by the Romans and made so splendid that Antony chose it as a gift to present to his beloved Cleopatra. Now only a small modern settlement remains, a little distance from the site of that famous " city of palms." Most of the palm trees have now disappeared, but banana groves make a welcome splash of green against the dusty background.

A few miles farther and we are at the banks of the River Jordan, which is here crossed by a steel bridge named after Lord Allenby. Each sect of the Christian church has here a different bathing-place, which each claims to be the exact spot where Jesus was baptized by John the Baptist. Willows, poplars, and various shrubs clothe the banks, but as we follow the muddy stream southward to the Dead Sea the vegetation takes on a sickly look.

Occupying the lowest part of that deep chasm through which the Jordan flows, the Dead Sea (*q.v.*) is almost 1,300 feet below the surface of the Mediterranean. It deserves its name, for it contains no animal life except of the lowest forms, and fish put into its water soon die. Yet this abode of desolation promises to become a valuable source of revenue, for it contains large amounts of potash and other salts, which are extracted by evaporation. The Jordan also serves an economic purpose, for it is harnessed to supply several cities with electricity.

Climbing back over the barren hills of Judea, we reach Bethlehem (*q.v.*), where Jesus was born. A few miles farther south, in the ancient city of Hebron, is the cave where Abraham, Isaac and Jacob are supposed to lie buried. About this place has been built a Moslem mosque, for the Mahomedans regard these patriarchs with reverence.

Passing to the north we cross Samaria and reach the fertile, well-watered and pleasant land of Galilee. Here, nestling among the hills, we find Nazareth (*q.v.*), where Jesus spent

**Extent.**—North to south, 265 miles ; east to west, from less than 10 to about 80 miles. Total area west of the River Jordan about 10,000 square miles ; population (estimated 1947) 1,933,670 (1,090,870 Mahomedans ; 614,240 Jews ; 146,160 Christians ; others 82,400).

**Physical Features.**—From the coastal plain along the Mediterranean the land rises towards the east, forming a rugged plateau intersected by deep valleys and broken mountain ranges, highest point, Jebel Jermak (3,934 feet) in Galilee. At the east the plateau drops steeply into the depression down which the River Jordan, rising on Mt. Hermon (9,400 feet) beyond the northern boundary, flows south through the Sea of Galilee to the Dead Sea (1,300 feet below sea-level).

**Products.**—Oranges, grapes ; olives and olive oil ; wine ; soap ; nuts, wheat, barley, millet, tobacco, water-melons; sheep, goats, camels ; hides and skins, wool ; salt, cement, potash.

**Chief Cities** (1946).—Tel-Aviv (183,000) ; Jerusalem (164,000) ; Haifa (145,000) ; Jaffa (102,000) ; Hebron, Nablus, Gaza, Lydda, Ramleh, Safad, Tiberius, Nazareth, Acre, Bethlehem, Jericho.

Photochrom

## IN THE TOWN OF CHRIST'S NATIVITY

This photograph of an old Arab astride his sturdy ass was taken in Bethlehem, the little Palestinian town where Jesus Christ was born some 1,900 years ago. There is nothing in the picture which would have been out of place in those far-off days, for Bethlehem until quite recently, has always been set in a quiet backwater of peace.

E.N.A

# CARRYING WATER IN PALESTINE

In Bethlehem, the birthplace of Jesus and of King David of Israel, young women carry jars of water balanced upon their heads, as is the custom among many Eastern races. The head-shawl and gown of this girl are embellished with coloured embroidery which she has no doubt worked with her own skilful fingers.

To face page 2481

His boyhood. Not far away to the east and north are the waters of the Sea of Galilee (Lake of Gennesareth or Tiberias). On these shores Jesus often walked, and here He met the fishermen who became His apostles. Now the region is quieter than it was in His day. Only a few scattered boats are seen on the waters, which were once covered with sails. With the exception of Tiberias, which has been rebuilt, the ring of cities whose stately buildings were reflected in its waters have fallen, leaving only heaps of ruins. But the lake has not lost its beauty. Its waters drain southward through the Jordan into the Dead Sea.

*Donald McLeish*

**PADDLING IN THE SEA OF GALILEE**

**Formed by an expansion of the River Jordan, the Sea of Galilee is 13 miles long and 8 miles wide. As we can learn from the Gospels, this sea or lake—it is known also as the Lake of Tiberias or Gennesareth—is subject to fierce and sudden storms, though in this picture it is in placid mood. On its shores are the remains of ancient cities such as Capernaum.**

Ascending one of the hills of Galilee and looking eastward, we see across the Jordan the heights of Gilead with their forests of oak and terebinth or turpentine trees.

To the south-west is the famous Plain of Esdraelon, the vast arena in which so many battles have taken place. Armies from the empires of the Nile and of the Euphrates, from the north and the south, from the east and the west, have here met in conflict. In the early days of Israel's history Barak and Gideon won here their splendid victories; and here

Saul met defeat against the Philistines, and Josiah against the Egyptians. Across this plain Jehu came driving so furiously to Jezreel; here the valiant Maccabees won freedom for the Jewish people; and in the Middle Ages many a Crusader died in the Plain of Esdraelon fighting for the Cross.

Napoleon's advance from Egypt was here checked by the Turks and British, and after three months' fighting he was forced back in the first retreat of his career. In the First World War (1914–18) the Allies won Palestine from the Turks

**ON THE BANKS OF THE SACRED RIVER JORDAN**

**This is the stream in which Christ was baptized by John the Baptist. In modern times guides have conducted many travellers through this region. The reach seen above is near the Dead Sea, into which the Jordan flows. The river occupies part of one of the world's most celebrated ' rift valleys ' (caused by the sinking of the earth's crust between two ' faults ').**

in this field that is supposed to be the Plain of Armageddon to which the Book of Revelation refers as the place where " the kings of the earth and of the whole world " are to gather for " the battle of the great Day of God Almighty," the Day of Judgement.

Today the Plain of Esdraelon is a scene of beauty, the home of prosperous Jewish agricultural colonies. This naturally fertile region, which through generations of neglect had become a land of pestilential swamps and barren wastes known as " the Valley of Death," has been reclaimed through the labour and sacrifice of Jewish pioneers and British administrators.

In material things Palestine is a poor country. Its natural resources are few. It has few minerals— no coal, no iron, no copper, no silver. Its forests have almost disappeared. Only in isolated spots is land productive. The ancient Israelites, coming to it from the wilderness, called it " a land flowing with milk and honey "; but it was only through patient toil that they won an abundance for their needs, and after many centuries of neglect much of the country has become a waste.

Even in Palestine's palmiest days water was so scanty as to be considered extremely precious. All through the Bible we find praise of water—of brooks and springs and wells. Rainfall was probably more abundant than today because of the greater number of trees, but seasons of drought often occurred even in those times. The rainfall is not evenly distributed throughout the year in Palestine. Practically all of it falls during the winter months, beginning in October or November and ending with the heavy showers of March and April. Much of the rain, too, percolates through the limestone rock and is thus wasted. The forests, which in ancient times helped to conserve the moisture, have almost disappeared, but large areas are now being reafforested.

Remarkable improvements have been made, especially in transportation. During the 1914–18 war the British built a double-track railway from Port Said to Haifa, which place has superseded Jaffa as the chief seaport and has a magnificent new harbour completed in 1933. This railway was extended during the Second World War to Beirut, and links up with the Turkish line to Istanbul, so that it is now possible to go by rail from Cairo to Istanbul. Other railways and excellent roads for motoring link all the chief towns.

Of the population of Palestine about three-fifths are Arabs (Mahomedans in faith), including many wandering shepherds. Jews form the greater part of the remainder.

In the settlement following the First World War, Palestine was taken from the Turkish Empire, and all the country west of the River Jordan was entrusted to Great Britain under a mandate from the League of Nations. Great Britain had already given a pledge (the Balfour Declaration) to do everything it could to aid the realization of the Zionists' dream of " establishing in Palestine a national home for the Jewish people."

Much has been done towards the realization of this dream. Not only has agriculture been developed, but a number of industries, of which there were practically none before the 1914–18 war, have been established. A striking instance of the progress due to Jewish activity is seen in the city of Tel-Aviv. Established in 1909 as a suburb of Jaffa and built on what was only a waste of sand-dunes, it has grown into a city of over 183,000. The River Jordan has been harnessed for power south of Lake Tiberias. There is a Hebrew University at Jerusalem, and many schools.

But the Arabs who lived in Palestine resented the coming of the Jews. Under the leadership of T. E. Lawrence (q.v.) they had played their gallant part in freeing the country from the Turks, and they had been given to understand that with the end of Turkish domination they would rule in their own land. Their ambitions were in direct conflict with those of the Jews, and both sides claimed that they were asking only what had been promised to them during the war.

*American Colony, Jerusalem*

**MODERN ARCHITECTURE IN PALESTINE**

Where once was a waste of sand-dunes now stands the modern city of Tel-Aviv. The Jewish architects have in many cases made striking departures in architecture from the conventional idea of a Palestinian city, as can be seen from this photograph taken at the junction of Allenby and Montefiore streets.

When the Nazi persecutions began in 1933 Jewish immigration increased, and the Arab community considered that its position was threatened by the influx of Jews from Central Europe. Rioting and strife culminated in an Arab revolt in 1936, and in 1937 a British proposal to partition Palestine was rejected by both Jew and Arab. In 1939 came the publication of the British Government's order which banned Jewish immigration after 1944. The massacre of the Jewish population of Europe under the Nazis left many displaced Jews, often the sole survivors of families, who felt themselves unable to remain in Europe. Other countries refused them entrance, and the Zionists declared that the British ban on immigration was illegal and opposed to the terms of the mandate.

While their recognized leaders counselled moderation, a minority of the Jews determined at the end of the Second World War to gain their ends by violence. Shipload after shipload of illegal immigrants tried to land, only to be intercepted by the Royal Navy and interned in Cyprus. Inside Palestine two groups of terrorists, the Irgun Zvai Leumi and the Stern gang, embarked on a campaign of murder and destruction against the Arabs and the British; and when Great Britain announced her intention of surrendering the Palestine mandate on May 15, 1948, whether or not a solution to the problem had been reached, a reign of terror began. Day after day British soldiers were murdered, bombs were thrown in the Arab quarters, and police posts were attacked. A wing of the King David Hotel in Jerusalem was blown up, with the loss of 91 lives. Two British sergeants were hanged after a mock trial as a " reprisal " for the execution of a Jewish terrorist.

As neither side would agree to the British proposals, the Palestine question was referred to the United Nations. A special committee was set up, while Great Britain made it clear that her forces would impose no solution on the country that had not been accepted equally by Jews and Arabs. By a majority of seven to three the committee, in August 1947, determined on partition of the country between the Jews and the Arabs.

Meanwhile, as the time approached for Britain to withdraw, Palestine became an armed camp. At midnight of the night preceding the expiry of the mandate, the Jews proclaimed the State of Israel, with the boundaries fixed in the United Nations partition recommendation, while the Arab Higher Committee for their part declared that the whole of Palestine was now an Arab state. With effect from the end of the mandate the neighbouring Arab nations, Syria and the Lebanon, Iraq, Transjordan, and Egypt, began a war on behalf of their countrymen in Palestine. The last British troops left at the end of June 1948.

The Jewish forces fought with Arab forces in the north, the east and the south. Here they advanced, there they were repelled. Then, in June 1948, the Swedish Count Folke Bernadotte, who had negotiated the last stages of the German armistice with the Allies in 1945, went to Palestine as United Nations mediator. An uneasy truce was declared, while the Count negotiated energetically with each side. Then, on September 17, a Jewish assassin's bullet struck him down.

**A SAMARITAN READING THE LAW**
A few families now remain in Palestine to represent the ancient Samaritan people. They recognize only the first five books of the Bible as sacred, and claim that the orthodox Jews have departed from the pure teachings of Moses.

A successor was appointed by the United Nations, who continued the negotiations for peace. Fighting again flared up, and Egyptian territory was invaded in January 1949 by the Jews, who achieved considerable military success in southern Palestine. A solution to please both sides seemed an impossibility. The new State of Israel had at once been recognized by the U.S.A., and later by other countries. In January 1949 Great Britain and France recognized the Israeli Government. Elections were held in February 1949, and Mr. Ben Gurion became Prime Minister of the Israeli Constituent Assembly, which met in Jerusalem. A few months later armistices were agreed between the Arab countries and the Israeli Government, Palestine remaining roughly divided between Israel and the Kingdom of Transjordan (*see* Jordan). In 1950 the Israeli Government proclaimed Jerusalem to be the capital of Israel.

**Palm.** The silhouette of a palm tree, with its tall, slender trunk surmounted by a crown of enormous leaves, is a sight which one could never forget or fail to recognize at first glance. The trunk, which may be 100 feet or more high, terminates at the top in a rosette of leaves radiating from it like the outspread fingers of the hand. It is this resemblance that gives the palm its name, from the Latin word *palma*, " palm of the hand."

Some palms, however, are mere shrubs. The dwarf palmettos have buried stems, and form low scrubby growths covering the ground like weeds, making, with their large prickly leaves, a well-nigh impenetrable thicket. Others, such as the rattan palm, have slender rope-like stems which climb like vines and often are several hundred feet long.

More than 1,500 species of palms have been discovered. They are found mostly in the Pacific

# SOME OF THE 1,500 SPECIES OF PALM

1. A native of Ceylon scaling the long, slender, leaning trunk of a coconut palm. This palm thrives on tropical coasts throughout the world. 2. One of the many fan palms from which fans and roof thatching are made. 3. An Arab gathering a meal of dates from a date palm in Algeria. 4. Looking down into the heart of a young sago palm; the pith is made into the sago of commerce. 5. Ropelike stems of rattan palms in Java. They run over other trees, or along the ground, and may grow several hundred feet long and are used for making ropes, mats and furniture.

islands, in Asia, America and Africa. Though they reach their greatest development in the rainy tropics, some species, such as the date palm (which is believed to be the palm of the Bible), grow in very arid regions, and others in the temperate zone.

Palm leaves are of two main types: fan-shaped (palmate), as in the common fan palm and palmetto; and feather-shaped (pinnate), as in the date and the coconut palms. In some species the leaves are 30 to 45 feet long and four to eight feet wide. The flowers are small and usually white, greenish, or yellow in colour, and are borne in clusters in the crown of leaves.

Next to the cereals and other members of the grass family the palms are the most useful of all plants. Their fruits, stems, and leaves are used in a number of manufactured products, besides furnishing food, shelter, and clothing for the natives of the regions in which they abound.

Among palm products are dates, a staple food of many desert peoples; palm-oil, derived from the fruits of the oil-palm (*Elaeis guineensis*) and other species, used in cooking, in soap-making, and as a lubricant; palm-wine, which is made from the sap of several species; sago and starch, from the pith of the sago palm (*Metroxylon*) and others; rattan, the thin flexible stems of various species of *Calamus;* and vegetable ivory, the nuts of the tagua or ivory palm (*Phytelephas macrocarpa*), from which buttons and various other small articles are manufactured. Valuable fibres used in making brushes, hats, and baskets are derived from palms, some of the commonest kinds being raffia, piassava, kitool, African fibre, palmetto, and coir or coconut fibre. Palms are the largest of all the monocotyledons and belong to the family *Palmaceae*.

## Palmyra.

It is a journey of 150 miles across the Syrian desert from Damascus to the ruins of Palmyra, the city from which Queen Zenobia 17 centuries ago held sway over a considerable kingdom on the eastern border of the Roman Empire, from northern Palestine to the Euphrates.

The famous " city of palms " can never have been more than a square mile in area, but the whole of that space was made beautiful. Through the centre, for nearly a mile, extended a quadruple colonnade of rosy-white limestone, 750 columns in all, each of them 55 feet high, and terminating in a triumphal arch. Beyond this, upon a terrace, stood the Temple of the Sun, its court surrounded by pillars intricately carved.

The wealth which made this beauty possible began to pour into Palmyra before the Christian era, when the oases in which the city stood became a trading post on the caravan route by which silks, perfumes and jewels of the East were brought to the Mediterranean world. The city's most splendid period extended from A.D. 130 to 270, when political importance was added to wealth by Rome's recognition of Palmyra as a valuable " buffer " state between her own possessions and the rising empire of Persia. Zenobia's husband, Odenathus, was made viceroy of the East, in return for military assistance against Persia. His glory was short-lived, for he was assassinated in 267, at the height of his success.

After her husband's death Zenobia sought to establish an independent empire for her son, but

**IN PALMYRA, CITY OF PALMS**
Though the once fair city of Palmyra has long since fallen into decay, its ruins testify to its former greatness. Among the temples which adorned it the largest was that of the Sun, the base of one of whose walls is seen here.

the story of her splendid defiance of Rome—which you may read in Chaucer's Monk's Tale—had a tragic ending. Her armies were no match for the troops of the soldier-emperor Aurelian, whose desert march to Palmyra was an achievement worthy of a Roman, and in 273 the queen was conquered. The city was destroyed, and thereafter the caravans took other routes.

Palmyra today is only a small town, but extensive ruins of the old city remain. Palmyra is the Tadmor of the Bible (2 Chron. viii, 4), which is said to have been built by Solomon.

## Pan.

In Greek mythology there is, perhaps, no more picturesque figure than Pan, the god of flocks and pastures, of fields and forests. He is represented as having horns, a goat's beard, pointed ears, a tail, and goat's feet. He led a merry life, dwelling in caves, wandering through wood and dale and over mountains, protecting flocks, hunting and fishing, and dancing with the nymphs.

According to legend, he fell in love with the beautiful nymph Syrinx, but, frightened at his appearance, she fled from him and was transformed into a reed by the gods. From this reed Pan made the instrument known as the syrinx or Pan's pipes.

The mischievous Pan took delight in coming upon travellers unexpectedly and exciting the sudden fear which has come to be called " panic." He is often represented as accompanied by goat-like beings much like himself, called satyrs. These were the fauns of Roman mythology, the companions of Faunus, who occupied a position similar to that of Pan. The worship of Pan was introduced into Athens from Arcadia, in southern Greece, in about the 5th century B.C., because of his supposed aid to the Athenians in the battle of Marathon.

In later times Pan came to be regarded as the god of universal Nature, through confusion of his name with another Greek word, *pan* meaning " all," and finally came to stand for all the Greek gods and for paganism itself. So a legend arose that when Christ was born a mighty voice proclaimed " Pan is dead! " thus heralding the end of the power of the old divinities.

**Panama.** Occupying the isthmus that connects North and South America, this Republic of Central America has an area of 28,576 square miles. It extends from Costa Rica in the west to Colombia in the East, the Caribbean Sea and the Pacific Ocean forming the northern and southern boundaries respectively. The country is cut in two by the Canal Zone, a strip of land five miles wide on each side of the Panama Canal, over which the United States exercises jurisdiction.

Low forest-covered mountains enclose wide valleys and plains in most of the Republic, though some of the peaks on the Costa Rican border are more than 11,000 feet high. The climate is hot and damp, and there are thick jungles in the lowlands. Large areas are uninhabited and almost unexplored; of the rest, only a small part is at present under cultivation.

Bananas are the main crop and chief export; coconuts, timber, sugar, cocoa and tobacco are also important. Excellent pasture lands support an extensive livestock industry. The forests yield various timbers, and rubber. Gold is mined. Other mineral deposits, such as manganese, silver, copper, and aluminium, have been little exploited. Pearl fishing is carried on at the Pearl Islands in the Gulf of Panama.

The capital is Panama City (population 111,000), and next in size is Colón (population 44,000). The only broad-gauge railway in the country connects these two towns; there are also some 50 miles of narrow-gauge line. Air services operate between Panama, the United States and other countries of Central and South America.

Formerly a department of the Republic of Colombia, with which it was united for 82 years, Panama achieved its independence by a bloodless revolution in 1903. In that year discussions were opened with Colombia by the United States Government with a view to transferring the rights of the French company engaged in building the Panama Canal to the United States. The Colombian Government rejected the terms offered by the United States; and the people of Panama, fearful lest the canal might be built in Nicaraguan territory, rebelled on November 3, 1903, the independence of the new republic being recognized by the United States 10 days later.

Panama took no active part in the Second World War, but leased to the United States air and naval bases for the protection of the Panama Canal. The population is 622,600.

## *How* MAN *beat* NATURE *at* PANAMA

*A waterway only fifty miles long and less than a thousand feet wide would not seem of great importance ; yet the Panama Canal is both a marvel of engineering and one of the world's greatest highways of trade.*

**Panama Canal.** Perhaps the most stupendous piece of work that has been done in America since the arrival there of Columbus was the building of the Panama Canal, and of all the stories in the world there are few more enthralling than this.

One chapter in this tale of adventure tells of Man's struggle against two deadly enemies—the *Anopheles* mosquito (q.v.), which carries the parasite that causes malaria, and the *Stegomyia* mosquito (later called *Aedes*), the carrier of yellow fever. For thousands of years these insects had helped to make an inpenetrable barrier; but at last scientists and engineers defeated them, and linked the Pacific with the Atlantic by means of a canal. Now, as you will read, steamships climb a water stairway over the intervening mountains; New York is nearer Australia by 3,000 miles; and the journey from Liverpool to Vancouver is 6,000 miles shorter.

The narrow Isthmus of Panama, only about 32 miles wide at its narrowest point, has been famous in history since the days when Balboa and Francis Drake first made their separate ways through its tropical forests and looked out on the Pacific Ocean. Old Panama on the Pacific side became one of the key-points of the world, and across the isthmus ran the road to Porto Bello, over which the treasure hunters of Spain carried their silver and gold to avoid the roundabout voyage by way of Cape Horn.

Until the end of the 19th century the true rulers of this region were not the kings of Spain or the seekers of gold, nor yet the buccaneers who haunted the surrounding seas, the famous Spanish Main. The kings of Panama, in fact, were those mosquitoes, holding the power of life and death over every man, woman, and child on the isthmus. In the power of those tiny creatures lay the destinies of this beautiful land. When a band of Scotsmen, in the 16th century, founded a settlement on the Gulf of Darien it was the mosquitoes, even more than the Spaniards, who laid siege to their camp and put them to rout. And it was the danger of insect-borne disease which caused the abandonment of the ancient plans for a Panama Canal, drawn up, at the order of the Spanish King Charles V, in 1529. When, nearly two centuries later, Europe first sent out engineers to dig the canal, those insects were reigning still; and today tons of corroded metal, and crumpled-up engines, and bars of iron that trees have picked up and twisted around their branches tell the tale of how the mosquitoes dealt with those engineering pioneers.

The heat of Panama is such as only tropical travellers know; at some seasons there are torrential rains; and so, in a country with unmade roads, with only the roughest tracks beaten by the tramping feet of centuries of passers-by, there was stagnant water everywhere. Moisture and warmth and a rich soil gave rise to luxuriant forests, tangled jungles of vegetation in which insects lived in myriads; and into the lakes and pools and marshes poured a stream of decay, of dead and dying animal and vegetable matter year after year, until it seemed natural that a city of 10,000 people, as Colón then was, should have 150,000 graves. And so Panama came to be unfit to live in.

The French engineer Ferdinand de Lesseps (1805–94), who had already dug the Suez Canal, opened to traffic in 1869, set out in 1881, as head of a French company and with a concession from the Republic of Colombia, to cut the American continents apart at the narrow Isthmus of Panama. There was a French consul there who advanced an engineer the money for a suit of clothes one day, and invited him to lunch the next; but the engineer did not come. He had died of yellow fever at three o'clock in the morning, and was buried at dawn in the new suit he had just bought.

There was another Frenchman, the first director-general of the canal, who spent £30,000 in building a house; before the house was finished his wife and son and daughter had died of yellow fever, and the director-general went back to France alone, a broken-hearted man. Another man took his place; he died of yellow fever. A thousand men were sent to dig, and almost every man was dead within a year—from yellow fever. Another thousand took their place, and before the first year ended the second thousand were nearly all dead, too. Sixty-nine men in every hundred died. So death went about in Panama, and it seemed that nothing could stop its march.

With 40,000 men and more than £50,000,000 spent, the great De Lesseps failed. His company went bankrupt, and a number of French public men were ruined in reputation by financial scandals connected with the "Panama Affair." De Lesseps died in Paris in 1894. His name is immortalized by his canal at Suez, but it is written across Panama in heaps of rusty iron and ruined machinery. There it lies in swamps and jungles, proclaiming to all the world the failure of human power against an invisible foe.

**WHERE THE ATLANTIC IS WEST OF THE PACIFIC**
Does this map seem puzzling when you first look at it? The Atlantic is on the west where the Pacific ought to be! Yet it is perfectly correct. The Isthmus of Panama, as you can see by the small map at the top left, curves toward the south-west at this point, placing the Atlantic end of the canal farther west than the Pacific termination. The heavy lines mark the boundaries of the zone controlled by the United States.

But if De Lesseps failed in the work at Panama, another Frenchman who stayed at home led the way to the discoveries in science which later enabled the task to be carried through to victory.

It was Louis Pasteur (q.v.) who, looking through his microscope, first set men searching for the invisible agents of death at Panama, and thus led to the discovery that the mosquitoes had destroyed hundreds of thousands of lives.

What Pasteur found was this: Man has arrayed against him myriads of smaller creatures which, often before he knows it, poison him and may destroy him. Sometimes these creatures live on a man's body, so that we call them parasites, because they live on others; sometimes they have smaller parasites which live on them, so that even a harmless insect may carry a poisonous parasite and pass it into the bloodstream of a man with its "bite" or puncture. This discovery by Pasteur, if it had been made earlier, would have saved the lives of many of

---

*CHIEF FACTS CONCERNING THE CANAL*

Work began May 4, 1904; canal opened Aug. 15, 1914.
Total length of canal 50·7 miles; bottom width of channel 300 to 1,000 feet; minimum depth 41 feet.
Length of each lock 1,000 feet; width 110 feet.
Height of Miraflores Lake, 55 feet above sea-level; of Gatun Lake, 85 feet above sea-level; of Madden Lake, 260 feet above sea-level.
Amount of earth and rock excavated before opening of the canal, 239,000,000 cubic yards. Total cost of the canal, including payments to Panama, the French Company, and for sanitation, over £73,000,000.
Time required for a vessel to pass through the canal, 7 to 8 hours; minimum time on record, 4 hours 10 minutes.
Distances saved: Liverpool to San Francisco 5,666 miles; Liverpool to Vancouver 6,000 miles; New York to San Francisco 7,873 miles, and to Yokohama 3,768 miles.

those Frenchmen who died in digging the canal. In addition to the work of the great Pasteur himself, credit is due to his countryman, Charles Laveran, who in 1880 first discovered the parasites which produce malaria; to the Britons, Sir Patrick Manson and Sir Ronald Ross; to the Italian zoologist Grassi; and to Walter Reed in the United States, who took a further step in this great work. So this knowledge—that malaria and yellow fever are mosquito-borne diseases, and they then could be conquered only by the elimination of the mosquitoes —came into the world.

For 70 years the United States had taken an interest in various projects for a canal to link the Pacific with the Atlantic. American opinion, however, had mostly favoured a projected route across Nicaragua.

The withdrawal of De Lesseps's company directed attention anew to the Panama route, and in 1903 the United States bought out the French rights for about £8,000,000. An additional payment to the new Republic of Panama, which had just broken free from Colombia, brought a confirmation of the transfer in 1904, the grant to the United States of the 10-miles-wide canal zone (552 square miles in all), and cleared away all obstacles to the commencement of active construction.

The task which the United States had assumed was to cut the continent in two at the narrow point from Panama to Colón. It sent 30,000, then 40,000, then nearly 50,000 men to do the work; and over this army of workers it placed two Army officers— Gen. G. W. Goethals as engineer in chief, and Col. William Gorgas as chief sanitary officer.

### How the Deadly Mosquitoes were Routed

Colonel Gorgas was worthy of that long line of scientists who have achieved the many triumphs of modern medicine. He began by arranging mosquito-proof screens for the houses, and ordered every household to cover up all vessels that held water. He drained lakes and swamps, and poured out the filth of ages to the sea. He drained every ditch and pond that could be drained. Over those that could not be drained he spread a film of oil, so that the larvae of the mosquitoes in the water could not breathe; and thus he sealed up the breeding places. He cut grass jungles to the ground, destroyed all vermin, and burned all rubbish. He raised the new buildings above the ground, and screened windows, doors and porches with fine wire screens. He similarly screened every train, and put hospital cars on them. He ordered alcohol out of the Canal Zone, and made it " prohibition " territory. The result of all these measures was that the mosquitoes were put to rout, and from one of the most unhealthy spots in the world the Isthmus of Panama became one of the healthiest.

Equally marvellous was the work done by General Goethals and his engineers and workmen, with their excavators, dredgers, and other machines, which excelled those of De Lesseps as much as the science of Gorgas exceeded that of the earlier French medical officers.

Henceforth for 10 years there was seen such a sight as the world perhaps had never witnessed since the building of the Pyramids or the Great Wall of China. The tropical sun beat down upon a vast panorama of industry. Swarming in the mighty cuttings were legions of perspiring labourers, white and black, some in shirt sleeves, some almost naked. Some toiled with pick, shovel, and crowbar, and others with drill and dynamite in the hard rock.

Overhead cable railways, and a network of railway lines, were everywhere. The derricks and cranes swung concrete blocks through the air and lowered them into place to form locks and embankments. Steam drills bored holes into solid rock at the rate of seven feet an hour. More than 100 steam shovels doing the work of 10,000 men dug up earth by 10-ton scoopfuls and dumped it into waiting railway trucks. One hundred and fifteen locomotives were engaged in hauling trains of these trucks to the dumps, and there a machine like a huge plough travelled from one end of a train to the other unloading 20 trucks, each carrying 600 tons, in less than 10 minutes, and performing the work of 400 labourers. The earth which was excavated amounted to more than 239 million tons.

### Stairway of Great Locks

Instead of cutting a sea-level canal through the mountain divide as the French had planned, the American plan was to leave the central section 85 feet above sea-level and to construct a water stairway of great locks by which ships could climb up one side of the divide and down the other end. Even with this advantage it was still necessary to make some cuttings more than 300 feet deep. The mountains were, therefore, blasted away.

Once there was an earthquake. Heavy rains brought terrific landslides, which often undid the work of months. The River Chagres was particularly troublesome because of its floods; but it was conquered by the construction at Gatun of one of the mightiest dams in the world, made of earth and rock, a structure a mile and a half long, half a mile wide at the base, and 100 feet wide at the top. This dam connects the hills at each side of the Chagres valley with a hill in the centre, creating Gatun Lake, which has an area of 164 square miles when the water is at normal level.

So for nearly 10 years the digging and dredging and building of concrete walls and locks went on. Then, on October 10, 1913, President Wilson, 4,000 miles away in Washington, pressed an electric button which sent a flash over wires and cables and set off a tremendous charge of dynamite that blew out a temporary dyke. A flood rushed through a rock-filled rift in the mountains, and the Panama Canal was a dream realized ! On August 15, 1914, just after the outbreak of the First World War, the first ship, the 9,000-ton Ancon, passed through the canal. The formal opening did not take place until six years later.

What is the canal like today? Imagine you are in a steamer just about to enter it. On your right you see the steel-concrete piers of Cristobal (Christopher), the new port of the Canal Zone; on your left the white houses and red roofs of Cristobal's twin city, Colón (Columbus), which, along with Panama City, flies the flag of the Panama Republic. Past the great bronze statue of Columbus you sail into the canal across the low coastal belt through a channel 500 feet wide and 41 feet deep, the minimum depth of the canal. The tropical forest has been pushed back, but you see it on each side, with its ferns, creepers, chattering monkeys, and

# CLEANSING A CITY IN THE PANAMA CANAL ZONE

One of the first tasks of the American engineers was to clean up the town. These two photographs show a section of Tenth Street, Colon, before and after paving. Paving gave it a new appearance and made the residents eager to keep it clean.

Colonel Gorgas, United States army doctor who was in charge of the fight for health in the Panama Canal zone, performed splendid work. He caused to be emptied every ditch and pond that could be drained ; others he had covered with a film of oil to kill the mosquito larvae. He destroyed all vermin, burned rubbish, screened windows, doors, and verandas of houses, and the windows of passenger carriages on trains, and had a hospital carriage attached to every train. From one of the most unhealthy spots in the world the Isthmus of Panama became one of the healthiest. The death rate for employees there during the 10 years which the Canal took to build was only 1·7 per cent. Continued sanitary precautions since the Canal was opened brought down the death rate to 0·6 per cent.

brilliantly coloured humming birds and blossoms. Then the shores begin to rise.

You sail seven miles, and suddenly the way is blocked by an enormous wall of concrete masonry, with a double steel gate in the middle. This is the entrance to the first of the three locks at Gatun. The right half of it opens in two leaves, seven feet in thickness and weighing perhaps 600 tons, and in your ship passes. Then you see that a central concrete partition, 600 feet wide, resembling a highway even to the lampposts, divides the canal into two sections, one for incoming the other for outgoing vessels.

The engines of your ship are stopped, and four electric locomotives on cog tracks on the canal walls—which are 50 feet wide at the bottom and eight feet wide at the top—slowly tow the ship into the lock by hawsers made fast to bow and stern. The gates close behind, shutting the vessel into the great chamber. Each lock is 1,000 feet long and 110 feet wide. From a huge unseen culvert water pours into the lock through great holes in the concrete floor, and your ship slowly rises until it is at the level of the next highest lock; then the gates open, and in you sail to the next lock. Twice the process is repeated, a half-hour being spent in each of the three locks, until the water stairway has lifted the ship to the 85-foot level of Gatun Lake. Here the engines start again, and you begin a 24-mile trip across this artificial lake.

Behind you to the right is the Gatun dam, holding in all those waters in this enormous elevated reser-

voir, which supplies water to the locks. At the centre of the dam is a concrete spillway to let the surplus waters escape through 14 gate-controlled openings into the lower Chagres, in order that the lake may be kept at the right level. Giant generators, run by this overflow, supply electricity for operating the hidden machinery of the locks and spillways. In 1935 another huge dam was completed across the upper Chagres at Alhajuila. Thus Madden Lake, 22 square miles in area, was formed, affording a reserve for Gatun Lake during the dry season. In 1940 a new set of locks, parallel to the existing ones, were begun, to provide an alternative route in case of damage.

Everywhere the scenery is entrancing. A palm-thatched hut perches on every hill-top, and groves of trees lift their heads above the waters. From Gatun Lake you sail into the Gaillard Cut, a great gash through the central divide, more than 300 feet wide at the bottom.

Eight miles more, and you begin to descend the water stairway. Through one lock at Pedro Miguel the ship drops down about 30 feet, to the level of Lake Miraflores, two miles wide; and later two more locks lower you to sea-level. From here you can see in the distance the new American port of Balboa, on the Pacific side. A tram-car line runs down the coast to Panama City. Then you steam 8½ miles through a 500-foot channel out into the deep waters of the Pacific.

The amount of sea-going trade which passes through the Canal increases year by year. It is

THE SPILLWAY AT GATUN DAM ON THE PANAMA CANAL

At the time of building, this was the largest dam in the world. It is nearly 1½ miles long measured at the crest, and half a mile thick at the base. At the surface of the water the dam is 400 feet thick. Twenty million cubic yards of material were required to build it. The concrete spillway shown in the photograph is 1,200 feet long and 300 feet wide, cut through a hill of rock in the centre of the dam. It allows the surplus water from Gatun Lake to empty out through the Chagres river into the Atlantic. Giant generators, run by this over-flow, supply electricity for operating the great locks at Gatun.

# THE GATUN LOCKS LET THROUGH A BATTLESHIP

Electric locomotives draw the ships through, thus avoiding the danger of damage to the locks, which would be almost certain if ships were allowed to proceed under their own power. This ship has entered the lock from the Atlantic side, and will be raised to the level shown by the blackened sides of the enclosure before proceeding into the next lock.

A 26,000-ton United States battleship is passing through one of the locks at Gatun, on the Panama Canal. Nearly all the world's ships are less than 600 feet long, and would thus pass through the locks, which are 1,000 feet in length, with room to spare. The width of the locks is 110 feet, which prevents a few of the largest ships from using the canal. On occasion, however, aircraft carriers and other very broad ships have passed through, with only a few inches to spare.

# HOW THE MIGHTY LOCKS OF THE PANAMA CANAL

The principles which are applied in the operation of the Panama locks are shown in this drawing. All vessels are towed into and through the locks by electric locomotives, which run on cog-rails on the tops of the lock walls. For each flight of locks there are two towing tracks, one on the side and one on the middle wall.

Usually four locomotives are required : two ahead, one on each wall, to pull ; and two behind, one on each wall, to keep the ship in the centre of the lock and to stop it when necessary. Each locomotive is so equipped that the towing line may be let out or taken in without actual motion of the locomotive. The lock

2492

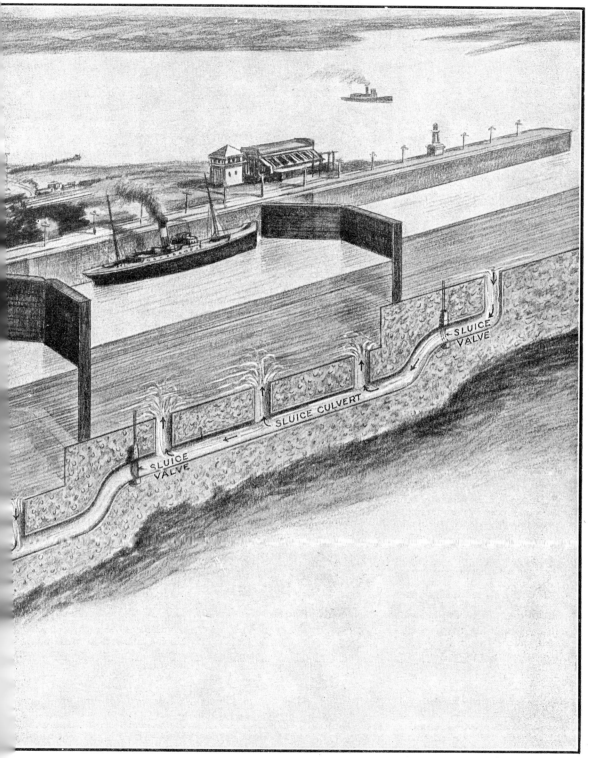

filled and emptied through a system of culverts. To fill a ck, the sluice valves at the upper end are opened, and the lower ves closed. The water flows through the culvert and up ough the holes in the floor into the lock chamber. To empty ck the upper valves are closed and the lower ones opened.

The water then flows out of the lock chamber by gravity, through the sluice culvert, and out into the lower lock or pool. The main culverts under the walls are 18 feet in diameter, while the smaller ones leading under the lock floor are three and a half feet across, thus allowing a rapid transfer of water.

P. A.-Reuters

**RARE GIANT PANDA IN LONDON'S ZOO**
Named Lien-Ho (Unity), this Giant Panda, long regarded as one of the world's rarest animals, was presented to the London Zoo by the Chinese Government in 1946. In the photograph on the left the quaint looking animal is enjoying a meal of bamboo-shoots, its favourite food. On the right it is being studied by its keeper and a young friend.

a polar bear when full grown; it is very hardy, living above the snow line in the mountains of Tibet and China. A peculiar feature of the Giant Panda is that it has developed a modification of the palm of its forepaw —a pad of flesh, which looks like a thumb, on to which the "fingers" are folded when it grasps a bamboo cane, its favourite food.

**Pandora.** According to the Greek legend, Pandora was the first woman on earth. When Prometheus stole the fire from heaven and bestowed it on mortals, Zeus caused a woman to be made from clay to bring trouble to Man.

estimated that about 10,000 vessels could pass through in a year; the actual number using the canal in recent years has been about 4,000 annually, and a total cargo of nearly 15 million tons is carried each year by these ships. A charge is made for every vessel passing through; in 1946 these tolls amounted to about £4,000,000.

**Panda.** This name is given to two animals. The ordinary Panda (*Aelurus fulgens*) is a small cat-bear which lives in the Himalayas. It is about 2½ feet long, but more than half of its length is accounted for by its bushy tail. Its fine, dense fur is chestnut-brown above and black beneath. More familiar to most people nowadays is the Giant Panda (*Aeluropoda melanoleucus*), long regarded as one of the world's rarest animals. It was first discovered by a French missionary in the bamboo jungles of Western China, during the winter of 1868–69, and in 1935 a specimen, called Ming, was exhibited at the London Zoo. Ming died in 1944, and was replaced by another, called Lien-Ho (meaning Unity). Lien-Ho, a great favourite, died in February 1950.

The Giant Panda is white, with black paws, a black saddle, black ears, and a black patch around each eye. Its exact place in the animal kingdom is by no means certain; but it is thought not to be a bear, though it looks like one. It weighs 22 stone, and in size is about half as big as

She was fashioned by Hephaestus, and each of the other gods contributed some gift, whence her name, which means "all-gifted." Aphrodite gave beauty, Hermes cunning and persuasion, Athene feminine accomplishments. Zeus sent her to Prometheus's brother, Epimetheus, who gladly accepted her as his wife, though Prometheus had cautioned him against her. Pandora brought with her a jar or box in which were all men's ills and troubles, and which she had been warned not to open. When she opened it they escaped and spread over the whole earth, Hope alone remaining.

Another story has it that the jar contained all blessings, which would have been preserved for Man had not Pandora opened it and allowed all but Hope to escape.

**Pansy.** The pansies and violas of our gardens are astonishing examples of the plant-breeders' art—as is immediately realized when you compare a cultivated pansy or a viola, having blooms more than two inches across, with the wild pansy or heartsease, *Viola tricolor*, of British fields, whose simple flower is a mere half-inch across.

Not only in size of flower but in colour has immense improvement been made, by long selection and cross-fertilization. And improvement has gone so far that whereas once upon a time a garden pansy always had velvety petals and the viola (or tufted pansy) had much daintier and more fragile

J. E. Tyler
**GARDEN PANSIES**
Perhaps none of the flowers of the old English garden is so popular as the pansy. Modern varieties are many-hued, but almost all have the dark markings seen here.